Systems Analysis and Design
Fourth Edition

Gary B. Shelly

Thomas J. Cashman

Harry J. Rosenblatt

COURSE TECHNOLOGY

25 THOMSON PLACE

BOSTON MA 02210

SHELLY
CASHMAN
SERIES®

Australia • Canada • Denmark • Japan • Mexico • New Zealand • Philippines • Puerto Rico • Singapore
South Africa • Spain • United Kingdom • United States

COURSE TECHNOLOGY

THOMSON LEARNING™

COPYRIGHT © 2001 Course Technology, a division of Thomson Learning.
Printed in the United States of America

Asia (excluding Japan)	Latin America	Canada
Thomson Learning	Thomson Learning	Nelson/Thomson Learning
60 Albert Street, #15-01	Seneca, 53	1120 Birchmount Road
Albert Complex	Colonia Polanco	Scarborough, Ontario
Singapore 189969	11560 Mexico D.F. Mexico	Canada M1K 5G4
Japan	South Africa	UK/Europe/Middle East
Thomson Learning	Thomson Learning	Thomson Learning
Palaceside Building 5F	Zonnebloem Building,	Berkshire House
1-1-1 Hitotsubashi, Chiyoda-ku	Constantia Square	168-173 High Holborn
Tokyo 100 0003 Japan	526 Sixteenth Road	London, WC1V 7AA United Kingdom
	P.O. Box 2459	
Australia/New Zealand	Halfway House, 1685	Spain
Nelson/Thomson Learning	South Africa	Thomson Learning
102 Dodds Street		Calle Magallanes, 25
South Melbourne, Victoria 3205		28015-MADRID
Australia		ESPANA

For more information, contact Course Technology, 25 Thomson Place, Boston, MA 02210.

Or visit our Internet site at www.course.com

For permission to use material from this product, contact us by
Tel (800) 730-2114
Fax (800) 730-2115
www.thomsonrights.com

Course Technology reserves the right to revise this publication and make changes from time to time in its content without notice.

PHOTO CREDITS: Chapter 1: *Figure 1-6* Space Shuttle launching, Courtesy of NASA; *Figure 1-8* State-of-the-Art server technology, Courtesy of IBM Corporation; *Figure 1-11* Motorola microchip, Bruce Forster/Stone; *Figure 1-15* Point of sale scanner, © 2000 PhotoDisc; **Chapter 2:** *Figure 2-6* Retina scanning device, Eric Bazin/Gamma Liaison; *Figure 2-8* Gateway smart forklifts, John Lund/Stone; *Figure 2-14* Interview , Bruce Ayres/Stone; *Figure 2-16* Oral Presentation, © Tom Carroll/International Stock; **Chapter 3:** *Figure 3-2* JAD team of users, managers, and IT professionals, Mark Richards/PhotoEdit; *Figure 3-12* Analysts in informal meeting, © 2000 PhotoDisc; *Figure 3-15* Worker observation photo, Richard Pasley/Stock Boston; *Figure 3-20* Professional using a handheld computer, Fisher/Thatcher/Stone; **Chapter 4:** *Figure 4-1* Systems analysts using visual aids, Jose Luis Pelez/The Stock Market; *Figure 4-15* Data entry work, AP/Wide World Photos; *Figure 4-22* Manufacturing environment, Spencer Grant/PhotoEdit; *Figure 4-40* Analyst and manager using decision tree, Spencer Grant/PhotoEdit; **Chapter 5:** *Figure 5-2* Auto dealership, Mark Segal/IndexStock; *Figure 5-6* Fitness center, Spencer Grant/PhotoEdit; *Figure 5-11* Fries basket, Jeff Baker; *Figure 5-30* Customers and service writers preparing work orders, © Mugshots/The Stock Market; **Chapter 6:** *Figure 6-2* Hotel reservations desk, Spencer Grant/PhotoEdit; *Figure 6-13* Magazines, Bonnie Kamin; *Figure 6-15* Wind tunnel, AP/Wide World Photos; *Figure 6-25* Automated data scanner, Courtesy of Symbol Technologies, Inc; *Figure 6-27* Airport tags, Tony Freeman/PhotoEdit; **Chapter 7:** *Figure 7-4* User at workstation displaying colorful user interface screen, Mark Richards/PhotoEdit; *Figure 7-19* Electronic customer signature, Al Cook/Stock Boston; *Figure 7-41* Shredder, Eric Kamp/IndexStock; *Figure 7-42* Diskless workstation, Andreas Pollok/Stone; **Chapter 8:** *Figure 8-19* Customer renting or returning a car, Michael Newman/PhotoEdit; *Figure 8-25* Faculty advisor with students, David Weintraub/Stock Boston; *Figure 8-32* Video rental checkout, David Young-Wolff/PhotoEdit; *Figure 8-41* Security system, Spencer Grant/PhotoEdit; **Chapter 9:** *Figure 9-4* Login and password, © 2000 PhotoDisc; *Figure 9-6* Kozmo.com shopper/delivery worker, AP/Wide World Photos; *Figure 9-40* Management presenting information to staff; Charles Gupton/Stone; **Chapter 10:** *Figure 10-5* Software engineering, Roger Tully/Stone; *Figure 10-21* Programmer and systems analyst participating in code review, © 2000 PhotoDisc; *Figure 10-23* IT staff members, users, and IT management in system testing, Stephen Marks Inc./The Image Bank; *Figure 10-24* Systems analyst preparing documentation, © 2000 PhotoDisc; **Chapter 11:** *Figure 11-1* Verifying product meets specifications, Lonnie Duka/Stone; *Figure 11-3* Trainer and trainee, Walter Hodges/Stone; *Figure 11-5* Training session, © 2000 Eyewire; *Figure 11-12* Users participating in the post-implementation phase, Fisher/Thatcher/Stone; **Chapter 12:** *Figure 12-1* NASA training, Jay Silverman Productions/The Image Bank; *Figure 12-2* Help desk staff and system user, © 2000 Eyewire; *Figure 12-4* Engineer analysing a system, AP/Wide World Photos; *Figure 12-17* Punch card, © Charles E. Rotkin/Corbis.

ISBN 0-7895-5957-9

5 6 7 8 9 10 BC 05 04 03 02

C O N T E N T S

PHASE 2
SYSTEMS ANALYSIS

CHAPTER 3
Requirements Modeling

CHAPTER 4
Data and Process Modeling

CHAPTER 5
Object Modeling

CHAPTER 6
Transition to Systems Design

PHASE 3
SYSTEMS DESIGN

CHAPTER 7
User Interface, Input, and Output Design

CHAPTER 8
Data Design

CHAPTER 9
Application Architecture

PHASE 4

SYSTEMS IMPLEMENTATION

CHAPTER 10
Application Development

CHAPTER 11
Installation and Evaluation

PHASE 5

SYSTEMS OPERATION
AND SUPPORT

CHAPTER 12
Systems Operation and Support

THE SYSTEMS ANALYSIS TOOLKIT

Part 1
Communication Tools

Part 2
Feasibility and Cost Analysis Tools

Part 3
Project Management Tools

Part 4
Alternative Systems Development Methodologies

PREFACE

The Shelly Cashman Series® offers the finest textbooks in computer education. *Systems Analysis and Design, Fourth Edition* continues with the innovation, quality, and reliability you have come to expect from this series. We are proud that our previous editions were best-sellers and we are confident that this edition will join its predecessors. This textbook emphasizes a practical approach to learning systems analysis and design. In it you will find an educationally sound and easy-to-follow pedagogy that artfully combines full-color pictures, drawings, and text to produce a visually appealing and straightforward presentation of systems analysis and design. The World Wide Web and the textbook integrate to offer students current information and links to Web-based resources, as well as a continuing Internet-based case study. These and other features provide you with the opportunity to deliver an exciting and dynamic systems analysis and design class.

OBJECTIVES OF THIS TEXTBOOK

Systems Analysis and Design, Fourth Edition is intended for a three-unit introductory systems analysis and design course. The objectives of this textbook are:

- To present a practical approach to systems analysis and design using a blend of traditional development with current technologies
- To define and describe in detail the five phases of the systems development life cycle (SDLC): systems planning, systems analysis, systems design, systems implementation, and systems operation and support
- To present the material in a visually appealing, full-color format and an exciting, easy-to-read style that invites students to learn
- To provide students with a comprehensive Systems Analysis Toolkit that highlights the importance of communications, economic analysis, and project planning skills across all phases of the SDLC, in addition to alternate development methodologies
- To give students an in-depth understanding of how information technology (IT) supports operational and business requirements in today's intensely competitive environment
- To provide examples of important IT developments and trends, using numerous screen shots of selected Web sites and Internet links
- To use the World Wide Web as an online information source and learning tool
- To teach real-world systems analysis and design skills in the context of solving realistic problems and present practical guidelines and tips for career success
- To provide a clear picture of how systems analysts interact with users, management, and other IT professionals in a typical business organization
- To offer interesting case studies and exercises that promote critical-thinking skills and encourage student participation

Detailed Coverage of Fundamental Topics

While providing broad coverage of the systems development life cycle, this textbook also presents topics that should be covered in any introductory systems analysis and design course. Such topics include business information systems concepts; mission statements; strategic planning; feasibility studies; fact-finding techniques; data flow diagrams; structured English; decision tables; decision trees; object-oriented analysis and design; enterprise computing; make or buy decisions;

employee empowerment; prototyping; CASE tools; systems flowcharts; the use of codes; reducing input errors; data security; automated design tools; entity-relationship diagrams; cardinality; normalization; UML notation; database design and management; traditional file organization; online versus batch processing; centralized versus distributed processing; LANs and WANs; client/server systems; software engineering; unit, link, and system testing; documentation; training; systems changeover; post-implementation evaluation; support activities; maintenance activities; capacity planning; communication tools; feasibility and cost analysis tools; and project management tools. Each of these topics is covered in detail and clearly linked to the appropriate phase or phases of the SDLC, so that students understand where they fit with the larger systems development life cycle.

DISTINGUISHING FEATURES

Systems Analysis and Design, Fourth Edition consists of the following distinguishing features:

A Proven Book

Based on our previous best-selling textbooks on systems analysis and design, this textbook evolved over the past eighteen years to ensure a presentation of the most current concepts, techniques, applications, and methodologies. More than three-quarter million students learned about systems analysis and design using the previous editions.

A Blend of Traditional Development with Current Technologies

This textbook does not present a theoretical view of systems analysis and design. Instead, we made every possible effort to teach the tools and techniques that systems analysts use in today's dynamic business world.

Numerous realistic examples support all text definitions, concepts, and techniques. We used examples and case studies from actual systems projects to teach students how to solve real-world problems. When students finish a systems analysis and design course using this book, they will know how to apply their skills in the real world of information technology and to complete IT projects successfully.

This textbook allows students to perform systems analysis and design tasks right from the start. Students begin applying concepts in Chapter 1 and continue performing systems analysis and design tasks in every following chapter.

Visually Appealing

In order to produce a visually appealing and easy-to-understand book, we used the latest technology, pictures, drawings, and text. Throughout the textbook, figures reinforce important points and the illustrations reflect the latest trends in systems analysis and design and simplify the more complex concepts. The color photos allow students to see examples of actual people, activities, and situations described in the textbook.

Nontechnical Language

This textbook assumes no previous systems analysis and design experience and requires no mathematics beyond the high school level. Drawing on the authors' many years of experience in teaching, consulting, management, and writing, we included numerous insights throughout the book. This provides continuity, simplicity, and practicality that students need and appreciate.

Continuing Case Studies in Every Chapter

In the fourth edition of this book, we provide up to six continuing case studies per chapter. When students complete their coursework and enter the workforce, they need to understand the specific business operations of a company and how the systems analyst role can differ from company to company. By providing case studies in every chapter, we offer students an opportunity to plan, analyze, design, implement, and support information systems involving human resources administration, health care, recreational facility management, and technology training. The SoftWear Limited case study provides an opportunity for students to work as members of a systems development team and complete the Your Turn assignments following in each chapter. The New Century Health Clinic and Ridgeway Company case studies allow students to work as systems analysts in realistic settings, and apply their knowledge and skills to develop new information systems. Brand-new to this edition, SCR Associates is an interactive Web-based case study of a fictional IT firm. For further information on this case study, please see the Web Enhancement section of this preface. All of these case studies allow students to apply the skills learned in the textbook.

Coverage of Object-Oriented Analysis and Design (OOAD)

With the increasing popularity of object-oriented programming languages, OOAD also has increased in popularity. Coverage of OOAD is provided in the text and presented as an alternate methodology within the overall framework of structured systems analysis and design. If a particular methodology approaches the systems development process in a different way, the authors explain the alternatives to the student. Data and process modeling for structured systems analysis and design is described in Chapter 4. Chapter 5 is devoted to object modeling, because of the vast differences between structured and object-oriented analysis and design.

Web Enhancements

Each of the previous editions introduced sound educational innovations that separated them from the rest of the market. *Systems Analysis and Design, Fourth Edition* continues the tradition by offering innovative, timely, and reliable Web enhancements that set a new standard for systems analysis and design textbooks. The purpose of the Web enhancements is to (1) provide students an interactive and fun learning opportunity, (2) provide up-to-date information on the Web and suggest Internet sites for additional exploration, and (3) provide examples of Web resources that relate to key subjects in the text. We integrated the Web enhancements into the textbook in four major ways:

- SCR Associates, an IT consulting firm, is an interactive case study that students can complete using the Web. Students login to the company intranet, read e-mail addressed to them, and perform assigned tasks in a realistic corporate setting.

- Numerous screen shots of actual Web sites show state-of-the-art IT technology and major trends.

- Throughout the text, margin annotations provide suggestions on how to obtain additional information via the Web on an important topic covered on the page.

- Learning games, based on the Key Terms, reinforce concepts the student learned in each chapter.

Systems Analyst's Toolkit

The Systems Analyst's Toolkit, which follows Chapter 12, presents communication skills, economic analysis tools, project planning skills, and alternate systems development methodologies that can be used across the five phases of the SDLC. Topics include guidelines for successful communications; feasibility and cost analysis methodologies; project management tools; rapid application development (RAD); Microsoft Solutions Framework (MSF); and Microsoft solutions architecture certification opportunities.

End of Chapter Material

This textbook contains the most comprehensive end of chapter material of any systems analysis and design textbook. This edition offers a Chapter Summary, Key Terms, Chapter Review, Discussion Topics, Chapter Assignments, Apply Your Knowledge, and Case Studies.

Software Bundling Opportunities

You can bundle Visible Analyst — Student Edition with the textbook so students can have their own copy for use in the lab, at home, or in a distance education environment. An evaluation copy of Visible Analyst — Student Edition is available on the Teaching Tools CD-ROM. Please see Visible Analyst — Student Edition in a later section for product and adoption information.

You can bundle a fully functional trial edition of Microsoft Visio Professional 2000 with this textbook so students can use their own copy in the lab at home or in a distance education environment to create network diagramming and design; directory services diagramming; database design and documentation; software development; Web site mapping; data flow diagramming; network diagrams and documentation; database diagrams and documentation; software diagrams and documentation; and Internet and intranet diagrams and documentation.

Other bundling opportunities exist with Microsoft Visual Basic 6.0, Oracle Designer, and custom combination packages. For more information, contact your Course Technology, Thomson Learning Sales Representative.

ORGANIZATION OF THIS TEXTBOOK

Systems Analysis and Design, Fourth Edition contains twelve chapters and the Systems Analyst's Toolkit. We organized the textbook so students will know clearly where they are and how their progress relates to the systems development life cycle process. We provide an introduction at the beginning of each SDLC phase, indicate the phase at the top of each page, and list objectives that describe the key skills and knowledge that students learn in the chapter. Within the chapter, we challenge students to practice their skills with What Do You Think? and Your Turn tasks. End of chapter material relates directly to the chapter objectives, so students can measure and track their progress.

VISIBLE ANALYST — STUDENT EDITION

The Visible Analyst — Student Edition, a powerful, integrated, application development tool, is available bundled with this textbook so that each student can own a copy at a fraction of the retail cost. Each copy of the software comes with a tutorial and two sample projects. The ISBN for the textbook/Visible Analyst bundle is 0-7895-6322-3.

Visible Analyst — Student Edition provides graphical analysis and design for structured, data, and object modeling, as well as construction in one affordable, easy-to-use package. It contains a powerful repository for storing and documenting data, processes, and objects as well as full analysis checking and extensive reporting capabilities. The Visible Analyst — Student Edition also generates Oracle and Access SQL DDL, XML DCD files, and includes an interface to Visual Basic.

Visible Analyst — Student Edition includes all the operational and functional capabilities of the commercial editions; however, there are certain constraints, including the following:

- Users may create only one project at a time (users also can access a sample project at the same time)

- Each project is limited to 10 diagrams per each type

- Each project is limited to 40 entities and classes

Adopting schools that bundle the Visible Analyst — Student Edition with this textbook can receive up to two free copies of the Visible Analyst — Student Edition from Visible Systems Corporation, one for each 15 copies sold to the bookstore. Schools can purchase additional copies of the Visible Analyst — Student Edition or the Visible Analyst — University Edition, a multiuser LAN version for computer laboratories, direct from Visible Systems at a minimal price. For more information on purchasing options please contact Visible Systems direct by phone at 800-333-8984, ext. 304, by e-mail at edusales@visible.com, or visit their web site at www.visible.com. For more information on the bundling options, please contact your Course Technology, Thomson Learning Sales Representative.

SHELLY CASHMAN SERIES TEACHING TOOLS

A comprehensive set of Teaching Tools accompanies this textbook in the form of a CD-ROM. The CD-ROM includes the Instructor's Manual and other teaching and testing aids. The CD-ROM (ISBN 0-7895-5969-2) is available through your Course Technology representative or by calling one of the following telephone numbers: Colleges and Universities, 1-800-648-7450; High Schools, 1-800-824-5179; Career Colleges, 1-800-477-3692; Canada, 1-800-268-2222; and Corporations and Government Agencies, 1-800-340-7450. The contents of the CD-ROM follow.

- **Instructor's Manual** The Instructor's Manual is made up of Microsoft Word files. The files include chapter objectives, lecture notes, answers to the end of chapter exercises, and a large test bank. You can modify the lecture notes or generate quizzes and exams from the test bank using your own word processing software. Where appropriate, solutions to laboratory assignments are embedded as icons.

- **Figures in the Book** Illustrations for most of the figures in the textbook are available. Use this ancillary to create a slide show from the illustrations for lecture or print transparencies for use in lectures with an overhead projector.

- **Course Test Manager** Course Test Manager is a powerful testing and assessment package that instructors can use to create and print tests from the large test bank. Instructors with access to a networked computer lab (LAN) can administer, grade, and track tests online. Students also can take online practice tests, which generate customized study guides that indicate where in the textbook students can find more information for each question.

- **Course Presenter** Course Presenter is a multimedia lecture presentation system that provides PowerPoint slides for every subject in each chapter. Use this system to present well-organized lectures that are interesting and knowledge-based. Fifteen presentation files are provided for the textbook, one for each chapter. Each file contains PowerPoint slides for every subject in each chapter, along with optional choices to show any figure in the chapter, as you introduce the material in class.

- **Course Syllabus** Any instructor who has been assigned a course at the last minute knows how difficult it is to create a course syllabus. For this reason, a sample syllabus is included that can be customized easily for a course.

- **Instructor's Lab Solutions** This ancillary contains the solutions for the Interactive Labs assessment quizzes.

- **Interactive Labs** Eighteen hands-on interactive labs that take the student from 10 to 15 minutes each to step through help solidify and reinforce mouse and keyboard usage, as well as computer concepts. Student assessment is available in each interactive lab by means of a Print button. The assessment requires students to answer true and false, multiple choice, and fill-in-the-blank questions.

- **Visible Analyst — Student Edition** A copy of this powerful CASE tool is available on the Teaching Tools CD-ROM for instructor evaluation only. For more information on Visible Analyst — Student Edition, see the discussion earlier in the preface.

- **Case Study Forms** A full set of systems development forms and templates is available on the Teaching Tools CD-ROM. Instructors can copy these files to a network folder, so students can use the forms and templates in the case study projects and assignments. This material also is available on the Shelly Cashman Web site at www.scsite.com/sad4e. The SCR Associates case has its own set of Web-based forms and templates, which are stored in the SCR forms library at www.scsite.com/sad4e/scr

- **Student Files** The documents needed to complete the SCR Associated case study. You can distribute the files on the Teaching Tools CD-ROM to your students over a network or you can have them follow the instructions on the inside back cover of this book to obtain a copy of the *Systems Analysis and Design* Data Disk.

DISTANCE LEARNING

Various distance learning options are available for your systems analysis and design course:

MyCourse.com

MyCourse.com is an online syllabus builder and course enhancement tool. Hosted by Course Technology, MyCourse.com adds value to your course by providing additional content that reinforces what students are learning.

Most importantly, MyCourse.com is flexible. You can choose how you want to organize the material — by date, by class session, or by using the default organization, which organizes content by chapter. MyCourse.com allows you to add your own materials, including hyperlinks, school logos, assignments, announcements, and other course content. If you are using more than one textbook, you can even build a course that includes all of your Course Technology texts in one easy-to-use site!

Start building your own course today! Just go to: www.mycourse.com/instructor

WebCT and Blackboard

For an additional charge you can create a distance learning course in either WebCT or Blackboard. Course Technology has partnered with WebCT and Blackboard to offer state-of-the-art Course Management tools and high-quality content so you can add an online component to your course or offer a full course outline. Course Technology provides robust content in addition to the content from your textbook — in essence, a pre-assembled course. You can select one of the following options: hosting courses at your school, WebCT, or Blackboard. Visit www.course.com/distancelearning for more information.

SHELLY CASHMAN ONLINE

Shelly Cashman Online is a World Wide Web service available to instructors and students of computer education. Visit Shelly Cashman Online at www.scsite.com. Shelly Cashman Online contains the following:

- **Series Information** Information on the Shelly Cashman Series products.

- **Teaching Resources** Designed for instructors teaching from and using Shelly Cashman Series textbooks and software. This area includes password-protected instructor materials that can be downloaded, course outlines, teaching tips, and much more.

- **Community** Opportunities to discuss your course and ideas with instructors in your field and the Shelly Cashman Series team.
- **Student Center** Dedicated to students learning about computers with Shelly Cashman Series textbooks and software. This area includes cool links, data that can be downloaded, and much more.

ACKNOWLEDGMENTS

The Shelly Cashman Series would not be the leading computer education series without the contributions of outstanding publishing professionals. First, and foremost among them is Becky Herrington, director of production and designer. She is the heart and soul of the Shelly Cashman Series, and it is only through her leadership, dedication, and tireless efforts that superior products are made possible. Becky created and produced the award-winning Windows series of books.

Under Becky's direction, the following individuals made significant contributions to these books: Doug Cowley, production manager; Ginny Harvey, series specialist; Ken Russo, senior Web designer; Mike Bodnar, associate production manager; Mark Norton, Web designer; Hector Arvizu, interior design and compositor; Meena Moest, production editor; Michelle French, and Christy Pardini, cover design and graphic artists; Jeanne Black, Quark expert; Cristina Haley, copyeditor and indexer; Nancy Lamm, proofreader; and Abby Reip, photo researcher.

Special thanks go to Richard Keaveny, associate publisher; Lora Wade, product manager; Francis Schurgot, Web product manager; Erin Roberts, associate product manager; Marc Ouellette, associate Web product manager; Erin Runyon, editorial assistant; Rachel VanKirk, product marketing manager; and Rose Marie Kuebbing, developmental editor.

We also would like to give special thanks to all the reviewers: Mike Michaelson, Palomar College; Robert Street Jr., Campbellsville University; Julia Tinsley, Indiana University, Kokomo; Kenneth Wallace, Craven Community College; and to the systems analysis students at College of the Albemarle who provided valuable comments and suggestions.

We hope you find using this textbook an enriching and rewarding experience.

Gary B. Shelly
Thomas J. Cashman
Harry J. Rosenblatt

NOTES TO THE STUDENT

SCR Associates is a fictional IT consulting firm that offers solutions and training for small- and medium-sized companies. As shown in the following figures, the SCR case is an interactive Web based case study, where you work as a newly-hired systems analyst assigned to a systems development team. SCR has a Web site, with information about the company, and a company intranet, where you can receive e-mail messages addressed to you and obtain other information. On the Internet, you can visit www.scsite.com/sad4e/scr for instructions about how to use your login name and password.

To Login

(1) Launch your browser; (2) type www.scsite.com/sad4e/scr in the Address bar of your browser (Figure 1); (3) read and follow the instructions on the Web page to enter your first and last name; (4) type scrteam in the password field; (5) click the Login button to enter the SCR Associates site (Figure 2).

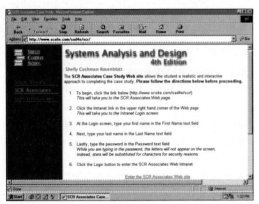

Figure 1

Figure 2

The Systems Analyst's Toolkit follows the text chapters, starting on page TK.1. All professionals, including systems analysts need a set of tools. The Toolkit provides four important cross-functional tools: communication tools, cost-benefit analysis tools, project management tools, and alternative systems development tools.

- Communication tools help you write effective reports, design and deliver powerful presentations, and conduct productive meetings.

- Feasibility and cost analysis tools provide valuable information about project feasibility and financial impact.

- Project management tools help you organize, plan, estimate, execute, and monitor IT projects.

- Alternative systems development methodologies explain two popular strategies: rapid application development (RAD) and Microsoft Solutions Framework (MSF).

You can use these flexible tools in several ways. For example, you can start by reviewing communication tools and cost-benefit analysis tools to prepare for the systems planning phase of the SDLC. On the other hand, you can wait until you need the skills for a specific case study or assignment, and use the tools at that time. Either way, make sure to study all the tools before the end of the course, because they are important to your success as a systems analyst. The following grid shows the four tools, and how they relate to the text chapters.

A star ★ indicates that you will need the tool to perform chapter tasks and assignments, and a bullet • indicates that the Toolkit information is desirable background.

SYSTEMS ANALYST'S TOOLKIT			
Part 1	Part 2	Part 3	Part 4
Communication Tools	Feasibility and Cost Analysis Tools	Project Management Tools	Alternative Systems Development Methodologies
Chapter 1 •	•	•	•
Chapter 2 ★	•	•	•
Chapter 3 ★	•	•	★
Chapter 4 ★	•	•	★
Chapter 5 ★	★	★	★
Chapter 6 ★	•	★	★
Chapter 7 ★	★	★	★
Chapter 8 ★	•	★	★
Chapter 9 ★	★	★	★
Chapter 10 ★	•	★	★
Chapter 11 ★	•	★	★
Chapter 12 ★	★	•	★

Systems Planning **PHASE 1**

Systems Analysis **PHASE 2**

Systems Design **PHASE 3**

Systems Implementation **PHASE 4**

Systems Operation and Support **PHASE 5**

Introduction to Systems Analysis and Design

Chapter 1 introduces you to the role of information technology in today's dynamic business environment. You will learn about the development of information systems, systems analysis and design concepts, the systems development life cycle, and various systems development methodologies, tools, and techniques. This chapter also describes the role of the information technology department and the people who work there.

INTRODUCTION

The headlines in Figure 1-1 mirror the dramatic changes in store for the business environment of the future. A global economy brings intense competition and constant change. Companies use information as a vital resource in the battle to increase productivity, deliver quality products and services, maintain customer loyalty, and make sound decisions. In a global marketplace, information technology often means the difference between success and failure.

OBJECTIVES

When you finish this chapter, you will be able to:

- Discuss the impact of information technology on business operations

- Define an information system and describe its components and characteristics

- Identify common types of information systems and explain who uses them

- Distinguish between structured analysis and object-oriented methodology

- Explain systems development techniques and tools, including modeling, prototyping, and CASE tools

- Describe the systems development life cycle

- Discuss the role of the information technology department and the systems analysts who work there

Enormous Internet Growth: No End in Sight

E-Commerce Is Changing the Way People Do Business

Companies Fight Hard for Talented IT People

an-
next
osal
thin

Internet Privacy Issues Spur Legal Battles

kely
ard.
om-

Customers Demand World-Class Support

Stocks: As board meeting

Brick-and-Mortar Companies Battle Dot-Com Firms

the loss. He has telegraphed his im-

Please see MA: A15

Mission-Critical Failures Can Sink Web-Based Companies

IT Revolution:
Is Your Web Site a Winner?

FIGURE 1-1 These headlines show how information technology has an enormous impact on business.

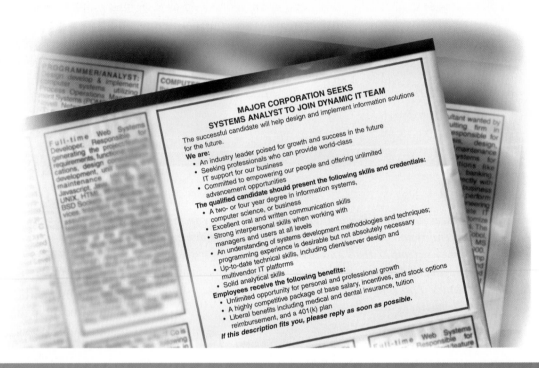

ON THE WEB

To learn more about Business Process Reengineering visit scsite.com/sad4e/more.htm, click Systems Analysis and Design Chapter 1 and then click the Business Process Reengineering link.

www.scsite.com

FIGURE 1-2   Would you be interested in this position?

Information technology (**IT**) is a combination of hardware, software, and telecommunications systems that support business operations, improve productivity, and help managers make decisions. To deal with the explosive growth in IT, employers must compete to hire the best and brightest people they can find. A key part of IT involves **systems analysis and design**, which is the process of developing **information systems** that effectively use hardware, software, data, processes, and people to support the company's business objectives.

A **systems analyst** working in the IT department plans, analyzes, and implements information systems. Would you apply for the systems analyst position described in Figure 1-2?

You can find many similar ads in newspapers, in magazines, or on IT company Web sites. Employment experts predict a shortage of qualified workers to fill IT positions, which creates a high demand for individuals with the right mix of skills, knowledge, and experience to fill those positions. Many IT companies list employment opportunities on their Web sites and aggressively recruit people for IT positions, as shown in Figure 1-3.

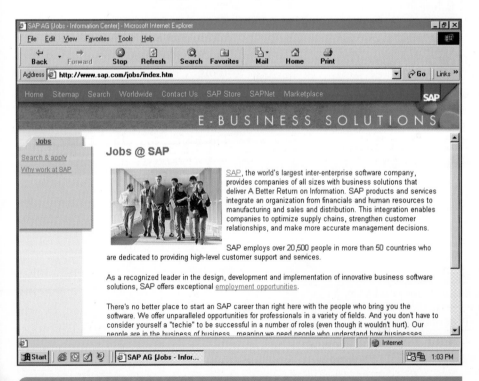

FIGURE 1-3   SAP, a leading software company, advertises employment opportunities on its Web site.

Business success depends on IT. According to an IBM study of more than 3,000 organizations, most companies use IT to serve their customers better, provide more access to information, respond more quickly to business changes, and increase employee productivity. The study confirmed that information systems must be aligned with customer expectations and business needs — not the other way around. The IBM study suggested that teams of IT professionals, managers, and users must build a shared business model, as shown in Figure 1-4.

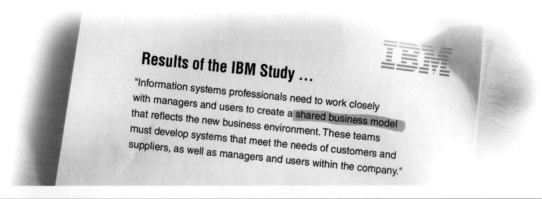

Results of the IBM Study ...

"Information systems professionals need to work closely with managers and users to create a shared business model that reflects the new business environment. These teams must develop systems that meet the needs of customers and suppliers, as well as managers and users within the company."

FIGURE 1-4   IBM's study suggests a strategy for systems development.

BUSINESS PROCESS MODELING

IT professionals must understand a company's business operations in order to design successful systems. Each business situation is different. For example, a retail store, an Internet auction site, and a hotel chain all have unique information systems requirements. Systems analysts use a process called **business process modeling** to represent a company's operations and information needs.

Business Profiles, Models, and Processes

A **business profile** defines a company's overall functions, processes, organization, products, services, customers, suppliers, competitors, constraints, and future direction. To understand a company's operations, systems analysts first develop a business profile and then create a series of business models. A **business model** graphically represents business functions that consist of business processes, such as sales, accounting, and purchasing, which perform specific tasks. A **business process** describes specific events, tasks, and desired results. Figure 1-5 shows a business process called HANDLE SALES ORDER that includes an event, three subprocesses, and a result. When companies attempt to simplify operations or reduce costs, they engage in **business process reengineering**.

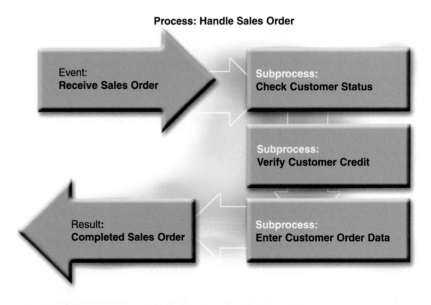

Process: Handle Sales Order

Event:
Receive Sales Order

Subprocess:
Check Customer Status

Subprocess:
Verify Customer Credit

Result:
Completed Sales Order

Subprocess:
Enter Customer Order Data

FIGURE 1-5   A business model might consist of an event, three subprocesses, and a result.

INFORMATION SYSTEM COMPONENTS

A **system** is a set of related components that produces specific results. For example, specialized systems manage the engine in your car, operate your microwave oven, and control an event as complex as the NASA launch shown in Figure 1-6. Companies support their business operations with information systems that manage data and information. When an information system is vital to the company's operations, it is called a **mission-critical system**.

FIGURE 1-6   Systems can be simple or complex. Imagine the systems used to launch the space shuttle into orbit and return it to Earth safely.

Every system requires some form of input data. For example, your car's engine receives data when you press down on the accelerator, and your microwave oven receives data when you press buttons to control cooking time and temperature. In an information system, **data** consists of basic facts that are the system's raw material. For example, Figure 1-7 shows a customer order entry system that assigns an order number and displays a blank order form. After a sales rep enters the input data (customer number, product code, and quantity ordered), the order entry system creates a customer order that contains the required information.

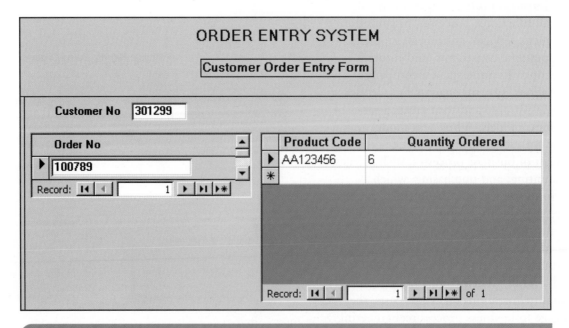

FIGURE 1-7   After a sales representative enters input data, the order entry system creates a sales order.

Information is data that has been changed into a useful form of output. The task of changing data into information is called **processing**. Powerful computers, such as the servers pictured in Figure 1-8, can process, access, and manage data today in ways that could not have been imagined 10 years ago.

An information system has five key components, as shown in Figure 1-9: hardware, software, data, processes, and people.

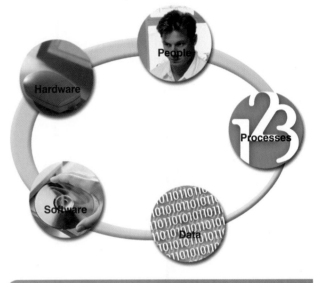

FIGURE 1-8 Multiple servers provide the power and speed that modern IT systems require.

FIGURE 1-9 Components of an information system.

Hardware

Hardware refers to the physical layer of the information system. Hardware includes computers, networks, communications equipment, scanners, digital capture devices, and other technology-based infrastructure.

Software

Software consists of system software and application software. **System software** controls the computer and includes the operating system, device drivers that communicate with hardware, and utilities that handle tasks such as converting data into a different format, virus protection, and creating backups. In a network environment, the **network operating system** (**NOS**) controls the flow of data, provides security, and manages network accounts. Either the hardware manufacturer supplies the system software, or a company purchases it from a vendor. System software also lets users access local or wide area networks, a company intranet, or the Internet.

Application software consists of programs that support users and enable companies to carry out business functions. Users increase their productivity with tools such as spreadsheets, word processors, and database management systems. Company-wide applications include payroll systems, order entry systems, and accounts receivable systems. When the company's IT department develops an information system, it is called an **in-house application**. An alternative to in-house development is purchasing a **software package** from an outside vendor that develops and sells information systems. A **horizontal system** is a basic system, such as an inventory or payroll program that can be adapted for use in many companies. A **vertical system** is designed to meet the unique requirements of a specific business or industry, such as a Web-based retailer or a video rental chain.

Most companies use a combination of in-house developed software and software packages. When planning information systems, companies must consider how newly acquired systems will interface with older systems, or **legacy systems**. For example, a new human resources information system might need to exchange data with an existing payroll application. For both systems to process data correctly, they must be able to exchange data.

Data

An information system transforms data into useful information. As shown in Figure 1-10, data about each employee and the employee's pay rate and deductions is stored in the EMPLOYEES table. Data about the employee's current hours worked and the pay period is stored in the PAYROLL table. The information system uses data from both tables to calculate the employee's gross pay and to produce a paycheck that subtracts taxes and deductions from total earnings.

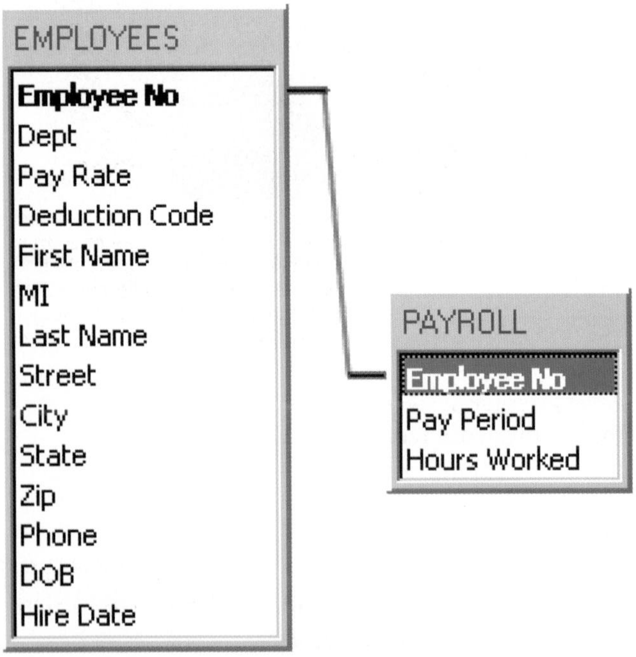

Processes

Processes, or **procedures**, describe the tasks that users, managers, and IT staff members perform. Processes necessary to support a specific business model are described in written documentation manuals and online reference materials.

People

The primary purpose of an information system is to provide valuable information to managers and users within and outside the company. **Users**, sometimes called **end users**, include employees, customers, vendors, and others who interact with an information system. Internal users include managers, technicians, sales reps, and corporate officers. External users include customers who track their orders on the company's Web site, suppliers who use a customer's system to plan their manufacturing schedules, and employees who log on to the company's intranet from home to check their e-mail messages. The success or failure of a system usually depends on whether users are satisfied with the system's output and operations.

Successful information systems also require the efforts of skilled professionals, such as systems analysts, programmers, and IT managers. Above all, information systems must fulfill business needs and support company objectives.

EMPLOYEES
- **Employee No**
- Dept
- Pay Rate
- Deduction Code
- First Name
- MI
- Last Name
- Street
- City
- State
- Zip
- Phone
- DOB
- Hire Date

PAYROLL
- **Employee No**
- Pay Period
- Hours Worked

FIGURE 1-10 An information system uses data stored in two tables to produce a paycheck.

BUSINESS INFORMATION SYSTEMS

A systems analyst must understand a company's business information systems needs. For example, the requirements of a Web-based music retailer are very different from those of a hotel chain or a truck manufacturer.

An analyst builds a business profile by investigating a company's mix of products and services and its ability to use the Internet to conduct business. The analyst also studies the interactivity among information systems, system boundaries, and specialized business information needs, as well as the company's size and future growth projections.

Categories of Companies

Traditionally, companies have been identified as production-oriented or service-oriented. A new category includes companies that depend on the Internet as a primary business channel.

Production-oriented companies primarily manufacture and sell products, such as the microchips shown in Figure 1-11. Motorola, Intel, and Compaq are examples of production-oriented companies. **Service-oriented** companies primarily offer information or services, or sell goods produced by others. AT&T, United Airlines, and Wal-Mart are examples of service companies. Some companies offer a mix of products, services, information, and technical resources to customers. For example, IBM reported in a recent financial statement that more than 58 percent of its total revenue was derived from the sale of software, services, and maintenance, compared with 42 percent from hardware sales. Although IBM still manufactures and sells technology products, it also operates an international consulting division, a leasing unit, and a financial services branch.

A new category of company is the **Internet-dependent firm**, which is often described as a **dot-com** (.com) company because it bases its primary business on a commercial Web site rather than using traditional business channels. Amazon.com and e-trade.com are examples of dot-com companies. At the other end of the spectrum are traditional companies, sometimes called **brick-and-mortar** companies because they conduct business from a physical location instead of from a Web site. In recent years, many Internet-based companies have enjoyed spectacular growth, and the value of their company stock has soared. Some observers are skeptical and wonder whether this momentum can continue, especially if a company lacks a solid record of profitability.

FIGURE 1-11 Motorola is an example of a production-oriented company that manufactures and sells microchips and a wide variety of technology products.

The Growth of E-Commerce

One of the faster-growing business sectors is Internet-based commerce, commonly called **e-commerce (electronic commerce)** or **I-commerce (Internet commerce)**. E-commerce includes both **B2C (Business-to-Consumer)** and **B2B (business-to-business)**. The demand for e-commerce systems will translate into career opportunities and new challenges for systems developers, another name for systems analysts. The October 4, 1999 issue of *INFOWORLD* magazine predicted that online retail sales would grow from $7.8 billion in 1999 to a staggering $108 billion in 2003. If that forecast is accurate, the trend will increase job opportunities for all IT professionals.

Advances in technology have greatly expanded the role of e-commerce in business. Some business analysts believe that the Internet is changing consumer buying habits and reshaping the economy. Many large and small businesses alike are developing strategies to survive in this new environment. To succeed in Web-based marketing, a company must offer an attractive user interface that is reliable, powerful, and secure.

E-commerce is changing traditional business models and creating new ones. For example, a common business model is a retail store that sells a product to a customer who physically visits the store. To carry out that same transaction on the Internet, however, the company must develop a different business model and deal with a different set of marketing, advertising, and profitability issues. Another e-commerce example is a company that takes a well-established business model, such as an auction, and extends it dramatically. Firms such as e-bay.com have transformed a traditional marketing concept into a new, enormously popular and successful method of buying goods and services.

ON THE WEB

For additional information on E-commerce visit scsite.com/sad4e/more.htm click Systems Analysis and Design Chapter 1 and then click the E-commerce link.

www.scsite.c

As more companies develop Web-based business models, new roles and opportunities for systems analysts will be created. The earliest e-commerce leaders were Internet start-up companies, such as Amazon.com and e-trade.com, but many traditional brick-and-mortar firms are beginning to capitalize on the Internet's enormous potential. Although they got off to a slow start in the e-commerce wars, many brick-and-mortar companies have substantial resources and world wide brand recognition. The September 18, 2000 issue of *INFOWORLD* magazine reported that "...brick-and-mortar powerhouses have been quietly incubating the next wave of e-commerce companies, ready to trounce their dot-com competition."

Characteristics of Information Systems

An analyst learns about an information system by asking questions about the system and how it supports business operations. As a systems analyst, you might ask the following questions as you complete your work:

1. Does this system interact with other systems? Figure 1-12 shows major business systems and communications links in a large company. The arrows in the figure show how data flows between the interactive systems. For example, a purchasing system generates orders that become input for a production system. Each system interacts with a finance system that monitors the company's profitability. A breakdown in any one system can affect company operations drastically. Reliable, secure communication links are vital when companies rely on telecommunications and the Internet for mission-critical systems.

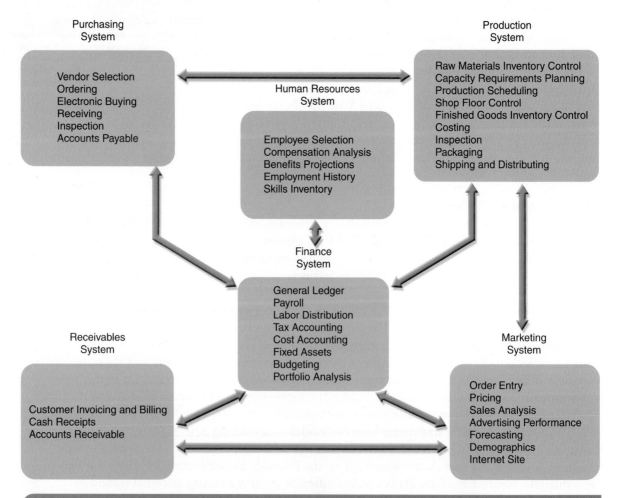

FIGURE 1-12   Arrows show the flow of data and information among typical business information systems and subsystems in an industrial company.

A company's information system also can interface with a system operated by another firm, such as when a payment is made by one company's accounts payable system to another company's accounts receivable system. This process, known as **electronic data interchange** (**EDI**), involves the computer-to-computer transfer of data between companies. EDI has expanded rapidly as companies form closer working relationships with their suppliers and customers. In the past, EDI was used mainly for processing transactions between two companies, such as purchasing or payments. Today, EDI can help a firm plan its production, adjust inventory levels, or stock up on raw materials using data that comes from another company's information systems.

2. What are the system's boundaries? A **system boundary** indicates where one system ends and another system begins. The boundary between two systems is not always clear-cut. For example, when are customer payments part of the accounts receivable system, and when are they included in the finance system? If customer payments need to be adjusted, must the adjustments take place in both systems? Who makes the adjustments? What processes and files are involved? Complex systems have many interfaces with other systems; the systems analyst must carefully plan and design these systems to design their boundaries correctly.

3. Will the system handle specialized business needs? Many firms require **specialized systems** for information management that is unique to their company or industry. At a college, for example, specialized systems handle class registration, classroom scheduling, and student grading. At a hospital, specialized systems manage patient admissions, room scheduling, and insurance billing. Firms in the banking, insurance, airlines, and telecommunications industries require complex systems to run their businesses. If a specialized system is available as a vertical software package, a company can purchase and customize the package. Otherwise, a company must develop specialized in-house systems.

4. What size is the company, and what growth is forecast? Large and small companies in the same industry have different information systems requirements. For example, banks range in size from local operations with one or two branches to multinational banks with branches in many states and foreign countries. All banks handle loan processing and checking accounts. A multinational bank, however, has a much higher volume of customers, transactions, and accounts. A large bank's systems are more complex because they consolidate information from banking centers around the world, handle currency exchange issues, and offer a wide array of products and services.

ON THE WEB

For an overview of Electronic Data Interchange visit scsite.com/sad4e/more.htm click Systems Analysis and Design Chapter 1 and then click the Electronic Data Interchange link.

www.scsite.c

TYPES OF BUSINESS INFORMATION SYSTEMS

Large companies require many different types of information systems. In the past, IT managers divided systems into categories based on the audience they served. Traditional categories included office systems (used by administrative staff), operational systems (used by operational personnel), management information systems (used by lower- and middle-level managers), and executive information systems (used by top managers). Other categories were decision support systems (used primarily by business planners) and expert systems (used by employees to control complex processes or diagnose problems).

Today, the traditional labels no longer apply. For example, all employees, including top managers, use office systems. Similarly, operational personnel often require information support from what formerly were called management information systems. Now, it is more useful to identify a system by its functions and features, rather than by its users. On that basis, today's systems include enterprise computing systems, transaction processing systems, business support systems, knowledge management systems, and user productivity systems.

Enterprise Computing Systems

Enterprise computing refers to information systems that support company-wide data management requirements. Airline reservation and credit card billing systems are examples of enterprise computing systems. Enterprise computing also can improve data security and reliability by imposing a company-wide framework for data access and storage. In many large companies, applications called **enterprise resource planning** (ERP) systems provide cost-effective data access for users and managers throughout the company. For example, a car rental company can use ERP to forecast customer demand for rental cars at hundreds of locations.

Many hardware and software vendors target the enterprise computing market and offer a wide array of products and services. Figure 1-13 shows a Web site maintained by Microsoft that is dedicated to enterprise computing marketing.

N THE WEB

r more detail on Enterprise esource Planning visit csite.com/sad4e/more.htm, ck Systems Analysis and esign Chapter 1 and then ck the Enterprise Resource lanning link.

w.scsite.com

FIGURE 1-13 Microsoft Corporation maintains a site dedicated to enterprise computing.

Transaction Processing Systems

Transaction processing (TP) systems and **online transaction processing** (OLTP) systems are called **operational systems** because they process data generated by day-to-day business operations. Examples of TP systems include customer billing, accounts receivable, and warranty claim processing.

TP captures necessary data and triggers a set of updates when a specific transaction occurs, such as a sales order. In the example shown in Figure 1-14, a single sales transaction must verify customer data, check the customer's credit status, post the invoice to the accounts receivable system, check to ensure that the requested item is in stock, adjust inventory data to reflect a sale, and update the sales activity file. TP systems typically involve very large amounts of data. To increase efficiency, TP systems process a set of transaction-related commands as a group rather than individually. TP systems also ensure that if any one element of a transaction fails, the system cannot process the rest of the transaction. This feature is known as **data integrity**. Most transaction processing systems are mission-critical systems that cannot be interrupted without severe disruption to the business.

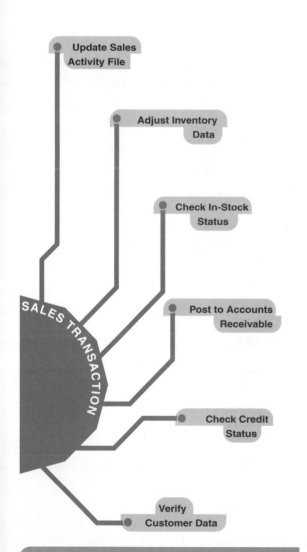

FIGURE 1-14 A single sales transaction consists of six separate tasks.

Business Support Systems

Business support systems (BSS) provide job-related information support to users at all levels of a company. These systems can analyze transactional data, generate information needed to manage and control business processes, and provide information that leads to better decision making.

Early business computer systems were operational systems that replaced manual tasks such as payroll processing. Companies soon realized that computers also could produce valuable information. The new systems were called **management information systems (MISs)** because primarily managers used them. Today, employees at all levels need information to perform their jobs, and they rely on information systems for that support.

An information system must generate timely and accurate records. For example, when a company sells merchandise to a customer, a transaction processing system records the sale, updates the customer's balance, and makes a deduction from inventory. A related business support system can highlight slow- or fast-moving items, customers with past due balances, and inventory items that need reordering. Managers, buyers, and inventory control specialists all use information to make better decisions. Large retail chains use point-of-sale scanners such as the one shown in Figure 1-15 to collect sales information that can be used to spot trends quickly, identify hot product items, and maintain a competitive edge.

An important feature of a business support system is decision support capability to conduct a **what-if analysis**. **Decision support** helps users make decisions by creating a business model and applying a set of variables. For example, a truck fleet dispatcher might run a series of what-if scenarios to determine the impact of increased demand or bad weather on the fleet's capability of delivering goods on time. Alternatively, a retailer might use what-if analysis to determine the price it must charge to increase profits by 10 percent assuming that volume and costs remain unchanged.

FIGURE 1-15 Scanners are used to input data into the system. They offer the advantages of accuracy and processing speed.

Knowledge Management Systems

Knowledge management systems are sometimes called **expert systems** because they simulate human reasoning by combining a knowledge base and inference rules that determine how the knowledge is applied. A **knowledge base** consisting of a large database allows users to find information by clicking menus, typing keywords, or entering text questions in normal English phrases. In a knowledge management system, logical rules named **inference rules** identify data patterns and relationships. For example, a data inquiry using the phrase *data screen* would produce different results than the phrase *screen data* because of the word order.

Figure 1-16 illustrates a technical support knowledge base in a Web site maintained by Novell for its customers and users. After a user enters a symptom, problem, or question, Novell's knowledge management system searches for a solution.

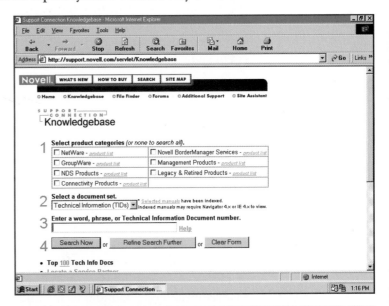

FIGURE 1-16 Novell's Web-based technical support includes a knowledge management system.

Knowledge management systems do not make decisions based on common sense or intuition as humans do. Many knowledge management systems use an approach called **fuzzy logic** that allows logical inferences to be drawn from imprecise relationships. Using fuzzy logic, values need not be black and white, like binary logic, but can be many shades of gray. For example, if you ask the Novell Knowledgebase (shown in Figure 1-16 on the previous page) to find information about user password administration, it will search the knowledge base for articles with those terms. Using fuzzy logic, the results will be displayed in priority order, with those that are presumably more relevant at the top of the list.

User Productivity Systems

User productivity systems provide employees at all organizational levels with a wide array of tools that can improve quality and job performance. Local and wide area networking, e-mail, voice mail, fax, video conferencing, word processing, automated calendars, database management, spreadsheets, desktop publishing, presentation graphics, company intranets, and Internet access throughout the company enhance user productivity.

When companies first installed word processing systems, managers expected to reduce the number of employees as office efficiency increased. That did not happen, primarily because the basic nature of clerical work changed. As the country shifted from an industrial to a service economy, companies required a new class of knowledge workers who needed constant access to information. This group grew rapidly as companies assigned more responsibility to employees at lower organizational levels. Relatively inexpensive hardware, powerful networks, corporate downsizing, and a move toward employee empowerment also have contributed to this trend. Today, administrative assistants and company presidents alike are networked, use their computer workstations, and share corporate data as they perform their jobs.

Information Systems Integration

Most large companies require systems that combine enterprise computing, transaction processing, business support, knowledge management, and user productivity features. For example, suppose an international customer has a problem with a product and makes a warranty claim. A customer service representative enters the claim into a transaction processing system. The transaction updates two other systems: a knowledge management system that has a history of product problems and warranty activity, and a quality control tracking system with decision support capabilities. A quality control engineer uses what-if analysis to determine if it would be less expensive to make certain design changes in the product that would reduce warranty claims. In this example, a transaction processing system is integrated with a knowledge management system and a business support system with decision support features.

ORGANIZATIONAL STRUCTURE

Corporate organizational structure has changed in recent years. As part of downsizing and business process reengineering, many companies reduced the number of management levels and delegated responsibility to operational personnel. Although the organization chart tends to be somewhat flatter, a traditional hierarchy still exists in most companies. In the typical organizational model shown in Figure 1-17, operational personnel report to lower- and middle-level managers, who in turn report to top managers. In a corporate structure, the top managers report to the board of directors that is elected by the company's shareholders. Although titles vary, distinct levels of responsibility exist. A systems analyst must understand the company's organizational model in order to recognize who is responsible for business processes and decisions and, hence, to be aware of what information is required by whom.

N THE WEB

learn more about User roductivity Systems visit site.com/sad4e/more.htm, ick Systems Analysis and esign Chapter 1 and then ick the User Productivity stems link.

w.scsite.com

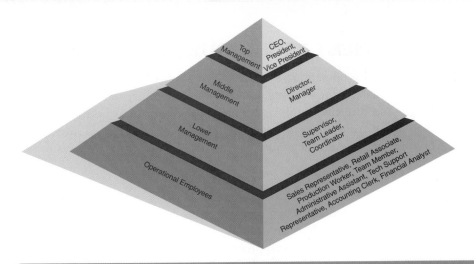

FIGURE 1-17 Organizational model of a typical company.

Top Management

Top managers develop long-range plans, called **strategic plans** that define the company's overall mission and goals. To carry out that task, top managers ask questions such as "How much should the company invest in information technology," or "How much will Internet sales grow in the next five years," or "Should the company build new factories or contract out the production functions?"

Strategic planning focuses on issues that affect the company's future survival and growth, including long-term IT plans. Top managers focus on the entire business enterprise and use information systems to set the company's course and direction. To develop a strategic plan, top managers also need information from outside the company, such as economic forecasts, technology trends, competitive threats, governmental issues, and shareholder concerns.

Middle Management

Middle managers focus their goals on a shorter time frame, usually ranging from one month to one year. They develop plans to achieve business objectives in a process called **tactical planning**. Middle managers delegate authority and responsibility to team leaders or supervisors and then provide direction, necessary resources, and feedback on performance as tasks are completed.

Middle managers need more detailed information than top managers, but somewhat less information than team leaders and supervisors. For example, a middle manager might review a weekly sales summary for a geographic region, whereas a sales team leader would need a daily report on customer activity. Middle managers also use business support systems, knowledge management systems, and user productivity systems to perform their jobs.

Lower Management

Supervisors and team leaders oversee operational employees and carry out day-to-day **operational plans**. They coordinate operational tasks, make necessary decisions, and ensure that the right tools, materials, and training are available. Like other managers, this group often needs decision support information, consults knowledge management systems, and relies on user productivity systems to carry out their day-to-day responsibilities.

Operational Employees

Operational employees primarily use TP systems to enter and receive data they need to perform their jobs. In many companies, operational employees also need information to handle tasks and make decisions that were assigned previously to supervisors. This trend, called **empowerment**, gives employees more responsibility and accountability. Many companies find that empowerment leads to better employee motivation and increased customer satisfaction.

SYSTEMS DEVELOPMENT TECHNIQUES AND TOOLS

In addition to understanding business operations, systems analysts must know how to use a variety of techniques, such as modeling, prototyping, and computer-aided systems engineering (CASE) tools, to plan, design, and implement information systems. They must be able to work in team environments where input from users, managers, and IT staff is synthesized into a design that will meet everyone's needs. And they must be able to use other software tools to illustrate accurately their designs and ideas.

Modeling

Modeling produces a graphical representation of a concept or process that systems developers can analyze, test, and modify. A systems analyst can describe and simplify an information system by using a set of business, data, object, network, and process models.

A **business model**, or **requirements model**, describes business functions that an information system must support. A **data model** describes data structures and design. An **object model** describes objects, which combine data and processes. A **network model** portrays the design and protocols of telecommunications links. A **process model** describes system logic and processes that programmers use to develop necessary code modules. Although the models might appear to overlap, they actually work together to describe the same environment from different points of view.

Modeling involves various techniques, such as data flow diagrams, entity-relationship diagrams, use cases, and unified modeling language. Those techniques are described in more detail in Chapters 3, 4, 5, and 8.

Prototyping

Prototyping involves the creation of an early working version of the information system or its components. Just as an aircraft manufacturer tests a new design in a wind tunnel, systems analysts construct and review prototypes for larger systems. Prototyping tests system concepts and provides an opportunity to examine input, output, and user interfaces before final decisions are made. The prototype can serve as an initial model that is used as a benchmark to evaluate the completed system, or the prototype itself can develop into the final version of the system. Either way, prototyping speeds up the development process significantly.

A possible disadvantage of prototyping is that important decisions might be made too early, before business or IT issues are thoroughly understood. If a prototype is based on careful fact-finding and modeling techniques, however, it can be an extremely valuable tool.

Computer-Aided Systems Engineering

Computer-aided systems engineering (CASE) is a technique that uses powerful programs, called **CASE tools**, to help systems analysts develop and maintain information systems. CASE tools provide an overall framework for systems development and support a wide variety of design methodologies, including structured analysis and object-oriented analysis.

Traditionally, systems developers differentiated between two CASE categories: upper CASE tools and lower CASE tools. **Upper CASE tools** support the modeling process and produce a logical design of the information system. **Lower CASE tools** speed the development process by generating source code based on the logical model. Today, many popular CASE tools combine upper and lower CASE features into a single product.

CASE tools can boost IT productivity and improve the quality of the finished product. For example, developers use CASE tools to maintain design integrity, manage a complex project, and generate a wide variety of business, process, and data models. Many CASE tools can build prototypes and generate code modules that speed up implementation. Figure 1-18 shows the Visible Systems Corporation Web site. Visible Systems is a leading vendor of CASE tools.

The Systems Analyst's Toolkit (Found at the back of this book) explains how systems developers use CASE tools, and provides suggestions and examples.

N THE WEB

r examples of CASE
ols visit scsite.com/
4e/more.htm, click
stems Analysis and Design
apter 1 and then click the
SE Tools link.

w.scsite

Joint Application Development and Rapid Application Development

In the past, the IT department typically developed information systems and contacted users only when their input was desired or needed. Unfortunately that approach often left large communication gaps between system developers and users. Over time, many companies discovered that systems development teams composed of IT staff, users, and managers could complete their work more rapidly and produce better results. Two methodologies became popular: **joint application development (JAD)** and **rapid application development (RAD)**. Both approaches use teams composed of users, managers, and IT staff to complete projects. JAD involves team-based fact-finding techniques, while RAD is more like a condensed version of the entire development process. JAD is described in more detail in Chapter 3, and RAD is explained in Part 4 of the Systems Analyst's Toolkit at the end of the book.

Other Systems Development Tools

In addition to CASE tools, a systems analyst uses various productivity tools to organize and structure the task of developing an information system. In addition to word processing, spreadsheets, graphics tools, and presentation software, analysts use special purpose charting tools. A popular example is VISIO, which is shown in Figure 1-19. A systems analyst can use Microsoft VISIO to draw flowcharts, data flow diagrams, entity-relationship diagrams, network diagrams, and business process diagrams, among others.

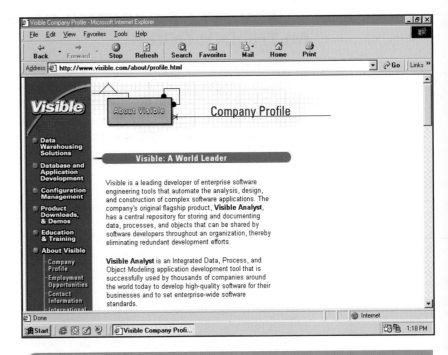

FIGURE 1-18 Visible Systems Corporation offers a variety of software engineering tools, including Visible Analyst, a popular CASE tool.

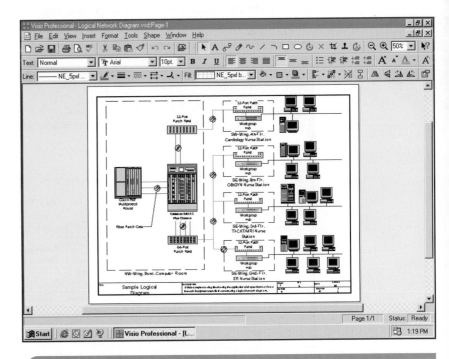

FIGURE 1-19 Microsoft VISIO is a popular multi-purpose charting tool. Shown here is a set of Microsoft VISIO modeling tools representing Cisco Systems hardware, which would be used in creating a network diagram.

OVERVIEW OF SYSTEMS DEVELOPMENT METHODOLOGIES

This section discusses the most popular methodologies for developing computer-based information systems. A popular, traditional method is called structured analysis, but a newer strategy called object-oriented analysis and design also is used widely. Each method offers many variations. Some organizations develop their own approaches or adopt methods offered by software vendors or consultants. Most IT experts agree that no single, best system development strategy exists. Instead, a systems analyst should understand the alternative methodologies and their strengths and weaknesses.

Structured Analysis

Structured analysis is a traditional systems development technique that is time-tested and easy to understand. Structured analysis evolved in a 1960s environment, where most systems were based on mainframe processing of individual data files. Because it describes the processes that transform data into useful information, structured analysis is called a **process-centered** technique. In addition to modeling the processes, structured analysis includes data organization and structure, relational database design, and user interface issues. Structured analysis uses a series of phases, called the **systems development life cycle (SDLC)** to plan, analyze, design, implement, and support an information system.

Structured analysis relies on a set of process models that graphically describe a system. Process modeling identifies the data flowing into a process, the business rules that transform the data, and the resulting output data flow. Figure 1-20 shows a simple process model that represents a school registration process with related input and output. Structured analysis is developing into a technique called information engineering. **Information engineering**, like enterprise computing, envisions the overall business enterprise and how corporate data and processes interact throughout the organization.

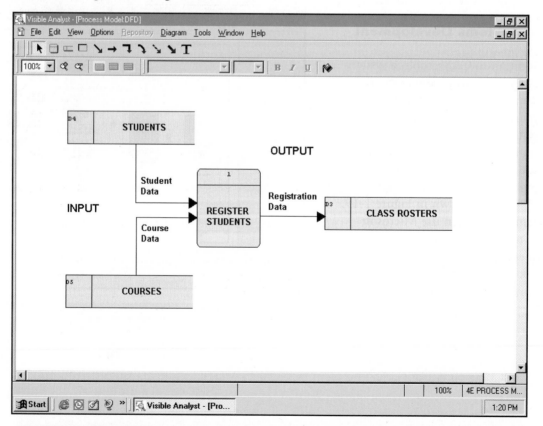

FIGURE 1-20   A process model for a school registration system shows a process that accepts input data from two sources and transforms it into output data.

Object-Oriented Analysis

Whereas structured analysis regards processes and data as separate components, **object-oriented (O-O) analysis** combines data and the processes that act on the data into things called objects. Systems analysts use O-O methods to model real-world business processes and operations. The result is a set of software objects that represent actual people, things, transactions, and events. Using an O-O programming language, a programmer then transforms the objects into reusable code and components.

An **object** is a member of a **class**, which is a collection of similar objects. Objects possess characteristics called **properties**, which it inherits from its class or possesses on its own. As shown in Figure 1-21, the class named PERSON includes INSTRUCTOR and STUDENT. Because the PERSON class has a property named *Address*, a STUDENT inherits an *Address* property. A STUDENT also has a property named *Major* that is not shared by other members of the PERSON class.

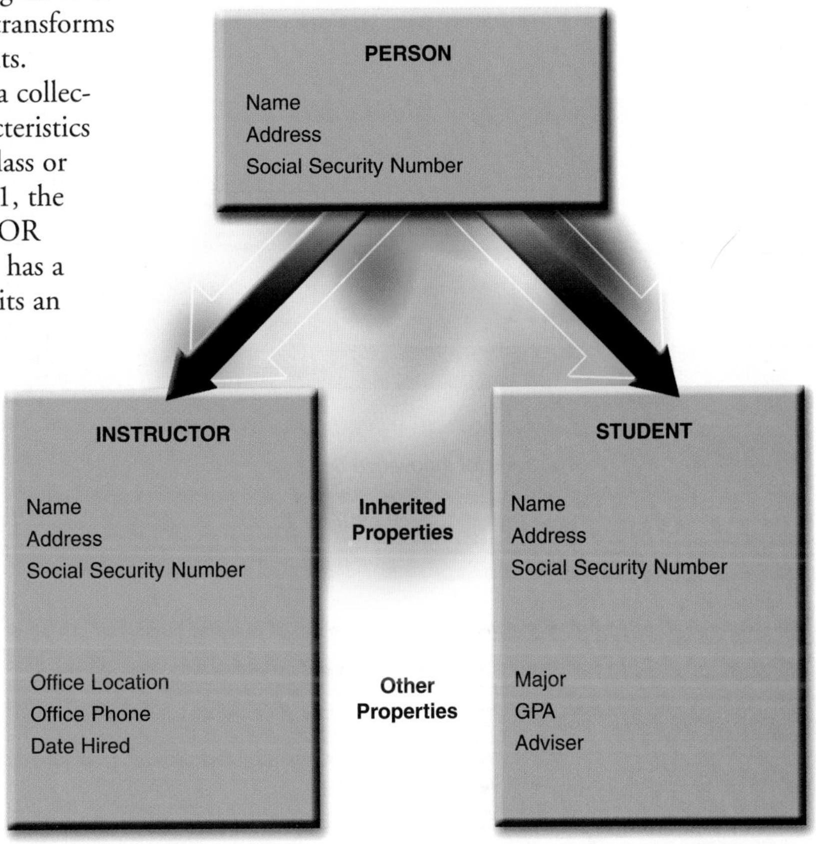

In O-O programming, built-in processes called **methods** can change an object's properties. For example, a sailboat object might have a property named sailing speed that can be changed by methods that raise and lower its sails. One object can send information to another object by using a **message**. A message can request specific behavior or information from the recipient. For example, if there is no wind, a sailboat owner object might send a "start the motor" message to the sailboat object. The owner object has the capability to send this message, and the sailboat object knows what actions to perform when it receives the message.

FIGURE 1-21 The PERSON class includes INSTRUCTOR and STUDENT objects, both have inherited properties and other properties.

O-O analysis uses object models to represent data, behavior, and by what means objects affect other objects. By describing the objects (data) and methods (processes) needed to support a business operation, a system developer can design reusable components that allow faster system implementation and decreased development cost.

Many analysts believe that, compared with structured analysis, O-O methods are more flexible, efficient, and realistic in today's dynamic business environment. Also, O-O analysis provides an easy transition to popular O-O programming languages, such as Java and C++. Chapter 5 covers O-O analysis and design and describes O-O terms, concepts, tools, and techniques in detail.

Other Development Strategies

In addition to structured analysis and O-O methodologies, you might encounter other systems development techniques created by individual companies. For example, Microsoft has developed an approach called **Microsoft Solutions Framework (MSF)**, as shown in Figure 1-22 that documents the experience of its own IT teams. MSF is described in more detail in Part 4 of the Systems Analyst's Toolkit.

Using MSF, you design a series of models, including a risk management model, a team model, and a process model, among others. Each model has a specific purpose and outputs that contribute to the overall design of the system. Although the Microsoft process differs from the SDLC phase-oriented approach, MSF developers do the same kind of planning, ask the same kinds of fact-finding questions, deal with the same kinds of design and implementation issues, and resolve the same kinds of problems. MSF uses O-O analysis and design concepts, but also examines a broader business and organizational context that surrounds the development of an information system.

Companies often choose to follow their own methodology. By using powerful CASE tools, an IT staff can apply a variety of techniques rather than being bound to a single, rigid methodology. For example, the Popkin Software CASE tool described in Figure 1-23 offers a complete set of analysis and modeling tools that support many methodologies and strategies. If a systems analyst needs additional choices, he or she can choose from an entire industry of IT software companies and consulting firms.

FIGURE 1-22 Microsoft Corporation offers a systems development methodology called Microsoft Solutions Framework (MSF) that relies on a set of concepts and models.

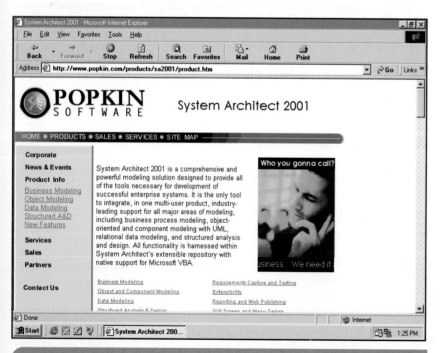

FIGURE 1-23 Popkin Software offers a CASE tool called System Architect 2001, which supports a wide variety of methodologies and strategies.

THE SYSTEMS DEVELOPMENT LIFE CYCLE

Structured analysis uses a technique called the systems development life cycle (SDLC) to plan and manage the systems development process. Although it is primarily identified with structured analysis, the SDLC describes activities and functions that systems developers typically perform, regardless of how those activities and functions fit into a particular methodology. The SDLC model includes the following steps:

1. Systems planning

2. Systems analysis

3. Systems design

4. Systems implementation

5. Systems operation and support

Traditionally, the SDLC is pictured as a **waterfall model** shown in Figure 1-24, where the result of each phase, often called an **end product** or **deliverable**, flows down into the next phase. In reality, the systems development process is dynamic, and constant change is common. Figure 1-25 represents an alternative model, where planning, analysis, and design interact. This **interactive model** depicts real-world practice and the constant dialog among users, managers, and systems developers.

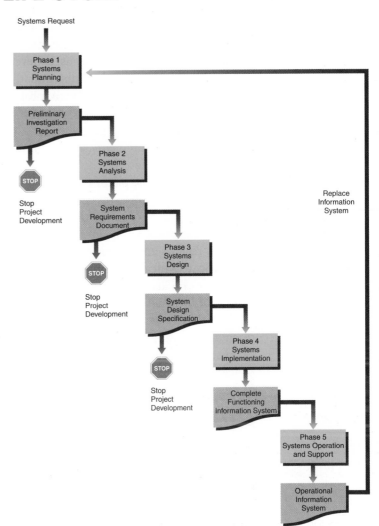

FIGURE 1-24 The phases and end products of the systems development life cycle (SDLC).

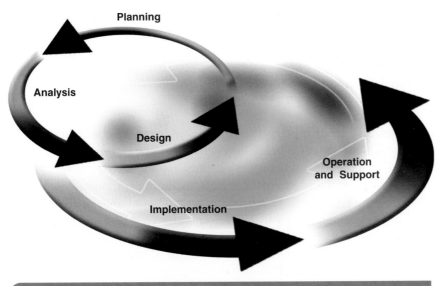

FIGURE 1-25 An alternative model of the SDLC that shows the interaction of planning, analysis, and design, which leads to implementation and then to operation and support.

ON THE WEB

For more information on the Systems Development Life Cycle (SDLC) visit scsite.com/sad4e/more.htm click Systems Analysis and Design Chapter 1 and then click the Systems Development Life Cycle (SDLC) link.

www.scsite.c

Systems Planning

Systems planning usually begins with a formal request to the IT department, called a **systems request** that describes problems or desired changes in an information system or a business process. In many companies today, IT systems planning is an integral part of overall business planning. When managers and users develop strategic, tactical, and operational plans, they include IT requirements that subsequently generate systems requests.

A systems request can come from a top manager, a planning team, a department head, or the IT department itself. The request can be very significant or relatively minor. A major request might involve a new information system or the replacement of an existing system that cannot handle current requirements. In contrast, a minor request might ask for a new feature or a change to the user interface.

The purpose of the planning phase is to identify clearly the nature and scope of the business opportunity or problem by performing a **preliminary investigation**, often called a **feasibility study**. The preliminary investigation is a critical step because the outcome will affect the entire development process. The end product, or deliverable, is a report that describes business considerations, reviews anticipated benefits and costs, and recommends a course of action based on economic, technical, and operational factors.

Suppose you are a systems analyst and you receive a request for system changes or improvements. Your first step is to determine whether it makes sense to launch a preliminary investigation at all. Often you will need to learn more about business operations before you can reach a conclusion. After an investigation, you might find that the system functions well, but that users need more training. In some situations, you might recommend a business process review, rather than an IT solution. In other cases, you might conclude that a full-scale systems review is necessary. If the development process continues, the next step is systems analysis.

Systems Analysis

The purpose of the systems analysis phase is to understand business requirements and build a logical model of the new system. The first step is **requirements modeling**, where you define and describe business processes. Requirements modeling continues the investigation that began during systems planning and involves various fact-finding techniques, such as interviews, surveys, observation, and sampling.

During the next tasks, **data modeling**, **process modeling**, and **object modeling**, you develop a logical model of business processes the system must support. The model consists of various types of diagrams, depending on the methodology being used.

The end product for the systems analysis phase is the system requirements document. The **system requirements document** describes management and user requirements, alternative plans and costs, and your recommendation.

Looking ahead to design and implementation, several possibilities exist: develop a new system in-house, purchase a commercial package, or modify an existing system.

Systems Design

The purpose of **systems design** is to create a blueprint for the new system that will satisfy all documented requirements, whether the system is being developed in-house or purchased as a package. During systems design, you identify all necessary outputs, inputs, interfaces, and processes. In addition, you design internal and external controls, including computer-based and manual features to guarantee that the system will be reliable, accurate, maintainable, and secure.

The design is documented in the **systems design specification** and presented to management and users for their review and approval. Management and user involvement is critical to avoid any misunderstandings about what the new system will do, how it will do it, and what it will cost.

Systems Implementation

During **systems implementation**, the new system is constructed. Whether the developers used structured analysis or O-O methods, the procedure is the same — programs are written, tested, and documented, and the system is installed. If the system was purchased as a package, systems analysts perform any necessary modifications and configurations. The objective of the implementation phase is to deliver a completely functioning and documented information system.

At the conclusion of this phase, the system is ready for use. Final preparations include converting data to the new system's files, training users, and performing the actual transition to the new system. The systems implementation phase also includes an assessment, called a **systems evaluation**, to determine whether the system operates properly and if costs and benefits are within expectations.

Systems Operation and Support

During **systems operation and support**, the IT staff maintains and enhances the system. **Maintenance** changes correct errors and adapt to changes in the environment, such as new tax rates. **Enhancements** provide new features and benefits. The objective during this phase is to maximize return on the IT investment. A well-designed system will be reliable, maintainable, and scalable. A **scalable** design can expand to meet new business requirements and volumes.

Information systems development is always a work in progress. Business processes change rapidly, and most information systems need to be replaced or significantly updated after several years of operation.

Systems Development Guidelines

As you gain experience as a systems analyst, you will develop your own style and techniques. Although each project is different, you should consider some basic guidelines as you build an information system:

1. Stick to an overall development plan. If you use an O-O methodology, follow a logical series of steps as you define the components. If you use the SDLC as a framework for systems development, complete the phases in sequence.

2. Ensure that users are involved in the development process, especially when identifying and modeling system requirements. Modeling and prototyping can help you understand user needs and develop a better system.

3. Identify major milestones for project review and assessment. At those milestones, managers and systems developers must decide whether to proceed with the project, redo certain tasks, return to an earlier phase, or terminate the project entirely. The SDLC model requires formal assessment of end products and deliverables. O-O analysis involves a continuous modeling process that also requires checkpoints and project review.

4. Establish interim checkpoints between major milestones to ensure that the project remains on schedule. Regardless of the development methodology, the systems analyst must keep the project on track and avoid surprises. Create a reasonable number of checkpoints — too many can be burdensome, but too few will not provide adequate control. An example of a checkpoint might be the completion of interviews conducted during a preliminary investigation.

5. Be flexible within the framework of your plan. Systems development is a dynamic process and overlap often exists between the phases of systems planning, analysis, design, and implementation. For example, when you investigate a systems request, you begin a fact-finding process that often carries over into the next phase. Similarly, you often start building process models before fact-finding is complete. The ability to overlap phases is especially important when you are working on a system that must be developed rapidly. The Systems Analyst's Toolkit describes project development strategies, such as JAD and RAD, and project management tools that can help you manage multiple tasks.

6. Provide accurate and reliable cost and benefit information. Managers want to know the cost of developing and operating a system. At the start of each phase, you must provide specific cost estimates. You should avoid a **project creep**, which describes a project that gradually expands and becomes more expensive.

WHAT DO YOU THINK?

Suppose you work in the IT department of Global Hotels, a multinational firm. Global Hotels runs several specialized business support systems, including a guest reservations system that was developed in-house to meet the requirements of a large company with worldwide operations. Global Hotels' reservations system has links to all major travel industry sites and the capability for guests to make reservations directly using the company's Web site.

Global Hotels just acquired Momma's, a regional chain of 20 motels in western Canada. Momma's uses a vertical reservations package suitable for small- to medium-sized businesses, and a generic accounting and finance package. Should Momma's use Global Hotels' information systems or continue with its own? In your answer, consider issues such as business profiles, business processes, system interactivity, EDI, e-commerce, and the characteristics of both information systems.

INFORMATION TECHNOLOGY DEPARTMENT

The **information technology (IT) department** develops and maintains a company's information systems. The structure of the IT department varies among companies, as does its name and placement within the organization. In a small firm, one person might handle all computer support activities and services, whereas a large corporation might require many people with specialized skills to provide information systems support. Figure 1-26 shows a typical IT organization in a company that has networked PCs, enterprise-wide databases, centralized processing, and a Web site. The IT group provides **technical support**, which includes six main functions: application development, systems support, user support, database administration, network administration, and Web support. These functions overlap considerably and often have different names in different companies.

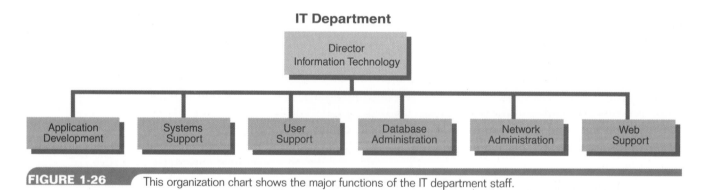

FIGURE 1-26 This organization chart shows the major functions of the IT department staff.

Application Development

Traditionally, IT departments had an **application development group** composed of systems analysts and programmers who handled information system design, development, and implementation. Today, many companies use development teams consisting of users, managers, and IT staff members for those same tasks. A popular model for information systems development is a project-oriented team using RAD or JAD, with IT professionals providing overall coordination, guidance, and technical support.

Systems Support

Systems support provides hardware and software support for enterprise computing systems, networks, transaction processing systems, and corporate IT infrastructure. The systems support group installs and supports operating systems, telecommunications software, and centralized database management systems. Systems support technicians also provide technical support to other groups in the IT department. If the company does not have a separate application development group, the systems support group also coordinates new system development.

User Support

User support provides users with technical information, training, and productivity support. The user support function usually is called a **help desk** or **information center (IC)**. A helpdesk staff trains users and managers on application software such as e-mail, word processors, spreadsheets, and graphics packages. User support specialists answer questions, troubleshoot problems, and serve as a clearinghouse for user problems and solutions.

In many companies, the user support team also installs and configures software applications that are used within the organization. Although user support specialists coordinate with other technical support areas, their primary focus is user productivity and support for user business processes.

Database Administration

In a large company, **database administration** involves database design, management, security, backup, and user access. In small- and medium-sized companies, IT support persons perform those roles in addition to other duties. Regardless of company size, mission-critical database applications require full-time attention and technical support.

Network Administration

Business operations often depend on networks that enable multiuser data access and processing. **Network administration** includes hardware and software maintenance, support, and security. In addition to controlling user access, network administrators install, configure, manage, monitor, and maintain network applications.

Web Support

Web support is the most recently created technical support function. Web support specialists, often called **webmasters**, support a company's Internet and intranet operations. Web support involves design and construction of Web pages, monitoring traffic, managing hardware and software, and linking Web-based applications to the company's existing information systems. Reliable, high quality Web support is especially critical to any company engaged in e-commerce.

THE SYSTEMS ANALYST POSITION

A systems analyst investigates, analyzes, designs, develops, installs, evaluates, and maintains a company's information systems. To perform those tasks, a systems analyst constantly interacts with users and managers within and outside the company. On large projects, the analyst works as a member of an IT department team; on smaller assignments, he or she might work alone.

Most companies assign systems analysts to the IT department, but analysts also can report to a specific user area such as marketing, sales, or accounting. As a member of a functional team, an analyst is better able to understand the needs of that group and how information systems support the department's mission. Smaller companies often use consultants to perform systems analysis work on an as-needed basis.

ON THE WEB

To find out more about Systems Analyst Positions visit scsite.com/sad4e/more.htm, click Systems Analysis and Design Chapter 1 and then click the Systems Analyst Positions link.

www.scsite.c

Responsibilities

The systems analyst's job overlaps business and technical issues. Analysts translate business requirements into practical IT projects that meet the company's needs. As systems developers, analysts perform a wide array of tasks, such as building business profiles, reviewing business processes, selecting hardware and software packages, designing information systems, training users, and planning e-commerce Web sites.

A systems analyst plans projects, develops schedules, and estimates costs. To keep managers and users informed, an analyst conducts meetings, delivers presentations, and writes memos, reports, and documentation. The Systems Analyst's Toolkit at the end of this text includes tools to help you with each of those important skills.

Required Skills and Background

A systems analyst needs solid technical knowledge, strong oral and written communication skills, good analytical ability, and an understanding of business operations and processes. Companies typically require that systems analysts have a college degree in information systems, computer science, business, or a closely related field, and IT experience often is required. For higher-level positions, many companies require a master's degree and additional experience.

A systems analyst needs good interpersonal skills to deal with people at all levels, from operational staff to senior executives, including people outside the company, such as software and hardware vendors, customers, and government officials.

Often an analyst must lead an IT development team. As a team leader, an analyst plans, estimates, and manages the project, and uses leadership and team-building skills to coach and motivate team members.

State-of-the-art knowledge is extremely important in a rapidly changing business and technical environment. The Internet offers numerous opportunities to update your knowledge and skills. Many Web sites, such as the one shown in Figure 1-27, offer free subscriptions and enable IT professionals to learn about the latest technical developments, exchange experiences, and ask questions.

Analysts also maintain their skills by attending training courses and workshops and by reading periodicals and books about IT issues and trends. Networking with colleagues is another way to keep up with new developments, and membership in professional associations also is important. A systems analyst, like any other professional, needs to manage his or her own career by developing knowledge and skills that are valuable and expected in the marketplace.

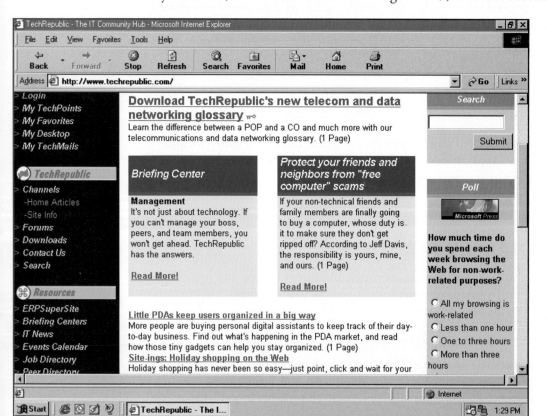

FIGURE 1-27 Example of a Web site that offers support for IT professionals, including forums, briefings, and technical information.

Certification Issues

In recent years, IT professionals have become interested in various types of certification offered by hardware and software companies. **Certification** does not guarantee competence or ability, but it does show that an individual demonstrates a certain level of knowledge and skill on a standardized test. Many companies regard certification as a credential to be considered during hiring or promotion. Certification is an excellent way for IT professionals to learn new skills and gain recognition for their efforts.

Career Opportunities

The demand for systems analysts is expected to remain strong well into the twenty-first century. Companies will need systems analysts to apply new information technology, and the explosion in e-commerce will fuel IT job growth. The systems analyst position is a challenging and rewarding one that can lead to a top management position. With an understanding of technical and business issues, a systems analyst has an unlimited horizon. Many companies have presidents and senior managers who started in IT departments as systems analysts.

The responsibilities of a systems analyst at a small firm are different from those at a large corporation. Would you be better off at a small or large company? Where will you find the best opportunity for experience and professional growth? Each person looks for different rewards in a job. What will be important to you?

JOB TITLES   First, do not rely on job titles alone. Some positions are called systems analysts, but involve only programming or technical support. In other cases, systems analyst responsibilities are found in positions titled computer specialist, programmer, programmer/analyst, systems designer, software engineer, and various others. Be sure the responsibilities of the job are stated clearly when you consider a position.

COMPANY ORGANIZATION   Find out all you can about the company and where the IT department fits in the organization chart. Where are IT functions performed, and by whom? A firm might have a central IT group, but decentralize the systems development function. This problem sometimes occurs in large conglomerates, where the parent company consolidates information that actually is developed and managed at the subsidiary level. Where would you rather work?

COMPANY SIZE   If you like more variety, then a smaller firm might suit you best. If you want to specialize, however, then consider a larger company with state-of-the-art systems. Although you might have more responsibility in a smaller company, the promotional opportunities and financial rewards often are greater in larger companies. You also might want to consider working as an independent consultant, either on your own or with others. Many consulting firms have been successful in offering their services to smaller business enterprises that do not have the expertise to handle systems development on their own.

CORPORATE CULTURE   In addition to having goals, methods, and information systems requirements, every firm has an underlying corporate culture. A **corporate culture** is the set of beliefs, rules, traditions, values, and attitudes that define a company and influence its way of doing business. To be successful, a systems analyst must understand the corporate culture and how it affects the way information is managed. Companies sometimes include statements about corporate culture in their mission statements, which are explained in Chapter 2.

SALARY, LOCATION, AND FUTURE GROWTH   Finally, consider salary, location, and the company's prospects for future growth and success. Think about your impressions of the company and the people you met during your interviews. Most important, review your short- and long-term goals very carefully before deciding which position is best for you.

W H A T   D O   Y O U   T H I N K ?

Lisa Jameson has two job offers. One is from Pembroke Boats, a builder of sailboats that employs 125 people in a small town in Ohio. Pembroke does not have an IT department and wants her to create one. The job position is called information coordinator, but she would be the only IT person.

The other offer, which pays about $7,500 more annually, is from Albemarle Express, a nation-wide trucking and warehousing firm located in Detroit. At Albemarle Express, Lisa would be a programmer-analyst, with the promise that if she does well in her position, she eventually will move into a systems analyst position and work on new systems development. Lisa has heard a rumor that another company might acquire Albemarle Express, but that rumor has occurred before and nothing has ever happened.

What should Lisa do, and why?

SOFTWEAR, LIMITED

SoftWear, Limited (SWL) is a continuing case study that illustrates the process of information systems development in a practical setting.

Background

SoftWear, Limited manufactures and sells casual and recreational clothing for men and women. SWL was formed about 10 years ago when a national firm sold the division during a corporate downsizing. A group of managers obtained financing and became owners of the company. With clever marketing, competitive pricing, and efficient production, SWL has grown to more than 450 employees, including the corporate headquarters and manufacturing plants. Last year, SWL had sales of $250 million.

Headquartered in Raleigh, North Carolina, the company employs 125 people, including officers, managers, and support staff. Another 35 salaried and 250 hourly people are employed at production facilities in Haskell, California, and Florence, Texas. The company also is in the process of building a new factory in Canada.

SWL maintains a Web site with information about the company and its products. SWL's Web site features text, graphics, and audio and allows customers to send e-mail, order products from the SoftWear catalog, and request special promotional items including beach umbrellas, hats, and T-shirts customized with the purchaser's logo. SWL also is studying other ways to use the Internet to boost product sales and expand its marketing efforts, including a special European promotion designed to increase awareness of SWL's Web site.

Organization

The headquarters includes the following departments: executive, operations, marketing, finance, and human resources. Figure 1-28 shows the organization chart of top-level management. Four vice presidents

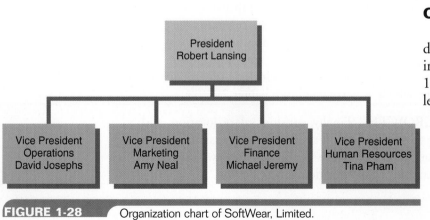

FIGURE 1-28   Organization chart of SoftWear, Limited.

Figure 1-29 shows a more detailed organization chart of the management positions within SWL. Notice that the director of information technology, Ann Hon, reports to Michael Jeremy, vice president of finance. The director of the payroll department, Amy Calico, also reports to Mr. Jeremy.

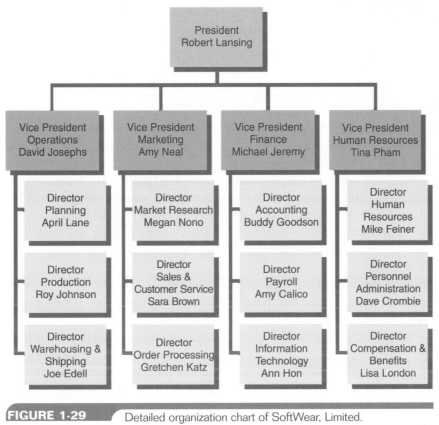

FIGURE 1-29 Detailed organization chart of SoftWear, Limited.

The IT department includes Ann Hon, the director; Jane Rossman, the systems support manager; Kerry Krauss, the user support manager; and Altovise Martin, the Web support manager. Figure 1-30 shows the organization of the IT department. At SWL, the systems support group also handles new systems development, network administration, and database administration.

Systems analysts and programmers report to Jane Rossman, systems support manager. Systems analysts primarily analyze and design information systems. Programmers primarily develop, test, and implement code necessary for systems development, enhancements, and maintenance. In addition to the current staff, SWL is planning to hire a programmer-analyst who will divide his or her time between systems analysis and programming duties.

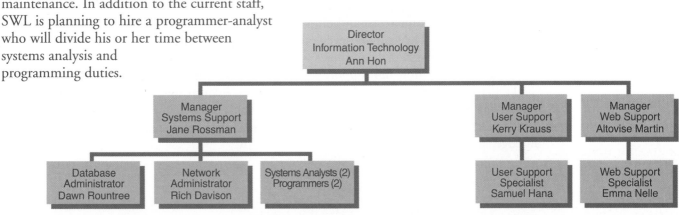

FIGURE 1-30 Organization chart of the IT department of SoftWear, Limited.

YOUR TURN

Write an employment ad for a new systems analyst position at SWL. Perform research on the Internet to locate examples of ads for systems analysts, and consider SWL's business profile when you write the ad.

The technical support staff members are responsible for the system software on all SWL computers. They also provide technical advice and guidance to the other groups within the IT department.

The operations staff is responsible for centralized IT functions, including SWL's mainframe computer, and provides network and database administration.

CHAPTER SUMMARY

In this chapter, you learned that information technology (IT) is a combination of hardware, software, and telecommunications systems that support business operations, improve productivity, and help managers make decisions. Systems analysis and design is the process of developing business information systems that transform data into useful information. A systems analyst starts with an overall business profile and creates a series of business models that represent business processes. The essential components of an information system are hardware, software, data, processes, and people. An information system can be developed in-house or purchased as a horizontal or vertical commercial package.

Companies are production oriented, service oriented, or a combination of the two. Internet-dependent firms opened up the vast potential of e-commerce, which is reshaping the economy. Four characteristics of business information systems that affect their design are interaction among two or more systems, the clarity of system boundaries, specialized information needs, and the company's size.

Based on their functions and features, information systems are identified as enterprise computing systems, transactional processing or operational systems, business support systems, knowledge management systems, or user productivity systems. In most companies, significant overlap and integration exists among the various types of information systems.

Organization structure typically includes top management, lower and middle management, and operational personnel. Top managers engage in strategic planning, which defines the overall mission and goals. Middle managers develop tactical plans to achieve short-term objectives. Lower managers use operational plans to carry out day-to-day tasks. Each organizational level has different responsibilities and different information needs.

Systems analysts use modeling, prototyping, and computer-aided software engineering (CASE) tools. Modeling produces a graphical representation of a concept or process, whereas prototyping involves the creation of an early working model of the information or its components. An analyst uses CASE tools to perform various systems development tasks.

Various development methodologies exist, including structured analysis, which treats data and processes as separate components, and object-oriented (O-O) analysis, which combines data and processes into objects. The systems development life cycle (SDLC) is a structured approach that consists of five phases: systems planning, systems analysis, systems design, systems implementation, and systems operation and support.

The IT department develops, maintains, and operates a company's information systems. A systems analyst investigates, analyzes, designs, develops, installs, evaluates, and maintains information systems. Systems analysts need a combination of technical and business knowledge, analytical ability, and communication skills.

Key Terms

application development group *1.22*
application software *1.5*
    B2B (business-to-business) *1.7*
    B2C (business-to-consumer) *1.7*
brick-and-mortar *1.7*
business model *1.3 1.14*
business process *1.3*
business process modeling *1.3*
business process reengineering *1.3*
business profile *1.3*
business support systems (BSS) *1.11*
    CASE tools *1.14*
certification *1.25*
class *1.17*
computer-aided systems engineering (CASE) *1.14*
corporate culture *1.25*
data *1.4*
data integrity *1.10*
data model *1.14*
data modeling *1.20*
database administration *1.23*
decision support *1.11*
deliverable *1.19*
dot-com *1.7*
e-commerce (electronic commerce) *1.7*
electronic data interchange (EDI) *1.9*
empowerment *1.13*
end product *1.19*
end users *1.6*
enhancements *1.21*
enterprise computing *1.10*
enterprise resource planning (ERP) *1.10*
expert systems *1.11*
feasibility study *1.20*
fuzzy logic *1.12*
hardware *1.5*
help desk *1.23*
horizontal system *1.5*
I-commerce (Internet commerce) *1.7*
in-house application *1.5*
inference rules *1.11*
information *1.5*
information center (IC) *1.23*
information engineering *1.16*
information systems *1.2*
information technology (IT) *1.2*
information technology (IT) department *1.22*
interactive model *1.19*
internet-dependent firm *1.7*
joint application development (JAD) *1.15*
knowledge base *1.11*
knowledge management systems *1.11*
legacy systems *1.6*
lower CASE tools *1.14*
maintenance *1.21*
management information systems (MISs) *1.11*
message *1.17*
methods *1.17*
Microsoft Solutions Framework (MSF) *1.18*

mission-critical system *1.4*
modeling *1.14*
network administration *1.23*
network model *1.14*
network operating system (NOS) *1.5*
object *1.17*
object model *1.14*
object modeling *1.20*
object-oriented (O-O) analysis *1.17*
online transaction processing (OLTP) *1.10*
operational plans *1.13*
operational systems *1.10*
preliminary investigation *1.20*
procedures *1.6*
processes *1.6*
processing *1.5*
process-centered *1.16*
process model *1.14*
process modeling *1.20*
production-oriented *1.7*
Project creep *1.21*
properties *1.17*
prototyping *1.14*
rapid application development (RAD) *1.15*
requirements model *1.14*
requirements modeling *1.20*
scalable *1.21*
service-oriented *1.7*
software *1.5*
software package *1.5*
specialized systems *1.9*
strategic plans *1.13*
structured analysis *1.16*
system *1.4*
system boundary *1.9*
system requirements document *1.20*
system software *1.5*
systems analysis and design *1.2*
systems analyst *1.2*
systems design *1.20*
systems design specification *1.20*
systems development life cycle (SDLC) *1.16*
systems evaluation *1.21*
systems implementation *1.20*
systems operation and support *1.21*
systems request *1.20*
systems support *1.23*
tactical planning *1.13*
technical support *1.22*
transaction processing (TP) *1.10*
upper CASE tools *1.14*
user productivity systems *1.12*
user support *1.23*
users *1.6*
vertical system *1.5*
waterfall model *1.19*
web support *1.23*
webmasters *1.23*
what-if analysis *1.11*

Chapter Review

1. What is information technology, and why is it important to a business?

2. Define business profiles, business models, and business processes.

3. Identify the main components of an information system.

4. Explain the difference between vertical and horizontal systems packages.

5. How do dot-com companies differ from brick-and-mortar companies?

6. Describe five types of information systems, and give an example of each.

7. Describe four organizational levels of a typical business and their information requirements.

8. Describe the phases of the systems development life cycle.

9. Explain the use of models, prototypes, and CASE tools in the systems development process.

10. What is objected-oriented analysis and how does it differ from structured analysis?

Discussion Topics

1. Some experts believe that the growth in e-commerce will cause states and local governments to lose a significant amount of sales tax revenue, unless Internet transactions are subject to sales tax. Do you agree? Why or why not?

2. Present an argument for and against the following proposition: Because IT managers must understand all phases of the business, a company should fill top management vacancies by promoting IT managers.

3. The head of the IT group in a company is often called the chief information officer (CIO) or chief technology officer (CTO). Should the CIO or CTO report to the company president, to the finance department where many of the information systems are used, or to someone or somewhere else? Why does it matter?

4. Computers perform many jobs that previously were performed by people. Will computer-based transactions and expanded e-commerce eventually replace person-to-person contact? From a customer's point of view, is this better? Why or why not?

Apply Your Knowledge

1 Low-Voltage Components

Situation:

You are the IT manager at Low-Voltage Components, a medium-sized firm that makes and sells specialized electrical cables to companies that manufacture electronic test equipment. Low-Voltage's largest customer, TX Industries, recently installed a computerized purchasing system and wants Low-Voltage to connect to the new system to receive purchase orders and production schedule forecasts. Low-Voltage currently has the following information systems: finance, accounts receivable, and accounts payable.

1. Should Low-Voltage develop an order entry system to connect with TX Industries' purchasing system? Why or why not?

2. What factors will affect the complexity of Low-Voltage's new order entry system?

3. What term describes the proposed computer-to-computer relationship between Low-Voltage and TX Industries?

4. Is Low-Voltage's proposed new system an operational system? Why or why not?

2 Systems Analyst Salaries

Situation:

As part of your job search, you decide to find out more about salaries and qualifications for systems analysts in the area where you would like to work. To increase your knowledge, search the Internet to perform the following research:

1. Find information about a career as a systems analyst.

2. Determine whether the Federal Bureau of Labor Statistics lists salary information for systems analysts. If so, summarize the information you find.

3. Find at least two online ads for systems analysts and list the employers, the qualifications, and the salaries, if mentioned.

4. Find at least one ad for an IT position that specifically mentions e-commerce.

3 MultiTech Interview

Situation:

You have an interview for an IT position with MultiTech, a large telecommunications company, and you want to learn more about the firm and its organizational structure. To prepare for the interview, you decide to review your knowledge about corporations, including the following questions:

1. What are the four organizational levels in a typical company?

2. How can you classify companies based on their mix of products and services?

3. What is empowerment?

4. What types of information systems might a large company use?

4 Rainbow's End Interview

Situation:

Your MultiTech interview seemed to go well, but you did not get the job. During the meeting, the interviewer mentioned that MultiTech uses structured analysis and relies heavily on modeling, prototyping, and CASE tools. Thinking back, you realize that you did not fully understand those terms. As you prepare for an interview with Rainbow's End, a large retail chain, you decide to review some IT terms and concepts. It is the day before the interview, and you are going through your notes about the following topics:

1. What is the main difference between structured analysis and O-O analysis?

2. What is a CASE tool and what does it do?

3. What is modeling and how is it done?

4. What is prototyping and why is it important?

Chapter Assignments

1. Contact at least three people at your school or a nearby company who use information systems. List the systems, the position titles of the users, and the business functions that the systems support.

2. Research newspaper or magazine articles to find computer companies whose stock is publicly traded. Choose a company in which you would like to invest and pretend to buy $1,000 of its stock. What is the current price per share? Why did you choose that company? Report each week to your class on how your stock is doing.

3. Use a software program to create an organization chart of your school's leadership or the leadership in a local company. You can use a drawing program, a chart tool such as MS Organization Chart, which is available in Microsoft Office programs, or you can draw it by hand.

4. In the early 1960s, the merger of the New York Central Railroad and the Pennsylvania Railroad created the largest railroad system in the United States. Unfortunately, the companies' two computer systems were not compatible and railroad operations were paralyzed for many months. Although the new company, Penn-Central, appeared to have a bright future, it declared bankruptcy only two years later. Do research to learn more about that event, or another instance where IT problems caused major financial damage to a corporation.

CASE STUDIES

Case Studies offer an opportunity for you to practice specific skills and knowledge learned in the chapter and provide practical experience for you as a systems analyst. Two of the case studies (New Century Health Clinic and Ridgeway Company) are continuing case studies that appear in each chapter. Additionally, one continuing case study (SCR Associates) utilizes the Internet to practice some of the topics covered in this chapter.

NEW CENTURY HEALTH CLINIC

Background

Five years ago, cardiologists Timothy Jones and Dolores Garcia decided to combine their individual practices in Fullerton, California, to form the New Century Health Clinic. They wanted to concentrate on preventive medicine by helping patients maintain health and fitness and by providing traditional medical care.

Dr. Jones recently asked you to work with him as an IT consultant. He wants you to help New Century develop an information system that will support the clinic's operations and future growth. During an initial meeting, he provided you with some background information and asked for your suggestions about how to get started.

At your desk, you begin to review New Century's situation. The clinic is located near a new shopping mall in a busy section of the city. New Century's staff includes four doctors, three registered nurses, four physical therapists, and six office staff workers. The clinic currently has a patient base of 3,500 patients from 275 different employers, many of which provide insurance coverage for employee wellness and health maintenance. Currently, New Century accepts 34 different insurance policies.

Anita Davenport, who has been with New Century since its inception, is the office manager. She supervises the staff, including Fred Brown, Susan Gifford, Tom Capaletti, Lisa Sung, and Carla Herrera.

Fred Brown handles office payroll, tax reporting, and profit distribution among the associates. Susan Gifford is responsible for the maintenance of patient records. Tom Capaletti handles most of the paperwork concerning insurance reporting and accounting. Lisa Sung has the primary responsibility for the appointment book, and her duties include making reminder calls to patients and preparing daily appointment lists. Carla Herrera primarily is concerned with ordering and organizing office and clinic supplies.

Each of the six office staff people has one or more primary responsibilities; however, all members of the staff help out whenever necessary with patient records, insurance processing, and appointment processing. In addition to their regular responsibilities, all six office workers are involved in the preparation of patient statements at the end of each month.

With this background information, you begin to prepare for your next meeting with Dr. Jones.

Assignments

1. Prepare an organization chart of New Century's office staff. You can use a drawing program, a chart tool such as Microsoft Organization Chart, which is available in Microsoft Office programs, or you can draw it by hand.

2. Identify at least three business processes that New Century performs, and explain who is responsible for the specific tasks.

3. Explain how New Century might use a transaction processing system, a business support system, and a user productivity system. For each type of system, provide a specific example, and explain how the system would benefit the clinic.

4. During the systems development process, should New Century consider any of the following: EDI, vertical and horizontal system packages, or the Internet? Explain your answers.

RIDGEWAY COMPANY

Background

Ridgeway Company develops and manages recreational facilities. The company currently owns several major operations and had revenues of approximately $75 million last year.

Ridgeway's top management includes George Ridgeway, president; Helen Hill, executive vice president; and three vice presidents who report directly to Ms. Hill — Luis Sanchez, vice president, finance; Trinh Lu, vice president, administration, research, and development; and Thomas McGee, vice president, operations. Bob Logan reports directly to the president in a staff capacity as the company's land development consultant.

Ridgeway Company recently acquired a large recreational complex that has a tennis club and a golf course. Now named the Ridgeway Country Club, its facilities include 20 lighted tennis courts, an 18-hole golf course, a pro shop that sells tennis and golfing supplies and related items, a clubhouse with a restaurant and bar, and other recreational facilities, including a swimming pool and an exercise room. Thomas McGee is the general manager of the Ridgeway Country Club.

Ridgeway recently purchased a minicomputer system to handle its information management requirements.

Linda Usher, information technology director, heads the IT department and reports to the vice president of finance. Reporting to Linda are the systems development manager, the operations manager, and the systems support manager.

Linda Usher recently met Bob Logan for lunch. Linda was surprised at the invitation, and Bob's secretary had given her no reason for this informal meeting. After some small talk, the discussion went like this:

Bob: I really need your help, Linda. Several months ago, I bought a new PC for my office. Believe me, I wasn't trying to get around your department. It's just that I know you folks are very busy, and I thought this was something I could do without bothering you.

Linda: You're not bothering me. What's on your mind?

Bob: All I needed was a program to help me keep track of how many members use each of Ridgeway Country Club's facilities. I figured it would help me predict future usage, spot trends, and point out potential problems of excess demand for certain facilities. For example, I'm sure we will need to build several additional tennis courts someday soon. I didn't think it would be a big deal to get a computer program to help me figure out how soon we'll need them.

Linda: What did you do next?

Bob: Well, the store where I bought the computer recommended a spreadsheet package that can handle statistics. They said it was very popular and would do exactly what I wanted. But it isn't working out. I had originally planned to keep track of weekly usage, but now I realize that in some cases I need daily or even hourly figures. And I can't get it to do the seasonal analyses I need. So now what should I do?

Linda: I'm sorry you're having trouble, Bob. Computers and programs are just tools. You still have to figure out exactly what you want to do before you can determine what tools you need to do it.

Bob: I see that now, Linda, but what I want to know is how I can salvage what I've already done. Do you have a few minutes this afternoon to look at what I've got on the computer and tell me how I can make it do what I want?

Linda: It isn't going to be that easy. Even with a small-scale system, we need to look at what you want to do, what kind of information you need, and what data you have available. Then we'll be able to determine what kind of program you need. Maybe there's a personal computer package that can do the job, or maybe we'll need to develop a specialized information system. That system might be able to run on your computer, or maybe it would run on Ridgeway's main computer system. I'm sure that by understanding your needs and doing a little research, we can solve your problem.

Assignments

1. What mistakes did Bob make?

2. Do you think Linda's assessment is correct? Do personal computer systems need the same kind of systems development life cycle as mainframe systems?

3. Prepare an organization chart of the top management at Ridgeway Company.

4. Add the organizational structure of the IT department to the organization chart.

ORIGINAL KAYAK ADVENTURES

Background

Original Kayak Adventures (OKA) offers guided eco-tours and kayak rentals along the Hudson River. John and Edie Caputo, who are avid kayakers and amateur naturalists, founded OKA two years ago.

The Caputos spent many weekends and vacations exploring the Hudson's numerous creeks and tributaries. John was a sales representative and Edie worked for a Web design firm. Two years ago, John's division was purchased by a rival company, which announced plans to move operations to another state. Rather than relocate, the Caputos decided to launch OKA. They reasoned that Edie could leave her job and work as a freelance Web designer, which would provide some income while John tried to build OKA into a profitable business. John and Edie are convinced that the eco-tourism market will expand greatly, and they look forward to sharing their experience and knowledge with others who enjoy nature and kayaking.

Original Kayak Adventures advertises in regional magazines and maintains a Web site, which Edie designed. Customers say that the site is attractive and informative, but the Caputos are not sure of its effectiveness in attracting new business. At this time, no other kayak rental firms operate within 20 miles of OKA's location.

So far, the Caputos' plan is working out well. OKA rents space at a nearby marina, where Edie runs the office and operates her Web design business. She also handles rentals when John is giving lessons or busy with a tour group. On summer weekends and holidays, Janet Jacobs, a local college student, handles telep

OKA's inventory includes 16 ren   d a large
assortment of accessories and safet   is considering
adding a selection of books and vi

OKA has three main business se   Most customers make advance reservations   t sometimes
there is room for last-minute cust   ons and
walk-in customers.

Reservations are entered in a lo   ess activity.
Edie also created a Microsoft Acc   s time, she
enters the reservation date, the re   er information
into a table, which is sorted by re   l list. For quick
reference, Edie also displays kaya   r-coded mag-
nets that show the available or re   the database,
Edie uses an inexpensive account

Although the OKA database h   noticed some
drawbacks. For example, reservat   etimes conflict
with John or Edie's availability. The Caputos also would like to get more information about rental patterns, customer profiles, advertising effectiveness, and future business opportunities. John and Edie have talked about updating the system, but they have been too busy to do so.

Handwritten note: CH 1 1) 1.34 2) 1.34 (1.A) 3) 1.33 4) 1.33

Assignments

1. Develop a business profile for Original Kayak Adventures. The profile should include information about OKA's main business segments, organization, resources, customers, and potential opportunity to engage in e-commerce.

2. List OKA's current functions and business processes. Draw a model of an OKA business process, including possible events, subprocesses, and results.

3. What types of information systems does OKA use? Do these systems support its current and future business objectives? Why or why not?

4. From an object-oriented viewpoint, the OKA treats reservations as a class. Based on the background information provided, what are some properties of reservation objects?

SCR ASSOCIATES

SCR Associates is an information technology consulting firm that offers IT solutions and training for small- and medium-sized companies. SCR's slogan is "We Know IT!"

Background

As a newly hired systems analyst, you will handle assignments, work on various SCR projects, and apply the skills you learned in the text. SCR needs an information system to manage training operations at the new SCR training center. The new system will be called TIMS (Training Information Management System).

The SCR case is available as an interactive, Web-based case study. You can log on to the Shelly Cashman Series site at www.scsite.com/sad4e/scr for instructions and assignments. If you prefer to complete the case study without using the Internet then you must download the data disk. See the inside back cover for instructions for downloading the data disk or see your instructor for more information on accessing the files required for this book.

Situation

This is your second day on the job as a systems analyst at SCR Associates. You spent most of yesterday filling out personnel forms and learning your way around the office. This morning, you sit at your desk and examine SCR's Web site. The site is a marketing tool, with attractive features and information about SCR, including the company's history, values, and services.

After exploring SCR's Web site, you click an icon to access the company intranet. After you enter your name and password, an opening screen displays. From here, you can check your e-mail or access various libraries where SCR data, forms, and resources are stored.

Before You Begin...

1. Review the summary of SCR's history, values, and services. Open the Document 1-1 from the data disk.

2. Review the list of SCR functions and organization. Open the Document 1-2 from the data disk.

3. Review the October 8 message from Smith, Campbell, and Richards welcoming new employees. Open the Document 1-3 from the data disk.

4. Review the October 9 message from Jesse Baker regarding a weekend work assignment. Open the Document 1-4 from the data disk.

ON THE WEB

The SCR case is available as an interactive, Web-based case study. You can log on to the Shelly Cashman Series site at www.scsite.com/sad4e/scr for instructions and assignments.

Assignments

1. Create an SCR organization chart.

2. Use the Internet to learn more about Visible Analyst and System Architect 2001 CASE tools, which SCR uses. List at least three features of each product. Write a brief memo describing your research.

3. Research newspapers, IT magazines, or other information sources to learn about recent developments in e-commerce. Write a brief memo describing your findings.

4. SCR has plenty of competition in the IT consulting field. Use the Internet to locate at least three other IT consulting firms, and write a brief memo that describes each firm, the services it offers, and whether e-commerce is mentioned.

Systems Planning

PHASE 1

Systems Analysis — PHASE 2

Systems Design — PHASE 3

Systems Implementation — PHASE 4

Systems Operation & Support — PHASE 5

Preliminary Investigation

Systems planning is the first of five phases in the systems development life cycle. In this chapter, you will learn about business and IT planning, and how systems projects get started and are reviewed initially.

Chapter 2 begins the study of the systems development life cycle (SDLC). Systems planning is the first phase in the SDLC. In this chapter, you will learn why it is important to understand business operations and requirements, how IT projects support a company's overall strategic plan, and how systems projects get started and are reviewed initially.

INTRODUCTION

During the systems planning phase, a systems analyst reviews systems projects and gains an understanding of the company's objectives, information requirements, and business operations.

The chapter begins with a discussion of strategic planning because IT professionals must understand, support, and help plan long-term company goals as well as day-to-day operations. You also will learn how the SDLC and CASE tools provide a framework for systems development.

Systems development typically begins with a systems request, followed by a preliminary investigation. You will learn how systems requests originate, how they are evaluated, and how to conduct a preliminary investigation. You also will learn about the fact-finding techniques that begin at this point and carry over into later development phases. Finally, you will examine the report to management, which concludes the systems planning phase.

OBJECTIVES

When you finish this chapter, you will be able to:

- Describe the strategic planning process, and why it is important to IT managers

- Explain the purpose of a mission statement

- Explain the SDLC as a framework for systems development and business modeling

- Explain the reasons for information systems projects and the factors that affect such projects

- Describe the initial review of systems requests and the role of the systems review committee

- Describe the internal and external factors that affect information systems projects

- Define operational feasibility, technical feasibility, and economic feasibility

- Describe the steps and end product of a preliminary investigation

N THE WEB

r an overview of Strategic
anning visit scsite.com/
d4e/more.htm, click
stems Analysis and Design
apter 2 and then click the
rategic Planning link.

w.scsite.com

THE IMPORTANCE OF STRATEGIC PLANNING

Strategic planning is the process of identifying long-term organizational goals, strategies, and resources. Strategic planning looks beyond day-to-day activities and focuses on a horizon that is 3, 5, 10, or 20 years in the future.

Overview of the Strategic Planning Process

Why does a systems analyst need to know about strategic planning? The answer might be found in an old story about two stonecutters who were hard at work when a passerby asked them what they were doing. "I am cutting stones," said the first worker. The second worker replied, "I am building a cathedral." So it is with information technology: One analyst might say, "I am using a CASE tool," whereas another might say, "I am helping the company succeed in a major new business venture." Systems analysts should focus on the larger, strategic role of IT as they carry out their day-to-day responsibilities.

During strategic planning, many companies ask a series of broadly worded questions that is called a **SWOT analysis** because it examines a company's strengths (**S**), weaknesses (**W**), opportunities (**O**), and threats (**T**). Each question leads to an IT-related issue, which in turn requires more review, analysis, and planning. For example:

- What are our major strengths, and how can we utilize them in the future? What must we do to strengthen our IT function, including our people and technology infrastructure?

- What are our major weaknesses, and how can we overcome them? How should we address weaknesses in IT resources and capability?

- What are our major opportunities, and how can we take full advantage of them? What IT plans do we have to support business opportunities?

- What major threats do we face, and what can we do about them? What can we do to deal with potential threats to IT success?

When a company performs a SWOT analysis, a long-term strategic plan emerges. The plan requires technical, financial, and human resources. Most important, the strategic plan requires information resources and technology that are supplied by IT professionals, including systems analysts.

From the Strategic Plan to Business Results

Figure 2-1 shows the strategic planning process. A company develops a mission statement based on the firm's purpose, values, and vision for the future. The mission statement is the foundation for major goals, shorter-term objectives, and day-to-day business operations.

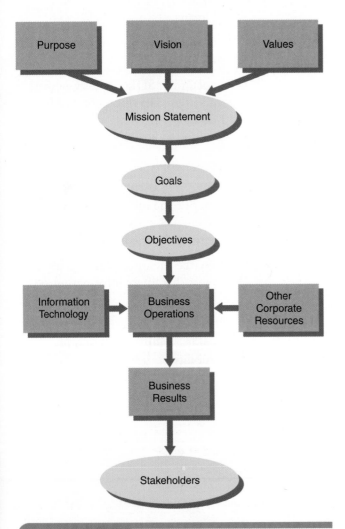

FIGURE 2-1   In the strategic planning process, a company's purpose, vision, and values shape its mission statement, which leads to goals, objectives, business operations, and results that affect company stakeholders.

A **mission statement** describes the company for its stakeholders and briefly states the company's overall purpose, products, services, and values. **Stakeholders** include anyone affected by the company's performance, such as customers, employees, suppliers, stockholders, and members of the community. Figure 2-2 shows examples of mission statements from several leading companies.

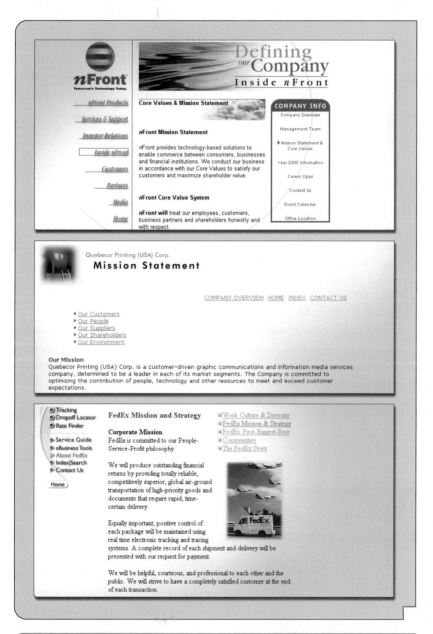

ON THE WEE

For examples of Mission
Statements visit
scsite.com/sad4e/more.ht
click Systems Analysis an
Design Chapter 2 and then
click the Mission Statemen
link.

www.scsite.c

FIGURE 2-2   Examples of mission statements from several companies.

The mission statement is just the starting point. Next, the company identifies a set of **goals** that will accomplish the mission. For example, the company might establish one-year, three-year, and five-year goals for expanding market share. To achieve those goals, the company develops a list of specific **objectives**, which have a shorter time frame. For example, if a goal is to increase Web-based orders by 30 percent next year, a company might set quarterly objectives with monthly milestones. Objectives also might include tactical plans, such as creating a new Web site and training a special customer support group to answer e-mail inquiries. Finally, the objectives are translated into day-to-day operations, using IT and other vital resources.

The Future

New industries, products, and services will require powerful information systems, and top managers will expect IT departments to support the business enterprise. E-commerce will continue to surge, and the business environment will be dynamic and challenging. To some firms, intense change will be threatening; to others it will represent an opportunity.

In the mid-1980s, Tom Peters wrote a popular book called *Thriving on Chaos* that became a standard guidebook for many corporations. Peters said that change will be constant and successful companies must reinvent their businesses and learn how to thrive on change. He accurately predicted global competition, rapidly changing markets, and the explosive growth of information technology. Today, top managers know they need powerful information systems to handle both the problems and opportunities of constant change.

A FRAMEWORK FOR SYSTEMS DEVELOPMENT

Although the SDLC is identified primarily with structured analysis, the SDLC phases provide a general framework for other methodologies as well. Regardless of the method the developer uses, he or she must start by learning about the business operations and information requirements. In many cases, a team of users, managers, and IT staff members develop a model of the business enterprise and the specific functions that the proposed system must support.

A Business Model Example

Suppose you are a systems analyst working in the IT department of an international hotel chain. The IT director favors the traditional SDLC as an overall framework for system development but also likes to use a CASE tool called System Architect 2001 (S/A 2001) to organize and guide the specific tasks. Because you have no experience with that tool, you decide to complete the S/A 2001 tutorial, which leads you through a series of screens similar to the ones in Figure 2-3.

N THE WEB

learn more about Future Trends visit scsite.com/ ad4e/more.htm, click ystems Analysis and Design hapter 2 and then click the uture IT Trends link.

w.scsite.com

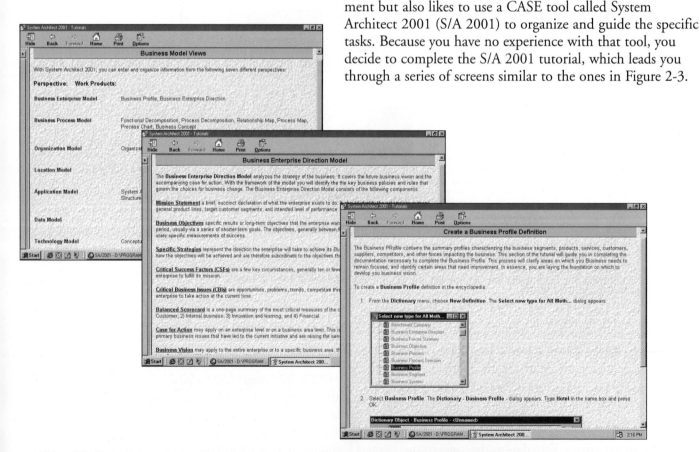

FIGURE 2-3   Tutorial screens from the System Architect 2001 CASE tool show examples of business process modeling.

As you work through the tutorial, you learn that you can model the business in various ways that include models of the overall enterprise, business processes, organization, locations, information system applications, company data, and necessary technology. You also find out that you can identify and document all sorts of background information, including the company's mission statement, objectives, strategies, critical success factors, and critical business issues. **Critical success factors** are vital objectives that must be achieved for the enterprise to fulfill its mission, and **critical business issues** are the key problems, opportunities, and constraints that affect and shape the firm's decisions. You learn that at some point in the systems development process, you will present a **case for action**, which is a summary of the project request and a specific recommendation.

This morning, the IT director asked you to work on a specific project. She and the marketing vice president want to know whether the current hotel reservation system can support a new business traveler incentive plan aimed at repeat business travelers. You know that S/A 2001 organizes all definitions and diagrams into storage areas called **encyclopedias.** When you investigate, you find that an encyclopedia for the reservation system already exists, as shown in Figure 2-4. As you begin to investigate the business enterprise, you see that several business objectives, critical business issues, and critical success factors have been identified and documented. This provides a starting point and a framework for your investigation.

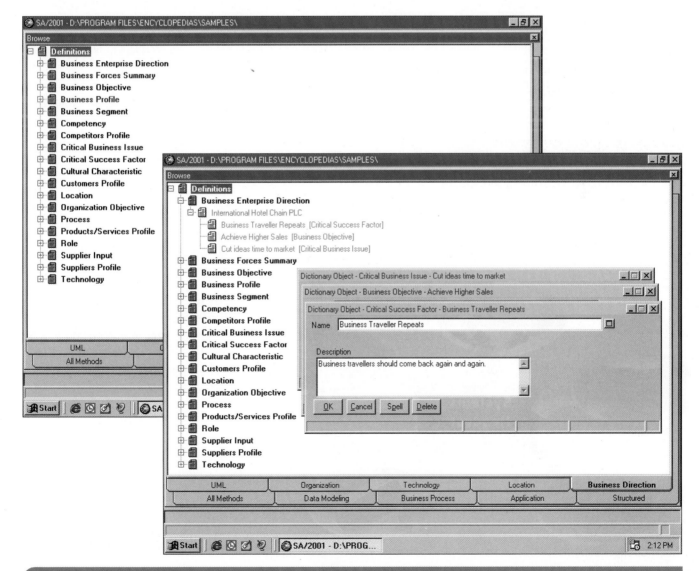

FIGURE 2-4 System Architect 2001 uses an encyclopedia to store diagrams and definitions for the sample reservations system.

N THE WEB

r additional information
n The Role Of The IT
epartment visit
 site.com/sad4e/more.htm,
ck Systems Analysis and
esign Chapter 2 and then
ck The Role Of The IT
epartment link.

w.scsite.com

The Role of the IT Department

In most successful companies, a close link exists between business operations and information technology. Ten years ago, the IT department commonly handled all aspects of systems development, and consulted users only when and if the department required user input. New approaches, such as joint application development (JAD) and rapid application development (RAD) are widely accepted, and today, you are more likely to see systems development teams of users, managers, and IT staff working together right from the start.

Even where team-oriented development is the norm, some companies see the role of the IT department as a gatekeeper, responsible for screening and evaluating systems requests. Should the IT department perform the initial evaluation, or should a cross-functional team do it? The answer depends on the company's size and organization, and whether IT is tightly integrated into business operations. In smaller companies or firms where there is only one person with IT skills, that person acts as a coordinator and consults closely with users and managers to evaluate systems requests.

W H A T   D O   Y O U   T H I N K ?

You are the IT director at Attaway Airlines, a small regional air carrier. You chair the company's systems review committee and you are currently dealing with strong disagreements about two key projects. Dan Esposito, the marketing manager, says it is vital to have a new computerized reservation system that can provide better customer service and reduce operational costs. Molly Kinnon, vice president of finance, is just as adamant that a new accounting system is needed immediately, because it will be very expensive to adjust the current system to new federal reporting requirements. Molly outranks Dan, and she is your boss. The next meeting, which promises to be a real showdown, is set for 9:00 a.m. tomorrow. How will you prepare for the meeting? What questions and issues should be discussed?

INFORMATION SYSTEMS PROJECTS

This section discusses reasons for systems projects, internal and external factors that affect systems projects, and systems request forms.

Reasons for Systems Projects

The starting point for a project is called a **systems request**, which is a formal way of asking for IT support. A systems request might propose enhancements for an existing system, the correction of problems, or the development of an entirely new information system.

As Figure 2-5 shows, the main reasons for systems requests are improved service to customers, better performance, more information, stronger controls, and reduced cost.

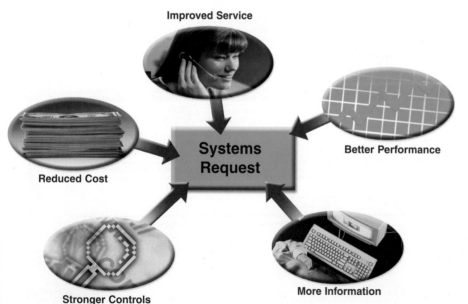

Improved Service

Better Performance

Systems Request

Reduced Cost

More Information

Stronger Controls

FIGURE 2-5   Five common reasons for systems requests.

IMPROVED SERVICE   Systems requests often are aimed at improving service to customers or users within the company. Allowing mutual fund investors to check their account balances on a Web site, storing data on rental car customer preferences, or creating an online college registration system are examples that provide valuable services and increased customer satisfaction.

BETTER PERFORMANCE   The current system might not meet performance requirements. For example, it might respond slowly to data inquiries at certain times, or be unable to support company growth. Performance limitations also result when a system that was designed for a specific hardware configuration becomes obsolete when new hardware is introduced.

MORE INFORMATION   The system might produce information that is insufficient, incomplete, or unable to support the company's changing information needs. For example, a system that tracks customer orders might not be capable of analyzing and predicting marketing trends. In the face of intense competition and rapid product development cycles, managers need the best possible information to make major decisions on planning, designing, and marketing new products and services.

STRONGER CONTROLS   A system must have effective controls to ensure that data is accurate and secure. Some common controls include passwords, various levels of user access, and **encryption**, or coding of data, so unauthorized users cannot easily read the data. Sophisticated controls include devices that scan a person's retina to use it as a fingerprint, as shown in Figure 2-6. Weak controls can allow data entry errors or unauthorized access. For example, if an invalid customer number is entered, the order system should reject the entry immediately and prompt the user to enter a valid number.

Controls must be effective without being excessive. If a system requires redundant data input or takes too long to verify every data item, internal users and customers might complain that the system is not user-friendly.

REDUCED COST   The current system could be expensive to operate or maintain as a result of technical problems, design weaknesses, or the changing demands of the business. It might be possible to adapt the system to newer technology or upgrade it. On the other hand, cost-benefit analysis might show that a new system would be more cost effective and provide better support for long-term objectives.

FIGURE 2-6   This retina scanning device is an example of a control technique.

Factors Affecting Systems Projects

Every business decision that a company makes is affected by internal and external factors, and IT systems projects are no exception. Figure 2-7 shows the main internal and external factors.

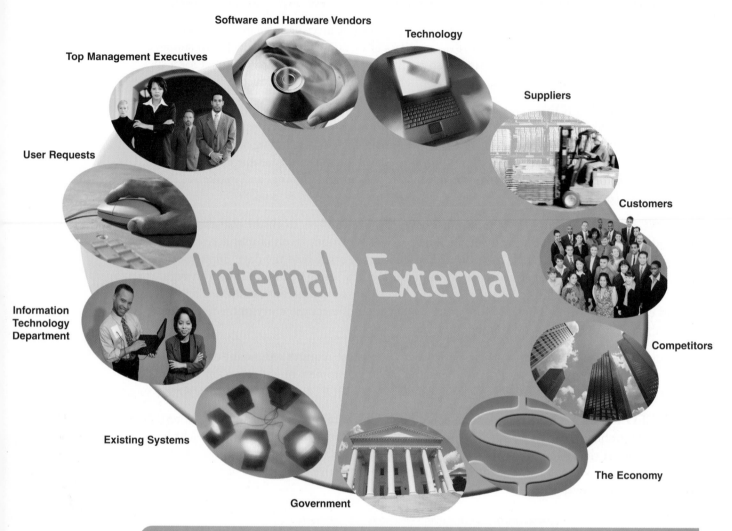

Software and Hardware Vendors

Technology

Top Management Executives

Suppliers

User Requests

Customers

Information Technology Department

Competitors

Existing Systems

The Economy

Government

Internal   External

FIGURE 2-7   Internal and external factors that affect IT systems projects.

USER REQUESTS   As users rely more heavily on information systems to perform their jobs, they are likely to request even more IT services and support. For example, sales reps might request improvements to the company's Web site, a more powerful sales analysis report, a network to link all sales locations, or an online system that allows customers to obtain the status of their orders instantly. Or, users might not be satisfied with the current system because it is difficult to learn or lacks flexibility. They might want information systems support for business requirements that did not even exist when the system was developed.

TOP MANAGEMENT DIRECTIVES   Directives from top managers are a prime source of major systems projects. Those directives often result from strategic business decisions that require new IT systems, more information for decision making, or better support for mission-critical information systems.

EXISTING SYSTEMS   Errors or problems in existing systems can trigger requests for systems projects. System errors must be corrected, but analysts often spend too much time reacting to day-to-day problems without looking at underlying causes. This approach can turn an information system into a patchwork of corrections and changes that cannot support the company's overall business needs.

INFORMATION TECHNOLOGY DEPARTMENT   Many systems project requests come from the IT department. IT staff members often make recommendations based on their knowledge of business operations and technology trends. IT proposals might be strictly technical matters, such as replacement of certain network components, or suggestions might be more business oriented, such as proposing a new reporting or data collection system.

THE ECONOMY   Economic activity has a powerful influence on corporate information management. In a period of economic expansion, firms need to be ready with scalable systems that can handle additional volume and growth. Predicting the business cycle is not an exact science, and careful research and planning is critically important.

TECHNOLOGY   Changing technology is a basic force in business and society in general. For example, the rapid growth of telecommunications has created entire new industries and technologies. Technology also dramatically reshapes existing business operations. For example, the success of scanner technology in supermarket checkout lanes resulted in universal bar coding that now affects virtually all products.

GOVERNMENT   Federal, state, and local government regulations affect the design of corporate information systems. For example, income tax reporting requirements must be designed into a payroll package. The debate about Internet sales tax issues could profoundly affect e-commerce, as well as traditional retail businesses.

SOFTWARE AND HARDWARE VENDORS   Most companies have a mix of software and hardware that must work together to support information systems requirements. As new versions of software or new hardware models appear, companies make decisions that affect existing systems and trigger systems requests.

COMPETITORS   Competition drives many information systems decisions. For example, if one cellular telephone provider offers a new type of digital service, other firms must match the plan in order to remain competitive. New product research and development, marketing, sales, and service all require IT support.

CUSTOMERS   Customer service is vitally important, and information systems that interact with customers receive top priority in most firms. Examples might include technical support systems, online inventory systems, and Web-based order entry systems. As shown in Figure 2-8, Gateway uses *smart* forklifts that read the UPC numbers as items are picked. Some believe that an automated warehouse is just as important as a successful Web site.

FIGURE 2-8   Gateway uses *smart* forklifts that can read bar codes.

SUPPLIERS   With the growth of electronic data interchange (EDI), relationships with suppliers are critically important. For example, an automobile company might require that suppliers code their parts in a certain manner to match the auto company's inventory control system. EDI also enables **just-in-time (JIT)** inventory systems, which rely on computer-to-computer data exchange to minimize unnecessary inventory.

Systems Request Forms

Many organizations use a special form for systems requests, similar to the sample shown in Figure 2-9. A properly designed form streamlines the process and ensures consistency. The form must be easy to understand and include clear instructions. It should include enough space for all required information and should indicate what supporting documents are needed. Some companies have designed online systems request forms that are filled in and submitted via e-mail.

When a systems request form is received, a systems analyst or IT manager examines it to determine what IT resources (staff and time) are required for the preliminary investigation. A designated manager or a committee then decides whether to proceed with a preliminary investigation.

In some cases, however, a system failure requires immediate attention, and there is no time for a formal request or a normal investigation. In urgent situations, an IT maintenance team attempts to restore operations immediately. When the system is back to normal, the team conducts a thorough review and prepares a systems request to cover the work that was performed.

EVALUATION OF SYSTEMS REQUESTS

In most organizations, the IT department receives more systems requests than it can handle. Many organizations assign responsibility for evaluating systems requests to a group of key managers and users. Many companies call this group a **systems review committee** or a **computer resources committee**. Regardless of the name, the objective is to use the combined judgment and experience of several managers to evaluate systems projects.

SWL   **REQUEST FOR INFORMATION SYSTEMS SERVICES**

Date: _____
Submitted by: _____ Title: _____
Department: _____ Location: _____
Phone: _____ e-mail: _____

REQUEST FOR:

[ ] Correction of system error
[ ] System enhancement
[ ] New system

URGENCY:

[ ] Immediate attention needed
[ ] Handle in normal priority sequence
[ ] Defer until new system is developed

DESCRIPTION OF REQUESTED SYSTEMS SERVICES:
(ATTACH ADDITIONAL DOCUMENTS AS NECESSARY)

(To be completed by the Information Technology Department)

[ ] Approved   Assigned to IT contact person: _____
User: _____
Urgency code (1 low to 5 high): _____

[ ] Modified (see attached notes)
[ ] Rejected (see attached statement)

Date _____   Action: _____

FIGURE 2-9   Sample systems request form.

Systems Review Committees

In some companies, one person instead of a committee is responsible for evaluating systems requests. This often is the case in smaller companies or firms where only one person has information technology skills. In that situation, the systems person must consult closely with users and managers throughout the company to ensure that business and operational needs are considered carefully.

In larger companies, instead of the company relying on a single person, a systems review committee provides a variety of experience and knowledge in evaluating systems requests. A typical committee consists of the IT director and several managers from other departments. Even where there is a committee, the IT director must act as a technical consultant to the committee to ensure that members are aware of crucial issues, problems, and opportunities. With a broader viewpoint, a committee can establish priorities more effectively than an individual, and one person's bias is less likely to affect a committee's decisions.

On the other hand, action on requests must wait until the committee meets. To avoid delay, committee members use memos, e-mail, and teleconferencing to communicate with each other. Another potential disadvantage of a committee is that members could favor projects requested by their own departments, and internal political differences can delay important decisions.

Evaluation of Projects

The systems review committee must evaluate the requests and set priorities. Suppose the committee receives four requests: a request from the marketing group to analyze current customer spending habits and forecast future trends, a request from the technical support group for a cellular link so service representatives can download technical data instantly, a request from the accounting department to redesign customer statements and allow access to them via the Internet, and a request from the production staff for an inventory control system that can exchange data with major suppliers directly.

With a limited staff, which of those projects should the committee consider for further study? What criteria should be applied? How should the committee decide the priorities? To answer those questions, the committee must assess the feasibility of each systems request.

Overview of Feasibility

A systems request must meet several tests to see whether it is worthwhile to proceed further. This series of tests is called a **feasibility study** and is a vital part of every systems project. As shown in Figure 2-10, a feasibility study uses three major yardsticks to measure, or predict a system's success: operational feasibility, technical feasibility, and economic feasibility.

Sometimes a feasibility study is quite simple and can be done in a few hours. If the request involves a new system or a major change, however, extensive fact-finding and investigation is required.

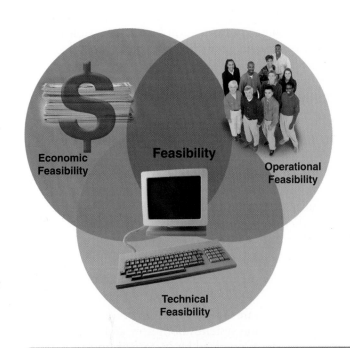

ON THE WE

To learn more about Feas[i]
Studies visit
scsite.com/sad4e/more.h[]
click Systems Analysis a[n]
Design Chapter 2 and the
click the Feasibility Studie[s]
link.

www.scsite.[]

FIGURE 2-10   A feasibility study includes tests for operational, technical, and economic feasibility.

Every systems request must pass an initial review to decide whether it deserves further study. How much effort needs to go into that decision? That depends on the request. For example, if a department wants an existing report sorted in a different order, the analyst can decide quickly whether the request is feasible. On the other hand, a proposal by the marketing department for a new market research system to predict sales trends requires more effort. In both cases, the systems analyst asks three important questions:

1. Is the proposal desirable in an operational sense? Is it a practical approach that will solve a problem or take advantage of an opportunity to achieve company goals?

2. Is the proposal technically feasible? Are the necessary technical resources and people available for the project?

3. Is the proposal economically desirable? What are the projected savings and costs? Are there other intangible factors, such as customer satisfaction or company image? Is the problem worth solving, and will the request result in a sound business investment?

Later in this chapter, you will learn some techniques to use in the fact-finding process, including the examination of company documents and organization charts, interviews with managers and users, and a review of current system documentation. If the systems request appears feasible, those tasks will begin now and then continue in the systems analysis phase.

OPERATIONAL FEASIBILITY   A system that has **operational feasibility** is one that will be used effectively after it has been developed. If users have difficulty with a new system, it will not produce the expected benefits. Operational feasibility depends on several vital issues. For example, consider the following questions:

- Does management support the project? Do users support the project? Is the current system well liked and effectively used? Do users see the need for change?

- Will the new system result in a workforce reduction? If so, what will happen to affected employees?

- Will the new system require training for users? If so, is the company prepared to provide the necessary resources for training current employees?

- Will users be involved in planning the new system right from the start?

- Will the new system place any new demands on users or require any operating changes? For example, will any information be less accessible or produced less frequently? Will performance decline in any way? If so, will an overall gain to the organization outweigh individual losses?

- Will customers experience adverse effects in any way, either temporarily or permanently? Will any risk to the company's image or goodwill result?

- Is the schedule for development of the system reasonable?

- Do any legal or ethical issues need to be considered?

TECHNICAL FEASIBILITY   A systems request has **technical feasibility** if the organization has the resources to develop or purchase, install, and operate the system. When assessing technical feasibility, an analyst must consider the following points:

- Does the company have the necessary hardware, software, and network resources? If not, can those resources be acquired without difficulty?

- Does the company have the needed technical expertise? If not, can it be acquired?

- Does the proposed platform have enough capacity for future needs? If not, can it be expanded?

- Will the hardware and software environment be reliable? Will it integrate with other company information systems, both now and in the future? Will it interface properly with external systems operated by customers and suppliers?

- Will the combination of hardware and software supply adequate performance? Do clear expectations and performance specifications exist?
- Will the system be able to handle future transaction volume and company growth?

ECONOMIC FEASIBILITY   A systems request has **economic feasibility** if the projected benefits of the proposed system outweigh the estimated costs involved in acquiring, installing, and operating it. Costs can be one time or continuing, and can incur at various times during project development and use.

When assessing costs, companies usually consider the **total cost of ownership** (TCO), which includes ongoing support and maintenance costs, as well as acquisition costs. To determine TCO, the analyst needs to estimate costs in each of the following areas:

- People, including IT staff and users
- Hardware and equipment
- Software, including in-house development as well as purchases from vendors
- Formal and informal training
- Licenses and fees
- Consulting expenses
- Facility costs
- The estimated cost of not developing the system or postponing the project

ON THE WE

To find out more about To
Cost Of Ownership (TCO)
scsite.com/sad4e/more.h
click Systems Analysis an
Design Chapter 2 and the
click the Total Cost Of
Ownership (TCO) link.

www.scsite.c

In addition to costs, you need to assess tangible and intangible benefits to the company. The systems review committee will use those figures, along with your cost estimates, to decide whether to pursue the project beyond the preliminary investigation phase.

Tangible benefits are benefits that can be measured in dollars. Tangible benefits result from a decrease in expenses, an increase in revenues, or both. Examples of tangible benefits include the following:

- A new scheduling system that reduces overtime
- An online package tracking system that improves service and decreases the need for clerical staff
- A sophisticated inventory control system that cuts excess inventory and eliminates production delays

Intangible benefits are difficult to measure in dollars but also should be identified. Examples of intangible benefits include the following:

- A user-friendly system that improves employee job satisfaction
- A sales tracking system that supplies better information for marketing decisions
- A new Web site that enhances the company's image

You also must consider the development timetable, because some benefits might occur as soon as the system is operational, but others might not take place until later.

The Systems Analyst's Toolkit contains tools to help you assess economic feasibility.

Determining Feasibility

The first step in the evaluation of a systems request is to make an initial determination of feasibility. Any request that is not feasible should be identified as soon as possible. For example, a request might require hardware or software that the company already rejected for other reasons. If so, the request will not fit the company's technical environment and should not be pursued further.

Even if the request is technically feasible, it might not be the best solution. For example, a request for a new report that is needed only once could require considerable design and programming effort. A better alternative might be to download the data to a personal computer-based software package and ask users to produce their own reports. In that case, a better investment is to train users instead of producing the reports for them.

You should keep in mind that systems requests that are not currently feasible can be resubmitted as new hardware, software, or expertise becomes available. Development costs might decrease, or the value of benefits might increase enough that a systems request eventually becomes feasible.

Conversely, an initially feasible project can be rejected later. As the project progresses, conditions often change. Acquisition costs might increase, and the project might become more expensive than anticipated. In addition, managers and users sometimes lose confidence in a project. For all those reasons, feasibility analysis is an ongoing task that must be performed throughout the systems development process.

Criteria Used to Evaluate Systems Requests

After rejecting systems requests that are not feasible, the systems review committee must establish priorities for the remaining items. Priority usually goes to projects that provide the greatest benefit, at the lowest cost, in the shortest period of time. Many factors, however, influence project evaluation. When assessing a project, a systems analyst should ask the following questions:

- Will the proposed system reduce costs? Where? When? How? How much?
- Will the system increase revenue for the company? Where? When? How? How much?
- Will the systems project result in more information or produce better results? How? Are the results measurable?
- Will the system serve customers better?
- Will the system serve the organization better?
- Can the project be implemented in a reasonable time period? How long will the results last?
- Are the necessary financial, human, and technical resources available?

Very few projects will score high in all areas. Some proposed systems might not reduce costs but will provide important new features. Other systems might reduce operating costs substantially but require the purchase or lease of additional hardware. Some systems might be very desirable but require several years of development before producing significant benefits.

Whenever possible, the analyst should evaluate a proposed project based on tangible factors. A **tangible factor** can be assigned an actual or approximate dollar value. A reduction of $8,000 in network maintenance is an example of a tangible factor.

Often, the evaluation involves intangible factors. In contrast to a tangible factor, it is difficult to assign a dollar value to an **intangible factor**. Enhancing the organization's image and improving customer service are examples of intangible factors. Intangible factors often weigh heavily in the decision for or against a systems project.

Discretionary and Non-discretionary Projects

Is the project absolutely necessary? Projects where management has a choice in implementing them are called **discretionary projects**. Projects where no choice exists are called **nondiscretionary projects**. Creating a new report for a user is an example of a discretionary project; adding a report required by a new federal law is an example of a nondiscretionary project.

WHAT DO YOU THINK?

Back at Attaway Airlines, the morning meeting ended with no agreement between Dan Esposito and Molly Kinnon. In fact, a new issue came up. Molly now says that the new accounting system is entitled to the highest priority because the federal government soon will require the reporting of certain types of company-paid health insurance premiums. Because the current system will not handle this report, she insists that the entire accounting system is a nondiscretionary project. As you might expect, Dan is upset. Can part of a project be nondiscretionary? What issues need to be discussed? The committee meets again tomorrow, and the members will look to you, as the IT director, for guidance.

If a particular project is not discretionary, is it really necessary for the systems review committee to evaluate it? Some people believe that waiting for committee approval delays critical nondiscretionary projects unnecessarily. Others believe that by submitting all systems requests to the systems review committee, the committee is kept aware of all projects that compete for the resources of the IT department. As a result, the committee assesses the priority of discretionary projects and can schedule them more realistically. Additionally, the committee might need to prioritize nondiscretionary projects when funds or staff are limited.

Many nondiscretionary projects are predictable. Examples include annual updates to payroll, tax percentages, or quarterly changes in reporting requirements for an insurance processing system. By planning ahead for predictable projects, the IT department manages its resources better and keeps the systems review committee fully informed without needing prior approval in every case.

PRELIMINARY INVESTIGATION OVERVIEW

A systems analyst conducts a preliminary investigation to study the systems request and recommend specific action. After obtaining an authorization to proceed, the analyst interacts with managers and users, as shown in the model in Figure 2-11. The analyst gathers facts about the problem or opportunity, project scope and constraints, project benefits, and estimated development time and costs. The end product of the preliminary investigation is a report to management.

Interaction with Managers and Users

Before beginning a preliminary investigation, a memo or an e-mail message should let people know about the investigation and explain your role. You should meet with key managers, users, and IT staff to describe the project, explain your responsibilities, answer questions, and invite comments. This starts an important dialog with users that will continue throughout the entire development process.

A systems project often produces significant changes in company operations. Employees may be curious, concerned, or even opposed to those changes. It is not surprising to encounter some user resistance during a preliminary investigation. Employee attitudes and reactions are important and must be considered.

FIGURE 2-11 Model of a preliminary investigation.

When interacting with users, you should be careful in your use of the word *problem*, because generally it has a negative meaning. When you ask users about *problems*, some will stress current system limitations rather than desirable new features or enhancements. Instead of focusing on difficulties, you should question users about additional capability they would like to have. Using this approach, you highlight ways to improve the user's job, you get a better understanding of operations, and you build better, more positive relationships with users.

STEPS IN THE PRELIMINARY INVESTIGATION

During a preliminary investigation, a systems analyst typically follows a series of steps, as shown in Figure 2-12. The exact procedure, however, depends on the nature of the request, the size of the project, and the degree of urgency.

Step 1: Understand the Problem or Opportunity

If the systems request involves a new information system or a substantial change in an existing system, systems analysts might need to develop a business profile that describes business processes and functions, as explained in Chapter 1. Even where the request involves relatively minor changes or enhancements, you need to understand how those modifications will affect business operations and other information systems. Often a change in one system has an unexpected effect on another system. When you analyze a systems request, you need to determine which departments, users, and business processes are involved.

In many cases, the systems request does not reveal the underlying problem, but only a symptom. For example, you might receive a request to investigate mainframe processing delays, and find improper scheduling practices, rather than hardware problems. Similarly, a request for analysis of customer complaints might disclose a lack of sales rep training, rather than problems with the product.

Step 1:	Understanding the problem or opportunity.
Step 2:	Define the project scope and constraints.
Step 3:	Perform fact-finding.
	• Analyze organizational charts.
	• Conduct interviews.
	• Review documentation.
	• Observe operation to obtain information.
	• Conduct a survey of people who use the system.
Step 4:	Estimate the project's benefits.
Step 5:	Estimate project development time and cost.
Step 6:	Present results and recommendations to management.

FIGURE 2-12   Steps in a preliminary investigation.

Step 2: Define the Project Scope and Constraints

Determining the **project scope** means to define the boundaries, or extent, of the project — being as specific as possible. For example, the statement, payroll is not being produced accurately is very general, compared with the statement, overtime pay is not being calculated correctly for production workers on the second shift at the Yorktown plant. Similarly, the statement, the project scope is to modify the accounts receivable system is not as specific as the statement, the project scope is to allow customers to inquire online about account balances and recent transactions.

Projects sometimes expand gradually, without specific authorization, in a process called **project creep**. To avoid this problem, you should define project scope as clearly as possible. You might want to use a graphical model that shows the systems, people, and business processes that will be affected. The scope of the project also establishes the boundaries of the preliminary investigation itself. A systems analyst should limit the focus to the problem at hand and avoid unnecessary expenditure of time and money.

Along with defining the scope of the project, you need to identify any constraints on the system. A **constraint**, or **requirement**, is a condition that the system must satisfy or an outcome that the system must achieve. A constraint can involve hardware, software, time, policy, law, or cost. System constraints also define project scope. For example, if the system must operate with existing hardware, that is a constraint that affects potential solutions. Other examples of constraints are: the order entry system must accept input from 15 remote sites; the human resources information system must produce statistics on hiring practices; and the new Web site must be operational by March 1. When examining constraints, you should identify their characteristics.

PRESENT VERSUS FUTURE CONSTRAINTS Is the constraint something that must be met as soon as the system is developed or modified, or is the constraint necessary at some future time?

INTERNAL VERSUS EXTERNAL CONSTRAINTS Is the constraint due to a requirement within the organization or does some external force, such as government regulations, impose it?

MANDATORY VERSUS DESIRABLE CONSTRAINTS Is the constraint mandatory? Is it absolutely essential that the constraint is met, or is it merely desirable? If desirable, how important is the constraint?

Examples of various types of constraints are shown in Figure 2-13. One common mistake is to list all constraints as mandatory, which results in increased development time and costs. Present, external, and mandatory constraints usually are fixed and must be met by the system when it is developed or modified. Constraints that are future, internal, or desirable often can be postponed.

Regardless of the type, all constraints should be identified as early as possible to avoid future problems and surprises.

CONSTRAINT	EXAMPLE
Present	The inventory system must be operational on January 1, 2002.
Future	The Web-based sales system must be able to handle transaction volume predicted for the next three years.
Internal	The human resources system must interface with the current accounting system.
External	The payroll system must produce output data in a form acceptable to the Internal Revenue Service.
Mandatory	The order entry system must run in a UNIX environment.
Desirable	The purchasing system should provide user-customizable screens. After further investigation, this is desirable only if adding this feature will not delay the project.

FIGURE 2-13 Examples of various types of constraints.

A clear definition of project scope and constraints avoids misunderstandings that arise when managers assume that the system will have a certain feature or support for a project, but later find that the feature is not included.

Step 3: Perform Fact-Finding

Fact-finding involves various techniques, which are described below. Depending on what information is needed to investigate the systems request, fact-finding might consume several hours, days, or weeks. For example, a change in a report format or data entry screen might require a single telephone call or e-mail message to a user, whereas a new inventory system would involve a series of interviews. During fact-finding, you might analyze organization charts, conduct interviews, review current documentation, observe operations, and carry out a user survey.

ANALYZE ORGANIZATION CHARTS In many instances you will not know the organizational structure of departments involved in the study. You should obtain organization charts to understand how the department functions and identify individuals you might want to interview. Organization charts often can be obtained from the company's human resources department. If such charts are unavailable, you should obtain the necessary information directly from department personnel and then construct your own charts. You can use an organization chart tool built into your word processor or a separate graphical tool, such as Microsoft Visio.

When organization charts are available, you should verify their accuracy. Keep in mind that organization charts show formal reporting relationships but not the informal alignment of a group, which also is important.

CONDUCT INTERVIEWS The primary method of obtaining information during the preliminary investigation is the interview, as shown in Figure 2-14. Remember that the purpose of the interview, and of the preliminary investigation itself, is to uncover facts, not to convince others that the project is justified. Your primary role in an interview is to ask effective questions and listen carefully. If you plan to talk to several people about the same topic, you should prepare a standard set of questions for all the interviews. Also be sure to include open-ended questions, such as "What else do you think I should know about the system?" or "Is there any other relevant information that we have not discussed?" You will learn more about interview techniques in Chapter 3, when you begin the systems analysis phase.

When conducting interviews during the preliminary investigation, you should interview managers and supervisors who have a broad knowledge of the system and can give you an overview of the business processes involved. Depending on the situation, you might talk to operational personnel to learn how the system functions on a day-to-day basis.

REVIEW CURRENT DOCUMENTATION Although interviews are an extremely important method of obtaining information, you also may want to investigate the current system documentation. The documentation might not be up-to-date, so you should check with users to confirm that you are receiving accurate and complete information.

N THE WEB

more information
Fact-finding visit
ite.com/sad4e/more.htm,
k Systems Analysis and
ign Chapter 2 and then
k the Fact-finding link.

w.scsite.com

FIGURE 2-14 The interview is the primary method of obtaining information.

OBSERVE OPERATIONS   Another fact-finding method is to observe the current system in operation. You might see how workers carry out typical tasks. You might choose to trace or follow the actual paths taken by input source documents or output reports. In addition to observing operations, you might want to sample the inputs or outputs of the system. Using simple statistical techniques described in the Systems Analyst's Toolkit, you can obtain valuable information about the nature and frequency of the problem.

CARRY OUT A USER SURVEY   Interviews can be time-consuming. Sometimes you can obtain information from a larger group by carrying out a user survey. In this case, you design a form that users complete and return to you for tabulation. A survey is not as flexible as a series of interviews, but it is less expensive, generally takes less time, and can involve a broad cross-section of people.

ON THE WE

To learn more about Effec
Communications visit
scsite.com/sad4e/more.h
click Systems Analysis an
Design Chapter 2 and the
click the Effective
Communications link.

www.scsite.c

Step 4: Determine Feasibility

At this point you have analyzed the problem or opportunity, defined project scope and constraints, performed fact-finding to learn about factors that might affect the project, and estimated the costs and benefits of the new system. Now you are ready to determine operational, technical, and economic feasibility.

Step 5: Estimate Time and Cost to Continue Development

To develop specific time and cost estimates for the next development phase, you should consider the following issues:

- What information must you obtain, and how will you gather and analyze the information?
- What sources of information will you use, and what difficulties will you encounter in obtaining the information?
- Will you conduct interviews? How many people will you interview, and how much time will you need to meet with the people and summarize their responses?
- Will you conduct a survey? Who will be involved? How much time will it take people to complete it? How much time will it take to prepare it and tabulate the results?
- How much will it cost to analyze the information gathered and to prepare a report with findings and recommendations?

In addition to time and cost figures for the next development phase, you should provide an estimate for the overall project, so managers can understand the full cost impact and timetable. Exact figures might not be available, but an estimated range of time and costs can be useful, particularly when forecasting a best versus worst scenario.

Step 6: Present Results and Recommendations to Management

At this stage, you have several alternatives. You might find that no action is necessary or that some other strategy, such as additional training, is needed. To solve a minor problem, you might implement a simple solution without performing further analysis. In other situations, you will recommend that the project proceed to the next development phase, which is systems analysis.

The final task in the preliminary investigation is to prepare a report to management. The report includes an evaluation of the systems request, an estimate of costs and benefits, and your recommendation. Part 1 of the Systems Analyst's Toolkit helps you achieve effective written and oral communications.

The format of the preliminary investigation report varies from one company to another. A typical report might include the seven sections shown in Figure 2-15.

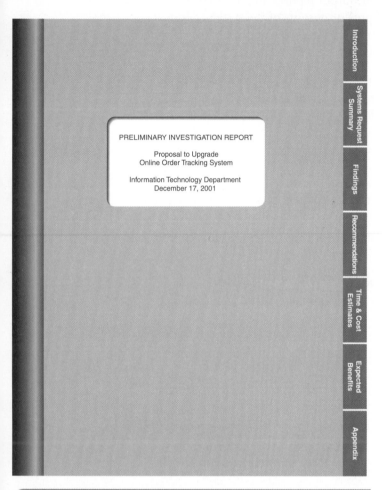

PRELIMINARY INVESTIGATION REPORT

Proposal to Upgrade
Online Order Tracking System

Information Technology Department
December 17, 2001

Introduction

Systems Request Summary

Findings

Recommendations

Time & Cost Estimates

Expected Benefits

Appendix

FIGURE 2-15 Sample of a preliminary investigation report.

1. *Introduction.* The first section is an overview of the report. The introduction contains a brief description of the system, the name of the person or group who performed the investigation, and the name of the person or group who initiated the investigation.

2. *Systems Request Summary.* The summary describes the basis of the systems request.

3. *Findings.* The findings section contains the results of your preliminary investigation, including a description of the project's scope, constraints, and feasibility.

4. *Recommendations.* Recommendations for further action, with specific reasons and justification, are explained in this section. Management will make the final decision, but the IT department's input is an important factor.

5. *Time and Cost Estimates.* This section describes the cost of acquiring and installing the system, and the total cost of ownership during the system's useful life.

6. *Expected Benefits.* Anticipated tangible and intangible benefits, and a timetable that shows when they are to occur is included in this section.

7. *Appendix.* An appendix is included in the report if you need to attach supporting information. For example, you might list the interviews you conducted, the documentation you reviewed, and other sources for the information you obtained. You do not need detailed reports of the interviews or other lengthy documentation. It is critical that you retain those documents to support your findings and for future reference.

In addition to a written report, you might be asked to give an oral presentation, as shown in Figure 2-16. Chapter 3 and Part 1 of the Systems Analyst's Toolkit provide suggestions on delivering presentations.

FIGURE 2-16 Oral presentations often are required during systems development, and systems analysts need to develop strong presentation skills.

SOFTWEAR, LIMITED

The management of SoftWear, Limited (SWL) outsources the company's payroll processing. A company called Business Information Systems (BIS) uses its own hardware and software to perform payroll processing for SWL and dozens of other companies. Contractual agreements between BIS and its customers identify specific information processing services and prices.

SWL's information technology department is located at the company headquarters in Raleigh and reports to the vice president of finance. The IT staff is responsible for SWL's mainframe computer and supports the company's Web site and the inventory, marketing, customer order entry, and accounting systems.

Robert Lansing, SWL's president, believes that IT support is vital to the company's strategic long-range plans, and approved increased IT budgets and expansion of the IT staff. In addition to the mainframe, the company networked personal computers in all offices and many shop floor locations and implemented a company intranet linking all SWL locations.

Even though it could handle its own payroll processing, SWL continues to use BIS for payroll services because BIS does a good job at a reasonable costs and it relieves SWL of this responsibility. Recently, problems with the system developed, and payroll department employees worked overtime to correct errors involving employee deductions.

SWL employees can make two types of voluntary payroll deductions. Starting in 1996, employees could contribute to the newly formed SWL credit union. To enroll or make changes, an employee must complete a deduction form. In 1998, the company gave employees an opportunity to purchase SWL company stock through payroll deductions. Employees enroll in the stock purchase plan or change their deductions by visiting the human resources department, which then sends a weekly list of transactions to the payroll department.

In addition to the credit union and stock purchase deductions, SWL employees soon may have other savings and investment choices. SWL's top management, with strong support from the vice president of human resources, may consider a new Employee Savings and Investment Plan (ESIP) that allows employees to purchase mutual funds, stocks, and other investments through regular payroll deductions. Under this new 401(k) plan, an outside investment firm, Court Street Securities, manages tax-sheltered deductions and services the individual accounts. Each employee maintains direct control over their investments using a 24-hour toll-free number or accessing the Court Street Securities Web site. Management expects to make a final decision about the new ESIP in several months.

Request for Information Technology Services

Tina Pham, vice president of human resources, learned that a number of SWL employees had complained about improper paycheck deductions, and she became concerned about employee morale. She decided to discuss the subject with Michael Jeremy, vice president of finance. At their meeting, he listened carefully and promised to look into the matter further.

That afternoon, Mr. Jeremy met with Amy Calico, director of payroll, to ask her about the problem as well as a recent increase in overtime pay in her group. Amy stated that the overtime became necessary because payroll operations recently required more time and effort. She also noted that, since this workload increase came about recently, she lacked the money in her budget to hire any additional people. She did not provide any specific explanation for the payroll deduction errors.

Mr. Jeremy then decided to ask the IT department to investigate the payroll system. He prepared a Request for Information Technology Services, as shown in Figure 2-17, and sent it to the IT department for action. In the request, he mentioned problems with the payroll system and requested help but did not identify the causes of the problems or propose a solution.

SWL REQUEST FOR INFORMATION TECHNOLOGY SERVICES

Date: _____September 18, 2001_____
Submitted by: ____Michael Jeremy____ Title: _Vice President - Finance____
Department: ____Finance____ Location: _Raleigh____
Phone: _____Ext. 239_____ e-mail: _mjeremy@swl.hq.fin.org___

REQUEST FOR:

[X] Correction of system error
[ ] System enhancement
[ ] New system

URGENCY:

[ ] Immediate attention needed
[X] Handle in normal priority sequence
[ ] Defer until new system is developed

DESCRIPTION OF REQUESTED SYSTEMS SERVICES:
(ATTACH ADDITIONAL DOCUMENTS AS NECESSARY)

I recently received several reports about incorrect deductions in employee paychecks. Also, I am concerned about overtime in the payroll department.

Amy Calico, director of payroll, tells me that the payroll system still requires a great deal of manual effort and that she needs more people to handle the workload properly.

I think there may be more to it than that, and I would like you to look into the situation. The purpose of using BIS, the outside service bureau, was to save money, not to incur additional expense. Also, I wonder where the errors are coming from. I thought we sent all the source data to BIS and they did the processing for us.

I would like you to find out what we need to do to eliminate the deduction errors and the payroll department overtime.

(To be completed by the Information Technology Department)

[ ] Approved   Assigned to IT contact person: _____
                User: _____
                Urgency code (1 low to 5 high): _____

[ ] Modified (see attached notes)
[ ] Rejected (see attached statement)

Date _____   Action: _____

FIGURE 2-17 Michael Jeremy's systems request.

Jane Rossman, manager of applications, normally receives systems requests and does an initial review to see whether a preliminary investigation is warranted. After a quick look at Mr. Jeremy's request, Jane decided to contact her boss, Ann Hon, director of information technology.

Because SWL does not have a formal systems review committee, Ann normally makes the initial decision on most systems requests. She always consults with other managers, if the proposal is significant or could affect their areas. After discussing the proposal, Jane and Ann decided that a preliminary investigation should start right away. Given that the system was eight years old and never received a major update, it seemed likely that they would find some problems that warranted attention.

Jane assigned Rick Williams, a systems analyst, to conduct a preliminary investigation of the payroll system. Ann sent the e-mail message shown in Figure 2-18 to Mr. Jeremy so he knew that Rick would start the preliminary investigation the following week.

Because the information technology department reports to him, Mr. Jeremy sent the memo shown in Figure 2-19 to all SWL departments. Although the memo gives few details, it explains that Rick Williams has been authorized to conduct a preliminary investigation and requests everyone's cooperation.

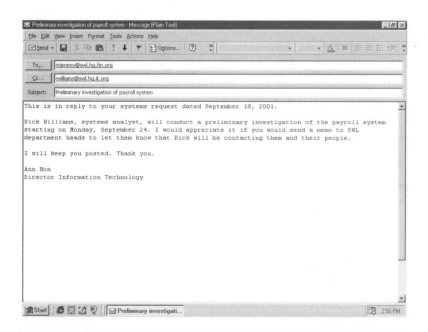

FIGURE 2-18 Ann Hon's e-mail message to Michael Jeremy.

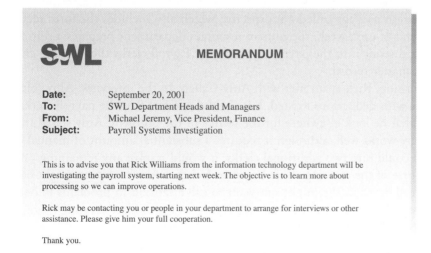

FIGURE 2-19 Michael Jeremy's memo announcing the start of the payroll system investigation.

Organization Charts

To begin his investigation, Rick met with Tina Pham, vice president of human resources. She gave Rick copies of job descriptions for all payroll department positions but did not have a current organization chart for that group.

After reviewing the descriptions, Rick visited Amy Calico, director of payroll. She explained how the payroll department was organized. She did not provide a formal chart, so Rick used Microsoft Visio to draw the chart shown in Figure 2-20.

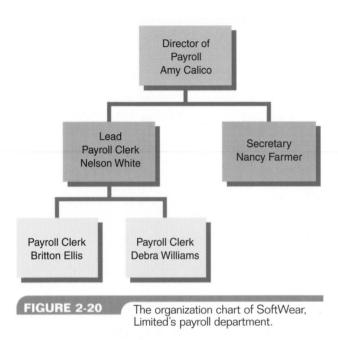

FIGURE 2-20 The organization chart of SoftWear, Limited's payroll department.

Interviews

Rick next decided to interview Michael Jeremy, Amy Calico, and Mike Feiner, director of human resources.

Mr. Jeremy provided an overview of the recent problems within the payroll system, including the costs of the current system. He had no specific data, but he believed, from what he had heard, that the majority of the errors involved stock purchases rather than credit union deductions.

Later that day, in his meeting with Mike Feiner, Rick found out more about the reported deduction errors. He learned that stock purchase enrollments and changes are handled differently from credit union deductions. For legal reasons, Mike explained, employees must complete a special form for stock purchase plan transactions. When enrolling or making changes, an employee visits the human resources department for a brochure and an information package called a prospectus, which also includes the form required to enroll. At the end of each week, the human resources department prepares a summary of deduction requests and sends it to the payroll department. Payroll clerks then file the changes with the employee's master record.

The next morning, Rick again met with Amy Calico. In the interview, Amy told Rick that some problems with deductions existed, but she did not feel that the payroll clerks were at fault. She suggested that he look elsewhere for the source of the problem. Amy stated that the payroll process generally works well, although it requires a substantial amount of manual effort. She said that if she could hire two additional clerks, it would resolve any remaining problems. During the course of the meeting, Rick began to feel that Amy's opinion might be somewhat biased. As payroll director, she might not want to call attention to problems in her department, and, Rick guessed, it involved other potential issues — such as her wanting more reports and wanting to expand her department. He made a mental note of those possibilities so that he could factor them in when considering her comments and assessment of the problem.

Current Documentation

After completing the three interviews, Rick reviewed his notes and decided to find out more about the actual sequence of operations in the current system. He studied the documentation and found that it provided step-by-step procedures for preparing the payroll. When he asked the payroll clerks about those procedures, he learned that some sections were outdated. The actual sequence of events is shown in Figure 2-21.

Step 1: A new SWL employee completes an employee master sheet and a W-4 form. The human resources department then enters the employee's status and pay rate. Copies of these forms are sent to the payroll department. The payroll department updates the employee master sheet whenever changes are received from the employee or the human resources department. Updates are made with various forms, including forms for credit union and employee stock purchase plan enrollment and changes.

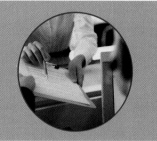

Step 2: On the last day of a weekly pay period, the payroll department prepares and distributes time sheets to all SWL departments. The time sheets list each employee, with codes for various status items such as regular pay, overtime, sick leave, vacation, jury duty, and personal leave.

Step 3: Department heads complete the time sheets on the first business day after the end of a pay period. The sheets then go to the payroll department, where they are reviewed. A payroll clerk enters pay rates and deduction information and forwards the time sheets to the BIS service bureau.

Step 4: BIS enters and processes the time sheet data, prints SWL paychecks, and prepares a payroll register.

Step 5: The checks, time sheets, and payroll register are returned to SWL. The payroll department distributes checks to each department, creates reports for credit union and stock purchase plan deductions, and then transfers necessary funds.

FIGURE 2-21   Sequence of events in payroll processing at SoftWear, Limited.

Rick also discovered that the payroll department never sees a copy of the form that an employee fills out in the human resources department when joining the stock purchase plan or changing deductions. Rick obtained a copy of the SWL stock purchase form from the human resources department and copies of several forms from the payroll department — including employee master sheets, employee time sheets, and credit union deduction forms. Rick put them in a file for later review.

During the preliminary investigation, Rick did not show concern with the detailed information on each form. He would review that information only after management authorized the IT department to continue with the systems analysis phase.

Presentation to Management

After Rick finished his investigation, he analyzed his findings, prepared a preliminary investigation report, and met with Jane and Ann to plan the presentation to management. Ann sent the report to Mr. Jeremy with a cover memo that announced the time and location of the presentation, as shown in Figure 2-22.

Figure 2-23 shows the preliminary investigation report that Rick prepared. Following the presentation to SWL's top managers and department heads, a question-and-answer session took place. The management group discussed the findings and recommendations and decided that the payroll system needed further analysis. The group also wanted to know if the BIS service bureau could handle the ESIP using their current arrangement. Ann replied that no clear answer could be given, and everyone agreed that the project scope should be broadened to include that question.

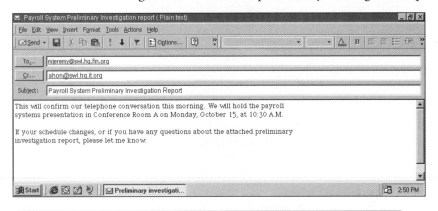

FIGURE 2-22 Cover message for the SWL Preliminary Investigation report.

PRELIMINARY INVESTIGATION REPORT
Subject: SWL Payroll Systems
October 8, 2001

INTRODUCTION
The information technology department completed a preliminary investigation of the payroll system. This investigation was the result of a systems request from Michael Jeremy, vice president of finance, on September 18, 2001.

SYSTEMS REQUEST SUMMARY
Two problems were mentioned in the request for information technology services: incorrect deductions from employee paychecks and payroll department overtime to perform manual processing tasks and make corrections.

PRELIMINARY INVESTIGATION FINDINGS
The following problems were found during the investigation:
1. Employee stock purchase deductions are reported to the payroll department in the form of a summary list from the human resources department. Data entry errors may occur during this process.

2. The payroll processing arrangement with Business Information Systems (BIS) requires a considerable amount of manual effort on SWL's part. The BIS system does not provide summary reports required for verification, reporting and application of total credit union and stock purchase plan deductions. These tasks are handled manually by payroll department staff at the end of each pay period.

3. Payroll overtime averages about six hours per week, plus an additional eight hours at the end of every month when stock purchase deductions are applied. This totals about 408 overtime hours. At an average base rate of $10.00, (calculated at time-and-a-half) the cost is $6,120 per year.

The following factors contribute to the payroll system problems:
1. The current payroll procedures were developed in 1991, when the company consisted of 75 employees, and did not change significantly. Today, more than 450 SWL people are covered by the payroll system, and some new options added, such as credit union and SWL stock purchase plan.

2. Several years ago, payroll clerks only had to copy pay rates from the employees master sheets to the weekly time sheets. Now, in addition to the pay rate, a clerk must handle employee deduction information.

PRELIMINARY INVESTIGATION REPORT
October 8, 2001
Page 2

RECOMMENDATIONS
The problems identified in this preliminary investigation will increase as SWL continues to grow. Also, it is unclear whether the current system can be modified to handle tasks that are now done manually.

Accordingly, the information technology department recommends that a system analysis project be performed. The analysis would include the following areas:
• Manual processing done at SoftWear, Limited
• Computer processing done by BIS service bureau

TIME AND COST ESTIMATES
We estimate that two weeks will be required for an analyst to perform the recommended systems analysis. Also, we will need to conduct approximately 20 hours of interviewing and discussions with people outside the information technology department. The following is an estimate of costs for performing the system analysis;

2.0 weeks	Systems Analyst	@$900/week	$1,800
0.5 weeks	Other SWL people	@$700/week (average)	$350
		Total	$2,150

If the systems development work continues on this project, total cost will depend on what approach is taken. If the current system can be modified, we estimate a total project effort of $15,000 to $20,000 over a three- to four-month period. If modification is not feasible, a revised cost estimate will be submitted for review.

EXPECTED BENEFITS
At the end of the systems analysis phase, the IT department will define, in detail, the problems that exist in the payroll system. We will propose solutions that will eliminate overtime costs, and reduce processing errors.

FIGURE 2-23 The preliminary investigation report on the payroll system.

CHAPTER SUMMARY

Systems planning is the first phase of the systems development life cycle. Effective information systems help an organization support its business processes and carry out its mission and serve its stakeholders. During strategic planning, a company examines its purpose, vision, and values and develops a mission statement, which leads to goals, objectives, day-to-day operations, and business results that affect company stakeholders.

Systems projects are initiated to improve performance, provide more information, reduce costs, strengthen controls, or provide better service. Various internal and external factors affect systems projects, such as user requests, top management directives, existing systems, the IT department, software and hardware vendors, technology, customers, competitors, the economy, and government.

During the preliminary investigation, the analyst evaluates the systems request and determines whether the project is operationally, technically, and economically feasible. Analysts evaluate systems requests on the basis of their expected costs and benefits, both tangible and intangible.

The steps in the preliminary investigation are to understand the problem or opportunity; define the project scope and constraints; perform fact-finding; estimate the project's benefits; estimate project development time and cost; and present results and recommendations to management. The report must include an estimate of time, staffing requirements, costs, benefits, and expected results for the next phase of the SDLC.

Key Terms

case for action (2.5)

computer resources committee (2.10)

constraint (2.17)

critical business issues (2.5)

critical success factors (2.5)

discretionary projects (2.14)

economic feasibility (2.13)

encryption (2.7)

encyclopedias (2.5)

feasibility study (2.11)

goals (2.3)

intangible benefits (2.13)

intangible factor (2.14)

just-in-time (JIT) (2.10)

mission statement (2.3)

nondiscretionary projects (2.14)

objectives (2.3)

operational feasibility (2.12)

preliminary investigation (2.15)

project creep (2.17)

project scope (2.17)

requirement (2.17)

stakeholders (2.3)

strategic planning (2.2)

SWOT analysis (2.2)

systems request (2.6)

systems review committee (2.10)

tangible benefits (2.13)

tangible factor (2.14)

technical feasibility (2.12)

total cost of ownership (TCO) (2.13)

Chapter Review

1. What is a goal? What is an objective? How are they different? How are they related?

2. What are five common reasons for systems requests?

3. What is the role of the systems review committee, and by what other names might the systems review committee be known?

4. What are some advantages and disadvantages of a systems committee approach?

5. What is feasibility? List and briefly discuss three kinds of feasibility.

6. What is project scope?

7. What is a constraint? In what three ways are constraints classified?

8. List and briefly describe the basic sections of the preliminary investigation report.

9. What is the purpose of the preliminary investigation?

10. How do tangible benefits differ from intangible benefits?

Discussion Topics

1. Directives from top management trigger many projects. Suppose that the vice president of marketing tells you to write a program to create mailing labels for a one time advertising promotion. As IT manager, you know that the labels are prepared more efficiently by simply exporting the data to a word processing program with a mail merge feature. How would you handle this situation?

2. The vice president of accounting says to you, the IT director, "This systems development life cycle stuff takes too long." She tells you that her people know what they are doing and that all systems requests coming from her department are necessary and important to the organization. She suggests that the IT department bypass the initial steps for any accounting department request and immediately get to work at the solution. What would you say to her?

3. One of your coworkers says, "Mission statements are nice, but they really don't change things down here in our department where the work gets done." How would you reply?

4. Would you, as an IT professional, risk your job to resist a strategic decision that you felt clearly was wrong?

Chapter Assignments

1. Use the Internet to find an example of a corporate mission statement.

2. Use the Internet to locate a consulting firm that helps companies develop strategic plans.

3. Pretend that you own a travel agency in a large city. You have many corporate clients, but growth has slowed somewhat. Some long-term employees are getting discouraged, but you feel that there might be a way to make technology work in your favor. Use your imagination and suggest at least one strength, weakness, opportunity, and threat that your business faces.

4. Write a mission statement and at least three goals for the travel agency described in Assignment 3.

Apply Your Knowledge

1 Last Chance Securities

Situation:

The IT director opened the department staff meeting today by saying "I've got some good news and some bad news. The good news is that management approved the payroll system project this morning. The new system will reduce clerical time and errors, improve morale in the payroll department, and avoid possible fines and penalties for noncompliance. The bad news is that the system must be installed by the end of December in order to meet new federal reporting rules, costs must be within the budgeted amount, the new system must interact with existing systems, and the vice president of finance insists on approving the final design."

1. Name the constraints and indicate whether each is present, future, internal, external, mandatory, or desirable.

2. It is important for everyone to agree on the scope of the payroll project. Explain how to define project scope.

3. Identify tangible and intangible benefits of the new payroll system.

4. What topics should be included in a report to management at the end of the preliminary investigation?

2 Way Out Bikes

Situation:

The owner of Way Out Bikes asked you for advice about acquiring an information system for her business. The company specializes in helping customers select exactly the right bicycle for their needs and lifestyle. Way Out cannot compete on price with mass merchandisers, but it seeks to offer value and expertise for which customers are willing to pay. You ask the owner whether she has long-range plans for the company, and she replies that she has not really thought beyond a one-year time frame.

1. Explain the concept of strategic planning to Way Out's owner.

2. Decide what else you might want to know about Way Out. Refer to the System Architect 2001 screen shown in Figure 2-24 to get some ideas, and list questions that you might want to ask the owner.

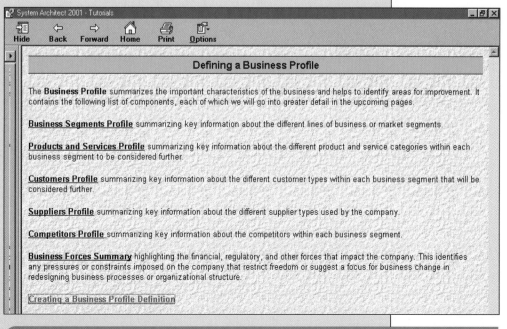

FIGURE 2-24 System Architect 2001 can help you define a business profile that summarizes the important characteristics of the business.

3. Draft a mission statement for Way Out.

4. Make a list of Way Out's stakeholders.

3 The Monday IT Department Staff Meeting

Situation:

Your boss, the IT manager, was ready to explode. "Why can't we get our priorities straight," he fumed. "Here we go again, working on a low-value project, just because it's a favorite of the marketing group. I wish we could get away from departmental politics! I want you to draft a memo that proposes a systems review committee for this company. Explain the advantages, but don't step on anyone's toes!"

1. Write a draft of the proposal, as your boss requested.

2. Write a memo to your boss explaining potential disadvantages of the committee approach.

3. Draft a set of ground rules for committee meetings. Try to suggest rules that will minimize political differences and focus on the overall benefit to the company.

4. Most people serve on a committee at some point in their lives. Write a brief memo describing your committee experiences, good or bad.

4 The Friday IT Department Staff Meeting

Situation:

By the end of the week, things quieted down. The IT staff discussed how to prioritize IT project requests, taking into account technical, operational, and economic feasibility. The IT manager asked for suggestions from the group.

1. Provide three examples of why a project might lack technical feasibility.

2. Provide three examples of why a project might lack operational feasibility.

3. Provide three examples of why a project might lack economic feasibility.

4. Devise a rating system for prioritizing systems requests.

CASE STUDIES

Case Studies offer an opportunity for you to practice specific skills and knowledge learned in the chapter and provide practical experience for you as a systems analyst. Two of the case studies (New Century Health Clinic and Ridgeway Company) are continuing case studies that appear in each chapter. Additionally, one continuing case study (SCR Associates) utilizes the Internet to practice some of the topics covered in this chapter.

NEW CENTURY HEALTH CLINIC

New Century Health Clinic's office manager, Anita Davenport, recently asked permission to hire an additional office clerk because she feels the current staff can no longer handle the growing workload. The associates discussed Anita's request during a recent meeting. They were not surprised that the office staff was feeling overwhelmed by the constantly growing workload.

Because the clinic was busier and more profitable than ever, they all agreed that New Century could afford to hire another office worker. Dr. Jones then came up with another idea. He suggested that they investigate the possibility of computerizing New Century's office systems. Dr. Jones said that a computerized system could keep track of patients, appointments, charges, and insurance claim processing and reduce paperwork. All the associates were enthusiastic about the possibilities and voted to follow up on the suggestion. Dr. Jones agreed to direct the project.

Because no member of the staff had computer experience, Dr. Jones decided to hire a consultant to study the current office systems and recommend a course of action. Several friends recommended you as a person who has considerable experience with computerized business applications.

Assignments

1. Dr. Jones arranged an introductory meeting between the associates of New Century Health Clinic and you to determine if mutual interest exists in pursuing the project. What should the associates try to learn about you? What should you try to learn in this meeting?

2. What kinds of questions would you ask to assess the initial feasibility of this project? Based on the information above, does the project seem feasible?

3. New Century Health Clinic management decided to contract for your services to perform a preliminary investigation. What will be your plan of action?

4. You begin the preliminary investigation. What information is needed? From whom will you obtain it? What techniques will you use in your fact-finding?

RIDGEWAY COMPANY

At Ridgeway Company, Senior Vice President Helen Hill, Vice President of Finance Luis Sanchez, and Director of Information Technology Linda Usher form the systems review committee that approves and schedules all IT projects.

Thomas McGee, vice president of operations, recently talked to Hill about the committee's work. "It just isn't fair," McGee began, "for the committee to have the power to turn down projects that one of my facility managers thinks is worthwhile. After all, Ridgeway runs all the facilities as separate profit centers. The Country Club pro shop, the golf course, the restaurant and bar, and the tennis club have separate budgets. When the information technology department does a project for one of them, the facility is charged for all development costs. My pro shop manager, Chris Connely, plans to submit a request for a computerized inventory system for the pro shop. We calculated the figures to prove that the system will save the shop and the company money in the long run. The pro shop can pay for the system development, but what's so frustrating is that after all our planning, the committee might say no. I can see why the committee needs the power to set priorities and schedules, but if we are willing to pay for a system, and if we believe the system is worthwhile, why should the committee veto it if they so choose?"

Assignments

1. Chris has asked you to help him with the systems request form. What are the reasons for the systems request? How would you describe the benefits of the new system? (Describe both tangible and intangible benefits.)

2. Review the criteria used to evaluate systems requests. Based on those criteria, does the computerized inventory system seem feasible? Explain the reasons for your answer.

3. Is a project that is good for the pro shop necessarily good for the company? For what valid reasons might the systems review committee turn down this project request?

4. How should Hill respond to McGee's complaint?

PEMBROKE IMPORTS

Four months ago, Pembroke Imports hired David Jackson away from an advertising agency, and ___ ___ ___ ___ ___ cently submitted a systems request to rede ___ ___ ___ ___ nnah Holt, the systems analyst assigned to c ___ ___ ___ son to determine the reasons for the requ ___ ___ s are much too unattractive and dull. "Pe ___ ___ have to show our customers that Pem ___ ___ es. The best place to start is with the mo ___ ___ ing more eye-catching, more artistic, mo ___ ___

H ___ ___ ng, Karen Alexander, who oversees the acc ___ ___ he monthly customer statements. Karen tol ___ ___ have been reported and no complaints fro ___ ___ been received. She assured Hannah that the ___ ___ d.

C ___ ___ Cecil Collier, the manager of customer rel ___ ___ having no problems with its customers. Sh ___ ___ which clearly showed that Pembroke Import's annual sales were increasing at a healthy pace.

[handwritten notes in margin:]
CH 2
1) 2.32 (2.6) (2.13)
2) 2.32 (2.10) (2.14)
3) 2.32 (2.11)
4) 2.32

Assignments

1. The chapter identifies five major reasons for systems projects. Has David made his systems request for one or more of those five reasons? If so, which one(s) and why? If not, why not?

2. Do you think this is a feasible project? Why or why not?

3. Of the three tests of feasibility — operational, technical, or economic — which would you perform first to measure the system project's feasibility? Why?

4. What should Hannah do next?

G. H. AMES & COMPANY

Kelly Tompkins, a systems analyst at G. H. Ames & Company, often is assigned responsibility for maintenance changes to the company's sales analysis system. She recently noticed an increase in the frequency of requests for fixes and additions to the system. Kelly mentioned this to her manager, Chris Lyle, who asked if the marketing department made any specific complaints about the system. When Kelly admitted that she was unaware of any such complaints, Chris said, "Then don't worry about it."

Assignments

1. If the frequency of fixes and enhancements on the sales analysis system is increasing, what are some possible causes?

2. Do you agree with Chris's decision? Why or why not? How else could Chris have responded to Kelly's concerns?

3. After further conversations with Kelly and a review of the systems requests, Chris agrees that it might be time for a major system upgrade. What factors affect this systems project and influenced Chris' decision?

5. Upon review, Chris assigns Kelly as the systems analyst on the project. What should be her next step?

SCR ASSOCIATES

SCR Associates is an information technology consulting firm that offers IT solutions and training for small- and medium-sized companies. SCR's slogan is "We Know IT!"

Background

As a newly hired systems analyst, you handle assignments, work on various SCR projects, and apply the skills you learned in the text. SCR needs an information system to manage training operations at the new SCR training center. The new system will be called TIMS (Training Information Management System).

The SCR case is available as an interactive, Web-based case study. You can log on to the Shelly Cashman Series site at www.scsite.com/sad4e/scr for instructions and assignments. If you prefer to complete the case study without using the Internet then you must download the data disk. See the inside back cover for instructions for downloading the data disk or see your instructor for more information on accessing the files required for this book.

Situation

In Part 2 you learn that SCR will expand its training business and open a new training center and that you will lead a systems development team. In this part of the case study, you will draft a strategic goal regarding the SCR training function, provide a recommendation for a systems review committee, describe the TIMS project scope and constraints, and prepare to conduct interviews.

Before You Begin ...

1. Review SCR's functions and organization. Open the Document 1-2 from the data disk.

2. Review the October 16 announcement to all SCR employees. Open the Document 2-1 from the data disk.

3. Review the October 17 message from Jesse Baker regarding the systems development team. Open the Document 2-2 from the data disk.

4. Review the October 19 message from Jesse Baker regarding training records. Open the Document 2-3 from the data disk. Open the Document 2-4 from the data disk.

Assignments

1. Draft a corporate goal for SCR that refers to the company's new training activity.

2. Decide whether or not SCR should have a systems review committee. Prepare a recommendation to Jesse Baker, together with your reasons.

3. Draft a specific statement of the project scope for the TIMS system and describe the constraints.

4. Identify the people you would like to interview to learn more about the new training activity, and prepare a list of the questions you plan to ask.

ON THE WEB

The SCR case is available as an interactive, Web-based case study. You can log on to the Shelly Cashman Series site at www.scsite.com/sad4e/scr for instructions and assignments.

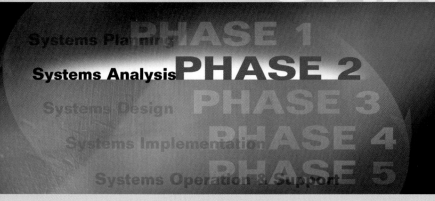

CHAPTER 3

Systems Planning PHASE 1

Systems Analysis PHASE 2

Systems Design PHASE 3

Systems Implementation PHASE 4

Systems Operation & Support PHASE 5

Requirements Modeling

Systems analysis is the second phase in the systems development life cycle. In the prior phase, systems planning, you conducted a preliminary investigation to learn more about the systems request. Now, in the systems analysis phase, your objective is to develop a logical, business-oriented model of the proposed system. You will learn about requirements modeling, data and process modeling, and object modeling. Before going on to the systems design phase, you also will consider the transition from logical to physical design.

Requirements modeling is the first of four chapters in the systems analysis phase. Chapter 3 describes the process of gathering facts about a systems project and creating models and documentation that will be used to design and develop the system.

INTRODUCTION

After an overview of the systems analysis phase, this chapter describes requirements modeling techniques and team-based methods that systems analysts use to visualize and document new systems. The chapter then discusses system requirements and fact-finding techniques, which include interviewing, documentation review, observation, surveys and questionnaires, sampling, and research.

OBJECTIVES

When you finish this chapter, you will be able to:

- Explain systems analysis phase activities and the end product of the systems analysis phase

- Describe joint application development (JAD)

- Describe the Unified Modeling Language (UML) and explain use case diagrams and sequence diagrams

- Explain how functional decomposition diagrams (FDD) are used during systems development

- List and describe system requirements, including outputs, inputs, processes, performance, and controls

- Explain the importance of scalability in system design

- Define total cost of ownership (TCO) and explain the concept

- Describe how to conduct a successful interview

- Explain when and how to use fact-finding techniques, including interviews, documentation review, observation, questionnaires, sampling, and research

- Develop effective documentation methods to use during systems development

SYSTEMS ANALYSIS PHASE OVERVIEW

The systems analysis phase includes the four activities shown in Figure 3-1: requirements modeling, data and process modeling, object modeling, and the transition to systems design. The overall objective is to understand the proposed project, ensure that it will support business requirements, and build a solid foundation for the systems design phase.

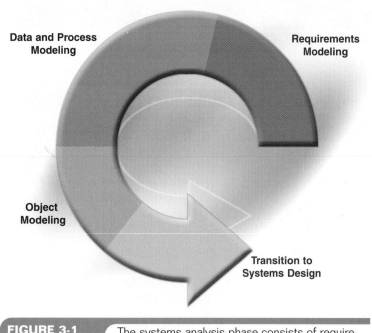

During systems analysis, you use models and other documentation tools to visualize and describe the proposed system. The first step, requirements modeling, is described in this chapter. **Requirements modeling** involves investigation and fact-finding to describe the current system and define the requirements for the new system. In Chapter 4, you will learn how to represent data and processes graphically. Chapter 5 describes object-oriented analysis and modeling, which was discussed briefly in Chapter 1. At the conclusion of the systems analysis phase, in Chapter 6, you prepare for systems design.

The end product of the systems analysis phase is a **system requirements document**, which is an overall design blueprint for the new system. In addition, each activity within the systems analysis phase has an end product and one or more milestones. Large systems projects require considerable effort to coordinate the people, tasks, timetables, and budgets. The Systems Analyst's Toolkit contains project management tools that can help monitor and control complex projects.

At this point in the systems development process, you must deal with a combination of concepts, facts, and people. To be successful, you must have both critical thinking and interpersonal skills. **Critical thinking skills** enable you to recognize the problem, analyze the elements, and communicate the results effectively. **Interpersonal skills** are especially important for a systems analyst who must work with people at all organizational levels and balance the sometimes conflicting needs of users.

FIGURE 3-1   The systems analysis phase consists of requirements modeling, data modeling, object modeling, and the transition to the systems design.

SYSTEMS DEVELOPMENT METHODS

The traditional model for systems development was an IT department that used structured analysis and consulted users when their input or approval was needed. Although the IT staff still has a central role and structured analysis remains a common method of systems development, many companies now use teams to develop information systems. For example, joint application development (JAD), which is discussed in this chapter, is a group-oriented technique for fact-finding and requirements modeling. Because it is not linked to a specific development methodology, systems developers use JAD when group input and interaction is desired.

Team-oriented methodologies that go beyond JAD and provide an overall framework for systems development include rapid application development (RAD) and Microsoft Solutions Framework (MSF), which are both described in the Systems Analyst's Toolkit.

Joint Application Development

Joint application development (JAD) is a popular systems development technique. In a traditional structured analysis process, the IT staff collects information from users and managers and develops the requirements for a new system. In contrast, using a JAD team approach (such as that shown in Figure 3-2), the company creates a task force of users, managers, and IT professionals that works together to gather information, discuss business needs, and define the new system requirements.

The JAD team usually meets over a period of days or weeks, in a special conference room or at an off-site location. Either way, JAD participants should be insulated from the distraction of day-to-day operations. The objective is to analyze the existing system, work on potential solutions, and agree on requirements for the new system.

The JAD group usually has a project leader, who needs strong interpersonal and organizational skills, and one or more members who document and record the results and decisions. Typical JAD participants and their roles are shown in Figure 3-3. IT staff members often serve as JAD project leaders, but that is not always the case. Systems analysts on the JAD team participate in discussions, ask questions, take notes, and provide support to the team. If CASE tools are available, analysts can develop models and enter documentation from the JAD session directly into the CASE tool.

FIGURE 3-2 A JAD team of users, managers, and IT professionals works together to identify and document requirements for a new system.

Typical JAD Participants and Roles	
JAD Participant	**Role**
JAD project leader	Develops an agenda, acts as a facilitator, and leads the JAD session
Top management	Provides enterprise-level authorization and support for the project
Managers	Provide department-level support for the project and understand how the project must support business functions and requirements
Users	Provide operational-level input on current operations, desired changes, input and output requirements, user interface issues, and how the project will support day-to-day tasks
Systems analysts and other IT staff members	Provide technical assistance and resources for JAD team members on issues such as security, backup, hardware, software, and network capability
Recorder	Documents results of JAD sessions and works with systems analysts to build system models and develop CASE tool documentation

FIGURE 3-3 Typical JAD participants and roles.

ON THE WEB

To learn more about Joint Application Development (JAD) visit scsite.com/sad4e/more.htm click Systems Analysis and Design Chapter 3 and then click the Joint Application Development (JAD) link.

www.scsite.c

A typical JAD session agenda is shown in Figure 3-4. The JAD process involves intensive effort by all team members. Because of the wide range of input and constant interaction among the participants, many companies believe that a JAD group produces the best possible definition of the new system.

Typical JAD Agenda	
Project leader	• Introduce all JAD team members • Discuss ground rules, goals, and objectives for the JAD sessions • Explain methods of documentation and use of CASE tools, if any
Top management (sometimes called the project owner or sponsor)	• Explain the reason for the project and express top management authorization and support
Project leader	• Provide overview of the current system and proposed project scope and constraints • Present outline of specific topics and issues to be investigated
Open discussion session, moderated by project leader	• Review the main business processes, tasks, user roles, input and output • Identify specific areas of agreement or disagreement • Break team into smaller groups to study specific issues and assign group leaders
JAD team members working in smaller group sessions, supported by IT staff	• Discuss and document all system requirements • Develop models and prototypes
Group leaders	• Report on results and assigned tasks and topics • Present issues that should be addressed by the overall JAD team
Open discussion session, moderated by project leader	• Review reports from small group sessions • Reach consensus on main issues • Document all topics
Project leader	• Present recap of JAD session • Prepare report that will be sent to JAD team members

FIGURE 3-4   Typical agenda for a JAD session.

Compared with traditional methods, JAD is more expensive and can be cumbersome if the group is too large relative to the size of the project. Many companies find, however, that JAD allows key users to participate effectively in the requirements modeling process. When properly used, JAD can result in a more accurate statement of system requirements, a better understanding of common goals, and a stronger commitment to the success of the new system.

MODELING TOOLS AND TECHNIQUES

Models help users, managers, and systems developers to understand current or new system designs. Modeling involves graphical methods and nontechnical language that represent the system at various stages of development. During requirements modeling, you can use the Unified Modeling Language to describe user interaction with the system, and functional decomposition diagrams to show the organization of business functions and processes. Modeling and fact-finding are closely related — fact-finding results translate into models that improve documentation and communication, and often lead to more fact-finding and modeling.

Unified Modeling Language

The **Unified Modeling Language** (UML) is a widely used method of visualizing and documenting software systems design. UML was created by Grady Booch, Ivar Jacobson, and James Rumbaugh in the early 1990s and soon became an IT industry standard. UML uses object-oriented design concepts, but it is independent of any specific programming language and is used to describe business processes and requirements generally.

UML provides various graphical tools and techniques, such as use case diagrams and sequence diagrams. During requirements modeling, a systems analyst can utilize such tools to represent the information system from a user's viewpoint. Use case diagrams, sequence dia-

ON THE WEB

For more detail on the Unified Modeling Language (UML) visit scsite.com/sad4e/more.ht click Systems Analysis an Design Chapter 3 and ther click the Unified Modeling Language (UML) link.

www.scsite.c

grams, and other UML concepts are discussed in more detail in Chapter 5, along with other object-oriented analysis methods. A brief description of each is given below.

USE CASE DIAGRAMS   During requirements modeling, systems analysts and users work together to document requirements and model system functions. A **use case diagram** visually represents the interaction between users and the information system.

In a use case diagram, the user becomes an **actor**, with a specific role that describes how he or she interacts with the system. Systems analysts can draw use case diagrams freehand or use CASE tools that integrate the use cases into the overall system design.

Figure 3-5 shows a simple use case diagram for a sales system where the actor is a customer and the use case involves a credit card validation that is performed by the system. Because use cases depict the system through the eyes of a user, common business language can be used to describe the transactions. For example, Figure 3-6 shows a table that documents the credit card validation use case. Figure 3-7 on the next page shows a student records system, with several use cases and actors.

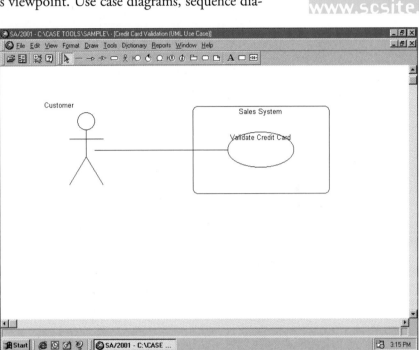

FIGURE 3-5   Use case diagram of a sales system where the actor is a customer and the use case involves a credit card validation.

Name of Use Case:	Credit card validation process
Name of use case:	Credit card validation process
Actor:	Customer
Description:	Describes the credit card validation process
Successful completion:	1. Customer clicks the input selector and enters credit card number and expiration date 2. System verifies card 3. System sends authorization message
Alternative:	1. Customer clicks the input selector and enters credit card number and expiration date 2. System rejects card 3. System sends rejection message
Precondition:	Customer has selected at least one item and has proceeded to checkout area
Postcondition:	Credit card information has been validated. Customer can continue with order
Assumptions:	None

FIGURE 3-6   A table documents the credit card validation use case shown in Figure 3-5.

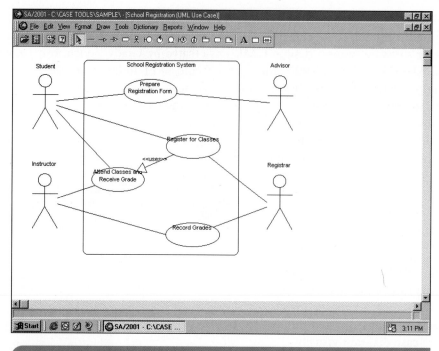

FIGURE 3-7   Use case diagram of a student records system.

SEQUENCE DIAGRAMS   **Sequence diagrams** show the timing of transactions between objects as they occur. A systems analyst might use a sequence diagram to show all possible outcomes, or focus on a single scenario. Figure 3-8 shows a simple sequence diagram of a successful credit card validation. The interaction proceeds from top to bottom, along a vertical timeline, while the horizontal arrows represent messages from one object to another.

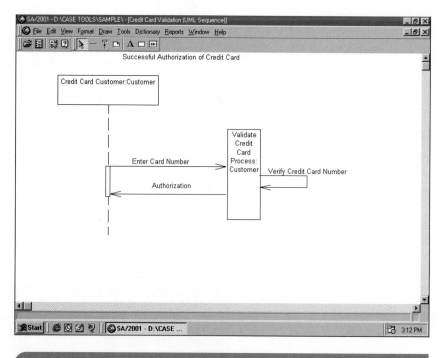

FIGURE 3-8   Sequence diagram of a successful credit card validation, showing how transactions proceed from top to bottom, along a vertical timeline.

Functional Decomposition Diagrams

A **functional decomposition diagram** (FDD) is a top-down representation of business functions and processes. Using an FDD, an analyst can show business functions and break them down into lower-level functions and processes. Creating an FDD is similar to drawing an organization chart — you start at the top and work your way down. Figure 3-9 shows a four-level FDD of a library system, drawn with the Visible Analyst CASE tool. FDDs can be used at several stages of systems development. During requirements modeling, analysts use FDDs to model business functions and show how they are organized into lower-level processes. Those processes are represented as logical symbols during data and process modeling and can translate into program modules during application development.

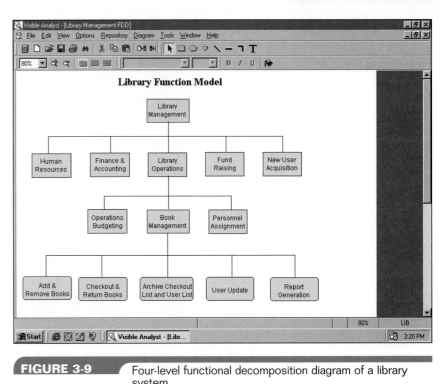

FIGURE 3-9 Four-level functional decomposition diagram of a library system.

SYSTEM REQUIREMENTS CHECKLIST

During requirements modeling, systems developers must identify and describe all system requirements. A **system requirement** is a characteristic or feature that must be included in an information system to satisfy business requirements and be acceptable to users. System requirements therefore serve as benchmarks to measure the overall acceptability of the finished system.

System requirements fall into five general categories: outputs, inputs, processes, performance, and controls. Typical examples of system requirements for each category are listed below.

Outputs

- The Web site must report online volume statistics every four hours, and hourly during peak periods.
- The inventory system must produce a daily report showing the part number, description, quantity on hand, quantity allocated, quantity available, and unit cost of all parts — sorted by part number.
- The contact management system must generate a daily reminder list for all sales reps.
- The purchasing system must provide suppliers with up-to-date specifications.
- The sales tracking system must produce a daily fast-moving-item report, listing all products that exceed the forecasted sales volume — grouped by style, color, size, and reorder status.
- The customer analysis system must produce a quarterly report that identifies changes in ordering patterns or trends, with statistical comparisons to the previous four quarters.

Inputs
- Manufacturing employees must swipe their ID cards into online data collection terminals that record labor costs and calculate production efficiency.
- The department head must enter overtime hours on a separate screen.
- Student grades must be entered on machine-scannable forms prepared by the instructor.
- Each input form must include date, time, product code, customer number, and quantity.
- Data entry screens must be uniform, except for background color, which can be changed by the user.
- A data entry person at the medical group must input patient services into the billing system.

Processes
- The student records system must allow record access by either the student name or the student number.
- As the final step in year-end processing, the payroll system must update employee salaries, bonuses, and benefits and produce tax data required by the IRS.
- The warehouse distribution system must analyze daily orders and create a routing pattern for delivery trucks that maximizes efficiency and reduces unnecessary mileage.
- The human resources system must interface properly with the existing payroll system.
- The video rental system must not execute new rental transactions for customers who have overdue tapes.
- The prescription system must automatically generate an insurance claim form.

Performance
- The system must support 25 users online simultaneously.
- Response time must not exceed four seconds.
- The system must be operational 7 days a week, 365 days a year.
- The accounts receivable system must prepare customer statements by the third business day of the following month.
- The student records system must produce class lists within five hours after the end of registration.
- The online inventory control system must flag all low-stock items within one hour after the quantity falls below a predetermined minimum.

Controls
- The system must provide log-on security at the operating system level and at the application level.
- An employee record must be added, changed, or deleted only by a member of the human resources department.
- The system must maintain separate levels of security for users and the system administrator.
- All transactions must have audit trails.
- The manager of the sales department must approve orders that exceed a customer's credit limit.
- The system must create an error log file that includes the error type, description, and time.

SCALABILITY AND TOTAL COST OF OWNERSHIP

In addition to the system requirements listed above, systems developers must consider future growth and demands on the system and the total cost of ownership, which includes all future operational and support costs.

Scalability

Scalability means the ability to adjust system capacity as business requirements change in the future. To ensure that the system will meet future requirements, you need information about current and future volume and growth for all outputs, inputs, and processes. For example, to create a Web site for customer orders, you need to know the estimated number of online customers, the periods of peak online activity, the number and types of data items required for each transaction, and the method of accessing and updating customer files.

Even to print customer statements, you need to know the number of active accounts and have a forecast for one, two, or five years, because that information affects future hardware decisions. In addition, with realistic volume projections, you can provide reliable cost estimates for related expenses such as postage and online charges. Similarly, for a motel chain reservation system, you might determine the frequency of online queries about room availability, the time required for each query, and the average response time. With that information, you could estimate server transaction volume and network requirements.

Transaction volume has a significant impact on operating costs. When volume exceeds the system's limitations, maintenance costs increase sharply. Volume can change dramatically if a company expands or goes into a new line of business. For example, a new Web-based marketing effort might require an additional server and 24-hour technical support.

Data storage also is an important concern. You need to determine how much data storage is required currently and predict future needs based on system activity and growth. Those requirements affect hardware, software, and network bandwidth needed to maintain system performance.

You also must consider data retention requirements and determine whether data can be deleted or archived on a specific timetable. You learn that a transaction file must be retained for five years. If the information is stored on tape cartridges, and you calculate that two cartridges are needed for each month's data, then the company will need 120 cartridges (2 cartridges per month × 12 months × 5 years).

Total Cost of Ownership

In addition to direct costs, systems developers must identify and document indirect expenses that contribute to the **total cost of ownership (TCO)**. That is especially important where the development team is assessing several alternatives. After considering the indirect (and, hence, sometimes hidden) costs, a system that seems inexpensive initially might actually turn out to be the most costly choice.

ON THE WEB

For additional information on Scalability visit scsite.com/sad4e/more.htm click Systems Analysis and Design Chapter 3 and then click the Scalability link.

www.scsite.c

Microsoft Solutions Framework (MSF) includes a TCO model that offers tools, methods, and guidelines to analyze and reduce TCO. On the Web site shown in Figure 3-10, Microsoft states that indirect costs have tripled over the last 10 years and account for almost 50 percent of total costs. Microsoft also points out that most indirect costs, such as end user peer- and self-support and downtime productivity losses, typically were not included in IT department budgets and were unaccounted for in most companies.

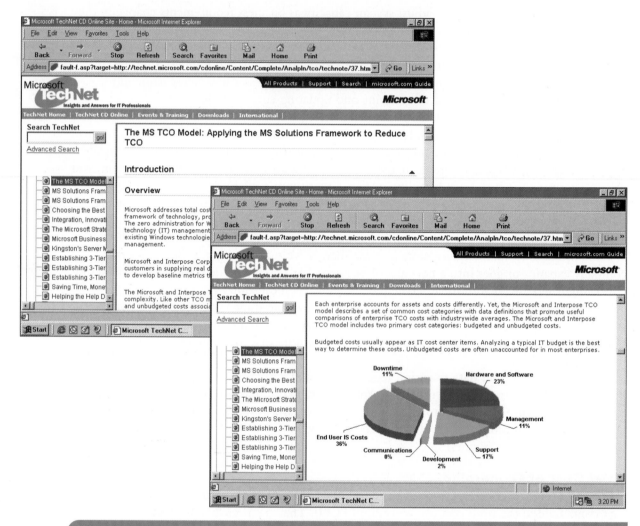

FIGURE 3-10 Microsoft Solutions Framework includes a total cost of ownership model that offers tools, methods, and guidelines to control TCO.

During requirements modeling, systems analysts should identify indirect costs and include them in TCO estimates. Even if accurate figures are unavailable, management should consider indirect costs that might increase TCO.

FACT-FINDING

Now that you understand the categories of system requirements, scalability, and TCO, the next step is to begin collecting information. Whether you are working on your own or as a member of a JAD team, during requirements modeling you will use various fact-finding techniques, including interviews, document review, observation, surveys and questionnaires, sampling, and research.

Overview

Although software can help you to gather and analyze facts, no program actually performs fact-finding for you. The first step is to identify the information you need. Typically, you begin by asking a series of questions, such as these: What business functions are supported by the current system? What strategic objectives and business requirements must be supported by the new system? What are the benefits and TCO of the proposed system? What transactions will the system process? What information do users and managers need from the system? Must the new system interface with legacy systems? What procedures could be eliminated by business process reengineering? What security issues exist? What risks are acceptable? What budget and timetable constraints will affect system development?

To obtain answers to those and similar questions, you must start with a fact-finding plan. You will develop a strategy, carry out fact-finding techniques, document the results, and prepare a system requirements document, which is presented to management.

Who, What, When, Where, and How?

Fact-finding involves answers to five familiar questions: *who, what, when, where,* and *how.* For each of those questions you also must ask another very important question: *why.* Some examples of these questions are:

1. *Who?* Who performs each of the procedures within the system? Why? Are the correct people performing the activity? Could other people perform the tasks more effectively?

2. *What?* What is being done? What procedures are being followed? Why is that process necessary? (Often, procedures are followed for many years and no one knows why. You should question why a procedure is being followed at all.)

3. *Where?* Where are operations being performed? Why? Where could they be performed? Could they be performed more efficiently elsewhere?

4. *When?* When is a procedure performed? Why is it being performed at this time? Is this the best time?

5. *How?* How is a procedure performed? Why is it performed in that manner? Could it be performed better, more efficiently, or less expensively in some other manner?

There is a difference between asking what is being done and what *could* or *should* be done. The sequence of the questions is very important, especially at this early stage of the development process. The systems analyst first must know what the current situation *is.* Only then can he or she tackle the question of what *should* be done. Figure 3-11 lists the basic questions and when they should be asked. Notice that the first two columns relate to the current system, but the third column focuses on the proposed system.

Current System		Proposed System
What is done?	Why is it done?	What should be done?
Where is it done?	Why is it done there?	Where should it be done?
When is it done?	Why is it done then?	When should it be done?
Who does it?	Why does this person do it?	Who should do it?
How is it done?	Why is it done this way?	How should it be done?

FIGURE 3-11 Sample questions during requirements modeling as the focus shifts from the current system to the proposed system.

The systems analysis phase can be especially challenging when a large system is involved. Business systems are never static — they change rapidly to meet the organization's needs. If revisions were made to a system, it might not resemble the original systems design at all. In some cases, the systems analyst must perform **reverse engineering** to find out how the original system functioned before it was modified. It is possible that several layers of changes were made at various times because of enhancements and maintenance.

INTERVIEWS

Systems analysts spend a great deal of time talking with people, both inside and outside the information technology department. Much of that time is spent conducting interviews, which are an important fact-finding technique. An **interview** is a planned meeting during which you obtain information from another person. You must have the skills needed to plan, conduct, and document interviews successfully. The interviewing process consists of these seven steps:

1. Determine the people to interview.

2. Establish objectives for the interview.

3. Develop interview questions.

4. Prepare for the interview.

5. Conduct the interview.

6. Document the interview.

7. Evaluate the interview.

Step 1: Determine the People to Interview

To get an accurate picture of the system, you must select the right people to interview and ask them the right questions. During the preliminary investigation, you talked mainly to middle managers or department heads. Now, during the systems analysis phase, you might need to interview people from all levels of the organization.

Although you can select your interview candidates from the formal organization charts that you reviewed earlier, you also must consider any informal structures that exist in the organization. Informal structures usually are based on interpersonal relationships and can develop from previous work assignments, physical proximity, unofficial procedures, or personal relationships such as the informal gathering shown in Figure 3-12. In an informal structure, some people have more influence or knowledge than appears on an organization chart. Your knowledge of the company's formal and informal structures helps you determine the people to interview during the systems analysis phase.

An analyst must consider informal structures in the organization when selecting interview candidates.

ON THE WE

For more resources on Interviewing Techniques v scsite.com/sad4e/more.h click Systems Analysis an Design Chapter 3 and the click the Interviewing Techniques link.

www.scsite.

Should you interview several people at the same time? Group interviews can save time and provide an opportunity to observe interaction among the participants. Group interviews also can present problems. One person might dominate the conversation, even when questions are addressed specifically to others. Organization level also can present a problem, as the presence of upper management in an interview can prevent lower-level employees from expressing themselves candidly.

Step 2: Establish Objectives for the Interview

After deciding on the people to interview, you must establish objectives for the session. First, you should determine the general areas to be discussed, and then list the facts you want to gather. You also should try to solicit ideas, suggestions, and opinions during the interview.

The objectives of an interview depend on the role of the person being interviewed. Upper-level managers can provide the big picture and help you to understand the system as a whole. Specific details about operations and business processes are best learned from people who actually work with the system on a daily basis.

In the early stages of systems analysis, interviews usually are general. As the fact-finding process continues, however, the interviews focus more on specific topics. Interview objectives also vary at different stages of the investigation. By setting specific objectives, you create a framework that helps you decide what questions to ask and how to phrase the questions.

Step 3: Develop Interview Questions

Creating a standard list of interview questions helps keep you on track and avoid unnecessary tangents. Also, if you interview several people who perform the same job, a standard question list allows you to compare their answers to the same questions. Although you have a list of specific questions, you might decide to depart from it because an answer to one question leads to another topic that you want to pursue. That question or topic then should be included in a revised set of questions used to conduct future interviews. If the question proves to be extremely important, you may need to return to a previous interviewee to query him or her on the topic.

The interview should consist of several different kinds of questions: open-ended, closed-ended, or questions with a range of responses. When you phrase your questions, you should avoid leading questions that suggest or favor a particular reply. For example, rather than asking, "What advantages do you see in the proposed system?" you might ask, "Do you see any advantages in the proposed system?"

OPEN-ENDED QUESTIONS   Open-ended questions encourage spontaneous and unstructured responses. Such questions are useful when you want to understand a larger process or draw out the interviewee's opinions, attitudes, or suggestions. Here are some examples of open-ended questions: Is the system operating properly? How is this task performed? Why do you perform the task that way? How are the checks reconciled? What added features would you like to have in the new billing system?

CLOSED-ENDED QUESTIONS   Closed-ended questions limit or restrict the response. You use closed-ended questions when you want information that is more specific or when you need to verify facts. Examples of closed-ended questions include the following: How many personal computers do you have in this department? Do you review the reports before they are sent out? How many hours of training does a clerk receive? Is the calculation procedure described in the manual? How many customers ordered products from the Web site last month?

RANGE-OF-RESPONSE QUESTIONS   **Range-of-response questions** are closed-ended questions that ask the person to evaluate something by providing limited answers to specific responses or on a numeric scale. This method makes it easier to tabulate the answers and interpret the results. Range-of-response questions might include these: On a scale of 1 to 10, with 1 the lowest and 10 the highest, how effective was your training? How would you rate the severity of the problem: low, medium, or high? Is the system shutdown something that occurs never, sometimes, often, usually, or always?

Step 4: Prepare for the Interview

After setting the objectives and developing the questions, you must prepare for the interview. Careful preparation is essential because this is an important meeting and not just a casual chat. Schedule a specific day and time for the meeting and place a reminder call to confirm the meeting. Remember that the interview is an interruption of the other person's routine. Business pressures might force a postponement of the meeting; when that occurs, you should schedule another appointment as soon as it is convenient for both of you. Remember to keep department managers informed of your meetings with their staff members. Sending a message to each department manager listing your planned appointments is a good way to keep them informed. Figure 3-13 is an example of such a message.

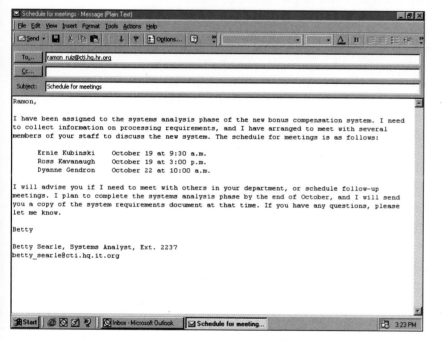

| FIGURE 3-13 | Sample message to a department head about interviews with people in his group. |

You should send a list of essential questions to an interviewee several days before the meeting, especially when detailed information is needed, so the person can prepare for the interview and minimize the need for a follow-up meeting. Figure 3-14 shows a sample memo that lists the primary interview questions, and confirms the date, time, location, and purpose of the interview.

If you have questions about documents, ask the interviewee to have samples available at the meeting. Your advance memo should include a list of the documents you want to discuss, if you know what they are. Otherwise, you can make a general request for documents, as the analyst did in her memo shown in Figure 3-14.

Two schools of thought exist about the best location for an interview. Some analysts believe that interviews should take place in the interviewee's office, whereas other analysts feel that a neutral location such as a conference room is better.

Supporters of interviews in the interviewee's office believe that is the best location because it makes the interviewee feel comfortable during the meeting. A second argument in favor of the interviewee's office is that the office is where he or she has the easiest access to supporting material that might be needed during the discussion. If you provide a complete list of topics in advance, however, the interviewee can bring the necessary items to a conference room or other location.

Supporters of neutral locations stress the importance of keeping interruptions to a minimum so both people can concentrate fully. In addition, an interview that is free of interruptions takes less time. If the meeting does take place in the interviewee's office, you should suggest tactfully that all calls be held until the conclusion of the interview.

MEMORANDUM

Date: October 12, 2001
To: Ross Kavanaugh, Compensation Manager
From: Betty Searle, Systems Analyst
Subject: Bonus Compensation System Meetings

I would like to confirm our meeting on October 19 at 3:00 P.M. in your office. As part of my information gathering for the new bonus compensation system, I need to know all details about the steps you and your staff perform in processing bonus compensation. I plan to ask the following questions:

1. What portion of bonus compensation processing is handled within your department?
2. What other areas of the company are responsible for different aspects of bonus compensation? How do these other areas interact with your department?
3. What procedures do you handle, and what specific steps are involved?
4. What improvements would you like to see in the bonus compensation processing when we implement this system on the computer?
5. Are portions of bonus compensation processing confidential? What special security requirements are needed?

If you have any written procedures, standard forms, or special calculations for the bonus compensation system, please have them available for me to review during our meeting. I will need my own copies of some of this material, but we can decide which material should be copied during our meeting.

Please contact me if something comes up and we have to reschedule our meeting.

FIGURE 3-14 Sample memo to interviewee to confirm a planned meeting.

Step 5: Conduct the Interview

After determining the people to interview, setting your objectives, and preparing the questions, you should develop a specific plan for the meeting. When conducting an interview, you should begin by introducing yourself, describing the project, and explaining your interview objectives.

During the interview, ask questions in the order in which you prepared them, and give the interviewee sufficient time to provide thoughtful answers.

Establishing a good rapport with the interviewee is important, especially if this is your first meeting. If the other person feels comfortable and at ease, you probably will receive more complete and candid answers. Your primary responsibility during an interview is to *listen carefully* to the answers. Analysts sometimes hear only what they expect to hear. You must concentrate on what is said and notice any nonverbal communication that takes place. This process is called **engaged listening**.

After asking a question, allow the person enough time to think about the question and arrive at an answer. Studies have shown that the maximum pause during a conversation is usually three to five seconds. After that interval, one person will begin talking. You will need to be patient and practice your skills in many actual interview situations to be successful.

When you finish asking your questions, summarize the main points covered in the interview and explain the next course of action. For example, mention that you will send a follow-up memo or that the interviewee should get back to you with certain information. When you conclude the interview, thank the person and encourage him or her to contact you with any questions or additional comments.

After an interview, you should summarize the session and seek a confirmation from the other person. By stating your understanding of the discussion, the interviewee can respond and correct you, if necessary. One good approach is to rephrase the interviewee's answers by saying, "If I understand you correctly, you are saying that ..."

Step 6: Document the Interview

Although taking notes during an interview has both advantages and disadvantages, the accepted view is that note taking should be kept to a minimum. Although you should write down a few notes to jog your memory after the interview, you should avoid writing everything that is said. Too much writing distracts the other person and makes it harder to establish a good rapport.

After conducting the interview, you must record the information quickly. You should set aside time right after the meeting to record the facts and evaluate the information. For that reason, try not to schedule back-to-back interviews. Studies have shown that 50 percent of a conversation is forgotten within 30 minutes. Therefore, you should use your notes to record the facts immediately so you will not forget them. You can summarize the facts by preparing a narrative describing what took place or by recording the answers you received next to each question on your prepared question list.

Tape recorders are effective tools for an interview; however, many people feel uncomfortable when recorders are present. Before using a recorder, you should discuss its use with the interviewee. Assure the interviewee that you will erase the tape after you transcribe your notes and that you will stop and rewind the tape anytime during the interview at his or her request. If you ask sensitive questions or the interviewee wants to answer a question without being recorded, explain that you will turn off the tape for a period of time during the interview.

Even with a tape recorder in use, you should listen carefully to the interviewee's responses so you can ask good follow-up questions. Otherwise, you might have to return for a second visit to ask the questions you missed the first time. Also, remember that each recorded interview takes twice the amount of time, because you must listen to or view the recorded meeting again after conducting the interview itself.

After the interview, send a memo to the interviewee expressing your appreciation for his or her time and cooperation. In the memo, you should note the date, time, location, purpose of the interview, and the main points you discussed so the interviewee has a written summary and can offer additions or corrections.

Step 7: Evaluate the Interview

In addition to recording the facts obtained in an interview, try to identify any possible biases. For example, an interviewee who tries to protect his or her own area or function might give incomplete answers or refrain from volunteering information. Or an interviewee with strong opinions about the current or future system might distort the facts. Some interviewees might answer your questions in an attempt to be helpful although they do not have the necessary experience to provide accurate information.

FastPak, the nation's fourth-largest overnight package service carrier, is headquartered in Fullerton, California. Jesse Evans is a systems analyst on an IT team that is studying ways to update FastPak's package tracking system. Jesse prepared well for her interview with Jason Tanya, FastPak's executive vice president. Mr. Tanya did not ask his assistant to hold his calls during the meeting, however. After several interruptions, Jesse tactfully suggested that she could come back another time, or perhaps that Mr. Tanya might ask his assistant to hold his calls. "No way," he replied. "I'm a very busy man and we'll just have to fit this in as we can, even if it takes all day." Jesse was unprepared for his response. What are her options? Is an analyst always in control of this kind of situation? Why or why not?

Unsuccessful Interviews

No matter how well you prepare for interviews, some are not successful. One of the main reasons could be that you and the interviewee did not get along well. Such a situation can be caused by several factors. For example, a misunderstanding or personality conflict could affect the interview negatively, or the interviewee might be afraid that the new system will eliminate or change his or her job.

In other cases, the interviewee might give only short or incomplete responses to your open-ended questions. If so, you should switch to closed-ended questions or questions with a range of responses, or try rephrasing your open-ended questions into those types of questions. If that still does not help, you should find a tactful way to conclude the meeting.

Continuing an unproductive interview is difficult. The interviewee could be more cooperative later, or you might find the information you seek elsewhere. If failure to obtain specific information will jeopardize the success of the project, inform your supervisor, who can help you decide what action to take. Your supervisor might contact the interviewee's supervisor, ask another systems analyst to interview the person, or find some other way to get the needed information.

OTHER FACT-FINDING TECHNIQUES

In addition to interviewing, systems analysts use other fact-finding techniques, including document review, observation, surveys and questionnaires, sampling, and research. Such techniques are used before interviewing begins to obtain a good overview, and to help develop better interview questions.

Document Review

Document review can help you understand how the current system is supposed to work. Remember that system documentation is sometimes out of date. Forms can change or be discontinued, and documented procedures often are modified or eliminated. You should obtain copies of actual forms and operating documents currently in use. You also should review blank copies of forms, as well as samples of actual completed forms. You usually can obtain document samples during interviews with the people who perform that procedure. If the system uses a software package, you should review the documentation for that software.

Observation

The **observation** of current operating procedures is another fact-finding technique. Seeing the system in action gives you additional perspective and a better understanding of system procedures. Personal observation also allows you to verify statements made in interviews and determine whether procedures really operate as they are described. Through observation, you might discover that neither the system documentation nor the interview statements are accurate.

Personal observation also can provide important advantages as the development process continues. For example, recommendations often are better accepted when they are based on personal observation of actual operations. Observation also can provide the knowledge needed to test or install future changes and can help build relationships with the users who will work with the new system.

Plan your observations in advance by preparing a checklist of specific tasks you want to observe and questions you want to ask. Consider the following issues when you prepare your list:

1. Ask sufficient questions to ensure that you have a complete understanding of the present system operation. A primary goal is to identify the methods of handling situations that are *not* covered by standard operating procedures. For example, what happens in a payroll system if an employee loses a time card? What is the procedure if an employee starts a shift 5 minutes late but then works 10 minutes overtime? Often, the rules for exceptions such as these are not written or formalized. Therefore, you must try to document any procedures for handling exceptions.

2. Observe all the steps in a transaction and note the documents, inputs, outputs, and processes involved.

3. Examine each form, record, and report. Determine the purpose each item of information serves.

4. Consider each user who works with the system and the following questions: What information does that person receive from other people? What information does this person generate? How is the information communicated? How often do interruptions occur? How much downtime occurs? How much support does the user require, and who provides it?

5. Talk to the people who receive current reports to see whether the reports are complete, timely, accurate, and in a useful form. Ask whether information can be eliminated or improved and whether people would like to receive additional information.

N THE WEB

additional information on Hawthorne Effect visit site.com/sad4e/more.htm, ck Systems Analysis and sign Chapter 3 and then ck the Hawthorne Effect link.

w.scsite.com

As you observe people at work, as shown in Figure 3-15, remain aware of a factor called the **Hawthorne Effect**. The name comes from a study performed in the Hawthorne plant of the Western Electric Company in the 1920s. The purpose of the study was to determine how various changes in the work environment affect employee productivity. The surprising result was that productivity improved during observation whether the conditions were made *better* or *worse*. Researchers concluded that productivity seemed to improve whenever the workers knew they were being observed.

FIGURE 3-15   In the Hawthorne study, worker productivity improved during observation. Always consider the Hawthorne Effect when observing the operation of an existing system.

ON THE WEB

To learn more about
Preparing Questionnaires
and Surveys visit
scsite.com/sad4e/more.htm
click Systems Analysis and
Design Chapter 3 and then
click the Preparing
Questionnaires and
Surveys link.

www.scsite.c

Thus, as you observe users, remember that normal operations might not always run as smoothly as your observations indicate. Operations also might run less smoothly because workers might be nervous during the observation. If possible, meet with workers and their supervisors to discuss your plans and objectives to help establish a good working relationship. In some situations, you might even participate in the work yourself to gain a personal understanding of the task or the environment.

Questionnaires and Surveys

In systems development projects where it is desirable to obtain input from a large number of people, a questionnaire can be a valuable tool. A **questionnaire**, also called a **survey**, is a document containing a number of standard questions that can be sent to many individuals.

Questionnaires are used to obtain information about workloads, reports received, volumes of transactions handled, types of job duties, difficulties, and opinions of how the job could be performed better or more efficiently. Figure 3-16 shows a sample questionnaire that includes several different question and response formats.

A typical questionnaire starts with a heading, which includes a title, a brief statement of purpose, the name and telephone number of the contact person, the deadline date for completion, and how and where to return the form. The heading usually is followed by general instructions that provide clear guidance on how to answer the questions. Headings also are used to introduce each main section or portion of the survey and include instructions when the type of question or response changes. A long questionnaire might end with a conclusion that thanks the participants and reminds them how to return the form.

PURCHASE REQUISITION QUESTIONNAIRE

Pat Kline, Vice President, Finance, has asked us to investigate the purchase requisition process to see if it can be improved. Your input concerning this requisition process will be very valuable. We would greatly appreciate it if you could complete the following questionnaire and return it by March 9 to Dana Juarez in information technology. If you have any questions, please call Dana at x2561.

A. **YOUR OBSERVATIONS**
Please answer each question by checking one box.

1. How many purchase requisitions did you process in the past five working days? _____

2. What percentage of your time is spent processing requisitions?
[ ] under 20%   [ ] 60–79%
[ ] 21–39%   [ ] 80% or more
[ ] 40–59%

3. Do you believe too many errors exist on requisitions?
[ ] yes
[ ] no

4. Out of every 100 requisitions you process, how many contain errors?
[ ] fewer than 5   [ ] 20 to 29
[ ] 5 to 9   [ ] 30 to 39
[ ] 10 to 14   [ ] 40 to 49
[ ] 15 to 19   [ ] 50 or more

5. What errors do you see most often on requisitions? (Place a 1 next to the most common error, place a 2 next to the second, etc.)
[ ] Incorrect charge number   [ ] Missing authorization
[ ] Missing charge information   [ ] Other (Please explain) _____
[ ] Arithmetic errors
[ ] Incorrect discount percent used

B. **YOUR SUGGESTIONS**
Please be specific, and give examples if possible.

1. If the currently used purchase requisition form were to be redesigned, what changes to the form would you recommend?
_____
_____
_____
_____
(Please attach another sheet if necessary)

2. Would you be interested in meeting with an information technology representative to discuss your ideas further? If so, please complete the following information:

Name _____ Department _____

Telephone _____ E-mail address _____

FIGURE 3-16 Sample questionnaire.

What about the issue of anonymity? Should people be asked to sign the questionnaire, or is it better to allow anonymous responses? The answer depends on two questions. First, does an analyst really need to know who the respondents are in order to match or correlate information? For example, it might be important to know what percentage of users need a certain software feature, but specific user names might not be relevant. Second, does the questionnaire include any sensitive or controversial topics? Many people do not want to be identified when answering a question such as "How well has your supervisor explained the system to you?" In such cases, anonymous responses might provide better information.

When designing a questionnaire, the most important rule of all is to make sure that your questions collect the right data in a form that you can use to further your fact-finding. Here are some additional ideas to keep in mind when designing your questionnaire:

- Keep the questionnaire brief and user-friendly.
- Provide clear instructions that will answer all anticipated questions.
- Arrange the questions in a logical order, going from easy to more complex topics.
- Phrase questions to avoid misunderstandings; use simple terms and wording.
- Try not to lead the response or use questions that give clues to expected answers.
- Limit the use of open-ended questions that are difficult to tabulate.
- Limit the use of questions that can raise concerns about job security or other negative issues.
- Include a section at the end of the questionnaire for general comments.
- Test the questionnaire whenever possible on a small test group before finalizing it and distributing to a large group.

Instead of using a paper form for your questionnaire, you can create a fill-in form and collect data on the Internet or a company intranet. For example, you can use Microsoft Word (as shown in Figure 3-17) to create several types of form fields such as text boxes, check boxes, and drop-down lists where users can click selections. Before you publish the form, you should protect it so that users can fill it in but cannot change the layout or design. Forms also can be automated, so that if a user answers no to question three, he or she goes directly to question eight, where the form-filling resumes.

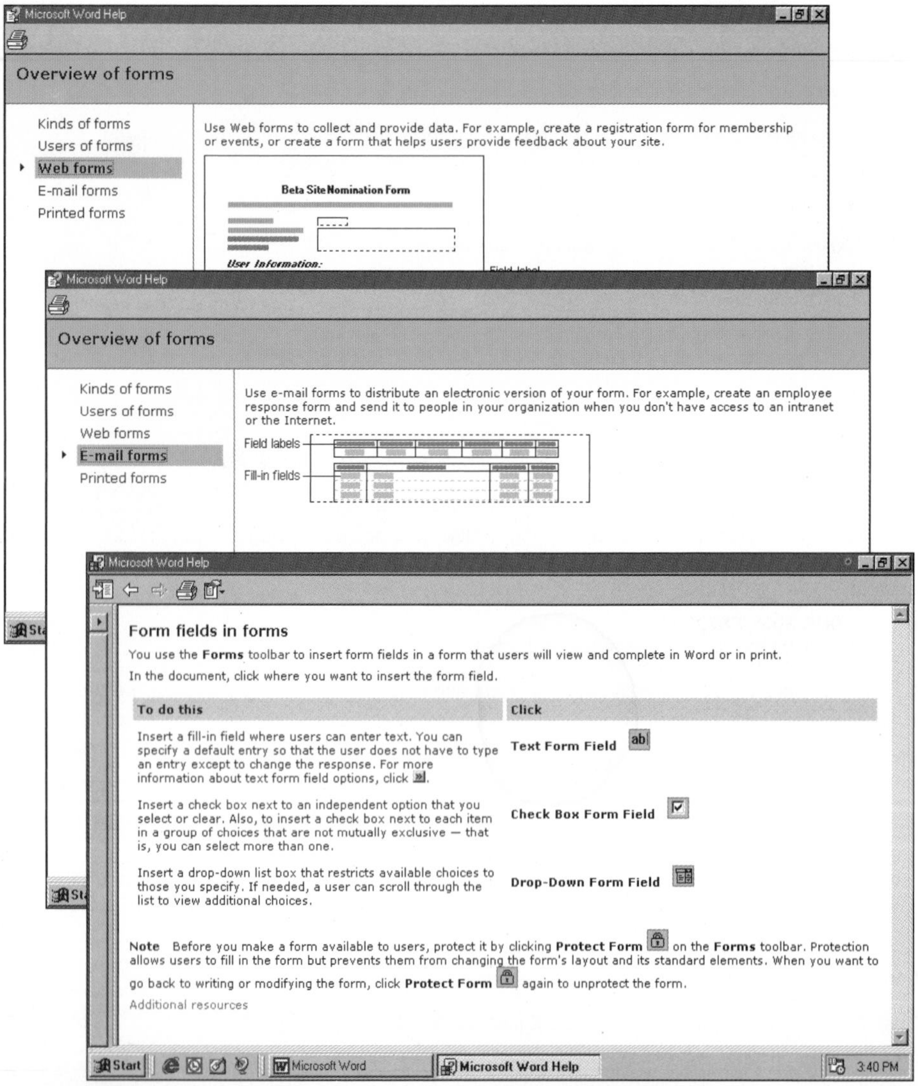

FIGURE 3-17   Microsoft Word enables you to create a fill-in form and collect data on the Internet or a company intranet.

Sampling

When studying an information system, you should collect examples of actual documents using a process called **sampling**. The samples might include records, reports, operational logs, data entry documents, complaint summaries, work requests, and various types of forms. Sampling techniques include systematic sampling, stratified sampling, and random sampling.

Suppose you have a list of 200 customers who complained about errors in their statements, and you want to review a representative sample of 20 customers. A **systematic sample** would select every tenth customer for review. If you want to ensure that the sample is balanced geographically, however, you could use a **stratified sample** to select five customers from each of four ZIP codes. Another example of stratified sampling is to select a certain percentage of transactions from each work shift, rather than a fixed number. Finally, a **random sample** selects any 20 customers.

The main objective of a sample is to ensure that it represents the overall population accurately. If you are analyzing inventory transactions, for example, you should select a sample of transactions that are typical of actual inventory operations and do not include unusual or unrelated examples. For instance, if a company performs special processing on the last business day of the month, that day is not a good time to sample *typical* daily operations.

You also should consider sampling when using interviews or questionnaires. Rather than interviewing everyone or sending a questionnaire to the entire group, you can use a sample of participants. You must use sound sampling techniques to reflect the overall population and obtain an accurate picture.

Research

Research is another important fact-finding technique. Your research can include reviewing journals, periodicals, and books to obtain background information, technical material, and news about industry trends and developments.

The Internet is an extremely valuable research tool. Most major hardware and software vendors maintain sites on the Web where you can obtain information about products and services offered by the company and send e-mail with specific questions to company representatives.

In addition to contacting specific firms, you can access Web sites maintained by publishers and independent firms that provide links to hundreds of hardware and software vendors, as shown in Figure 3-18. Such sites are one-stop information centers where IT professionals can find information, share ideas, and keep posted on developments in technology.

ON THE WEB

For additional information on Sampling visit scsite.com/sad4e/more.htm click Systems Analysis and Design Chapter 3 and then click the Sampling link.

www.scsite.co

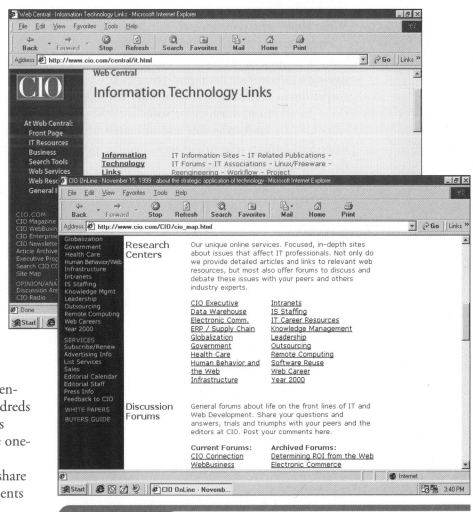

FIGURE 3-18 Example of Web site maintained by *CIO* magazine with various features for information technology professionals.

Using the Internet, you also can access information from federal and state governments, as well as from publishers, universities, and libraries around the world. Finally, **newsgroups** are good resources for exchanging information with other professionals, seeking answers to questions, and monitoring discussions that are of interest to you. In addition to electronic research, you can attend professional meetings, seminars, and discussions with other IT professionals, which can be very helpful in problem solving.

Research also can involve **site visits**, where the objective is to observe a system in use at another location. If you are studying your firm's human resources information system, for example, you might want to see how another company's system works. Site visits also are important when considering the purchase of a software package. If the software vendor suggests possible sites to visit, be aware that such sites might constitute a biased sample. A single site visit seldom gives you true pictures, so you should try to visit more than one installation.

Before a site visit, prepare just as you would for an interview. Contact the appropriate manager and explain the purpose of your visit. Decide what questions you will ask and what processes you will observe. During your visit, observe how the system works and note any problems or limitations. You also will want to learn about the support provided by the vendor, the quality of the system documentation, and so on.

Interviews vs. Questionnaires

When you must ask a series of identical questions to many individuals, a questionnaire is very useful. On the other hand, if you require information from only a few people, then you probably should interview each person individually. Is it better to interview or use a questionnaire? What about situations that do not fall neatly into either category?

The interview is more familiar and personal than a questionnaire. People who are unwilling to put critical or controversial comments in writing might talk more freely in person. Moreover, during a face-to-face interview, you can react immediately to anything the interviewee says. If surprising or confusing statements are made, you can pursue the topic with additional questions. In addition, during a personal interview, you can watch for clues to help you determine if responses are knowledgeable and unbiased. Participation in an interview can contribute to improved human relations as well, because people who are asked for their opinions often view the project more favorably.

Interviewing, however, is a costly and time-consuming process. In addition to the meeting itself, both people must prepare, and the interviewer has to do follow-up work. When a number of interviews are planned, the total cost can be quite substantial. The personal interview usually is the most expensive fact-finding technique.

In contrast, a questionnaire gives many people the opportunity to provide input and suggestions. Questionnaire recipients can answer the questions at their convenience and do not have to set aside a block of time for an interview. If the questionnaire allows anonymous responses, people might offer more candid responses than they would in an interview.

Preparing a good questionnaire, however, like a good interview, requires skill and time. If a question is misinterpreted, you cannot clarify the meaning as you can in a face-to-face interview. Furthermore, unless questionnaires are designed well, recipients might view them as intrusive, time-consuming, and impersonal. As an analyst, you should select the technique that will work best in a particular situation.

Ann Ellis is a systems analyst at CyberStuff, a large company that sells computer hardware and software via telephone, mail order, and the Internet. CyberStuff processes several thousand transactions per week on a three-shift operation and employs 50 full-time and 125 part-time employees. Lately, the billing department has experienced an increase in the number of customer complaints about incorrect bills. During the preliminary investigation, Ann learned that some CyberStuff representatives did not follow established order entry procedures. She feels that with more information, she might find a pattern and identify a solution for the problem.

Ann is not sure how to proceed. She came to you, her supervisor, with two separate questions. First, is a questionnaire the best approach, or would interviews be better? Second, whether she uses interviews, a questionnaire, or both techniques, should she select the participants at random, include an equal number of people from each shift, or use some other approach? As Ann's supervisor, what would you suggest, and why?

DOCUMENTATION

Keeping accurate records of interviews, facts, ideas, and observations is essential to successful systems development. The ability to manage information is the mark of a successful systems analyst and an important skill for all IT professionals.

The Need for Recording the Facts

As you gather information, the importance of a single item can be overlooked or complex system details can be forgotten. The basic rule is to *write it down*. You should document your work according to the following principles: record information as soon as you obtain it; use the simplest recording method possible; record your findings in such a way that they can be understood by someone else; and organize your documentation so related material is located easily.

Often, systems analysts use special forms for describing a system, recording interviews, and summarizing documents. One type of documentation is a **narrative list** with simple statements about what is occurring, apparent problems, and suggestions for improvement. Other forms of documentation that are described in Chapter 4 include data flow diagrams, flowcharts, sample forms, and screen captures.

Software Tools

Many software programs are available to help you record and document information. Some examples are described here.

CASE TOOLS   You can use CASE tools at every stage of systems development. This chapter contains several examples of CASE tool features. The Systems Analyst's Toolkit contains a section that describes other features and capabilities of CASE tools.

WORD PROCESSING   Using the features of a powerful word processing program, such as Microsoft Word or Corel WordPerfect, you can create reports, summaries, tables, and forms. In addition to standard document preparation, the program can help you organize a presentation with templates, bookmarks, annotations, revision control, and an index. You can consult the program's help system for more information about those and other features. You also can create fill-in forms to conduct surveys and questionnaires, as described earlier in this chapter.

ON THE WEB

For more detail on Documentation visit scsite.com/sad4e/more.htm click Systems Analysis and Design Chapter 3 and then click the Documentation lin

www.scsite.c

SPREADSHEETS   A spreadsheet program, such as Microsoft Excel or Corel Quattro Pro, can help you track and manage numerical data or financial information. You also can generate graphs and charts that display the data and show possible patterns, and you can use the statistical functions in a spreadsheet to tabulate and analyze questionnaire data. A graphical format often is used in quality control analysis because it highlights problems and their possible causes, and it is effective when presenting results to management.

A common tool for showing the distribution of questionnaire or sampling results is a vertical bar chart called a histogram. Most spreadsheet programs can create histograms and other charts that can display data you have collected. Figure 3-19 displays a typical histogram that might have resulted from the questionnaire shown in Figure 3-16.

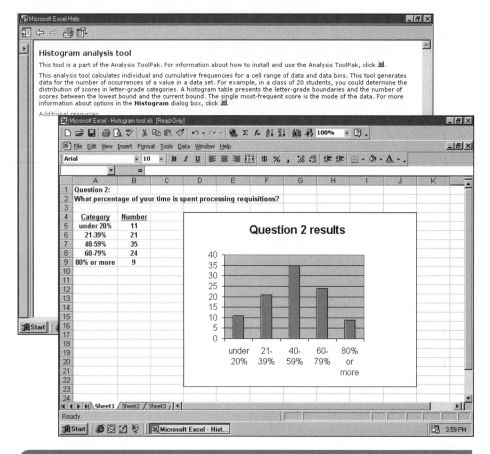

FIGURE 3-19   A histogram using Microsoft Excel displays results from the sample questionnaire shown in Figure 3-16.

DATABASES   A database program allows you to manage information about events, observations, and samples. You could use a database package, such as Microsoft Access or Corel Paradox to manage the details of a complex project, create queries to retrieve specific information, and generate reports.

PRESENTATION GRAPHICS   A presentation graphics package, such as Microsoft PowerPoint or Corel Presentations, is a powerful tool for organizing and developing your formal presentation. Presentation graphics programs enable you to create organization charts that can be used in a preliminary investigation and later during requirements modeling. These high-quality charts also can be included in written reports and management presentations.

PERSONAL INFORMATION
MANAGERS   A busy analyst needs to
keep track of meetings, interviews, appointments, and deadlines that are weeks or
months in the future. A **personal information manager (PIM)**, such as Microsoft
Outlook, Corel Sidekick, or Lotus
Organizer, can help manage those tasks and
provide a personal calendar and a to-do list,
with priorities and the capability to check
off completed items. Many IT professionals
use handheld computers like the ones
shown in Figure 3-20 to manage calendars,
schedules, appointments, and telephone
lists.

PREVIEW OF DATA, PROCESS, AND OBJECT MODELING

At the conclusion of requirements modeling, systems developers should have a clear
understanding of business processes and
system requirements. The resulting set of
models and documentation should include
substantial input from users and managers.

FIGURE 3-20   Many IT professionals use handheld computers to manage
calendars, schedules, appointments, and telephone lists.

The next step is to understand and model the logical design of the system. Data and process
modeling, which is described in Chapter 4, uses a structured analysis approach. Structured
analysis looks at the system in terms of data and the processes that act on that data. Object
modeling, which is explained in Chapter 5, views the system as a collection of objects that
contain data and processes.

IT professionals have differing views about systems development methodologies, and no
universally accepted approach exists. By studying both structured analysis and object-oriented
methods, you gain valuable knowledge, skills, and perspective. You then can use that information to determine what method, or combination of methods, is best for the different situations
you will face in your career.

SOFTWEAR, LIMITED

In Chapter 2, you learned that SWL's vice president of finance, Michael Jeremy, submitted a request for information systems services to investigate problems with the company's payroll system. Jane Rossman, the manager of applications, assigned systems analyst Rick Williams to conduct a preliminary investigation to study the payroll system's problems.

Rick's investigation revealed several problems, including input errors and a need for manual preparation of various reports. The payroll department often is working overtime to correct those errors and produce the required reports.

The information technology department recommended conducting an analysis to investigate the problem areas in the payroll system, and Mr. Jeremy approved the study. Now, as the systems analysis phase begins, the next step is requirements modeling.

Human Resources Department Interview

During the preliminary investigation phase, Rick prepared the organization chart of the payroll department shown in Figure 3-21. He also prepared the organization chart of the human resources department shown in Figure 3-22.

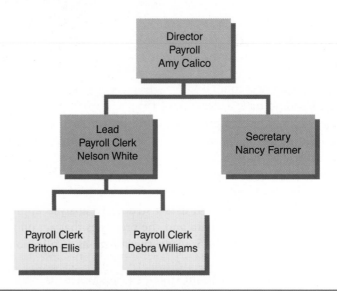

| **FIGURE 3-21** | Payroll department organization chart. |

Rick learned that some errors occurred in employee stock purchase deductions, so he decided to study that process. He knew that the human resources department initiates stock purchase deductions. He reviewed the organization chart and decided to interview Meredith Rider, manager of human resources administration. Meredith is responsible for completing the personnel records of newly hired employees and sending the forms to the payroll department.

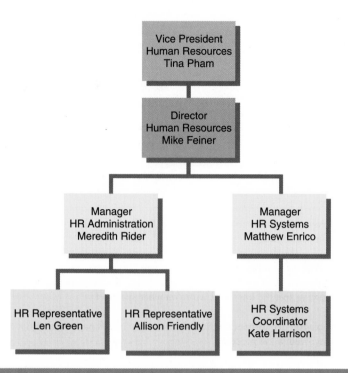

FIGURE 3-22 Human resources department organization chart.

Before arranging any interviews, Rick sent the memo shown in Figure 3-23 to the human resources director, Mike Feiner, to keep him posted. Then Rick called Meredith to make an appointment and sent her the confirmation memo shown in Figure 3-24 on the next page that describes the topics and requested copies of related forms.

SWL   **MEMORANDUM**

Date: October 17, 2001
To: Mike Feiner, Director of Human Resources
From: Rick Williams, Systems Analyst
Subject: Payroll System Investigation

The information technology department currently is investigating improvements to the payroll system. We are interested especially in problems relating to the employee stock purchase plan.

I plan to meet with Meredith Rider to discuss this topic. I also may need to meet with other people in your department, and I will keep you informed.

Thank you for your assistance.

FIGURE 3-23 Rick Williams's memo announcing the start of the payroll system investigation.

MEMORANDUM

Date: October 18, 2001
To: Meredith Rider, Manager of Human Resources Administration
From: Rick Williams, Systems Analyst
Subject: Payroll System Investigation

Confirming our telephone conversation this morning, I will plan to meet you on Monday, October 22 at 10:00 A.M. in your office.

I would like to discuss the procedures you follow for handling employee payroll information, including voluntary deductions for the credit union and the SWL stock purchase plan. I would like to discuss the following specific questions with you when we meet:

1. How is the payroll department notified of a new employee's pay rate and status, and what forms are involved in the process?

2. What is the procedure for handling changes in the initial information, and how is the payroll department notified of these changes?

3. Do employees use a standard enrollment form to sign up for the SWL stock purchase plan?

4. What is the procedure for submitting stock purchase deduction information to the payroll department, and what forms are involved in the process?

When we meet, I would like to have blank copies of any standard forms that are used and samples of the forms filled in with typical data. Thank you for you assistance. I'll look forward to meeting you next Monday.

FIGURE 3-24 Rick Williams's memo to Meredith Rider regarding preparation for the interview.

In the interview, Meredith explained that when employees are hired, they complete a Payroll Master Record Form (Form PR-1) that includes personal data and other required information. The human resources department completes the form by adding pay rate and other data and then sends a copy of the PR-1 form to the payroll department. Meredith gave Rick a blank copy of a PR-1 form shown in Figure 3-25. She explained that because payroll and personnel information is confidential, she could not give Rick a completed form.

SWL PAYROLL MASTER RECORD FORM

Social Security number _____

Name _____
              last   first   middle

Address _____
              street   city   state   zip

Telephone_____

EMERGENCY CONTACT:

Name _____
              last   first   middle

Address _____
              street   city   state   zip

Telephone_____

(FOR PAYROLL DEPARTMENT USE ONLY)

Department _____ Location _____

Job title_____

Pay rate _____ per _____

Status   ☐ Exempt   ☐ Nonexempt

         ☐ W4 submitted   ☐ Citizenship Information

         ☐ Insurance forms OK   ☐ Employee Handbook

         ☐ Orientation complete ☐ Credit Union brochure

Federal income tax exemptions _____

Form checked by _____

(Form PR-1)

FIGURE 3-25 Sample employee Payroll Master Record Form (Form PR-1).

When an employee's pay rate or status changes, the human resources department completes the Payroll Status Change Form (Form PR-2) shown in Figure 3-26 and sends a copy to the payroll department. The payroll department files that form with the employee's PR-1.

SWL **PAYROLL STATUS CHANGE FORM**

FOR HUMAN RESOURCES DEPARTMENT USE ONLY

SSN ____________ Dept. and Location ____________

Name ______________________________
last first middle

Pay rate change ☐ Old ____ per ____ New ____ per ____

Status change ☐ Old ________ New ________

Position change ☐ Old ________ New ________

Effective date of change ____________

____________________ Date ____________
By: Human Resources Department

(Form PR-2)

FIGURE 3-26 Payroll Status Change Form (Form PR-2).

SWL **PAYROLL DEDUCTION CHANGE FORM**

Please print clearly

Social Security Number ____________ Date ____________

Name ______________________________
last first middle

W4 exemption change ☐ Old ________ New ________

Credit Union change ☐ Old ________ New ________

Employee signature ____________ Date ____________

(FOR HUMAN RESOURCES DEPARTMENT USE ONLY)

Effective date of change ____________ ____________________
By: Human Resources Department

(Form PR-3)

FIGURE 3-27 Payroll Deduction Change Form (Form PR-3).

Meredith also explained that after completing a 90-day probationary period, employees are allowed to participate in the SWL Credit Union. An employee submits the Payroll Deduction Change Form (Form PR-3) shown in Figure 3-27 to the human resources department, and from there it is forwarded to the payroll department.

SWL also has an Employee Stock Purchase Plan. An individual must be employed for 180 days to be eligible for the plan. The employee receives a brochure and prospectus, and then he or she completes the Employee Stock Purchase Plan Form (Form PR-4) shown in Figure 3-28 to enroll. The human resources department completes the weekly report of all stock plan enrollments and changes on a PR-5 form shown in Figure 3-29 and then sends a copy to the payroll department.

The payroll department records the information on a card that is filed with the employee's master record.

SWL

EMPLOYEE STOCK PURCHASE PLAN
Enrollment and Change Form

To be completed by Employee
(Please print clearly)

I, _____ , hereby acknowledge that I have received a brochure and prospectus on the common stock of SoftWear, Limited (SWL) and that I understand the terms and conditions by which SWL stock is offered to employees.

I understand that an account will be established in my name, and stock will be purchased through payroll deductions. I also understand that my ownership rights in SWL stock purchased for this account are subject to the provisions of the Stock Ownership Plan (the Plan), and I agree to the terms thereof.

I understand that I may change or discontinue my contributions at any time, and that I am entitled to a return of my contributions with thirty days written notice.

I wish to contribute a total of $ _____ per week to the Plan. I understand that deductions will be invested monthly on a pro rata basis pursuant to the SWL systems and procedures manual.

_____ SSN _____ Date _____
(Employee signature)

(Form PR-4)

FIGURE 3-28   Employee Stock Purchase Plan Form (Form PR-4)

SWL

EMPLOYEE STOCK PURCHASE PLAN
WEEKLY DEDUCTION SUMMARY REPORT

Week ending _____   (Form PR-5)

Code: N = New C = Change	SSN	Employee Name	Deduction Amount

FIGURE 3-29   Employee Stock Purchase Plan Weekly Deduction Summary Report (Form PR-5).

After the interview with Meredith, Rick sent the follow-up memo shown in Figure 3-30 and attached a copy of the interview documentation shown in Figure 3-31.

MEMORANDUM

Date: October 23, 2001
To: Meredith Rider
From: Rick Williams
Subject: Payroll System Investigation

Thank you for meeting with me on October 22 and explaining the procedures involved in preparing and submitting employee information for the payroll system.

I have attached a summary of the interview and my observations about the information flow in the current system.

Please examine the interview summary and give me your comments, including any additions or corrections. We will be submitting a final recommendation in two weeks, so I would like to have your input by October 30.

I appreciate the time you spent with me. If you have any other questions, please let me know.

Attachment: Interview Summary

FIGURE 3-30 Follow-up memo from Rick Williams to Meredith Rider and request for her comments on the interview summary.

Payroll Department Interview

Rick's next interview was with the lead payroll clerk, Nelson White. During the interview, Nelson confirmed that when an employee is hired, a PR-1 form is completed in the human resources department. This is form then forwarded to payroll, where it is filed. He explained that each week the payroll department sends a time sheet to every SWL department manager. The time sheet lists each employee, with space to record regular hours, vacation, sick leave, jury duty, and other codes for accounting purposes.

After each pay period, SWL managers complete their departmental time sheets and return them to the payroll department. Payroll then enters the pay rate and deduction information and delivers the sheets to Business Information Systems (BIS), the service bureau that prepares SWL's payroll.

After the payroll is run, a BIS employee returns the time sheets, paychecks, and the payroll register to SWL. The director of payroll, Amy Calico, sends the paychecks to SWL department heads for distribution to employees.

Nelson uses the weekly payroll register to prepare a report of credit union deductions and a check to the credit union for the total amount deducted. Stock purchases, on the other hand, are processed monthly, based on the stock's closing price on the last business day of the month. Using the weekly payroll registers, Nelson manually prepares a monthly report of employee stock purchases and forwards a copy of the report and a funds transfer authorization to Carolina National Bank, which is SWL's stock transfer agent.

INTERVIEW DOCUMENTATION

Name of System: Payroll   **Page** 1 of 1
Date: October 23, 2001
Prepared by: Rick Williams
Title: Systems Analyst
Purpose: Interview Summary: Meredith Rider, Manager of Human Resources Administration
Location: Raleigh

Five basic forms are used by the human resources department that relate to the payroll system:
1. Payroll Master Record Form (Form PR-1)
2. Payroll Status Change Form (Form PR-2)
3. Payroll Deduction Change Form (Form PR-3)
4. Employee Stock Purchase Enrollment and Change Form (Form PR-4)
5. Employee Stock Purchase Plan Weekly Deduction Summary Report (Form PR-5)

When an employee is hired, the following takes place:
1. The human resources department prepares a Payroll Master Record Form (Form PR-1), with employee data, including Social Security number, name, address, telephone, emergency contact, and information about the position, title, and initial pay rate.
2. A copy of this form is sent to the payroll department, where it is filed and maintained.
3. Subsequent pay rate or status changes are submitted by the human resources department to the payroll department on a Payroll Status Change Form (Form PR-2). Payroll then files these change forms with the employee's PR-1 form.

After 90 days of employment, the employee is eligible to join the SWL Credit Union.
1. To enroll, or to make changes in existing deductions, the employee goes to the human resources department and completes a Payroll Deduction Change Form (Form PR-3) .The human resources department sends the form to payroll, where it is filed with the employee's Payroll Master Record Form (Form PR-1).

After 180 days of employment, the employee is eligible to enroll in the SWL Stock Purchase Plan.
1. To enroll, an employee completes an Employee Stock Purchase Plan Enrollment and Change Form (Form PR-4).
2. The human resources department prepares an Employee Stock Purchase Plan Weekly Deduction Summary Report (Form PR-5) and sends it to the payroll department, with copies of the PR-4 forms, which then are filed with the employee's PR-1 form.

Changes in employee status that affect payroll involve the following forms:
1. Pay rate   PR-2
2. Status (exempt vs. nonexempt)   PR-2
3. Federal tax exemptions   PR-3
4. Credit Union deductions   PR-3
5. Employee Stock Purchase Plan deductions   PR-3

When an employee changes Credit Union deductions or federal tax exemptions:
1. The employee completes a Payroll Deduction Change Form (Form PR-3).
2. The form is forwarded to the payroll department.
3. The form is filed with the employee's PR-1 form.

I have identified several problems with the current procedures:
1. Data errors can occur when the human resources staff prepares the weekly summary of employee stock purchase deductions, and no system verification takes place until incorrect deductions are reported.
2. The system performs no verification of employment dates, and it is possible that the 90- and 180-day eligibility periods are applied incorrectly.
3. The filing of the PR-2, PR-3, and PR-4 forms with the Payroll Master Record Forms in the payroll department could lead to problems. If any of the forms are lost or misfiled, incorrect data is entered into the system.

FIGURE 3-31   Documentation of the interview with Meredith Rider.

Rick asked Nelson why BIS did not produce a report on employee stock purchase deductions. Nelson replied that although the payroll is run weekly, the stock deductions are invested only once a month. Because the two cycles do not match, the BIS system could not handle the task.

Nelson then referred Rick to the *SWL Systems and Procedures Manual* page that describes how monthly Employee Stock Purchase Plan investment amounts are calculated, as shown in Figure 3-32. After blanking out the employee's name and Social Security number, Nelson also gave Rick a sample of three monthly deduction registers, as shown in Figure 3-33. Rick began to see why it was taking so much effort to prepare the reports. The process that Nelson described provided much more detail than the general description that Rick had received during the preliminary investigation from Amy Calico, payroll director.

SoftWear, Limited   Payroll
Systems and Procedures Manual   Page 29

VII.   Employee Stock Purchase Plan

          The human resources department will notify the payroll department of the weekly deduction that the employee has specified on the Employee Stock Purchase Plan Enrollment and Change Form and send a copy of the Employee Stock Purchase Plan Enrollment and Change Form (Form PR-4) and the Employee Stock Purchase Plan Weekly Deduction Summary Report (Form PR-5) to the payroll department.

          Deduction will be made weekly and then invested on a monthly basis. The payroll department will calculate the proper monthly investment amount on a pro rata basis, as follows:

     A.   A nominal per diem deduction rate will be established by dividing the weekly deduction by 7, rounded to 3 decimal places.

     B.   The monthly Plan investment will be the number of calendar days in the month times the nominal per diem rate, rounded to 2 decimal places. For example:

          Weekly deduction: $20.00 / 7 = 2.8571 = $2.857 per diem
          Month of January = 31 times 2.857 = 88.567 = $88.57

     C.   At the end of each month, the payroll department will prepare a monthly deduction register (Form PR-6) that shows individual employee deductions by week, and a monthly total.

FIGURE 3-32   Sample page from *SWL Systems and Procedures Manual.*

SWL

**EMPLOYEE STOCK PURCHASE PLAN
MONTHLY DEDUCTION REGISTER**

(Form PR-6)   Period: July, 2001

Name	SSN	Week Ending Date	Weekly Deduction	Monthly Investment
		7/6/01	23.00	
		7/13/01	23.00	
		7/20/01	23.00	
		7/27/01	23.00	98.58

SWL

**EMPLOYEE STOCK PURCHASE PLAN
MONTHLY DEDUCTION REGISTER**

(Form PR-6)   Period: August, 2001

Name	SSN	Week Ending Date	Weekly Deduction	Monthly Investment
		8/3/01	23.00	
		8/10/01	23.00	
		8/17/01	23.00	
		8/24/01	23.00	
		8/31/01	23.00	101.87

SWL

**EMPLOYEE STOCK PURCHASE PLAN
MONTHLY DEDUCTION REGISTER**

(Form PR-6)   Period: September, 2001

Name	SSN	Week Ending Date	Weekly Deduction	Monthly Investment
		9/7/01	23.00	
		9/14/01	23.00	
		9/21/01	23.00	
		9/28/01	23.00	98.58

FIGURE 3-33   Sample of the Monthly Deduction Register for the Employee Stock Purchase Plan for July, August, and September 2001, showing the weekly deduction and monthly investment amounts.

BIS Interview

Rick decided that he should talk with someone at the BIS service bureau to find out more about its operations. He learned from Nelson that Linda DeMarco was BIS's customer relations manager, so he scheduled an appointment with her.

When Rick arrived at BIS, Linda greeted him warmly. She explained that she had planned to meet with members of SWL's payroll department within the next month or two to discuss the latest developments. Because Rick was now working on SWL's payroll system, however, this meeting would save her a trip. Rick temporarily abandoned his interview plan and asked Linda what she had in mind.

"The payroll system that your company is using, which we call GAPP, for Generalized Automated Payroll Program, was originally developed here at BIS in 1991," Linda began. "In fact, SoftWear, Limited was one of our very first customers. We've worked together for a long time, and we are very committed to your firm. As you know, GAPP was modified and updated many times since 1991. But let's face it, even with the patches, GAPP is an antique! Anyway, I have some exciting news. A few months ago, our company decided to develop a new, state-of-the-art payroll system. We are going to call it CHIPS, for Comprehensive High-powered Interactive Payroll System. I am really looking forward to working with your company when you switch over to CHIPS," Linda said.

Rick took a few moments to consider this surprising development. He then asked what would happen with GAPP. Linda stated that GAPP would be available to customers for another year or two, but that BIS would make no further enhancements to that system. Using BIS resources to maintain an obsolete system would not make sense, she explained.

Rick had hoped that some changes to the BIS payroll system would solve the manual deduction reporting problems payroll system. He now realized that was impossible, so he decided to learn more about CHIPS.

Rick described the problem with the mismatched deduction cycles and asked if CHIPS would handle that. Linda said that she already had looked into the matter. She pointed out that SWL was their only customer with more than one deduction application cycle. From BIS's point of view, programming CHIPS to handle multiple cycle reports did not make sense. Linda suggested that perhaps a special add-on module could be written, once CHIPS was up and running. BIS could do that kind of job on a contract basis, she added.

Rick then asked when the new system would be available and what the cost would be. Linda stated that current plans were to begin offering CHIPS sometime in the following year. She explained that the system was still in development, and she could not be more specific about timetables and costs. She was sure, however that the monthly fee for CHIPS would not increase more than 30 percent above the current GAPP charges.

As Rick was preparing to leave, Linda urged him to keep in touch. In the next few months, she explained, plans for CHIPS would become more specific, and she would be able to answer all his questions.

New Developments

When Rick returned from his meeting with Linda, he immediately went to his manager, Jane Rossman. After he described his visit to BIS, Jane telephoned Ann Hon, director of information technology. Within the hour, Jane and Rick held a meeting with Ann in her office. Rick repeated the details of his visit, and Ann asked for his opinion on how the developments at BIS would affect SWL's current systems analysis.

Rick explained that one of the problems — possible input errors when transferring data from the human resources summary list — might be solved easily by developing a new form or procedure. Nevertheless, he saw no obvious solutions for the stock purchase deduction problems, except to change the scope of the payroll project.

Jane, Rick, and Ann then analyzed the situation. They all agreed that because of the upcoming changes at BIS, the current payroll system project would produce very limited results and should be expanded in scope. They totaled the costs of the SWL project to that point and prepared estimates for a detailed investigation of the entire payroll system in order to meet SWL's current and future needs.

Later that week, Ann met with Michael Jeremy, vice president of finance, to discuss the situation and present her proposal to go forward with an expanded analysis. Before she even started, however, Mr. Jeremy filled her in on the latest announcement from SWL's top management: the company had decided to move forward with the new Employee Savings and Investment Plan (ESIP) under consideration. He said that in December, Robert Lansing, SWL's president, would announce a target date of April 1, 2002, for the new ESIP plan. Mr. Jeremy explained that the new plan would be a 401(k) plan with tax advantages for employees.

Facing the new constraints on top of the existing payroll system problems, it looked like SWL would need a new payroll system after all.

The Revised Project

Jane Rossman assigned Carla Moore, a programmer-analyst, to work with Rick Williams on the revised system project. Because they now had to determine the requirements for the complete payroll system, Rick and Carla conducted follow-up interviews with Nelson White and Meredith Rider, as well as Allison Friendly, a human resources representative, and both payroll clerks, Britton Ellis and Debra Williams. During the payroll department interviews, the payroll staff prepared samples of all the existing payroll reports. At the end of the fact-finding process, Rick and Carla decided to prepare the functional decomposition diagram shown in Figure 3-34. The diagram shows the main functions identified during the interviews.

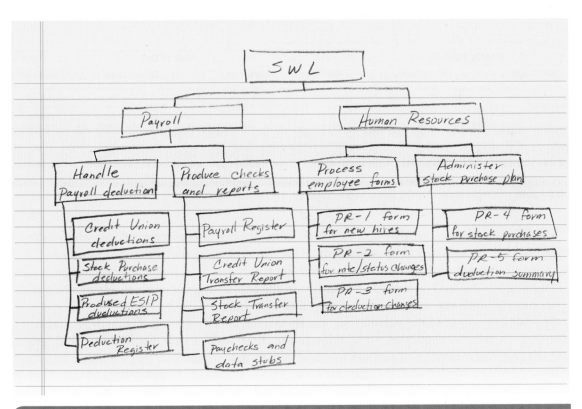

FIGURE 3-34 A functional decomposition diagram shows the main functions that were identified during the interviews.

The Payroll Register report is shown in Figure 3-35. On the report, each employee is listed on a separate line, along with his or her earnings, deductions, and net pay. BIS creates three copies of this report each week. One copy is sent to Michael Jeremy, and one copy goes to Amy Calico. The third copy is used by the payroll department for determining SWL's obligation for tax withholding and FICA payments and for applying credit union and stock purchase plan deductions. BIS also prints three copies of the Employee Compensation Record shown in Figure 3-36, which shows year-to-date payroll information for each employee.

SWL   **PAYROLL REGISTER**

Week Ending _____   *Page 1*

Employee Data		Earnings			Deductions					Net Pay	
Name	SSN	Regular Pay	Overtime Pay	Total Pay	Federal Tax	State Tax	FICA	Credit Union	Stock Plan	Net Amount	Check Number

FIGURE 3-35   Sample page of SWL Payroll Register report.

SWL   **EMPLOYEE COMPENSATION RECORD**

Name _____   SSN _____

Week Ending	Weekly Payroll										Year to Date								
	Earnings			Deductions					Net Pay		Earnings			Deductions					Net Pay
	Reg. Pay	OT Pay	Total Pay	Fed. Tax	State Tax	FICA	Credit Union	Stock Plan	Net Pay	Check No.	Reg. Pay	OT Pay	Total Pay	Fed. Tax	State Tax	FICA	Credit Union	Stock Plan	Net Amount
08/03/01	352.00		352.00	45.00	7.40	22.40	10.00	9.20	258.00	011917	10,912.00		10,912.00	1,395.00	229.40	694.40	310.00	285.20	7,998.00
08/10/01	352.00		352.00	45.00	7.40	22.40	10.00	9.20	258.00	016175	11,264.00		11,264.00	1,440.00	236.80	716.80	320.00	294.40	8,256.00
08/17/01	352.00		352.00	45.00	7.40	22.40	10.00	9.20	258.00	020342	11,616.00		11,616.00	1,485.00	244.20	739.20	330.00	303.60	8,514.00
08/24/01	352.00		352.00	45.00	7.40	22.40	10.00	9.20	258.00	030919	11,968.00		11,968.00	1,530.00	251.60	761.60	340.00	312.80	8,772.00
08/31/01	352.00		352.00	45.00	7.40	22.40	10.00	9.20	258.00	041313	12,320.00		12,320.00	1,575.00	259.00	784.00	350.00	322.00	9,030.00

FIGURE 3-36   Sample page of SWL Employee Compensation Record report.

Mr. Jeremy receives a weekly overtime report from BIS that lists every employee who worked overtime that week. When Carla asked him about that report, he stated that he consulted it occasionally but admitted that he did not need the report every week. He also receives an accounting report, but he routinely forwards it to the accounting department. He mentioned that an overall financial summary was more valuable to him.

Another key output of the payroll system is the payroll check shown in Figure 3-37 that is distributed weekly to employees. In addition to the check itself, a stub lists hours worked, gross pay, all deductions from gross pay, net pay, and year-to-date totals.

SOFTWEAR, LIMITED
999 Technology Plaza
Raleigh, NC 29991

SWL

55-555/5555
1234567

No. _____
Date _____

Pay to the Order of _____ $ _____

_____ Dollars

(Not Negotiable)

Carolina Bank
999 Ninth Street
Raleigh, NC 29999

_____
1234>>567>>8888

Week Ending _____

	This Period	Year-to-Date Totals
EARNINGS		
Regular pay		
Overtime pay		
Total pay		
DEDUCTIONS		
Federal tax		
State tax		
FICA		
Credit Union		
Stock Plan		
Net pay		

FIGURE 3-37 Sample SWL employee paycheck and stub.

YOUR TURN

1. When Rick Williams met with Meredith Rider, he asked for copies of actual reports and completed forms that contain confidential information. When developing a new system, can a systems analyst be trusted with confidential information? What are the pros and cons of giving an analyst simulated copies of forms and reports that contain fictitious data?

2. When Rick met with Linda DeMarco of the BIS service bureau, he abandoned his planned list of questions after she started to explain the developments at BIS. What questions do you suppose were on his original list?

3. Assume that you were with Rick at the meeting with Linda. Draft a follow-up message to her that describes the interview.

CHAPTER SUMMARY

The systems analysis phase includes four activities: requirements modeling, data and process modeling, object modeling, and the transition to systems design. The overall objective is to understand the proposed project, ensure that it will support business requirements, and build a solid foundation for the systems design phase.

During requirements modeling, you identify the business-related requirements for the new information system, including outputs, inputs, processes, performance, and controls. You consider scalability to ensure that the system can support future growth and expansion. You also estimate total cost of ownership (TCO) to identify all costs, including indirect costs.

Joint application development (JAD) is a popular, team-based approach to fact-finding and requirements modeling. JAD involves an interactive group of users, managers, and IT professionals who participate in requirements modeling and develop a greater commitment to the project and to their common goals.

Systems analysts use various tools and techniques to model system requirements. Unified Modeling Language (UML) is a widely used method of visualizing and documenting software design through the eyes of the business user. UML tools include use case diagrams and sequence diagrams to represent actors, their roles, and the sequence of transactions that occurs. A functional decomposition diagram (FDD) is used to represent business functions and processes.

The fact-finding process includes interviewing, document review, observation, questionnaires, sampling, and research. Successful interviewing requires good planning and strong interpersonal and communication skills. The systems analyst must decide on the people to interview, set interview objectives, and prepare for, conduct, and analyze interviews. The analyst also might find it helpful to use one or more software tools during fact-finding.

Systems analysts should carefully record and document factual information as it is collected, and various software tools can help an analyst visualize and describe an information system. The chapter concluded with a preview of data, process, and object modeling.

Key Terms

actor (*3.5*)
closed-ended questions (*3.13*)
critical thinking skills (*3.2*)
document review (*3.17*)
engaged listening (*3.15*)
functional decomposition diagram (FDD) (*3.7*)
Hawthorne Effect (*3.18*)
interpersonal skills (*3.2*)
interview (*3.12*)
joint application development (JAD) (*3.3*)
narrative list (*3.23*)
newsgroups (*3.22*)
observation (*3.18*)
open-ended questions (*3.13*)
personal information manager (PIM) (*3.25*)
questionnaire (*3.19*)
random sample (*3.21*)

range-of-response questions (*3.14*)
requirements modeling (*3.2*)
research (*3.21*)
reverse engineering (*3.12*)
sampling (*3.21*)
scalability (*3.9*)
sequence diagrams (*3.6*)
site visits (*3.22*)
stratified sample (*3.21*)
survey (*3.19*)
system requirement (*3.7*)
system requirements document (*3.2*)
systematic sample (*3.21*)
total cost of ownership (TCO) (*3.9*)
Unified Modeling Language (UML) (*3.5*)
use case diagram (*3.5*)

Chapter Review

1. Systems analysis consists of obtaining answers to what five questions? What additional question is asked in the process of answering each of those five questions?

2. What is a system requirement? Into what categories can system requirements be classified?

3. What is JAD, how does it differ from traditional methods of fact-finding, and what are some advantages and potential disadvantages of using JAD?

4. What is total cost of ownership (TCO), and why is it important?

5. What are the three different types of questions? How do those different questions affect the answers given?

6. What are three types of sampling, and why would you use them?

7. What is the Hawthorne Effect? Why is it significant?

   Answer the following question after you complete the rapid application development (RAD) section in Part 4 of the Systems Analyst's Toolkit.

8. What is RAD, what are the four RAD phases, and what takes place during each phase?

   Answer the following questions after you complete the presentations section in Part 1 of the Systems Analyst's Toolkit.

9. To what three different audiences might you have to give a presentation? How would the presentation differ for each? If only one presentation is given with all interested parties in attendance, to whom should the presentation primarily be addressed?

10. How should you react if your hands shake while you are giving a presentation, or if you are nervous when people are looking at you?

Discussion Topics

1. A group meeting sometimes is suggested as a useful compromise between interviews and questionnaires. In such a group meeting, one systems analyst meets with and asks questions of a number of users at one time. Discuss the advantages and disadvantages of such a group meeting.

2. JAD requires strong interpersonal and communication skills on the part of the systems analyst. Are those skills different from the ones that an analyst needs when conducting one-to-one interviews? Explain your answer.

3. Review magazines or textbooks to find examples of each of the following types of visual aids: bar chart, pie chart, line chart, table, diagram, and bulleted list of key points. How effective do you think each aid is? Find at least one example that you feel could be improved. Discuss its shortcomings and prepare an improved version of it.

4. Review the presentations section in Part 1 of the Systems Analyst's Toolkit, then attend a speech or presentation and analyze its effectiveness. Consider the speaker's delivery and how he or she organized the material, used visual aids, and handled audience questions. Describe specifically how the speech or presentation was most effective, as well as how it could have been improved.

Apply Your Knowledge

1 Elmwood College

Situation:

The school is considering a new system that will speed up the registration process. As a systems analyst, you are asked to develop a plan for fact-finding.

1. List all the possible techniques that you might use.

2. Describe an advantage for each technique.

3. Suppose the development budget is tight. How might that affect the fact-finding process?

4. What are the five important questions to use during fact-finding?

2 JAD Session 1

Situation:

You are an IT advisor to a JAD team that is studying a new inventory system. The proposed system will provide more information and faster updates, and will automatically monitor fast- or slow-moving items. Some controversy exists about whether to use an on-site or off-site location for the JAD sessions.

1. How would you advise the project leader?

2. Who should be on the JAD team, and what would be their roles as team members?

3. The JAD project leader asked for advice about how to get the first session started. How would you reply?

4. You invited the senior vice president to the opening JAD session, but she says she is quite busy and might not be able to attend unless it is really important. What would you say to her?

3 JAD Session 2

Situation:

The JAD team wants you to draw up a checklist of requirements for the new system.

1. List the five main categories of system requirements.

2. Use your imagination and provide at least one example per category of a system requirement that might be appropriate for an inventory system.

3. The project leader wants you to explain scalability to the team. How will you do that?

4. Several managers on the team have heard of TCO but are not quite sure what it is. How will you explain it to them?

Better Hardware Marketing System

Situation:

Your boss, the IT director, wants you to explain UML to a group of company managers and users who will serve on a systems development team for the new marketing system.

1. Describe UML and how it can be used during systems development.

2. Explain use case diagrams to the group, and provide a simple example.

3. Explain sequence diagrams to the group, and provide a simple example.

4. During the meeting, a manager asks you to explain why it is desirable to describe the system though the eyes of a user. How would you answer?

Chapter Assignments

1. Design a questionnaire to learn more about the registration process at your school or how customers place orders at a local business. Apply the guidelines and skills described in this chapter.

2. Use Microsoft Word or another word processing program to design a simple form, using the program's form-filling feature.

3. Use the Internet to find information about JAD. Summarize the information for your class.

4. Use the Internet to find a Web site that contains current IT industry news, information, and links. Bookmark the site and print a copy of the initial screen.

CASE STUDIES

Case Studies offer an opportunity for you to practice specific skills and knowledge learned in the chapter and provide practical experience for you as a systems analyst. Two of the case studies (New Century Health Clinic and Ridgeway Company) are continuing case studies that appear in each chapter. Additionally, one continuing case study (SCR Associates) utilizes the Internet to practice some of the topics covered in this chapter.

NEW CENTURY HEALTH CLINIC

New Century Health Clinic has decided to computerize its office systems. The associates hired you, a local computer consultant, to perform a preliminary investigation. You had several meetings with Dr. Tim Jones to discuss the various office records and accounting systems. Anita Davenport, New Century's office manager, participated in those meetings.

In a report to the associates at the end of your investigation, you recommended conducting a detailed analysis of the patient record system, the patient and insurance billing systems, and the patient scheduling system. You believe that New Century would benefit most from implementing those three systems. Although the systems could be developed independently, you recommended analyzing all three systems together because of the significant interaction among them.

You presented your findings and recommendations at a late afternoon meeting of the associates. After answering several questions, you left the meeting so they could discuss the matter privately. Dr. Jones began the discussion by stating that he was impressed with your knowledge and professionalism, as well as your report and presentation.

Dr. Jones recommended accepting your proposal and hiring you immediately to conduct the systems analysis phase. Dr. Garcia, however, was not as enthusiastic and pointed out that such a study would certainly disrupt office procedures. The staff already had more work than they could handle, she argued, and taking time to answer your questions would only make the situation worse. Dr. Jones countered that the office workload was going to increase in any event, and that it was important to find a long-term solution to the problem. After some additional discussion, Dr. Garcia finally agreed with Dr. Jones's assessment. The next morning, Dr. Jones called you and asked you to go ahead with the systems analysis phase of the project.

CH3

1) 3.45 sys requirements (3.7)

2) 3.45 (3.9) compare scalability

3) 3.45 (3.19 - 3.20)

4) 3.45 (3.37) (3.7)

prepared in Chapter 1 for New Century.

...rview during the systems analysis phase.

...interviews you will conduct.

...individual you will interview.

...structor regarding how to accomplish this. One

...tion gained from each of the interviews.

...aire to a sample of New Century patients to find ...surance and scheduling procedures. Design a ...as in this chapter, and decide what sample of

RIDGEWAY COMPANY

During requirements modeling for the new membership billing system, Linda Usher, IT director, conducted a series of interviews, reviewed company records, observed business operations, and analyzed a sample of Ridgeway Country Club member charges. Linda's objective was to learn about the proposed system and develop a list of system requirements. The following information is the result of her fact-finding efforts.

Membership at Ridgeway is limited to 2,000 full members with unlimited privileges and 1,000 social members who are permitted to use only the clubhouse and swimming pools. A waiting list exists for both types of membership. A full member buys a share in the club and pays monthly dues of $300. Social members pay monthly dues of $100. A name and address file of all members is maintained on index cards in the corporate accounting department.

Thomas McGee is the general manager and manages Ridgeway's operations. At his suggestion, management decided to develop a new membership billing system for Ridgeway. The current system functions as follows.

Two types of sales forms currently are used. Members and their guests use one sales form for recording tennis and golf lessons, purchases in the pro shop, and recording the rounds of golf played. This sales form is a pressure-sensitive form that has two parts: the member is given the top copy, and the second copy is forwarded to the corporate accounting department. The second sales form is used for purchases made in the restaurant and bar. This form also is pressure sensitive, but in this case, the bottom copy is given to the member, and the top copy is sent to Ridgeway's accounting department.

Members must sign both types of sales forms and place their member numbers on the form. The accounting department receives the sales slips and posts them to an account ledger for each member of the club. Posted on each account line is the date of the charge, a description of the charge including where the charge occurred, the amount of the charge, and the running balance.

The charges on the account ledger appear on a monthly statement sent to each member. The statement also includes the member's monthly dues. Each member is required to make a minimum amount of purchases each month: $100 for a full member and $35 for a social member. If a member's purchases for the month exceed the minimum, the member pays the amount of the purchases. Otherwise, the member pays the minimum amount. Members make an average of 10 charges per month. Only the statement is mailed to the member. Corporate accounting retains copies of charge slips for one year in case a member questions a charge.

A monthly summary sales report is sent to Ridgeway's headquarters. The report shows total sales by club area (pro shop, restaurant, and tennis lessons) and an overall total. Thomas McGee receives three reports on a monthly basis:

- A daily sales report that shows total sales in the restaurant, the bar, and the pro shop — broken down by day. The report also shows overall totals for the month for the three operations and a grand total.
- A monthly member sales report that lists all members alphabetically and their total purchases for the month.
- An exception report that lists alphabetically all members who made no purchases during the month.

Assignments

1. List the system requirements for the new membership billing system. Assume that Linda can add her own ideas to achieve more effective outputs, inputs, processes, performance, and controls. Include at least one example for each catagory.

2. Are there scalability issues that Linda Usher should consider? What are they?

3. If Linda wants to conduct a survey of members to obtain their input, what type of sampling should she use? Why?

4. Draw an FDD that shows the main operations described in the fact statement.

BAXTER COMMUNITY COLLEGE — PART 1

Baxter Community College is a two-year school in New Jersey. Twice a year, the records office at Baxter mails requests for donations to the alumni. The staff uses a word processing merge file to create personalized letters, but the data on past contributions and other alumni information is stored manually. The registrar, Mary Louise, recently submitted a systems request asking the college's IT department to develop a computerized alumni information system. Baxter Community College does not have a formal systems review committee, and each department head has an individual budget for routine information services.

Todd Wagner, a systems analyst, was assigned to perform a preliminary investigation. After reading his report, Mary asked him to proceed with the systems analysis phase, saying that a formal presentation was unnecessary. Todd has scheduled an interview tomorrow with her, and he asked you to help him prepare for the meeting.

Assignments
1. Make a list of the topics that you think Todd should cover during the interview.

2. Prepare a list of specific questions that Todd should ask. Include open-ended, closed-ended, and range-of-response questions.

3. Conduct interviews in class, with half the students assuming Todd's role and the other half playing the registrar.

4. Document the information covered during the interviews.

BAXTER COMMUNITY COLLEGE — PART 2

Todd Wagner completed the systems analysis work and prepared a recommendation for a new alumni system with online update and query features. He discussed his ideas with Penny Binns, the IT department head, and several coworkers. They all felt that Todd had excellent ideas. Todd then prepared and sent the final report for the systems analysis phase.

Before completing this part of the case, you should review the presentations section in the Systems Analyst's Toolkit.

This time, Mary Louise, the registrar, wanted a formal presentation. She requested that the college president and all the administrative vice presidents receive invitations to attend. The registrar wanted to ensure that she would have support for the new alumni system.

Unfortunately, Todd's car would not start the morning of the presentation. Therefore, he arrived 12 minutes late for the presentation and was out of breath and disorganized. He immediately apologized and began to set out his notes. He then noticed that an easel was not in the room to hold his flip charts. Consequently, he moved a table closer to the front wall, placed the flip chart on the table, propped it against the wall, and began his presentation.

The flip chart was not very steady in that position, however, so Todd stood next to it to hold it. In order to flip to the next chart, Todd had to juggle the entire flip chart. He was so busy with the charts that he did not notice that people in the back of the room strained to see them. The registrar finally interrupted to point out that not everyone was able to see the charts. Todd rushed out of the room to find an easel. When he finally returned with an easel, he found that several of the attendees had left. He did finish the presentation but with little of his original enthusiasm.

Assignments

1. List every mistake that Todd made.

2. For each mistake listed, describe what Todd should have done differently.

3. What might Mary Louise have done to help Todd?

4. What do you think Todd should do next to try to salvage the project?

TARGET INDUSTRIES

Michelle Quinn recently was hired as a systems analyst at Target Industries. The new position was a promotion for her, because she was a programmer at her previous job. Michelle's first assignment at Target was a preliminary investigation about improvements to an existing computer system. Michelle's boss was very pleased with her work and assigned her to work on the systems analysis phase.

During the preliminary investigation, Michelle had a brief interview with Raymond Morgan, who is the most knowledgeable person about existing system procedures at Target. Now, she needed a more detailed interview with Raymond to learn about system operations. Michelle was nervous about her ability to remember the details, so she hid a small tape recorder in her purse and switched it on just before the interview. That night at home, Michelle replayed the tape many times, transcribing everything Raymond said. The next day at work she wrote up the interview documentation based on those transcribed interview notes and then erased the tape.

Assignments

1. What do you think of Michelle's actions?

2. What would you have done in that situation?

3. What are the disadvantages to using a tape recorder to record the interview?

4. What else might Michelle have done to ensure that she understood and retained the information revealed during the interview?

SCR ASSOCIATES

SCR Associates is an information technology consulting firm that offers IT solutions and training for small- and medium-sized companies. SCR's slogan is "We Know IT!"

Background

As a newly hired systems analyst, you will handle assignments, work on various SCR projects, and apply the skills you learned in the text. SCR needs an information system to manage training operations at the new SCR training center. The new system will be called TIMS (Training Information Management System).

The SCR case is available as an interactive, Web-based case study. You can log on to the Shelly Cashman Series site at www.scsite.com/sad4e/scr for instructions and assignments. If you prefer to complete the case study without using the Internet then you must download the data disk. See the inside back cover for instructions for downloading the data disk or see your instructor for more information on accessing the files required for this book.

Situation

In Part 3 of the case, you will arrange a JAD session, engage in fact-finding activities, develop requirements models, and identify requirements for the new system.

Before You Begin ...

1. Review the October 25 message from Jesse Baker regarding a questionnaire. Open the Document 3-1 from the data disk.

2. Review the October 26 message from Jesse Baker regarding sampling. Open the Document 3-2 from the data disk.

3. Review the November 2 JAD session summary. Open the Document 3-3 from the data disk.

Assignments

1. Assume that you have approval from the group managers to have their people join a JAD session for three days next week. Send a message to the JAD team members, with a brief explanation of JAD methods and a proposed agenda.

2. Design a questionnaire for former and potential students in SCR's training classes. Apply the guidelines and skills described in this chapter. Also, reply to Jesse Baker's e-mail message about sampling. Write a brief memo with your recommendation and your reasons.

3. Read the JAD session summary and prepare a list of system requirements. Include outputs, inputs, processes, performance, and controls.

4. Based on your understanding of the proposed training function, draw an FDD that shows of the main functions of the training information management system.

CHAPTER 4

PHASE 1 Systems Planning

Systems Analysis **PHASE 2**

Systems Design PHASE 3

Systems Implementation PHASE 4

Systems Operation & Support PHASE 5

Data and Process Modeling

Structured analysis describes a system in terms of its inputs, outputs, data, and processes. During structured analysis, systems analysts use data and process modeling to show how system processes transform data into useful information. The end product of structured analysis is a logical model, which also is called a business model because it must support business operations and meet the needs of managers and users. A logical model shows what the system must do, regardless of how it will be accomplished physically. Later, in the systems design phase, the analyst builds a set of physical models that describe how the system will function.

Structured analysis involves three main tools: data flow diagrams, a data dictionary, and process descriptions. Systems analysts also use CASE tools to develop data and process models and document the system design.

INTRODUCTION

During the requirements modeling process described in Chapter 3, you used fact-finding techniques to gather and record data about the current system and user requirements. Now, in Chapters 4 and 5, you will learn about the next steps in the systems analysis phase. You will use structured analysis and objected-oriented techniques to document the system requirements, analyze them, and develop a logical model of the system that you present to management. In the final stage of systems analysis, explained in Chapter 6, you learn how to evaluate various development alternatives, develop the system requirements proposal, and prepare for the systems design phase.

OBJECTIVES

When you finish this chapter, you will be able to:

- Describe data and process modeling concepts and tools

- Explain how structured analysis describes an information system

- Describe the symbols used in data flow diagrams and explain the rules for their use

- Explain the sequence of data flow diagrams, from general to specific

- Explain how to level and balance a set of data flow diagrams

- Draw a complete set of data flow diagrams for an information system

- Describe how a data dictionary is used and what it contains

- Use process description tools, including structured English, decision tables, and decision trees

- Explain the interaction among data flow diagrams, the data dictionary, and process description

- Describe the relationship between logical and physical models

This is the second of four chapters in the systems analysis phase. It explains how to represent system data and processes graphically.

N THE WEB ▶

learn more about
D Symbols visit
site.com/sad4e/more.htm,
k Systems Analysis and
sign Chapter 4 and then
k the DFD Symbols link.

w.scsite.com

DATA FLOW DIAGRAMS

In the Systems Analyst's Toolkit, you learn how to use visual aids to help explain a concept, as shown in Figure 4-1. During the systems analysis phase, you learn how to create a visual model of the information system using a set of data flow diagrams.

A **data flow diagram (DFD)** shows how data moves through an information system but does not show program logic or processing steps. DFDs represent a logical model that shows *what* the system does, not *how* it does it. That distinction is important because focusing on implementation issues at this point would restrict your search for the most effective system design.

FIGURE 4-1   Systems analysts often use visual aids during presentations.

DFD Symbols

DFDs use four basic symbols that represent processes, data flows, data stores, and external entities. Several different versions of DFD symbols exist, but they all serve the same purpose. This text uses a popular version called the **Gane and Sarson** symbol set for all of its examples. Another popular symbol set is the **Yourdon** symbol set. Figure 4-2 shows examples of both versions. Symbols are referenced in the text using all capital letters for the symbol name.

PROCESS SYMBOL A **process** receives input data and produces output that has a different content, form, or both. For instance, the process for calculating pay uses two inputs (pay rate and hours worked) to produce one output (total pay). Processes can be very simple or quite complex. In a typical company, processes might include calculating sales trends, filing online insurance claims, ordering inventory from a supplier's system, or verifying e-mail addresses for Web customers. Processes contain the **business logic**, also called **business rules** that transform the data and produce the required results.

The symbol for a process is a rectangle with rounded corners. The name of the process appears inside the rectangle. The process name identifies a specific function and consists of a verb (and an adjective, if necessary) followed by a singular noun. Examples of process names are APPLY RENT PAYMENT, CALCULATE COMMISSION, ASSIGN FINAL GRADE, VERIFY ORDER, and FILL ORDER.

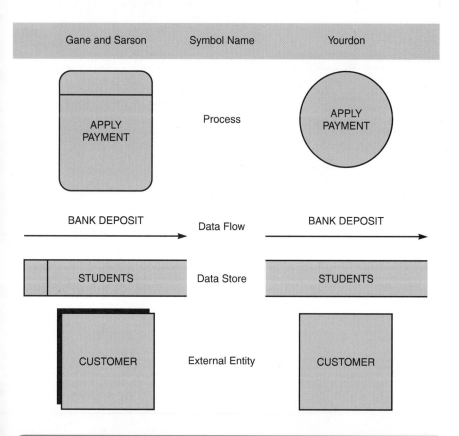

FIGURE 4-2   Data flow diagram symbols, symbol names, and examples from the Gane and Sarson and Yourdon symbol sets.

Processing details are not shown in a DFD. For example, you might have a process named DEPOSIT PAYMENT. The process symbol does not reveal the business logic for the DEPOSIT PAYMENT process. To document the logic, you create a process description, which is explained later in this chapter.

In DFDs, a process appears as a **black box**, where the inputs, outputs, and general function of the process are known, but the underlying details are not shown. A black box approach shows an information system in a series of increasingly detailed pictures. You use that technique to zoom in and explode each process without confusing the overall view of the system.

DATA FLOW SYMBOL A **data flow** is a path for data to move from one part of the information system to another. A data flow in a DFD represents one or more data items. For example, a data flow could represent a single data item (such as a student ID number) or it could represent a *set* of data (such as a class roster with student ID numbers, names, and registration dates for a specific class). The diagram does not show the structure and detailed contents of a data flow. Those elements are defined in the data dictionary, which is described later in this chapter.

The symbol for a data flow is a line with a single or double arrowhead. The data flow name appears above, below, or alongside the line. A data flow name consists of a singular noun and an adjective, if needed. Examples of data flow names are DEPOSIT, INVOICE PAYMENT, STUDENT GRADE, ORDER, and COMMISSION. Exceptions to the singular name rule are data flow names, such as GRADING PARAMETERS, where a singular name could mislead you into thinking a single parameter or single item of data exists.

Figure 4-3 shows typical examples of data flow and process symbol Iconnections. Because a process changes data from one form into another, at least one data flow *must enter* and one data flow *must exit* each process symbol, as they do in the CREATE INVOICE process. A process symbol can have more than one outgoing data flow, as shown in the GRADE STUDENT WORK process, or more than one incoming data flow, as shown in the CALCULATE GROSS PAY process. A process also can connect to any other symbol, including another process symbol, as shown by the connection between VERIFY ORDER and ASSEMBLE ORDER in Figure 4-3. Therefore, a data flow *must* have a process symbol on at least one end.

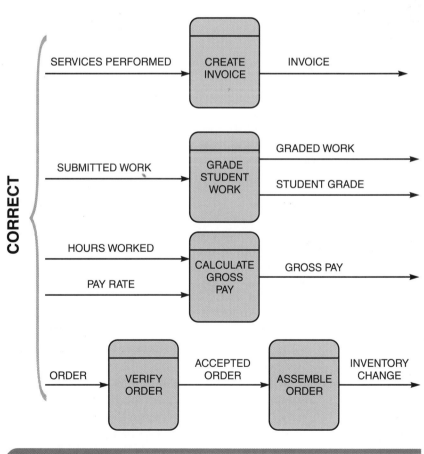

FIGURE 4-3 Examples of correct combinations of data flow and process symbols.

Figure 4-4 shows three data flow and process combinations that you must avoid. The APPLY INSURANCE PREMIUM process, for instance, has no input data flow. Because it has no input, the process is called a **spontaneous generation** process. The CALCULATE GROSS PAY is a **black hole** process, which is a process that has no output. A **gray hole** is a process that has at least one input and one output, but the input obviously is insufficient to generate the output shown. For example, a date of birth input is not sufficient to produce a final grade output in the CALCULATE GRADE process.

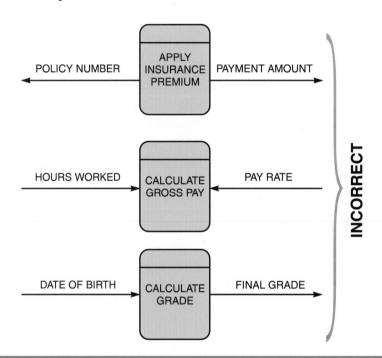

FIGURE 4-4 Examples of incorrect combinations of data flow and process symbols: APPLY INSURANCE PREMIUM has no inputs and is called a spontaneous generation process. CALCULATE GROSS PAY has no outputs and is called a black hole process. CALCULATE GRADE has an input that is obviously unable to produce the output. This process is called a gray hole.

Spontaneous generation, black holes, and gray holes are logically not possible in a DFD because a process must act on input, shown by an incoming data flow, and produce output, represented by an outgoing data flow.

DATA STORE SYMBOL A **data store**, or a **data repository**, is used in a DFD to represent a situation in which the system must retain data because one or more processes need to use the stored data at a later time. For instance, instructors need to store student scores on tests and assignments during the semester so they can assign final grades at the end of the term. In a payroll example, you store employee salary and deduction data during the year so you can report total earnings and withholdings at the end of the year. The DFD does not show the detailed contents of a data store; the specific structure and data elements are defined in the data dictionary (which we discuss later in this chapter).

The physical characteristics of a data store are unimportant because you are concerned only with a logical model. Also, the length of time that the data is stored is unimportant — it can be a matter of seconds while a transaction is processed or a period of months while data is accumulated for year-end processing. What is important is that a process needs access to the data at some later time.

In a DFD, the Gane and Sarson symbol for a data store is a flat rectangle that is open on the right side and closed on the left side. The name of the data store appears between the lines and identifies the data it contains. A data store name is a plural name consisting of a noun and adjectives, if needed. Examples of data store names are STUDENTS, ACCOUNTS RECEIVABLE, PRODUCTS, DAILY PAYMENTS, PURCHASE ORDERS, OUTSTANDING CHECKS, INSURANCE POLICIES, and EMPLOYEES. Exceptions to the plural name rule are collective nouns that represent multiple occurrences of objects. For example, GRADEBOOK represents a group of students and their scores.

A data store must be connected to a process with a data flow. Figure 4-5 illustrates typical examples of data stores. In each case, the data store has at least one incoming and one outgoing data flow and is connected to a process symbol with a data flow.

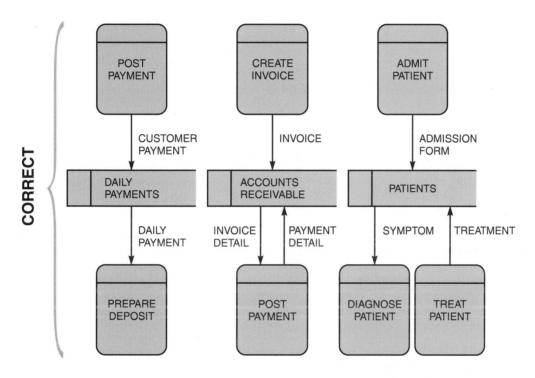

FIGURE 4-5   Examples of correct uses of data store symbols in a data flow diagram.

Violations of the rule that a data store must have at least one incoming and one outgoing data flow are shown in Figure 4-6. In the first example, two data stores are connected incorrectly (without a process in between them and missing an incoming data flow on one and the outgoing data flow on the other), and in the second and third examples, the data stores lack either an outgoing or incoming data flow.

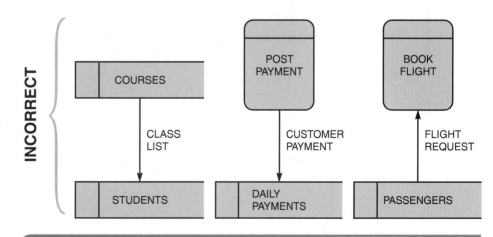

FIGURE 4-6   Examples of incorrect uses of data store symbols: two data stores cannot be connected by a data flow without an intervening process, and each data store should have an outgoing and incoming data flow.

EXTERNAL ENTITY SYMBOL An external entity is a person, department, outside organization, or other information system that provides data to the system or receives output from the system. The symbol for an external entity is a rectangle, which usually is shaded to make it look three-dimensional. The name of the external entity appears inside the square.

External entities show the boundaries of the information system and how the information system interacts with the outside world. For example, a customer submitting an order is an external entity because the customer supplies data to the order system. Other examples of external entities include a patient who supplies medical data, a homeowner who receives a property tax bill, a warehouse that supplies a list of items in stock, and an accounts payable system that receives data from the company's purchasing system.

External entities also are called **terminators**, because they are data origins or final destinations. Systems analysts call an external entity that supplies data to the system a **source**, and an external entity that receives data from the system a **sink**. An external entity name is the singular form of a department, outside organization, other information system, or person. Examples of external entity names are CUSTOMER, STUDENT, EMPLOYEE, MEMBER, SALES REP, WAREHOUSE, ACCOUNTING, BANK, INTERNAL REVENUE SERVICE, PAYROLL SYSTEM, and GENERAL LEDGER SYSTEM. An external entity might be a source or a sink or both, as shown in Figure 4-7. An external entity must be connected to a process by a data flow. Figure 4-8 shows violations of this rule.

With an understanding of the proper use of DFD symbols, you are ready to construct diagrams that use these symbols. Figure 4-9 shows a summary of the rules for using DFD symbols.

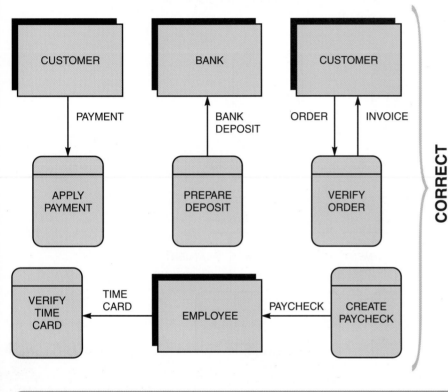

FIGURE 4-7 Examples of correct uses of external entities in a data flow diagram.

Context Diagrams

During requirements modeling, you used interviews, questionnaires, and other techniques to gather facts about the system, and you learned how the various people, departments, data, and processes fit together to support business operations. Now you are ready to create a graphical model of the information system based on your fact-finding results.

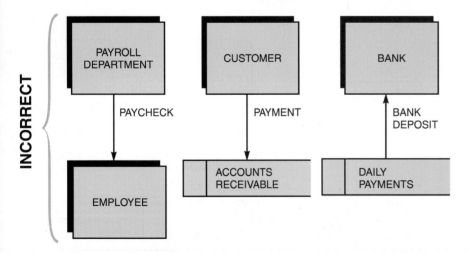

FIGURE 4-8 Examples of incorrect uses of external entity symbols. An external entity must be connected by a data flow to a process, and not directly to a data store or to another external entity.

DATA FLOW THAT CONNECTS	OKAY TO USE?	
	YES	NO
A process to another process	☑	☐
A process to an external entity	☑	☐
A process to a data store	☑	☐
An entity to another entity	☐	☑
An entity to a data store	☐	☑
A data store to another data store	☐	☑

FIGURE 4-9 Rules for connecting processes, data stores, and external entities in a DFD.

To learn how to construct DFDs, you will use examples of three information systems. The simplest example is a grading system that instructors use to assign final grades based on the scores the students receive during the term. The second example is an order system that a company uses to enter orders and apply payments against a customer's balance. The third example is a manufacturing system that handles a company's production.

The first step in constructing a set of DFDs is to draw a context diagram. A **context diagram** is a top-level view of an information system that shows the system's boundaries and scope. To draw a context diagram, you start by placing a single process symbol in the center of the page. The symbol represents the entire information system, and you identify it as process 0. Then you place the external entities around the perimeter of the page and use data flows to connect the entities to the central process. You do not show any data stores in a context diagram because data stores are internal to the system.

How do you know what external entities and data flows to place in the context diagram? You begin by reviewing the system requirements to identify all external data sources and destinations. During that process, you record the name of the external entities, the name and content of the data flows, and the direction of the data flows. If you do that carefully, and you did a good job of fact-finding in the previous stage, you should have no difficulty drawing the context diagram.

Figure 4-10 shows the context diagram for the grading system. The GRADING SYSTEM process is at the center of the diagram. The three external entities (STUDENT RECORDS SYSTEM, STUDENT, and INSTRUCTOR) are placed around the central process. Interaction among the central process and the external entities involves six different data flows. The STUDENT RECORDS SYSTEM external entity supplies data through the CLASS ROSTER data flow and receives data through the FINAL GRADE data flow. The STUDENT external entity supplies data through the SUBMITTED WORK data flow and receives data through the GRADED WORK data flow. Finally, the INSTRUCTOR external entity supplies data through the GRADING PARAMETERS data flow and receives data through the GRADE REPORT data flow.

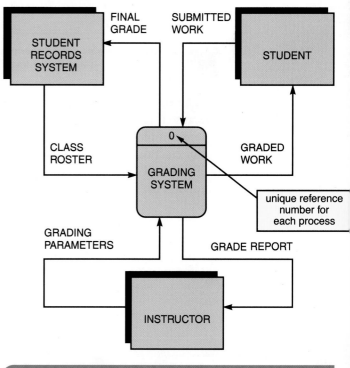

FIGURE 4-10 Context diagram DFD for the grading system.

The context diagram for an order system is shown in Figure 4-11. Notice that the ORDER SYSTEM process is at the center of the diagram and five external entities surround the process. Three of the external entities, SALES REP, BANK, and ACCOUNTING, have single incoming data flows for COMMISSION, BANK DEPOSIT, and CASH RECEIPTS ENTRY, respectively. The WAREHOUSE external entity has one incoming data flow — PICKING LIST — that is, a report that shows the items ordered and their quantity, location, and sequence to pick from the warehouse. The WAREHOUSE external entity has one outgoing data flow, COMPLETED ORDER. Finally, the CUSTOMER external entity has two outgoing data flows, ORDER and PAYMENT, and two incoming data flows, ORDER REJECT NOTICE and INVOICE.

N THE WEB

r samples of Context
agrams visit scsite.com/
.d4e/more.htm, click
stems Analysis and Design
apter 4 and then click the
ontext Diagrams link.

w.scsite.com

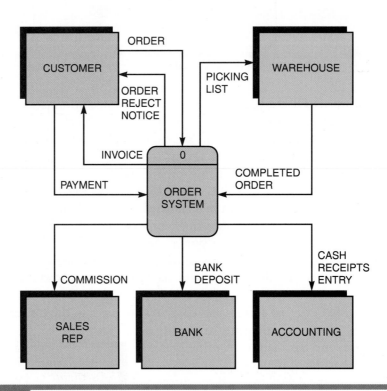

FIGURE 4-11   Context diagram DFD for an order system.

The context diagram for the order system appears more complex than the grading system because it has two more external entities and three more data flows. What makes one system more complex than another is the number of components, the number of levels, and the degree of interaction among its processes, external entities, data stores, and data flows.

Figure 4-12 shows the context diagram for the manufacturing system. The information system supports the company's entire production; it has 13 external entities and 18 data flows.

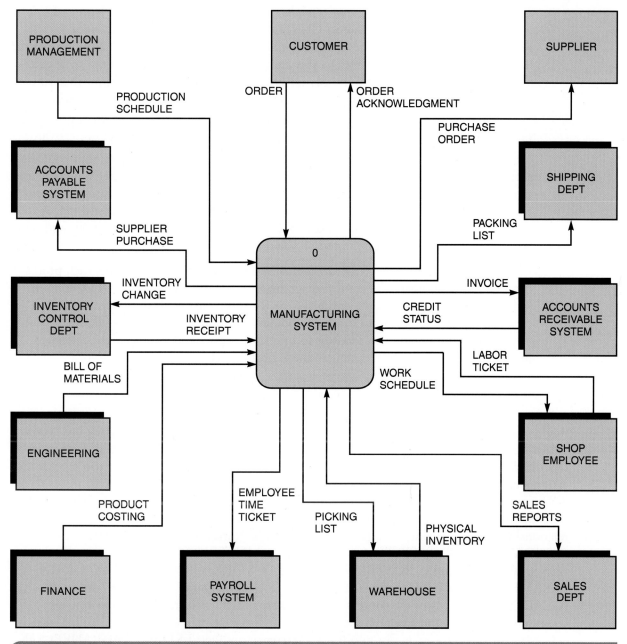

FIGURE 4-12 Context diagram DFD for a manufacturing system.

Conventions for DFDs

The DFDs shown in Figures 4-10 on page 4.7 through 4-12 follow **conventions**, or rules you should use when constructing DFDs. The conventions include the following:

1. *Each context diagram must fit on one page.*

2. *The process name in the context diagram should be the name of the information system.* For example, the process names in Figures 4-10 through 4-12 are GRADING SYSTEM, ORDER SYSTEM, and MANUFACTURING SYSTEM. The system name is used as the process name because the context diagram shows the entire information system and its boundaries. For processes in lower-level DFDs, use a verb followed by a descriptive noun, such as UPDATE INVENTORY, CALCULATE OVERTIME, or PRODUCE REPORT.

3. *Use unique names within each set of symbols.* For instance, the diagram in Figure 4-12 uses only one external entity named CUSTOMER and only one data flow named PURCHASE ORDER. Whenever you see the external entity CUSTOMER on one of the other manufacturing system's DFDs, you know that you are dealing with the same external entity. Whenever the PURCHASE ORDER data flow appears, you know that you are dealing with the same data flow. The naming convention also applies to data stores.

4. *Do not cross lines.* One way to achieve that goal is to restrict the number of symbols in any DFD. On lower-level diagrams with multiple processes, you should not have more than nine process symbols. Including more than nine symbols usually is a signal that your diagram is too complex and that you should reconsider your analysis. Another way to avoid crossing lines is to duplicate an external entity or data store. When duplicating a symbol on a diagram, make sure to document the duplication to avoid possible confusion. A special notation, such as an asterisk, next to the symbol name and inside the duplicated symbols signifies that they are duplicated on the diagram.

5. *Use a unique reference number for each process symbol.* In addition to a name, each process has a reference number. The context diagram, which is the highest-level DFD, contains process 0, which represents the entire system. To show the details inside process 0, you create a DFD named diagram 0, which contains additional processes. As you work your way through the system, you identify additional processes and assign unique reference numbers to them, until you complete the logical model.

Diagram 0

A context diagram provides the most general view of an information system and contains a single process symbol, which is like a black box. To show the detail inside the black box, you create DFD diagram 0. **Diagram 0** (the digit zero, and not the letter O) zooms in on the context diagram and shows major processes, data flows, and data stores. Diagram 0 also repeats the external entities and data flows that appear in the context diagram.

When you expand the context diagram into DFD diagram 0, you must retain all the connections that flow into and out of process 0. The grading system in Figure 4-13 shows the relationship between a context diagram and diagram 0. Notice that the three external entities (STUDENT RECORDS SYSTEM, STUDENT, and INSTRUCTOR) and the six data flows (FINAL GRADE, CLASS ROSTER, SUBMITTED WORK, GRADED WORK, GRADING PARAMETERS, and GRADE REPORT) appear in both diagrams. In addition, process 0 (GRADING SYSTEM) in the context diagram is expanded in diagram 0 to show four processes, one data store, and five new data flows.

Notice that each process in diagram 0 has a reference number: ESTABLISH GRADEBOOK is 1, ASSIGN FINAL GRADE is 2, GRADE STUDENT WORK is 3, and PRODUCE GRADE REPORT is 4. These reference numbers are important because they identify a series of DFDs. If more detail were needed for ESTABLISH GRADEBOOK, for example, you would draw a diagram 1, because GRADEBOOK is process 1.

The process numbers do not suggest that the processes are accomplished in a sequential order. Each process always is considered to be available, active, and awaiting data to be processed. If processes must be performed in a specific sequence, you document the information in the process descriptions (discussed later in this chapter), not in the DFD.

The FINAL GRADE data flow output from the ASSIGN FINAL GRADE process is a diverging data flow that becomes an input to the STUDENT RECORDS SYSTEM external entity and to the GRADEBOOK data store. A **diverging data flow** is a data flow in which the same data travels to two or more different locations. In that situation, a diverging data flow is the best way to show the flow rather than showing two identical data flows, which could be misleading.

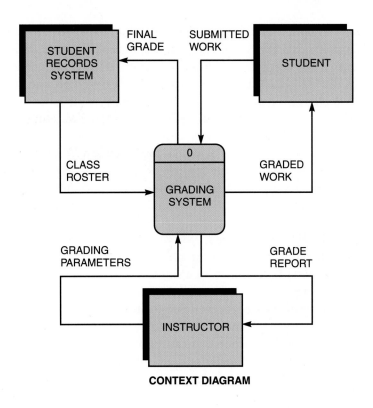

CONTEXT DIAGRAM

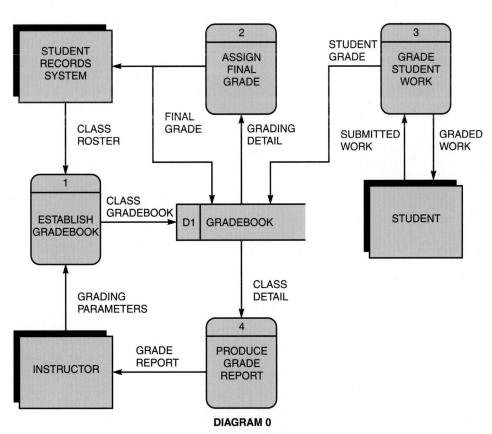

DIAGRAM 0

FIGURE 4-13   Context diagram and diagram 0 for the grading system.

If the same data flows in both directions, you can use a double-headed arrow to connect the symbols. To identify specific data flows into and out of a symbol, however, you use separate data flow symbols with single arrowheads. For example, in Figure 4-13 on the previous page the separate data flows (SUBMITTED WORK and GRADED WORK) go into and out of the GRADE STUDENT WORK process.

Because diagram 0 is a more detailed or expanded version of process 0 on the context diagram, diagram 0 is called an **exploded** view of process 0. You also can refer to diagram 0 as a **partitioned** or **decomposed** view of process 0. When you explode a DFD, the higher-level diagram is called the **parent** diagram, and the lower-level diagram is referred to as the **child** diagram. The grading system is simple enough that you do not need any additional DFDs to model the system. At that point, the four processes, the one data store, and the 10 data flows can be documented in the data dictionary.

When you create a set of DFDs for a system, you break the processing logic down into smaller units, called functional primitives that programmers will use to develop code. A **functional primitive** is a process that consists of a single function that is not exploded further. For example, each of the four processes in Figure 4-13 is a functional primitive. You document the logic for a functional primitive in a process description in the data dictionary. Later, when the logical design is implemented as a physical system, programmers will transform each functional primitive into a unit of program code that carries out the required processing steps. Deciding whether to explode a process further or determine that it is a functional primitive is largely a matter of experience, judgment, and interaction with programmers who must translate the logical design into code.

Figure 4-14 shows the diagram 0 for the order system. Process 0 on the order system's context diagram is exploded to show three processes (FILL ORDER, CREATE INVOICE, and APPLY PAYMENT), one data store (ACCOUNTS RECEIVABLE), two new data flows (INVOICE DETAIL and PAYMENT DETAIL), and one diverging data flow (INVOICE). Figure 4-15 shows how large companies use powerful, flexible order systems to support their business.

To ensure your understanding of what is being modeled in the DFD shown in Figure 4-14, the following walkthrough will guide you.

FIGURE 4-14 Diagram 0 DFD for the order system.

Large companies depend on powerful order entry systems to handle thousands of daily orders and to maintain a high level of customer service and satisfaction.

1. A CUSTOMER submits an ORDER. Depending on the processing logic, the FILL ORDER process either sends an ORDER REJECT NOTICE back to the customer or sends a PICKING LIST to the WAREHOUSE.

2. A COMPLETED ORDER from the WAREHOUSE is input to the CREATE INVOICE process, which outputs an INVOICE to both the CUSTOMER process and the ACCOUNTS RECEIVABLE data store.

3. A CUSTOMER makes a PAYMENT that is processed by APPLY PAYMENT. APPLY PAYMENT requires INVOICE DETAIL input from the ACCOUNTS RECEIVABLE data store along with the PAYMENT. APPLY PAYMENT also outputs PAYMENT DETAIL back to the ACCOUNTS RECEIVABLE data store and outputs COMMISSION to the SALES DEPT, BANK DEPOSIT to the BANK, and CASH RECEIPTS ENTRY to ACCOUNTING.

The walkthrough of diagram 0 illustrates the basic requirements of the order system. To learn more, you would examine the detailed description of each separate process. Notice that the CREATE INVOICE process is a functional primitive, but the other two processes shown in Figure 4-14 are not functional primitives because each has a more detailed DFD. (You cannot however, tell that from the DFD; you just have to look and see if there are other exploded views for the individual processes.)

Lower-Level Diagrams

When lower-level diagrams, also called child diagrams, are needed to show detail, it is essential that they be leveled and balanced. **Leveling** is the process of drawing a series of increasingly detailed diagrams, until the desired degree of detail is reached. **Balancing** maintains consistency among the entire series of diagrams, including input and output data flows, data definition, and process descriptions.

Figures 4-16 and 4-17 provide an example of leveling and balancing when a lower-level diagram is exploded from a parent diagram. The DFDs were created using Visible Analyst, a popular CASE tool.

Figure 4-16 shows PROCESS 0, which has two input flows and two output flows. The process itself appears as a black box, with no detail. In Figure 4-17, PROCESS 0 is exploded to show three subprocesses and five internal data flows. Notice that the details of process 0 are shown inside the dashed line, just as if the box had a transparent case. The DFDs in Figures 4-16 and 4-17 are leveled and balanced. Each of the internal processes is numbered to show that it is a child of the parent process, and the four data flows into and out of PROCESS 0 are maintained.

One advantage of using a CASE tool to draw DFDs is that the program will track input and output data flows and alert you to improper balancing.

LEVELING Leveling displays the information system as a single process, and then shows more detail until all processes are functional primitives. At that point, analysts describe the set of DFDs as leveled. Leveling also is called exploding, partitioning, or decomposing. Because analysts create DFDs as a series of top-down pictures of an information system, each lower level provides additional details.

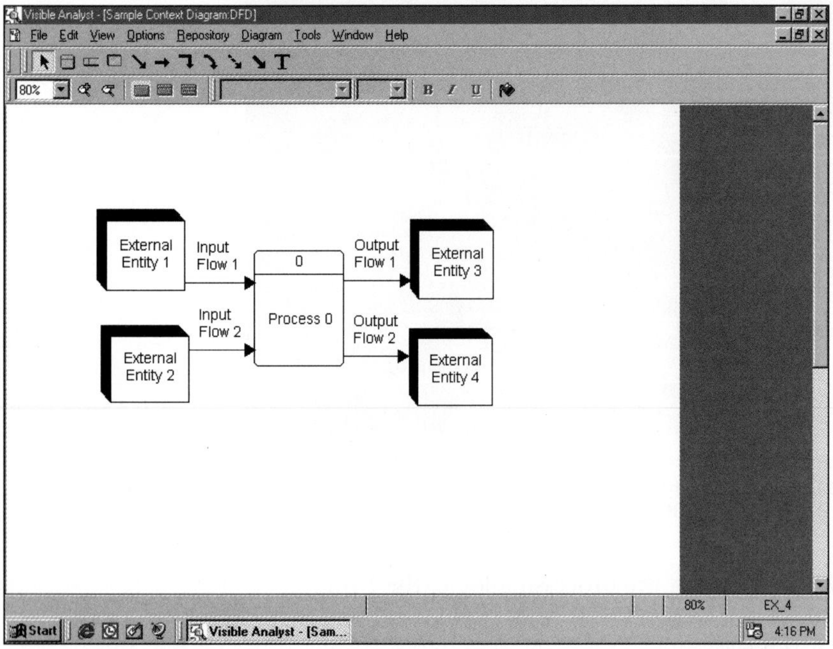

FIGURE 4-16   Example of a parent DFD diagram, showing process 0 as a black box.

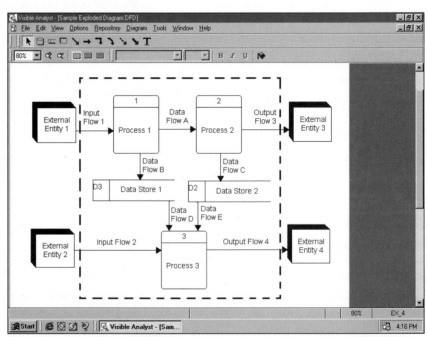

FIGURE 4-17   In the next level of detail, the process 0 black box reveals three processes, two data stores, and five internal data flows — all of which are shown inside the dashed line.

Now consider the example of the leveling of diagram 0. The exploded version of FILL ORDER from diagram 0 in Figure 4-14 on page 4.12 is shown in Figure 4-18. The new DFD is called diagram 1 because it is the decomposition of the FILL ORDER process, which has a reference number of 1.

Figure 4-18 shows the exploded version of the FILL ORDER process. FILL ORDER consists of three detailed processes: VERIFY ORDER, PREPARE REJECT NOTICE, and ASSEMBLE ORDER. All processes on more detailed DFDs are numbered using a decimal notation consisting of the parent's reference number, a decimal point, and a sequence number within the new diagram. The parent process of diagram 1 is process 1, so the processes in Figure 4-18 have reference numbers of 1.1, 1.2, and 1.3. If process 1.3, ASSEMBLE ORDER, is decomposed further, then it would appear in diagram 1.3 and the processes in diagram 1.3 would be numbered as 1.3.1, 1.3.2, 1.3.3, and so on. This numbering technique makes it easy to link all DFDs in an orderly fashion.

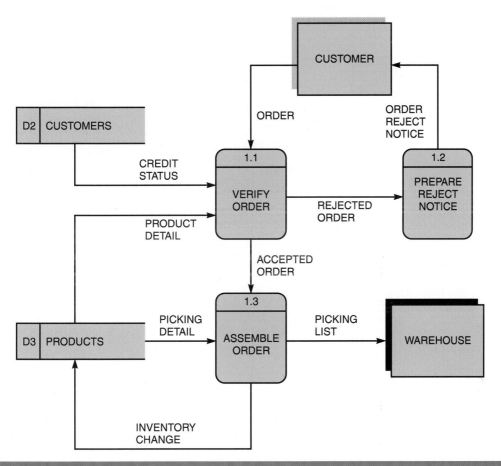

FIGURE 4-18 Diagram 1 DFD, detail of FILL ORDER, for the order system.

Under the leveling concept, the context diagram represents the highest-level view of an information system, followed by diagram 0, which shows more detail. The grading system that we were examining earlier, which is relatively simple, is completely represented by a context diagram and a diagram 0. The order system is more complex and includes an additional level of DFDs. Larger information systems, such as the manufacturing system, might require an analyst to work though many DFD levels to reach the system's functional primitive processes.

Not all processes are exploded to the same number of levels. The order system diagram 0 shown in Figure 4-14 has one functional primitive process, CREATE INVOICE, and two other processes that an analyst would explode to an additional level. It is not necessary to explode all processes down to exactly the same level — the main objective is to continue until you reach functional primitives that can be translated into units of program code. Most systems analysts find that developing a set of DFDs requires trying various designs until they find the best overall solution.

Figure 4-19 is equivalent to Figure 4-18 and is a common way of showing DFDs below the context diagram level. The difference between these two diagrams is that in Figure 4-19 the analyst has not drawn the CUSTOMER and WAREHOUSE external entities. As a result, the data flows are missing a DFD symbol at one end. Many analysts draw DFDs that way because they feel the missing symbols are not required, and removing them simplifies the diagram. Because the missing symbols appear on the parent, you can refer to that diagram if you need to know the source or destination of the data flows.

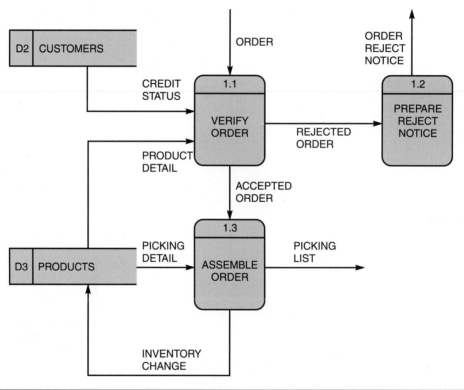

FIGURE 4-19   Diagram 1 DFD, detail of FILL ORDER, for the order system. In contrast to the DFD in Figure 4-18, this diagram does not show the symbols that connect to data flows entering or leaving FILL ORDER on diagram 0.

On the other hand, some analysts prefer to show all the symbols. Either approach is acceptable, as long as you are consistent. You should follow whichever approach your instructor suggests or the method your company adopts as a standard.

When constructing DFDs, you might run into a special situation concerning data stores. Sometimes a data store has output data flows only, which means that the information system accesses the data but does not change it in any way. In that case, the data store is updated by some other system. For example, the CUSTOMERS data store shown in Figure 4-18 provides credit status input to the order system but is not maintained by that system. Another one-way data store example is a tax table that contains a series of tax rates.

BALANCING Effective DFDs are accurate, clear, and consistent. One way to gain consistency is to define each functional primitive with a process description and see that each data store, data flow, external entity, and process is defined in the data dictionary (discussed in a later section). To achieve consistency, you also must balance your DFDs properly.

A **balanced** set of DFDs preserves the input and output data flows of the parent on the child DFD. Figure 4-19 shows a balanced DFD; it has the same input and output flows as its parent process, FILL ORDER, as shown in Figure 4-14. The ORDER data flow provides input to both FILL ORDER and diagram 1, and the PICKING LIST and ORDER REJECT NOTICE data flows serve as output from both FILL ORDER and diagram 1. Because the DFDs do not show data dictionary entries, you would need to verify that all processes, data flows, and data stores are properly documented in the data dictionary to ensure that the DFD is consistent.

DATA STORES Figure 4-20 shows the order system's diagram 3, which is the detail of process 3, APPLY PAYMENT. The data store DAILY PAYMENTS appears on that diagram, but it did not appear on diagram 0. Why? When drawing DFDs, you show a data store only when two or more processes use that data store. The DAILY PAYMENTS data store was internal to PROCESS 3, so the analyst did not show it on diagram 0. When you explode PROCESS 3 into DFD diagram 3, however, you see that three processes (POST PAYMENT, DEPOSIT PAYMENT, and PREPARE ACCOUNTING ENTRY) all require the use of the DAILY PAYMENTS data.

Strategies for Developing DFDs

What about an overall strategy for developing a set of DFDs? A set of DFDs is a graphical, top-down model, so most analysts first create the context diagram, then diagram 0, then all the child diagrams for diagram 0, and so on.

Other analysts, however, follow an alternative bottom-up strategy. With a bottom-up strategy, you first identify all functional primitives, data stores, external entities, and data flows. Then you group processes with other related symbols to develop the lowest-level diagrams. Next, you group those diagrams in a logical way to form the next higher level. You continue to work your way up until you reach diagram 0.

Regardless of which strategy you use, you should apply the suggestions and guidelines discussed in this chapter. The main objective is to ensure that your model is accurate and easy to understand. Reviewing data and process models with users allows you to obtain their feedback and approval for the logical design of the system.

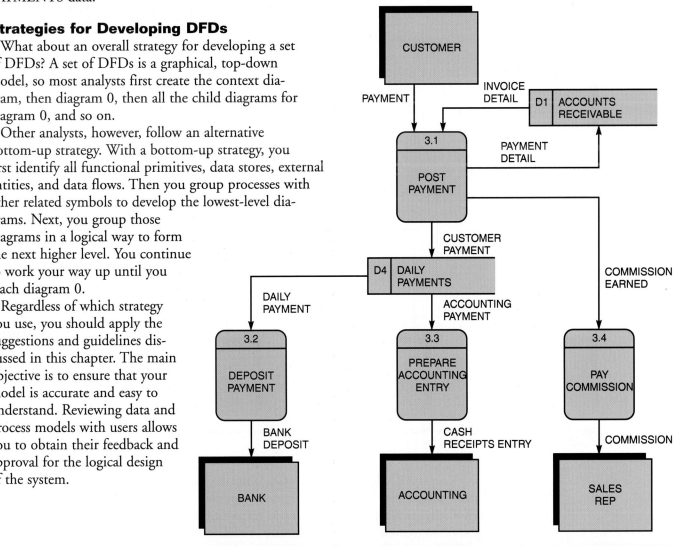

FIGURE 4-20   Diagram 3 DFD, detail of APPLY PAYMENT, for the order system.

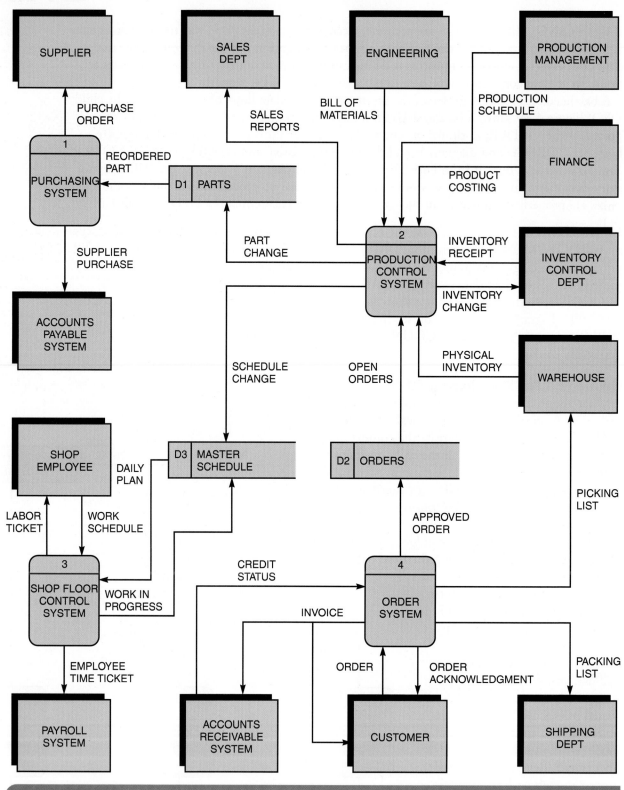

FIGURE 4-21 Diagram 0 for the manufacturing system.

Now review Figure 4-21, which shows diagram 0 for the manufacturing system. In a large system such as this, each process in diagram 0 actually represents an entire system. Using a diagram 0 is just one of dozens of acceptable ways for you to partition a large system into its component systems. As you do so, remember the general rule of thumb that a diagram should have no more than nine process symbols. Figure 4-21 has only four process symbols, so you can imagine how complicated a diagram would be with nine or more processes.

The manufacturing system is an example of a highly complex system with many processes, data stores, and data flows. As shown in Figure 4-22, any highly complex system requires many interactive processes and data sources to produce products efficiently. In such cases, you might use a combination of the top-down and the bottom-up strategies. You might begin with a bottom-up approach, encounter problems, and have to work your way back down before continuing up again. Alternatively, you could start at the top, working your way down and then back up repeatedly. In either case, you will find that diagramming is an iterative process.

If users and other analysts who review your DFDs find them correct and simple to follow, you have chosen the proper strategy. The best approach depends on your personal preferences and the circumstances of the information system you are modeling.

FIGURE 4-22 Manufacturing systems require many interactive processes and data sources to produce the right product at the right time.

WHAT DO YOU THINK?

You are the IT director at a large midwestern university. As part of a training program, you decide to draw a DFD that includes some obvious mistakes, to see whether your newly hired junior analysts can find them. You came up with the diagram 0 DFD shown in Figure 4-23. Based on the rules explained in this chapter, how many problems should the analysts find?

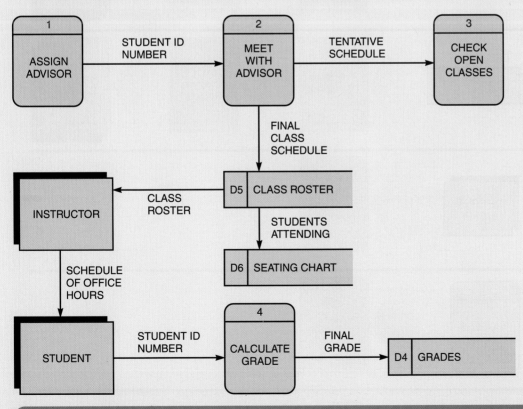

FIGURE 4-23 What are the mistakes in this diagram 0 DFD?

DATA DICTIONARY

A set of DFDs produces a logical model of the system, but the details within those DFDs are documented separately in a data dictionary, which is the second component of structured analysis.

A **data dictionary**, or data repository, is a central storehouse of information about the system's data. An analyst uses the data dictionary to collect, document, and organize specific facts about the system, including the contents of data flows, data stores, external entities, and processes. The data dictionary also defines and describes all data elements and meaningful combinations of data elements. A **data element**, or **data item** or **field**, is the smallest piece of data that has meaning within an information system. Examples of data elements are student grade, salary, Social Security number, account balance, and company name. Data elements are combined into records or **data structures**. A **record** is a meaningful combination of related data elements that is included in a data flow or retained in a data store. For example, an auto parts store inventory record might include part number, description, supplier code, minimum and maximum stock levels, cost, and list price.

Figure 4-24 shows a data dictionary and the items that are defined during structured analysis. Significant relationships exist among these items. Notice that the data stores and data flows are based on data structures that are composed of data elements. Data flows are connected to data stores, external entities, and processes. Accurately documenting these relationships in a data dictionary is essential so the data dictionary is consistent with the DFDs.

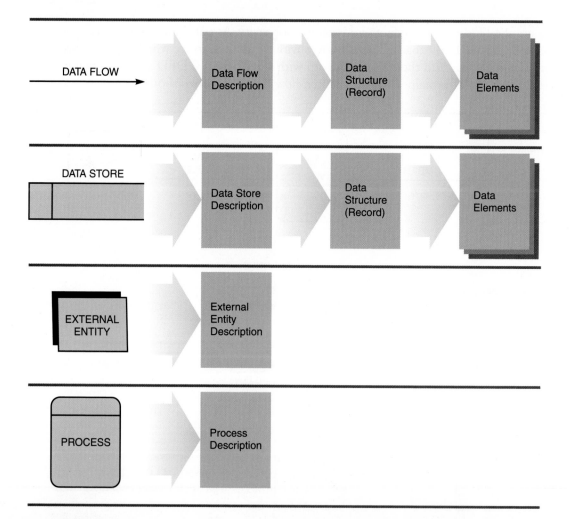

FIGURE 4-24   Contents of the data dictionary, including data flows, data stores, data structures and records, data elements, external entities, and processes.

Documenting the Data Elements

You must document every data element in the data dictionary. Some analysts like to record their notes on forms such as the one shown in Figure 4-25, which documents a SOCIAL SECURITY NUMBER data element. Others prefer to enter the information directly into a CASE tool. Several of the DFDs and data dictionary entries that appear in this chapter were created using a popular CASE tool called Visible Analyst. Although other CASE tools might use other terms or display the information differently, the objective is the same: to provide clear, comprehensive information about the data and processes that make up the system.

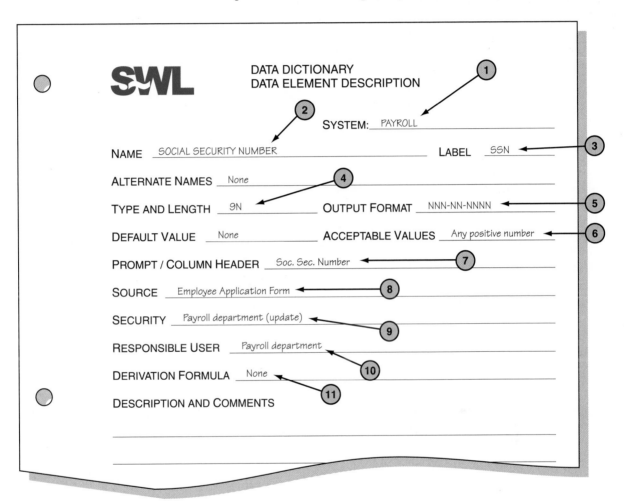

FIGURE 4-25 Using a manual form, the analyst has recorded information for a data element named SOCIAL SECURITY NUMBER. Later, the analyst will create a data dictionary entry using a CASE tool.

1. Manual documentation entries often indicate which system is involved. This is not necessary with a CASE tool because all information is stored in one file that is named for the system.
2. The data element has a standard name that provides consistency throughout the data dictionary.
3. The data element can have a label that usually is an abbreviation of the name.
4. This entry indicates that the data element consists of nine numeric characters.
5. An output format shows how the data will be displayed on the screen and in printed reports.
6. Depending on the data element, very strict limits might be placed on acceptable values, or none at all.
7. This entry is a standard way to refer to the data element in reports or interactive dialog with the user.
8. The data comes from the employee's job application.
9. This entry indicates that only the payroll department has authority to update or change this data.
10. This entry indicates the individual or department responsible for entering and changing data.
11. This entry indicates that this data does not need to be derived or calculated from other system data.

In Figure 4-26, two sample screens show how the SOCIAL SECURITY NUMBER data element might be recorded in the Visible Analyst data dictionary.

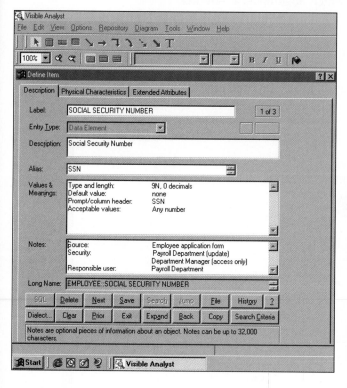

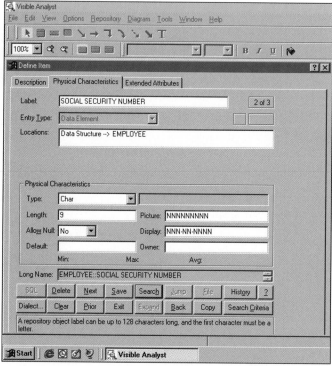

FIGURE 4-26 Two Visible Analyst screens that describe the data element named SOCIAL SECURITY NUMBER. Notice that many of the items were entered from the manual form shown in Figure 4-25 on the previous page.

Regardless of the terminology or method, the following attributes usually are recorded and described in the data dictionary:

Data element name or label. The standard name for the data element; it should be meaningful to users.

Alternate name(s). Any name(s) other than the standard data element name; these names are called **synonyms** or **aliases**. For example, if you have a data element named CURRENT BALANCE, various users might refer to it by alternate names such as OUTSTANDING BALANCE, CUSTOMER BALANCE, RECEIVABLE BALANCE, or AMOUNT OWED.

Type and length. **Type** refers to whether the data element contains numeric, alphabetic, or character values. **Length** is the maximum number of characters for an alphabetic or character data element or the maximum number of digits and number of decimal positions for a numeric data element. In addition to text and numeric data, sounds and images also can be stored in digital form. In some systems, these binary data objects are managed and processed just as traditional data elements are. For example, an employee record might include a digitized photo image of the person.

Output format. The arrangement of the data element when users see it printed on reports or displayed on the screen. For example, a telephone number that is stored as 9195559999 has an output format of (919) 555-9999.

Default value. The value for the data element if a value otherwise is not entered for it. For example, all new customers might have a default value of $500 for the CREDIT LIMIT data element.

Prompt, column header, or field caption. The default display screen prompt or report column heading when the information system outputs the data element.

Source. The specification for the origination point for the data element's values. The source could be a specific form, a department or outside organization, another information system, or the result of a calculation.

Security. Identification for the individual or department that has access or update privileges for each data element. For example, only a credit manager has the authority to change a credit limit, while sales reps are authorized to access data in a read-only mode.

Responsible user(s). Identification of the user(s) responsible for entering and changing values for the data element.

Acceptable values and data validation. Specification of the data element's **domain**, which is the set of values permitted for the data element; these values can be either specifically listed or referenced in a table, or selected from a specified range of values. You also would indicate if a value for the data element is optional. Some data elements have additional **validity rules**. For example, an employee's salary must be within the range defined for the employee's job classification.

Derivation formula. If the data element's value is the result of a calculation, then you show the formula for the data element, including significant digits and rounding operations, if any.

Description or comments. Part of the data element's documentation that allows you to provide additional definitions, descriptions, or notes.

Documenting the Data Flows

In addition to documenting each data element, you must document all data flows in the data dictionary. Figure 4-27 on the next page shows a definition for a data flow named COMMISSION. The information on the manual form at the top was entered into the CASE tool data dictionary at the bottom of Figure 4-27.

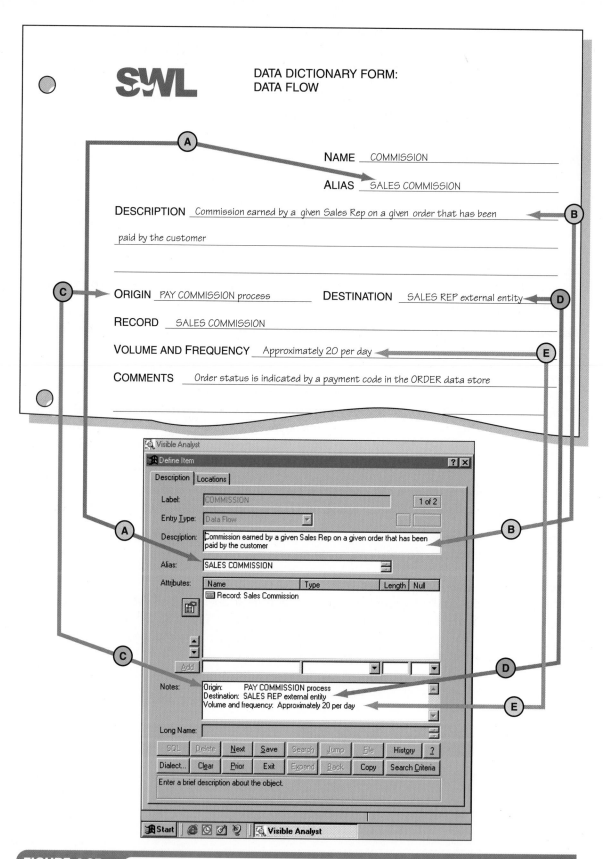

FIGURE 4-27 The data flow named COMMISSION is described in a manual data dictionary form, then entered into a Visible Analyst data dictionary.

Although terms can vary, the typical attributes are as follows:

Data flow name or label. The data flow name as it appears on the DFDs.

Alternate name(s). Aliases for the DFD data flow name(s).

Description. Describes the data flow and its purpose.

Origin. The DFD beginning, or source, for the data flow; the origin can be a process, a data store, or an external entity.

Destination. The DFD ending point(s) for the data flow; the destination can be a process, a data store, or an external entity.

Record. Each data flow represents a group of related data elements called a record or data structure. In most data dictionaries, records are defined separately from the data flows and data stores. When records are defined, more than one data flow or data store can use the same record, if necessary.

Volume and frequency. Describes the expected number of occurrences for the data flow per unit of time. For example, if a company has 300 employees, a TIME CARD data flow would involve 300 transactions and records each week, as employees submit their work hour data.

Documenting the Data Stores

You must document every DFD data store in the data dictionary. Figure 4-28 shows the definition of a data store named PRODUCTS.

Typical characteristics of a data store are as follows:

Data store name or label. The data store name as it appears on the DFDs.

Alternate name(s). Aliases for the DFD data store name.

Description. Describes the data store and its purpose.

Input data flows. The standard DFD names for the data flows entering the data store.

Output data flows. The standard DFD names for the data flows leaving the data store.

Record. The record name in the data dictionary for the data store.

Volume and frequency. Describes the estimated number of records stored in the data store; specifies any growth and changes statistics for the data store.

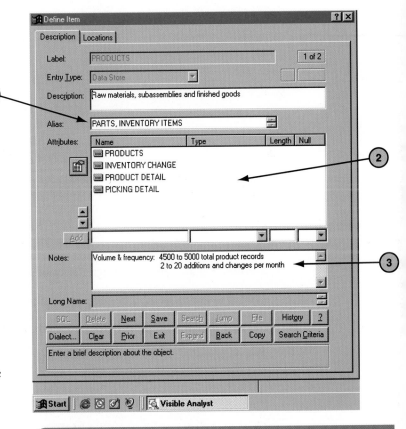

FIGURE 4-28 Visible Analyst screen that documents a data store named PRODUCTS.

1. Data elements in the PRODUCTS data store. This data store has two alternative names, or aliases.

2. For consistency, the data element names are standardized throughout the data dictionary.

3. It is important to document these estimates, because they will affect design decisions in subsequent SDLC phases.

Documenting the Processes

You must document every process, as shown in Figure 4-29. Your documentation includes a description of the process's characteristics and, for functional primitives, a process description, which is a model that documents the processing steps and business logic.

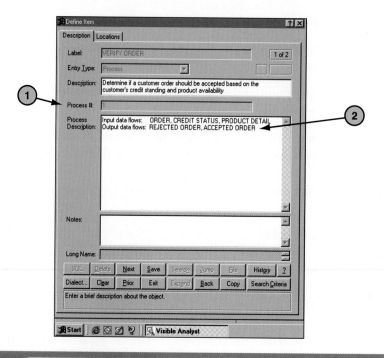

Visible Analyst screen that describes a process named VERIFY ORDER.

1. The process number identifies this process. Any subprocesses are numbered 1.1, 1.2, 1.3, and so on.
2. These data flows will be described specifically elsewhere in the data dictionary.

Following are typical characteristics of a process:

Process name or label. The process name as it appears on the DFDs.

Purpose or description. A brief statement of the process's general purpose.

Process number. A reference number that identifies the process and indicates relationships among various levels in the system.

Input data flows. The standard DFD names for the data flows entering the process.

Output data flows. The standard DFD names for the data flows leaving the process.

Process description. This section is filled in only if the process is a functional primitive. For functional primitives the process description documents the processing steps and business logic. You will learn how to write process descriptions in the next section.

Documenting the External Entities

By documenting all external entities, the data dictionary can serve as a complete documentation package. Figure 4-30 shows a definition for an entity named WAREHOUSE.

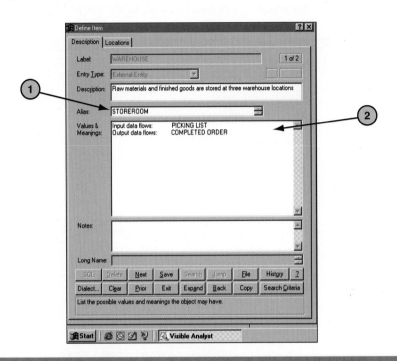

FIGURE 4-30	Visible Analyst screen that documents an external entity named WAREHOUSE.

1. The external entity can have an alternative name, or alias, if properly documented.
2. For consistency, these data flow names are standardized throughout the data dictionary.

Typical characteristics of an external entity include the following.

External entity name. The external entity name as it appears on the DFDs.

Alternate name(s). Any aliases for the external entity name.

Description. Describe the external entity and its purpose.

Input data flows. The standard DFD names for the input data flows to the external entity.

Output data flows. The standard DFD names for the data flows leaving the external entity.

Documenting the Records

A record is a data structure that contains a set of related data elements that are stored and processed together. Data flows and data stores consist of records that you must document in the data dictionary. You define characteristics of each record, as shown in Figure 4-31.

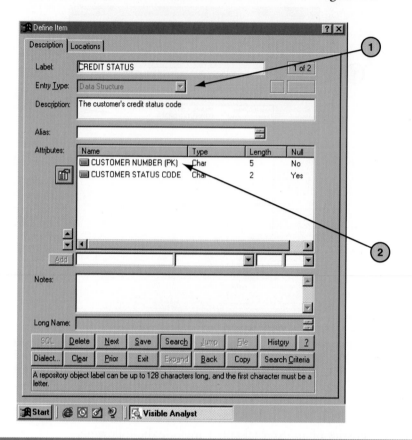

FIGURE 4-31   Visible Analyst screen that documents a record named CREDIT STATUS.

1. The Visible Analyst tool defines a data structure as a group of related data elements that also can be referred to as a record.
2. The (PK) notation indicates that the CUSTOMER NUMBER is a primary key.

Typical characteristics of a record include the following.

Record or data structure name. The record name as it appears in the related data flow and data store entries in the data dictionary.

Alternate name(s). Any aliases for the record name.

Definition or description. A brief definition of the record.

Record content or composition. A list of all the data elements included in the record. The data element names must match exactly what you entered in the data dictionary. Identify any data element that will serve as a primary key. A **primary key** is a data element in a record that uniquely identifies that record. A primary key can consist of one data element or a combination of two or more data elements. The CREDIT STATUS record shown in Figure 4-31, for example, has a primary key of CUSTOMER NUMBER (PK is used to identify the primary key), which distinguishes one customer's record from all other customer records. In a video store, you might need to use a primary key based on a combination of two fields, such as MOVIE NUMBER and COPY NUMBER, to identify each individual tape.

Data Dictionary Reports

The data dictionary serves as the central storehouse of documentation for an information system. In addition to describing each data element, data flow, data store, record, external entity, and process, the data dictionary documents the relationships among these components. You can obtain many valuable reports from a data dictionary, including the following:

- An alphabetized list of all data elements by name
- A report by user departments of data elements that must be updated by each department
- A report of all data flows and data stores that use a particular data element
- Detailed reports showing all characteristics of data elements, records, data flows, processes, or any other selected item stored in the data dictionary

ON THE WEB

To learn more about Modular Design visit scsite.com/sad4e/more.ht▶ click Systems Analysis and Design Chapter 4 and then click the Modular Design li▶

www.scsite.c

PROCESS DESCRIPTION TOOLS

A **process description** documents the details of a functional primitive, which represents a specific set of processing steps and business logic. Using a set of process description tools, you create a model that is accurate, complete, and concise. Typical process description tools include structured English, decision tables, and decision trees. When you analyze a functional primitive, you break the processing steps down into smaller units in a process called modular design.

FIGURE 4-32 Sequence structure.

Modular Design

Modular design is based on combinations of three **logical structures**, sometimes called **control structures**, which serve as building blocks for the process. Notice that each logical structure has a single entry and exit point. The three structures are called sequence, selection, and iteration. A rectangle represents a step or process, a diamond shape represents a condition or decision, and the logic follows the lines in the direction indicated by the arrows.

1. **Sequence.** The completion of steps in sequential order, one after another, as shown in Figure 4-32. One or more of the steps might represent a subprocess that contains additional logical structures.

2. **Selection.** The completion of one of two or more process steps based on the results of a test or condition. In the example shown in Figure 4-33, the system tests the input, and if the hours are greater than 40, it performs the CALCULATE OVERTIME PAY process.

3. **Iteration.** The completion of a process step that is repeated until a specific condition changes, as shown in Figure 4-34. An example of iteration is a process that continues to print paychecks until it reaches the end of the payroll file. Iteration also is called **repetition** or **looping**.

Sequence, selection, and iteration structures can be combined in various ways to describe processing logic.

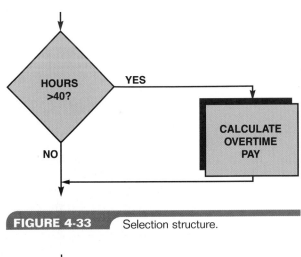

FIGURE 4-33 Selection structure.

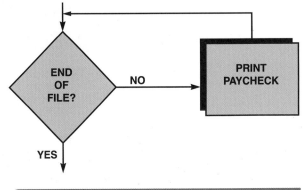

FIGURE 4-34 Iteration structure.

Structured English

Structured English is a subset of standard English that describes logical processes clearly and accurately. When you use structured English, you must conform to the following rules:

- Use only the three building blocks of sequence, selection, and iteration.

- Use indentation for readability.

- Use a limited vocabulary, including standard terms used in the data dictionary and specific words that describe the processing rules.

An example of structured English appears in Figure 4-35, which shows the VERIFY ORDER process that was illustrated earlier in Figure 4-29 on page 4.26. In Figure 4-35, structured English was added to describe the processing logic.

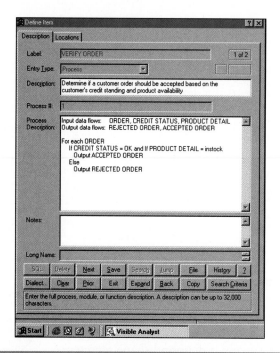

FIGURE 4-35 The VERIFY ORDER process description documents the logic rules and processing steps.

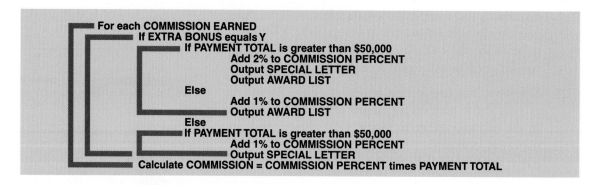

FIGURE 4-36 Sample structured English process description. Structured English is an organized way of describing what actions are taken on data. This structured English example describes a commission calculation policy.

Structured English might look familiar to programming students because it resembles pseudocode, which is used in program design. Although the techniques are similar, the primary purpose of structured English is to describe the underlying business logic, while programmers, who are concerned with coding, mainly use pseudocode as a shorthand notation for the actual code.

Figure 4-36 shows another example of structured English. Notice that the capitalized words are all terms from the data dictionary to ensure consistency between process descriptions and the data dictionary. The other terms, such as *for, each, if,* and *output,* describe the processing logic. Following these structured English rules ensures that your process descriptions are understandable to users who must confirm that the process is correct, as well as to other analysts and programmers who must design the information system from your descriptions.

Decision Tables

A **decision table** shows a logical structure, with all possible combinations of conditions and resulting actions. Analysts often use decision tables, in addition to structured English, to describe a logical process and ensure that they have not overlooked any logical possibility.

A simple example of a decision table is based on the VERIFY ORDER process shown in Figure 4-35. When documenting a process, it is important to consider every conceivable outcome to ensure that you have overlooked nothing. From the structured English description, we know that an accepted order requires that credit status is OK and the product is in stock. Otherwise, the order is rejected. The decision table shown in Figure 4-37 shows all the possibilities. To create a decision table, follow the steps indicated in the figure.

Because each condition has two possible values, the number of rules doubles each time you add a condition. For example, one condition creates only two rules, two conditions create four rules, three conditions create eight rules, and so on. As shown in Figure 4-37, four possible combinations exist, but only one rule — rule 1 — permits an accepted order output.

ON THE WEB

For more information about Decision Tables visit scsite.com/sad4e/more.htm click Systems Analysis and Design Chapter 4 and then click the Decision Tables lin

www.scsite.c

VERIFY ORDER Process				
Based On	1	2	3	4
Credit status is OK	Y	Y	N	N
Product is in stock	Y	N	Y	N
Accept order	X			
Reject order		X	X	X

FIGURE 4-37 Example of a simple decision table showing the processing logic of the VERIFY ORDER process.

1. Place a heading at the top left that names the table.
2. Enter the conditions under the heading, with one condition per line, to represent the customer status and availability of products.
3. Enter all potential combinations of Y/N (for yes and no) for the conditions. Each column represents a numbered possibility called a rule.
4. Place an X in the action entries area for each rule to indicate whether to accept or reject the order.

A more complex situation is presented in Figure 4-38. In the example, the credit manager can waive the credit status requirement in certain situations. To ensure that all possibilities are covered, notice that the first condition provides an equal number of Ys and Ns, the second condition alternates Y and N pairs, and the third condition alternates single Ys and Ns.

The first table in Figure 4-38 shows eight rules. Because some rules are duplicates, however, the table can be simplified. To reduce the number of rules, you must look closely at each combination of conditions and actions. If you have rules with three conditions, only one or two of them may control the outcome, and the other conditions do not matter. You can indicate that with dashes (–) as shown in the second table in Figure 4-38. Then you can combine and renumber the rules, as shown in the final table.

VERIFY ORDER Process with Credit Waiver (Initial version)								
	1	2	3	4	5	6	7	8
Credit status is OK	Y	Y	Y	Y	N	N	N	N
Product is in stock	Y	Y	N	N	Y	Y	N	N
Waiver from credit manager	Y	N	Y	N	Y	N	Y	N
Accept order	X	X			X			
Reject order			X	X		X	X	X

VERIFY ORDER Process with Credit Waiver (With rules marked for combination)								
	1	2	3	4	5	6	7	8
Credit status is OK	Y	Y	-	-	N	N	-	-
Product is in stock	Y	Y	N	N	Y	Y	N	N
Waiver from credit manager	-	-	-	-	Y	N	-	-
Accept order	X	X			X			
Reject order			X	X		X	X	X

VERIFY ORDER Process with Credit Waiver (After rule combination and simplification)				
	1 (Combines previous 1, 2)	2 (Previous 5)	3 (Previous 6)	4 (Combines previous 3, 4, 7, 8)
Credit status is OK	Y	N	N	-
Product is in stock	Y	Y	Y	N
Waiver from credit manager	-	Y	N	-
Accept order	X	X		
Reject order			X	X

FIGURE 4-38   A more complex example of a decision table for the VERIFY ORDER process showing the results of rule combination and simplification.

1. Because the product is not in stock, the other conditions do not matter.
2. Because the other conditions are met, the waiver does not matter.

In the example, rules 1 and 2 can be combined because credit status is OK, and the waiver is not needed. Rules 3, 4, 7, and 8 also can be combined because the product is not in stock, and credit status does not matter. The result is that instead of eight possibilities, only four logical rules are created that control the VERIFY ORDER process.

In addition to multiple conditions, decision tables can have more than two possible out-comes. An example is presented in the PAY COMMISSION decision table shown in Figure 4-39. Here only two conditions exist: Was an extra bonus given, and did the payment total exceed $50,000? Based on these two conditions, four possible actions can occur, as shown in the table.

PAY COMMISSION	1	2	3	4
EXTRA BONUS	Y	Y	N	N
PAYMENT TOTAL > $50,000	Y	N	Y	N
Add 2% to COMMISSION PERCENT	X			
Add 1% to COMMISSION PERCENT		X	X	
Output SPECIAL LETTER	X		X	
Output AWARD LIST	X	X		

FIGURE 4-39   Sample decision table based on the commission calculation policy described in structured English in Figure 4-32 on page 4.29. For example, if the payment total is more than $50,000 but no extra bonus is to be paid, the policy is to add 1 percent to the commission percent and to output a special letter to the sales representative.

Decision tables often are the best way to describe a complex set of conditions. Many analysts use decision tables because they are easy to construct and understand, and programmers find it easy to work from a decision table when developing code.

Decision Trees

A **decision tree** is a graphical representation of the conditions, actions, and rules found in a decision table. Decision trees show the logic structure in a horizontal form that resembles a tree with the roots at the left and the branches to the right. Like flowcharts, decision trees are effective ways to present the system to management, as shown in Figure 4-40. Decision trees and decision tables are considered equivalent, but in different forms — a graphic versus a table.

FIGURE 4-40   Analysts and managers use graphical representations, including flowcharts and decision trees, to show the process under consideration.

Figure 4-41 shows the same PAY COMMISSION conditions and actions shown in Figure 4-39 on the previous page. A decision tree is read from left to right, with the conditions along the various branches and the actions at the far right. Because the example has two conditions with four resulting sets of actions, the example has four terminating branches at the right side of the tree.

Whether to use a decision table or a decision tree often is a matter of personal preference. A decision table might be a better way to handle complex combinations of conditions. On the other hand, a decision tree is an effective way to describe a relatively simple process.

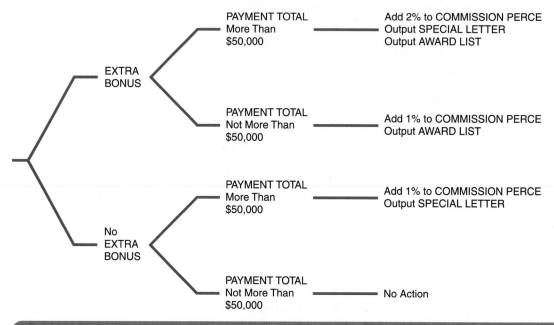

FIGURE 4-41   Sample decision tree process description. Similar to a decision table, a decision tree illustrates the action to be taken based on certain conditions but presents it graphically. This decision tree is based on the commission calculation policy described in structured English in Figure 4-36 on page 4.31. For example, if the payment total is more than $50,000 but no extra bonus is to be paid, the policy is to add 1 percent to the commission percent and to output a special letter to the sales representative.

N THE WEB

an overview of Logical sus Physical Models visit ite.com/sad4e/more.htm, k Systems Analysis and sign Chapter 4 and then k the Logical Versus sical Models link.

w.scsite.com

LOGICAL VERSUS PHYSICAL MODELS

While structured analysis tools are used to develop a logical model for a new information system, such tools also can be used to develop physical models of an information system. A physical model shows how the system's requirements are implemented. During the systems design phase, you create a physical model of the new information system that follows from the logical model and involves operational tasks and techniques.

Sequence of Models

What is the relationship between logical and physical models? Think back to the beginning of the systems analysis phase, when you were trying to understand the existing system. Rather than starting with a logical model, you first studied the physical operations of the existing system to understand how the current tasks were carried out. Many systems analysts create a physical model of the current system and then develop a logical model of the current system before tackling a logical model of the new system. Performing that extra step allows them to understand the current system better.

Four-Model Approach

If you follow this sequence when you develop an information system, you will develop a total of four models: a physical model of the current system, a logical model of the current system, a logical model of the new system, and a physical model of the new system. The major benefit of the four-model approach is that you will have a better grasp of the current system functions before making any modifications or improvements. That is important because mistakes made early in systems development will affect later SDLC phases and can result in unhappy users and additional costs. Taking additional steps to avoid these potentially costly mistakes can prove to be well worth the effort. Another advantage is that the requirements of a new information system often are quite similar to the current information system, especially where the proposal is based on new computer technology rather than a large number of new requirements. Adapting the current system logical model to the new system logical model in these cases is a straightforward process.

The major disadvantage of the four-model approach is the added time and cost needed to develop a logical and physical model of the current system. Most projects have very tight schedules that might not allow time to create the current system models. Additionally, users and managers want to see progress on the new system; spending too much time on the current system seems counterproductive. Finally, if you truly know the new system's requirements, then spending time documenting a system that is being replaced might not be necessary or wise.

WHAT DO YOU THINK?

In the SWL case study that follows, Rick Williams and Carla Moore are working on the logical model of SWL's payroll system, using DFDs, a data dictionary, and process descriptions. At some point while working on the logical model of the system, Rick considers some new enrollment forms that the human resources department might use to implement the Employee Savings and Investment Plan (ESIP). Was the subject of forms identified as a physical implementation issue? Is Rick going off on a tangent by considering *how* something will be done, instead of sticking to *what* will be done?

SOFTWEAR, LIMITED

Rick Williams, a systems analyst, and Carla Moore, a programmer/analyst, continued their work on the SWL payroll system project. After completing detailed interviews and other fact-finding activities, Rick and Carla now understand how the current system operates and the new requirements desired by users. They are ready to organize and document their findings by preparing a logical model of the payroll system.

Data Flow Diagrams

Rick and Carla reviewed the collected set of requirements and decided that the first step is to prepare a context diagram. Rick was most familiar with the payroll system, so he prepared the diagram shown in Figure 4-42. On a Friday afternoon, Rick walked Carla through the diagram and asked for her comments.

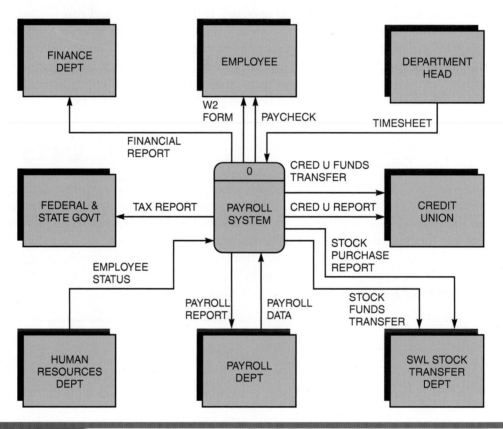

FIGURE 4-42   Initial version of context diagram for SoftWear, Limited's payroll system.

The diagram shows how the two analysts understood the system. They knew that an employee received a paycheck each week, based on a timesheet submitted by the department head, and that each employee receives a W-2 form at the end of the year. They knew that the human resources department prepares employee status changes, and the payroll department enters the pay rate information. The diagram also noted the output of state and federal government reports and internal reports to SWL's finance and payroll departments. The credit union and the SWL stock transfer department reports and fund transfers also were included.

Carla, however, was not sure that they had covered everything. They both decided that it was a good idea to review the system requirements over the weekend and discuss the diagram again on Monday.

The weekend review turned out to be a wise strategy. When she reviewed her interview documentation, Carla discovered that the payroll department enters the timesheet data received from department heads, as well as the pay rate information. So she removed the department head entity symbol and changed the existing input data flow from the payroll department, calling it PAY DETAIL.

After studying his notes, Rick also detected an error: The payroll system produces a report for the accounting department, and that report is not shown on the diagram. They also realized that federal and state reporting requirements were different, so it would be more accurate to treat them as two separate entities. Rick revised the context diagram to reflect these changes, as shown in Figure 4-43.

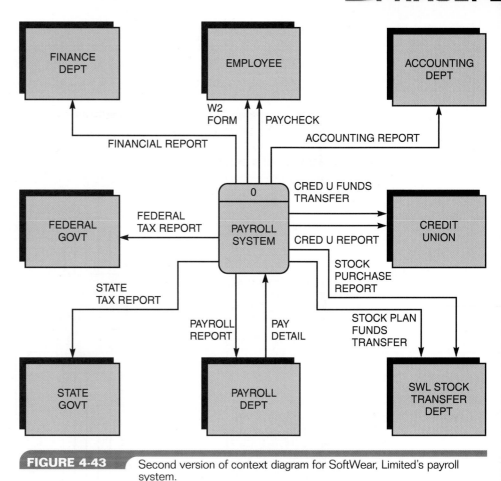

FIGURE 4-43 Second version of context diagram for SoftWear, Limited's payroll system.

Rick and Carla were comfortable with the context diagram and scheduled a meeting for the next day with Amy Calico, director of the payroll department, to discuss the diagram. In preparation for the meeting, they brainstormed their ideas about the payroll system's major processes, data stores, and data flows, and reviewed the system's requirements one more time.

The next day, Rick and Carla presented the context diagram to Amy, who had several suggestions. Amy noted that the human resources department generates employee status changes, including job title, pay rate, and exempt status. But the human resources group does not enter the data directly into the payroll system. Instead, all employee changes are sent to the payroll department for entry. Amy had several other comments:

- Periodic changes in state and federal government tax rates should be shown as inputs to the payroll system.
- All reports, except for a financial summary, should be distributed to the accounting department instead of to the finance department. The accounting department also should receive a copy of the payroll report. Rick and Carla both recalled that Mr. Jeremy wanted the change.
- The bank returns cleared payroll checks to the payroll department once a month. Amy reminded the analysts that the payroll system handles the reconciliation of payroll checks.
- The human resources department would be setting up additional ESIP deduction choices for employees under a new 401(k) plan. Human resources also would receive ESIP reports from the payroll system.

Rick and Carla admitted that they had not considered the ESIP reports when they constructed the diagram. After discussing it, they agreed that the new functions should be shown in the diagram. Following the meeting, Rick and Carla prepared the final version of the payroll system context diagram shown in Figure 4-44 with all the suggested changes.

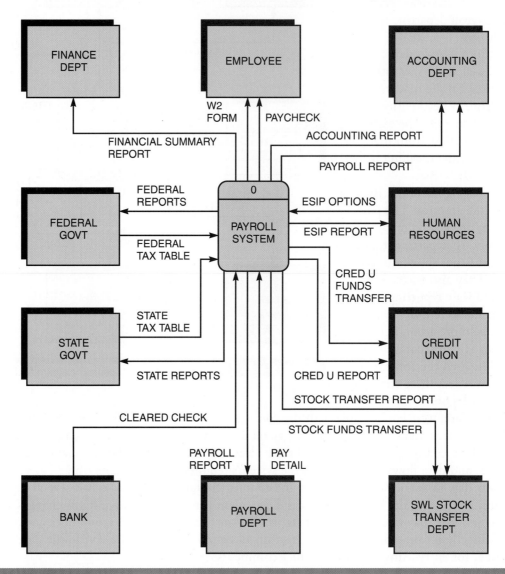

FIGURE 4-44   Final context diagram for SoftWear, Limited's payroll system.

While their conversation with Amy Calico was still fresh in her mind, Carla proposed that they construct the diagram 0 DFD. After going through several draft versions, they were able to complete the diagram 0 shown in Figure 4-45. They decided that the major processes were the check reconciliation subsystem, the pay employee subsystem, the payroll accounting subsystem, and a subsystem that would handle all voluntary deductions, which they called the ESIP deduction subsystem.

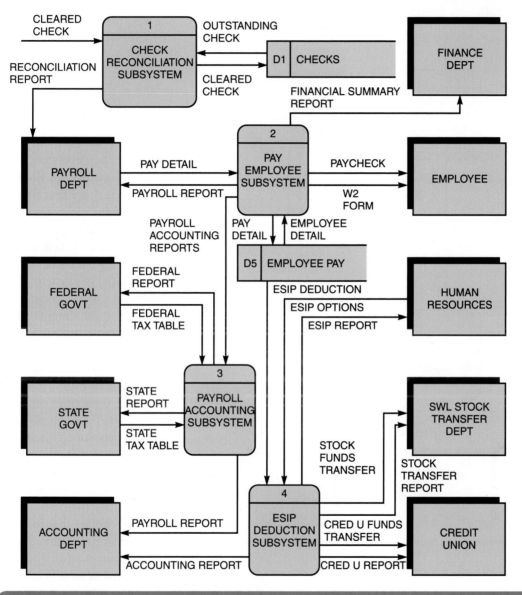

FIGURE 4-45   Diagram 0 DFD for SoftWear, Limited's payroll system.

Over the next few days, Rick concentrated on partitioning the pay employee subsystem and the ESIP subsystem, while Carla developed the lower-level diagrams for the other two subsystems.

At that point, Rick considered the problem of applying certain deductions on a monthly cycle, even though the deductions were made weekly. To provide flexibility, he decided to use two separate processes, as shown in Figure 4-46. When he finished, his diagram 4 DFD contained the two processes EXTRACT DEDUCTION and APPLY DEDUCTION, as well as a local data store, UNAPPLIED DEDUCTIONS. Several local data flows also were included. The first process, EXTRACT DEDUCTION, would deduct the proper amount in each pay period. The deductions would be held in the temporary data store and then applied in the APPLY DEDUCTION process on a weekly or monthly basis, depending on the type of deduction. Rick decided that those processes were functional primitives and he did not need to partition them further. That task completed the logical model of the new SWL payroll system.

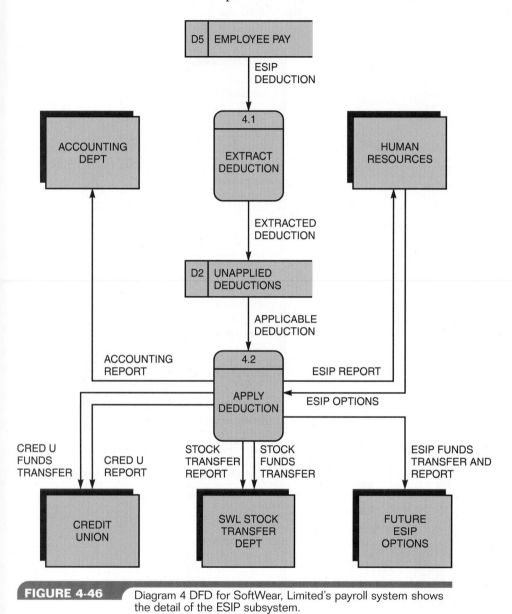

Rick and Carla also considered the physical design of the ESIP deduction subsystem that would be completed later. They knew that it would be necessary to add some new forms and to redesign others. They saw that the human resources department would need a new form for enrollments or deduction changes for the credit union, SWL stock purchase plan, or any new ESIP choices that might be offered in the future. The payroll department then could use the form as its official

FIGURE 4-46 Diagram 4 DFD for SoftWear, Limited's payroll system shows the detail of the ESIP subsystem.

notification. To provide for future expansion and add flexibility, the human resources department also would need a form to notify payroll of any new type of deduction, with a deduction code, the name of the deduction, and the payroll cycle involved. Rick anticipated that the new system would eliminate problems with improper deductions, while adding flexibility and reducing maintenance costs.

Data Dictionary and Process Descriptions

As they constructed the DFDs for the payroll system, Rick and Carla also developed the data dictionary entries with supporting process descriptions.

Using the Visible Analyst CASE tool, Rick documented the PROCESS 4 ESIP
DEDUCTION SUBSYSTEM as shown in Figure 4-47. Then he defined the data flow called
ESIP REPORT that originates in the APPLY DEDUCTION process and connects to the
HUMAN RESOURCES entity, as shown in Figure 4-48. He also documented the ESIP
OPTIONS record as shown in Figure 4-49, which consists of eight data elements.

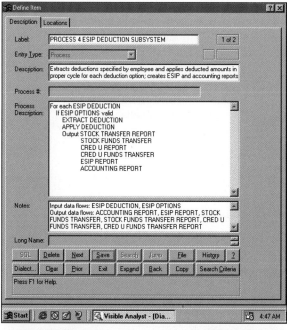

FIGURE 4-47   Data dictionary definition
for the PROCESS 4 ESIP
DEDUCTION SUBSYSTEM.

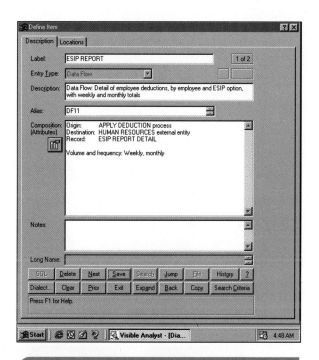

FIGURE 4-48   Data dictionary definition for the
ESIP REPORT data flow.

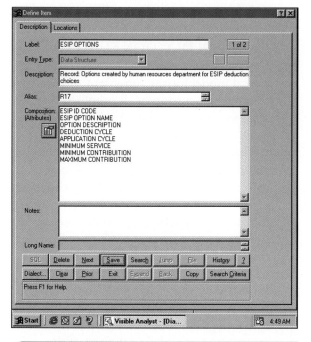

FIGURE 4-49   Data dictionary definition for the
ESIP OPTIONS record.

Carla prepared the process description for EXTRACT DEDUCTION as shown in Figure 4-50. Notice that she numbered the process 4.1, because it was exploded from process 4. The two analysts also completed the descriptions for the data element EXTRACTED DEDUCTION as shown in Figure 4-51, and the ESIP ID CODE as shown in Figure 4-52. They spent the next two days documenting the rest of the data flows and external entities for the ESIP DEDUCTION SUBSYSTEM, along with data elements and records.

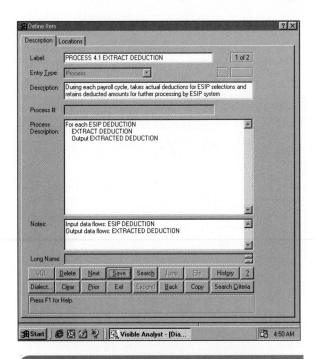

FIGURE 4-50 Data dictionary definition for PROCESS 4.1 EXTRACT DEDUCTION.

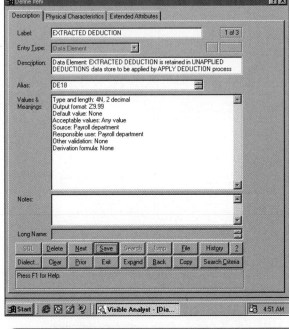

FIGURE 4-51 Data dictionary definition for the data element EXTRACTED DEDUCTION.

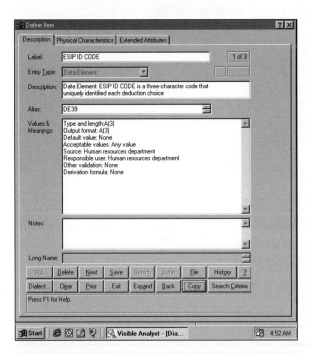

FIGURE 4-52 Data dictionary definition for the data element ESIP ID CODE.

After completing the documentation of the ESIP DEDUCTION SUBSYSTEM, Carla and Rick met with Amy to review the logical model for the subsystem. After a thorough discussion of all proposed changes and processing, Amy approved the model.

Rick and Carla continued their analysis and documentation of the payroll system over the next several days. As they completed a model of a portion of the information system, they would meet with the appropriate users at SWL to review the model, obtain user input, make necessary adjustments to the model, and obtain the users' approval. After Rick and Carla finished the complete payroll information system logical model, they turned their attention to completing the rest of the system requirements document.

Suppose that you are working with Rick and Carla when a new systems request comes in. SWL's vice president of marketing, Amy Neal, wants to change the catalog mailing program and provide a reward for customers who use the Internet.

Amy's plan specifies that customers will remain on SWL's mailing list if they either requested a catalog, ordered from SWL in the last two years, or signed the guest register on SWL's new Web site. To encourage Internet visitors, customers who register on the Web site also will receive a special discount certificate.

To document the requirements, Rick wants you to design a decision table. Initially, it appears to have eight rules, but you notice that some of those rules are duplicates, or might not be realistic combinations.

1. Design the decision table with all possibilities.

2. Simplify the table by combining rules where appropriate.

3. Draw a decision tree that reflects Amy Neal's policy.

4. Create a set of structured English statements to show the policy.

CHAPTER SUMMARY

This chapter examines data and process modeling, which is a structured analysis technique. You use data and process modeling to construct a logical model for an information system of any size or level of complexity. Data and process modeling has three main components: DFDs, the data dictionary, and process descriptions.

DFDs graphically show the movement and transformation of data in the information system. DFDs use four symbols: The process symbol transforms data; the data flow symbol shows data movement; the data store symbol shows data at rest; and the external entity symbol represents someone or something connected to the information system. Various rules and techniques are used to name, number, arrange, and annotate the set of DFDs to make them consistent and understandable.

A set of DFDs is like a pyramid with the context diagram at the top. The context diagram represents the information system's scope and its external connections but not its internal workings. Diagram 0 displays the information system's major processes, data stores, and data flows and is the exploded version of the context diagram's process symbol, which represents the entire information system. Lower-level DFDs show additional detail of the information system through the leveling technique of numbering and partitioning. Leveling continues until you reach the functional primitive processes, which are not decomposed further and are documented with process descriptions. All diagrams must be balanced to ensure their consistency and accuracy.

The data dictionary is the central documentation tool for structured analysis. All data elements, data flows, data stores, processes, external entities, and records are documented in the data dictionary. Consolidating documentation in one location allows you to verify the information system's accuracy and consistency more easily and generate a variety of useful reports.

Each functional primitive process is documented using structured English, decision tables, and decision trees. Structured English uses a subset of standard English that defines each process with combinations of the basic building blocks of sequence, selection, and iteration. You also can document the logic by using decision tables or decision trees.

Key Terms

aliases (*4.22*)
balanced (*4.17*)
balancing (*4.13*)
black box (*4.3*)
black hole (*4.4*)
business logic (*4.2*)
business model (*4.1*)
business rules (*4.2*)
child (*4.12*)
context diagram (*4.7*)
control structures (*4.29*)
conventions (*4.9*)
data and process modeling (*4.1*)
data dictionary (*4.20*)
data element (*4.20*)
data flow (*4.3*)
data flow diagram (DFD) (*4.2*)
data item (*4.20*)
data repository (*4.4*)
data store (*4.4*)
data structures (*4.20*)
decision table (*4.30*)
decision tree (*4.33*)
decomposed (*4.12*)
diagram 0 (*4.10*)
diverging data flow (*4.10*)
domain (*4.23*)
exploded (*4.12*)

field (*4.20*)
functional primitive (*4.12*)
Gane and Sarson (*4.2*)
gray hole (*4.4*)
length (*4.22*)
leveling (*4.13*)
logical model (*4.1*)
logical structures (*4.29*)
looping (*4.29*)
modular design (*4.29*)
parent (*4.12*)
partitioned (*4.12*)
physical models (*4.1*)
primary key (*4.28*)
process (*4.2*)
process description (*4.29*)
record (*4.20*)
repetition (*4.29*)
sink (*4.6*)
spontaneous generation (*4.4*)
structured analysis (*4.1*)
structured English (*4.30*)
source (*4.6*)
synonyms (*4.22*)
terminators (*4.6*)
type (*4.22*)
validity rules (*4.23*)
Yourdon (*4.2*)

Chapter Review

1. Describe structured analysis and name the three main data and process modeling techniques.

2. Define and draw Gane and Sarson symbols used for processes, data flows, data stores, and entities.

3. Give four examples of typical names for processes, data flows, data stores, and entities.

4. What is the relationship between a context diagram and diagram 0, and which symbol is *not* used in a context diagram?

5. What is meant by an exploded DFD?

6. Describe a data dictionary, and give examples of how and when it is used.

7. Explain the DFD leveling technique.

8. What is a balanced DFD?

9. Describe the steps in creating a decision table.

10. What is structured English?

Discussion Topics

1. Suppose you were assigned to develop a logical model of the registration system at a school or college. Would you be better off to use a top-down approach, or would a bottom-up strategy be better? What would influence your decision?

2. Some systems analysts find it better to start with a decision table, then construct a decision tree. Others believe it is easier to do it in the reverse order. Which do you prefer? Why?

3. A systems analyst attended a weeklong workshop on structured analysis. When she returned to her job, she told her boss that structured analysis was not worth the time to learn and use on the job. Her view was that it was too academic and had too much new terminology to be useful in a practical setting. Do you agree or disagree? Defend your position.

4. This chapter describes a black box concept that allows more detail to be shown as a process is exploded. Can the concept be applied in business management generally, or is it limited to information systems design? Provide reasons and examples with your answer.

Apply Your Knowledge

1 Digital Consulting

Situation:

You are a senior systems analyst at Digital Consulting, a growing IT consulting firm. You are leading the development team for a major client. You need to explain structured analysis to your two newly hired junior analysts (Sara and Mike) before meeting with the client tomorrow afternoon.

1. Describe the rules for creating a context diagram.

2. Make a basic list of dos and don'ts when developing DFDs.

3. Explain the importance of leveling and balancing.

4. Create a simple example of a system with several entities and processes, and ask Sara and Mike to draw a context diagram and a diagram 0 DFD. Prepare sample answers for them.

2 Precision Tools

Situation:

Precision Tools sells a line of high-quality woodworking tools. When customers place orders on the company's Web site, the system checks to see if the items are in stock, issues a status message to the customer, and generates a shipping order to the warehouse, which fills the order. When the order is shipped, the customer is billed. The system also produces various reports.

1. Draw a context diagram for the order system.

2. Draw DFD diagram 0 for the order system.

3. Name four attributes that you can use to define a process in the order system.

4. Name four attributes that you can use to define an entity in the order system.

3 Claremont School

Situation:

The Claremont School course catalog reads as follows: "To enroll in CIS 288, which is an advanced course, a student must complete two prerequisites — CIS 110 and CIS 286. A student who completes either one of these prerequisites and obtains the instructor's permission, however, will be allowed to take CIS 288."

1. Create a decision table that describes the Claremont School course catalog regarding eligibility for CIS 288. Show all possible rules.

2. Simplify the table you just created. Describe the results.

3. Draw a simplified decision tree to represent the Claremont School catalog. Describe the results.

4. Why might you use a decision tree rather than a decision table?

City Bus Lines

Situation:

City Bus Lines is developing an information system that will monitor passenger traffic, peak travel hours, and equipment requirements. The IT manager wants you to document a process that will determine if extra busses are needed on a route, and automatically assign them if all other routes are operating on schedule. During peak periods, however, a dispatcher will be allowed to override the system and shift busses from one route to another.

1. Create a decision table that describes the bus transfer process.

2. Draw a decision tree that describes the bus transfer process.

3. Name four attributes that you can use to define a data flow in the bus information system.

4. Name four attributes that you can use to define a data store in the bus information system.

Chapter Assignments

1. Draw a context diagram and a diagram 0 DFD that represents the registration system at your school or an imaginary school.

2. On the Internet, locate at least three firms that offer CASE tools. Write e-mail messages to the companies to find out whether they offer demonstration copies or student versions of their products.

3. Suppose that you want to demonstrate a decision table to someone who has never seen one. Think of an example, with two or three conditions, from everyday life. Draw a decision table that captures all possible outcomes.

4. Draw a simplified decision tree that represents the City Bus Lines policy.

CASE STUDIES

Case Studies offer an opportunity for you to practice specific skills and knowledge learned in the chapter and provide practical experience for you as a systems analyst. Two of the case studies (New Century Health Clinic and Ridgeway Company) are continuing case studies that appear in each chapter. Additionally, one continuing case study (SCR Associates) utilizes the Internet to practice some of the topics covered in this chapter.

NEW CENTURY HEALTH CLINIC

You began the systems analysis phase at New Century Health Clinic by completing a series of interviews, reviewing existing reports, and observing office operations. (You can obtain a complete, "standard" set of summaries through your instructor, or on the Internet at www.scsite.com/sad4e.)

As you learned, the doctors, nurses, and physical therapists provide services and perform various medical procedures. All procedures are coded according to *Current Procedure Terminology*, which is published by the American Medical Association. The procedure codes consist of five numeric digits and a two-digit suffix, and are used for all billing and insurance claims.

From your fact-finding, you determined that seven reports are required at the clinic. The first report is the daily appointment list for each provider. The list shows all scheduled appointment times, patient names, and services to be performed, including the procedure code and description. A second daily report is the call list, which shows the patients who are to be reminded of their next day's appointments. The call list includes the patient name, telephone number, appointment time, and provider name. The third report is the weekly provider report that lists each of the providers and the weekly charges generated, plus a month-to-date (MTD) and a year-to-date (YTD) summary.

The fourth report is the statement — a preprinted form that is produced monthly and mailed in a window envelope. Statement header information includes the statement date, head of household name and address, the previous month's balance, the total household charges MTD, the total payments MTD, and the current balance. The bottom section of the statement lists all activity for the month in date order. For each service performed, a line shows the patient's name, the service date, the procedure code and description, and the charge. The statement also shows the date and amount of all payments and insurance claims. When an insurance payment is received, the source and amount are noted on the form. If the claim is denied or only partially paid, a code is used to explain the reason. A running balance appears at the far right of each activity line.

The associates also require two insurance reports: the weekly Insurance Company Report and

to these six reports, the office staff would like
ostcards for sending reminders to patients
nt. Reminders usually are mailed twice
s you gathered and prepare a system require-
of the proposed system. Your tools will include
s.

CH 4
1) 4.6

2) 4.10

·y's information system.

·y. Be sure to show subsystems for handling
·rance processing, report processing, and

needed for the system. Under each data store,

5. Prepare a data dictionary entry and process description for one of the system's functional primitives.

RIDGEWAY COMPANY

Review the facts presented in the Ridgeway Company case studies in Chapters 2 and 3. Use that information to complete the following tasks.

Assignments

1. Prepare the context diagram for the billing system.

2. Prepare the diagram 0 DFD for the billing system.

3. If any processes on diagram 0 need to be partitioned, prepare the second-level diagrams for those processes.

4. For each data store, list the data elements that would be found in that data store.

SCR ASSOCIATES

SCR Associates is an information technology consulting firm that offers IT solutions and training for small- and medium-sized companies. SCR's slogan is "We Know IT!"

Background

As a newly hired systems analyst, you will handle assignments, work on various SCR projects, and apply the skills you learned in the text.

The SCR case is available as an interactive, Web-based case study. You can log on to the Shelly Cashman Series site at www.scsite.com/sad4e/scr for instructions and assignments. If you prefer to complete the case study without using the Internet then you must download the data disk. See the inside back cover for instructions for downloading the data disk or see your instructor for more information on accessing the files required for this book.

Situation

In the previous assignment for SCR Associates, you completed requirements modeling for the new training information management system (TIMS). In this assignment, you will perform data and process modeling. You will create DFDs, develop a data dictionary, use decision tables and decision trees.

Before You Begin ...

1. Review the November 12 message from Jesse Baker regarding DFDs. Open the Document 4-1 from the data disk.

2. Review the November 14 message from Jesse Baker regarding CASE tools. Open the Document 4-2 from the data disk.

3. Review the November 16 message from Jesse Baker regarding course fee discounts. Open the Document 4-3 from the data disk.

4. Review the JAD session summary. Open the Document 3-3 from the data disk.

Assignments

1. Using Jesse Baker's November 12 message and the JAD session summary as a guide, draw a context diagram and a diagram 0 DFD for the TIMS system.

2. Draw a lower-level DFD for each process you identify in diagram 0 DFD.

3. Perform Internet research on CASE tools and write a brief memo responding to Jesse Baker's November 14 message.

4. Draw a decision tree that represents the example you suggested in Chapter Assignment 3.

ON THE WEB

The SCR case is available as an interactive, Web-based case study. You can log on to the Shelly Cashman Series site at www.scsite.com/sad4e/scr for instructions and assignments.

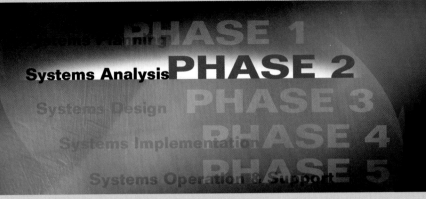

Object Modeling

INTRODUCTION

In Chapter 4, you learned how to use structured analysis techniques to develop a data and process model of the proposed system. Now, in Chapter 5, you will learn about object-oriented analysis, which is another way to view and model the system requirements. In this chapter you use object-oriented methods to document, analyze, and model the information system. In Chapter 6, which concludes the systems analysis phase, you will evaluate alternatives, develop the system requirements document, learn about prototyping, and prepare for the systems design phase of the SDLC.

OBJECTIVES

When you finish this chapter, you will be able to:

- Explain how object-oriented analysis can be used to describe an information system

- Define object modeling terms and concepts, including objects, attributes, methods, messages, classes, and instances

- Explain relationships among objects, including dependency, association, aggregation, and inheritance

- Draw an object relationship diagram

- Describe Unified Modeling Language (UML) tools and techniques, including use cases, use case diagrams, class diagrams, sequence diagrams, state transition diagrams, and activity diagrams

- Explain the advantages of using CASE tools in developing the object model

- Explain how to organize the object model

N THE WEB

r an overview of
bject-Oriented Terms
d Concepts visit
csite.com/sad4e/more.htm,
ck Systems Analysis and
esign Chapter 5 and then
ck the Object-Oriented
rms and Concepts link.

w.scsite.com

OBJECT-ORIENTED TERMS AND CONCEPTS

Object-oriented analysis describes an information system by identifying things called objects. An **object** represents a real person, place, event, or transaction. For example, when a patient makes an appointment to see a doctor, the patient is an object, the doctor is an object, and the appointment itself is an object.

Object-oriented analysis is a popular approach that sees a system from the viewpoint of the objects themselves as they function and interact with the system. The end product of object-oriented analysis is an **object model**, which represents the information system in terms of objects and object-oriented concepts. Later, during the implementation phase of the SDLC, systems analysts and programmers transform the objects into program code modules. A modular approach saves money and time, because the modules can be optimized, tested, and reused.

Overview

In Chapter 3, you learned that the Unified Modeling Language (UML) is a widely used method of visualizing and documenting an information system. In this chapter, you use the UML to develop object models. Your first step is to understand basic object-oriented terms, including objects, attributes, methods, messages, classes, and instances. In this chapter, you will learn how systems analysts use those terms to describe an information system.

An object represents a person, place, event, or transaction that is significant to the information system. In Chapter 4, you created DFDs that treated data and processes separately. An object, however, includes data *and* the processes that affect that data. For example, a customer object has a name, an address, an account number, and a current balance. Customer objects also can perform specific tasks, such as placing an order, paying a bill, and changing their address.

An object has certain **attributes**, which are characteristics that describe the object. For example, if you own a vehicle, it has attributes such as make, model, and color. An object also has **methods**, which are tasks or functions that the object performs when it receives a **message**, or command, to do so. For example, your vehicle performs a method called *turn on wipers* when you send a message by moving the proper control. Figure 5-1 shows examples of attributes, methods, and messages for a vehicle object.

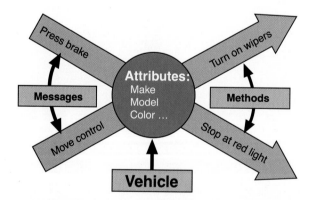

FIGURE 5-1   A vehicle object has attributes, can perform methods, and receive messages.

A **class** is a group of similar objects. For example, PT Cruisers belong to a class called CAR. An **instance** is a specific member of a class. *Your* red 2001 PT Cruiser, therefore, is an instance of the CAR class. At an auto dealership, like the one in Figure 5-2, you might observe many instances of the CAR class, the TRUCK class, the MINIVAN class, and the SPORT UTILITY VEHICLE class, among others.

Although the term *object* usually refers to a particular instance, systems analysts sometimes use the term to refer to a class of objects. Usually the meaning is understood from the context and the way the term is used.

FIGURE 5-2 At an auto dealership you can observe many instances of the CAR class, the TRUCK class, the MINIVAN class, and the SPORT UTILITY VEHICLE class.

Objects

Consider how the UML describes a family with parents and children. The UML represents an object as a rectangle with the object name at the top, followed by the object's attributes and methods.

Figure 5-3 shows a CHILD object with certain attributes such as name, age, sex, and hair color. If the family has three children, there are three instances of the CHILD object. A CHILD object performs certain methods, such as picking up toys, eating dinner, and playing with siblings. To signal the CHILD object to perform those tasks, you send certain messages that the CHILD object could understand. For example, the DINNER'S READY message tells a CHILD object to come to the table and eat a meal, while the SHARE WITH YOUR BROTHER/SISTER message tells a CHILD object to cooperate with other CHILD objects.

ON THE WEB

For more examples and discussion of Objects visit scsite.com/sad4e/more.ht click Systems Analysis and Design Chapter 5 and then click the Objects link.

www.scsite.c

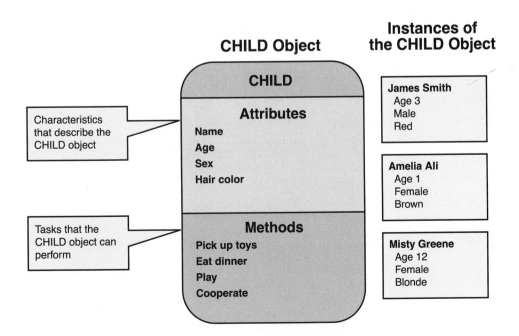

FIGURE 5-3 The CHILD object includes four attributes and four methods. James Smith, Amelia Ali, and Misty Greene are instances of the CHILD object.

Continuing with the family example, the PARENT object in Figure 5-4 possesses the same attributes as the CHILD object and an additional attribute defining the parent as a biological, step-, or adoptive parent. The PARENT object also can perform methods, such as reading a bedtime story, driving the car pool van, or preparing a school lunch. The message GOOD NIGHT tells the PARENT object to read a bedtime story, while the message DRIVE signals that it is the PARENT object's turn to drive the car pool van.

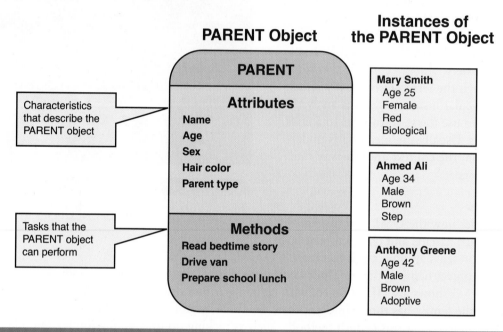

FIGURE 5-4 The PARENT object includes five attributes and three methods. Mary Smith, Ahmed Ali, and Anthony Greene are instances of the PARENT object.

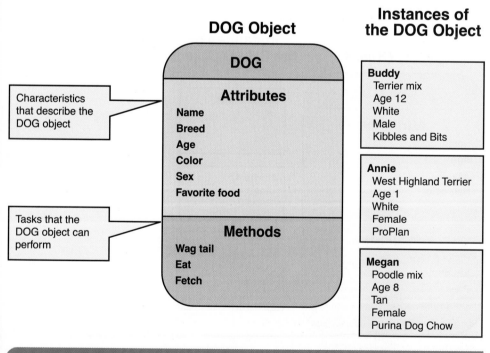

The family also might have a DOG object, as shown in Figure 5-5. That object can have attributes such as name, breed, age, color, sex, and favorite food. The DOG object can perform methods such as wagging its tail, eating, and fetching things. The message GOOD DOG, when directed to the DOG object, signals it to wag its tail. Similarly the DINNER'S READY message signals the DOG object to run to its bowl and eat.

FIGURE 5-5 The DOG object includes six attributes and three methods. Buddy, Annie, and Megan are instances of the DOG object.

Now consider an example of a fitness center, as shown in Figure 5-6, and the objects that interact with the fitness center's enrollment system. A typical fitness center might have students, instructors, fitness-class schedules, and a registration process.

STUDENT and INSTRUCTOR objects are shown in Figure 5-7. Each STUDENT object has the following attributes: student number, name, address, telephone, date of birth, fitness record, and status. In addition, a STUDENT can add a fitness-class; drop a fitness-class; change an address, telephone, or status; and update his or her fitness record.

The INSTRUCTOR object in Figure 5-7 has the following attributes: instructor number, name, address, telephone, fitness-classes taught, availability, private lesson fee, and status. An INSTRUCTOR object can teach a fitness-class, and change his or her availability, address, telephone, private lesson fee, or status.

FIGURE 5-6 A typical fitness center might have students, instructors, fitness-class schedules, and a registration process.

STUDENT Object

STUDENT

Attributes

Student number
Name
Address
Telephone
Date of birth
Fitness record
Status

Methods

Add fitness-class
Drop fitness-class
Change address
Change telephone
Change status
Update fitness record

INSTRUCTOR Object

INSTRUCTOR

Attributes

Instructor number
Name
Address
Telephone
Fitness-classes taught
Availability
Private lesson fee
Status

Methods

Teach fitness-class
Change availability
Change address
Change telephone
Change private lesson fee
Change status

FIGURE 5-7 The STUDENT object includes seven attributes and six methods. The INSTRUCTOR object includes eight attributes and six methods.

The FITNESS-CLASS SCHEDULE object shown in Figure 5-8 includes data about fitness-classes, including fitness-class number, date, time, type, location, instructor number, and maximum enrollment. The FITNESS-CLASS SCHEDULE object includes the methods that can add or delete a fitness-class, or change a fitness-class date, time, instructor, location, or enrollment.

The REGISTRATION RECORD object shown in Figure 5-9 includes the student number, fitness-class number, registration date, fee, and status. The REGISTRATION RECORD object includes methods to add a REGISTRATION instance when a student enrolls, or drop a REGISTRATION instance if the fitness-class is canceled or for nonpayment. Notice that if a student registers for three fitness-classes, the result is three instances of the REGISTRATION RECORD object. The REGISTRATION RECORD object also includes a method of notifying students and instructors of information.

Attributes

If objects are similar to nouns, attributes are similar to adjectives that describe the characteristics of an object. How many attributes are needed? The answer depends on the business requirements of the information system and its users. Even a relatively simple object, such as an inventory item, might have a part number, description, supplier, quantity on hand, minimum stock level, maximum stock level, reorder time, and so on. Some objects might have a few attributes; others might have dozens.

Systems analysts define an object's attributes during the systems design process. In an object-oriented system, objects can inherit, or acquire, certain attributes from other objects. When you learn about relationships between objects and classes, you will understand how that occurs.

Objects can have a specific attribute called a **state**. The state of an object is an adjective that describes the object's current status. For example, as shown in Figure 5-10, a student can be a FUTURE student, a CURRENT student, or a PAST student. Similarly, a fitness-class can be OPEN, CLOSED, or CANCELED; and a bank account can be ACTIVE, INACTIVE, CLOSED, or FROZEN.

FITNESS-CLASS SCHEDULE Object

FITNESS-CLASS SCHEDULE

Attributes

Fitness-class number
Date
Time
Type
Location
Instructor number
Maximum enrollment

Methods

Add fitness-class
Delete fitness-class
Change date
Change time
Change instructor
Change location
Change enrollment

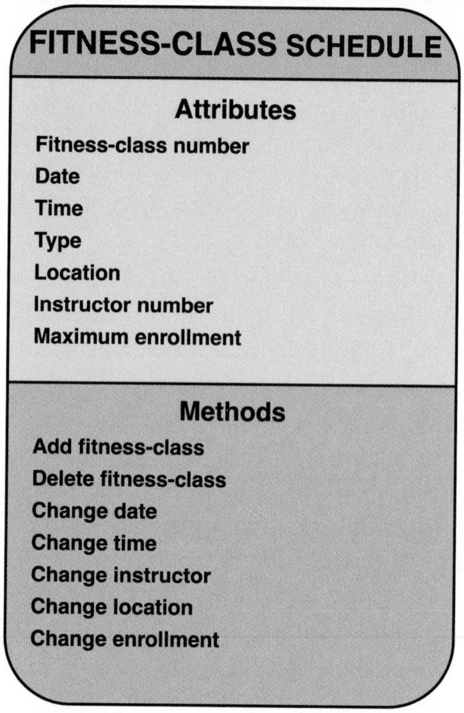

FIGURE 5-8 The FITNESS-CLASS SCHEDULE object includes seven attributes and seven methods.

REGISTRATION RECORD Object

REGISTRATION RECORD

Attributes

Student number
Fitness-class number
Registration date
Fee
Status

Methods

Add student
Drop student
Notify instructor of add
Notify instructor of drop
Notify all of fitness-class cancellations

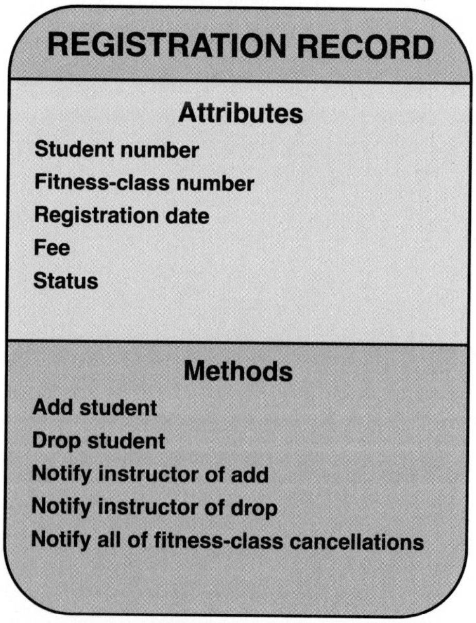

FIGURE 5-9 The REGISTRATION object includes five attributes and five methods.

STUDENT Object

State	Status
Future	Registered, but has not started to attend
Current	Registered, attending one or more fitness-classes
Past	Attended one or more fitness-classes in the past

FITNESS-CLASS Object

State	Status
Open	Fitness-class is open for enrollment
Closed	Fitness-class has reached maximum enrollment
Canceled	Fitness-class has been canceled

BANK ACCOUNT Object

State	Status
Active	Account is open and meets standards for activity
Inactive	Account is dormant for specified period of time
Closed	Account was closed
Frozen	Assets have been legally attached

FIGURE 5-10 An object's *state* is an attribute that indicates the object's status.

FIGURE 5-11 In a fast-food restaurant, preparing more fries is a common task.

Methods

A method defines specific tasks that an object can perform. Just as objects are similar to nouns and attributes are similar to adjectives, methods resemble verbs that describe *what* and *how* an object does something.

Consider a server who prepares fries in a fast-food restaurant, as shown in Figure 5-11. When a systems analyst describes the operation in UML terms, as shown in Figure 5-12, the server performs a method called MORE FRIES. The MORE FRIES method includes the steps required to heat the oil, fill the fry basket with frozen potato strips, lower it into the hot oil, check for readiness, remove the basket when ready and drain the oil, pour the fries into a warming tray, and add salt.

Figure 5-13 on the next page shows another example of a method. At the fitness center, an ADD STUDENT method adds a new instance of the STUDENT class. Notice that nine steps are required to add the new instance and record the necessary data.

Method: MORE FRIES	Steps:
	1. Heat oil
	2. Fill fry basket with frozen potato strips
	3. Lower basket into hot oil
	4. Check for readiness
	5. When ready raise basket and let drain
	6. Pour fries into warming tray
	7. Add salt

FIGURE 5-12 The MORE FRIES method requires the server to perform seven specific steps.

Method:	Steps:
ADD STUDENT	**1. Add a new student instance**
	2. Record STUDENT number
	3. Record student name
	4. Record student address
	5. Record student telephone number
	6. Record student date of birth
	7. Record sex of student
	8. Record state of student
	9. Save new student data

FIGURE 5-13   In the fitness center example, the ADD STUDENT method requires nine specific steps.

When a method creates a new instance of an object (such as adding a new student, fitness-class, or instructor) it is called a **constructor method**. A method that changes existing data is called an **update method**. For example, an update method changes a student's address when the CHANGE ADDRESS message is received. A **query method** is any method that provides information about an object's attributes. Just as you can send a query to a database, a query method called FITNESS-CLASS LISTING creates a list of all students registered in a specific fitness-class.

Messages

A message is a command that tells an object to perform a certain method. For example, the message ADD directs the STUDENT class to add a STUDENT instance. The STUDENT class understands that it should add the student number, name, and other data about that student, as shown in Figure 5-14. Similarly, a message named DELETE tells the STUDENT class to delete a STUDENT instance.

The same message to two different objects can produce different results. The concept that a message gives different meanings to different objects is called **polymorphism**. For example, in Figure 5-15, the message GOOD NIGHT signals the PARENT object to read a bedtime story, but the same message to the DOG object tells the dog to sleep. The GOOD NIGHT message to the CHILD object signals it to request a drink of water or a five-minute reprieve.

Message: ADD
Tells the STUDENT class to perform all the steps needed to add a STUDENT instance.

Message: DELETE
Tells the STUDENT class to perform all the steps needed to delete a STUDENT instance.

STUDENT

Attributes
Student number
Name
Address
Telephone
Date of birth
Fitness record
Status

Methods
Add student
Delete student
Add fitness-class
Drop fitness-class
Change address
Change telephone
Change status
Update fitness record

FIGURE 5-14   The message ADD signals the STUDENT class to perform the ADD STUDENT method. The message DELETE signals the STUDENT class to perform the DELETE STUDENT method.

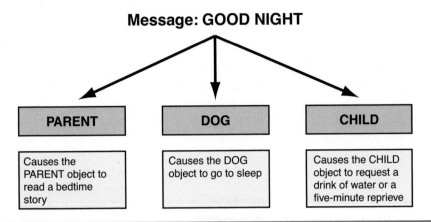

Message: GOOD NIGHT

PARENT	DOG	CHILD
Causes the PARENT object to read a bedtime story	Causes the DOG object to go to sleep	Causes the CHILD object to request a drink of water or a five-minute reprieve

FIGURE 5-15 In an example of polymorphism, the message GOOD NIGHT produces different results, depending on which object receives it.

You can view an object as a **black box**, because a message to the object triggers changes within the object without specifying how the changes must be carried out. A gas pump is an example of a black box. When you select the economy grade at a pump, you do not need to think about how the pump determines the correct price and selects the right fuel, as long as it does so properly.

The black box concept is an example of **encapsulation**, which means that all data and methods are self-contained. A black box does not want or need outside interference. By limiting access to internal processes, an object prevents its internal code from being altered by another object or process. Encapsulation allows objects to be used as modular components anywhere in the system, because objects send and receive messages but do not alter the internal methods of other objects.

Object-oriented designs typically are implemented with object-oriented programming languages. A major advantage of O-O designs is that systems analysts can save time and avoid errors by using modular objects, and programmers can translate the designs into code, working with reusable program modules that have been tested and verified. For example, in Figure 5-16, a specific SALES TRANSACTION object sends a message to an instance of the CUSTOMER class. Notice that the SALES TRANSACTION object and CUSTOMER class could be reused, with minor modifications, in other sales-oriented systems where many of the attributes and methods are similar.

Message: UPDATE BALANCE

SALES TRANSACTION → CUSTOMER

FIGURE 5-16 In a sales system, a specific SALES TRANSACTION sends a message to an instance of the CUSTOMER class.

Classes

An object belongs to a group or category called a class. All objects within a class share common attributes and methods. Objects within a class can be grouped into **subclasses**, which are more specific categories within a class. For example, TRUCK objects represent a subclass within the VEHICLE class, along with other subclasses called CAR, MINIVAN, and SCHOOL BUS, as shown in Figure 5-17. Notice that all four subclasses share common traits of the VEHICLE class, such as make, model, year, weight, and color. Each subclass also can possess traits that are uncommon, such as a load limit for the TRUCK or an emergency exit location for the SCHOOL BUS.

In the fitness center example shown in Figure 5-18, INSTRUCTOR objects represent a subclass within the EMPLOYEE class. The EMPLOYEE class also can contain MANAGER and OFFICE STAFF subclasses, because a manager and staff members are employees. All INSTRUCTOR, MANAGER, and OFFICE STAFF objects contain similar information (such as employee number, name, title, and pay rate) and perform similar tasks (such as getting hired and changing an address or telephone number).

A class can belong to a more general category called a **superclass**. For example, a NOVEL class belongs to a superclass called BOOK, because all novels are books. The NOVEL class can have subclasses called HARDCOVER and PAPERBACK. Similarly, as shown in Figure 5-19, the EMPLOYEE class belongs to the PERSON superclass, because every employee is a person, and the INSTRUCTOR class is a subclass of EMPLOYEE.

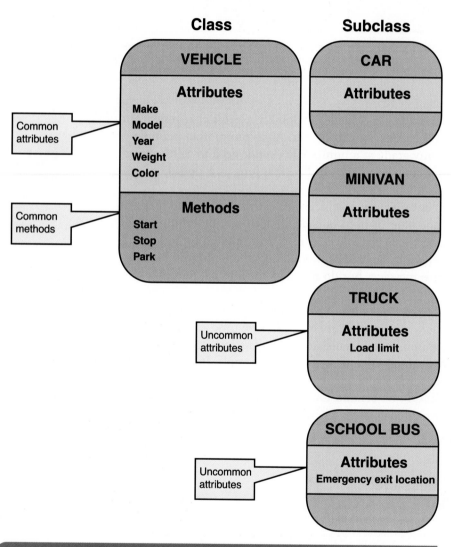

FIGURE 5-17   The VEHICLE class includes common attributes and methods. CAR, TRUCK, MINIVAN, and SCHOOL BUS are instances of the VEHICLE class.

RELATIONSHIPS AMONG OBJECTS AND CLASSES

Relationships enable objects to communicate and interact as they perform business functions and transactions required by the system. Relationships describe what objects need to know about each other, how objects respond to changes in other objects, and the effects of membership in classes, superclasses, and subclasses. Some relationships are stronger than others (just as a relationship between family members is stronger than one between casual acquaintances). Types of relationships, from weakest to strongest, include dependency, association, aggregation, and inheritance.

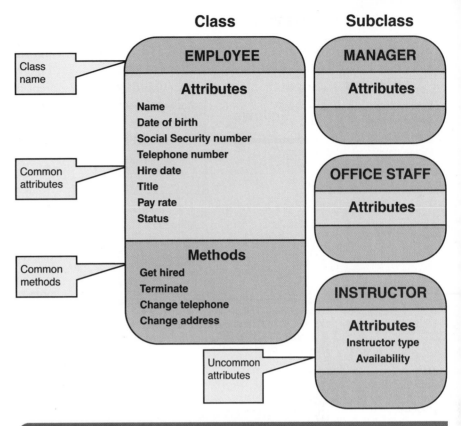

FIGURE 5-18 The fitness center EMPLOYEE class includes common attributes and methods. MANAGER, OFFICE STAFF, and INSTRUCTOR are subclasses within the EMPLOYEE class.

ON THE WEB

To learn more about Relationships Between Objects and Classes visit scsite.com/sad4e/more.htm, click Systems Analysis and Design Chapter 5 and then click the Relationships Between Objects and Classes link.

www.scsite.com

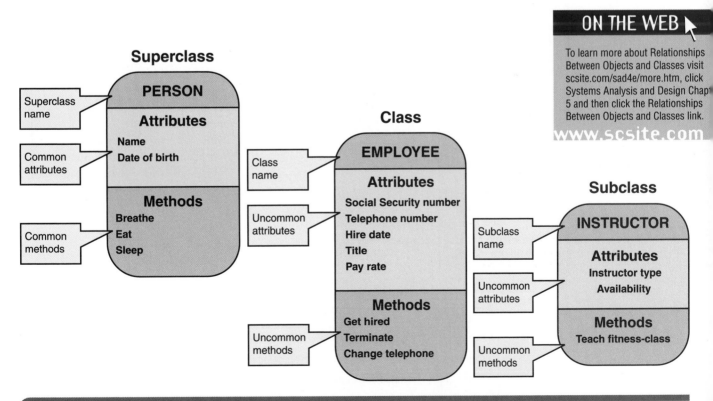

FIGURE 5-19 At the fitness center, the PERSON superclass includes common attributes and methods. EMPLOYEE is a class within the PERSON superclass. INSTRUCTOR is a subclass within the EMPLOYEE class.

Dependency

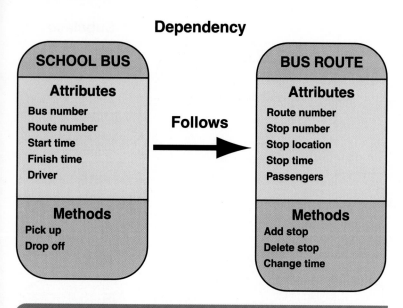

FIGURE 5-20 A *dependency* relationship exists between the SCHOOL BUS and the BUS ROUTE objects. Any change in the BUS ROUTE object will affect the SCHOOL BUS object.

Dependency

Dependency occurs when one object must be informed about another. In the example in Figure 5-20, the SCHOOL BUS object must be kept informed about the BUS ROUTE object in order to make the correct stops at the correct time. Any change in the BUS ROUTE object will affect the SCHOOL BUS object.

Association

An **association** relationship is stronger than a dependency and occurs when certain attributes of one object are determined by its interaction with another object, as shown in Figure 5-21. For example, when a student enrolls in one or more fitness-classes in the REGISTRATION RECORD object, the student's status, or state, in the STUDENT object becomes CURRENT. If a student drops all fitness-classes in the REGISTRATION RECORD object, the student's state in the STUDENT object becomes PAST.

Association

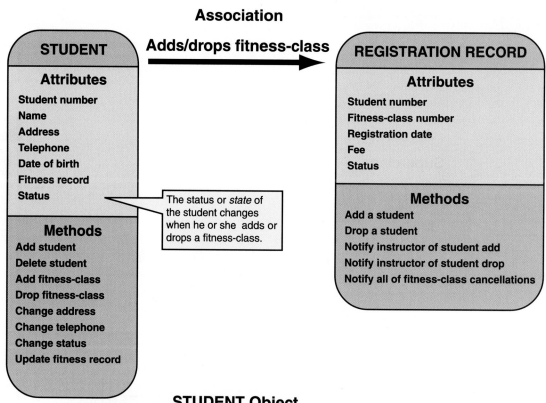

FIGURE 5-21 An *association* relationship exists between the STUDENT and the REGISTRATION RECORD object. Changes in the REGISTRATION RECORD object can affect the status of the STUDENT object.

Aggregation

An **aggregation** relationship exists when an object forms *part of* another object. For example, an EMPLOYEE object has specific attributes and methods. As shown in Figure 5-22, however, an EMPLOYEE object also belongs to a DEPARTMENT object, which has its own attributes and methods. The aggregation relationship between an EMPLOYEE and a DEPARTMENT is stronger than an association or a dependency, because all members of the DEPARTMENT must be instances of the EMPLOYEE object.

Inheritance

Inheritance enables an object to derive one or more of its attributes from another object. In the example in Figure 5-23, the INSTRUCTOR object inherits many traits from the EMPLOYEE object, including SOCIAL SECURITY NUMBER, TELEPHONE NUMBER, and HIRE DATE. The INSTRUCTOR object also can possess additional attributes, such as TYPE OF INSTRUCTOR. Because all employees share certain attributes, those attributes are assumed through inheritance and do not need to be repeated in the INSTRUCTOR object.

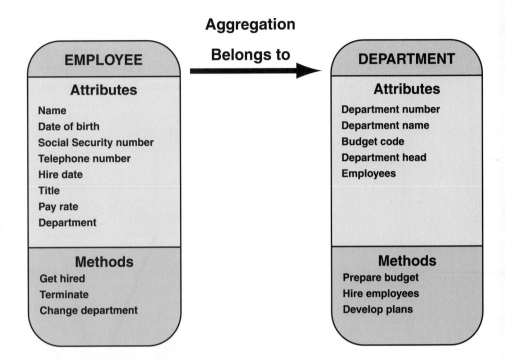

FIGURE 5-22 An *aggregation* relationship exists between the DEPARTMENT and EMPLOYEE objects. All members of the DEPARTMENT are part of the EMPLOYEE object.

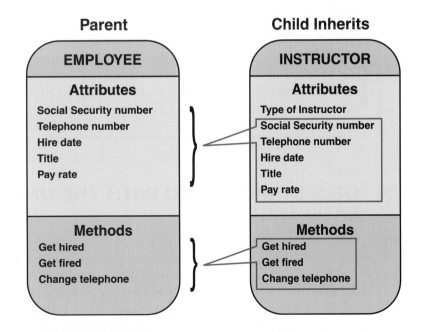

FIGURE 5-23 An inheritance relationship exists between the INSTRUCTOR and EMPLOYEE objects. The INSTRUCTOR object inherits characteristics from the EMPLOYEE class and can have additional attributes of its own.

Object Relationship Diagram

After you identify the objects, classes, and relationships, you are ready to prepare an object relationship diagram that will provide an overview of the system. You will use that model as a guide as you continue to develop additional diagrams and documentation. Figure 5-24 shows an object relationship diagram for the fitness center. Notice that the model shows the objects and how they interact to perform business functions and transactions.

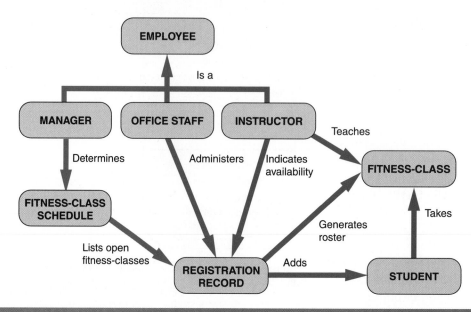

FIGURE 5-24 Object relationship diagram for the fitness center.

W H A T   D O   Y O U   T H I N K ?

One of your responsibilities at Cyber Associates, an IT consulting firm, is to assign new systems analysts to various tasks and projects. Some of the senior people believe that inexperienced analysts should start with object-oriented techniques, which are easier to learn and apply. Others think that an analyst should learn structured analysis first, and then proceed to object-oriented skills. What is your viewpoint, and why?

N THE WEB

learn more
out the UML visit
site.com/sad4e/more.htm,
ck Systems Analysis and
sign Chapter 5 and then
ck the UML link.

w.scsite.com

OBJECT MODELING WITH THE UNIFIED MODELING LANGUAGE

Just as structured analysis uses DFDs to model data and processes, systems analysts use the Unified Modeling Language (UML) to describe object-oriented systems.

In Chapter 3, you learned that the UML is a popular technique for documenting and modeling a system. The UML uses a set of symbols to represent graphically the various components and relationships within a system. Although the UML can be used for business process modeling and requirements modeling, it is mainly used to support object-oriented system analysis and to develop object models.

In 1997, the Object Management Group (OMG), an industry group concerned with object-oriented issues and trends, adopted the UML as an object modeling standard. You can learn more about the OMG by visiting its Web site shown in Figure 5-25.

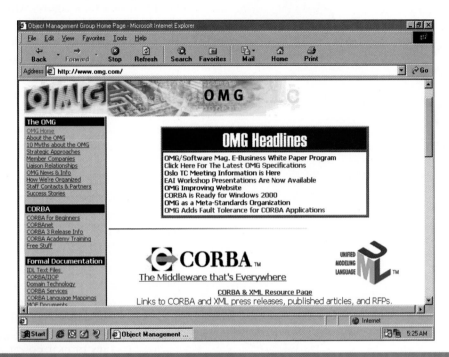

FIGURE 5-25 The Object Management Group (OMG) is an industry association concerned with object-oriented issues and standards.

The UML consists of various diagrams that use common symbols and notation. This integrated approach makes it easier to create, read, and utilize UML diagrams. In this chapter, we use the UML to describe use cases, use case diagrams, class diagrams, sequence diagrams, state transition diagrams, and activity diagrams.

Use Case Modeling

A **use case** represents the steps in a specific business function or process. An external entity, called an **actor**, initiates a use case by requesting the system to perform a function or process. For example, in a medical office system, a PATIENT (actor) can MAKE AN APPOINTMENT (use case), as shown in Figure 5-26.

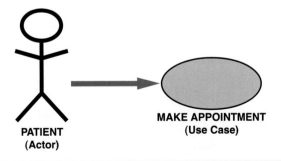

FIGURE 5-26 In a medical office system, a PATIENT (actor) can MAKE APPOINTMENT (use case).

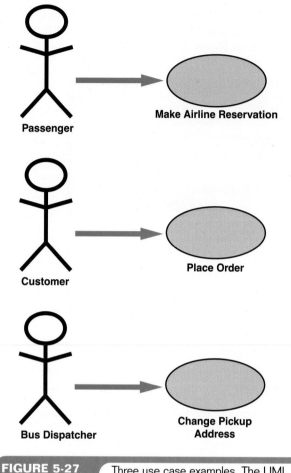

Notice that the UML symbol for a use case is an oval with a label that describes the action or event. The actor is shown as a stick figure, with a label that identifies the actor's role. The line from the actor to the use case is called an association because it links a particular actor to a use case. Figure 5-27 shows use case examples of a passenger making an airline reservation, a customer entering an order, and a bus dispatcher changing a student's pickup address.

Use cases also can interact with other use cases. When the outcome of one use case is incorporated by another use case, we say that the second case **uses** the first case. The UML indicates the relationship with a hollow-headed arrow that *points at* the use case being used. Figure 5-28 shows an example where a student adds a fitness-class and PRODUCE FITNESS-CLASS ROSTER *uses* the results of ADD FITNESS-CLASS to generate a new fitness-class roster. Similarly, if an instructor changes his or her availability, UPDATE INSTRUCTOR INFORMATION *uses* the CHANGE AVAILABILITY use case to update the INSTRUCTOR object.

FIGURE 5-27 Three use case examples. The UML symbol for a use case is an oval. The actor is shown as a stick figure.

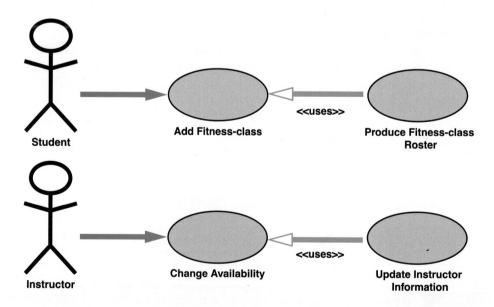

FIGURE 5-28 When a student adds a fitness-class, PRODUCE FITNESS-CLASS ROSTER *uses* the results of ADD FITNESS-CLASS to generate a new fitness-class roster. When an instructor changes his or her availability, UPDATE INSTRUCTOR INFORMATION *uses* the CHANGE AVAILABILITY use case to update the instructor object.

Add New Student Use Case

Add New Student

Name:	Add New Student
Actor:	Student/Manager
Description:	Describes the process used to add a student to a fitness-class
Successful completion:	1. Manager checks FITNESS-CLASS SCHEDULE object for availability 2. Manager notifies student 3. Fitness-class is open and student pays fee 4. Manager registers student
Alternative:	1. Manager checks FITNESS-CLASS SCHEDULE object for availability 2. Fitness-class is full 3. Manager notifies student
Precondition:	Student requests fitness-class
Postcondition:	Student is enrolled in fitness-class and fees have been paid
Assumptions:	None

Cancel Fitness-class Use Case

Cancel Fitness-class

Name:	Cancel Fitness-class
Actor:	Manager
Description:	Describes the process used to cancel a fitness-class
Successful completion:	1. Manager notifies FITNESS-CLASS SCHEDULE object of canceled class 2. FITNESS-CLASS SCHEDULE object produces letters notifying students enrolled in the fitness-class of the cancellation 3. Manager refunds fees to students 4. Manager notifies INSTRUCTOR object of canceled fitness-class
Alternative:	None
Precondition:	Fitness-class has been canceled
Postcondition:	Students have been notified of cancellation and refunds have been made
Assumptions:	None

FIGURE 5-29 The ADD NEW STUDENT use case description documents the process used to add a current student into an existing fitness-class. The CANCEL FITNESS-CLASS use case description documents the process used to cancel a fitness-class, refund fees, and notify students.

FIGURE 5-30
A typical auto service department might involve customers, service writers who prepare work orders and invoices, and mechanics who perform the work.

ON THE WEB

For more information about Use Case Diagrams visit scsite.com/sad4e/more.htm, click Systems Analysis and Design Chapter 5 and then click the Use Case Diagrams link.

www.scsite.com

To create use cases, you start by reviewing the information that you gathered during the requirements modeling phase. Your objective is to identify the actors and the functions or transactions they initiate. For each use case, you also develop a **use case description** in the form of a table. A use case description documents the name of the use case, the actor, a description of the use case, a step-by-step list of the tasks and actions required for successful completion, a description of alternative courses of action, preconditions, postconditions, and assumptions. Figure 5-29 on the previous page shows examples of the ADD NEW STUDENT use case and the CANCEL FITNESS-CLASS use case.

When you identify use cases, try to group all the related transactions into a single use case. For example, when a hotel customer reserves a room, the reservation system blocks a room, updates the occupancy forecast, and sends the customer a confirmation. Those events are all part of a single use case called RESERVE ROOM, and the specific actions are step-by-step tasks within the use case.

Use Case Diagrams

A **use case diagram** is a visual summary of several related use cases within a system orsubsystem. Consider an auto service department, as shown in Figure 5-30. The operation involves customers, service writers who prepare work orders and invoices, and mechanics who perform the work. Figure 5-31 shows a possible use case diagram for the auto service department.

Use Case Diagram: Auto Service Department

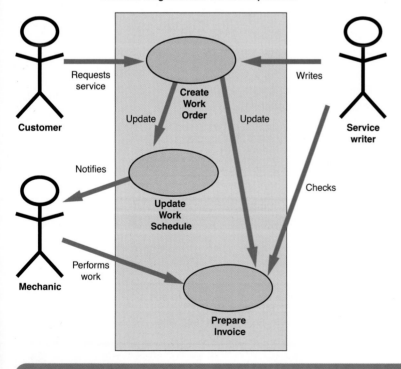

FIGURE 5-31
A use case diagram to handle work at an auto service department.

When you create a use case diagram, the first step is to identify the system boundary, which is represented by a rectangle. The **system boundary** shows what is included in the system (inside the rectangle) and what is not included in the system (outside the rectangle). After you identify the system boundary, you place the use cases on the diagram, add the actors, and show the relationships.

Figure 5-32 shows a use case diagram for a school bus system that creates a new bus route, and Figure 5-33 shows a use case diagram to schedule a new fitness-class at the fitness center.

Class Diagrams

A **class diagram** represents a detailed view of a single use case, shows the classes that participate in the use case, and documents the relationship among the classes. Like a DFD, a class diagram is a logical model, which evolves into a physical model and finally becomes a functioning information system. In structured analysis, entities, data stores, and processes are transformed into data structures and program code. Similarly, class diagrams evolve into code modules, data objects, and other system components.

The first step is to review the use case and identify the classes that participate in the underlying business transaction. In a class diagram, each class appears as a rectangle, with the class name at the top, followed by the class's attributes and methods. Lines show relationships between classes and have labels identifying the action that relates the two classes.

Use Case Diagram: Create Bus Route

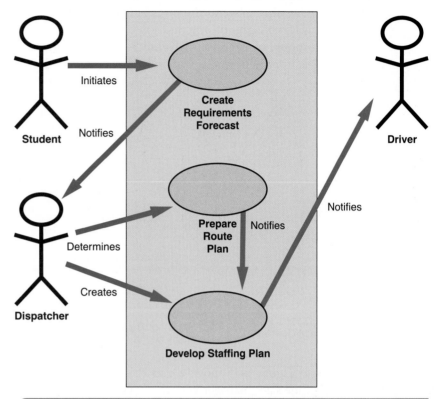

FIGURE 5-32   A use case diagram to create a school bus route.

Use Case Diagram: Schedule New Fitness-class

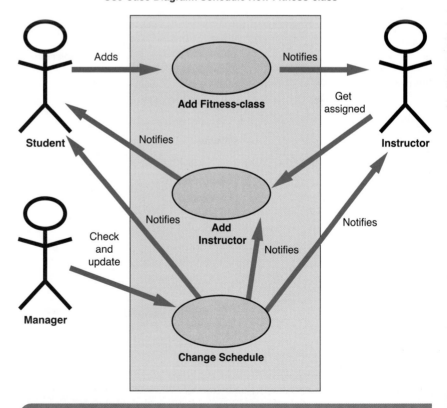

FIGURE 5-33   A use case diagram to schedule a new fitness-class at the fitness center.

The class diagram also includes a concept called **cardinality**, which describes how instances of one class relate to instances of another class. For example, an employee might have earned no vacation days or one vacation day or many vacation days. Similarly, an employee might have no spouse or one spouse. Figure 5-34 shows various UML notations and examples. Cardinality also is important during structured analysis data design, which is discussed in Chapter 8.

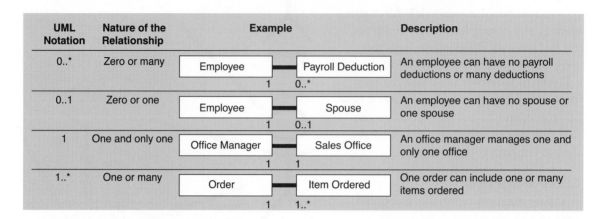

UML Notation	Nature of the Relationship	Example		Description
0..*	Zero or many	Employee	Payroll Deduction	An employee can have no payroll deductions or many deductions
0..1	Zero or one	Employee	Spouse	An employee can have no spouse or one spouse
1	One and only one	Office Manager	Sales Office	An office manager manages one and only one office
1..*	One or many	Order	Item Ordered	One order can include one or many items ordered

FIGURE 5-34   UML notations indicate the nature of the relationship between instances of one class and instances of another class.

Figure 5-35 shows a class diagram for a sales order use case. Notice that the sales office has one sales manager who can have anywhere from zero to many sales reps. Each sales rep can have anywhere from zero to many customers, but each customer has only one sales rep.

In Figure 5-36, a class diagram for a Web-based airline reservation use case includes four classes. Notice that a RESERVATION can include one or more FLIGHTS, and one PASSEN-GER makes one or more RESERVATIONS.

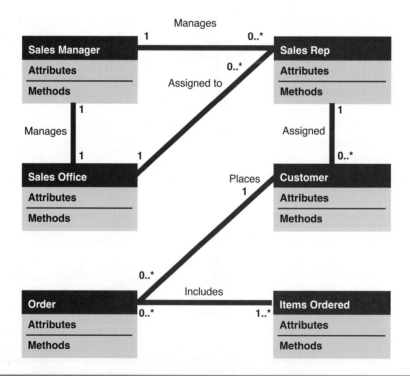

FIGURE 5-35   Class diagram for a sales order use case (attributes and methods omitted for clarity).

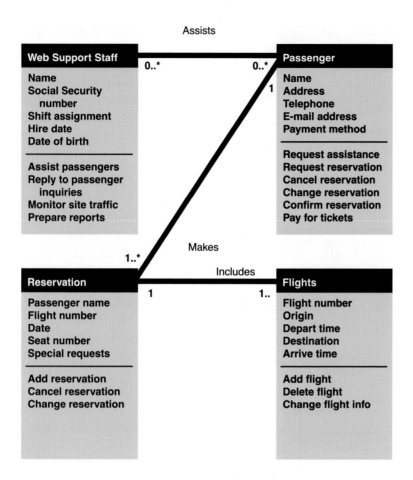

FIGURE 5-36 Class diagram for an airline reservation use case.

Sequence Diagrams

A **sequence diagram** is a dynamic model of a use case, showing the interaction among classes during a specified time period. A sequence diagram graphically documents the use case by showing the classes, the messages, and the timing of the messages. Sequence diagrams include symbols that represent classes, lifelines, messages, and focuses.

CLASSES A class is identified by a rectangle with the name inside. Classes that send or receive messages are shown at the top of the sequence diagram.

LIFELINES A lifeline is identified by a dashed line, as shown in Figure 5-37. The **lifeline** represents the time during which the object above it is able to interact with the other objects in the use case. An *X* marks the end of *the lifeline*.

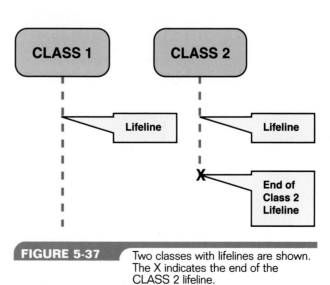

FIGURE 5-37 Two classes with lifelines are shown. The X indicates the end of the CLASS 2 lifeline.

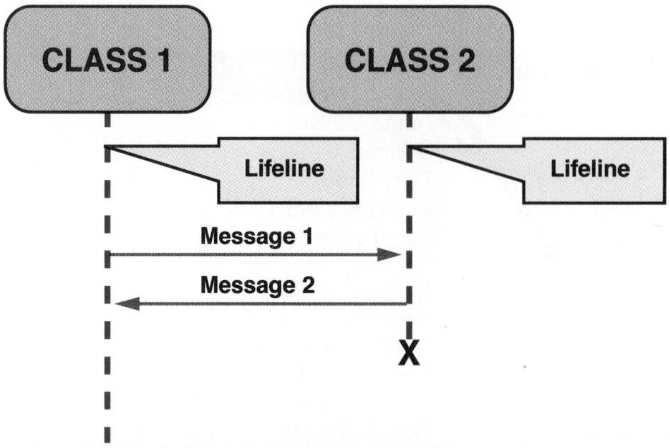

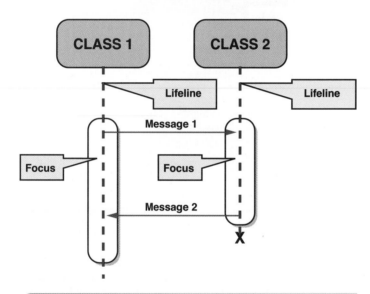

FIGURE 5-38 Two messages are shown. Each message is represented by a line with a label that describes the message.

FIGURE 5-39 Each class has a focus that shows the period when messages are sent or received.

MESSAGES A message is identified by a line showing direction that runs between two objects, as shown in Figure 5-38. The label shows the name of the message and can include additional information about the contents.

FOCUSES A **focus** is identified by a narrow vertical rectangle that covers the lifeline, as shown in Figure 5-39. The focus indicates when an object sends or receives a message.

Using the fitness center example, Figure 5-40 shows a sequence diagram for the ADD NEW STUDENT use case. Notice that the vertical position of each message indicates the timing of the message. The ADD NEW STUDENT use case description is documented in Figure 5-29 on page 5.17.

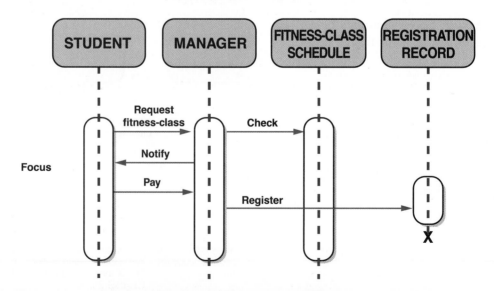

FIGURE 5-40 The sequence diagram for the ADD NEW STUDENT use case. The use case description for ADD NEW STUDENT is shown in Figure 5-29.

State Transition Diagrams

Earlier in this chapter you learned that *state* refers to an object's current status. A **state transition** diagram shows how an object changes from one state to another, depending on events that affect the object. All possible states must be documented in the state transition diagram, as shown in Figure 5-41. A bank account, for example, could be opened as a NEW account, change to an ACTIVE account, and eventually become a CLOSED or FORMER account. Another possible state for a bank account could be FROZEN, if the account's assets are legally attached.

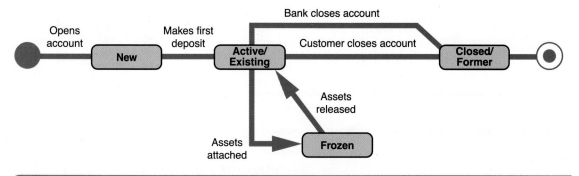

FIGURE 5-41 An example of a state transition diagram for a bank account.

In a state transition diagram, the states appear as rounded rectangles with the state names inside. The small oval to the left is the initial state, or the point where the object first interacts with the system. Reading from left to right, the lines show direction and describe the action or event that causes a transition from one state to another. The circle at the right with a hollow border is the final state.

In the example shown in Figure 5-42, a FUTURE student attends a fitness-class and becomes a CURRENT student, and a CURRENT student completes a fitness-class or drops the fitness-class and becomes a PAST student.

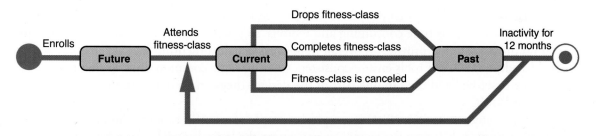

FIGURE 5-42 An example of a state transition diagram showing student status at the fitness center. Notice that former students who re-enroll after 12 months of inactivity are treated as new students.

Activity Diagrams

An **activity diagram** resembles a horizontal flow chart that shows the actions and events as they occur. Activity diagrams show the order in which the actions take place and identify the outcomes. Figure 5-43 shows an activity diagram for a cash withdrawal at an ATM machine. Notice that the customer initiates the activity by inserting an ATM card and requesting cash. Activity diagrams also can display multiple use cases in the form of a grid, where classes are shown as vertical bars and actions appear as horizontal arrows.

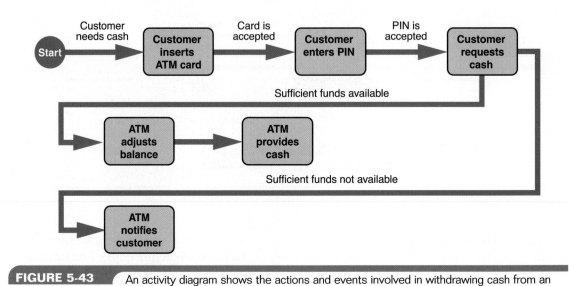

FIGURE 5-43 An activity diagram shows the actions and events involved in withdrawing cash from an ATM machine.

Sequence diagrams, state transition diagrams, and activity diagrams are dynamic modeling tools that can help a systems analyst understand how objects behave and interact with the system.

CASE Tools

Object modeling requires many types of diagrams to represent the proposed system. Creating the diagrams by hand is time consuming and tedious, so systems analysts rely on CASE tools to speed up the process and provide an overall framework for documenting the system components. In addition, CASE tools ensure consistency and provide common links so that once objects are described and used in one part of the design, they can be reused multiple times without further effort.

System Architect 2001 (SA/2001) is a typical example of a CASE tool that builds and updates a data repository, called an encyclopedia, as you create the logical model. Using SA/2001, a systems analyst can document the steps in a use case and define the events in a state transition diagram, as shown in Figure 5-44.

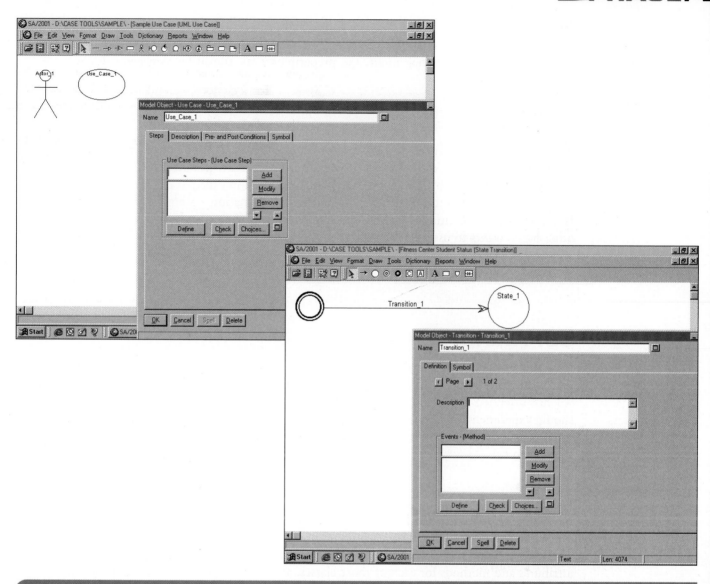

FIGURE 5-44 System Architect 2001 helps an analyst document use cases and state transition diagrams.

CASE tools speed up the development process, ensure consistency, and provide common links so that objects can be described in one part of the design and reused in other areas of the model.

ORGANIZING THE OBJECT MODEL

In this chapter, you learned how to use object-oriented tools and techniques to build a logical model of the information system. Now you are ready to organize your diagrams and documentation so the object model is easily read and understood. You should organize your use cases and use case diagrams so they can be linked to the appropriate class, state transition, sequence, and activity diagrams. Those diagrams will form the foundation for the systems design, so accuracy is important. Remember that it is much easier to repair a diagram now than to change the software later.

When you are sure your diagrams are correct, you can proceed to the tasks described in Chapter 6, including evaluating alternatives, creating the systems requirement document, delivering a presentation to management, and preparing for the transition to systems design.

WHAT DO YOU THINK?

Jack Forester and Lisa Turner are systems analysts in the IT department of TravelBiz, a nationwide travel agency that specializes in business travel. TravelBiz has decided to expand into the vacation travel market by launching a new business division called TravelFun. The IT director assigned Jack and Lisa to create a flexible, efficient information system for the new division. Jack wants to use traditional analysis and modeling techniques for the project. Lisa, on the other hand, wants to use an object-oriented methodology. Which approach would you suggest and why?

SOFTWEAR, LIMITED

Rick Williams, a systems analyst, and Carla Moore, a programmer/analyst, completed a set of DFDs representing a data and process model of the SWL payroll system project. Rick had recently attended a workshop on object modeling techniques, and suggested that he and Carla should experiment with object-oriented analysis. After he explained the concepts and techniques to Carla, she agreed that it was a good opportunity to gain some experience, and they decided to give it a try.

Classes

Rick and Carla began by reviewing the data they had collected earlier, during requirements modeling. They studied the DFDs and the data dictionary, and they identified the people, events, and transactions that they would represent as classes. They identified employees, human resources transactions, time sheet entries, payroll actions, and stock transfers. They defined attributes and methods for each of those classes, as shown in Figure 5-45. When they were finished, they reviewed the results. They noticed that the structured DFDs did not show a department head as an entity. Rick remembered that department heads submitted time sheets to the payroll department, and the payroll clerks actually entered the data into the system. Because they were looking at the system in a different way, they decided to include department heads as a subclass of the EMPLOYEE class.

EMPLOYEE

Employee number
Employee name
Address
Telephone number
Date of birth
Sex
Title, rate of pay
Deductions
State

___

Add new
Change name
Change address
Change telephone
Change deductions
Change state

HR TRANSACTION

Employee number
Employee name
State

___

Add new
Change state
Notify

TIME SHEET ENTRY

Employee number
Week ending date
Hours worked

___

Add new
Correct hours
Generate report

PAYROLL ACTION

Employee number
Hours worked
Overtime hours
Rate of pay
Overtime rate
Deductions
Contributions
Federal tax withheld
State tax withheld
Local tax withheld

___

Generate checks
Change deductions
Change contributions
Change federal rate
Change local rate
Change state rate
Change rate of pay
Generate W-2
Notify
Calculate

STOCK TRANSFER

Employee number
Stock holdings
Stock contribution

___

Purchase stock
Sell stock
Change contribution
Generate report

DEPT HEAD

Employee number
Employee name
Address
Telephone number
Date of birth
Sex
Title, rate of pay
Deductions
State

___

Add new
Change name
Change address
Change telephone
Change deductions
Change state
Manages work
Submits time sheets

FIGURE 5-45   SWL payroll system classes.

Use Cases

The next step was for Rick and Carla to define the use cases. They decided to list all situations that involved the EMPLOYEE object. They realized that a new employee gets hired, an employee gets promoted, an employee gets a raise; an employee gets fired, an employee retires, an employee changes his or her name, and an employee requests a contributions change.

They also decided to create use cases for the PAYROLL ACTION object. The scenarios included these: change an employee's deductions, change an employee's contributions, change the federal tax rate, change the state tax rate, change the local tax rate, calculate weekly gross pay, calculate weekly taxes, calculate weekly contributions, generate weekly paychecks, and notify the stock transfer department of change in contributions.

Next, they identified the actors involved in each use case. Rick suggested that EMPLOYEE and DEPARTMENT HEAD were needed, and Carla added the PAYROLL CLERK. After they defined the use cases and the actors, they started to create a description for each use case. They created a table for each use case showing the use case name, actors, description, successful completion, alternatives, preconditions, postconditions, and assumptions.

Creating use case descriptions was hard work, and they found that they had to return frequently to their documentation and fact-finding results. The first batch of use case descriptions involved the EMPLOYEE actor, as shown in Figure 5-46. The use cases were GET HIRED and RECEIVE RAISE. Then they created use case descriptions for RECEIVE PROMOTION and TERMINATE, which are shown in Figure 5-47. Carla thought that the descriptions had given them plenty of practice, so they agreed to go on to the next step.

Get Hired Use Case

Name:	Get Hired
Actor:	Employee
Description:	Describes the process used to add a new hire
Successful completion:	1. Employee gets hired 2. Employee fills out new hire package 3. Human resources department enters employee data and completes the HR transaction
Alternative:	None
Precondition:	Employee has been approved for hire
Postcondition:	Employee has been enrolled in benefits programs and is in active employee status
Assumptions:	Employee accepts position and begins service

Receive Raise Use Case

Name:	Receive Raise
Actor:	Employee
Description:	Describes the change to an employee's pay rate
Successful completion:	1. Employee gets a raise 2. Human resources department changes employee data to the employee object and the human resources records
Alternative:	None
Precondition:	Employee has been approved for a raise
Postcondition:	Employee's pay rate is changed on all records
Assumptions:	None

FIGURE 5-46 Use case descriptions for GET HIRED and RECEIVE RAISE use cases.

Receive Promotion Use Case

Name:	Receive Promotion
Actor:	Employee
Description:	Describes change to employee title
Successful completion:	1. Employee gets promoted 2. Human resources department changes employee data and completes HR transaction
Alternative:	None
Precondition:	Employee has been approved for promotion
Postcondition:	Employee title is changed
Assumptions:	Employee accepts position

Terminate Use Case

Name:	Terminate
Actor:	Employee
Description:	Describes termination process
Successful completion:	1. Employee terminates 2. Human resources department changes employee data and completes HR transaction 3. Employee issued final paycheck and benefits
Alternative:	None
Precondition:	Termination approved for employee
Postcondition:	Employees status is changed on all records
Assumptions:	None

FIGURE 5-47 Use case descriptions for RECEIVE PROMOTION and TERMINATE use cases.

Now they were ready to develop a use case diagram that would provide a visual summary of related use cases. Rick suggested that they try to limit the use cases to three or four per diagram to make the final package easy to read. They decided to document an employee contribution change, and they created the use case diagram shown in Figure 5-48 on the next page. Their diagram included three related use cases inside a system boundary: REQUEST CONTRIBUTION CHANGE, NOTIFY PAYROLL, and NOTIFY STOCK TRANSFER. The use case diagram depicts the EMPLOYEE actor initiating a change in the contribution amount.

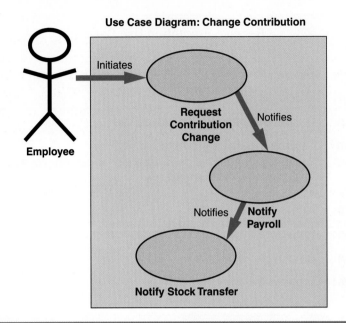

FIGURE 5-48   Use case diagram for the CHANGE CONTRIBUTION scenario.

Next, they decided to create a use case diagram to describe how the payroll is generated. Their use case diagram is shown in Figure 5-49. The diagram includes three use cases: CREATE TIMESHEET ENTRY, CALCULATE PAYROLL, and GENERATE PAYCHECK. In their diagram, the DEPARTMENT HEAD actor creates a new instance of the CREATE TIMESHEET ENTRY object, which notifies the CALCULATE PAYROLL use case, which is initiated by the PAYROLL CLERK. The GENERATE PAYCHECK use case then issues a paycheck to the EMPLOYEE actor.

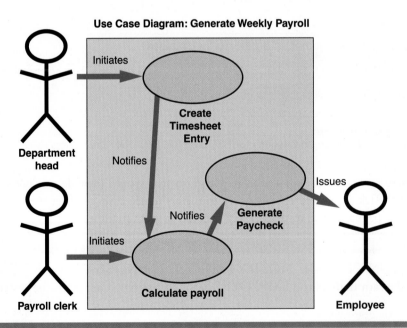

FIGURE 5-49   Use case diagram for the GENERATE WEEKLY PAYROLL scenario.

Class Diagrams

The use cases and use case diagrams helped Rick and Carla understand how the various objects and classes interacted. At this point, Carla suggested that they construct class diagrams for each use case. The class diagrams document the classes and relationships involved in an individual use case. They agreed to start with the GENERATE PAYROLL use case, because it was quite complex and would test their new skills. When they finished, they saw that the class diagram included five classes and several different types of relationships. Their class diagram is shown in Figure 5-50.

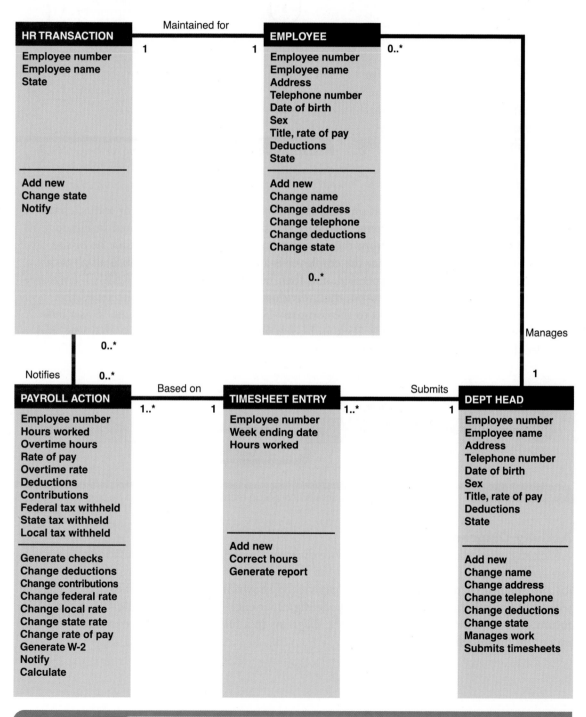

FIGURE 5-50 The GENERATE PAYROLL class diagram includes four classes and various types of relationships among the classes.

Sequence Diagrams

Next, the pair decided to create a sequence diagram. Carla was eager to see how a sequence diagram would help them visualize the time frame in which events occur. They created a diagram for the CHANGE CONTRIBUTIONS method in the EMPLOYEE object. The sequence diagram in Figure 5-51 shows the steps that occur when an employee changes benefits contributions. Notice that the diagram includes the messages sent and the lifeline of the objects. Rick and Carla were satisfied that they could create sequence diagrams easily, and they decided to move on to the state transition diagram.

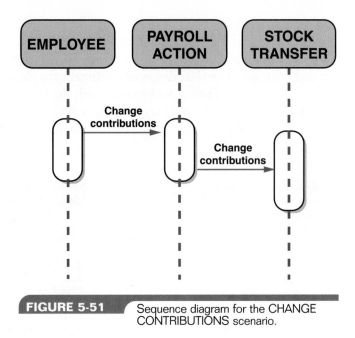

FIGURE 5-51 Sequence diagram for the CHANGE CONTRIBUTIONS scenario.

State Transition Diagram

Rick explained that a state transition diagram shows how an object's state, or status, changes as a result of various actions or events. The state transition diagram they created in Figure 5-52 shows the status of an employee from the time the employee is hired to the time he or she quits, is fired, or retires. Notice that the employee is a FUTURE employee until all physicals are passed and all paperwork is processed, and then he or she becomes a CURRENT employee. Once employment ends for any reason, the individual becomes a PAST employee. At this point, even if the employee returns to the company later on he or she will come in as a new instance of the EMPLOYEE object. Rick and Carla were surprised at how easy that was, and they decided to try an activity diagram.

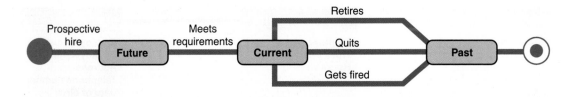

FIGURE 5-52 State transition diagram shows changes in employee status caused by actions and events.

Activity Diagram

Rick suggested that they create an activity diagram showing some of the situations they had explored in detail. Their diagram showed the interaction between objects during certain scenarios and enabled them to visualize system activity, as shown in Figure 5-53. They agreed that the technique gave them additional object modeling experience that would be valuable in the future. At that point, they packaged all the diagrams in a folder and saved the overall object model for future reference.

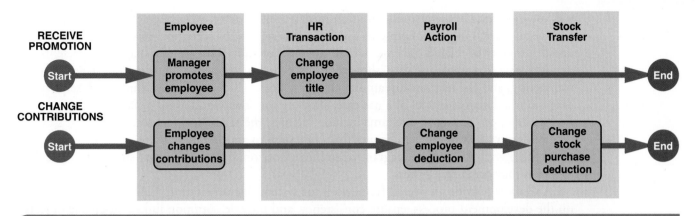

PHASE 2

FIGURE 5-53 Activity diagram shows the RECEIVE PROMOTION scenario and the CHANGE CONTRIBUTIONS scenario.

YOUR TURN

Rick is interested in your views on the future of object-oriented analysis and design. He is scheduled to make a presentation on the topic next week at a meeting of IT professionals. He asked you to do some research, using the Internet and industry publications, and send him an e-mail message describing the current use of object-oriented analysis and trends for the future.

CHAPTER SUMMARY

This chapter introduces object modeling, which is a popular technique that describes a system in terms of objects. Objects represent real people, places, events, and transactions. Unlike structured analysis, which treats data and processes separately, objects include data and processes that can affect the data. During the implementation process, systems analysts and programmers transform objects into program code modules that can be optimized, tested, and reused as often as necessary.

Object-oriented terms include classes, attributes, instances, messages, and methods. Classes include objects that have similar attributes, or characteristics. Individual members of a class are called object instances. Objects within a class can be grouped into subclasses, which are more specific categories within the class. A class also can belong to a more general category called a superclass.

Objects can send messages, or commands that require other objects to perform certain methods, or tasks. The concept that a message gives different meanings to different objects is called polymorphism. An object resembles a black box, with encapsulated, or self-contained, data and methods. Various relationships exist between objects, including dependency, association, aggregation, and inheritance. After you identify the objects, classes, and relationships, you prepare an object relationship diagram that shows the objects and how they interact to perform business functions and transactions.

The Unified Modeling Language (UML) is a widely used method of visualizing and documenting an information system. UML techniques include use cases, use case diagrams, class diagrams, sequence diagrams, state transition diagrams, and activity diagrams.

A use case describes a business situation initiated by an actor, who interacts with the information system. Each use case represents a specific transaction, or scenario. A use case diagram is a visual summary of related use cases within a system or subsystem. A class diagram represents a detailed view of a single use case, showing the classes that participate in the underlying business transaction, and the relationship among class instances, which is called cardinality. A sequence diagram is a dynamic model of a use case, showing the interaction among classes during a specified time period. Sequence diagrams include lifelines, messages, and focuses. A state transition diagram shows how an object changes from one state to another, depending on events that affect the object. An activity diagram resembles a horizontal flow chart that shows actions and events as they occur in a system.

CASE tools provide an overall framework for system documentation. CASE tools can speed up the development process, ensure consistency, and provide common links that enable objects to be reused.

At the end of the object modeling process, you organize your use cases and use case diagrams, and link them to class, sequence, state transition, and activity diagrams.

Key Terms

activity diagram (5.24)	methods (5.2)
actor (5.15)	object (5.2)
aggregation (5.13)	object model (5.2)
association (5.12)	polymorphism (5.8)
attributes (5.2)	query method (5.8)
black box (5.9)	relationships (5.11)
cardinality (5.20)	sequence diagram (5.21)
class (5.3)	state (5.6)
class diagram (5.19)	state transition (5.23)
constructor method (5.8)	subclasses (5.10)
dependency (5.12)	superclass (5.10)
encapsulation (5.9)	system boundary (5.19)
focus (5.22)	update method (5.8)
inheritance (5.13)	use case (5.15)
instance (5.3)	use case description (5.18)
lifeline (5.21)	use case diagram (5.18)
message (5.2)	uses (5.16)

Chapter Review

1. What is object-oriented analysis, and what are some advantages of using this technique?

2. Define an object and give an example.

3. Define an attribute and give an example.

4. Define a method and give an example.

5. Define encapsulation and explain the benefits it provides.

6. Define polymorphism and give an example.

7. Define a class, subclass, and superclass and give examples.

8. Define an actor and give an example.

9. Define a use case and a use case diagram, and give examples.

10. Define the term black box, and explain why it is an important concept in object-oriented analysis.

Discussion Topics

1. The chapter mentioned that systems analysts and programmers transform objects into program code modules that can be optimized, tested, and reused. Modular design is a very popular design concept in many industries. What other examples of modular design can you suggest?

2. You are an IT consultant and you are asked to create a new system for a small real estate brokerage firm. Your only experience is with traditional data and process modeling techniques. This time, you decide to try an object-oriented approach. How will you begin? How are the tasks different from traditional structured analysis?

3. You are creating a system for a bowling alley to manage information about its leagues. During the modeling process, you create a state transition diagram for an object called LEAGUE BOWLERS. What are the possible states of a league bowler and what happens to a bowler who quits the league and rejoins the following season?

4. A debate is raging at the IT consulting firm where you work. Some staff members believe that it is harder for experienced analysts to learn object-modeling techniques, because the analysts are accustomed to thinking about data and processes as separate entities. Others believe that solid analytical skills are easily transferable and do not see a problem in crossing over to the newer approach. What do you think, and why?

Apply Your Knowledge

1 Post Office

Situation:
Consider a typical post office and the processes involved in selling stamps, renting post office boxes, and delivering mail to postal customers.

1. Identify possible actors and use cases involved in post office functions.

2. Create a use case diagram for the post office system.

3. Select one of the use cases and create a class diagram.

4. Create a sequence diagram for the use case you selected.

2 New Branch School District

Situation:
The New Branch School District operates a fleet of 40 buses that serve approximately 1,000 students in grades K–12. The bus operation involves 30 regular routes, plus special routes for activities, athletic events, and summer sessions. The district employs 12 full-time drivers and 25 to 30 part-time drivers. A dispatcher coordinates the staffing and routes and relays messages to drivers regarding students and parents who call about pickup and drop-off arrangements.

1. Identify possible actors and use cases involved in school bus operations.

2. Create a use case diagram for the school bus system.

3. Create a sequence diagram for the use case you selected.

4. Create a state transition diagram that describes typical student states and how they change based on specific actions and events.

3 Pleasant Creek Community College Registration System

Situation:

Pleasant Creek Community College has a typical school registration process. Student support services include faculty advisors and tutors. The administration has asked you, as IT manager, to develop an object-oriented model for a new registration system.

1. List possible objects in the new registration system, including their attributes and methods.

2. Identify possible use cases and actors.

3. Create a use case diagram that shows how students register.

4. Create a state transition diagram that describes typical student states and how they change based on specific actions and events.

4 Student Bookstore at Pleasant Creek Community College

Situation:

The bookstore staff at Pleasant Creek Community College works hard to satisfy students, instructors, and the school's business office. Instructors specify textbooks for particular courses, and the bookstore orders the textbooks and sells them to students. The bookstore wants you to develop an object-oriented model for a new bookstore information management system.

1. List possible objects in the bookstore operation, including their attributes and methods.

2. Identify possible use cases and actors.

3. Select one of the use cases that you identified in Step 2 and create a sequence diagram.

4. Create an object relationship diagram that provides an overview of the system, including how textbooks are selected by instructors, approved by a department head, and sold to students by the bookstore.

Chapter Assignments

1. Search the Internet for information about the history and development of UML.

2. Contact the IT staff at your school or at a local business to learn whether the organization uses object-oriented programming languages. If so, determine what languages and versions are used, and why they were selected.

3. Search the Internet for information about groups and organizations that support and discuss object-oriented methods and issues.

4. Search the Internet for information about CASE tools that provide UML support.

CASE STUDIES

Case Studies offer an opportunity for you to practice specific skills and knowledge learned in the chapter and provide practical experience for you as a systems analyst. Two of the case studies (New Century Health Clinic and Ridgeway Company) are continuing case studies that appear in each chapter. Additionally, one continuing case study (SCR Associates) utilizes the Internet to practice some of the topics covered in this chapter.

NEW CENTURY HEALTH CLINIC

You began the systems analysis phase at New Century Health Clinic by completing a series of interviews, reviewing existing reports, and observing office operations. Then, in Chapter 4, you acquired more information and developed a set of DFDs, process descriptions, and a data dictionary.

Now you decide to practice the object modeling skills you learned in this chapter. Start by going back to Chapter 4 and reviewing the New Century factual material and interview results. (You can obtain a complete, "standard" set of interview summaries from your instructor or from the Internet at www.scsite.com/sad4e.) Then complete the following tasks.

Assignments

1. Identify possible use cases and actors, and create a use case diagram for the New Century Health Clinic system.

2. Select one of the use cases and create a class diagram.

3. Create a sequence diagram for the use case that you selected.

4. Create a state transition diagram that describes typical patient states and how they change based on specific actions and events.

RIDGEWAY COMPANY

Review the facts presented in the Ridgeway Company case study in Chapters 2 and 3 and review the DFDs you developed in Chapter 4. Use that information to complete the following tasks.

Assignments

1. Identify possible use cases and actors, and create a use case diagram for the Ridgeway Country Club information system.

2. Select one of the use cases and create a class diagram.

3. Create an object relationship diagram for the system.

4. Create a state transition diagram that describes typical member states and how they change based on specific actions and events.

SCR ASSOCIATES

SCR Associates is an information technology consulting firm that offers IT solutions and training for small- and medium-sized companies. SCR's slogan is "We Know IT!"

Background

As a newly hired systems analyst, you will handle assignments, work on various SCR projects, and apply the skills you learned in the text. SCR needs an information system to manage training operations at the new SCR training center. The new system will be called TIMS (Training Information Management System).

The SCR case is available as an interactive, Web-based case study. You can log on to the Shelly Cashman Series site at www.scsite.com/sad4e/scr for instructions and assignments. If you prefer to complete the case study without using the Internet then you must download the data disk. See the inside back cover for instructions for downloading the data disk or see your instructor for more information on accessing the files required for this book.

Situation

In Part 5 of the SCR case, you will apply your object modeling skills and create various diagrams and documentation for the new TIMS system. You will review background material and develop an object-oriented logical model of the proposed system.

ON THE WEB ▶

The SCR case is available as an interactive, Web-based case study. You can log on to the Shelly Cashman Series site at www.scsite.com/sad4e/scr for instructions and assignments.

Before You Begin ...

1. Review the November 21 message from Jesse Baker regarding object-oriented analysis. Open the Document 4-1 from the data disk.

2. Review the JAD session summary. Open the Document 3-3 from the data disk.

Assignments

1. Identify possible use cases and actors, and create a use case diagram for the TIMS system.

2. Select one of the use cases and create a class diagram.

3. Create a sequence diagram for the use case that you selected.

4. Create a state transition diagram that describes typical student states and how they change based on specific actions and events.

PHASE 1
Systems Analysis **PHASE 2**
Systems Design **PHASE 3**
Systems Implementation **PHASE 4**
Systems Operation & Support **PHASE 5**

Transition to Systems Design

Chapter 6 is the final chapter in the systems analysis phase. In this chapter, you will learn about evaluating software alternatives, preparing the system requirements document, prototyping, and preparing for the transition to the next SDLC phase — systems design.

INTRODUCTION

The main objective of the systems analysis phase is to build a logical model of the new information system. In Chapters 3, 4, and 5, you learned about requirements modeling, data and process modeling, and object modeling. Chapter 6 describes the remaining activities in the systems analysis phase, which include evaluation of alternative solutions, preparation of the system requirements document, and presentation of the system requirements document to management. The chapter also describes the transition to systems design, prototyping, design guidelines, and the use of codes.

OBJECTIVES

When you finish this chapter, you will be able to:

- Evaluate software alternatives and development strategies

- Explain advantages and disadvantages of developing in-house software versus purchasing and customizing a software package

- Describe how companies use outsourcing and user applications

- List the steps in purchasing and evaluating a software package

- Explain the differences between a request for proposal (RFP) and a request for quotation (RFQ)

- Describe the system requirements document and the presentation to management at the end of the systems analysis phase

- Explain the transition from systems analysis to systems design, and the difference between logical and physical design

- Explain the importance of prototyping and describe various prototyping methods, tools, and techniques

- Discuss the systems design process and provide guidelines for system design

- Create and use appropriate codes during systems design and development

EVALUATING SOFTWARE ALTERNATIVES

Earlier in the systems analysis phase, you investigated the current system and developed a logical model for the proposed system. Now, as you prepare for the transition to the systems design phase, you will examine software alternatives and select an overall strategy for the proposed system.

Companies can acquire software by developing an in-house system, buying a commercial software package, or customizing a software package. Although many factors influence this decision, the most important consideration is total cost of ownership (TCO), which was explained in Chapter 3. The steps in system development are shown in Figure 6-1.

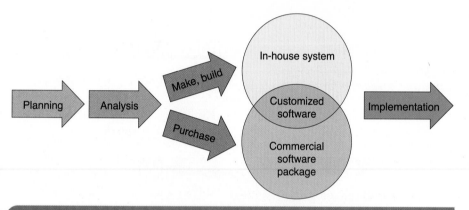

The choice between developing in-house software and purchasing software often is called a **make or buy**, or **build or buy** decision. The company's IT department makes, builds, and develops **in-house software**, whereas a **software package** is purchased or leased from another firm. The package might be a standard commercial program or a customized package designed specifically for the purchaser. Companies that develop software for sale are called **software vendors**. A firm that enhances a commercial package by adding custom features

FIGURE 6-1   Depending on which alternative is selected, a company might develop a system in-house or purchase and possibly customize a commercial package.

and configuring it for a particular industry is called a **value-added reseller (VAR)**.

Software packages are available for every type of business activity. A software package that can be used by many different types of organizations is called a **horizontal application**. An accounting package is a good example of a horizontal application because it can be utilized by many different businesses.

In contrast, a software package developed to handle information requirements for a specific type of business is called a **vertical application**. For example, organizations with special system

N THE WEB

examples of Vertical
plications visit scsite.com/
4e/more.htm, click
stems Analysis and Design
apter 6 and then click the
tical Applications link.

w.scsite.com

requirements include colleges, banks, hospitals, insurance companies, construction companies, real estate firms, and airlines. A hotel chain might use a vertical application for its guest reservation system, as shown in Figure 6-2, and use horizontal applications for basic business needs, such as payroll processing and accounts payable.

FIGURE 6-2   Hotel chains require vertical applications to support reservation systems and information needs that are unique to the hotel industry.

Of the software acquisition options available — developing in-house, buying a software package, or customizing a software package — each has advantages, disadvantages, and cost considerations, as shown in Figure 6-3. Those software acquisition options are described in detail in the next three sections.

Reasons for In-House Development Software	Reasons for Purchasing a Software Package
Satisfy unique requirements	Lower costs
Minimize changes in business procedures and policies	Requires less time to implement
Meet constraints of existing systems	Proven reliability and performance benchmarks
Meet constraints of existing technology	Implementation by other companies
Develop internal resources and capabilities	Requires less technical development staff Future upgrade provided by the vendor

FIGURE 6-3 Companies consider a number of factors in deciding whether to develop a system in-house or purchase a commercial package.

Developing Software In-House

With an enormous variety of software packages available to handle horizontal and vertical business operations, why would a firm choose to develop its own software? Typically, companies choose in-house development to satisfy unique business requirements, to minimize changes in business procedures and policies, to meet constraints of existing systems and existing technology, and to develop internal resources and capabilities.

SATISFY UNIQUE BUSINESS REQUIREMENTS Companies often decide to develop software in-house because no commercially available software package can meet their unique business requirements. A college, for example, needs a course scheduling system based on curriculum requirements, student demand, classroom space, and available instructors. A package delivery company needs a system to identify the best combination of routes and loading patterns for the company's fleet of delivery trucks. If existing software packages cannot handle those requirements, then in-house developed software might be the only choice.

MINIMIZE CHANGES IN BUSINESS PROCEDURES AND POLICIES A company also might choose to develop its own software if available packages will require changes in current business operations or processes. While installing a new software package almost always requires some degree of change in how a company does business, if the installation of a purchased package will be too disruptive, then the organization might decide to develop its own software instead.

MEET CONSTRAINTS OF EXISTING SYSTEMS Any new software installed must work with existing systems. For example, if a new budgeting system must interface with an existing accounting system, finding a software package that works correctly with the existing accounting system might prove difficult. If so, a company could develop its own software to ensure that the new system will interface with the old system.

MEET CONSTRAINTS OF EXISTING TECHNOLOGY Another reason to develop software in-house is that the new system must work with existing hardware and legacy systems. That could require a custom design not commercially available. Some companies have older microcomputer workstations that cannot handle graphics-intensive software or high-speed Internet access. In that situation, the company either must upgrade the environment or develop in-house software that can operate within the constraints of the existing hardware. As a systems analyst, you addressed the issue of technical feasibility during the preliminary investigation. Now, in the systems analysis phase, you must examine the advantages and disadvantages of in-house software development to decide whether it is justifiable.

DEVELOP INTERNAL RESOURCES AND CAPABILITIES   Many firms feel that in-house IT resources and capabilities provide a competitive advantage because they can respond quickly when business problems or opportunities arise. By designing a system in-house, companies can develop and train an IT staff that understands the organization's business functions and information support needs.

Purchasing a Software Package

During the systems analysis phase, you should investigate whether a commercially available software package could satisfy system requirements. Advantages of purchasing a software package over developing software in-house include lower costs, less time to implement, proven reliability and performance benchmarks, less technical development staff, future upgrades provided by the vendor, and the ability to use other companies who have already implemented the software as resources.

LOWER COSTS   Because many companies use software packages, software vendors spread the development costs over many customers. Compared to software developed in-house, a software package almost always is less expensive — particularly in terms of initial investment.

LESS TIME TO IMPLEMENT   When you purchase a package, it already has been designed, programmed, tested, and documented. Therefore, the in-house time normally spent on those tasks is eliminated. Of course, you still must install the software and integrate it into your systems environment, which can take a significant amount of time.

PROVEN RELIABILITY AND PERFORMANCE BENCHMARKS   If the package has been on the market for any length of time, any major problems probably have already been detected and corrected by the vendor. If the product is popular, it almost certainly has been rated and evaluated by independent reviewers.

LESS TECHNICAL DEVELOPMENT STAFF   Companies that use commercial software packages often are able to reduce the number of programmers and systems analysts on the IT staff. Using commercial software also means that the IT staff can concentrate on systems whose requirements cannot be satisfied by software packages.

FUTURE UPGRADES PROVIDED BY THE VENDOR   Software vendors regularly upgrade software packages by adding improvements and enhancements to create a new version or release. A new release of a software package, for example, can include drivers to support a new laser printer or a new type of data storage technology. In many cases, the vendor receives input and suggestions from current users when planning future upgrades.

OTHER COMPANIES AS RESOURCES   Using a commercial software package means you can contact users in other companies to get their impressions and input about the software package. You might be able to try the package or make a site visit to observe the system in operation before making a purchase decision. If a company decides to install a new software release, the upgrade must be planned and coordinated carefully, just as with any other system change. Upgrades generally are less expensive than buying the entire package or acquiring new software because vendors usually offer a lower price to current users. If you have modified the package, however, you must make similar modifications for any upgrades that you install later.

Customizing Software Packages

If you do not find a software package that satisfies your specific requirements, you can develop your own software package or acquire a package that you can customize to meet your needs. Three ways to customize a software package are as follows:

1. You can purchase a basic package that vendors will customize to suit your needs. Many vendors offer basic packages in a standard version with add-on components that are configured individually. A vendor offers options when the standard application will not satisfy all customers. A human resources information system is a typical example, because each company handles employee compensation and benefits differently.

2. You can negotiate directly with the software vendor to make enhancements to meet your needs by paying for the changes.

3. You can purchase the package and make your own modifications. That option is attractive when the product comes close to satisfying your requirements and the vendor will not (or cannot) make the requested changes. A disadvantage of that approach is that systems analysts and programmers might be unfamiliar with the software and will need time to learn the package and make the modifications correctly.

Additionally, some advantages of purchasing a standard package can be lost if the product must be customized. If the vendor does the customizing, the modified package will cost more, take longer to obtain, and might be less reliable. Although vendors regularly upgrade their standard software packages, they might not upgrade a customized version. In addition, if the modifications are done by the company purchasing the software, when a new release of the package becomes available, the company might have to modify the new version.

Other Software Alternatives

Thus far, we have discussed three primary software alternatives: developing in-house software, buying a software package, and customizing a software package. Other possibilities include using an application service provider, outsourcing, and developing end-user applications.

APPLICATION SERVICE PROVIDERS A new category of software supplier is the **application service provider (ASP)**. An ASP delivers applications, or access to applications, by charging a usage or subscription fee. An ASP provides more than a license to use the software; it rents an operational package to the customer. If a company uses an ASP to supply a transaction processing package, for example, the company does not have to design, develop, implement, and maintain the package. The service that the ASP provides is called **application hosting**. As shown in Figure 6-4 on the next page, Microsoft believes that *software as a service* represents a new model for hosting commerce, business, and knowledge management application services.

ASPs represent a growing trend, with the Internet serving as a logical and popular delivery channel. Many large firms, such as SAP have entered the ASP marketplace by offering applications on a rental basis, as reported in the *INFOWORLD* magazine article shown in Figure 6-4.

ON THE WEB

To learn more about ASPs
scsite.com/sad4e/more.htm
click Systems Analysis and
Design Chapter 6 and then
click the ASPs link.

www.scsite.c

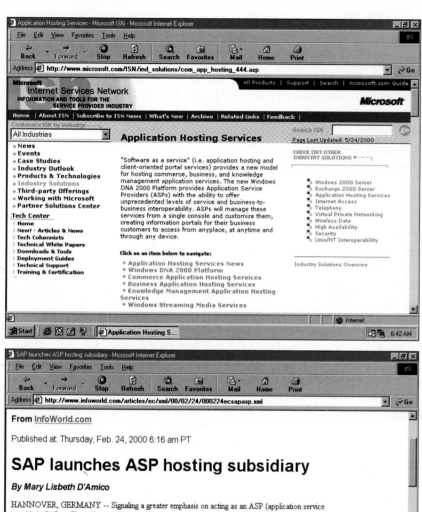

N THE WEB

r more information
out Outsourcing visit
site.com/sad4e/more.htm,
ck Systems Analysis and
sign Chapter 6 and then
ck the Outsourcing link.

w.scsite.com

FIGURE 6-4   Microsoft believes that software as a service represents a new model for application services. Many large firms, such as SAP, compete in the ASP marketplace by offering applications on a rental basis.

OUTSOURCING   **Outsourcing** is the use of outside companies called **service providers** to handle a portion of a company's IT workload on a temporary or long-term basis. Like ASPs, outsourcing also is a popular trend, as shown in Figure 6-5. Many firms outsource IT work as a way of controlling costs and dealing with rapid technological change. According to an estimate in the January 17, 2000, issue of *INFOWORLD*, companies report outsourcing savings of 20 to 40 percent compared with performing the same services in-house. Service providers usually concentrate on specific functions such as hardware, software and network support, or business services such as payroll processing and billing.

Outsourcing can be especially attractive to a company whose volume fluctuates widely, such as a defense contractor. In some situations, a company outsources application development or customization tasks to an IT consulting firm if the company lacks the time or expertise to handle the work on its own. Outsourcing relieves the company of the responsibility of adding IT staff in busy times and downsizing when the workload lightens.

Outsourcing also involves some concerns. A company must turn over internal data to an external service provider and trust the provider to maintain quality. In addition, as the author of the *INFOWORLD* article shown in Figure 6-5 points out, a company must plan outsourcing carefully to avoid lost revenue, added expenses, and potential litigation.

Companies often require additional programmers, systems analysts, and other technical personnel to handle peak workloads on a short-term basis. Rather than extra staff, companies can get assistance from a **contract personnel firm**, which supplies technical help for a specific period of time at a set rate. A company also might turn to a contract personnel firm, or an IT consultant, when it needs people with specialized skills or knowledge for a short-term project.

Outsourcing strategies can include everything from a temporary arrangement with a payroll service to a long-term contract with a **systems management** or **facilities management** firm that provides IT support for an entire operation. A major disadvantage of outsourcing is that it raises employee concerns about job security. Talented people usually prefer positions where the firm is committed to in-house IT development.

USER APPLICATIONS Business requirements sometimes can be fulfilled by a user application, rather than a formal information system or commercial package. **User applications** utilize standard business software, such as Microsoft Office 2000, which has been configured in a specific manner to enhance user productivity. For example, to help a sales rep respond rapidly to customer price requests, an IT support person can set up a form letter with links to a spreadsheet that calculates incentives and discounts. In addition to configuring the software, the IT staff can create a **user interface**, which includes screens, commands, controls, and features that enable users to interact more effectively with the application. User interface design is described in Chapter 7.

In some situations, user applications offer a simple, low-cost solution. Most IT departments have a backlog of projects, and IT solutions for individuals or small groups do not always receive a high priority. At the same time, application software is more powerful, flexible, and user-friendly than ever. Companies such as Microsoft and Corel offer software suites and integrated applications that can exchange data

FIGURE 6-5 Outsourcing IT functions is a growing trend, and many companies, including IBM, offer outsourcing services. Outsourcing is an attractive alternative, but a company must plan and prepare an outsourcing project carefully to avoid potential problems, as the *INFOWORLD* article indicates.

with programs that include tutorials, Wizards, and Help features to guide less experienced users who know what they need to do but do not know how to make it happen.

Many companies empower lower-level employees by providing more access to data and more powerful data management tools. Empowerment also makes the IT department more productive because it can spend less time responding to the daily concerns of users and more time on high-impact systems development projects that support strategic business goals. In most large and medium-sized companies, a **help desk**, or **information center** (**IC**), within the IT department is responsible for supporting users. The IC staff provides hotline assistance, training, and guidance to users who need support.

Once they learn an application, many users can perform tasks that once required a programmer. Some user applications have powerful screen generators and report writers that allow users to design their own data entry forms and reports. For example, as shown in Figure 6-6, Microsoft Access includes Form Wizard and Report Wizard tools that ask a series of questions, and then create the form or report. Those design tools allow users to design specific input and output views that meet their operational needs — with little or no assistance required from the IT staff.

Users typically require spreadsheets, database management programs, and other software packages to meet their information needs. If user applications access corporate data, you must provide appropriate controls to ensure data security and integrity. For example, some files are read-only so users can view, but not change, the data. For security reasons, companies usually restrict user applications to PC-based systems within a user's department.

Selecting a Software Alternative

The company must decide whether to develop the software in-house, customize a software package, purchase a software package, or select some combination of these solutions. The decision affects the remaining SDLC phases and your involvement as a systems analyst. The decision to develop software in-house, for example, can require more participation from the systems analyst than choosing a commercial package. Management usually makes a determination after you present your written recommendations and deliver a formal presentation, which is described later in the chapter. Figure 6-7 illustrates how systems analysts are involved in various software alternatives.

If management decides to develop the system in-house, the systems design phase of the SDLC can begin. During systems design, described in Chapters 7, 8, and 9, you will develop the physical design for the system.

If management decides to buy a software package, you will perform a series of five steps: evaluate the information system requirements, identify potential software vendors, evaluate software package alternatives, make the purchase, and install the software package. Those steps are described in detail in the next section.

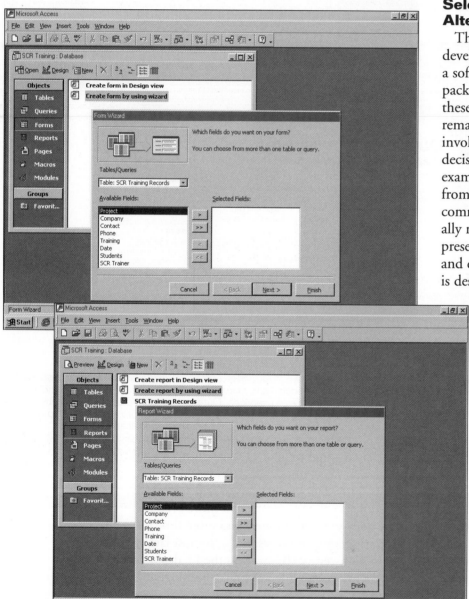

FIGURE 6-6 Microsoft Access includes Form Wizard and Report Wizard tools that ask a series of questions, and then create a form or report.

If management decides to customize a software package, you will follow the same five steps described in buying a package, with one major difference. Because your system will require additional features or capabilities, you must design the specific changes, just as you would for an in-house developed project. So even though you are purchasing a package, you also must work through the systems design phase of the SDLC to design the modifications. Customizing a software package requires a combination of tasks, because you are purchasing *and* redesigning an essential part of the system.

HIGH	In-house developed software
	In-house customizations of a software package
	In-house software developed by contract personnel
Degree of systems analyst involvement	End-user computing
	Outsource a customized software package
	Software vendor customizes its software package
	Software vendor enhances its software package
LOW	Software package used without modification

FIGURE 6-7 A systems analyst's involvement depends on which alternative is selected.

STEPS IN EVALUATING AND PURCHASING SOFTWARE PACKAGES

Step 1: Evaluate the Information System Requirements

Based on your analysis of the system requirements, you must identify the system's key features, estimate volume and future growth, specify any hardware constraints, and prepare a request for proposal or quotation.

IDENTIFY THE KEY FEATURES OF THE SYSTEM Evaluating system requirements involves highlighting any critical features the system must have. For example, if a company operates nationwide, then its payroll system must be capable of deducting any applicable state income taxes. To be acceptable, a software package would have to include this essential feature.

ESTIMATE VOLUME AND FUTURE GROWTH You need to know the current volume of transactions and processing and then forecast changes over a three-to-five-year period. Figure 6-8 shows a one-year volume estimate for an order entry system based on current procedures and a one-year estimate factoring in the addition of a Web-based sales site. Notice that the Web site will handle almost twice as many orders while the number of sales reps is reduced by more than half. Volume figures are constraints for both the software package and the hardware required. You must make sure that the package and the hardware can handle future transaction volumes and data storage requirements.

ONLINE ORDER ENTRY SYSTEM Estimated Activity During Next 12-Month Period			
	Current Level	Future Growth Based on Existing Order Entry Procedures	Future Growth Assuming New Web Site Is Operational
Customers	36,500	40,150	63,875
Daily Orders	1,435	1,579	2,811
Daily Order Lines	7,715	7,893	12,556
Sales Reps	29	32	12
Order Entry Support Staff	2	4	3
Products	600	650	900

FIGURE 6-8 Volume estimate for an order entry system showing current activity and how future growth would be affected by Web-based sales.

SPECIFY ANY HARDWARE CONSTRAINTS   As noted, the software must run properly on your current or proposed hardware platform. Whenever possible, you should make decisions about software first because software is the main element in any system — it is the part with which people work and directly affects the system's usability.

PREPARE A REQUEST FOR PROPOSAL OR QUOTATION   To obtain the information you need to make a decision, you should prepare a request for proposal or a request for quotation. The two documents are similar but used in different situations, based on whether or not you have selected a specific software product.

Typically, a **request for proposal (RFP)** is a written list of features and specifications given to prospective vendors when you have not identified a specific product or package to use. Based on the RFP, vendors can decide if they have a product that will meet your needs and then respond with suggestions and alternatives. RFPs vary in size and complexity, just like the systems they describe. An RFP for a large system can contain dozens of pages with unique requirements and features. You can use an RFP to designate some features as essential and others as desirable. An RFP also requests specific pricing and payment terms. Figure 6-9 shows an example of a page from an RFP.

ON THE WEB

To learn more about RFPs and RFQs visit scsite.com/sad4e/more.htm, click Systems Analysis and Design Chapter 6 and then click the RFPs and RFQs link.

www.scsite.com

SWL   **REQUEST FOR PROPOSAL**
ACCOUNTS PAYABLE SYSTEM

Features	Standard Feature	Comments
1. Interface to general ledger	✔	
2. Matching to receiving documents	✔	
3. Matching to purchase documents	✔	
4. Automatic check printing	✔	
5. Recurring payments		Planned For Next Release
6. Flexible payment selection	✔	
7. Checking statement reconciliation		Will Do On Custom Basis
8. Consolidated check preparation	✔	
9. Duplicate invoice check		No Plans For This Feature
10. Manual check processing	✔	

Reports		
1. Vendor listing	✔	By Vendor Name
2. Invoice register	✔	
3. Check register	✔	
4. Cash requirements	✔	Weekly And Monthly
5. Detail aging	✔	30, 60, 90, 120 + Days
6. Form 1099 reports		Planned For Next Release
7. Account distribution	✔	
8. Bank statement reconciliation		Will Do On Custom Basis

FIGURE 6-9   Among other things, an RFP requires a vendor to indicate whether its product supports specific features and reports. Although the package shown does not offer all the features requested in the RFP, the vendor plans to provide some of the features in future versions. Information on pricing and terms appears in another section of the document.

On the other hand, you can use a **request for quotation** (**RFQ**) when you already know the specific product or package you want and you need to obtain price quotations or bids. RFQs can involve outright purchase or a variety of leasing options and can include maintenance or technical support terms. You can think of an RFQ as a shortened version of an RFP, because the RFQ refers to a specific product and does not contain a set of detailed specifications. With both methods, the objective is to obtain vendor replies that are clear, comparable, and responsive so you can make a well-informed selection decision.

In today's fast-paced IT marketplace, traditional methods for obtaining RFQs are often too slow. The InfoQuote Web site shown in Figure 6-10 offers a meeting place where sellers can list their products and buyers can obtain an instant quote on a package such as the vehicle information management system shown in the example.

Step 2: Identify Potential Software Vendors

The next step is to contact potential vendors. If the software runs on personal computers, you might purchase the package from a commercial software vendor. Preparing an RFP will help the vendor's sales representatives identify possible solutions.

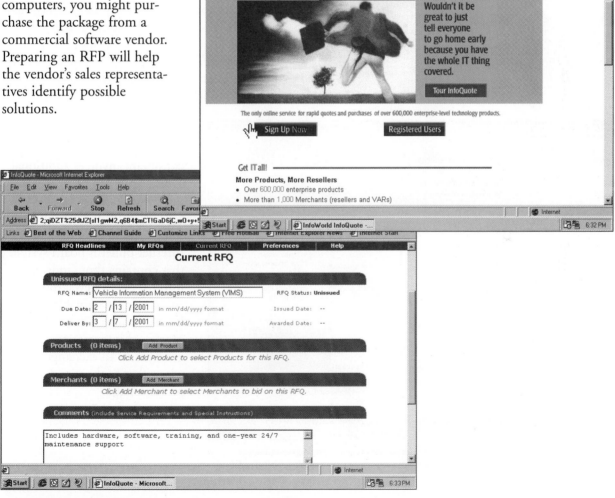

FIGURE 6-10 InfoQuote is an online service that offers instant quotes on more than 600,000 products from more than 1,000 merchants.

If software will run on a mainframe computer, or as an enterprise-wide application, you probably will not purchase it from a retail source. Instead, you can identify popular products and strategies by contacting software vendors, industry sources, and IT consultants. The Internet is a primary marketplace for all IT products, and you can expect to find descriptive information on the Web about all major vendors and their products. In addition, firms such as IDEAS International offer services to help you select and configure a system, as shown in Figure 6-11.

If you need to identify vertical applications for specific industries, you can research industry trade journals or Web sites to find reviews for industry-specific software. Industry trade groups often can direct you to companies that offer specific software solutions. Figure 6-12 shows an example of an IT firm that creates specialized software solutions for many industries, including hospitality, automotive, retailing, and medical.

Another approach is to work with a consulting firm. Many IT consultants offer specialized services that help companies select software packages. A major advantage of using a consultant is that you can tap into broad experience that is difficult for any one company to acquire. Consultants can be located by contacting professional organizations, industry sources, or simply by searching the Internet. Using a consultant involves additional expense but can prevent even more costly mistakes.

Another valuable resource is the Usenet. The **Usenet** is an Internet bulletin board system that contains thousands of forums, called **newsgroups** that cover every imaginable topic. Usenet groups are excellent sources of information and good places to exchange ideas with other analysts and IT professionals.

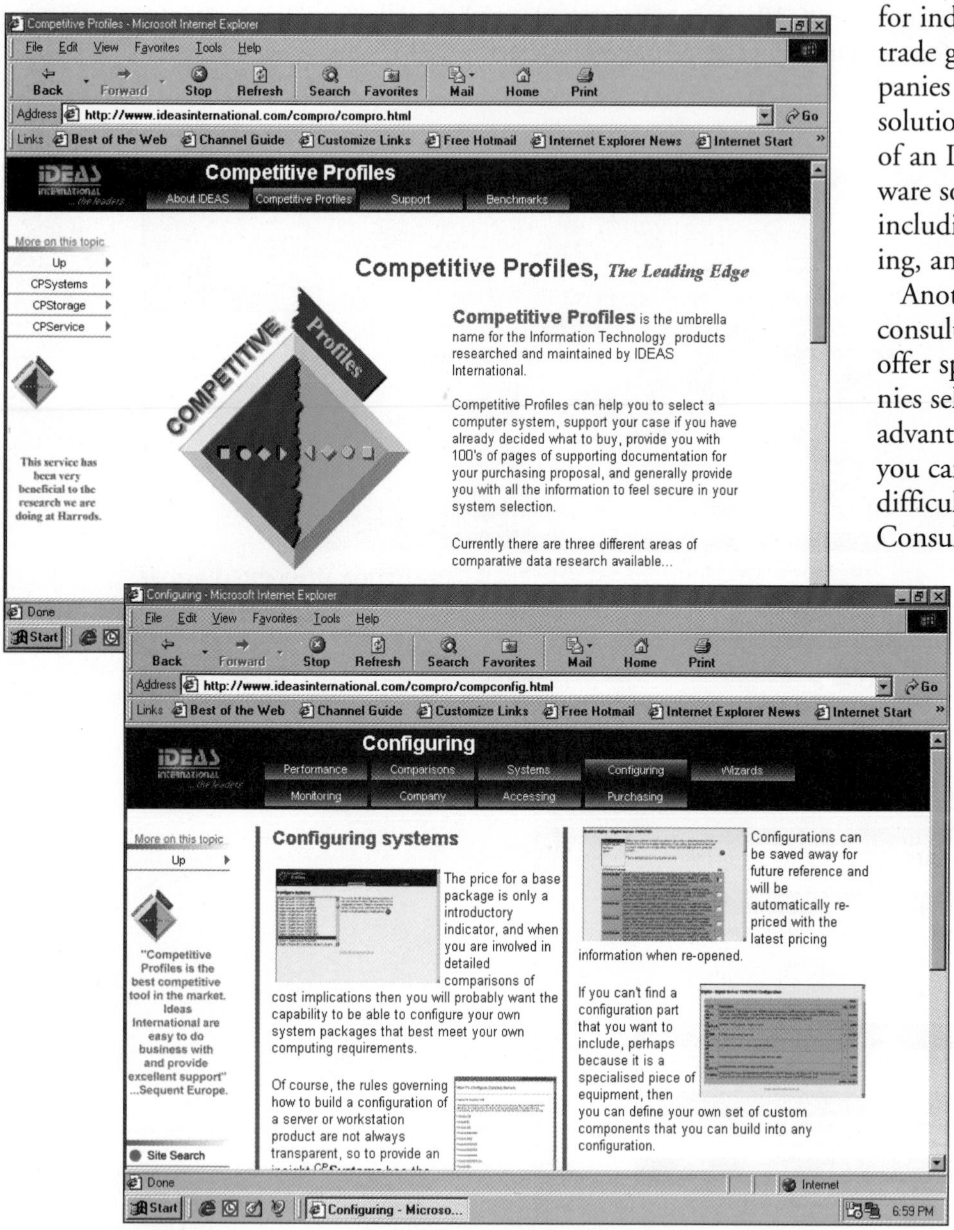

FIGURE 6-11 Firms such as IDEAS International offer services to help you select and configure a system.

Step 3: Evaluate Software Package Alternatives

After identifying possible software packages, you must compare them and select one to fit the company's needs. First you should obtain information about the packages from as many sources as possible, including vendor presentations and literature, product documentation, trade publications, and companies that perform software testing and evaluation. To learn more about particular software packages, search the Internet using keywords that describe the application. Web sites maintained by consultants and software publishers often include product references and links to vendors. As part of the evaluation process, you will obtain information from existing users, test the application, and benchmark the package if necessary.

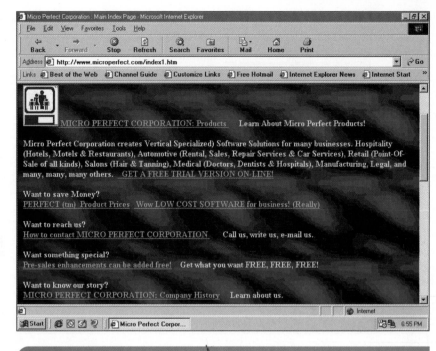

FIGURE 6-12   Micro Perfect Corporation is an example of an IT consulting firm that develops industry-specific software solutions for customers.

EXISTING USERS   You can contact existing users of the software package to obtain feedback and learn about their experiences. For personal computer packages, ask your retail source for references, or contact the software company directly. For minicomputer and mainframe software packages, software vendors typically supply user references. User references are important because you need to know whether the software package has worked well for companies like yours. Vendors, however, usually have satisfied clients on their reference lists, so do not be surprised if you receive mostly positive feedback from that source.

TESTING   If possible, ask users in your organization to try the software package. For horizontal applications or a small system, using a demonstration copy to enter a few sample transactions could be an acceptable test. For vertical applications or large systems, a team of IT staff and users might need several days or weeks to perform tests.

BENCHMARKING   To determine whether a package can handle a certain transaction volume efficiently, you can perform a **benchmark** test. A benchmark measures the time a package takes to process a certain number of transactions. For example, a benchmark can consist of measuring the time needed to post 1,000 sales transactions. If you are considering two or more packages, benchmark testing is a good way to measure relative performance.

Many IT publications publish regular reviews of individual packages, including benchmark tests, and often have annual surveys covering various categories of software. Some of the publications shown in Figure 6-13 also offer online versions and additional Web-based features, search capability, and IT links.

ON THE WEB

For background on Benchmarking visit scsite.com/sad4e/more.htm click Systems Analysis and Design Chapter 6 and then click the Benchmarking link

www.scsite.c

FIGURE 6-13   Many IT publications provide specialized information, reviews of individual software packages, and benchmark tests. These reviews are important to the systems analyst because they can provide an unbiased opinion of the package.

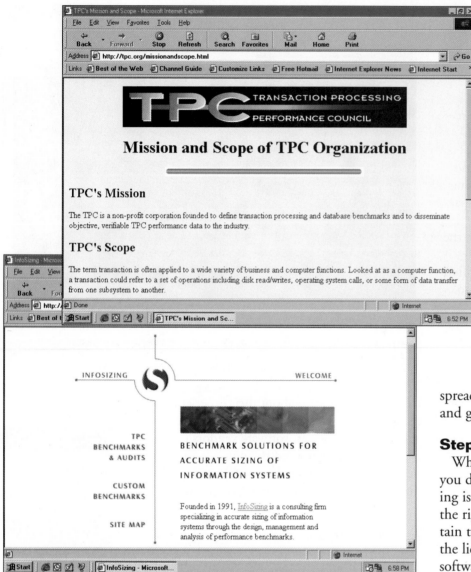

FIGURE 6-14 The Transaction Processing Performance Council (TPC) is an example of a nonprofit organization that publishes standards and reports for its members and the general public, while InfoSizing is an IT consulting firm that offers analysis of performance benchmarks.

You also can obtain information from independent firms that benchmark various software packages and sell comparative analyses of the results, as shown in Figure 6-14. The Transaction Processing Performance Council (TPC) is an example of a nonprofit organization that publishes standards and reports for its members and the general public, while InfoSizing is an IT consulting firm that offers analysis of performance benchmarks.

Finally, you should match each package against the RFP features and rank the choices. If some features are more important than others, give them a higher weight. You can use a spreadsheet to perform the calculations and graph the results.

Step 4: Make the Purchase

When you purchase software, usually you do not own it — what you are buying is a **software license** that gives you the right to use the software under certain terms and conditions. For example, the license would allow you to use the software only on a single computer, a specified number of computers, a network, or an entire site, depending on the terms of the license agreement.

Other license restrictions could prohibit you from making the software available to others or modifying the program. For personal computer users, software license terms and conditions usually cannot be modified. For minicomputer and mainframe users, terms of the license agreement can be negotiated and should be reviewed carefully by management and the legal department.

Although most software packages are purchased, some vendors offer leasing as a financial alternative. For example, IBM provides flexible leasing programs for software and hardware through a special financial services group. If a customer does decide to lease, a **lease agreement** describes the time period, terms, and payments. Another alternative, discussed earlier in the chapter, is to investigate whether the package is available through an ASP for a rental or subscription fee.

As part of the acquisition strategy, you should consider a **maintenance agreement**, which allows you to contact the vendor for assistance when you have system problems or questions. The agreement might provide full support for a period of time or list specific charges for particular services.

Many personal computer packages provide a mail-in registration card that entitles users to free technical support for a period of time. Sometimes support is offered with a charge per occurrence, or per minute or hour of technical support time. Some software vendors also contact registered owners whenever a new release is available and usually offer the new release at a reduced price. For most minicomputer and mainframe packages, a maintenance agreement gives you the right to obtain new releases of the package at no charge or at a reduced rate.

Step 5: Install the Software Package

After purchasing the software package, the final step is installation. For small systems, installation can take one day or less. For large systems or network installations, the process can require considerable time and effort. Your installation strategy should be planned well in advance, especially if any disruption of normal business operations is expected. If the software package is customized, then the task will be more complex and difficult.

Before you can use the new software package, you must complete all implementation steps, including loading, configuring, and testing the software; training users; and converting data files to the new system's format. Chapters 10 and 11 discuss implementation strategies and techniques in more detail.

Evaluation and Selection Teams

Most companies use a combination of in-house developed software, software packages, outsourcing, and end-user systems. Even a single system can use a mix of software alternatives. For example, a company purchases a standard software package to process its payroll, and then develop its own software to handle the interface between the payroll package and the company's in-house manufacturing cost analysis system.

The evaluation and selection of alternatives is not a simple process. The objective is to obtain the product with the lowest total cost of ownership, but actual cost and performance can be difficult to measure. With a large number of choices, how do you select the best alternative?

When selecting hardware and software, systems analysts often work as an **evaluation and selection team**. A team approach ensures that critical factors are not overlooked and that a sound choice is made. The evaluation and selection team also must include users, who will participate in the selection process and feel a sense of ownership in the new system.

The primary objective of the evaluation and selection team is to eliminate system alternatives that will not work, rank the system alternatives that will work, and then present the viable alternatives to management for a final decision.

WHAT DO YOU THINK?

Doug's Sporting Goods sells hunting and fishing supplies. The company has grown considerably in the last two years. Doug Sawyer, the company's founder and president, wants to develop a customer order entry system and hired your IT consulting firm to advise him about software alternatives. Doug is leaning toward in-house development because he does not want to depend on outside vendors and suppliers for technical support and upgrades. Doug also says that he is not interested in selling on the Web, but that could change in the future.

Doug wants to meet with you tomorrow to make a decision. What will you say to Doug at the meeting?

COMPLETION OF SYSTEMS ANALYSIS

To complete the systems analysis phase, you must prepare the system requirements document and your presentation to management. In addition to the information that follows, the Systems Analyst's Toolkit includes a section with guidelines and suggestions for preparing the written report and the presentation to management.

System Requirements Document

The **system requirements document**, or **software requirements specification**, contains the requirements for the new system, describes the alternatives that were considered, and makes a specific recommendation to management. This important document is the starting point for measuring the performance, accuracy, and completeness of the finished system before entering the systems design phase.

The system requirements document is like a contract that identifies what must be delivered, by the systems developers, to users; therefore you should write the system requirements document in language that users can understand so they can offer input, suggest improvements, and approve the final version.

Because the system requirements document can be lengthy, you should format and organize it so it is easy to read and use. The system requirements document should include a cover page and a detailed table of contents. You also can add an index and a glossary of terms to make the document easier to use. The content of the system requirements document will depend on the company and the complexity of the system. The Systems Analyst's Toolkit provides guidance and offers suggestions to help you create the system requirements document.

Presentation to Management

The presentation to management at the end of the systems analysis phase is one of the most critical milestones in the systems development process. At this point, managers make key decisions that affect the future development of the system.

Prior to the management presentation, you might give two other presentations: one to the principal individuals in the IT department to keep them posted, and another presentation to users to answer their questions and seek their approval. The system requirements document is the basis for all three presentations, and you should distribute the document, or a summary, in advance so the recipients can review it.

When preparing your presentation, you should review the guidelines and suggestions in the Systems Analyst's Toolkit, which will help you design and deliver a successful presentation. In addition to the techniques found in the Toolkit, also keep the following suggestions in mind:

- Begin your presentation with a brief overview of the purpose and primary objectives of the system project.
- Summarize the primary viable alternatives. For each alternative, describe the costs, advantages, and disadvantages.
- Explain why the evaluation and selection team chose the recommended alternative.
- Allow time for discussion and for questions and answers.
- Obtain a final decision from management or agree on a timetable for the next step in the process.

The object of the management presentation is to obtain approval for the development of the system and to gain management's full support, including necessary financial resources. Management will probably choose one of five alternatives: develop an in-house system, modify the current system, purchase or customize a software package, perform additional systems analysis work, or stop all further work. Depending on their decision, your next task as a systems analyst will be one of the following:

1. **Develop an in-house system.** Begin the systems design phase for the new system.

2. **Modify the current system.** Begin the systems design phase for the modified system.

3. **Purchase or customize a software package.** Negotiate the purchase terms with the software vendor for management approval. Then, if the package will be used without modification, you can begin planning the systems implementation phase. If you must make modifications to the package, your next step is to start the systems design phase. If the vendor will make the modifications, then your next step is to start planning the testing and documentation of the modifications as part of the systems implementation phase.

4. **Perform additional systems analysis work.** Management might want you to investigate certain alternatives further, explore alternatives not examined, reduce the project scope because of cost constraints, or expand the project scope based on new developments. If necessary, you will perform the additional work and schedule a follow-up presentation.

5. **Stop all further work.** The decision might be based on your recommendation, a shift in priorities or costs, or for other reasons. Whatever the reason, if that is management's decision, then you have no additional tasks for the project other than to file all your research in a logical location so that it can be retrieved if the project is reopened in the future.

After the presentation and management decision, you will begin a variety of tasks, depending on the strategy chosen. If you are developing an in-house system or modifying a package, you will build a model of the proposed system and start designing the system's output, input, files, and data structures. The following sections describe several tools and techniques that can assist you in that process, including prototyping, CASE tools, and alternative graphical tools.

TRANSITION TO SYSTEMS DESIGN

If management decides to develop the system in-house, then the next phase of the SDLC — the systems design phase — can begin. In a smaller company, you might be assigned full responsibility for the project. In a large IT group, you could work as a member of a development team even though you had not participated in the earlier SDLC phases.

When systems design begins, it is essential to have an accurate and understandable system requirements document. Your document contains the design for the new system and is the starting point for the systems design phase. Errors, omissions, ambiguities, and other problems will affect the quality and completeness of the finished product. As you proceed to the next phase, you must be certain that you performed a thorough and accurate systems analysis and communicated the results in your system requirements document.

Systems Design Overview

The **logical design** of an information system defines the functions and features of the system and the relationships among its components. The logical design includes the output that must be produced by the system, the input needed by the system, and the processes that must be performed by the system without regard to how tasks will be accomplished *physically*. Because the logical design defines the necessary, or *essential*, requirements of a system, it also is known as the **essential model**.

As previously discussed, a logical design defines *what* must take place, not *how* it is to be accomplished. Logical designs, thus, do not address the actual methods of implementation. The logical design for a customer system, for example, describes the data that must be entered, specifies that records must be displayed in customer number order, and explains what information to produce for a customer status report. Specifications for the actual input, or entry, of data, the sort method, the physical process of creating the report, and the exact format of the report are not part of the logical design.

In contrast, the **physical design** of an information system is a plan for the actual implementation of the system. The physical design is built on the system's logical design and describes the implementation of a specific set of system components. In the customer system, for example, the physical design describes actual processes of entering, verifying, and storing data; the physical layout of data files; the sorting procedures; the exact format of reports; and so on. Whereas logical design is concerned with *what* the system must accomplish, physical design is concerned with *how* the system will meet those requirements.

The logical design is completed during the systems analysis phase of the SDLC. To create the logical design, you investigated, analyzed, and documented the input, processing, and output requirements and constraints. Now, in the systems design phase, you are ready to begin work on the physical design of the system.

The Relationship between Analysis and Design

Because logical and physical designs are related so closely, good systems design is impossible without careful, accurate systems analysis. In fact, the design phase typically cannot begin until the analysis work is complete. Although some overlap is possible, it is much better to finish the analysis phase before moving on to systems design.

During systems design, you should return to the analysis phase only in very limited situations. You might return to fact-finding, for example, if you discover that you overlooked an important fact, if users have significant new needs, or if legal or governmental requirements change. You might return to requirements analysis if you encounter unforeseen design issues or problems. Such cases are the exception to the rule, however. If an analyst develops a pattern of returning to prior phases, it could indicate that the earlier work was inaccurate or incomplete.

FIGURE 6-15 Wind tunnel testing is a typical example of prototyping.

PROTOTYPING

A **prototype** is an early, rapidly constructed working version of the proposed information system. Prototyping is common in manufacturing, where engineers use a model to resolve problems before production begins, as shown in the wind tunnel testing in Figure 6-15.

User input and approval is essential at every stage of the systems development process. Prototyping allows users to examine a model that accurately represents system outputs, inputs, interfaces, and processes. Users can *test-drive* the model and either approve it or request changes. In some situations, the prototype evolves into the final version of the information system; in other cases, the prototype is intended only to validate user requirements and is discarded afterward.

Approaches to Prototyping

Prototyping involves a repetitive sequence of analysis, design, modeling, and testing. The end product of **system prototyping** is a full-featured, working model of the information system, ready for implementation, as shown in Figure 6-16. Rapid application development (RAD), which is described in Part 4 of the Systems Analyst's Toolkit, relies heavily on system prototyping. Using RAD methods, a team of users, managers, and IT staff members works together to develop a model of the information system that evolves into the completed system. The RAD team defines, analyzes, designs, and tests prototypes using a highly interactive process.

Planning → Analysis → Design → SYSTEM PROTOTYPE → Implementation

FIGURE 6-16 The end product of prototyping is a working model of the information system, ready for implementation.

Systems analysts also use prototyping to verify user requirements, after which the prototype is discarded and implementation continues, as shown in Figure 6-17. The approach is called **design prototyping**, or **throwaway prototyping**. In this case, the prototyping objectives are more limited, but no less important. The end product of design prototyping is a user-approved design prototype that documents and benchmarks the features of the finished system.

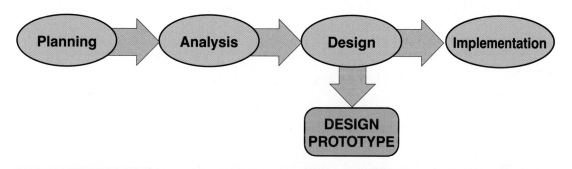

Planning → Analysis → Design → Implementation

Design → DESIGN PROTOTYPE

FIGURE 6-17 The end product of throwaway prototyping is a user-approved design prototype that documents and benchmarks the features of the finished system.

Design prototyping makes it possible to capture user input and approval while continuing to develop the system within the framework of the SDLC. Systems analysts typically use design prototyping as they construct outputs, inputs, and user interfaces, as discussed in Chapter 7.

Whenever possible, you should allow users to experiment with a prototype and provide feedback on how well it meets their needs. This approach can increase development costs, but the expense will be offset by lower costs during subsequent SDLC phases. Prototyping offers many benefits, including the following:

- Users and systems developers can avoid misunderstandings.
- System developers can create accurate specifications for the finished system based on the prototype.
- Managers can evaluate a working model more effectively than a paper specification.
- Systems analysts can use a prototype to develop testing and training procedures before the finished system is available.
- Prototyping reduces the risk and potential financial exposure that occur when a finished system fails to support business needs.

Although most systems analysts believe that the advantages of prototyping far outweigh any disadvantages, you should consider the following potential problems:

- The rapid pace of development can create quality problems, which are not discovered until the finished system is operational.
- Other system requirements, such as reliability and maintainability, cannot adequately be tested using a prototype.
- In very complex systems, the prototype becomes unwieldy and difficult to manage.

Prototyping Tools

Systems analysts can use powerful tools to develop prototypes. Most prototyping is done using CASE tools, application generators, report generators, screen generators, and fourth-generation languages (4GLs). In combination, the tools provide a framework for rapid, efficient software development, called a **fourth-generation environment**, as shown in Figure 6-18.

In a fourth-generation environment, the development tools are highly interactive. For example, systems analysts use CASE tools to create a series of diagrams and definitions, which generate a data dictionary automatically. The data dictionary organizes and documents all data elements and interacts with application, screen, and report generators to produce a system prototype. Because 4GLs are object-oriented programming languages (OOPL), they are especially valuable in implementing an object-oriented system design.

When creating prototypes, a systems analyst should consider how application generators, report generators, and screen generators can cut development time and reduce expense.

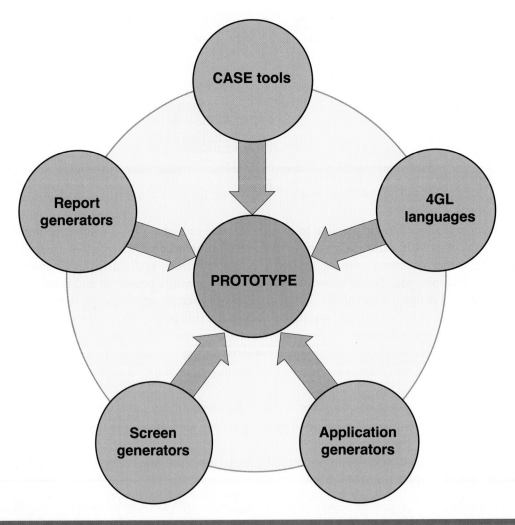

FIGURE 6-18   A fourth-generation environment provides a framework for rapid, efficient software development.

APPLICATION GENERATORS   An **application generator**, also called a **code generator**, allows you to develop computer programs rapidly by translating a logical model directly into **fourth-generation language (4GL)** code. As shown in Figure 6-19, Popkin's System Architect offers a 4GL interface that uses information stored in the data repository to generate applications in languages such as Delphi, PowerBuilder, or Microsoft Visual Basic.

Another application development approach is to use Microsoft Visual Basic, Visual C++, or Visual J++, which are popular Windows-based tools that use a menu-driven environment to generate program code. Languages such as C++ and Java are called **event driven** (because a programmer specifies the actions that the program must perform when certain events occur) and **nonprocedural** (because the programmer does not write a series of instructions that the program follows from start to finish). In contrast, COBOL is an example of a **procedural** language that requires the programmer to create code for each processing step. Some CASE tools, such as Visible Analyst, can generate programs in COBOL, as shown in Figure 6-19.

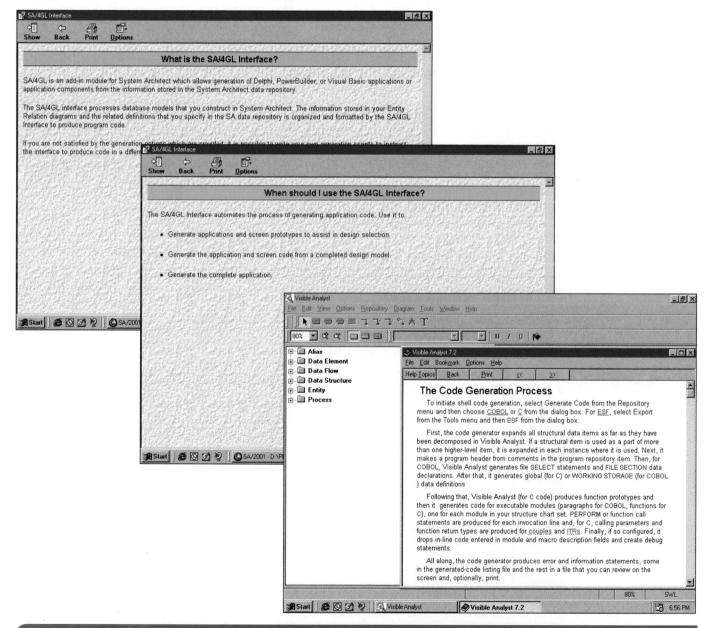

FIGURE 6-19   Application generators can create applications from information stored in the data repository. Popkin's System Architect offers a 4GL interface that can generate applications in Delphi, PowerBuilder, or Visual Basic languages. The Visible Analyst code generator can create applications in COBOL and other languages.

ON THE WEB

For examples of Screen Generators visit scsite.com/ad4e/more.htm, click Systems Analysis and Design Chapter 6 and then click the Screen Generators link.

www.scsite.com

REPORT GENERATORS   A **report generator**, also called a **report writer**, is a tool for designing formatted reports rapidly. Figure 6-20 shows three popular report writers. Using a report writer, you can modify the report design easily at any time in the design process. When you are satisfied with the report layout, the report writer creates a report definition similar to a printer spacing chart, and program code that actually produces the report. You also can input sample field values to create a **mock-up report** that users can review before final report design decisions are made.

SCREEN GENERATORS   A **screen generator**, or **form generator**, is an interactive software tool that helps you design a custom interface, create screen forms, and handle data entry format and procedures. The screen generator allows you to control how the screen will display captions, data fields, data, and other visual attributes. Modern CASE tools usually include a screen generator that interacts with the data dictionary. Figure 6-21 shows how Popkin's System Architect CASE tool is used to generate a screen layout. Notice that the top view lists five steps. The systems analyst creates a graphic layout, selects a 4GL development environment, and specifies a file name for the output. After System Architect generates the screen, a systems analyst can modify the design if necessary, as shown in the bottom view.

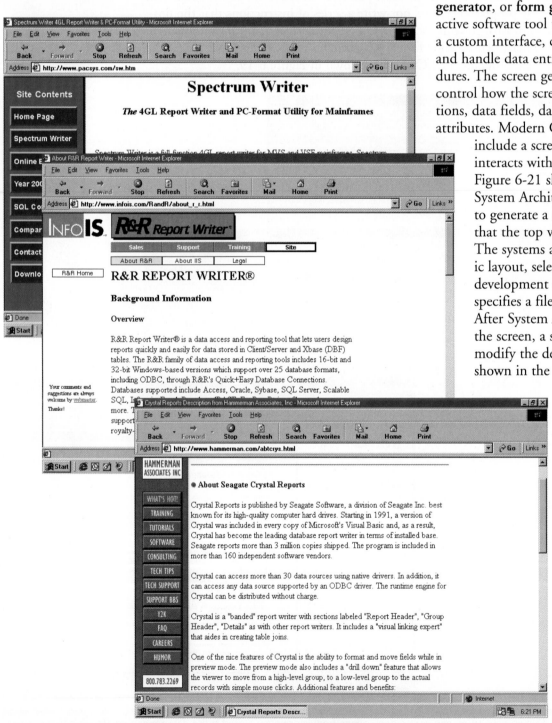

FIGURE 6-20   Three examples of report writers that can design formatted reports rapidly.

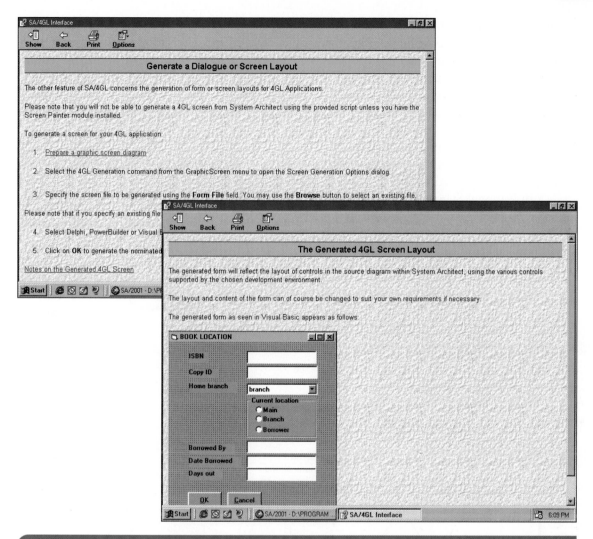

FIGURE 6-21 A screen generator allows you to control how the screen will display captions, data fields, data, and other visual attributes.

Limitations of Prototypes

The final version of the system typically demands higher-level performance than the prototype can provide. A prototype is a functioning system, but it is less efficient than a fully developed system. Because it is a model, rather than a completed system, the prototype will have slower processing speeds and response times. The prototype also might lack security requirements, exception and error handling procedures, and other required functions. Despite those limitations, systems developers can upgrade the prototype into the final information system by adding the necessary capability. Otherwise, the prototype is discarded and the remaining SDLC phases are completed. Even when it does not evolve into the finished system, the prototype greatly helps to ensure that the final product will meet all requirements. Satisfying system requirements is the ultimate goal of systems development, and prototyping is an extremely valuable tool during the process.

Other Modeling Tools

As you proceed from logical design to physical design, you continue to use DFDs, object modeling tools, CASE tools, and the prototyping tools described in this chapter. You also should know about systems flowcharts, which are another method of describing the physical design of a system.

For many years, systems flowcharts were used to display the major processes, inputs, and outputs of a system. A **systems flowchart** is primarily a physical modeling tool that uses various symbols to identify input and output operations, represent data or files, and show media such as disks, documents, and reports. Some systems analysts still use systems flowcharts because they are easy to construct and understand, but you are more likely to see them on older, file-oriented designs. Most systems flowcharts use a standard set of symbols developed by the American National Standards Institute (ANSI). Figure 6-22 shows the ANSI symbols. The right part of the figure shows how they are used in a systems flowchart for an order system.

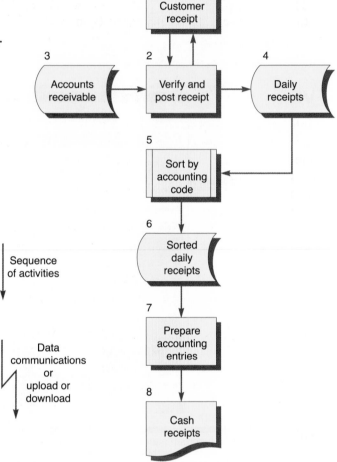

FIGURE 6-22 Using standard ANSI symbols, a systems flowchart shows how an order system handles customer payments. Lines with arrowheads indicate the flow of data, just as they do in data flow diagrams. The flow of data and processing steps generally occurs from top to bottom and left to right.

The order system flowchart in Figure 6-22 shows how a customer payment is posted and processed. Lines with arrowheads indicate the flow of data, just as they do in data flow diagrams. The flow of data and processing steps generally occurs from top to bottom.

Each symbol's shape indicates its purpose. The symbols are numbered for easier reference. In Figure 6-22, symbols 1, 3, 4, 6, and 8 represent data or files stored in specific form or physical media. Symbol 1 is a workstation symbol. Symbols 3, 4, and 6 are disk symbols, and symbol 8 is a document or report symbol. The other three symbols — 2, 5, and 7 — identify major processes that transform the data or files into another form. Symbols 2 and 7 are process symbols that represent programs, and symbol 5 is a predefined process symbol that represents a system utility program. Figure 6-22 shows three major processing steps that are completed in sequence:

- The first step (symbol 2) verifies terminal-entered customer receipts (symbol 1) by reading from the accounts receivable file (symbol 3), reporting back to the workstation on the validity of the receipt, and then posting the valid receipts to the daily receipts file (symbol 4).
- The second step (symbol 5) sorts the daily receipts into accounting code sequence and then creates the sorted daily receipts file (symbol 6).
- The third step (symbol 7) reads the sorted daily receipts and then consolidates information to produce the cash receipts report (symbol 8).

OVERVIEW OF SYSTEMS DESIGN

An information system has five basic components: data, people, processes, hardware, and software. Interaction among the components has a major impact on the design process, so the systems analyst must understand the entire logical design of the system before beginning the physical design of any one component.

The first step is to review the system requirements document, which is especially important if you did not work on the previous phase or if a substantial amount of time passed since the analysis phase was completed. After you review the system requirements, you are ready to start the actual design process. What should you do first, and why?

The best place to begin is with the user interface, which affects the overall interaction between the user and the system. As you develop the user interface, you will move into specific input and output design tasks. Then you will work on data design and systems architecture for the system.

Because the components of a system are interdependent, the design phase is not a series of clearly defined steps. Although you might start with one component, it is not unusual to work on several components at the same time. For example, making a decision to change a report format might require other changes in data design or input screens.

The final step in systems design is to prepare a system design specification report and present your results to management. Those tasks and other systems design activities are listed and described in Figure 6-23.

Step	Activity	Description
1	**Review system requirements.**	Become familiar with the logical design.
2	**Design the system.**	
	• User interface	Design an overall user interface, including screens, commands, controls, and features that enable users to interact with an application.
	• Input processes	Determine how data will be input to the system and design necessary source documents.
	• Input and output formats and reports	Design the physical layout for each input and output screen and printed report.
	• Data	Determine how data will be organized, stored, maintained, updated, accessed, and used.
	• System architecture	Determine processing strategies and methods, client/server interaction, network configuration, and Internet/intranet interface issues.
3	**Present the systems design.**	Create the systems design specification document, in which you describe the proposed system design, the anticipated benefits of the system and the estimated development and implementation costs.

FIGURE 6-23 The systems design phase consists of three main steps.

Systems Design Objectives

The goal of **systems design** is to build a system that is effective, reliable, and maintainable. To be effective, the system must satisfy the defined requirements and constraints. The system also must be accepted by users who use it to support the organization's business objectives.

A system is reliable if it adequately handles errors, such as input errors, processing errors, hardware failures, or human mistakes. Ideally, *all* errors can be prevented. Unfortunately, no system is completely foolproof, whether it is a payroll system, a telephone switching system, an Internet access system, or a space shuttle navigation system. A more realistic approach to building a reliable system is to plan for errors, detect them as early as possible, allow for their correction, and prevent them from damaging the system itself.

A system is maintainable if it is well designed, flexible, and developed with future modifications in mind. No matter how well a system is designed and implemented, at some point it will need to be modified. Modifications will be necessary to correct problems, to adapt to changing user requirements, to enhance the system, or to take advantage of changing technology. Your systems design must be capable of handling future modifications or the system soon will be outdated and fail to meet requirements.

Systems Design Considerations

Good design results in systems that are effective, reliable, and maintainable. As shown in Figure 6-24, design considerations involve users, data, and processing.

Systems Design Considerations
User Considerations
• Consider points where users interact with the system
• Anticipate future user, system and organizational needs
Data Considerations
• Enter data where and when it occurs
• Verify data where it is input
• Use automated data entry methods whenever possible
• Control access for data entry
• Report every instance of entry and change of data
• Enter data only once
Processing Considerations
• Use a modular design
• Design independent modules that perform a single function

FIGURE 6-24 Good design results in systems that are effective, reliable, and maintainable. Design considerations involve users, data, and processing.

USER CONSIDERATIONS Of the many issues you must consider during systems design, your most important goal is to make the system acceptable to users, or user-friendly. Throughout the design process, the essential factor to consider is how decisions will affect users. Always remember that you are designing the system for the user, and keep these basic points in mind:

Carefully consider any point where users receive output from, or provide input to, the system. Above all, the user interface must be easy to learn and use. Input processes should be well documented, easy to follow, intuitive, and forgiving of errors. Output should be attractive and easy to understand, with an appropriate level of detail.

Anticipate future needs of the users, the system, and the organization. Suppose that an employee master file contains a one-character field to indicate each employee's category. The field currently has two valid values: *F* indicates a full-time employee, and *P* indicates a part-time employee. Depending on the field value, either FULL-TIME or PART-TIME will print as the value on various reports. While those two values could be programmed, or **hardcoded**, into the report programs, designing a separate table with category codes and captions is a better choice. The hardcoded solution is straightforward, but if the organization adds another value, such as *X* for FLEXTIME, a programmer would have to change all the report programs. If a separate table for codes and captions is used, it can be changed easily without requiring modifications to the reports.

You must provide flexibility. Suppose that a user wants a screen display of all customer balances that exceed $5,000 in an accounts receivable system. How should you design that feature? The program could be hardcoded to check customer balances against a fixed value of 5,000, which is a simple solution for the programmer and the user because extra keystrokes or commands are not entered to produce the display. That approach, however, is inflexible. For instance, if a user later needs a list of customers whose balances exceed $7,500 rather than $5,000, the existing system cannot provide the information. To accommodate the request, the programmer would have to change and retest the program and rewrite new documentation.

On the other hand, you could design the program to produce a report of all customers whose balance exceeds a specific amount entered by the user. For example, if a user wants to display customers with balances of more than $7,500, he or she can enter the number 7,500 in a parameter query. A **parameter** is a value that the user enters whenever the query is run, which provides flexibility, enables users to access information easily, and costs less.

A good system design can combine both approaches. In that example, you could design the program to accept a variable amount entered by the user but start with a default value of 5,000. Then users can press the ENTER key to accept the default value, or enter another value. Often the best design strategy is to come up with several alternatives, so users can decide what will work best for them. Again, always remember to design the system with the user in mind.

WHAT DO YOU THINK?

Experienced analysts sometimes complain that users request many reports but use only a small portion of the data. In many offices you see in-boxes filled with reports and stacks of reports sitting on desks. Why? Suppose you are interviewing users about what reports they want or need. What questions would you ask? What if users could design most of their own reports without assistance from the IT staff, by using a powerful, user-friendly report writer program? Do you think they would request as many reports or the same types of reports? What are the pros and cons of giving users total control over output?

DATA CONSIDERATIONS Data entry and storage considerations are important parts of the system design. Here are some guidelines to follow:

Data should be entered into the system where and when it occurs because delays cause data errors. For example, employees in the receiving department should enter data about incoming shipments when the shipments arrive, and sales clerks should enter data about new orders when they take the orders.

Data should be verified when it is entered, to catch errors immediately. The input design should specify a data type, such as numeric, alphabetic, or character, and a range of acceptable values for each data entry item. If an incorrect data value is entered, the system should recognize and flag it immediately. The system also should allow corrections at any time. Some errors, for example, are corrected easiest right at entry while the original source documents are at hand or the customer is on the telephone. Other errors may need further investigation, so users must be able to correct errors at a later time.

FIGURE 6-25   Automated data entry methods, such as the scanner shown above, reduce input errors and improve employee productivity.

Automated methods of data entry should be used whenever possible. Receiving department employees in many companies, for example, use scanners to capture data about merchandise received. Automated data entry methods, such as the scanner shown in Figure 6-25, reduce input errors and improve employee productivity.

Access for data entry should be controlled and all entries or changes to critical data values should be reported. Dollar fields and many volume fields are considered critical data fields. Examples of critical volumes include the number of checks processed, the number of medical prescriptions dispensed, or the number of insurance premium payments received. Reports that trace the entry of and changes to critical data values are called **audit trails** and are essential in every system.

Every instance of entry and change to data should be logged. For example, the system should record when a customer's credit limit was established, and by whom, which is necessary to construct the history of a transaction.

Data should be entered into a system only once. If input data for a payroll system also is needed for a human resources system, you should design a program interface between the systems so data can be transferred automatically.

Data duplication should be avoided. In an inventory file, for example, the suppliers' addresses should not be stored with every part record. Otherwise, the address of a vendor who supplies 100 different parts is repeated 100 times in the data file. Additionally, if the vendor's address changes, all 100 parts records must be updated. Data duplication also can produce inconsistencies. If those 100 stored addresses for the vendor are not identical, how would a user know which version is correct?

PROCESSING CONSIDERATIONS   In addition to the issues affecting users and data, you should consider the following guidelines in your processing design:

Use a modular design. In a modular design, you create individual processing components, called modules, that connect to a higher-level program or process. In a traditional, structured design, each module represents a specific process or subprocess shown on a DFD and documented in a process description. If you are using an object-oriented design, object classes are represented by code modules when implementing the design with an OOPL. You will learn more about modular design in Chapter 10, which describes application development.

Design modules that perform a single function are easier to understand, implement, and maintain. Independent modules also provide greater flexibility because they can be developed and tested individually, and then combined at a later point in the development process. Modular design is especially helpful when developing large-scale systems because separate teams of analysts and programmers can work on different areas of the project, and then integrate the modules to create a finished system.

Design Trade-offs

You will find that design goals often conflict with each other. In the systems design phase, you must analyze alternatives and weigh trade-offs constantly. To make a system easier to use, for example, programming requirements might be more complex. Making a system more flexible might increase maintenance requirements. Meeting one user's requirements could make it harder to satisfy another user's needs.

Most design trade-off decisions that you will face come down to the basic conflict of *quality versus cost*. Although every project has budget and financial constraints, you should avoid decisions that achieve short-term savings but might mean higher costs later. For example, if you try to reduce implementation costs by cutting back on system testing or user training, you can create higher operational costs in the future. If necessary, you should document and explain the situations carefully to management, and discuss the possible risks. Each trade-off must be considered individually, and the final result must be acceptable to users, the systems staff, and company management.

DESIGNING AND USING CODES

A **code** is a set of letters or numbers that represents a data item. Codes can be used to simplify output, input, and data formats. During systems design, you review existing codes and develop new ones that will be used to store and access data efficiently.

Overview of Codes

Because codes often are used to represent data you encounter them constantly in your everyday life. Student numbers, for example, are unique codes used in a school registration system to identify students. Three students with the name John Turner might be enrolled at your school, but only one is student number 268960.

Your ZIP code is another common example. A ZIP code contains multiple items of information compressed into nine digits. The first digit identifies one of ten geographical areas of the United States. The combination of the next three digits identifies a major city or major distribution point. The fifth digit identifies an individual post office, an area within a city, or a specific delivery unit. The last four digits identify a post office box or a specific street address.

For example, consider the ZIP code 27906-2624 shown in Figure 6-26. The first digit, 2, indicates a broad geographical area in the eastern United States. The digits, 790, indicate Elizabeth City, North Carolina. The fifth digit, 6, identifies the post office that services the College of the Albemarle. The last four digits, 2624, identify the post office box for the college.

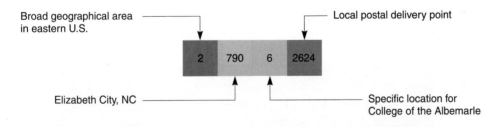

Broad geographical area
in eastern U.S.

Local postal delivery point

2 790 6 2624

Elizabeth City, NC

Specific location for
College of the Albemarle

FIGURE 6-26 — A ZIP code is an example of a significant digit code that uses subgroups to provide information.

As you can imagine, codes serve many useful purposes. Because codes often are shorter than the data they represent, they save storage space and costs, reduce data transmission time, and decrease data entry time. For example, ZIP codes are used to classify and sort mail efficiently. Codes also can be used to reveal or conceal information. The last two digits of a seven-digit part number, for example, can represent the supplier number; or the coded wholesale price on a retail price tag is known to salespeople but generally not to customers.

Finally, codes can reduce data input errors in situations when the coded data is easier to remember and enter than the original source data, when only certain valid codes are allowed, and when something within the code itself can provide immediate verification that the entry is correct.

Because users must deal with coded data, the coding methods must be acceptable to them. If you plan to use new codes or change existing ones, you first should obtain comments and feedback from users.

Types of Coding

1. **Sequence codes** are numbers or letters assigned in a specific order. Sequence codes contain no additional information other than an indication of order of entry into the system. For example, a human resource system issues consecutive employee numbers to identify employees. Because the codes are assigned in the order in which employees are hired, you can use the code to see that employee number 584 was hired after employee number 433. The code, however, does not indicate the starting date of either person's employment.

2. **Block sequence codes** use blocks of numbers for different classifications. College course numbers usually are assigned using a block sequence code. 100-level courses, such as Chemistry 110 and Mathematics 125, are freshman-level courses, whereas course numbers in the 200s indicate sophomore-level courses. Within a particular block, the sequence of numbers can have some additional meaning, such as when English 151 is the prerequisite for English 152.

3. **Alphabetic codes** use alphabet letters to distinguish one item from another based on a category, an abbreviation, or an easy-to-remember value, called a mnemonic code. Many classification codes fit more than one of the following definitions:

    a. **Category codes** identify a group of related items. For example, a local department store uses a two-character category code to identify the department in which a product is sold: GN for gardening supplies, HW for hardware, and EL for electronics.

    b. **Abbreviation codes** are alphabetic abbreviations. For example, standard state codes include NY for New York, ME for Maine, and MN for Minnesota. Some abbreviation codes are called **mnemonic codes** because they use a specific combination of letters that are easy to remember. Many three-character airport codes such as those pictured in Figure 6-27 are mnemonic codes: LAX represents Los Angeles International Airport, DFW is Dallas/Ft. Worth Airport, and JFK is John F. Kennedy International Airport. Some airport codes are not mnemonic, such as ORD, which designates Chicago O'Hare International Airport, or HPN, which identifies the airport in White Plains, New York.

FIGURE 6-27 Codes are used to identify and rate baggage in the airline industry. Codes are machine-readable using the bar code that is printed when the baggage is checked. Airline employees recognize the unique three-character code that identifies the destination. A bar code reader scans a code that also represents the employee number who checked in the baggage, the passenger's name, and other pertinent information. Note that some codes are mnemonic; others are not.

4. **Significant digit codes** distinguish items by using a series of subgroups of digits. ZIP codes, for example, are significant digit codes. Other such codes include inventory location codes that consist of a two-digit warehouse code, followed by a one-digit floor number code, a two-digit section code, a one-digit aisle number, and a two-digit bin number code. Figure 6-28 illustrates the inventory location code 11205327. What looks like a large eight-digit number is actually five separate numbers, each of which has significance.

5. **Derivation codes** combine data from different item attributes, or characteristics, to build the code. Most magazine subscription codes are derivation codes. One popular magazine's subscriber code consists of the subscriber's five-digit ZIP code, followed by the first, third, and fourth letters of

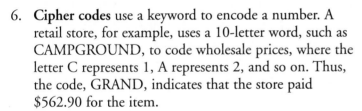

FIGURE 6-28 | Sample of a code that uses significant digits to pinpoint the location of an inventory item.

the subscriber's last name, the last two digits of the subscriber's house number, and the first, third, and fourth letters of the subscriber's street name. The magazine's subscriber code for one particular subscriber is shown in Figure 6-29.

6. **Cipher codes** use a keyword to encode a number. A retail store, for example, uses a 10-letter word, such as CAMPGROUND, to code wholesale prices, where the letter C represents 1, A represents 2, and so on. Thus, the code, GRAND, indicates that the store paid $562.90 for the item.

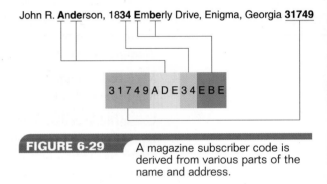

FIGURE 6-29 | A magazine subscriber code is derived from various parts of the name and address.

7. **Action codes** indicate what action is to be taken with an associated item. For example, a computerized query/update program requires you to enter a student number and an action code to act on the record in a certain manner; the action code *D* indicates that you want to display the student's record, *A* indicates that you want to add a record for the student number, and *X* indicates that you want to exit the program.

8. **Self-checking codes** use a check digit to verify the validity of a numeric code. One method of using a four-digit self-checking code is to calculate a check digit by multiplying the first digit by 1, the second digit by 2, and so on. Then, those products are summed. If the sum contains more than one digit, the digits in the sum are added and the adding of the sum is repeated as many times as necessary until the result is a one-digit answer. That final answer is the check digit appended to the numeric code. The code 1302-6 is valid because the result of the calculation is 6, which matches the given check digit, as shown in Figure 6-30. Figure 6-30 also shows the erroneous code 7198-3. At least one of the five digits in the code is wrong because the calculation result is 5, which does not match the given check digit 3.

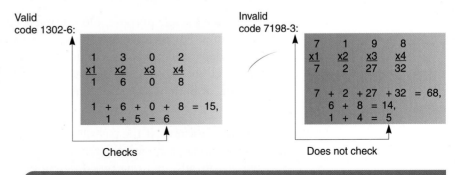

FIGURE 6-30 | The first code is valid and it checks, but in the second code the check digit is invalid.

You could build a useful code by using a combination of two or more coding schemes, but simpler coding schemes usually work better.

Developing a Code

Devising a code with too many features makes it difficult to remember, decipher, and verify. Keep the following suggestions in mind when developing a code:

1. Keep codes concise. Do not create codes that are longer than necessary. For example, if you need a code to identify each of 250 customers, you will not need a six-digit code.

2. Allow for expansion. A coding scheme must allow for reasonable growth in the number of assigned codes. If the company currently has eight warehouses, you should not use a one-digit code for the warehouse number. If three more warehouses are added, the code must be increased to two digits or changed to a character code in order to identify each location. The rule also applies to using a single letter as a character code; you might need more than 26 codes in the future.

3. Keep codes stable. Codes that have to be changed cause major problems when they are implemented and replace the old codes. During the changeover period, you will have to change all the stored occurrences of a particular code and all documents containing the old code, as users switch to the new code. Usually, both the old and new codes are used for an interim period, and special procedures are required to handle the two codes. For example, when area codes change, you can use either area code for a certain time period.

4. Make codes unique. Codes used for identification purposes must be unique to have meaning. If the code HW can indicate hardware or housewares, the code is not very useful.

5. Use **sortable** codes. If products with three-digit codes in the 100s or the 300s are of one type, while products with codes in the 200s are a different type, a simple sort will not group all the products of one type together. In addition, be careful that single-digit character codes will sort properly with double-digit codes — in some cases you must add a leading zero (01, 02, 03, and so on) to ensure that codes sort correctly.

6. Avoid confusing codes. Do not code some part numbers with two letters, a hyphen, and one digit, and others with one letter, a hyphen, and two digits. Avoid allowing both letters and numbers to occupy the same positions within a code because some of those are easily confused. It is easy to confuse the number zero (0) and the uppercase letter O, or the number one (1) with the lowercase letter L (l) or uppercase letter I. For example, the five-character code 5Z081 easily can be misread as 5ZO8I, or 52081, or, even totally incorrectly, as S2OBI.

7. Make codes meaningful. Codes must be easy to remember, useful for users, convenient to use, and easy to encode and interpret. Using SW as a code for the southwest sales region, for example, has far more meaning than the code 14. Using ENG as the code for the English department is easier to interpret and remember than either XQA or 132.

8. Use a code for a single purpose. Do not use a single code to classify two or more unrelated attributes. For example, if you use a single code to identify the combination of an employee's department *and* the employee's insurance plan type, users will have difficulty identifying all the subscribers of a particular plan, or all the workers in a particular department, or both. A separate code for each separate characteristic makes much more sense.

9. Keep codes consistent. If the payroll system already is using two-digit codes for departments, do not create a new, different coding scheme for the personnel system. If those two systems already are using two different coding schemes, you should try to convince the users of the two systems to adopt a single and consistent department-coding scheme.

SOFTWEAR, LIMITED

Systems analyst Rick Williams and programmer/analyst Carla Moore continued to work on a logical model of the payroll system. Meanwhile, the information systems department recently purchased and installed Visible Analyst, a CASE toolkit that supports logical and physical modeling. Rick and Carla traveled to Massachusetts to attend a one-week workshop to learn how to use the package.

After returning from their trip, Rick and Carla decided to create the logical model for the payroll system with Visible Analyst. They felt that the time spent now would pay off in later phases of the project. Rick and Carla used the manual DFDs they created in Chapter 4 to create computerized DFDs using Visible Analyst. Now all related items for the new system are stored in the CASE tool.

Over the next month, Rick and Carla looked at various alternatives and spent their time evaluating the potential solutions. They determined that the best solution was to purchase a payroll package, but the ESIP processing was so unique that none of the available software packages would handle SWL's specific requirements. They concluded that SWL should purchase a payroll package and develop the ESIP system in-house. Jane Rossman and Ann Hon agreed with their recommendation.

The systems analysts completed work on the logical model, alternative evaluations, and cost and time estimates and then prepared the system requirements document for the payroll system. The document was printed and distributed and a management presentation was scheduled at the end of the following week.

At this point, the IT team members were confident that they had done a good job. They had worked closely with SWL users throughout the development process and received user approval on important portions of the document as it was being prepared. They developed visual aids, rehearsed the presentation, and then tried to anticipate questions that management might ask.

Carla gave the management presentation. She recommended that SWL purchase a payroll package sold by Pacific Software Solutions and that ESIP processing be developed in-house to interface with the payroll package.

During the presentation, Carla and Rick answered questions on several points, including the economic analysis they had done. Michael Jeremy, vice president of finance, was especially interested in the method they used to calculate payback analysis, return on investment, and net present value for the new system.

SWL's president, Robert Lansing, arrived for the last part of the presentation. When the presentation ended, he asked the top managers how they felt about the project, and they indicated support for the proposal made by the IT department. The next step was to negotiate a contract with Pacific Software Solutions and for Rick and Carla to begin systems design for the ESIP processing component.

YOUR TURN

Although the presentation was successful, Rick and Carla both feel that the IT department should have a checklist to serve as a suggested model to help IT staff people who must prepare management presentations. They asked you to suggest a list of dos and don'ts for presentations. They also want you to review the DFDs that they prepared using Visible Analyst to see if you have any suggestions for improvement. If you have access to a copier, make a copy of the DFDs shown in Chapter 4, and then write your notes directly on the diagrams. Otherwise, you can present a brief memo listing your comments.

CHAPTER SUMMARY

In this chapter, you studied the evaluation of software alternatives, the preparation and presentation of the system requirements document, and the transition to the systems design phase of the SDLC.

The most important software alternatives are in-house systems, software packages, and customized software packages. Compared with developing an in-house system, an existing commercial software package is an attractive alternative, because a package generally costs less, takes less time to implement, has fewer errors, has a proven track record, requires fewer systems developers, and is upgraded frequently. In-house development might be the best choice when a software package cannot meet system requirements or constraints. A customized software package also might be an appropriate alternative in those situations.

The process of acquiring software involves a series of steps: evaluate the needs, identify all possible solutions, evaluate the feasible solutions, make the purchase, and install the product. In addition to the three main alternatives, you also can consider outsourcing and user applications as possible solutions.

The system requirements document is the end product of the systems analysis phase. The document details all system requirements and constraints, recommends the best solution, and provides cost and time estimates for future development work. The system requirements document is the basis for the management presentation. At this point, the firm might decide to develop an in-house system, modify the current system, purchase or customize a software package, perform additional systems analysis work, or stop all further work.

As you prepared for the transition from the systems analysis to systems activities, you learned that a prototype is a working model of the proposed system that you can use to verify the system requirements with users or as a basis for the new system.

You learned that a set of interactive tools, called a 4GL environment, can help you construct the prototype. A 4GL environment includes screen generators, report writers, application or code generators, and fourth-generation languages — all of which interact with a data dictionary developed with CASE tools. You also learned that systems flowcharts sometimes can represent the physical model of an information system.

You reviewed a set of systems design guidelines and suggestions, including user considerations, data considerations, and processing considerations.

Finally, you learned that a code is a set of letters or numbers used to represent data in a system. By using codes, you can speed up data entry, reduce data storage space, and reduce transmission time. Codes also can be used to reveal or to conceal information. The main types of codes are sequence codes, block sequence codes, classification codes, alphabetic codes (including category codes, abbreviation codes, and mnemonic codes), significant digit codes, derivation codes, cipher codes, action codes, and self-checking codes.

Key Terms

abbreviation codes (6.30)
action codes (6.31)
alphabetic codes (6.30)
application generator (6.21)
application hosting (6.5)
application service provider (ASP) (6.5)
audit trails (6.28)
benchmark (6.13)
block sequence codes (6.30)
build or buy (6.2)
category codes (6.30)
cipher codes (6.31)
code (6.29)
code generator (6.21)
contract personnel firm (6.6)
derivation codes (6.31)
design prototyping (6.19)
essential model (6.17)
evaluation and selection team (6.15)
event driven (6.21)
facilities management (6.6)
form generator (6.22)
fourth-generation environment (6.20)
fourth-generation language (4GL) (6.21)
hardcoded (6.26)
help desk (6.7)
horizontal application (6.2)
in-house software (6.2)
information center (IC) (6.7)
lease agreement (6.14)
logical design (6.17)
maintenance agreement (6.14)
make or buy (6.2)
mnemonic codes (6.30)

mock-up report (6.22)
newsgroups (6.12)
nonprocedural (6.21)
outsourcing (6.6)
parameter (6.27)
physical design (6.18)
procedural (6.21)
prototype (6.18)
report generator (6.22)
report writer (6.22)
request for proposal (RFP) (6.10)
request for quotation (RFQ) (6.11)
screen generator (6.22)
self-checking codes (6.31)
sequence codes (6.30)
service providers (6.6)
significant digit codes (6.31)
software change control (6.40)
software license (6.14)
software package (6.2)
software requirements specification (6.16)
software vendors (6.2)
sortable (6.32)
system prototyping (6.19)
system requirements document (6.16)
systems design (6.26)
systems flowchart (6.24)
systems management (6.6)
throwaway prototyping (6.19)
Usenet (6.12)
user applications (6.7)
user interface (6.7)
value-added reseller (VAR) (6.2)
vertical application (6.2)

Chapter Review

1. Explain the difference between horizontal application software and vertical application software.

2. What is the most common reason for a company to choose to develop its own information system? Give two other reasons why a company might choose the in-house approach.

3. Discuss four advantages of buying a software package.

4. What is an RFP, and how does it differ from an RFQ?

5. What is the purpose of a benchmark test?

6. Explain software licenses, lease agreements, and maintenance agreements.

7. What decisions might management reach at the end of the systems analysis phase, and what would be the next step in each case?

8. What is a prototype, and how do systems developers use prototyping?

9. What is a 4GL environment?

10. What is a code? List and describe each of the common coding schemes.

Discussion Topics

1. Suppose you tried to explain the concept of throwaway prototyping to a manager, and she responded by asking, "So, is the prototyping a waste of time and money?" How would you reply?

2. For many years, IT professionals said that COBOL was outdated. Yet many firms still have a large investment in older COBOL programs, and they spent substantial amounts of money to make older programs Y2K compliant. What are the pros and cons of continuing to operate COBOL-based software in the post-Y2K era? To obtain more information, do some research on the Internet, or locate a company that still uses COBOL.

3. Select a specific type of vertical application software to investigate. Visit local computer stores and use the Internet to determine what software packages are available. Describe the common features of those packages and the features that distinguish one product from another.

4. Select a specific type of horizontal application software to investigate. Visit local computer stores and use the Internet to determine what software packages are available. Describe the common features of those packages and the features that distinguish one product from another.

Apply Your Knowledge

1 Top Sail Realty

Situation:

Top Sail Realty is one of the largest time-sharing and rental brokers for vacation cottages along the North Carolina coast. After 10 successful years of matching up owners and renters, Top Sail decided to acquire a computerized reservation and booking system. Top Sail's owner read an article about software packages, and she asked you, as an IT consultant, for your advice.

1. Do you consider the reservations system a horizontal or a vertical application? Give reasons for your answer.

2. When you evaluate software packages, what steps will you follow?

3. If you identify one or more software packages that look promising, what will you do next?

4. What other issues can arise during the purchase and implementation of a package system?

2 One Way Movers, Inc.

Situation:

As IT manager at One Way, you scheduled a management presentation next week. You prepared and distributed a systems requirement document, and you anticipate some intense questioning at the meeting.

1. When planning your presentation, what are some techniques you will use?

2. Based on the suggestions in the Systems Analyst's Toolkit, what visual aids can you use during your presentation?

3. In deciding on your proposal, what options does management have?

4. If management decides to purchase or customize a software package, what steps will you take?

3 Tangible Investments Corporation

Situation:

Tangible Investments Corporation needs a new customer billing system. As project leader, you decided to create a prototype that users can evaluate before the final design is implemented. You plan to use a traditional structured analysis methodology. To prepare for your meeting with top management tomorrow, you need to review the following topics.

1. Explain the main purpose of prototyping.

2. Explain why prototypes might or might not evolve into the final version of the system.

3. Describe the tools typically used in developing prototypes.

4. List at least three advantages and three disadvantages of prototyping.

4 Western Wear Outfitters

Situation:

Western Wear is a mail-order firm that offers an extensive selection of casual and recreational clothing for men and women. Western Wear launched a new Web site, and the company decided to develop a new set of product codes. Currently, 650 different products exist, with the possibility of adding more in the future. Many products come in various sizes, styles, and colors. The marketing manager asked you to develop an individualized product code that can identify a specific item and its characteristics. Your initial reaction is that it can be done, but the code might be fairly complex. Back in your office, you review the text material on codes and give the matter some thought.

1. Design a code scheme that will meet the marketing manager's stated requirements.

2. Write a brief memo to the marketing manager suggesting at least one alternative to the code she proposed, and state your reasons.

3. Suggest a code scheme that will identify each Western Wear customer.

4. Suggest a code scheme that will identify each specific order.

Chapter Assignments

1. The text mentions several firms and organizations that offer IT benchmarking. Locate another benchmarking firm on the Internet, and write up a description of the services it offers.

2. Go to Part 2 of the Systems Analyst's Toolkit and review the concept of net present value (NPV). Determine the NPV for the following: An information system will cost $95,000 to implement over a one-year period and will produce no savings during that year. When the system goes online, the company will save $30,000 during the first year of operation. For the next four years, the savings will be $20,000 per year. Assuming a 12 percent discount rate, what is the NPV of the system?

3. Visit the IT department at your school or at a local company and determine whether the information systems were developed in-house or purchased as software packages. If packages were acquired, determine what customizing was done, if any. Write a brief memo describing the results of your visit.

4. Think of all the places where codes are used, including catalogs, stores, and other businesses. Perform research to identify as many codes as possible (at least 10). Write up a list of the coding scheme and explain how each one operates.

CASE STUDIES

Case Studies offer an opportunity for you to practice specific skills and knowledge learned in the chapter and provide practical experience for you as a systems analyst. Two of the case studies (New Century Health Clinic and Ridgeway Company) are continuing case studies that appear in each chapter. Additionally, one continuing case study (SCR Associates) utilizes the Internet to practice some of the topics covered in this chapter.

NEW CENTURY HEALTH CLINIC

Based on your earlier recommendations, New Century decided to continue the systems development process for a new information system that would improve operations, decrease costs, and provide better service to patients.

Now, at the end of the systems analysis phase, you are ready to prepare a system requirements document and give a presentation to the New Century associates. Many of the proposed system's advantages were described during the fact-finding process. Those include smoother operation, better efficiency, and more user-friendly procedures for patients and New Century staff.

You also must examine tangible costs and benefits to determine the economic feasibility of several alternatives. If New Century decides to go ahead with the development process, the main options are to develop the system in-house or purchase a vertical package and configure it to meet New Century's needs. You have studied those choices and put together some preliminary figures.

You know that New Century's current workload requires three hours of office staff overtime per week at a base rate of $8.50 per hour. In addition, based on current projections, New Century will need to add another full-time clerical position in about six months. Neither the overtime nor the additional job will be needed if New Century implements the new system. The current manual system also causes an average of three errors per day, and each error takes about 20 minutes to correct. The new system should eliminate those errors.

Based on your research, you estimate by working full-time you could complete the project in about 12 weeks. Your consulting rate, which New Century agreed to, is $30 per hour. If you design the new system as a database application, you can expect to spend about $2,500 for a networked commercial package. After the system is operational and the staff is trained, you hope that New Century can handle routine maintenance tasks without your assistance.

As an alternative to in-house development, a vertical software package is available for about $9,000. The vendor offers a lease-purchase package of $3,000 down, followed by two annual installments of $3,000 each. If New Century buys the package, it would take you about four weeks to install, configure, and test it, working full-time. The vendor provides free support during the first year of operation, but then New Century must sign a technical support agreement at an annual cost of $500. Although the package contains many of the features that New Century wants, most of the reports are predesigned and it would be difficult to modify their layouts.

No matter which approach is selected, New Century probably will need you to provide about 10 hours of initial training and support each week for the first three months of operation. After the new system is operational, it will need routine maintenance, file backups, and updating. Those tasks will require about four hours per week and can be performed by a clinic staff member. In both cases, the necessary hardware and network installation will cost about $5,000. In your view, the useful life of the system will be about five years, including the year in which the system becomes operational.

Assignments

You scheduled a presentation to New Century in one week, and must submit a system requirements document during the presentation. Prepare both the written documentation and the presentation. (To give a successful presentation, you will need to learn the skills described in the Systems Analyst's Toolkit.) Your oral and written presentation must include the following:

1. Provide an overview of the proposed system, including costs and benefits, with an explanation of the various cost-and-benefit types and categories.

2. Develop an economic feasibility analysis, using payback analysis, ROI, and present value (assume a discount rate of 10 percent).

3. Prepare a data and process model, including a context diagram and diagram 0.

4. Prepare an object model, including use case diagrams for the major business functions.

5. Provide a brief explanation of the various alternatives that should be investigated if development continues, including in-house development and any other possible strategies.

You may wish to include other material to help your audience understand the new system and make a decision on the next step.

Presentation Rules

The following presentation rules should be considered:
- Use suitable visual aids.
- Use presentation software, if you wish.
- Distribute handouts before, during, or after the presentation.
- Follow the guidelines in the Systems Analyst's Toolkit.
- Keep your presentation length to 30 minutes, including 5 minutes for questions.

Rules for the System Requirements Document

Consider the following rules while preparing the system requirements document:

- Follow the guidelines in the Systems Analyst's Toolkit.
- Pay special attention to the reports section and the description of the various sections of the systems analysis report.
- Include any charts, graphs, or other helpful visual information in the document.
- Spell check and carefully proofread everything you submit.

RIDGEWAY COMPANY

Thomas McGee asked you to give a presentation on the new membership billing system to Ridgeway's management team. Before you complete the assignments, review the Ridgeway Company requirements that were described in Chapters 2 and 3.

Assignments

1. Prepare a short overview of the proposed system, including possible costs and benefits.

2. Write a brief explanation of the various alternatives that should be investigated if development continues, including in-house development and any other possible strategies.

3. Based on the suggestions in the Systems Analyst's Toolkit, what visual aids can you use during your presentation?

4. Consider the nature of Ridgeway's operations, including its business functions, customers, employees, and locations. Suggest at least three code schemes that Ridgeway could implement during the systems design phase of the SDLC. Explain the reasons for your suggestions.

CUTTING EDGE

Part 3 of the Systems Analyst's Toolkit discusses **software change control**, which is the process of managing and controlling changes after management approves the system requirements document. You should review the material about this topic now, before completing the Cutting Edge case.

Cutting Edge is a company that develops and sells accounting software tailored to specific businesses and industries. Product manager Michelle Kellogg is leading a development team working on a specialized package for homebuilders. The systems analysis phase was completed on March 6. The package is scheduled for release on August 1.

On April 1, Michelle received a request from Cutting Edge's CEO for a new feature to be added to the package. She asked Michelle to analyze the change and determine its impact on the project.

Michelle reviewed the results at a meeting on April 15. Adding the new feature to the package now increases the development cost by $28,000 and delays the release date by one month. Michelle also evaluated a second alternative: develop the package without the requested change and add the feature in a follow-up release, which requires two additional months to complete and costs $66,000.

Assignments

1. Because the project is in the systems design phase and no programming has been started, why would incorporating the requested change add one month and $28,000 to the project?

2. If the change were delayed until after the initial release of the package, why would it require two additional months and $66,000 more to implement a new version with the desired feature?

3. What are the advantages and disadvantages of each alternative?

4. Suppose you are Michelle and you must recommend action on the change request. What factors would you consider, and what would you recommend?

SCR ASSOCIATES

SCR Associates is an information technology consulting firm that offers IT solutions and training for small- and medium-sized companies. SCR's slogan is "We Know IT!"

Background

As a newly hired systems analyst, you will handle assignments, work on various SCR projects, and apply the skills you learned in the text. SCR needs an information system to manage training operations at the new SCR training center. The new system will be called TIMS (Training Information Management System).

The SCR case is available as an interactive, Web-based case study. You can log on to the Shelly Cashman Series site at www.scsite.com/sad4e/scr for instructions and assignments. If you prefer to complete the case study without using the Internet then you must download the data disk. See the inside back cover for instructions for downloading the data disk or see your instructor for more information on accessing the files required for this book.

Situation

In Part 6 of the SCR case, you evaluate software alternatives and development strategies for the new TIMS system; also, you prepare for the transition from systems analysis to systems design.

Before You Begin ...

1. Review the December 3 message from Jesse Baker regarding the object model presentation. Open the Document 6-1 from the data disk.

2. Review the December 4 message from Jesse Baker regarding evaluation of alternatives, cost-benefit analysis, RAD, and prototyping. Open the Document 6-2 from the data disk.

3. Review the December 5 message from Jesse Baker regarding a presentation. Open the Document 6-3 from the data disk.

4. Review the sample of questionnaire results. Open the Document 6-4 from the data disk.

5. Read the material on RAD in Part 4 of the Systems Analyst's Toolkit.

6. Read the material on cost-benefit analysis in Part 2 of the Systems Analyst's Toolkit.

7. Review the November 9 summary of cost-benefit data. Open the Document 6-5 from the data disk.

Assignments

1. Research the Internet to locate vertical software packages for training operations. Report your results in a memo.

2. Jesse Baker wants you to analyze in-house development of TIMS. Use the summary of questionnaire results (Document 6-3 on the data disk) and the information in the cost-benefit summary (Document 6-4 on the data disk) to create a detailed three-year cost-benefit worksheet. Then use the worksheet data to calculate payback, ROI, and NPV for the TIMS project. Summarize your findings in a brief memo to Jesse Baker.

3. Would you recommend a RAD approach for completing the development of the TIMS system? Write a memo that briefly discusses the pros and cons of RAD, together with your recommendation and reasons.

4. Develop a plan for prototyping during the design phase of TIMS.

ON THE WEB

The SCR case is available as an interactive, Web-based case study. You can log on to the Shelly Cashman Series site at www.scsite.com/sad4e/scr for instructions and assignments.

Systems Planning **PHASE 1**

Systems Analysis **PHASE 2**

Systems Design **PHASE 3**

Systems Implementation **PHASE 4**

Systems Operation & Support **PHASE 5**

User Interface, Input, and Output Design

PHASE 3: SYSTEMS DESIGN

Systems design is the third phase in the systems development life cycle. In the previous phase, systems analysis, you developed a logical model of the system and considered various software strategies and implementation alternatives. Now you are ready to begin the physical design of the system that will meet the specifications described in the system requirements document

This is the first of three chapters in the systems design phase of the SDLC. During systems design, you construct a physical model of the information system based on the logical model you developed in the systems analysis phase. In this chapter, you will focus on how to design the user interfaces, input procedures, and output required to support business requirements.

INTRODUCTION

User interface, input, and output design begins the systems design phase of the SDLC. This chapter begins with user interface design concepts, including functions, layout, and usability. The chapter then covers input procedures, controls, and formats. The chapter concludes with a discussion of output design, including printed reports and other system outputs.

After the logical model is constructed, systems analysts turn their attention to the physical design. A key design element is the **user interface**, which describes how users interact with the system. When developing older, processing-centered systems, analysts typically designed all the printed and screen output first, then worked on the inputs necessary to produce the results. Often, the user interface mainly consisted of **process-control** screens that allowed the user to send commands to the system. That approach worked well with traditional systems that transformed input data into specific output information.

OBJECTIVES

When you finish this chapter, you will be able to:

- Explain the concept of user interface design and human-computer interaction

- Define user-centered interface design principles

- Describe guidelines for user interface design

- Describe user interface controls

- Explain input design concepts, techniques, and methods

- Describe guidelines for data entry screen design and validation checks for reducing input errors

- Design effective source documents and input controls

- Discuss output design issues and various types of output

- Design various types of printed reports, and suggest necessary output control and security

ON THE WEB

or an overview of User
nterface Design visit
csite.com/sad4e/more.htm,
lick Systems Analysis and
esign Chapter 7 and then
lick the User Interface
esign link.

ww.scsite.com

As information management evolved from centralized data processing to dynamic, enterprise-wide systems, the primary focus also shifted — from the IT department to the users themselves. The IT group became an enabler of information technology, rather than a supplier of information. Today, the main focus is on users within and outside the company, how they communicate with the information system, and how the system supports the firm's business operations. Figure 7-1 shows a model of a traditional, processing-centered information system, while Figure 7-2 shows a modern, user-centered system.

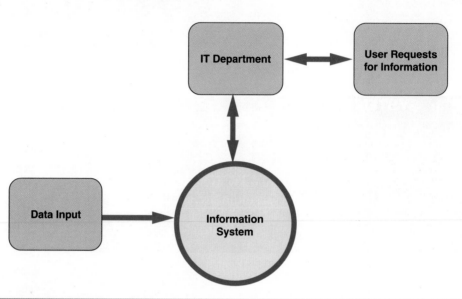

FIGURE 7-1   Model of a traditional, processing-centered information system.

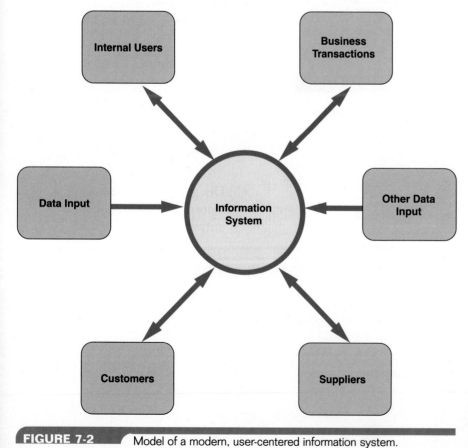

FIGURE 7-2   Model of a modern, user-centered information system.

USER INTERFACE DESIGN

In a **user-centered** system, the distinction blurs between input, output, and the interface itself. Most users work with a varied mix of input, screen output, and data queries as they perform their day-to-day job functions. Because all those tasks require interaction with the computer system, the user interface is a logical starting point in the systems design phase. Many firms, including IBM, offer consulting services and software solutions to help companies develop successful user interfaces, as shown in Figure 7-3.

User interface design requires an understanding of human-computer interaction and user-centered design principles, discussed in the next section. Input and output design topics are covered later in this chapter.

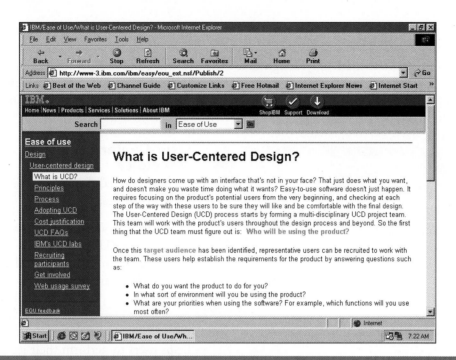

FIGURE 7-3 IBM offers consulting services and software solutions to help companies develop successful user interfaces.

Human-Computer Interaction

A user interface is based on basic principles of human-computer interaction. **Human-computer interaction (HCI)** describes the relationship between computers and people who use them to perform business-related tasks, as shown in Figure 7-4. HCI concepts apply to everything from a PC desktop to the main menu for a global network. In its broadest sense, a user interface includes all the communications and instructions necessary to enter input to the system, and to obtain output in the form of screen displays or printed reports.

FIGURE 7-4 A user interface is based on basic principles of human-computer interaction, which describes the relationship between computers and people who use them to perform business-related tasks.

As a systems analyst, you will design user interfaces for in-house developed software and customize interfaces for various commercial packages and user productivity applications. Your main objective is to create a user-friendly design that is easy to learn and use. As IBM points out on its Web site shown in Figure 7-5, "In a complex world, easy hits the spot." IBM notes that it pays to make ease of use a priority right from the start, because each dollar spent up front saves $10 later on.

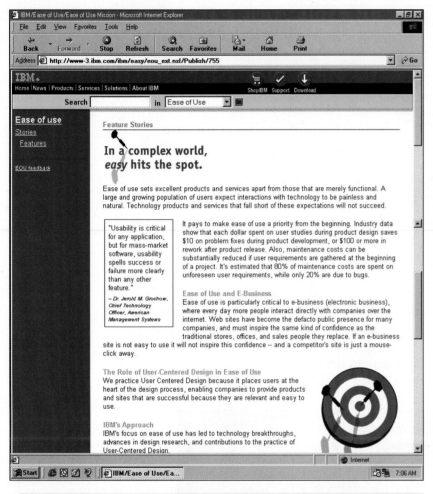

FIGURE 7-5   As IBM points out, ease of use sets excellent products apart from those that are merely functional.

User-Centered Design Principles

User-centered design involves eight basic principles:

UNDERSTAND THE UNDERLYING BUSINESS FUNCTIONS   The interface designer must understand the underlying business functions and how the system supports individual, departmental, and enterprise goals. The overall objective is to design an interface that helps users to perform their jobs. A good starting point might be to analyze a functional decomposition diagram (FDD). As you learned in Chapter 3, an FDD is a graphical representation of business functions that starts with major functions, then breaks them down into several levels of detail. An FDD can provide a checklist of user tasks that you must include in the interface design.

MAXIMIZE GRAPHICAL EFFECTIVENESS   Studies show that people learn better visually. The immense popularity of Microsoft Windows is largely the result of a graphical user interface that is easy to learn and use. A **graphical user interface** (GUI) uses graphical objects and techniques that allow users to communicate with the system. Now that GUIs have become universal in application packages, users expect in-house software also to have GUIs. A well-designed GUI can help users learn a new system rapidly, and work with the system effectively.

PROFILE THE SYSTEM'S USERS   A systems analyst should understand user experience, knowledge, and skill levels. If a wide range of capability exists, the interface should be flexible enough to accommodate novices as well as experienced users.

THINK LIKE A USER   To develop an interface driven by user requirements, the designer must learn to think like a user and see the system through a user's eyes.

USE PROTOTYPING   From a user's viewpoint, the interface is the most critical part of the system design because it is where he or she interacts with the system — perhaps for many hours each day. It is essential to construct models, mock-ups, and prototypes for user approval. The interface designer should obtain as much feedback as possible, as early as possible. You can present screen mock-ups to users as a succession of **storyboards**, which are sketches that show the general screen layout and design. Users must test all aspects of the interface design and provide feedback to the designers.

DESIGN A COMPREHENSIVE INTERFACE

The user interface should include all tasks, commands, and communications between users and the information system. The screen shown in Figure 7-6 shows the main options for a student registration system at a school. In a GUI environment, a user can display and work with multiple windows on a single screen. The windows can contain processing options, data options, or both. To make the interface even more powerful, the user can have several programs open at once and data can be transferred between them. Because GUIs are used for data entry as well as for process control, they must follow the guidelines for good data entry screen design discussed later in this chapter.

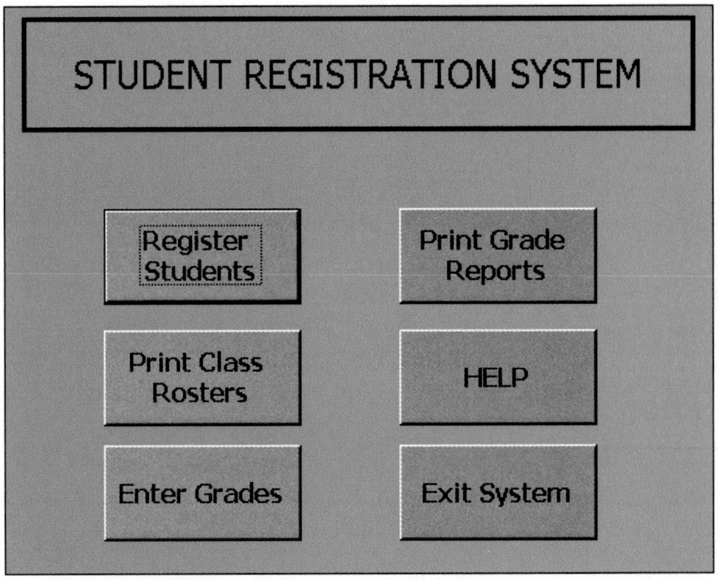

CONTINUE THE FEEDBACK PROCESS

Even after the system is operational, it is important to monitor system usage and solicit user suggestions. You can determine if system features are being used as intended by observing and surveying users. Sometimes, full-scale operations highlight problems that were not apparent when the prototype was tested. Based on user feedback, Help screens might need revision and design changes to allow the system to reach its full potential.

DOCUMENT THE INTERFACE DESIGN You should document all screen designs for later use by programmers. If you are using a CASE tool or screen generator, number the screen designs and save them in a hierarchy similar to a menu tree. User-approved sketches and storyboards also can be used to document the user interface.

By applying basic user-centered design principles, a systems analyst can plan, design, and deliver a successful user interface.

User Interface Design Guidelines

Good user interface design is based on a combination of ergonomics, aesthetics, and interface technology. **Ergonomics** describes how people work, learn, and interact with computers; **aesthetics** focuses on how an interface can be made attractive and easy to use; and **interface technology** provides the operational structure required to carry out the design objectives.

Systems analysts should consider various guidelines when designing a user interface, including the following topics:

FOCUS ON BASIC OBJECTIVES

- Facilitate the system design objectives, rather than calling attention to the interface.
- Create a design that is easy to learn and remember.
- Design the interface to improve user efficiency and productivity.
- Write commands, actions, and system responses that are consistent and predictable.
- Minimize data entry problems.
- Correct errors easily.
- Create a logical and attractive layout.

STUDENT REGISTRATION SYSTEM

Register Students | Print Grade Reports
Print Class Rosters | HELP
Enter Grades | Exit System

FIGURE 7-6 An example of an initial screen for a student registration system at a school.

BUILD AN INTERFACE THAT IS EASY TO LEARN AND USE

- Label clearly all controls, buttons, and icons.
- Select only those images that users can understand easily, if you use images to identify icons or controls. For example, Figure 7-7 shows three control buttons, but only the printer image has an obvious meaning.
- Provide on-screen instructions that are logical, concise, and clear. In Figure 7-8, the top message is hard to understand, but the bottom message is unmistakable.
- Show all commands in a list of menu items, but dim any commands that are not currently available.
- Make it easy to return to one or more levels in the menu structure.

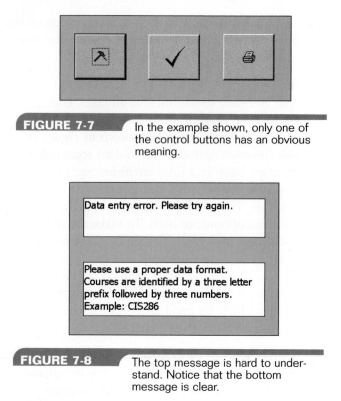

FIGURE 7-7 In the example shown, only one of the control buttons has an obvious meaning.

Data entry error. Please try again.

Please use a proper data format. Courses are identified by a three letter prefix followed by three numbers. Example: CIS286

FIGURE 7-8 The top message is hard to understand. Notice that the bottom message is clear.

PROVIDE FEATURES THAT PROMOTE EFFICIENCY

- Organize tasks, commands, and functions in groups that resemble actual business operations. You should group functions and submenu items in a multilevel menu hierarchy, or tree, that is logical and reflects how users typically perform the tasks. Figure 7-9 shows an example of a menu hierarchy for an order tracking system.
- Create alphabetical menu lists or place the selections used frequently at the top of the menu list. No universally accepted approach to menu item placement exists. The best strategy is to design a prototype and obtain feedback from users. Some applications, such as Microsoft Word 2000, even allow menus to show recently used commands first. Some users might accept that design, but others might find it distracting.

Customer Order Tracking System

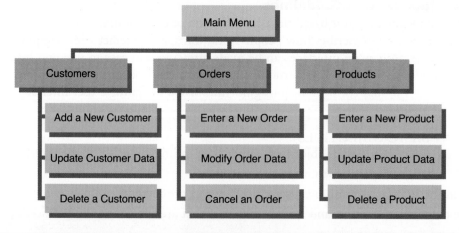

FIGURE 7-9 Tasks, commands, and functions should be organized in logical groups, such as this menu hierarchy for a customer order tracking system.

- Provide shortcuts so experienced users can avoid multiple menu levels. You can create shortcuts using hotkeys that allow a user to press the ALT key + the underlined letter of a command.

- Use default values if the majority of values in a field are the same. For example, if 90 percent of the firm's customers live in Albuquerque, use *Albuquerque* as the default value in the City field.

- Use a duplicate value function that enables users to insert into a field in the new record the value from the same field in the previous record.

- Provide a fast-find feature that displays a list of possible values as soon as users enter the first few letters.

- Use a natural language feature that allows users to type commands or requests in normal English phrases. For example, natural language queries can be used with a Help system that lets you ask a question and receive a response, as shown in the Microsoft PowerPoint example in Figure 7-10. Most users like natural language features because they do not have to memorize a series of complex commands and syntax. Natural language technology still is evolving and is being used in many Internet browsers and search engines. Figure 7-11 shows a Web site for PLS (Personal Librarian Software), a leading supplier of information retrieval software that supports natural language queries. PLS is owned by America Online (AOL). A Help system using PLS allows users to search for topics using natural language queries.

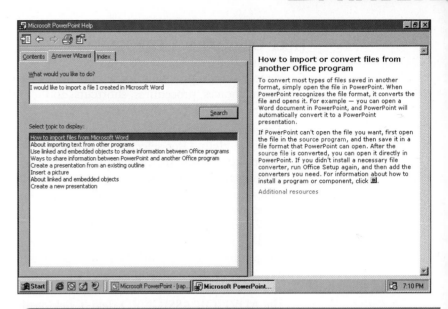

FIGURE 7-10 The Microsoft PowerPoint Help system allows users to type commands or requests in normal English phrases.

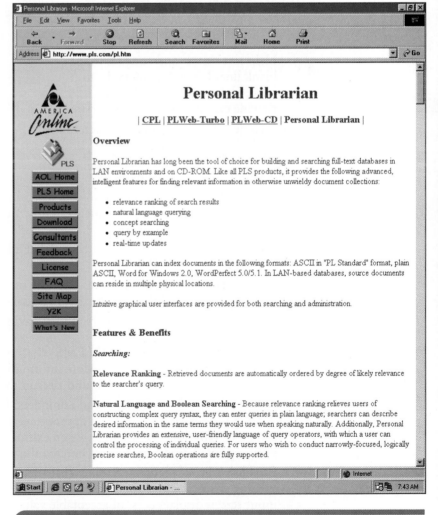

FIGURE 7-11 PLS is a leading supplier of information retrieval software, such as Personal Librarian, that supports natural language queries.

MAKE IT EASY FOR USERS TO OBTAIN HELP OR CORRECT ERRORS

- Ensure that Help is always available. Help screens should provide information about menu choices, procedures, shortcuts, and errors.

- Provide user-selected Help and context-sensitive Help. **User-selected** Help displays information when the user requests it. By making appropriate choices through the menus and submenus, the user eventually reaches a screen with the desired information. Figure 7-12 shows the main Help screen for the student registration system. **Context-sensitive** Help offers assistance for the task in progress. Figure 7-13 shows a Help screen that displays if a user requests Help while entering data into the ADVISOR ASSIGNED field. Clicking the Close button returns the user to the current task.

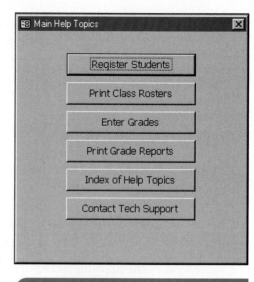

FIGURE 7-12 The main Help screen for the student registration system.

- Provide a direct route for users to return to the point from where Help was requested. Title every Help screen to identify the topic, and keep Help text simple and concise. Insert blank lines between paragraphs to make Help easier to read, and provide examples where appropriate.

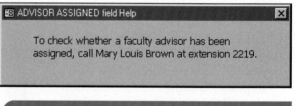

FIGURE 7-13 A context-sensitive Help screen that displays if a user requests help while entering data into the ADVISOR ASSIGNED field. Clicking the Close button returns the user to the task.

- Include contact information, such as a telephone extension or e-mail address if a department or Help desk is responsible for assisting users.

- Require user confirmation before data deletion (*Are you sure?*) and provide a method of recovering data that is deleted inadvertently. Build in safeguards that prevent critical data from being changed or erased.

- Provide an Undo key or a menu choice that allows the user to eradicate the results of the most recent command or action.

- Highlight the erroneous part and allow the user to make the correction without retyping the entire command if an error exists in a user-entered command.

- Use hypertext links to assist users as they navigate through Help topics.

MINIMIZE INPUT DATA PROBLEMS

- Provide data validation checks. More information on data validation techniques is provided in the section on input design found later in this chapter.

- Display event-driven messages and reminders. Just as context-sensitive Help is important to users, it is desirable to display an appropriate message when it is time for the user to perform a certain task. For example, when exiting the system, a message might ask users if they want a printed report of the data entered during the recent session.

- Establish a list of predefined values that users can click to select. Predefined values prevent spelling errors, avoid inappropriate data in a field, and make the user's job easier — the input screen displays a list of acceptable values and the user simply points and clicks the choice.

- Build in rules that enforce data integrity. For example, if the user tries to enter an order for a new customer, the customer must be added before the system will accept the order data.

- Use **input masks**, which are templates or patterns that make it easier for users to enter data. Microsoft Access 2000 provides standard input masks for fields such as dates, telephone numbers, ZIP codes, and Social Security numbers. In addition, you can create custom input masks for any type of data, as shown in Figure 7-14. Notice that the mask can manipulate the input data and apply a specific format. For example, if a user enters text in lowercase, the input mask >*LLLLLLLL* will convert the data to capital letters.

PROVIDE FEEDBACK TO USERS

- Display messages at a logical place on the screen, and be consistent.

- Alert users to lengthy processing times or delays. Give users an on-screen progress report, especially if the delay is lengthy.

- Allow messages to remain on the screen long enough for users to read them. In some cases, the screen should display messages until the user takes some action.

- Let the user know whether the task or operation was successful or not. For example, use messages such as *Update completed, All records have been posted,* or *ID Number not found.*

- Provide a text explanation if you use an icon or image on a control button for the user to identify the control button when moving the insertion point over the icon or image.

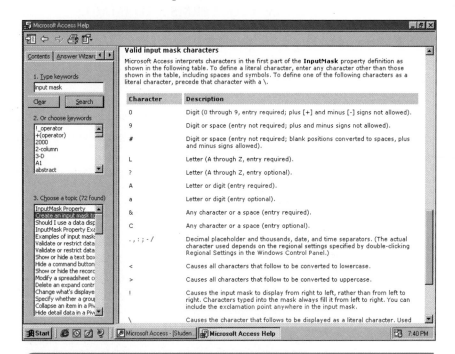

FIGURE 7-14 You can create custom input masks for any type of data or field values in this example using Microsoft Access 2000.

- Use messages that are specific, understandable, and professional. Avoid messages that are cute, cryptic, or vague, such as: *ERROR!, Unacceptable value,* or *Error DE4-16.* Better examples are: *Enter a number between 1 and 5; Customer number must be numeric - please reenter;* or *Call the Accounting Department, Ext. 239 for assistance.*

CREATE AN ATTRACTIVE LAYOUT AND DESIGN

- Use appropriate colors to highlight different areas of the screen; avoid gaudy and bright colors.

- Use special effects sparingly. For example, animation and sound might make screens interesting, but special effects can be distracting and you should use them carefully.

- Use hyperlinks that allow users to jump to related topics.

- Group related objects and information. Visualize the screen the way a user will see it, and simulate the tasks that the user will perform.

- Screen density is important. Keep screen displays uncluttered, with enough white space to create an attractive, readable design.

- Display titles, messages, and instructions in a consistent manner and in the same general locations on all screens.

- Use consistent terminology. For example, do not use the terms *delete, cancel,* and *erase* to indicate the same action. Similarly, the same sound should always signal the same event.

- Ensure that commands will always have the same effect. For example, if the *BACK* control button returns a user to the prior screen, the *BACK* command should always perform that function throughout the application.
- Ensure that similar mouse actions will produce the same results throughout the application. The results of pointing, clicking, and double-clicking should be consistent and predictable.
- Require the user to confirm data entry by pressing the ENTER key or TAB key at the end of a fill-in field, even if the data does not completely fill the field.

USE FAMILIAR TERMS AND IMAGES

- Remember that users are accustomed to a pattern of *red = stop*, *yellow = caution*, and *green = go*. Stick to that pattern and use it when appropriate to reinforce on-screen instructions.
- Provide a keystroke alternative for each menu command, with easy-to-remember letters, such as <u>F</u>ile, <u>E</u>xit, and <u>H</u>elp.
- Use familiar commands if possible, such as *Cut, Copy,* and *Paste.*
- Provide a Windows look and feel in your interface design if users are familiar with Windows-based applications.
- Avoid complex terms and technical jargon; instead, use select terms that come from everyday business processes and the vocabulary of a typical user.

User Interface Controls

The designer can include many control features, such as menu bars, toolbars, dialog boxes, text boxes, toggle buttons, list boxes, scroll bars, drop-down list boxes, option buttons, check boxes, command buttons, spin bars, and calendars among others. Figure 7-15 shows a data entry screen for the student registration system. The screen design uses several features that are described in the following section.

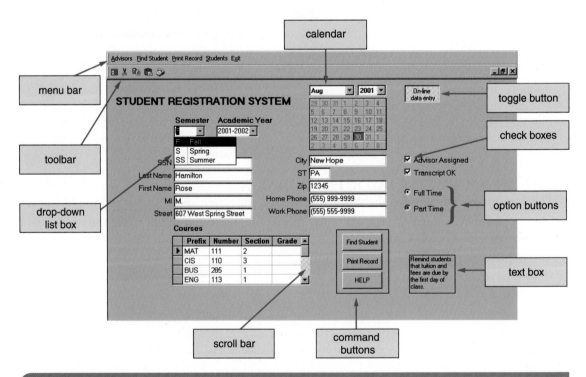

FIGURE 7-15 A data entry screen for the student registration system. This screen uses several design features that are described in the text.

The main menu options display at the top of the screen on a **menu bar**. Some software packages allow you to create customized menu bars and toolbars. You can add a shortcut feature that lets a user select a menu command either by clicking the desired choice or by pressing the ALT key and the underlined letter.

A **toolbar** contains icons or buttons that represent shortcuts for executing common commands. The commands might be navigation shortcuts or can trigger other actions. For example, users can press the telephone dialer button to autodial the telephone number in a selected field. When a user clicks the Find Student command button in Figure 7-15, a dialog box opens with instructions, as shown in Figure 7-16. A **dialog box** allows a user to enter information about a task that the system will perform. A **text box** can display messages or provide a place for a user to enter data. A **toggle button** is used to represent on or off status — clicking the toggle button switches to the other status. A **list box** displays a list of choices that the user can select. If the list does not fit in the box, a **scroll bar** allows the user to move through the available choices. A **drop-down list box** displays the current selection; when the user clicks the arrow, a list of the available choices displays. **Option buttons**, or **radio buttons**, represent groups of options. The user can select only one option at a time; selected options contain a black dot. A **check box** is used to select one or more choices from a group. Selected options are represented by a check mark or an X. **Command buttons** initiate an action such as printing a form or requesting Help. A **spin bar** allows a user to flip through various choices that appear in a window. A **calendar control** allows the user to select a date that the system will display and store as a field value.

Screen design requires a sense of aesthetics as well as technical skills. You should design screens that are attractive, easy to use, and workable. You also should obtain user feedback early and often as the design process continues. The opening screen is especially important because it introduces the application and allows users to view the main options. When designing an opening screen, you can use a main form that functions as a switchboard. A **switchboard** uses command buttons that enable users to navigate the system and select from groups of related tasks. Figure 7-17 shows the switchboard and a data entry screen for a project management system. Notice the drop-down list box that allows users to enter a status code simply by clicking a selection.

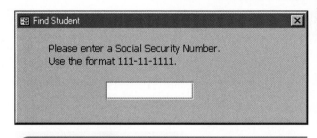

FIGURE 7-16 When a user clicks the Find Student command button, a dialog box displays with instructions.

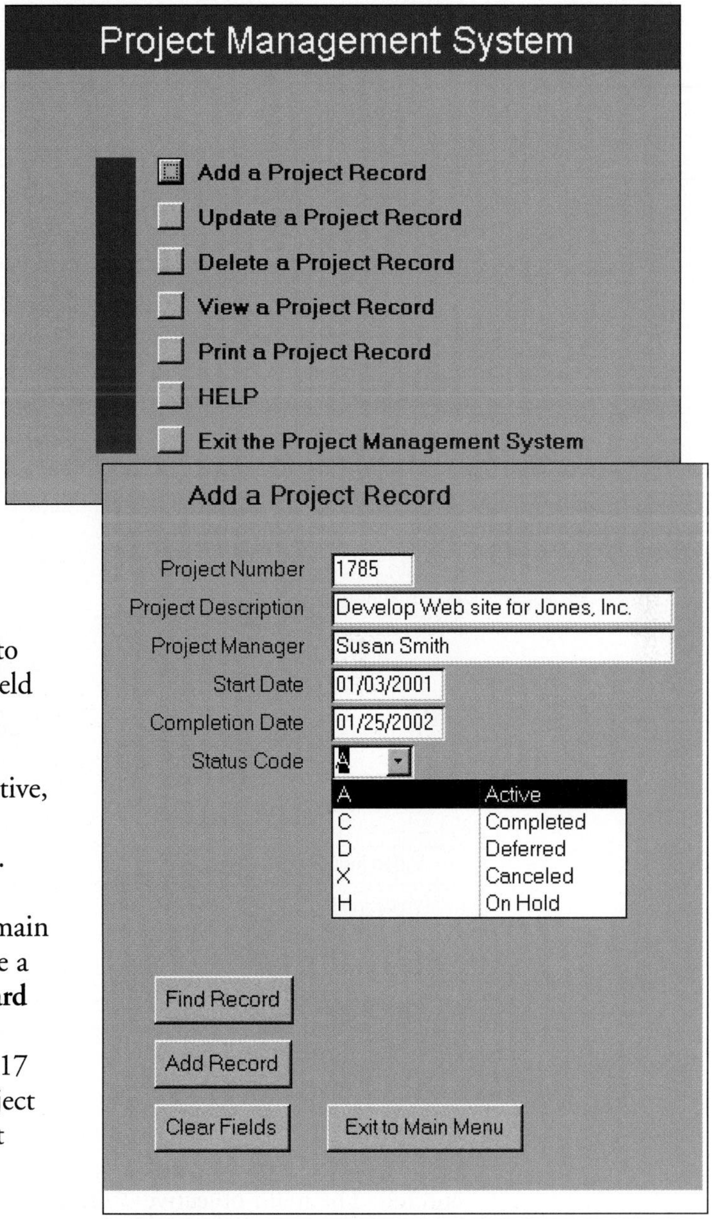

FIGURE 7-17 An example of a switchboard and a data entry form for a project management system.

N THE WEB

or more information
out Input Design visit
-site.com/sad4e/more.htm,
ck Systems Analysis and
esign Chapter 7 and then
ck the Input Design link.

w.scsite.com

INPUT DESIGN

Input technology has changed dramatically in recent years. Today, many input devices and techniques are available, as shown in Figure 7-18. Businesses use the technology to speed up the input process, reduce costs, and capture data in new forms, such as the digital signature shown in Figure 7-19.

Input Device	Description
Biological feedback device	Device that creates a digital image of biological data such as fingerprints or retina patterns.
Data collection device	Fixed or portable devices that can read data on-site; fixed devices include ATMs and warehouse inventory control points; portable devices include terminals used by package delivery drivers, some of which can capture and store a signature digitally.
Digital camera	Device that records photographs in digital form rather than using traditional film; the resulting data file can be stored, displayed, or manipulated by the computer.
Electronic whiteboard	Electronic version of standard whiteboard that uses scanners to record and store text or graphics that are written or drawn on the board.
Graphic input device	Includes light pens, digitizers, and graphics tablets that allow drawings to be translated into digital form that can be processed by a computer.
Handheld computer pen	Electronic device, also called a stylus, that allows users to form characters on the screen of a handheld computer. Handwriting recognition software translated the characters into computer-readable input.
Internet workstation	Enables the user to provide input to Web-based intranet or Internet recipients; can be integrated with information system output or personal computer applications.
Keyboard	Most common input device.
MICR (magnetic ink character recognition)	Technology used primarily in the banking industry to read magnetic ink characters printed on checks.
Mouse	Pointing device that allows the user to move the insertion point to a specific location on the screen and select options.
Scanner/optical recognition	Various devices that read printed bar codes, characters, or images.
Telephone	Technology that allows users to press telephone buttons or speak selected words to choose options in a system, such as electronic funds transfer, shop-at-home purchases, or registration for college courses.
Terminal	Device that might be dumb (screen and keyboard only) or intelligent (screen, keyboard, independent processing).
Touch screen	Sensors that allow users to interface with the computer and select options by touching specific locations on the screen.
Video input	Video camera input, in digital form, that can be stored and replayed later.
Voice input device	Device that allows users to enter data and issue commands using spoken words; also can be used in connection with telephone input, so a user can press, or say, a number to select a processing option.

FIGURE 7-18   Common types of input devices.

No matter how data enters an information system, the quality of the output is only as good as the quality of the input. The concept, sometimes known as **garbage in**, **garbage out** (**GIGO**), is familiar to IT professionals, who know that the best time to avoid problems is when the data is entered. The main objective of input design is to ensure the quality, accuracy, and timeliness of input data.

During input design, you determine how data will be captured and entered into the system. **Data capture** is the identification and recording of source data. **Data entry** is the process of converting source data into computer-readable form and entering it into the information system.

Input design has six main objectives:

1. To select a suitable input and data entry method

2. To reduce input volume

3. To design attractive data entry screens

4. To use validation checks to reduce input errors

5. To design required source documents

6. To develop effective input controls

Input and Data Entry Methods

Input processes should be efficient, timely, and logical. Systems analysts apply business process engineering techniques when studying transactions and business operations to determine how and when data should enter the system. Usually, the first decision is whether to use batch or online input methods. Each method has advantages and disadvantages, and the systems analyst must consider the following factors:

FIGURE 7-19 A customer's signature can be stored in digital form and entered into the information system.

BATCH INPUT Using **batch input**, data entry is performed on a specified time schedule, such as daily, weekly, monthly, or longer. For example, batch input occurs when a payroll department collects time cards at the end of the week and enters the data as a **batch**. Another example is a school that enters all grades for the academic term in a batch.

ONLINE INPUT Although batch input is used in specific situations, most business activity requires **online data entry**. The online method offers major advantages, including the immediate validation and availability of data. A popular online input method is **source data automation**, which combines online data entry and automated data capture using input devices such as **magnetic data strips**, or **swipe scanners**. Source data automation is fast, accurate, and does not require human involvement in the translation process.

Many large companies use a combination of source data automation and a powerful communication network to manage global operations instantly. Some common examples of source data automation are:

- Businesses that use point-of-sale (POS) terminals equipped with bar code scanners and magnetic swipe scanners to input credit card data.

- Automatic teller machines (ATMs) that read data strips on bank cards.

- Factory employees who use magnetic ID cards to clock on and off specific jobs so the company can track production costs accurately.

- Hospitals that imprint bar codes on patient identification bracelets and use portable scanners when gathering data on patient treatment and medication.

- Retail stores that use portable bar code scanners to log new shipments and update inventory data.

- Libraries that use handheld scanners to read optical strips on books.

TRADEOFFS Although online input offers many advantages, it does have some disadvantages. For example, unless source data automation is used, manual data entry is slower and more expensive than batch input because it is performed at the time the transaction occurs and often done when computer demand is at its highest.

ON THE WEB

For examples of Input and Data Entry Methods visit scsite.com/sad4e/more.htm click Systems Analysis and Design Chapter 7 and then click the Input and Data Entry Methods link.

www.scsite.c

The decision to use batch or online input depends on business requirements. For example, hotel reservations must be entered and processed immediately, but hotels can enter their monthly performance figures in a batch. In fact, some input occurs naturally in batches. A cable TV provider, for example, receives customer payments in batches when the mail arrives.

Input Volume

To reduce input volume, you must reduce the number of data items required for each transaction. Data capture and data entry require time and effort, so when you reduce input volume, you avoid unnecessary labor costs, get the data into the system more quickly, and decrease the number of errors. The following guidelines will help reduce input volume:

1. Input necessary data only. Do not input a data item unless it is needed by the system. A completed order form, for example, might contain the name of the clerk who took the order. If that data is not needed by the system, the user should not enter it.

2. Do not input data that the user can retrieve from system files or calculate from other data. In the order system example shown in Figure 7-20, the system generates an order number and logs the current date and time. Then the user enters a customer ID. If the entry is valid, the system displays the customer name so the user can verify it. The user then enters the item and quantity. Note that the description, price, extended price, total price, sales tax, and grand total are retrieved automatically or calculated by the system.

3. Do not input constant data. If orders are in batches with the same date, then a user should enter the order date only once for the first order in the batch. If orders are entered online, then the user can retrieve the order date automatically using the current system date.

4. Use codes. You learned in Chapter 6 that codes are shorter than the data they represent and that coded input can reduce data entry time. In the order system example in Figure 7-20, the CUSTOMER ID and ITEM fields are codes.

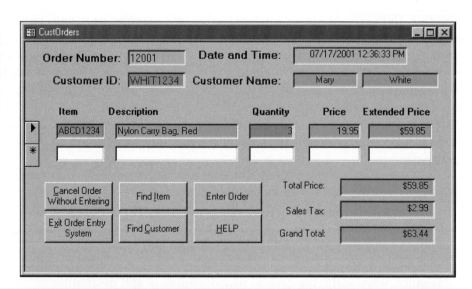

FIGURE 7-20 In this data screen for customer orders, the system generates an order number and logs the current date and time. The user enters a customer ID. If the entry is valid, the system displays the customer name so the user can verify it. The user then enters the item and quantity. Note that the description, price, extended price, total price, sales tax, and grand total are retrieved automatically or calculated by the system.

Designing Data Entry Screens

Some users work with many features of the user interface; others spend most of their time entering data. This section discusses interface guidelines and concepts that primarily relate to systematic data entry. Notice that many of the guidelines are based on general principles of interface design discussed earlier in this chapter.

The most effective method of online data entry is **form filling**, in which a blank form that duplicates or resembles the source document is completed on the screen. The user enters the data and then moves to the next field.

1. Restrict user access to screen locations where data is entered. When the screen in Figure 7-20 displays, the system should position the insertion point in the first data entry location. After the operator enters a CUSTOMER ID, the insertion point should move automatically to the entry location for the next field (ITEM). A user should be able to position the insertion point only in places where data is entered on the form.

2. Provide a descriptive caption for every field, and show the user where to enter the data and the required or maximum field size. Typically, white boxes show the location and length of each field. Other methods used to indicate field locations are video highlighting, underscores, special symbols, or a combination of these features.

3. Display a sample format if a user must enter values in a field in a specific format. For example, provide an on-screen instruction to let users know that the date format is MMDDYY, and provide an example if the user must enter **separators**, such as slashes. It is better to use an input mask, so users simply can enter 112702 to represent November 27, 2002.

4. Require an ending keystroke for every field. Pressing the ENTER key or the TAB key should signify the end of a field entry. Avoid a design that moves automatically to the next item when the field is full. The latter approach requires an ending keystroke *only* when the data entered is less than the maximum field length. It is confusing to use two different data entry procedures.

5. Do not require users to type leading zeroes for numeric fields. For example, if the project number is 45, the operator should type 45 instead of 045 before pressing the ENTER key. An exception to that rule might occur when entering a date, where a leading zero is needed to identify single-digit months.

6. Do not require users to type trailing zeroes for numbers that include decimals. For example, when a user types a value of 98, the system should interpret the value as 98.00 if the field has been formatted to include numbers with two decimal places. The decimal point is needed *only* to indicate nonzero decimal places, such as 98.76.

7. Display default values so operators can press the ENTER key to accept the suggested value. If the default value is not appropriate, the operator can change it.

8. Use a default value when a field value will be constant for successive records or throughout the data entry session. For example, if records are input in order by date, the date used in the first transaction should be used as the default date until a new date is entered, at which time the new date becomes the default value.

9. Display a list of acceptable values for fields, and provide meaningful error messages if the user enters an unacceptable value. An even better method, which was described in the user interface design section, is to provide a drop-down list box containing acceptable values that allows the user to select a value by clicking.

10. Provide a way to leave the data entry screen at any time without entering the current record. In Figure 7-20 on page 7.14, clicking the Cancel Order Without Entering button cancels the current order and moves the insertion point back to the beginning of the form.

11. Provide users with an opportunity to confirm the accuracy of input data before entering it by displaying a message such as, *Add this record? (Y/N)*. A positive response *(Y)* adds the record, clears the entry fields, and positions the insertion point in the first field so the user can input another record. If the response is negative *(N)*, the current record is not added and the user can correct the errors.

12. Provide a means for users to move among fields on the form in a standard order or in any order they choose. For example, in the form shown in Figure 7-20, pressing the TAB key moves the insertion point to the next field, and pressing the SHIFT + TAB keys together moves the insertion point to the previous field. In a graphical user interface (GUI), the user can override the standard field order and select field locations with the mouse or cursor keys.

13. Design the screen form layout to match the layout of the source document. If the source document fields start at the top of the form and run down in a column, the input screen should use the same design.

14. Allow users to add, change, delete, and view records. Figure 7-20 shows a screen that can be used for entering orders, finding items, and finding customers. After the operator enters a customer identification code, the order form displays current values for all appropriate fields. Then the operator can view the data, make changes, enter the order, or cancel without ordering. Messages such as: *Apply these changes? (Y/N)* or *Delete this record? (Y/N)* should require users to confirm the actions. Highlighting the letter *N* as a default response will avoid problems if the user presses the ENTER key by mistake.

15. Provide a method to allow users to search for specific information, as shown in Figure 7-20.

Input Errors

Reducing the number of input errors improves data quality. One way to reduce input errors is to eliminate unnecessary data entry, as discussed earlier in the chapter. For example, a user cannot misspell a customer name if it is not entered, or entered automatically based on the user entering the customer ID. Similarly, an outdated item price cannot be used if the item price is retrieved from a master file instead of being entered manually.

The best defense against incorrect data is to identify and correct errors before they enter the system by using data validation checks. A **data validation check** improves input quality by testing the data and rejecting any entry that fails to meet specified conditions. You can design at least eight types of data validation checks into the input process.

1. **Sequence checks** are used when the data must be in some predetermined sequence. If the user must enter work orders in numerical sequence, for example, then an out-of-sequence order number indicates an error, or must enter transactions chronologically, then a transaction with an out-of-sequence date indicates an error.

2. **Existence checks** are used for mandatory data items. For example, if an employee record requires a Social Security number, an existence check would not allow the user to save the record until he or she enters a suitable value in the SSN field.

3. **Data type checks** test to ensure that a data item fits the required data type. For example, a numeric field must have only numbers or numeric symbols, and an alphabetic field can contain only the characters A through Z or the characters a through z.

4. **Range checks** test data items to verify that they fall between a specified minimum and maximum value. The daily hours worked by an employee, for example, must fall within the range of 0 to 24. When the validation check involves a minimum or a maximum value, but not both, it is called a **limit check**. Checking that a payment amount is greater than zero, but not specifying a maximum value, is an example of a limit check.

5. **Reasonableness checks** identify values that are questionable, but not necessarily wrong. For example, input payment values of $.05 and $5,000,000.00 both pass a simple limit check for a payment value greater than zero, and yet both values could be errors. Similarly, an hours worked value of 24 passes a 0 to 24 range check, but the value seems unlikely and the system should verify it using a reasonableness check.

6. **Validity checks** are used for data items that must have certain values. For example, if an inventory system has 20 valid item classes, then any input item that does not match one of the valid classes will fail the check. Verifying that a customer number on an order matches a customer number in the customer file is another type of validity check. Because the value entered must refer to another value, that type of check also is called **referential integrity**, which is discussed in more detail in Chapter 8. Another validity check might verify that a new customer number does *not* match a number already stored in the customer master file.

7. **Combination checks** are performed on two or more fields to ensure that they are consistent or reasonable when considered together. Even though all the fields involved in a combination check might pass their individual validation checks, the combination of the field values might be inconsistent or unreasonable. For example, if an order input for 30 units of a particular item has an input discount rate applicable only for purchases of 100 or more units, then the combination is invalid; either the input order quantity or the input discount rate is incorrect.

8. **Batch controls** are totals used to verify batch input. Batch controls might check data items such as record counts and numeric field totals. For example, before entering a batch of orders, a user might calculate the total number of orders and the sum of all the order quantities. When the batch of orders is entered, the order system also calculates the same two totals. If the system totals do not match the input totals, then a data entry error has occurred. Unlike the other validation checks, batch controls do not identify specific errors. For example, if the sum of all the order quantities does not match the batch control total, you know only that one or more orders in that batch was entered incorrectly or not input. The batch control totals often are called **hash totals**, because they are not meaningful numbers themselves, but are useful for comparison purposes.

Source Documents

A **source document** is a form used to request and collect input data, trigger or authorize an input action, and provide a record of the original transaction. During the input design stage, you develop source documents that are easy to complete and inexpensive.

Consider a time when you struggled to complete a poorly designed form. You might have encountered insufficient space, confusing instructions, or poor organization, all symptoms of incorrect **form layout**. Good form layout makes the form easy to complete and provides enough space, both vertically and horizontally, for users to enter the data. A form should indicate data entry positions clearly using blank lines or boxes and descriptive captions. Figure 7-21 on the next page shows several techniques used for line and boxed captions on source documents, and an example of check boxes that are effective when a user must select choices from a list.

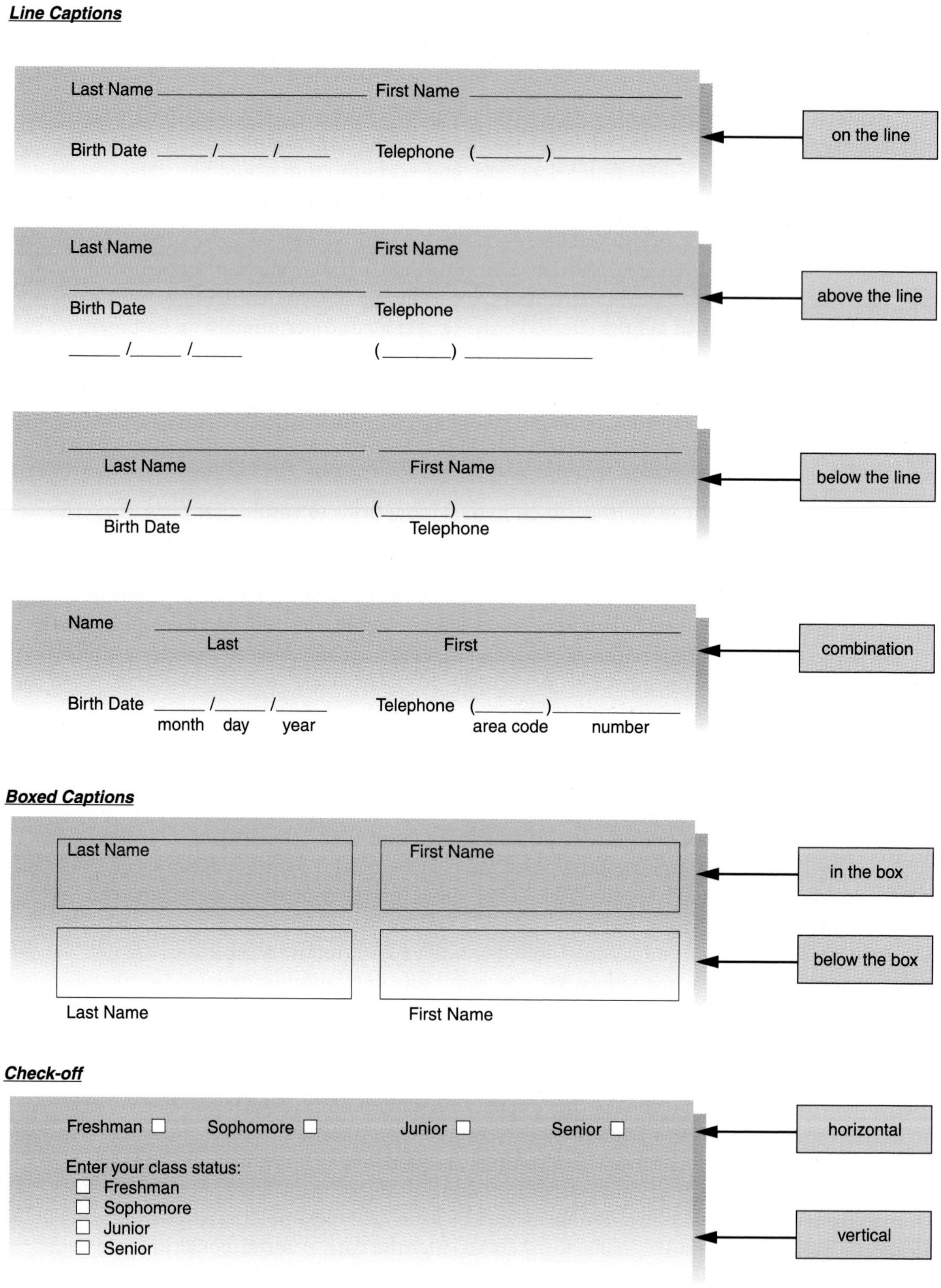

Line Captions

Last Name _____ First Name _____

Birth Date _____ / _____ / _____ Telephone (_____)_____ ← on the line

Last Name

First Name

_____ _____

Birth Date Telephone ← above the line

_____ / _____ / _____ (_____) _____

_____ _____

Last Name First Name ← below the line

_____ / _____ / _____ (_____) _____

Birth Date Telephone

Name _____ _____

Last First ← combination

Birth Date _____ / _____ / _____ Telephone (_____)_____

month day year   area code   number

Boxed Captions

Last Name	First Name	
		← in the box

		← below the box
Last Name	First Name	

Check-off

Freshman ☐   Sophomore ☐   Junior ☐   Senior ☐   ← horizontal

Enter your class status:
☐ Freshman
☐ Sophomore
☐ Junior   ← vertical
☐ Senior

FIGURE 7-21   Examples of caption techniques for source documents.

The sequence of information on a form also is important. Source documents typically include most of the zones shown in Figure 7-22. The **heading zone** usually contains the company name or logo and the title and number of the form. The **control zone** contains codes, identification information, numbers, and dates that are used for storing completed forms. The **instruction zone** contains instructions for completing the form. The main part of the form, called the **body zone**, usually takes up at least half of the space on the form and contains captions and areas for entering variable data. If totals are included on the form, they appear in the **totals zone**. Finally, the **authorization zone** contains any required signatures.

Information should flow on a form from left to right and top to bottom to match the way users read documents naturally. That layout makes the form easy to use for the individual who completes the form, and for users who enter data into the system using the completed form. For example, compare the two different layouts for a hypothetical form shown in Figure 7-23. Notice that the top diagram is confusing, while the bottom one is logical and easy to follow.

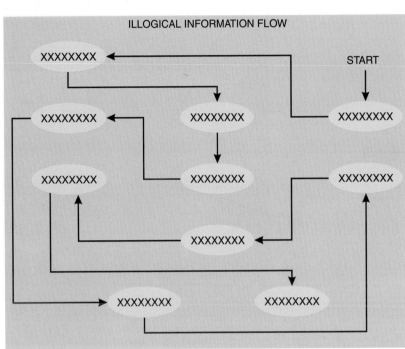

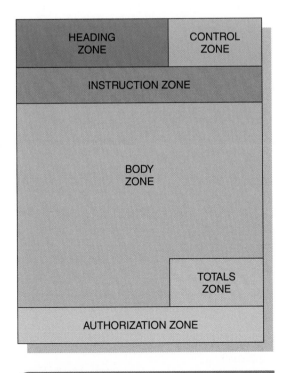

FIGURE 7-22   Source document zones.

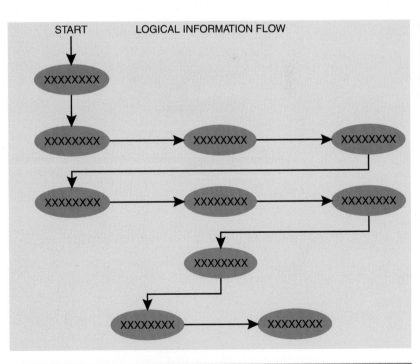

FIGURE 7-23   Two different layouts for a hypothetical form. Notice that the top diagram is confusing, while the bottom one is logical and easy to follow.

Figure 7-24 shows a source document for a video club membership application, and Figure 7-25 shows a multipage source document for a dog license. Both forms follow the recommended top to bottom, left to right layout. Notice that the two-part dog license application also serves as a receipt; the top (white) copy is retained as the source document and the bottom (yellow) copy is returned to the applicant.

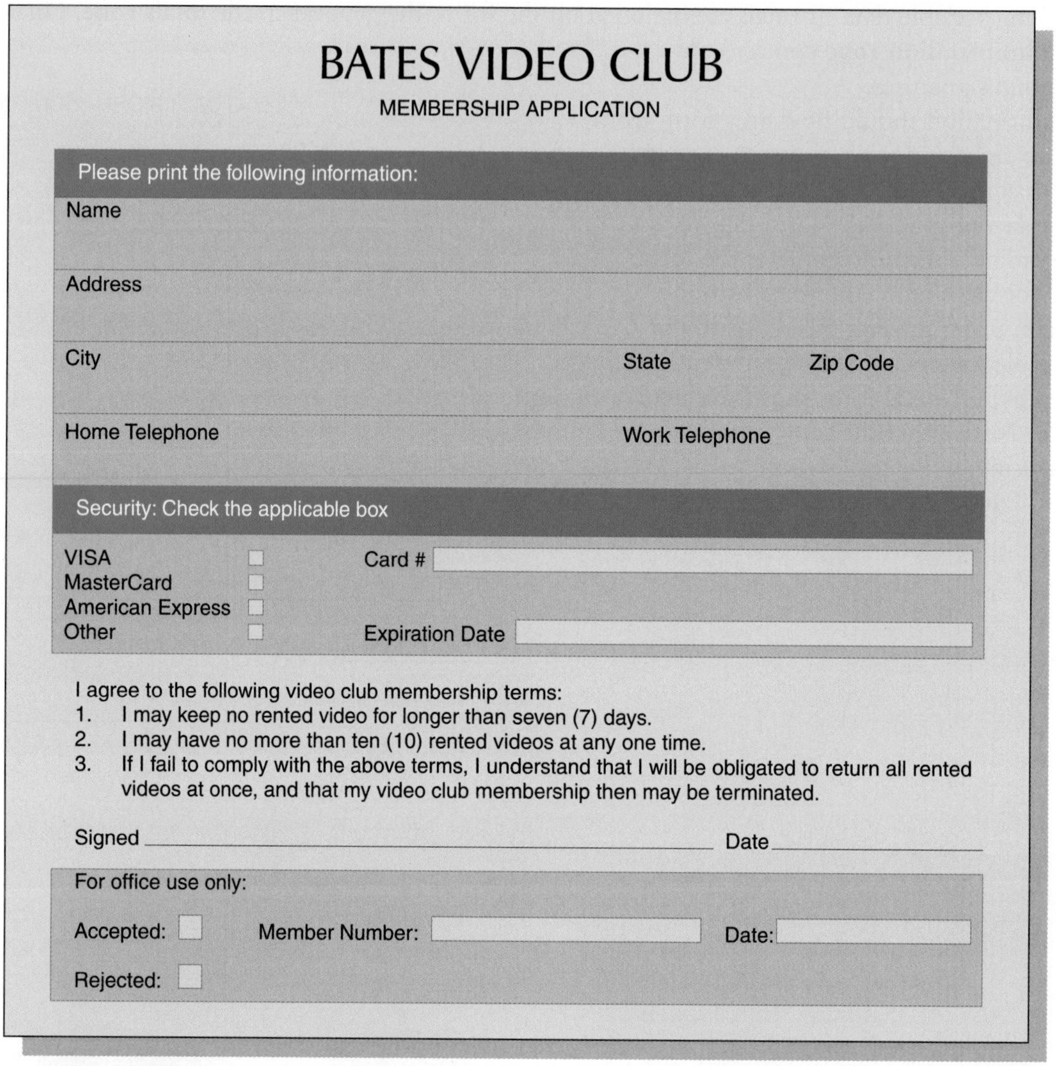

BATES VIDEO CLUB
MEMBERSHIP APPLICATION

Please print the following information:

Name

Address

City   State   Zip Code

Home Telephone   Work Telephone

Security: Check the applicable box

VISA   ☐   Card #
MasterCard   ☐
American Express   ☐
Other   ☐   Expiration Date

I agree to the following video club membership terms:
1. I may keep no rented video for longer than seven (7) days.
2. I may have no more than ten (10) rented videos at any one time.
3. If I fail to comply with the above terms, I understand that I will be obligated to return all rented videos at once, and that my video club membership then may be terminated.

Signed _____ Date _____

For office use only:

Accepted: ☐   Member Number: _____   Date: _____

Rejected: ☐

FIGURE 7-24   Source document for a video club membership application.

DOG LICENSE
2002

PARKER COUNTY
STATE OF MICHIGAN

LICENSE NUMBER:
00001

THIS LICENSE EXPIRES:
DECEMBER 31, 2002

__________ City

__________ Twnshp

Received of ____________________ Telephone __________
(Name of Dog Owner)

____
(Complete Mailing Address of Dog Owner)

the sum of $________, amount due for DOG LICENSE for one dog, hereinafter described, which, upon compliance with the Dog Law of 1979 and all Amendments thereto, you are authorized to keep without further payment, until this license expires. State law requires all dogs 6 months and older to have a current license.

Beagle . . . . [ ]	Doberman . . . . . [ ]	Poodle . . . . [ ]	Dog's Name ________
Boxer . . . . [ ]	Hound . . . . [ ]	Samoyed . . . . . . [ ]	
Bull. . . . . [ ]	Labrador . . . . . . [ ]	Setter. . . . . [ ]	Color ________
Chihuahua . . . . . [ ]	Pekinese . . . . . . [ ]	Shepherd . . . . . . [ ]	
Cockapoo. . . . . . [ ]	Pointer . . . . [ ]	Spaniel. . . . . [ ]	Age ______ Today's Date ______
Collie . . . . [ ]	Police . . . . [ ]	Terrier. . . . . [ ]	
Dachshund. . . . . [ ]	Pomeranian . . . . [ ]	Weimaraner . . . . [ ]	Rabies Vac. No. ____ Expires ______
Other. . . . . [ ]			Veterinarian ________

[ ] MALE, $7.50 [ ] FEMALE, $15.00 [ ] ALTERED, $5.00

FIGURE 7-25 Multipage source document for a dog license that serves as an application and a receipt.

Application for Free InfoWorld Subscription

NEW SUBSCRIBERS ONLY! Apply online at: www.iwsubscribe.com

Form: 1

A MAILING ADDRESS

If military: please specify branch and base. If government: please specify division.

NAME

TITLE

COMPANY NAME

DIVISION / DEPT / MAIL STOP

MAILING ADDRESS

CITY / STATE / ZIP / POSTAL CODE

Is the mailing address your home address? ❑ 1. Yes ❑ 2. No
If yes, are your home and business address the same? ❑ 1. Yes ❑ 2. No

COMPANY PHYSICAL ADDRESS: (NO P.O. BOXES)
REQUIRED IF MAILING ADDRESS IS NOT YOUR COMPANY PHYSICAL LOCATION

PHYSICAL ADDRESS

CITY / STATE / ZIP / POSTAL CODE

6 OVER THE COURSE OF ONE YEAR, DO YOU BUY, SPECIFY, RECOMMEND, OR APPROVE THE PURCHASE OF THE FOLLOWING PRODUCTS OR SERVICES WORTH: (PLEASE SELECT THE CORRECT LETTER CODE FOR THE DOLLAR AMOUNT, AND WRITE THAT LETTER IN THE CORRESPONDING BOX):

NOTE: IF YOU CANNOT DISTINGUISH BETWEEN THIS AND OTHER LOCATION(S), PUT RESPONSE IN THE FIRST COLUMN.

CONSULTANTS: PLEASE INCLUDE WHAT YOU RECOMMEND FOR YOUR CLIENTS AS WELL AS WHAT YOU BUY FOR YOUR OWN BUSINESS.

A. $50,000,000 or more
B. $30,000,000 to $49,999,999
C. $20,000,000 to $29,999,999
D. $10,000,000 to $19,999,999
E. $5,000,000 to $9,999,999
F. $2,500,000 to $4,999,999
G. $1,000,000 to $2,499,999
H. $600,000 to $999,999
I. $400,000 to $599,999
J. $100,000 to $399,999
K. $50,000 to $99,999
L. Less than $49,999
M. None

Product category	For this location: (write code in box)	For other locations: (write code in box)
Large systems	01. ☐	08. ☐
Client computers	02. ☐	09. ☐
Networking / Telecom (including servers)	03. ☐	10. ☐
Internet / Intranet / Extranet	04. ☐	11. ☐
Peripheral equipment	05. ☐	12. ☐
Software	06. ☐	13. ☐
Service / support	07. ☐	14. ☐

FIGURE 7-26 Paper-based subscription application for *INFOWORLD*.

Layout and design also is important on Web-based forms. Compare the paper-based subscription application for *INFOWORLD* in Figure 7-26 to the online form shown in Figure 7-27 on the next page. Notice that the Web-based form uses drop-down list boxes and input masks to make it easier for the subscriber to fill out.

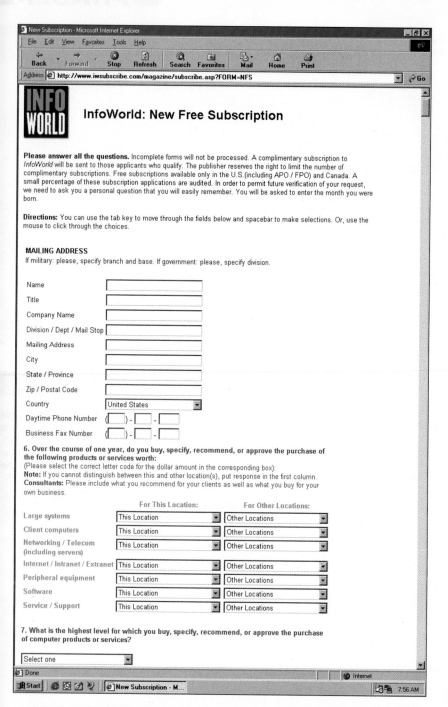

FIGURE 7-27 Notice that the Web-based subscription form for *INFOWORLD* uses drop-down list boxes and input masks to make it easier for the subscriber.

Input Control

Input control includes the necessary measures to ensure that input data is correct, complete, and secure. You must focus on input control during every phase of input design, starting with source documents that promote data accuracy and quality. When a batch input method is used, the computer can produce an input log file that identifies and documents the data entered.

Every piece of information should be traceable back to the input data that produced it. That means that you must provide an **audit trail** that records the source of each data item and when it entered the system. In addition to recording the original source, an audit trail must show how and when data is accessed or changed, and by whom. All those actions must be logged in an audit trail file and monitored carefully.

A company must have procedures for handling source documents to ensure that data is not lost before it enters the system. All source documents that originate from outside the organization should be logged when they are received. Whenever source documents pass between departments, the transfer should be recorded.

Data security protects data from loss or damage and recovers data when it is lost or damaged. Once data is entered, the company should store source documents in a safe location for some specified length of time. The company should have a **records retention policy** that meets all legal requirements and business needs.

Audit trail files and reports should be stored and saved. Then, if a data file is damaged, you can use the information to reconstruct the lost data. Data security also involves protecting data from unauthorized access. System sign-on procedures should prevent unauthorized individuals from entering the system and users should change their passwords regularly. Having several levels of access also is advisable. For example, a data entry person might be allowed to *view* a credit limit, but not *change* it. Sensitive data can be **encrypted**, or coded, in a process called **encryption**, so only users with decoding software can read it.

When should a systems analyst decide a design issue, and when should users be allowed to select what works best for them? The field of ergonomics is concerned with improving the work environment and studying how users interact with their environment. Does ergonomics also include studying the effect on users of input screens?

Suppose you are a systems analyst working on the input design for a new order entry system at Boolean Toys, a fast-growing developer of software for preschool children. You have been told that users request many reports, but use only a small portion of the data from the reports. In many offices you see in-boxes filled with reports and you also see stacks of reports sitting on desks. Should you interview users about what reports they want or need? What questions would you ask? What if Boolean's users could design most of their own reports without assistance from the IT staff by using a powerful, user-friendly report generator program? Do you think they would request as many reports or the same types of reports? What are the pros and cons of giving users total control over output?

OUTPUT DESIGN ISSUES

Before designing output, ask yourself several questions:
- What is the purpose of the output?
- Who wants the information, why it is it needed, and how will it be used?
- What specific information will be included?
- Will the output be printed, viewed on-screen, or both?
- When will the information be provided, and how often must it be updated?
- Do security or confidentiality issues exist?

The design process should not begin until you have answered those questions. Some of that information probably was gathered during the systems analysis phase. To complete your understanding, you should meet with users to find out exactly what kind of output is needed. You can use prototypes and mock-ups to obtain feedback throughout the design process. Your answers will affect your output design strategies, as you will see in the next section.

Types of Output

Although most system output is printed in reports (which is discussed in the next section) or displayed on screens, new technology has had an enormous impact on how people communicate and obtain information. The change especially is true in business information systems that require significant user interaction.

ON THE WE

For more information abc
Printed Report Design vis
scsite.com/sad4e/more.h
click Systems Analysis a
Design Chapter 7 and the
click the Printed Report
Design link.

www.scsite.

Figure 7-28 shows that, in addition to traditional printed and screen output, information is delivered to users by means of the Internet, e-mail, audio output, automated facsimile systems, computer output microfilm, and other specialized methods. The type of output and the technology needed usually is decided during the systems analysis phase, based on user requirements. Now, in the systems design phase, you must design the actual reports, screen forms, and other output delivery methods.

Information Delivery Method	Description
Audio	Audio output consists of speech or sounds that can be stored digitally and reproduced as audible information.
Automated facsimile	Automated facsimile systems allow users to request and receive specific information by facsimile.
Computer output microfilm (COM)	Computer output microfilm (COM) records information as images on microfilm rolls or microfiche sheets.
E-mail	E-mail, or electronic messaging systems, support internal and external business communications using local or wide area networks, including the Internet.
Internet-based	The Internet has profoundly affected business communications and changed the way business is conducted. Companies today depend on Web-based information delivery to support business operations, to manage the enterprise, and to provide an information infrastructure.
Other specialized devices	Diverse business operations require specialized applications, including point-of-sale terminals, ATMs, special-purpose printers, plotters, digital photos, and visual displays on machines and appliances.
Printer	Prints text and graphics on various types of paper.
Screen	Displays text and graphics on computer monitor or terminal.

FIGURE 7-28 Common information delivery methods.

INTERNET-BASED INFORMATION DELIVERY   Millions of firms use the Internet to reach new customers and markets around the world. To support the explosive growth in e-commerce, Web designers must provide user-friendly screen interfaces that display output and accept input from customers. For example, a business can link its inventory system to its Web site so the output from the inventory system is displayed as an online catalog. Customers visiting the site can review the items, obtain current prices, and check product availability. Another example of Web-based output is a system that provides customized responses to product or technical questions. When a user enters a product inquiry or requests technical support, the system responds with appropriate information from an on-site knowledge base.

E-MAIL   E-mail, or electronic messaging, has become an essential means of internal and external business communication. Employees send and receive e-mail on local or wide area networks, including the Internet. Companies send new product information to customers via e-mail, and financial services companies use e-mail messages to confirm online stock trades. Employees use e-mail to exchange documents, data, schedules, and share business-related information they need to perform their jobs. In many firms, e-mail has virtually replaced traditional memos and printed correspondence.

AUDIO OUTPUT   Audio output can be attached to an e-mail message or inserted as an audio clip in a document as shown in Figure 7-29. In addition, many firms use automated systems to handle voice transactions and provide information to customers. For example, using a Touch-Tone™ telephone, a customer can confirm an airline seat assignment, check a credit card balance, or find out the current price of a mutual fund.

AUTOMATED FACSIMILE SYSTEMS

Some firms use **automated facsimile**, sometimes called **faxback** systems, to allow a customer to request a fax using e-mail, the company Web site, or by telephone. The response is transmitted in a matter of seconds back to the user's fax machine. A computer firm, for example, might allow customers to request technical updates, information on new device drivers, or product assistance via fax. That type of automated output is available 24 hours a day and provides an immediate response to a customer.

COMPUTER OUTPUT MICRO-FILM (COM)

Computer output microfilm (COM) systems, such as microfilm and microfiche, capture an image of a document and produce film output. Users then can retrieve, view, and print the images. **Microfilm** records the images on a roll of film, and **microfiche** records images using a small sheet of film. COM systems are especially important where it is necessary to show a signature, date stamp, or other visual feature of a document.

SPECIALIZED FORMS OF OUTPUT

An incredibly diverse marketplace requires a variety of specialized output. Consider the following examples:

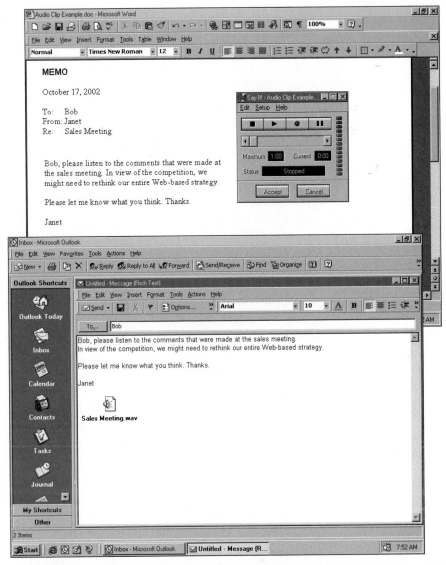

FIGURE 7-29   Audio output can be attached to an e-mail message or inserted as an audio clip in a Microsoft Word 2000 document.

- Retail point-of-sale terminals that handle computer-based credit card transactions, print receipts, and update inventory records.

- Automatic teller machines (ATMs) that process bank transactions and print deposit and withdrawal slips.

- Special-purpose printers that produce labels, photos, driver's licenses and, in some states, lottery tickets.

- Plotters that produce high-quality images such as blueprints, maps, and electronic circuit diagrams.

- Digitized photos that companies can print on employee identification cards.

- Programmable devices such as television sets, VCRs, and microwave ovens that produce visual output displays.

In today's interconnected world, output from one system often becomes input into another system. For example, within a company, production data from the manufacturing system becomes input to the inventory system. The same company might transmit employee W-2 tax data to the IRS system electronically. A company employee might use tax preparation software to file a tax return electronically, receive a refund deposited directly into his or her bank account, and see the deposit reflected on the bank's information system.

Although digital technology has opened new horizons in business communications, printed output still is the most common type of output, and there are specific considerations that apply to it. For those reasons, printed output is discussed in its own section which follows.

PRINTED OUTPUT

Although many organizations strive to reduce the flow of paper and printed reports, few firms have been able to eliminate printed output totally. Because they are portable, printed reports are convenient, and even necessary in some situations. Many users find it handy to view screen output, then print out the information they need for a discussion or business meeting. Printed output also is used in **turnaround documents**, which are output documents that are later entered back into the same or another information system. Your telephone or utility bill, for example, might be a turnaround document printed by the company's billing system. When you return the bill with your payment, the bill is scanned into the company's accounts receivable system to record your payment accurately.

Reports, like any other element of the user-computer interface, should be attractive, professional, and easy to use. Systems analysts should realize that printed output is highly visible, and managers sometimes judge an entire project by the quality of the reports they receive.

Types of Reports

To be useful, a report must include the information that a user needs. From a user's point of view, a report with too little information is of no value. Too much information, however, can make a report confusing and difficult to understand. When designing reports, the essential goal is to match the report to the user's specific information needs. Depending on their job functions, users might need one or more of the reports described below.

06/28/02	EMPLOYEE HOURS WEEK ENDING DATE: 06/28/02				PAGE 1
SHOP NUMBER	EMPLOYEE NAME	POSITION	REGULAR HOURS	OVERTIME HOURS	TOTAL HOURS
8	Andres, Marguerite	Clerk	20.0	0.0	20.0
8	Bogema, Michelle	Clerk	12.5	0.0	12.5
8	Davenport, Kim	Asst Mgr	40.0	5.0	45.0
8	Lemka, Susan	Clerk	32.7	0.0	32.7
8	Linquist, Linda	Clerk	16.0	0.0	16.0
8	Ramirez, Rudy	Manager	40.0	8.5	48.5
8	Ullery, Ruth	Clerk	20.0	0.0	20.0
11	Byrum, Cheri	Clerk	15.0	0.0	15.0
11	Byrum, Mary	Clerk	15.0	0.0	15.0
11	Deal, JoAnn	Clerk	4.8	0.0	4.8
11	Gadzinski, Barbara	Manager	40.0	10.0	50.0
11	Huyhn, Loc	Clerk	20.0	0.0	20.0
11	Schuller, Monica	Clerk	10.0	0.0	10.0
11	Stites, Carol	Clerk	40.0	12.0	52.0
11	Thompson, Mary Kay	Asst Mgr	40.0	1.5	41.5
17	De Martini, Jennifer	Clerk	40.0	8.4	48.4
17	Haff, Lisa	Manager	40.0	0.0	40.0
17	Rittenbery, Sandra	Clerk	40.0	11.0	51.0
17	Wyer, Elizabeth	Clerk	20.0	0.0	20.0
17	Zeigler, Cecille	Clerk	32.0	0.0	32.0

detail lines

FIGURE 7-30 A detail report, with one printed line per employee.

DETAIL REPORTS   A **detail report** produces one or more lines of output for each record processed. Each line of output printed is called a **detail line**. Figure 7-30 shows a simple detail report of employee hours for a chain of retail shops. Notice that one detail line prints for each employee. All the fields in the record do not have to be printed, nor do the fields have to be printed in the sequence in which they appear in the record. An employee paycheck that has multiple output lines for a single record is another example of a detail report.

A well-designed detail report should provide totals for numeric fields. Notice that the report shown in Figure 7-30 lacks subtotals and grand totals for regular hours, overtime hours, and total hours. Figure 7-31 shows the same report with subtotals and grand totals added. In the example, the SHOP NUMBER field is called a **control field** because it controls the output. When the value of a control field changes, a control break occurs. A **control break** usually causes specific actions, such as printing subtotals for a group of records. That type of detail report is called a **control break report**. To produce a control break report, the records must be arranged, or sorted, in control field order. The sorting can be done by the report program itself, or in a previous procedure.

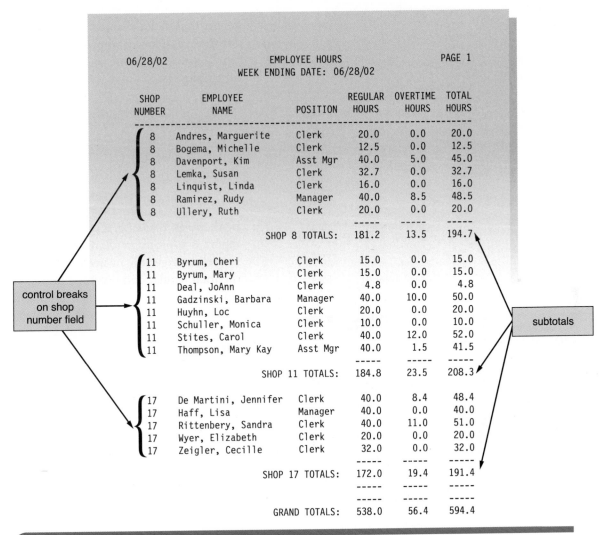

| FIGURE 7-31 | This detail report contains the same data as Figure 7-30, but provides much more information. Control breaks are used to separate the data for each shop, with subtotals and grand totals for numeric fields. |

Because it contains one or more lines for each record, a detail report can be quite lengthy. Consider, for example, a large auto parts business. If the firm stocks 3,000 parts, then the detail report would include 3,000 detail lines on approximately 50 printed pages. A user who wants to locate any part in short supply has to examine 3,000 detail lines to find the critical items. A much better alternative is to produce an exception report.

EXCEPTION REPORTS   An **exception report** displays only those records that meet a specific condition or conditions. Exception reports are useful when the user wants information only on records that might require action, but does not need to know the details. For example, a credit manager might use an exception report to identify only those customers with past due accounts, or a customer service manager might want a report on all packages that were not delivered within a specified time period. Figure 7-32 shows an exception report that includes information only for those employees who worked overtime, instead of listing information for all employees.

```
06/28/02                    OVERTIME REPORT                  PAGE 1
                      WEEK ENDING DATE:  06/28/02

         SHOP                               EMPLOYEE        OVERTIME
        NUMBER      POSITION                  NAME           HOURS
        -----------------------------------------------------------
          8         Asst Mgr        Davenport, Kim            5.0
                    Manager         Ramirez, Rudy             8.5
                                                             -----

                                       SHOP 8 TOTAL:         13.5

          11        Manager         Gadzinski, Barbara       10.0
                    Clerk           Stites, Carol            12.0
                    Asst Mgr        Thompson, Mary Kay        1.5
                                                             -----

                                      SHOP 11 TOTAL:         23.5

          17        Clerk           De Martini, Jennifer      8.4
                    Clerk           Rittenbery, Sandra       11.0
                                                             -----

                                      SHOP 17 TOTAL:         19.4
                                                             -----
                                                             -----

                                       GRAND TOTAL:          56.4
```

FIGURE 7-32   An exception report that shows information *only* for the employees who worked overtime.

SUMMARY REPORTS   Upper-level managers often want to see total figures and do not need supporting details. A sales manager, for example, might want to know total sales for each sales representative, but not want a detail report listing every sale made by them. In that case, a **summary report** is appropriate. Similarly, a personnel manager might need to know the total regular and overtime hours worked by employees in each shop but might not be interested in the number of hours worked by each employee. For the personnel manager, a summary report such as the one shown in Figure 7-33 would be useful. Generally, reports used by individuals at higher levels in the organization include less detail than reports used by lower-level employees.

User Involvement

Printed reports are an important way of delivering information to users, so recipients should approve all report designs in advance. To avoid problems, you should submit each design for approval as you complete it, rather than waiting until you finish all report designs.

```
06/28/02            EMPLOYEE HOURS SUMMARY          PAGE 1
                   WEEK ENDING DATE: 06/28/02

         SHOP        REGULAR      OVERTIME     TOTAL
        NUMBER        HOURS        HOURS       HOURS
        ---------------------------------------------
          8          181.2         13.5        194.7

          11         184.8         23.5        208.3

          17         172.0         19.4        191.4
                     ----------------------------------
        TOTALS:      538.0         56.4        594.4
```

FIGURE 7-33   A summary report lists subtotals and grand totals.

When designing a report, you should prepare a mock-up, or prototype, for users to review. The mock-up should include sample field values, with enough records to show all the design features. Depending on the type of printed output, you can use a word processor, a report generator, or a printer spacing chart to create mock-up reports.

Report Design Principles

Printed reports must be attractive, professional, and easy to read. Good report design, like any other aspect of the user interface, requires effort and attention to detail.

To produce a well-designed report, the analyst must consider several topics, including report headers and footers, page headers and footers, column headings and alignment, column spacing, field order, and grouping of detail lines. Figure 7-34 shows an example of those design features.

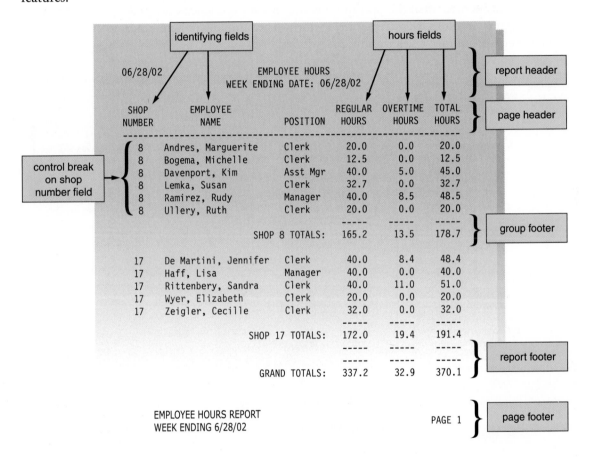

FIGURE 7-34 The Employee Hours report is a detail report with control breaks. Subtotals and grand totals are included for appropriate numeric fields. Notice that a report header identifies the report and the printing date, a page header contains the column headings, a group footer contains subtotals for each shop, a report footer contains the grand totals, and a page footer identifies the report, the date, and the page number.

REPORT HEADERS AND FOOTERS Every report should have a report header and a report footer. The **report header**, which appears at the beginning of the report, identifies the report, and contains the report title, date, and other necessary information. The **report footer**, which appears at the end of the report, can include grand totals for numeric fields and other end-of-report information, as shown in Figure 7-34.

PAGE HEADERS AND FOOTERS   Every page should include a **page header**, which appears at the top of the page that includes the column headings that identify the data. The headings should be short but descriptive. Avoid abbreviations unless you know that users will understand them clearly. Either a page header or a **page footer**, which appears at the bottom of the page, is used to display the name of the report and the page number.

COLUMN HEADING ALIGNMENT   Figure 7-35 shows several column heading alignment options. In Example 1, the left-justified column headings do not work well with numeric fields because the amount 1.25 would print past the right edge of the AMOUNT heading. In Example 2, the right-justified headings cause a problem with alphanumeric fields, because none of the characters in a short name would print under any part of the NAME heading. Centering headings over *maximum* field widths, as shown in Example 3, is not ideal when many of the actual values are shorter than the maximum width. Most experienced designers prefer Example 4, which centers headings over *average* field widths or Example 5, where headings are left-justified over alphanumeric fields and right-justified over numeric fields.

Example 1: Column headings are left-justified over maximum field widths.	NAME XXXXXXXXXXXXXXXXXXXXXXXXX	NUMBER ZZZ9	AMOUNT ZZZ,ZZ9.99
Example 2: Column headings are right-justified over maximum field widths.	NAME XXXXXXXXXXXXXXXXXXXXXXXXX	NUMBER ZZZ9	AMOUNT ZZZ,ZZ9.99
Example 3: Column headings are centered over maximum field widths.	NAME XXXXXXXXXXXXXXXXXXXXXXXXX	NUMBER ZZZ9	AMOUNT ZZZ,ZZ9.99
Example 4: Column headings are centered over average field widths.	NAME XXXXXXXXXXXXXXXXXXXXXXXXX	NUMBER ZZZ9	AMOUNT ZZZ,ZZ9.99
Example 5: Column headings are left-justified over alphanumeric fields and right-justified over numeric fields.	NAME XXXXXXXXXXXXXXXXXXXXXXXXX	NUMBER ZZZ9	AMOUNT ZZZ,ZZ9.99

FIGURE 7-35   Five different column heading alignment options.

Some designers use a combination of alignment techniques by centering headings for alphanumeric fields over average field widths, right-justifying headings over shorter numeric fields, and centering headings over average widths for larger numeric fields.

COLUMN SPACING   You should space columns of information carefully. A crowded report is hard to read, and large gaps between columns make it difficult for the eye to follow a line.

FIELD ORDER   Fields should be displayed and grouped in a logical order. The report shown in Figure 7-34 on the previous page, for example, shows detail lines printed in alphabetical order within shop number, so the shop number is in the left column, followed by the employee name. The employee position relates to the name, so the items are printed together. The hours information also is grouped.

GROUPING DETAIL LINES   Often, it is meaningful to arrange detail lines in groups, based on a control field. For example, using the department number as a control field, individual employees can be grouped by department. You can print a **group header** above the first detail line and a **group footer** after the last detail line in a group, as shown in Figure 7-34 on page 7.29. In a group footer, you can include a subtotal, an average, or a count of the records in that group.

Report Design Example

Although the Employee Hours report shown in Figure 7-34 follows many of the design guidelines discussed, you could still improve it. Too much detail is on the page, forcing users to search for the information they need. Can you see any material that you could eliminate?

If most employees do not work overtime, then overtime hours should stand out. You can do that by not printing 0.0 when overtime hours are zero. Repeating the shop number for each employee also is unnecessary, because the employees are grouped by shop number. Another way to avoid repeating the shop number is to use a group header to identify each shop, and eliminate the SHOP NUMBER field altogether. Finally, most of the employees in a shop are clerks. The manager and assistant manager titles would stand out better if the word Clerk were not printed for all clerical employees. Those changes have been made in Figure 7-36. The EMPLOYEE NAME and POSITION columns also were exchanged to avoid a large gap between names and the REGULAR HOURS column.

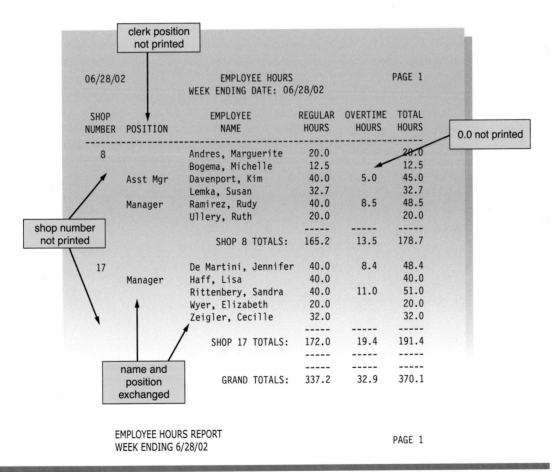

```
06/28/02                    EMPLOYEE HOURS              PAGE 1
                    WEEK ENDING DATE: 06/28/02

   SHOP                   EMPLOYEE     REGULAR  OVERTIME  TOTAL
  NUMBER  POSITION          NAME        HOURS    HOURS    HOURS
--------------------------------------------------------------
    8               Andres, Marguerite   20.0             20.0
                    Bogema, Michelle     12.5             12.5
          Asst Mgr  Davenport, Kim       40.0     5.0     45.0
                    Lemka, Susan         32.7             32.7
          Manager   Ramirez, Rudy        40.0     8.5     48.5
                    Ullery, Ruth         20.0             20.0
                                        -----   -----    -----
                    SHOP 8 TOTALS:      165.2    13.5    178.7

   17               De Martini, Jennifer 40.0     8.4     48.4
          Manager   Haff, Lisa           40.0             40.0
                    Rittenbery, Sandra   40.0    11.0     51.0
                    Wyer, Elizabeth      20.0             20.0
                    Zeigler, Cecille     32.0             32.0
                                        -----   -----    -----
                    SHOP 17 TOTALS:     172.0    19.4    191.4
                                        -----   -----    -----
                                        -----   -----    -----
                    GRAND TOTALS:       337.2    32.9    370.1
```

clerk position not printed

0.0 not printed

shop number not printed

name and position exchanged

EMPLOYEE HOURS REPORT
WEEK ENDING 6/28/02

PAGE 1

FIGURE 7-36   An improved version of the Employee Hours report shown in Figure 7-34.

SYSTEM DOCUMENTATION

NAME OF SYSTEM	DATE	PAGE 1 OF 1
Payroll	April 26, 2002	
ANALYST	PURPOSE OF DOCUMENTATION	
S. Schaffner	Report Analysis-Employee Hours Report	

FIELD	FIELD TYPE	FIELD LENGTH
Shop Number	Numeric	2
Employee Position	Alphanumeric	8
Employee Name	Alphanumeric	20
Regular Hours	Numeric	3 (1 decimal position)
Overtime Hours	Numeric	3 (1 decimal position)
Total Hours	Numeric	3 (1 decimal position)

COMMENTS
1. Week ending date is printed at the top of the report.
2. Shop number is printed only for the first employee detail line for a shop and for the first employee detail line on a page.
3. Employee Position is printed only for nonclerks. If Employee Position is equal to "Clerk" eight blank characters are printed.
4. Only nonzero Overtime Hours are printed. If Overtime Hours is equal to 0.0, four blank characters are printed.

SORT SEQUENCE
Detail lines are in order by employee name within shop number.

TOTALS REQUIRED
1. Shop totals for regular, overtime, and total hours are printed and identified by shop number.
2. Grand totals for regular, overtime, and total hours are printed.

MEDIA
The report is printed on single-ply, standard white stock paper.

FREQUENCY
The report is printed weekly on the first working day of the week on or before 10:00 a.m. of the second working day of the month.

DISTRIBUTION
The report is delivered to the personnel director no later than 11:00 a.m. of the second working day of each week.

ATTACHMENTS
Printer spacing chart and mock-up report are attached.

FIGURE 7-37 The report analysis form for the Employee Hours report shown in Figure 7-36 on the previous page.

Other Design Issues

Good design standards produce reports that are uniform and consistent. When a system produces multiple reports, each report should share common design elements. For example, the date and page numbers should print in the same place on each report page. Abbreviations used in reports should be consistent. When indicating a numeric value, it is confusing for one report to use #, another *NO*, and a third *NUM*. Items in a report also should be consistent. If one report prints inventory location as shelf number followed by bin number, then printing bin number followed by shelf number on another report creates confusion.

Most of the design principles for plain paper reports also apply to reports on preprinted forms, except that heading information usually is preprinted for reports such as invoices and monthly statements. The same functional and aesthetic design principles also apply to preprinted forms. You should make column headings short but descriptive and avoid nonstandard abbreviations. Use reasonable spacing between columns for better readability. The order and placement of printed fields should be logical, and totals should be identified clearly.

When designing a preprinted form, you should contact the forms vendor for advice on paper sizes, type styles and sizes, paper and ink colors, field placement, and other important form details. Your goal is to design a form that is attractive, readable, and useful, at a reasonable price.

After a report design is approved, you should document the design in a **report analysis form**, which contains information about the fields, data types and lengths, report frequency and distribution, and other comments. Figure 7-37 shows a report analysis form for the Employee Hours report.

Designing Character-Based Reports

Today, most reports are designed in a graphical environment with a choice of typefaces and scalable fonts, which gives the designer more freedom than a character-based environment. Some information systems, still use character-based reports that are produced on high-speed impact printers. Those reports often are printed on **greenbar** paper stock, which uses alternating green and white bands that make the report easier to read.

PRINTER SPACING CHARTS   Although less common now, in the current era of graphical design, printer spacing charts still are used to design new character-based reports and modify existing ones. A **printer spacing chart** is a grid of rows and columns that represents the lines and positions on a page of printer paper. Most high-speed impact printers can print up to 132 characters per line, so printer spacing charts must include at least that many positions.

On a printer spacing chart, you indicate print positions for variable information by entering format codes to specify output requirements and field sizes. In Figure 7-38 on the next page, the third and fifth lines on the printer spacing chart show variable output specifications for the detail lines. The first output field on line 3 is a 15-character field named LAST NAME. The format specification for that field is written as XXXXXXXXXXXXXXX. The second output field, FIRST NAME, has 10 characters, so the format specification is written as XXXXXXXXXX. You also can write long, alphanumeric formats by marking the first and last positions with an X and connecting the Xs with a dashed line. For example, you can indicate the FIRST NAME field as X---------X.

The third field on the detail line is a two-digit field named AGE. In Figure 7-38, the format is written as Z9; the Z indicates that any leading zero in the age is to be suppressed. The fourth field is a six-digit field named BIRTH DATE; its format is Z9/99/99.

Notice that the specification for the fifth line is identical to that of the third line. The information was repeated to indicate the line spacing desired. The fourth line was left blank to tell the programmer to double-space the detail lines. The detail line specifications appear on consecutive lines to indicate single-spacing.

The wavy vertical lines drawn under each output field below the fifth line indicate that detail line output continues using the same format. Thus, a third detail line with the same format specifications would be printed on line 7 of the report, a fourth on line 9, and so on. In addition to showing line spacing, you must show detail line information when other output, such as totals, will follow that line. If reports span multiple pages, you should prepare charts for the following pages if they differ from the first report page.

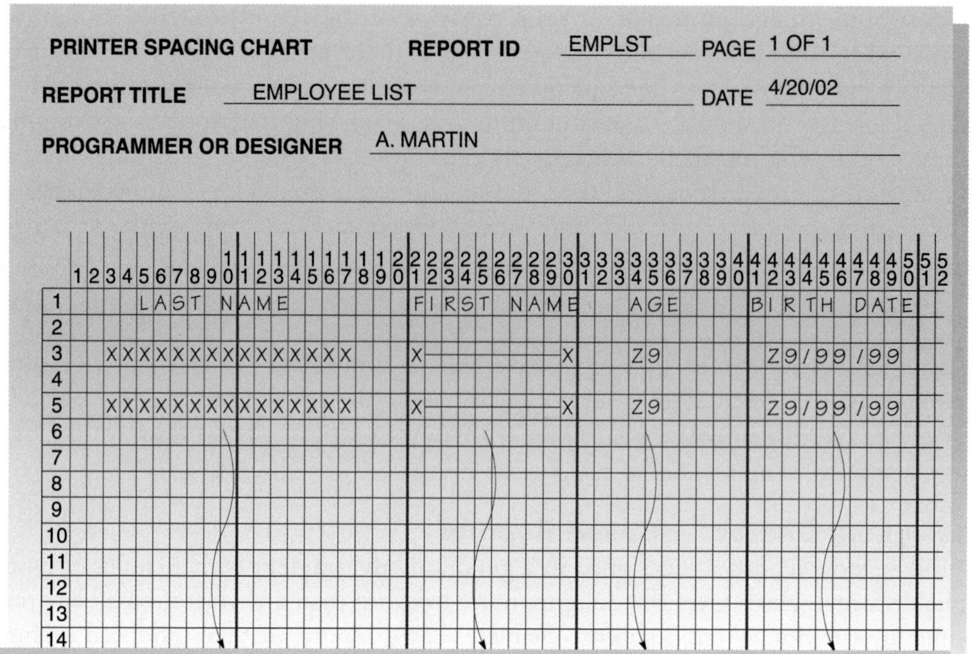

```
PRINTER SPACING CHART          REPORT ID     EMPLST     PAGE 1 OF 1

REPORT TITLE    EMPLOYEE LIST                           DATE 4/20/02

PROGRAMMER OR DESIGNER    A. MARTIN
```

	LAST NAME	FIRST NAME	AGE	BIRTH DATE
1	LAST NAME	FIRST NAME	AGE	BIRTH DATE
3	XXXXXXXXXXXXXXX	X———X	Z9	Z9/99/99
5	XXXXXXXXXXXXXXX	X———X	Z9	Z9/99/99

```
LAST NAME        FIRST NAME    AGE    BIRTH DATE
Christophersen   George        39     10/27/61
Stein            Josephine     82      2/05/19
Caviggiola       Robert        10     12/13/90
Warner           Mary Ann      23      4/30/78
```

FIGURE 7-38 A printer spacing chart and report sample, with both constant and variable information.

WHAT DO YOU THINK?

Lynn Jennings is the IT manager at Lazy Eddie, a chain that specializes in beanbag chairs and recliners. She asked Jan Lauten, a senior systems analyst, to review the large number of printed reports that are distributed to Lazy Eddie's 35 store managers. "Jan, I just can't believe that our people really read all of those reports," Lynn said. "We constantly add new reports, and we never seem to eliminate the old ones. Sometimes I think all we're doing is keeping the paper companies in business!" Jan replied, "I agree, but what can we do? The managers say they want the reports, but I always see them stacked on top of file cabinets. I've never seen anyone read a report."

"I have an idea," Lynn said. "I want you to come up with a procedure that requires users to review and justify their information needs to see if they really use the reports we send them. You could design a form that asks if the information still is required, and why. Try to get users to decide if a report is worth the cost of producing it. Do you think you can do it?"

"Sure I can," Jan replied. When Jan returned to her office, she wondered where to begin.

What advice would you give to Jan?

Printing Volume and Time Requirements

Technological advances have resulted in printers that are faster, better, and less expensive than their predecessors. Powerful laser printers are the standard for business printing because they offer speed, excellent quality, and graphical output. Impact printers, still are used for multiple form output and certain high-speed applications.

Although printed output is necessary in many situations, a high volume of reports can significantly increase a system's TCO (Total Cost of Ownership). Paper is expensive to purchase, print, store, and dispose of, and printed information is outdated quickly. Printed output can include a three-page document for one user, or a 500-page inventory report for another.

As a systems analyst, you must determine if printing resources can handle the system's requirements. Although technology advances have made high-speed printing relatively inexpensive, every printer has specific capacities and limitations. Efficient printing operations, timely delivery of finished reports, and accurate forecasts of paper and storage needs all depend on accurate estimates of print volumes and times.

LENGTH CALCULATIONS   After completing a report design, it is important to estimate the length of the printed output. For example, consider the employee hours report shown in Figure 7-36 on page 7.31. Assume that the company has a total of 380 employees in six shops. The paper will have 66 lines per page. Six lines are reserved for the top and bottom margins, leaving 60 printed lines per page. In the report, every page begins with six lines of heading information (report heading and page heading), leaving 54 lines per page for printing employee detail lines, shop (group) footing lines, and grand total footing lines.

Because there are 380 employees, 380 detail lines will print. Each of the six shops has three footing lines, for a total of 18 shop footing lines. Finally, the grand total requires three additional lines. The complete report will include 401 detail and total lines. At 54 lines per page, the report will require 7.4 pages. Therefore, the final estimate for the paper requirements for the weekly report is eight printed pages per week. Figure 7-39 shows those volume calculations.

CALCULATING THE LENGTH OF THE REPORT

	66	total lines available per page of stock paper
-	6	lines reserved for top and bottom margins
-	6	lines per page for 2 title lines, 1 blank line, 2 column heading lines, and 1 hyphen line
	54	available detail lines per page
	3	lines per shop for 1 line with hyphens, 1 line of shop totals, and 1 blank line
X	6	shops
	18	shop footing lines
+	3	lines per report for 2 lines with hyphens and 1 line of grand totals
	21	footing lines
+	380	detail lines
	401	report lines
÷	54	lines per page
	7.4	printed pages

FIGURE 7-39   Report volume calculations for the Employee Hours report shown in Figure 7-36.

TIME CALCULATIONS   You also can estimate the time required to print the report. Laser printers are rated in **ppm**, which represents the number of **pages per minute**. For example, at 16 ppm, a laser printer would print the eight-page Employee Hours report in about 30 seconds. Companies also use high-speed **line printers**, which are impact printers commonly used for internal reports such as payroll or inventory listings. If the Employee Hours report were printed on a line printer with a speed of 2,000 lines per minute, you would divide 401 lines by 2,000 lines per minute, for a total time of .20 minutes, or 12 seconds of printing time.

CALCULATING THE LENGTH OF THE REPORT

66	total lines available per page of stock paper
- 6	lines reserved for top and bottom margins
- 6	lines per page for 2 page heading lines, 1 blank line, 2 column heading lines, and 1 blank line
54	available detail lines per page
2,100,000	detail lines
÷ 54	detail lines per page

38,889 printed pages

CALCULATING THE TIME TO PRINT THE REPORT
LINE PRINTER AT 2000 LINES PER MINUTE

4	printed heading lines per page
x 38,889	pages
155,556	printed heading lines
+ 2,100,000	printed detail lines
2,255,556	printed lines
÷ 2,000	lines printed per minute

1,128 minutes = 18.8 hours of printer usage

LASER PRINTER AT 16 PPM

38,889	pages
÷ 16	pages per minute

2,431 minutes = 40.5 hours of printer usage

FIGURE 7-40 Report length calculations for a monthly report for 2,100,000 customer accounts.

N THE WEB

r an overview of Output
ntrol and Security visit
site.com/sad4e/more.htm,
ck Systems Analysis and
sign Chapter 7 and then
ck the Output Control and
curity link.

Figure 7-40 shows the paper requirements and printer time calculations for a much larger report. The example dramatically shows the value of volume and time estimates. Imagine the problems that might occur when the report is printed for the first time if no one estimated that it would take nearly 19 hours to print 38,889 pages.

Both of the time calculation examples are for reports printed on plain paper. If special forms are used, the calculation process is similar, but you must add a time factor for loading and unloading the forms.

Output Control and Security

Output must be accurate, complete, current, and secure. Companies use various **output control** methods to maintain output integrity and security. For example, every report should include an appropriate title, report number or code, printing date, and time period covered. Reports should have pages that are numbered consecutively, identified as *Page xx of xx*, and the end of the report should be labeled clearly. Control totals and record counts should be reconciled against input totals and counts. Reports should be selected at random for a thorough check of correctness and completeness. All processing errors or interruptions must be logged so they can be analyzed.

Output security protects privacy rights and shields the organization's proprietary data from theft or unauthorized access. To ensure output security, you must perform several important tasks. First, limit the number of printed copies and use a tracking procedure to account for each copy. When printed output is distributed from a central location, you should use specific procedures to ensure that the output is delivered to authorized recipients only. That is especially true when reports contain sensitive information, such as payroll data. All sensitive reports should be stored in secure areas. All pages of confidential reports should be labeled appropriately.

As shown in Figure 7-41, it is important to shred sensitive reports, out-of-date reports, and output from aborted print runs. Blank check forms must be stored in a secure location and be inventoried regularly to verify that no forms are missing. If signature stamps are used, they must be stored in a secure location away from the forms storage location.

In most organizations, the IT department is responsible for output control and security measures. Systems analysts must be concerned with security issues as they design, implement, and support information systems. Whenever possible, security should be designed into the system by using passwords, shielding sensitive data, and controlling user access. Physical security will always be necessary, especially in the case of printed output that is tangible and can be viewed and handled easily.

As part of the trend toward enterprise-wide data management, many companies have installed diskless workstations, which offer security advantages. A **diskless workstation** as shown in Figure 7-42, is a network terminal that supports a full-featured user interface, but limits the printing or copying of data, except to certain network resources that can be monitored and controlled more easily.

FIGURE 7-41 To maintain output security, it is important to shred sensitive reports, out-of-date reports, and output from aborted print runs.

FIGURE 7-42 A diskless workstation supports a full-featured user interface, but can limit the printing or copying of data

SOFTWEAR, LIMITED

SoftWear, Limited decided to use the payroll package developed by Pacific Software Solutions and customize it by adding its own ESIP system to handle SWL's Employee Savings and Investment Plan.

Because most of the payroll requirements would be handled by Pacific's payroll package, the IT team decided that Carla Moore would work on the new ESIP modules, and Rick Williams would concentrate on the rest of the payroll system. A new systems analyst, Becky Evans, was assigned to help Rick with the payroll package.

Pacific Software Solutions offered free training for new customers, so Rick and Becky attended a three-day train-the-trainer workshop at Pacific's site in Los Angeles. When they returned, they began developing a one-day training session for SWL users, including people from the accounting, payroll, and human resources departments. The initial training would include the features and processing functions of the new payroll package that was scheduled to arrive the following week.

In the meantime, as Carla began to design the user interface for the ESIP system, she realized that she would need to develop two new source documents: an ESIP Option form and an ESIP Deduction Authorization form. She also planned to design a main switchboard and all necessary screen forms.

Carla started by designing the ESIP Option Form that could be used for adding new ESIP options and modifying existing ones when authorized by the vice president of human resources. She included an ESIP ID code, an ESIP option name, and other information as shown in Figure 7-43. For each field, she established a range of acceptable values.

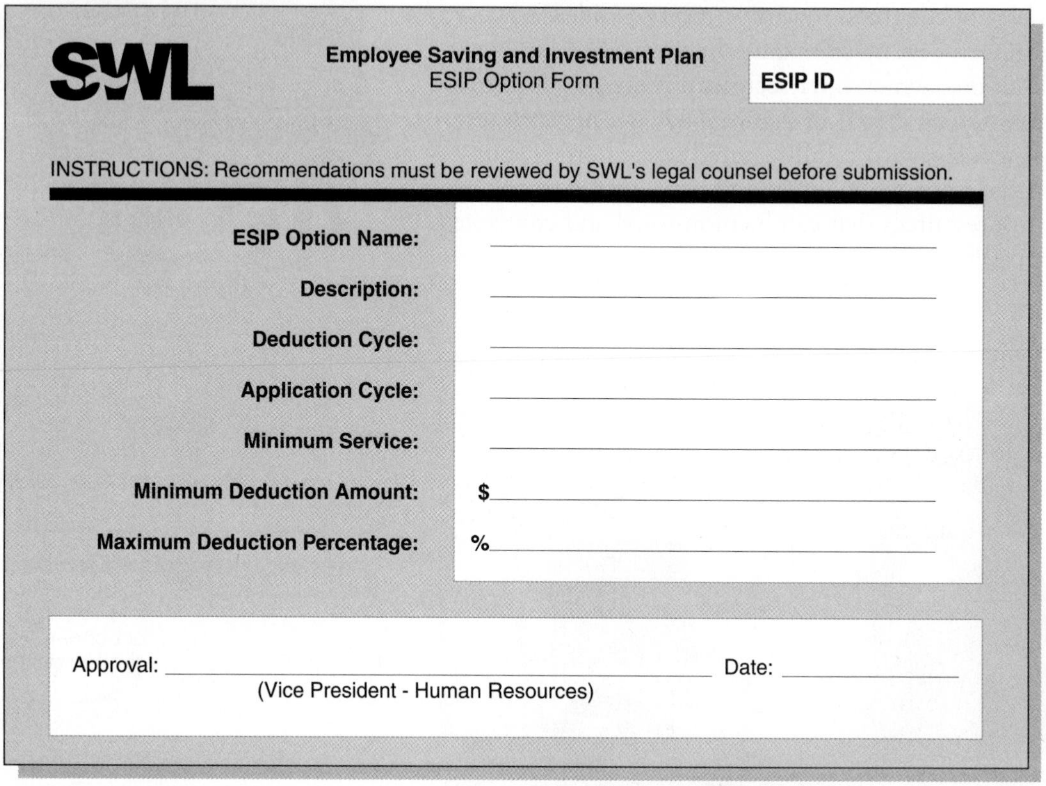

SWL

Employee Saving and Investment Plan
ESIP Option Form

ESIP ID _____

INSTRUCTIONS: Recommendations must be reviewed by SWL's legal counsel before submission.

ESIP Option Name: _____

Description: _____

Deduction Cycle: _____

Application Cycle: _____

Minimum Service: _____

Minimum Deduction Amount: $_____

Maximum Deduction Percentage: %_____

Approval: _____ Date: _____
(Vice President - Human Resources)

FIGURE 7-43   The design for a source document to add or change ESIP options.

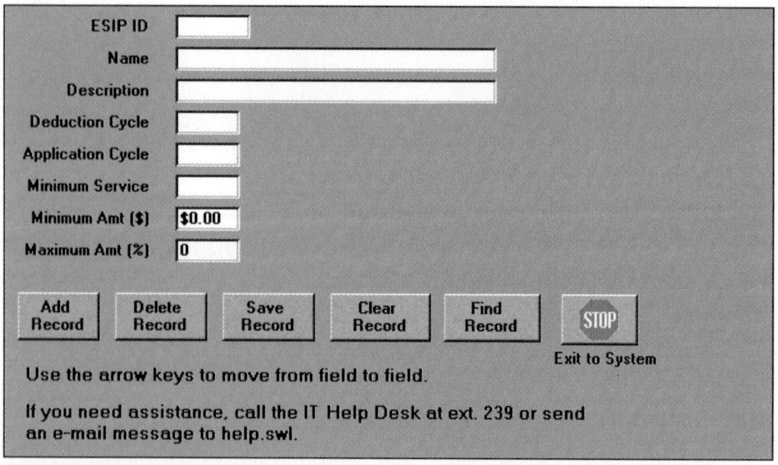

ESIP ID [   ]
Name [   ]
Description [   ]
Deduction Cycle [   ]
Application Cycle [   ]
Minimum Service [   ]
Minimum Amt ($) [$0.00]
Maximum Amt (%) [0]

| Add Record | Delete Record | Save Record | Clear Record | Find Record | STOP |

Exit to System

Use the arrow keys to move from field to field.

If you need assistance, call the IT Help Desk at ext. 239 or send an e-mail message to help.swl.

FIGURE 7-44   Data entry screen for adding and changing ESIP options.

Next, Carla worked on a data entry screen based on the ESIP Option Form. Using SWL's existing screen design standards, she quickly developed the screen shown in Figure 7-44. Carla decided that she could make the screen more useful if users could view data on existing options. The user could add, delete, or find a record by entering the appropriate action codes.

Instead of waiting until all input design was finished, Carla decided to create mock-ups to show Tina Pham, vice president of human resources and Mike Feiner, director of human resources. Figure 7-45 shows the two mock-ups. Carla reasoned that if any comments or suggestions were offered, they also would apply to other input screens.

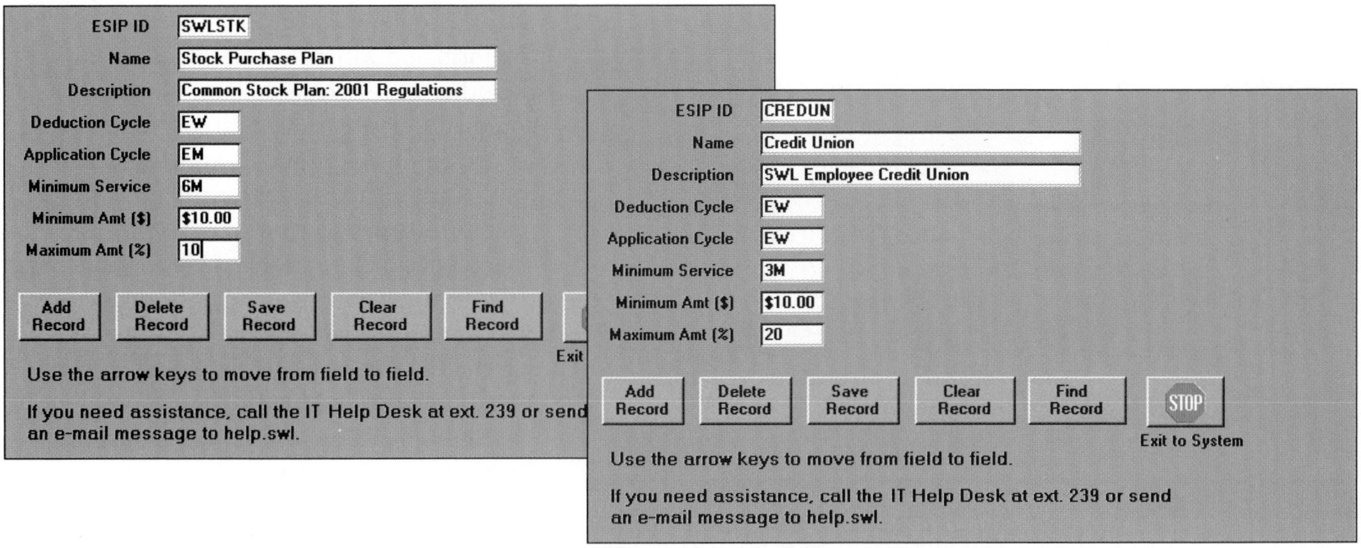

FIGURE 7-45 Carla's mock-up screens, with actual data, to obtain user approval.

The ESIP Deduction Authorization Form was more complicated than the ESIP Option Form because it required more data and signatures. It took several hours for Carla to design the form shown in Figure 7-46. She divided the form into three sections: the employee completes the information in the top section; human resources complete the middle section; and payroll representatives complete the bottom section.

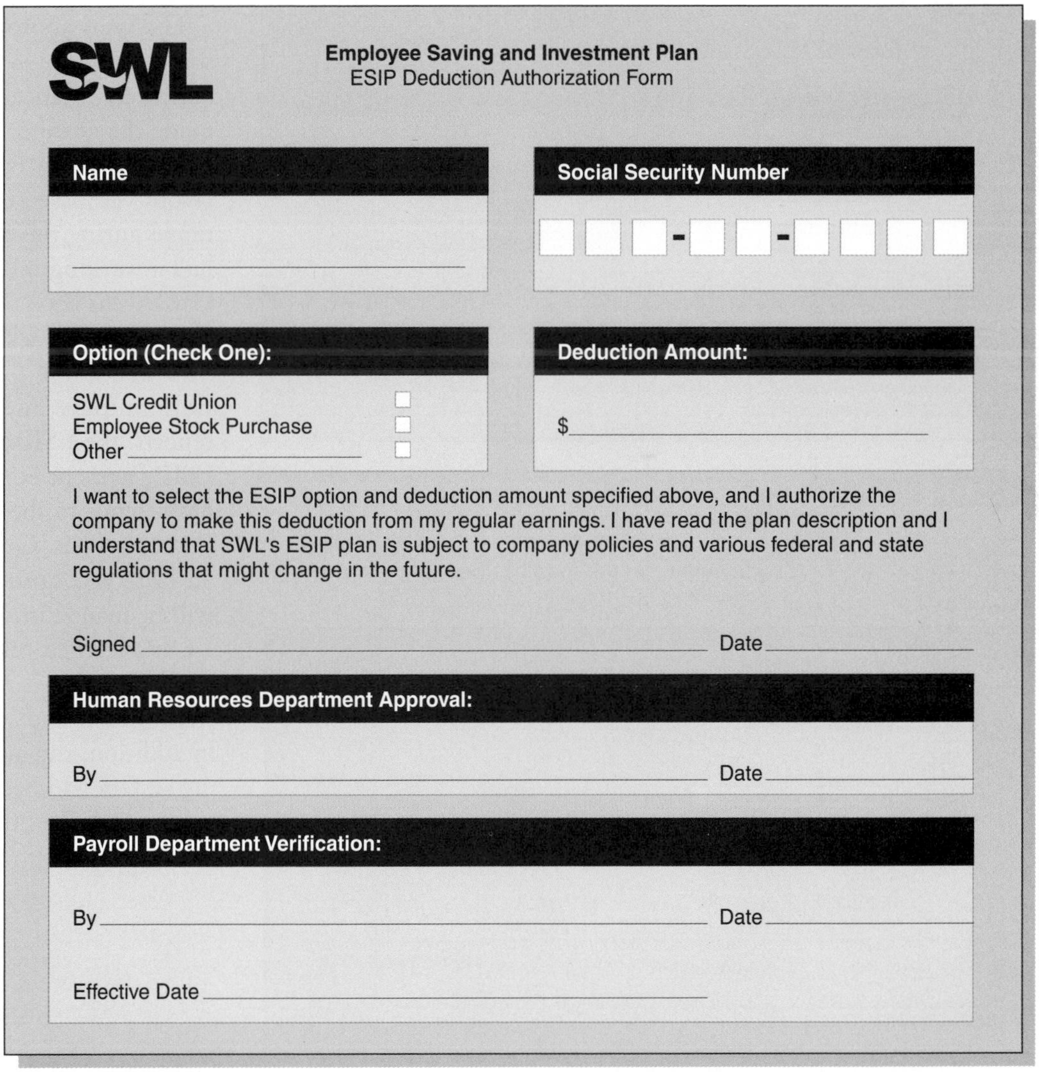

SWL

Employee Saving and Investment Plan
ESIP Deduction Authorization Form

Name

Social Security Number

___ - __ - ____

Option (Check One):

SWL Credit Union ☐
Employee Stock Purchase ☐
Other ________ ☐

Deduction Amount:

$________

I want to select the ESIP option and deduction amount specified above, and I authorize the company to make this deduction from my regular earnings. I have read the plan description and I understand that SWL's ESIP plan is subject to company policies and various federal and state regulations that might change in the future.

Signed ________ Date ________

Human Resources Department Approval:

By ________ Date ________

Payroll Department Verification:

By ________ Date ________

Effective Date ________

FIGURE 7-46 The design for the ESIP Deduction Authorization Form.

| FIGURE 7-47 | Data entry screen for ESIP deductions. Here, the user has entered an employee Social Security number and is about to press the ENTER key. Notice that the form has several command buttons, including a STOP button that exits the program. |

| FIGURE 7-48 | After the user presses the ENTER key, the system retrieves the employee name and displays it so the user can verify it. Notice that the user must check a box to verify that the form has been signed properly. |

| FIGURE 7-49 | In this step, the user has entered an employee stock purchase deduction of $10.00 and the current date and is ready to save the record. |

Carla designed a data entry screen based on the form and made the screen consistent with the other ESIP screen designs. Now a user could add, delete, save, clear, or find a record by clicking the appropriate command buttons. Carla also provided instructions to the operator for exiting from the system.

Carla decided to create a series of mock-ups to show users how the new ESIP deduction screen would work. Figure 7-47 shows the screen after the user has entered an employee's Social Security number. In Figure 7-48, the system has retrieved the employee's name, Sean Fitzpatrick, so the user can verify it against the source document. Figure 7-49 shows that the user has entered the stock purchase plan code, SWLSTK, and the system has supplied the name. Finally, the user enters the $10.00 deduction and the current date.

The users approved the new design, with one suggestion — the system date should be added automatically as the entry date. Carla made the change and designed the switchboard shown in Figure 7-50. The switchboard layout was based on comments that users made during the design process. Now that she had a working model of the input system, Carla went back to the users to show them the complete package.

At that point, Carla started to work on the ESIP outputs. She had to design several reports: the ESIP Deduction Register, the ESIP Payment Summary, and the checks that SWL sends to the credit union and the Stock Purchase Plan. Carla also needed to develop an ESIP accounting summary as a file that will be loaded into the accounting system.

Carla learned that standard SWL company checks were used to make the payments to the credit union and stock purchase department. In addition, the output entry to the accounting system had been specified by the accounting department in a standard format for all entries into that system.

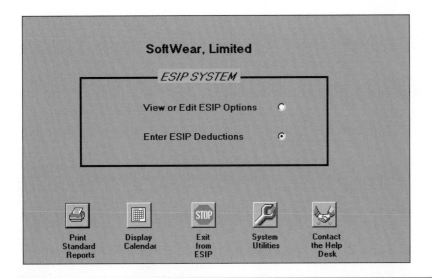

FIGURE 7-50 The ESIP switchboard includes option buttons and command buttons to select various processing choices.

To prepare the new ESIP Deduction Register, Carla reviewed the documentation from the systems analysis phase to make sure that she understood the logical design and the available data fields.

Carla decided to use a monthly format because accounting would apply some deductions on a monthly cycle. She started her design with a standard SWL report heading. Then she added a control heading and footing for each employee's Social Security number. The total of employee deductions would be compared with the transferred ESIP funds to make sure that they matched. After preparing a rough layout, Carla used a report generator (Microsoft Access) to create the design shown in Figure 7-51. Then she prepared the mock-up report shown in Figure 7-52 on the next page, using test data for the month of April 2002.

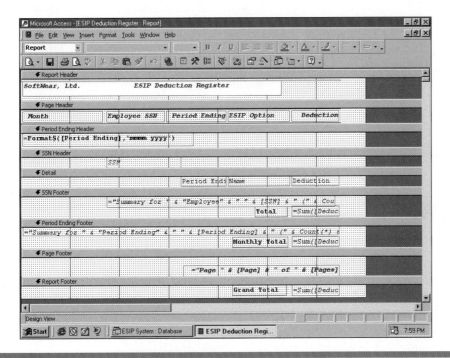

FIGURE 7-51 The layout for the ESIP Deduction Register that Carla created. Notice that SSN is a control break field. An SSN header introduces the group of detail records and an SSN footer includes subtotals for the group.

```
SoftWear, Limited          ESIP Deduction Register

 Month              Employee SSN      Period Ending  ESIP Option          Deduction
 April 2002
                    000-00-0000
                                      04/05/2002  Stock Purchase           $15.00
                                      04/05/2002  Credit Union             $20.00
                                      04/12/2002  Credit Union             $20.00
                                      04/12/2002  Stock Purchase           $15.00
                                      04/19/2002  Stock Purchase           $15.00
                                      04/19/2002  Credit Union             $25.00
                                      04/26/2002  Stock Purchase           $15.00
                                      04/26/2002  Credit Union             $20.00

                    Summary for Employee = 000000000 (8 detail records)
                                          Total                          $145.00

                    123-45-6789
                                      04/05/2002  Stock Purchase           $10.00
                                      04/05/2002  Credit Union             $30.00
                                      04/12/2002  Stock Purchase           $10.00
                                      04/12/2002  Credit Union             $30.00
                                      04/19/2002  Stock Purchase           $10.00
                                      04/19/2002  Credit Union             $30.00
                                      04/26/2002  Credit Union             $30.00
                                      04/26/2002  Stock Purchase           $10.00

                    Summary for Employee = 123456789 (8 detail records)
                                          Total                          $160.00

                    999-99-9999
                                      04/05/2002  ESIP: Option 1            $9.99
                                      04/12/2002  ESIP: Option 1            $9.99
                                      04/19/2002  ESIP: Option 1            $9.99
                                      04/26/2002  ESIP: Option 1            $9.99

                    Summary for Employee = 999999999 (4 detail records)
                                          Total                           $39.96

        Summary for 'Period Ending' = 04/26/2002 (20 detail records)
                                   Monthly Total                        $344.96
                                   Grand Total                          $344.96
```

FIGURE 7-52   Mock-up report for the ESIP Deduction Register.

When Carla showed the mock-up report to Mike Feiner, director of human resources, he said that he wanted to see the data grouped by the type of ESIP deduction with the appropriate subtotals. Carla was able to modify the report to satisfy his request. Figure 7-53 shows the revised mock-up report that she sent to Mike, which he later approved. Carla also sent the mock-up report to Amy Calico, director of payroll. Several days later, she received an e-mail message from Amy that approved the version without any changes.

```
SoftWear, Limited        ESIP Deduction Register by ESIP Option

Name                    SSN              Period Ending        Deduction

Credit Union            000-00-0000         04/05/2002          $20.00
                        000-00-0000         04/12/2002          $20.00
                        000-00-0000         04/19/2002          $25.00
                        000-00-0000         04/26/2002          $20.00
                        123-45-6789         04/05/2002          $30.00
                        123-45-6789         04/12/2002          $30.00
                        123-45-6789         04/19/2002          $30.00
                        123-45-6789         04/26/2002          $30.00
                                      ESIP Option Total        $205.00


ESIP: Option 1          999-99-9999         04/05/2002           $9.99
                        999-99-9999         04/12/2002           $9.99
                        999-99-9999         04/19/2002           $9.99
                        999-99-9999         04/26/2002           $9.99
                                      ESIP Option Total         $39.96


Stock Purchase Plan     000-00-0000         04/05/2002          $15.00
                        000-00-0000         04/12/2002          $15.00
                        000-00-0000         04/19/2002          $15.00
                        000-00-0000         04/26/2002          $15.00
                        123-45-6789         04/05/2002          $10.00
                        123-45-6789         04/12/2002          $10.00
                        123-45-6789         04/19/2002          $10.00
                        123-45-6789         04/26/2002          $10.00
                                      ESIP Option Total        $100.00

                                          Grand Total:         $344.96
```

FIGURE 7-53 Version 2 of the ESIP Deduction Register as requested by Mike Feiner. Notice that detail lines now are grouped by ESIP option, rather than employee SSN.

During the systems analysis phase, Carla learned that the accounting department required a control report to show the ESIP deduction amounts that were not yet applied. The control report is used to verify the amount of the checks or fund transfers SWL makes to the Credit Union and Stock Purchase Plan. The accounting department needs the control report to verify the accounting system outputs and balance the ESIP deduction totals against the payroll system's Payroll Register report.

Figure 7-54 shows a mock-up of the ESIP Payment Summary report. Carla met with Buddy Goodson, director of accounting, to review the design. Buddy was pleased with the report and felt it would be acceptable to the company's outside auditors. Buddy met with the auditing firm later that week and secured the team's approval.

```
SoftWear, Limited          ESIP Payment Summary Report

Last Deduction Period in Month: 04/26/2002

ESIP Code              Name                        Deduction

CREDUN                 Credit Union                 $205.00

ESIP01                 ESIP: Option 1                $39.96

SWLSTK                 Stock Purchase Plan          $100.00


                                    Grand Total:    $344.96
```

FIGURE 7-54 Mock-up of the ESIP Payment Summary Report.

YOUR TURN

Carla Moore asked you for some help. Initially, she believed that the new ESIP Deduction Authorization form could handle all current and future deductions, including the employee stock purchase plan. SWL's legal counsel, however, says that the Employee Stock Purchase Plan requires a separate enrollment and change form because of governmental regulations.

Carla wants you to design a new source document for the stock purchase plan and a matching data entry screen. You should start by reviewing the existing stock purchase form, which is shown in Figure 3-28 on page 3.31.

CHAPTER SUMMARY

In this chapter, you began your study of the systems design phase. The purpose of systems design is to create a physical model of the system that satisfies the logical design requirements that were defined during the systems analysis phase. The chapter began with a discussion of human-computer interaction concepts and graphical user interfaces (GUIs), which use graphical objects and techniques that allow users to communicate with the system.

You learned that user-centered design principles are used to understand the business functions, maximize graphical effectiveness, profile the system's users, think like a user, use prototyping, design a comprehensive interface, continue the feedback process, and document the interface design.

The chapter listed several interface design guidelines, which suggested that you focus on basic objectives, make the interface easy to learn and use, provide features that promote efficiency, make it easy for users to obtain Help and correct errors, minimize input data problems, provide feedback to users, create an attractive layout and design, and use familiar terms and images.

You learned that an interface can include various controls, including menu bars, toolbars, drop-down menus, dialog boxes, toggle buttons, list boxes, option buttons, check boxes, command buttons, and spin bars. Controls are placed on a main switchboard, which is like a graphical version of a main menu.

During input design, you learned about batch and online input methods. Input design includes selecting appropriate input media and methods, developing efficient input procedures, reducing input volume, and avoiding input errors. In carrying out those tasks, the systems analyst must consider three key procedures: data capture, data entry, and input methods. Data capture involves identifying and recording source data. Data entry involves converting source data into a computer-readable form and entering it into the system. A wide variety of input media is available, including optical, voice, and magnetic recognition devices; special-purpose terminals; and graphical input devices.

An effective way to reduce input errors is to reduce input volume. You also can reduce errors by using well-designed data entry screens, and by using data validation checks that verify data sequence, existence, range and limit, reasonableness, validity, combination, and batch controls.

You learned about source document design and the various zones in a source document, including the heading zone, the control zone, the instruction zone, the body zone, the totals zone, and the authorization zone. Next, you learned about input control, including audit trails, data security, and records retention policies.

The section on output included a discussion of output design issues and a description of various types of output, such as Web-based information delivery, audio output, automated facsimile and faxback systems, e-mail, and other specialized forms of output.

You learned about various types of printed reports, including detail, exception, and summary reports. The chapter also described the features and sections of reports, including control fields, control breaks, report headers and footers, page headers and footers, and group headers and footers. Examples of report design were presented, along with suggestions about designing character-based reports. You learned how to estimate printing volume and time.

Finally, you learned about output control and the various measures you can take to achieve adequate output control to ensure that information is correct, complete, and secure.

Key Terms

aesthetics (*7.5*)
audit trail (*7.22*)
authorization zone (*7.19*)
automated facsimile (*7.25*)
batch (*7.13*)
batch controls (*7.17*)
batch input (*7.13*)
body zone (*7.19*)
calendar control (*7.11*)
check box (*7.11*)
combination checks (*7.17*)
command buttons (*7.11*)
context-sensitive (*7.8*)
control break (*7.27*)
control break report (*7.27*)
control field (*7.27*)
control zone (*7.19*)
data capture (*7.13*)
data entry (*7.13*)
data security (*7.22*)
data type checks (*7.16*)
data validation checks (*7.16*)
detail line (*7.27*)
detail report (*7.27*)
dialog box (*7.11*)
diskless workstation (*7.37*)
drop-down list box (*7.11*)
encrypted (*7.22*)
encryption (*7.22*)
ergonomics (*7.5*)
exception report (*7.28*)
existence checks (*7.16*)
faxback (*7.25*)
form filling (*7.15*)
form layout (*7.17*)
garbage in garbage out (GIGO) (*7.12*)
graphical user interface (GUI) (*7.4*)
greenbar (*7.33*)
group footer (*7.31*)
group header (*7.31*)
hash totals (*7.17*)
heading zone (*7.19*)
human-computer interaction (HCI) (*7.3*)
input control (*7.22*)
input masks (*7.9*)

instruction zone (*7.19*)
interface technology (*7.5*)
limit check (*7.17*)
line printers (*7.35*)
list box (*7.11*)
magnetic data strips (*7.13*)
menu bar (*7.11*)
microfiche (*7.25*)
microfilm (*7.25*)
online data entry (*7.13*)
option buttons (*7.11*)
output control (*7.36*)
output security (*7.36*)
page footer (*7.30*)
page header (*7.30*)
ppm (pages per minute) (*7.35*)
printer spacing chart (*7.33*)
process-control (*7.1*)
radio buttons (*7.11*)
range checks (*7.17*)
reasonableness checks (*7.17*)
records retention policy (*7.22*)
referential integrity (*7.17*)
report analysis form (*7.33*)
report footer (*7.29*)
report header (*7.29*)
scroll bar (*7.11*)
separators (*7.15*)
sequence checks (*7.16*)
source data automation (*7.13*)
source document (*7.17*)
spin bar (*7.11*)
storyboards (*7.5*)
summary report (*7.28*)
swipe scanners (*7.13*)
switchboard (*7.11*)
text box (*7.11*)
toggle button (*7.11*)
toolbar (*7.11*)
totals zone (*7.19*)
turnaround documents (*7.26*)
user-centered (*7.2*)
user interface (*7.1*)
user-selected (*7.8*)
validity checks (*7.17*)

Chapter Review

1. Explain the concept of human-computer interaction (HCI).

2. Describe eight principles for a user-centered interface design.

3. Explain each of the data validation checks mentioned in this chapter.

4. Describe six types of user interface controls, and provide an example of how you could use each type in a data entry screen.

5. Explain the concept of a GUI and a switchboard. How does a GUI design differ from a character-based screen design?

6. Explain batch and online input methods. Define source data automation and provide an example.

7. Provide six guidelines for reducing input volume.

8. List and describe various types of output, including technology-based forms of information delivery.

9. Define detail reports, exception reports, and summary reports. Explain the concept of a control field and how it is used to produce a control-break report.

10. On a printer spacing chart, how do you indicate the following objects: constant fields, variable fields, and line spacing?

Discussion Topics

1. Some systems analysts maintain that source documents are unnecessary. They say that all input can be entered directly into the system, without wasting time in an intermediate step. Do you agree? Can you think of any situations where source documents are essential?

2. Some systems analysts argue, "Give users what they ask for. If they want lots of reports and reams of data, then that is what you should provide. Otherwise, they will feel that you are trying to tell them how to do their jobs." Others say, "Systems analysts should let users know what information can be obtained from the system. If you listen to users, you'll never get anywhere, because they really don't know what they want and don't understand information systems." What do you think of these arguments?

3. Suppose your company employs 75 technical support representatives who travel constantly and work at customer sites. Your task is to design an information system that provides technical data and information to the field team. What types of output and information delivery would you suggest for the system?

4. A user interface can be quite restrictive. For example, the interface design might not allow a user to exit to a Windows desktop or to log on to the Internet. Should a user interface include such restrictions? Why or why not?

Apply Your Knowledge

1 North Shore Boat Sales

Situation:

North Shore Boat Sales sells new and used boats and operates a Web-based boat brokerage business in Toronto. The company has grown and North Shore needs a new information system to manage the inventory, the brokerage operation, and information about prospective buyers and sellers. Don Robinson, the owner, asked you to design samples of the computer screens and reports that the new system might produce.

1. Design a switchboard that includes the main information management functions that North Shore might require. Create a storyboard with a design layout that allows customers to perform the following functions: obtain information about new boats, obtain information about used boats, send an e-mail to North Shore, learn more about the company, or review links to other marine-related sites.

2. Prospective buyers might want to search for boats by type, size, price range, or manufacturer. Develop a screen design that would permit those choices.

3. Suggest reports that might be useful to North Shore's management.

4. Suggest the general layout for a Web-based source document that prospective sellers could use to describe their boats. The information should include boat type (sail or power), manufacturer, year, length, type of engine, hull color, and asking price.

2 Terrier News

Situation:

Terrier News is a monthly newsletter devoted to various breeds of terriers and topics of interest to terrier owners and breeders. Annie West, the editor and publisher, asked you to help her design a system to enter and manage the hundreds of classified ads that Terrier News publishes. Some ads are for dogs wanted; some are for dogs for sale; and some offer products and services.

1. Design a suitable source document for ads that are telephoned or mailed in.

2. Explain user-centered design principles in a brief memo to Annie.

3. Suggest at least four user interface design guidelines that could be used for the new system.

4. Suggest several types of controls that might be used on the switchboard you plan to design. Explain why you chose each control, and create a storyboard that shows the switchboard layout.

3 Sky-High Internet Services

Situation:

Sky-High Internet Services is a leading Internet service provider in a metropolitan area. The new customer billing system has caused an increase in complaints. Tammy Jones, the office manager, asked you to investigate the situation. After interviewing data entry operators and observing the online data input process, you are fairly certain that most errors occur when data is entered.

1. Write a brief memo to Tammy explaining the importance of data validation during the input process.

2. Suggest at least three specific data validation checks that might help reduce input errors.

3. Would a batch input system offer any advantages? Write a brief memo to Tammy stating your views.

4. Suppose that Sky-High is predicting 25 percent annual growth, on a current base of 90,000 customers. If the growth pattern holds, how many customers will Sky-High have in three years? If it takes about 12 minutes to enter a new customer into the system, how many additional data entry operators will be needed to handle the growth next year? Assume that an operator works about 2,000 hours per year. Also assume a 30 percent annual attrition rate for existing customers.

4 Castle Point Antique Auction

Situation:

Castle Point Antique Auction operates a successful Web site that offers an auction forum for buyers and sellers of fine antiques. Monica Creighton, the owner, asked you to help her design some new documents and reports.

1. Suggest the general layout for a Web-based source document that prospective bidders would submit. The information should include user ID, password, name, address, telephone, e-mail address, item number, bid offered, and method of payment (money order, check, American Express, MasterCard, or Visa).

2. Suggest the general layout for a Web-based source document that prospective sellers could use to describe their antiques. The information should include the user ID, password, item, dimensions, origin, condition, and asking price.

3. Write a brief memo to Monica explaining the difference between detail reports, exception reports, and summary reports. Suggest at least one example of each type of report that she might want to consider.

4. Suppose Castle Point wants to print a catalog of current items. How long would it take to print a list of 2,500 items, at five items per page, on a laser printer rated at 20 ppm?

Chapter Assignments

1. Search the Web to find an example of an attractive user interface. Document your research and discuss it with your class.

2. Examine various application software packages to find example of good (or bad) user interface design. Document your research and discuss it with your class.

3. Search your own files or review other sources to find good (or bad) examples of source document design. Document your research and discuss it with your class.

4. Visit the administrative office at your school, or a local company. Ask to see examples of output documents, such as computer-printed invoices, form letters, or class rosters. Analyze the design and appearance of each document, and try to identify at least one possible improvement for each.

CASE STUDIES

Case Studies offer an opportunity for you to practice specific skills and knowledge learned in the chapter and provide practical experience for you as a systems analyst. Two of the case studies (New Century Health Clinic and Ridgeway Company) are continuing case studies that appear in each chapter. Additionally, one continuing case study (SCR Associates) utilizes the Internet to practice some of the topics covered in this chapter.

NEW CENTURY HEALTH CLINIC

Based on what you have learned in this chapter, complete the following assignments.

The associates at New Century Health Clinic approved your recommendations for a new computer system. Your next step is to develop a design for the new system, including a user interface, inputs, and outputs.

Assignments

1. Determine the data required for a new patient. Design an input source document that will be used to capture the data and a data entry screen to input the information.

2. What data validation checks would the clinic need for the new patient data entry screen? Write a brief memo with your recommendations.

3. Design the daily appointment list and a monthly statement using a printer spacing chart or graph paper. Include a mock-up report and a report analysis form for each report.

4. Dr. Jones has asked you to create a monthly Claim Status Summary report. He wants you to include the insurance company number, the patient number and name, the procedure date, the procedure code and description, the fee, the date the claim was filed, the amount of the claim, the amount of reimbursement, and the amount remaining unpaid. He wants you to group the data by insurance company number, with subtotals by company and grand totals, for each numeric field. When you design the report, make sure to include printer spacing charts, a mock-up report, and a report analysis form.

RIDGEWAY COMPANY

Thomas McGee, vice president of operations for the Ridgeway Company, recently requested three new reports.

1. A monthly report showing daily sales totals at the pro shop, restaurant, and bar that will print in date order for each facility.

2. A monthly report showing the charge total for each member, with details of each charge, printed in member number order.

3. A report listing each member who made no charges during the month, printed in member number order.

The following information is available on a billing record.

Field	Description
CHARGE DATE	8 numeric digits, YYYYMMDD form
CHARGE AMOUNT	6 numeric digits, including 2 decimal positions
CHARGE LOCATION CODE	1 numeric digit: 1 = restaurant, 2 = bar, 3 = pro shop
CHARGE DESCRIPTION	25 characters
MEMBER NUMBER	4 numeric digits
MEMBER LAST NAME	18 characters
MEMBER FIRST NAME	15 characters

Assignments

1. Design each of the three management reports using printer spacing charts or graph paper. Include any record groups and subtotals that are required.

2. Suppose Thomas wants a further breakdown in the second report, so that members and their purchases are listed under each of the operations (pro shop, restaurant, and bar). What modifications do you need to make in the report design?

3. Classify each report (detail, exception, summary) and explain the reasons for your choices.

4. Thomas decides that he wants the second report (monthly sales total by member) printed in order of highest to lowest sales. What modifications do you need to make in the report design?

BATES VIDEO CLUB

The Bates Video Club has hired you to design two online data entry screens. Based on what you have learned in this chapter, complete the following assignments.

Assignments

1. Design a data entry screen for entering new members, using the source document shown in Figure 7-24 on page 7.20.

2. You were not consulted when the membership application form shown in Figure 7-24 was designed originally. Do you have any suggestions that might improve the design?

3. The owner of Bates Video Club also would like you to design a video rental input screen. In addition to the video data, the video rental form must include the following fields: Member Number, Name, and Date.

4. Suggest at least three data validation checks that might help reduce input errors for the video rental system.

SCR ASSOCIATES

SCR Associates is an information technology consulting firm that offers IT solutions and training for small- and medium-sized companies. SCR's slogan is "We Know IT!"

Background

As a newly hired systems analyst, you will handle assignments, work on various SCR projects, and apply the skills you learned in the text. SCR needs an information system to manage training operations at the new SCR training center. The new system will be called TIMS (Training Information Management System).

The SCR case is available as an interactive, Web-based case study. You can log on to the Shelly Cashman Series site at www.scsite.com/sad4e/scr for instructions and assignments. If you prefer to complete the case study without using the Internet then you must download the data disk. See the inside back cover for instructions for downloading the data disk or see your instructor for more information on accessing the files required for this book.

Situation

In Part 7 of the SCR case, you will develop a user interface, prepare input and output designs, and develop source documents for the new TIMS system.

Before You Begin ...

1. Review the December 18 message from Jesse Baker regarding the decision to move forward with the TIMS system design process. Open the Document 7-1 from the data disk.

2. Review the December 19 message from Jesse Baker regarding specific design tasks and target dates. Open the Document 7-2 from the data disk.

Assignments

1. Review the guidelines for user interface design. Then design a switchboard with a main menu and control buttons that allow users to select five areas: students, instructors, courses, course schedules, and course rosters. When the user enters an area, he or she should have a choice of adding, updating, or deleting. A user also should be able to obtain context-sensitive and specific Help from the switchboard and from lower-level menus and forms. Prepare storyboards that show the proposed screens.

2. Review the guidelines for effective data entry screen design and data validation checks. Then suggest features that should be included in the design.

3. Review the guidelines for source document designs. Prepare designs for two source documents — one for an SCR mail-in form that students can use to register for courses by mail, and one that can be used as a Web-based course registration form.

4. Review the guidelines for report design. Design a detail report that will display a list of all SCR courses in alphabetical order, with the course name and the instructor name in a group header; the Social Security number, name, and telephone number of each current student in the detail section; and the student count in a group footer.

ON THE WEB

The SCR case is available as an interactive, Web-based case study. You can log on to the Shelly Cashman Series site at www.scsite.com/sad4e/scr for instructions and assignments.

CHAPTER 8

PHASE 1 Systems Planning
PHASE 2 Systems Analysis
Systems Design PHASE 3
PHASE 4 Systems Implementation
PHASE 5 Systems Operation & Support

Data Design

In this, the second of three chapters in the systems design phase of the SDLC, you will focus on data design and management issues that are necessary to construct the physical model of the information system.

INTRODUCTION

In the systems analysis phase, you created data flow diagrams and identified data elements, data flows, and data stores to build a logical design for the information system. In this part of the systems design phase, you will develop a physical plan for data organization, storage, and retrieval.

This chapter begins with a review of data design concepts and terminology, then discusses relationships among data objects and how to draw entity-relationship diagrams that describe those associations. You also will learn how to use normalization concepts to build an effective database design. The chapter concludes with a discussion of physical design issues, logical and physical records, data storage formats, and data controls.

OBJECTIVES

When you finish this chapter, you will be able to:

- Explain data design concepts and data structures

- Describe file processing systems and various types of files

- Describe database systems, their characteristics, and advantages

- Define the components of a database management system (DBMS)

- Explain the concepts of data warehousing and data mining

- Understand data design terminology, including entities, fields, common fields, records, files, tables, and key fields

- Explain data relationships and draw an entity-relationship diagram

- Define cardinality, cardinality notation, and crow's foot notation

- Explain normalization, including examples of first, second, and third normal form

- Describe hierarchical, network, relational, and object-oriented database models

- Differentiate between logical and physical records, and discuss data storage formats and date fields

- Explain data control measures

ON THE WEB

or an overview of Database
Management Systems
(DBMSs) visit scsite.com/
ad4e/more.htm, click
Systems Analysis and Design
Chapter 8 and then click the
Database Management
Systems (DBMSs) link.

ww.scsite.com

DATA DESIGN CONCEPTS

Before constructing an information system, a systems analyst must understand basic data design concepts, including how data is structured and the characteristics of file-oriented and database systems. A systems analyst also must understand data warehousing, data mining, and the components of a database management system.

Data Structures

A **file** contains data about people, places, things, or events that interact with the information system. For example, a file might consist of data about customers, products, orders, or suppliers. Depending on business requirements, an information system can be designed as a file-oriented system or a database system.

AUTO REPAIR SHOP

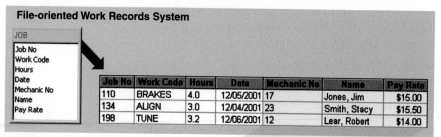

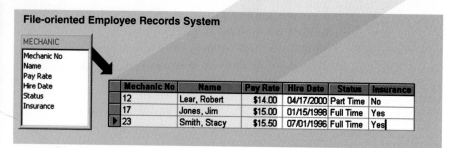

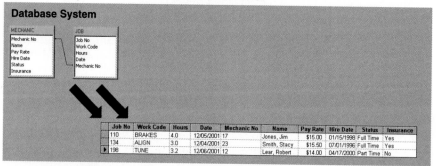

A **file-oriented** system processes one or more individual data files using a method called **file processing**. In the example shown in Figure 8-1, an auto repair shop might use two separate file-oriented systems: a Work Records system that maintains a JOB data file, and an Employee Records system that maintains a MECHANIC data file. Notice that some information is duplicated in both data files.

A **database** consists of linked data files, also called **tables**, that form an overall data structure. Compared to file processing, a database environment offers greater flexibility and efficiency. For example, Figure 8-2 shows a database that links the MECHANIC file and the JOB file. Notice that the database design avoids duplication — the MECHANIC and JOB files become components of a larger data structure. A **database management system** (**DBMS**) is a collection of tools, features, and interfaces that enables users to add, update, manage, access, and analyze data in a database.

File processing systems still exist to handle specific applications, but most information systems today are designed as databases. The pros and cons of file processing compared with database systems are discussed in the following section.

FIGURE 8-1   An auto repair shop maintains a JOB data file for its Work Records system and a MECHANIC data file for its Employee Records system. Notice that some data about employees is duplicated in both files.

FIGURE 8-2   A database design for the auto repair shop links the two data files and avoids duplication. Notice that the Mechanic No field provides a link between the two data files.

Overview of File Processing

Some systems use file processing to handle large volumes of structured data on a regular basis. Many older systems utilized file-processing designs because that approach was well suited to mainframe hardware and batch input. Although less common today, file processing can be more efficient and cost less than a DBMS in certain situations. For example, consider a credit card company that posts thousands of daily transactions from a TRANSACTION file to customer balances stored in a CUSTOMER file, as shown in Figure 8-3. For that relatively simple process, file processing is highly effective.

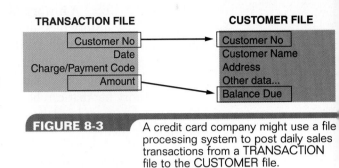

FIGURE 8-3 A credit card company might use a file processing system to post daily sales transactions from a TRANSACTION file to the CUSTOMER file.

In a typical file processing environment, a company might have three departments, each with its own information system and data files. Several potential problems exist in a file-processing environment. The first problem is **data redundancy**, which means that data common to two or more information systems is stored in several places. Data redundancy requires more storage space, and maintaining and updating data in several locations is expensive. Secondly, **data integrity** problems can occur if updates are not applied in every file. Changing the data in only one of the systems will cause inconsistent data and result in incorrect information in the second system. The third problem is the **rigid data structure** of a typical file-processing environment. Businesses must make decisions based on company-wide data, and managers often require information from multiple business units and departments. In a file-processing environment, that means retrieving information from independent, file-based systems, which is slow and inefficient.

A file-oriented information system uses various types of files, including master files, table files, transaction files, work files, security files, and history files.

MASTER FILES A **master file** stores relatively permanent data about an entity. For example, a PRODUCT master file contains one logical record for each product the company sells. The quantity-on-hand field in each record might change daily, but the number of file records does not change unless the company adds a new product or discontinues an old one. Master files might include data for customers, sales representatives, students, employees, or patients.

TABLE FILES A **table file** contains reference data used by the information system. As with master files, table files are relatively permanent and are not updated by the information system. Examples of table files include tax tables and postage rate tables.

TRANSACTION FILES A **transaction file** stores records that contain day-to-day business and operational data. A transaction file is an input file that updates a master file; after the update is completed, the transaction file has served its purpose. Unless they are saved for security or backup reasons, transaction files are temporary files. An example of a transaction file is a charges and payments file that updates a customer balance file.

WORK FILES A **work file** is a temporary file created by an information system for a single task. Most often a work file is created by one process in the information system and used by another process within the same system. Work files also are called **scratch files**. Work files can contain copies of master file records or various other records that are needed temporarily. Example of work files include sorted files and report files that hold output reports until they are printed.

SECURITY FILES A **security file** is created and saved for backup and recovery purposes. Examples of security files include audit trail files and backups of master, table, and transaction files. New security files must be created regularly to replace outdated files.

HISTORY FILES   A **history file** is a file copy created and saved for historical or archiving purposes. New history files, unlike new security files, do not replace the old files. In some cases, inactive master file records are deleted periodically and added to a special history file. For example, records for students who have not registered for any course in the last two semesters might be deleted from the active student master file and added to an inactive student file, which is a type of history file that can be used for queries or reports. If an inactive student registers again, his or her data record is deleted from the inactive student file and added back to the active student master file.

Overview of Database Systems

A properly designed database offers a solution to the problems of file processing. (Keep in mind, however, that a poorly designed database can actually create more problems.) A database provides an overall framework that avoids data redundancy and supports a real-time, dynamic environment.

In a file-processing environment, data files are designed to fit individual business systems. In contrast, in a database environment, several systems can be built around a single database. Figure 8-4 shows a database environment with a database serving five separate information systems.

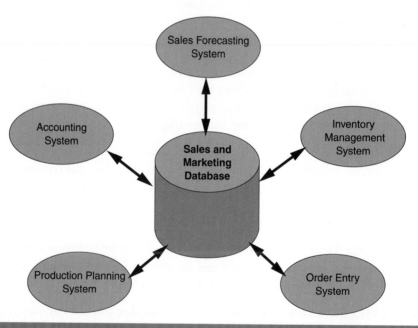

FIGURE 8-4   A typical database environment might consist of a database serving five separate business systems.

From a user's point of view, the main advantage of a DBMS is that it offers timely, interactive, and flexible data access. Specific DBMS advantages include the following:

- *Scalability.* **Scalability** means that a system can be expanded, modified, or downsized easily to meet the rapidly changing needs of a business enterprise.

- *Better support for client/server systems.* In a **client/server** system, processing is distributed throughout the organization. Client/server systems require the power and flexibility of a database design. You will learn more about client/server systems in Chapter 9.

- *Economy of scale.* Database design allows better utilization of hardware. If a company maintains an enterprise-wide database, processing is less expensive using a powerful mainframe server instead of using several smaller computers. The inherent efficiency of high-volume processing on larger computers is called **economy of scale.**

- *Sharing of data.* Data can be shared across the enterprise, allowing more users to access more data. Because the database design is flexible, users can view the same information in different ways. Users are empowered because they have access to the information they need to do their jobs.
- *Balancing conflicting requirements.* Typically, a DBMS is managed by a person called a **database administrator** (**DBA**), who assesses overall requirements and maintains the database for the benefit of the entire organization rather than a single department or user.
- *Enforcement of standards.* Effective database administration ensures that standards for data names, formats, and documentation are followed uniformly throughout the organization.
- *Controlled redundancy.* Because the data is stored in a single database, data items do not need to be duplicated in separate files for various systems. Even where some duplication might be desirable for performance reasons, the database approach allows control of the redundancy.
- *Security.* The DBA can define authorization procedures to ensure that only legitimate users can access the database and can allow different users to have different levels of access. Most DBMSs provide sophisticated security support.
- *Increased programmer productivity.* Programmers do not have to create the underlying file structure for a database. That allows them to concentrate on logical design and, therefore, a new database application can be developed more quickly than a file-oriented system.
- *Data independence.* Systems that interact with a DBMS are relatively independent of how the physical data is maintained. That design provides the DBA flexibility to alter data structures without modifying information systems that use the data.

Although a DBMS has many advantages, there are some tradeoffs. Because DBMSs are powerful, they require more expensive hardware, software, and data networks capable of supporting a multiuser environment. In addition, a DBMS is more complex than a file processing system, therefore the learning curve for systems analysts, database administrators, and users usually is steeper, which increases TCO (Total Cost of Ownership). Finally, procedures for security, backup, and recovery are more complicated and critical in a database environment. When a company maintains all vital data resources in a database, a DBMS failure seriously disrupts business operations.

Although the trend is toward enterprise-wide database design, many companies still use a combination of centralized DBMSs and smaller, department-level data management systems. Why is this so? Most large businesses view data as a company-wide resource that must be accessible to users throughout the company. At the same time, other factors encourage a decentralized design, including network expense; a reluctance to move away from smaller, more flexible systems; and a realization that enterprise-wide DBMSs can be highly complex and expensive to maintain. The compromise, in many cases, is a client/server design, where processing is shared by several computers. Client/server systems are described in Chapter 9. As with many design decisions, the best solution depends on the individual circumstances.

DBMS Components

A DBMS provides an interface between a database and users who need to access the data. Although users are concerned primarily with an easy-to-use interface and support for their business requirements, a systems analyst must understand all of the components of a DBMS. In addition to interfaces for users, database administrators, and related systems, a DBMS also has a data manipulation language, a schema, and a physical data repository, as shown in Figure 8-5 on the next page.

**INTERFACES FOR USERS, DATABASE ADMIN-
ISTRATORS, AND RELATED SYSTEMS** When
users, database administrators, and related information systems request data and services, the DBMS
processes the request, manipulates the data, and provides a response.

- *Users.* Users typically work with predefined
  queries and switchboard commands, but also
  use query languages to access stored data. A
  query language allows a user to specify a
  task without specifying how the task will
  be accomplished. Some query languages
  use natural language commands that
  resemble ordinary English sentences.
  With a **query-by-example (QBE)** language, the user provides an
  example of the data
  requested. Many database
  programs also generate
  **SQL (Structured Query
  Language)**, which is a
  query language that
  allows PC users to com-
  municate with servers
  and mainframe comput-
  ers. Figure 8-6 shows a
  QBE request for all Bright Silver Metallic or
  Black 2001 PT Cruisers with roof racks. The
  QBE request generates the SQL commands
  shown at the bottom of Figure 8-6.

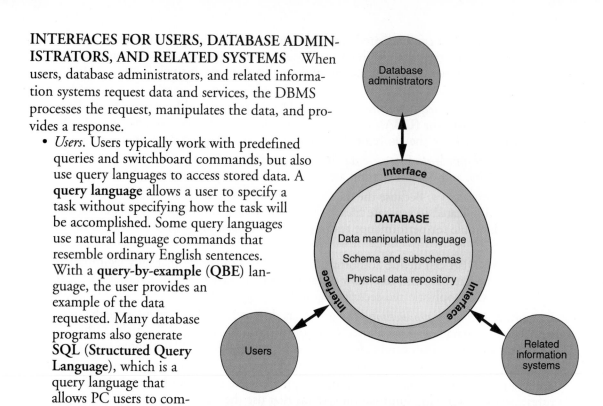

FIGURE 8-5 In addition to interfaces for users, database
administrators, and related information systems, a
DBMS also has a data manipulation language, a
schema, and a physical data repository.

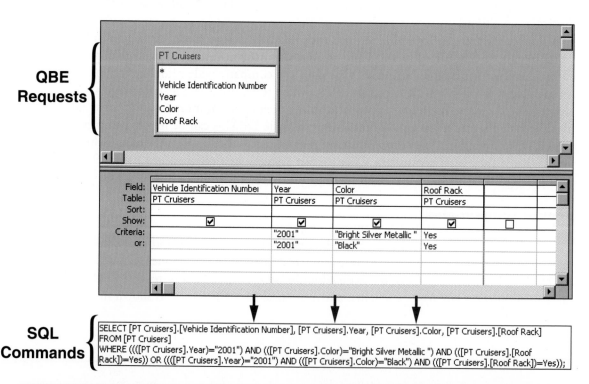

FIGURE 8-6 Using QBE, a user can request a list of all Bright Silver Metallic or Black 2001 PT
Cruisers with roof racks. The QBE request generates the SQL commands shown.

- *Database administrators.* A DBA is responsible for DBMS management and support. DBAs are concerned with data security and integrity, preventing unauthorized access, providing backup and recovery, audit trails, maintaining the database, and supporting user needs. Most DBMSs provide utility programs to assist the DBA in creating and updating data structures, collecting and reporting patterns of database usage, and detecting and reporting database irregularities.

- *Related information systems.* A DBMS might support several related information systems that provide input to, and require specific data from, the DBMS. For example, a database might support five separate systems, as shown in Figure 8.4 on page 8.4. Unlike a user interface, no human intervention is required for two-way communication between the DBMS and the related systems.

DATA MANIPULATION LANGUAGE   A **data manipulation language (DML)** controls database operations, including storing, retrieving, updating, and deleting data. Most commercial DBMSs, such as Oracle and IBM's DB/2 use a DML. Some database products, such as Microsoft Access, also provide an easy-to-use graphical environment that enables users to control operations with menu-driven commands.

SCHEMA   The complete definition of a database, including descriptions of all fields, records, and relationships, is called a **schema.** You also can define one or more subschemas. A **subschema** is a view of the database used by one or more systems or users. A subschema defines only those portions of the database that a particular system or user needs or is allowed to access. For example, to protect individual privacy, you might not want to allow a project management system to retrieve employee pay rates. In that case, the project management system subschema would not include the pay rate field. Database designers also use subschemas to restrict the level of access permitted. For example, specific users, systems, or locations might be permitted to create, retrieve, update, or delete data, depending on their needs and the company's security policies.

PHYSICAL DATA REPOSITORY   In Chapter 4, you learned about a data dictionary, which describes all data elements included in the logical design. At this stage of the systems development process, the data dictionary is transformed into a physical data repository, which also contains the schema and subschemas. The physical repository might be centralized, or distributed at several locations. Physical design issues are discussed further in Chapter 9, where system architecture is described.

Data Warehousing

Many large companies use software packages that gather and store data in special configurations called data warehouses. A **data warehouse** is an integrated collection of data that can support management analysis and decision making. For example, in a typical company, data is generated by transaction-based systems, such as order entry, inventory, accounts receivable, and payroll. If a user wants to know the customer number on sales order 4071, he or she can retrieve the data easily from the order entry system.

On the other hand, suppose that a user wants to see May sales results for the sales rep assigned to a specific customer, as shown in Figure 8-7 on the next page. Although the information systems are interactive, it is difficult for a user to extract specific data that spans several systems and time frames; the average user might need assistance from the IT staff.

ON THE WE

To learn more about Data Warehousing visit scsite.c sad4e/more.htm, click Systems Analysis and Des Chapter 8 and then click t Data Warehousing link.

www.scsite.

Rather than accessing separate systems, a data warehouse stores transaction data in a format that allows users to access, combine, and analyze the data. A data warehouse allows users to specify certain **dimensions,** or characteristics. In a consumer products data warehouse, dimensions might include time, customer, and sales representative. By selecting values for each characteristic, a user can obtain multidimensional information from the stored data.

N THE WEB

r more information
out Data Mining visit
site.com/sad4e/more.htm,
ck Systems Analysis and
sign Chapter 8 and then
ck the Data Mining link.

w.scsite.com

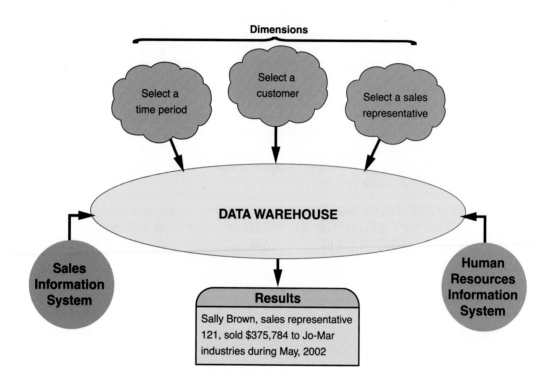

FIGURE 8-7   A data warehouse might store data from several information systems. By selecting values, a user can obtain multidimensional information from the stored data.

Data Mining

Data mining software looks for meaningful patterns and relationships among data. For example, data mining software could help a consumer products firm identify potential customers based on their prior purchases. Many firms, including the examples in Figure 8-8, offer data mining products.

The enormous growth in e-commerce has focused attention on data mining as a tool to analyze Web visitor behavior and traffic trends. In the March 7, 2000, edition of *INFOWORLD*, Michael Lattig reported that IBM and two business partners, Hyperion and WebTrends, were offering solutions to companies trying to make sense of business-relevant data. In the article, *INFOWORLD* quotes a Hyperion executive as saying, "E-businesses are starting to get held accountable for showing business results beyond simply counting clicks ... and we share the same vision that customers can't do e-business without analysis." The statement went on to say that, "The idea is that we are going to offer customers unparalleled opportunities for analytics in understanding Web visitor behavior, and also merge and correlate that capability with critical corporate databases."

Microsoft also is an active competitor in the data mining field, and has announced the release of software specifications that provide a standard interface for integrating data mining tools and capabilities into e-commerce applications.

FIGURE 8-8   Several examples of data mining products.

DATA DESIGN TERMINOLOGY

Using the data design concepts discussed in the previous section, a systems analyst can select a strategy and begin to construct a data management system. The first step is to understand data design terminology.

Definitions

Figure 8-9 shows a table with fields and records that describe an entity called CUSTOMER.

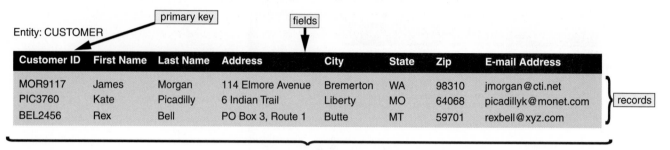

CUSTOMER TABLE

FIGURE 8-9 A file or table for an entity named CUSTOMER includes records, fields, and a primary key.

ENTITY   An **entity** is a person, place, thing, or event for which data is collected and maintained. For example, an online sales system includes entities named CUSTOMER, ORDER, PRODUCT, and SUPPLIER. When you prepared DFDs during the systems analysis phase, you identified various entities and data stores. Now you will consider the relationships among the entities.

FIELD   A **field**, also called an **attribute**, is a single characteristic or fact about an entity. In the example shown in Figure 8-9, the entity named CUSTOMER has fields to store data about each customer, such as First Name, Last Name, and Address. A **common field** is an attribute that appears in more than one entity. Common fields can be used to link entities in various types of relationships.

RECORD   A **record**, also called a **tuple** (rhymes with couple), is a set of related fields that describes one instance, or member of an entity, such as one customer, one order, or one product. A record might have one or dozens of fields, depending on what information is needed.

FILE AND TABLE   Records are grouped into files or tables, depending on the data design model.

In a file-oriented system, a set of related records forms a file that contains data about a person, place, thing, or event, as you learned earlier in this chapter. For example, if an inventory system tracks 1,500 products, the PRODUCT file has 1,500 records — one record for each product. Often, data in files can be structured, or organized, in a manner that speeds up processing in a file-oriented system.

In a database environment, a set of related records is grouped into a table that stores data about a specific entity. Tables are shown as two-dimensional structures that consist of vertical columns representing fields and horizontal rows for records. For example, a sales database system might have separate tables called CUSTOMER, ORDER, PRODUCT, and SUPPLIER.

Although they can have different meanings in a specific context, the terms *file* and *table* often can be used interchangeably.

Key Fields

During the systems design phase, you use **key fields** to organize, access, and maintain data structures. The four types of keys are primary keys, candidate keys, foreign keys, and secondary keys.

PRIMARY KEYS   A **primary key** is a field or combination of fields that uniquely and minimally identifies a particular member of an entity. For example, in a customer table the customer number is a unique primary key because no two customers can have the same customer number. That key also is minimal because it contains no information beyond what is needed to identify the customer. In Figure 8-9, Customer ID is an example of a primary key based on a single field.

A primary key also can be composed of two or more fields. For example, if a student registers for three courses, his or her student number will appear in three records in the registration system. If one of those courses has 20 students, 20 separate records will exist for that course number — one record for each student who registered.

In the registration file, neither the student number nor the course ID is unique, so neither field can be a primary key. To identify a specific student in a specific course, the primary key must be a combination of student number and course ID. In that case, the primary key is a **combination** key, or a **multivalued key**.

Figure 8-10 shows four different tables. The first three tables have single-field primary keys. Notice that in the fourth table, however, the primary key is a combination of two foreign key fields: STUDENT-NUMBER and COURSE-ID.

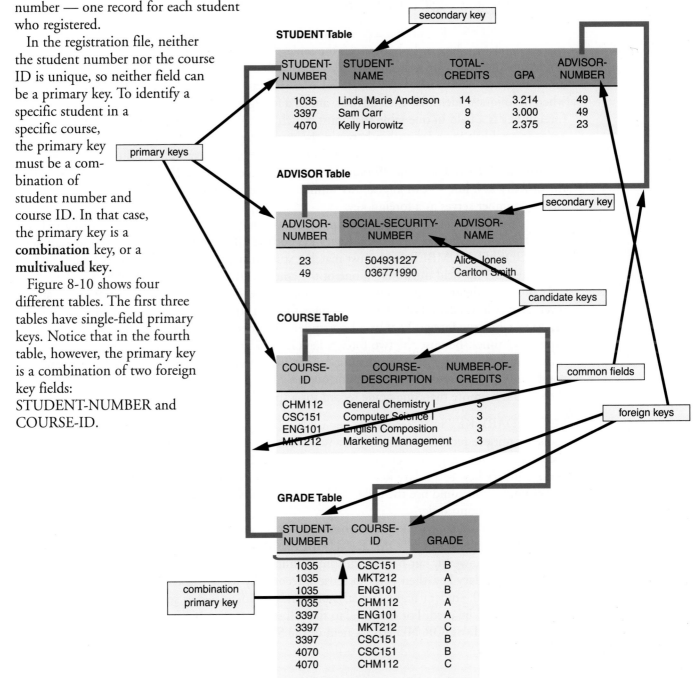

FIGURE 8-10   Examples of common fields, primary keys, candidate keys, foreign keys, and secondary keys.

CANDIDATE KEYS   Sometimes you have a choice of fields or field combinations to use as the primary key. Any field that could serve as a primary key is called a **candidate key**. For example, if every employee has a unique employee number, then you could use either the employee number or the Social Security number as a primary key. Because you can designate only one field as a primary key, you should select the field that contains the least amount of data and is the easiest to use. Any field that is not a primary key or a candidate key is called a **nonkey field**.

The primary keys shown in Figure 8-10 on the previous page also are candidate keys. Two other candidate keys exist: the SOCIAL-SECURITY-NUMBER field in the ADVISOR table and the COURSE-DESCRIPTION field in the COURSE table.

FOREIGN KEYS   Recall that a common field exists in more than one table and can be used to form a relationship, or link, between the tables. For example, in Figure 8-10, the ADVISOR-NUMBER field appears in both the STUDENT table and the ADVISOR table and joins the tables together. Notice that ADVISOR-NUMBER is a primary key in the ADVISOR table, where it uniquely identifies each advisor, and is a foreign key in the STUDENT table. A **foreign key** is a field in one table that must match a primary key value in another table in order to establish the relationship between the two tables.

Unlike a primary key, a foreign key need not be unique. For example, Carlton Smith has advisor number 49. The value 49 must be a unique value in the ADVISOR table because it is the primary key, but 49 can appear any number of times in the STUDENT table, where the advisor number serves as a foreign key.

Figure 8-10 also shows how two foreign keys can combine to form a primary key in another table. The two fields that form the primary key for the GRADE table also are both foreign keys: the STUDENT-NUMBER field must match a student number in the STUDENT table and the COURSE-ID field must match one of the course IDs in the COURSE table.

As shown in Figure 8-10, foreign keys are not unique. A particular advisor number can appear several times in the STUDENT table — once for each student assigned to that advisor. In the GRADE table, the foreign keys based on student numbers and course IDs can appear any number of times. Because the two foreign keys form a unique primary key, however, only one combination of a specific student and a specific course can exist. For example, only one combined instance of student 1035 and course CSC151 can exist in the GRADE table, or else there could be more than one grade record for a specific student in a specific course.

SECONDARY KEYS   A **secondary key** is a field or combination of fields that can be used to access or retrieve records. Secondary key values are not unique. For example, if you need to access records for only those customers in a specific ZIP code, you would use the ZIP code field as a secondary key. Secondary keys also can be used to sort or display records in a certain order. For example, you could use the GPA field in a STUDENT file to display records for all students in grade point order.

The need for a secondary key arises because a table can have only one primary key. In a CUSTOMER file the CUSTOMER-NUMBER is the primary key. You might know a customer's name, however, but not the customer's number. If you assign the CUSTOMER-NAME field as a secondary key, then you can retrieve records by using the CUSTOMER-NAME field.

In Figure 8-10, student name and advisor names are identified as secondary keys, but other fields also could be used. For example, to find all students who have a particular advisor, you could use the ADVISOR-NUMBER field in the STUDENT file as a secondary key.

Referential Integrity

In Chapter 7, you learned that validity checks can help avoid data input errors. One type of validity check, called **referential integrity**, is a set of rules that avoids data inconsistency and quality problems. In a relational database, referential integrity means that a foreign key value cannot be entered in one table unless it matches an existing primary key in another table. For example, referential integrity would prevent you from entering a customer order in an order table unless that customer already exists in the customer table. Without referential integrity, you might have an order called an **orphan**, because it had no related customer.

In the example shown in Figure 8-10 on page 8-11, referential integrity will not allow a user to enter an advisor number (foreign key value) in the STUDENT table unless a valid advisor number (primary key value) already exists in the ADVISOR table.

Referential integrity also can prevent the deletion of a record if the record has a primary key that matches foreign keys in another table. For example, suppose that an advisor resigns to accept a position at another school. You cannot delete the advisor from the ADVISOR table while records in the STUDENT file still refer to that advisor number. Otherwise, the STUDENT records would be orphans. To avoid the problem, students must be reassigned to other advisors by changing the value in the ADVISOR-NUMBER field; then the advisor record can be deleted.

When creating a relational database, you can build referential integrity into the design. Figure 8-11 shows a Microsoft Access screen that identifies a common field and allows the user to enforce referential integrity rules.

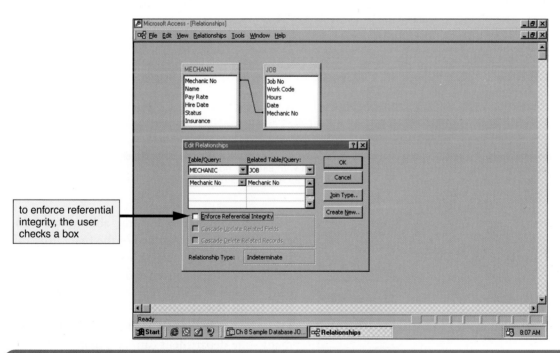

to enforce referential integrity, the user checks a box

FIGURE 8-11 Microsoft Access allows a user to specify that referential integrity rules will be enforced in a relational database design.

DATA RELATIONSHIPS

Recall that an entity is a person, place, thing, or event for which data is collected. A **relationship** is a logical link between entities based on how they interact. For example, a relationship exists between the entities PRODUCT and WAREHOUSE because products are stored in warehouses.

ON THE WEB

For an overview of Referential Integrity visit scsite.com/sad4e/more.ht click Systems Analysis and Design Chapter 8 and then click the Referential Integrity link.

www.scsite.c

Entity-Relationship Diagrams

An **entity-relationship diagram (ERD)** is a graphical model of the information system that depicts the relationships among system entities. Figure 8-12 shows the basic format of an ERD. Each entity is represented as a rectangle, and a diamond represents the **relation**, or relationship, that connects the entities. The entity rectangles are labeled with singular nouns and the relationship diamonds are labeled with active verbs. For example, in Figure 8-12, a doctor treats a patient. You also might say that a patient is *treated* by a doctor, but it is better to use the active voice. Some CASE tools permit two relationships — one in each direction.

Unlike data flow diagrams and systems flowcharts, entity-relationship diagrams do not depict data or information flows. An ERD has no arrowheads. One of the entities must be positioned above or to the left of the other entity, but that positioning does not imply a superior/inferior relationship between the entities or a flow from the first entity to the second entity.

Three main types of relationships can exist between entities. A **one-to-one relationship**, abbreviated **1:1**, exists when exactly one of the second entity occurs for each instance of the first entity. ERDs for several possible 1:1 entity relationships are shown in Figure 8-13. A number 1 is placed alongside each of the two lines connecting a rectangle to the diamond to indicate the 1:1 relationship.

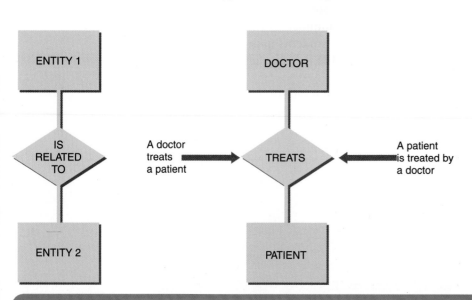

FIGURE 8-12 In an entity-relationship diagram, entities are labeled with singular nouns and relationships are labeled with verbs. The ERD is interpreted as a simple English sentence.

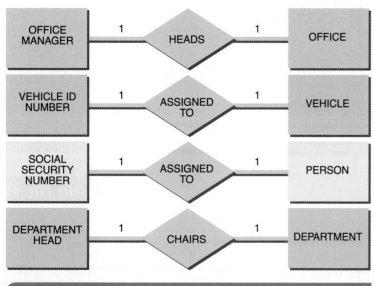

FIGURE 8-13 One-to-one (1:1) relationships.

A **one-to-many relationship**, abbreviated **1:M**, exists when one occurrence of the first entity can be related to many occurrences of the second entity, but each occurrence of the second entity can be associated with only one occurrence of the first entity. For example, the relationship between DEPARTMENT and EMPLOYEE is one-to-many: one department can have many employees, but each employee works in only one department. Several possible 1:M entity-relationship diagrams are shown in Figure 8-14. The line connecting the many entity to the relationship is labeled with the letter M, whereas the number 1 labels the other connecting line. In some software programs, the many side of the relationship is shown as an infinity symbol (∞) or a crow's foot notation, which is explained later in this section.

How many is *many*? The first 1:M relationship shown in Figure 8-14 shows the entities INDIVIDUAL and AUTOMOBILE. One automobile is owned by one individual, but one person might own twenty automobiles, or one, or even none. Thus, *many* can mean any number, including zero. Typically, however, an automobile has one and only one owner.

A **many-to-many relationship**, abbreviated **M:N**, exists when one instance of the first entity can be related to many instances of the second entity, and one instance of the second entity can be related to many instances of the first entity. The relationship between STUDENT and CLASS, for example, is many-to-many — one student can take many classes, and one class can have many students enrolled. Figure 8-15 shows several M:N entity-relationships. One of the lines connecting an entity to a relation is labeled with the letter M; the letter N labels the connection between the other entity and the relation.

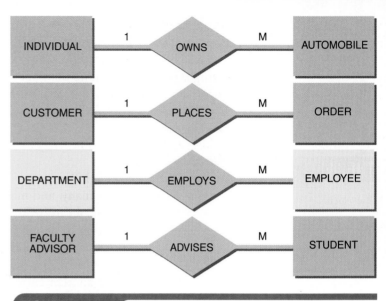

FIGURE 8-14   One-to-many (1:M) relationships.

Notice that an M:N relationship is different from 1:1 or 1:M relationships because the event or transaction that links the two entities is actually a third entity, called an **associative entity** that has its own set of attributes and characteristics. In the first example in Figure 8-15, the

ENROLLS IN relation represents a REGISTRATION entity that records each instance of a specific student enrolling in a specific course. Similarly, the RESERVES SEAT ON relation represents a RESERVATION entity that records each instance of a specific passenger reserving a seat on a specific flight. In the third example, the LISTS relation represents an ORDER-LINE entity that records each instance of a specific product listed in each specific order. When you create the tables and record designs for a M:N relationship, you must include a table and a record design for each associative entity.

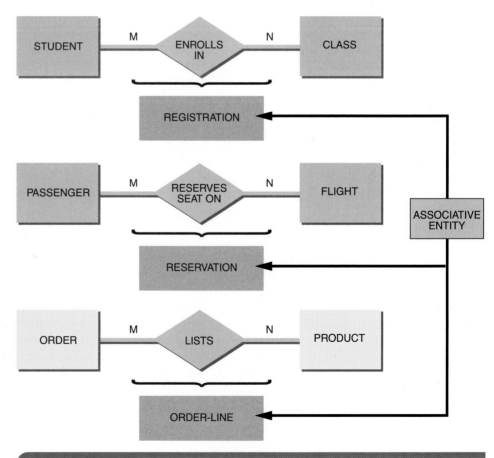

FIGURE 8-15   Many-to-many (M:N) relationships. Notice that the event or transaction that links the two entities is an associative entity with its own set of attributes and characteristics.

A complete ERD shows all system entities and relationships. Figure 8-16 has five entities: SALES REP, CUSTOMER, ORDER, PRODUCT, and WAREHOUSE and the relationship between SALES REP and CUSTOMER is one-to-many. In some organizations, however, a customer might be served by more than one sales rep, in which case the relationship changes to a many-to-many relationship. The relationship between WAREHOUSE and PRODUCT is one-to-many, but the relationship is many-to-many if the company stores multiple products in multiple warehouses.

Cardinality

Figures 8-13, 8-14, and 8-15 on pages 8.14 and 8.15 describe various relationships among entities: one-to-one, one-to-many, and many-to-many. The nature of those relations also is called cardinality. As an analyst, you must understand cardinality in order to design files and databases that accurately reflect all relationships among entities.

Cardinality describes how instances of one entity relate to instances of another entity. In a specific relationship, an entity can be mandatory, which means that it always is required, or optional. If an entity is mandatory, only one instance might be allowed in a relationship, or many instances might be permitted. For example, consider the relationship between two entities: CUSTOMER and ORDER. One customer can have one order, many orders, or none, but each order must have one and only one customer.

ON THE WEB

For an overview of Cardinality visit scsite.com/sad4e/more.htm, click Systems Analysis and Design Chapter 8 and then click the Cardinality link.

www.scsite.com

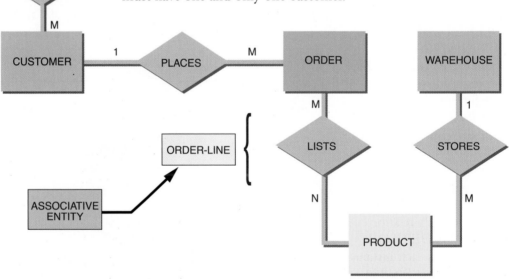

FIGURE 8-16   An entity-relationship diagram for SALES REP, CUSTOMER, ORDER, PRODUCT, and WAREHOUSE.

Several different types of **cardinality notation** can be used to show relationships between entities. One common method is called **crow's foot notation** because of the shapes, which include circles, bars, and symbols that indicate various possibilities. A single bar indicates one, a double bar indicates one and only one, a circle indicates zero, and a crow's foot indicates many. Figure 8-17 shows the cardinality symbol, the meaning, and the UML representation. As you learned in Chapter 5, UML notations can be used to indicate the nature of the relationship between instances of one class and instances of another class, as shown in Figure 5-34 on page 5.20.

In Figure 8-17, four examples of cardinality notation are shown. In the first example, one and only one CUSTOMER can place anywhere from zero to many of the ORDER entity. In the second example, one and only one ORDER can include one ITEM ORDERED or many. In the third example, one and only one EMPLOYEE can have one SPOUSE or none. In the fourth example, one EMPLOYEE, or many employees, or none, can be assigned to one PROJECT, or many projects, or none.

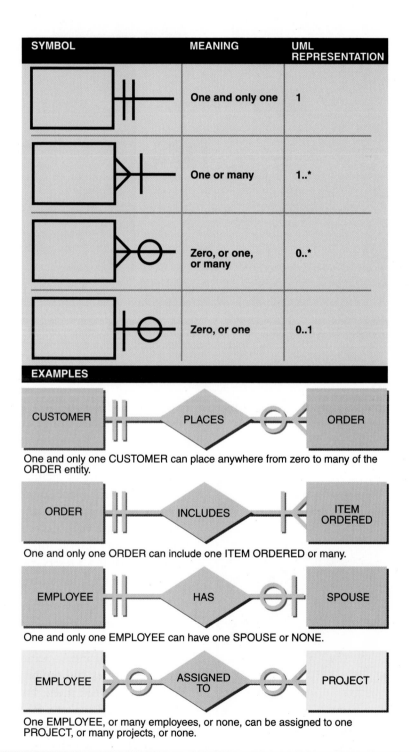

FIGURE 8-17   Crow's foot notation is a common method of indicating cardinality, as shown at the top of the figure. The four examples show how you can use various symbols to describe the relationship between two entities.

Most CASE products support the drawing of ERDs from entities in the data repository. Figure 8-18 shows part of a library system ERD drawn using the Visible Analyst CASE tool. Notice that crow's foot notation is used to show the nature of the relationships, which are described in both directions.

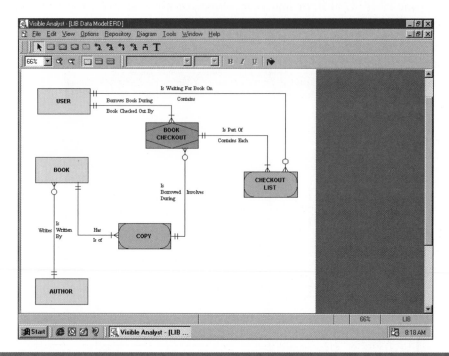

FIGURE 8-18   Visible Analyst includes an example ERD for a library system in its tutorial for new users. Notice that crow's foot notation has been used and relationships are described in both directions.

Creating an ERD

Entity-relationship diagrams are easy to construct if you use the following four steps:

1. *Identify the entities.* Review your DFDs and list the people, places, things, or events for which data is collected. Ensure that you identify all data stores. For example, consider the rental car company shown in Figure 8-19. People might include customers and employees; places might include rental locations and return points; things would include vehicles, rental contracts, and customer reservations; events would include making a reservation, executing a rental contract, and returning a car.

2. *Determine all significant events, transactions, or activities that occur between two or more entities.* The task requires you to analyze the business operations and identify the entities and the nature of the relationship between them. For example, a CUSTOMER makes a RESERVATION and a LOCATION has various VEHICLES available for rental.

FIGURE 8-19   When a customer rents or returns a car, several entities are involved, including the customer, the reservation, the vehicle, and the location.

3. *Analyze the nature of the interaction.* Does the interaction involve one instance of the entity or many? Is the pattern always the same or does it depend on some factor? For example, consider the relationship between CUSTOMER and RESERVATION. One and only one customer can have one, many, or no reservations — but each reservation must have one and only one customer. In addition, a LOCATION can have one VEHICLE, or many, or none — but each vehicle must have one and only one assigned location.

4. *Draw the ERD.* You can draw the ERD manually or by using a CASE tool. Study the diagram carefully to ensure that all entities and relationships are shown accurately. If you are using a type of cardinality notation, ensure that you have used the correct symbols to indicate the nature of each relationship.

Now that you understand database elements and their relationships, you can start designing records and constructing data files and tables. The first step is the normalization of your record designs, which is described next.

NORMALIZATION

Normalization is a process by which you identify and correct inherent problems and complexities in your record designs. A **record design** specifies the fields and identifies the primary key, if any, for all records in a particular file or table. Working with a set of initial record designs, you use normalization to develop an overall database design that is simple, flexible, and free of data redundancy.

The normalization process typically involves three stages: first normal form, second normal form, and third normal form. The three normal forms constitute a progression in which a record design in first normal form is better than one that is unnormalized; a record design in second normal form is better yet; and a record in third normal form represents the best design.

Record Designs

Designing records is easier if you use a standard method of showing the record structure, fields, and primary keys. The examples in the following sections show record designs starting with the name of the file or table, followed by a parenthetical expression that contains the field names separated by commas. The primary key field(s) is underlined. Repeating groups of fields, which are explained in the next section, are enclosed within a second set of parentheses. The format looks like this:

NAME (<u>FIELD 1</u>, FIELD 2, FIELD 3, (REPEATING FIELD 4, REPEATING FIELD 5))

First Normal Form

A record is in **first normal form** (1NF) if it does not contain a repeating group. A **repeating group** is a set of data items that can occur any number of times in a single record. You can think of a repeating group as a set of subsidiary records contained within the main record. For example, consider the ORDER records shown in Figure 8-20 on the next page. In addition to the order number and date, the record contains repetitions of the product number, description, and number ordered. An **unnormalized** record is one that contains a repeating group, which means that a single record has multiple occurrences of particular field, each occurrence having different values. Figure 8-20 shows an unnormalized record.

)N THE WEB

or more information bout Normalization visit csite.com/sad4e/more.htm, lick Systems Analysis and esign Chapter 8 and then lick the Normalization link.

w.scsite.com

ORDER

Primary key (ORDER-NUM) — Primary key for repeating group (PRODUCT-NUM)

RECORD#	<u>ORDER-NUM</u>	ORDER-DATE	PRODUCT-NUM	PRODUCT-DESC	NUM-ORDERED
1	40311	03111999	304	All-purpose gadget	7
			633	Trangam	1
			684	Super gismo	4
2	40312	03111999	128	Steel widget	12
			304	All-purpose gadget	3
3	40313	03121999	304	All-purpose gadget	144

repeating groups

FIGURE 8-20 The unnormalized ORDER record design. Records 1 and 2 have repeating groups because they contain several products. ORDER-NUM is the primary key, and PRODUCT-NUM serves as primary key for the repeating group.

The record design shown in Figure 8-20 is unnormalized because it contains a repeating group of three fields. Following the notation guidelines, you can describe the record as follows:

ORDER (<u>ORDER-NUM</u>, ORDER-DATE, (<u>PRODUCT-NUM</u>, PRODUCT-DESC, NUM-ORDERED))

The notation indicates that the ORDER record design contains five fields, which are listed within the outer parentheses. The ORDER-NUM field is underlined to show that it is the primary key. The PRODUCT-NUM, PRODUCT-DESC, and NUM-ORDERED fields are enclosed within an inner set of parentheses to indicate that they are fields within a repeating group. Notice that PRODUCT-NUM also is underlined because it acts as the primary key of the repeating group. If a customer orders three different products in one order, then the fields PRODUCT-NUM, PRODUCT-DESC, and NUM-ORDERED repeat three times, as shown in Figure 8-20.

To convert an unnormalized record to 1NF, you must expand the primary key to include the key of the repeating group, then remove the repeating group. For example, in the ORDER record, the repeating group consists of three fields: PRODUCT-NUM, PRODUCT-DESC, and NUM-ORDERED. Of the three fields, only PRODUCT-NUM can be a primary key because it uniquely identifies each instance of the repeating group.

When you expand the primary key of ORDER record to include PRODUCT-NUM, you eliminate the repeating group and the ORDER record is now in 1NF, as shown:

ORDER (<u>ORDER-NUM</u>, ORDER-DATE, <u>PRODUCT-NUM</u>, PRODUCT-DESC, NUM-ORDERED)

When you eliminate the repeating group, additional records emerge — one for each combination of an order and a product. The result is more records, but a greatly simplified record design. Figure 8-21 shows the 1NF form for the ORDER records. Notice that the repeating group for order 40311 has become three separate records and the repeating group for order 40312 has become two separate records. In 1NF, each record stores data about a specific product located in a specific order.

The primary key of the 1NF design cannot be the ORDER-NUM field, because the order number does not uniquely identify each product in a multiple item order. Similarly, PRODUCT-NUM cannot be the primary key, because it appears more than once if several orders include the same product. Because each record must reflect a specific product in a specific order, you need a combination of ORDER-NUM and PRODUCT-NUM to identify a single record uniquely. Therefore, the combination of ORDER-NUM and PRODUCT-NUM is the primary key.

ORDER RECORD#	ORDER-NUM	ORDER-DATE	PRODUCT-NUM	PRODUCT-DESC	NUM-ORDERED
1	40311	03111999	304	All-purpose gadget	7
2	40311	03111999	633	Trangam	1
3	40311	03111999	684	Super gismo	4
4	40312	03111999	128	Steel widget	12
5	40312	03111999	304	All-purpose gadget	3
6	40313	03121999	304	All-purpose gadget	144

Combination primary key (over ORDER-NUM and PRODUCT-NUM)

repeating groups have been eliminated

FIGURE 8-21 The ORDER records as they appear in 1NF. Repeating groups have been eliminated. The repeating group for order 40311 has become three separate records, and the repeating group for order 40312 has become two separate records. The primary key is a combination of ORDER-NUM and PRODUCT-NUM.

Second Normal Form

To understand second normal form (2NF), you first must understand the concept of functional dependence. The field X is **functionally dependent** on the field Y if the value of X depends on the value of Y. For example, an order date is dependent on an order number; for a particular order number, there is only one value for the order date. In contrast, the product description is not dependent on the order number. For a particular order number, there might be several product descriptions — one for each item ordered.

A record design is in **second normal form** (2NF) if it is in 1NF and if all fields that are not part of the primary key are dependent on the entire primary key. If any field in a 1NF record depends on only one of the fields in a combination primary key, then the record is not in 2NF. A 1NF record with a primary key that is a single field is automatically in 2NF.

Now reexamine the 1NF design for the ORDER record:

ORDER (<u>ORDER-NUM</u>, ORDER-DATE, <u>PRODUCT-NUM</u>, PRODUCT-DESC, NUM-ORDERED)

The primary key is the combination of the order number and the product number. The NUM-ORDERED field depends on the entire primary key. For the number ordered to be meaningful, you need to know the product number and a specific order number. The ORDER-DATE field depends only on the order number, which is a part of the primary key and the PRODUCT-DESC field depends only on the product number, which is another part of the primary key. Because all fields are not entirely dependent on the primary key, the record design is not in 2NF.

Why is it important to move from 1NF to 2NF? Four kinds of problems are found with records in 1NF that do not exist in 2NF. First, consider the work necessary to change a particular product's description. Suppose 1,000 current orders exist for product number 304. Changing the product description involves modifying 1,000 records for product number 304. Updating all 1,000 records would be cumbersome and expensive.

Second, 1NF records can contain inconsistent data. Nothing prevents product number 304 from having two or more different product descriptions in two or more different records. In fact, if product number 304 appeared in 30 order records, 30 different product descriptions could exist for the same product number.

The third problem arises when you want to add a new product for your customers to order. Because the primary key must include an order number and a product number, you need values for both fields in order to add a record. What value do you use for the order number when you want to add a new product that has not been ordered by any customer? You could use a dummy order number, then replace it with a real order number when the product is ordered to solve the problem, but that solution also creates difficulties.

The fourth problem concerns deletions. If all the related records are deleted once an order is filled and paid for, what happens if you delete the only record that contains product number 633? The information about that product number and its description is lost.

A standard process exists for converting a record design from 1NF to 2NF. First, create a new record design for each field in the primary key. Then, create new record designs for all combinations of primary key fields taken two at a time, three at a time, and so on, until you have a record with the entire original primary key. For each new record, designate a field (or a combination of fields) as a primary key. In our sample 1NF record, you begin by creating the following three partial records:

> ORDER (<u>ORDER-NUM</u>,...)
> PRODUCT (<u>PRODUCT-NUM</u>,...)
> ORDER-LINE (<u>ORDER-NUM</u>, <u>PRODUCT-NUM</u>,...)

Finally, place each of the remaining fields with its appropriate primary key, which is the minimal key on which it depends. Give each record a name. When you have finished placing all the fields, remove any record that has had no additional field placed into it. The remaining records are the 2NF version of your original record design. For the example record, the process yields:

> ORDER (<u>ORDER-NUM</u>, ORDER-DATE)

> PRODUCT (<u>PRODUCT-NUM</u>, PRODUCT-DESC)

> ORDER-LINE (<u>ORDER-NUM</u>, <u>PRODUCT-NUM</u>, NUM-ORDERED)

Instead of one 1NF record design, you now have three records that are in 2NF. The records then are assigned new, descriptive names: ORDER, PRODUCT, and ORDER-LINE, respectively. The 2NF versions are shown in Figure 8-22.

Has the 2NF design eliminated all potential problems? To change a product description, now you change just one PRODUCT record. Multiple, inconsistent values for the product description are impossible because the description appears in only one location. To add a new product, you simply create a new PRODUCT record, instead of creating a dummy order record. When you remove the last ORDER-LINE record for a particular product number, you do not lose that product number and its description because the PRODUCT record still exists. The four potential problems are eliminated and the three 2NF record designs are superior to both the original unnormalized record and the 1NF record design.

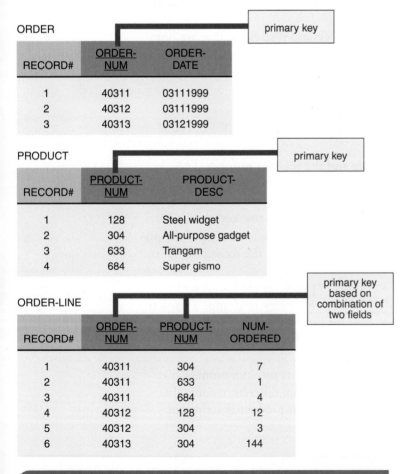

ORDER

RECORD#	ORDER- NUM	ORDER- DATE
1	40311	03111999
2	40312	03111999
3	40313	03121999

primary key

PRODUCT

RECORD#	PRODUCT- NUM	PRODUCT- DESC
1	128	Steel widget
2	304	All-purpose gadget
3	633	Trangam
4	684	Super gismo

primary key

ORDER-LINE

primary key based on combination of two fields

RECORD#	ORDER- NUM	PRODUCT- NUM	NUM- ORDERED
1	40311	304	7
2	40311	633	1
3	40311	684	4
4	40312	128	12
5	40312	304	3
6	40313	304	144

FIGURE 8-22 ORDER, PRODUCT, and ORDER-LINE tables in 2NF. All fields are functionally dependent on the entire primary key.

Third Normal Form

When all tables are in 3NF, a database design avoids redundancy and data integrity problems. A popular rule of thumb is that a design is in 3NF if every nonkey field depends on the key, the whole key, and nothing but the key.

Consider the following CUSTOMER record design, as shown in Figure 8-23:

CUSTOMER (<u>CUSTOMER-NUM</u>, CUSTOMER-NAME, ADDRESS, SALES-REP-NUM, SALES-REP-NAME)

The record is in 1NF because it has no repeating groups. The record also is in 2NF because the primary key is a single field. But the design still has four potential problems similar to the four 1NF problems described earlier. Changing the name of a sales rep still requires changing every record in which that sales rep name appears. Nothing about the design prohibits a particular sales rep from having

> in 2NF, the nonkey field SALES-REP-NAME is functionally dependent on another nonkey field SALES-REP-NUM

CUSTOMER IN 2NF

RECORD#	CUSTOMER-NUM	CUSTOMER-NAME	ADDRESS	SALES-REP-NUM	SALES-REP-NAME
1	108	Benedict, Louise	San Diego, CA	41	Kaplan, James
2	233	Corelli, Helen	Nashua, NH	22	McBride, Jon
3	254	Gomez, J.P.	Butte, MT	38	Stein, Ellen
4	431	Lee, M.	Snow Camp, NC	74	Roman, Harold
5	779	Paulski, Diane	Lead, SD	38	Stein, Ellen
6	800	Zuider, Z.	Greer, SC	74	Roman, Harold

FIGURE 8-23   2NF record design for the CUSTOMER data.

different names in different records. In addition, because the sales rep name is part of the CUSTOMER record, you must create a dummy CUSTOMER record to add a new sales rep who has not yet been assigned any customers. Finally, if you delete all the records for customers of sales rep number 22, you will lose that sales rep's number and name.

Those potential problems are caused because the record design is not in 3NF. A record design is in **third normal form (3NF)** if it is in 2NF and if no nonkey field is dependent on another nonkey field. Remember that a nonkey field is a field that is not a candidate key for the primary key. The CUSTOMER record example is not in 3NF because one nonkey field, SALES-REP-NAME, depends on another nonkey field, SALES-REP-NUM.

To convert the record to 3NF, you must remove all fields from the 2NF record that depend on another nonkey field and place them in a new record that uses the nonkey field as a primary key. In our CUSTOMER record example, the SALES-REP-NAME field depends on another field, SALES-REP-NUM, which is not part of the primary key. Therefore, to reach 3NF, you must remove SALES-REP-NAME and place it into a new record that uses SALES-REP-NUM as the primary key. As shown in Figure 8-24, the third normal form produces two separate records:

CUSTOMER (<u>CUSTOMER-NUM</u>, CUSTOMER-NAME, ADDRESS, SALES-REP-NUM)

SALES-REP (<u>SALES-REP-NUM</u>, SALES-REP-NAME)

CUSTOMER IN 3NF

RECORD#	CUSTOMER-NUM	CUSTOMER-NAME	ADDRESS	SALES-REP-NUM
1	108	Benedict, Louise	San Diego, CA	41
2	233	Corelli, Helen	Nashua, NH	22
3	254	Gomez, J.P.	Butte, MT	38
4	431	Lee, M.	Snow Camp, NC	74
5	779	Paulski, Diane	Lead, SD	38
6	800	Zuider, Z.	Greer, SC	74

> in 3NF, no nonkey field is dependent on another nonkey field

SALES-REP IN 3NF

RECORD#	SALES-REP-NUM	SALES-REP-NAME
1	22	McBride, Jon
2	38	Stein, Ellen
3	41	Kaplan, James
4	74	Roman, Harold

FIGURE 8-24   When CUSTOMER data is transformed from 2NF to 3NF, the result is two records: CUSTOMER and SALES-REP.

A Normalization Example

To show the normalization process, consider the familiar situation shown in Figure 8-25, which is a system with three entities: ADVISOR, STUDENT, and COURSE, as shown in the ERD in Figure 8-26.

The initial design of the record for the STUDENT entity includes the student number, student name, total credits taken, grade point average (GPA), advisor number, advisor name, and, for every course the student has taken, the course number, course description, and grade received.

FIGURE 8-25   A faculty advisor, who represents an entity, can advise many students, each of whom can register for one or many courses.

Figure 8-27 shows three unnormalized STUDENT records. The STUDENT record design can be written as:

> STUDENT (<u>STUDENT-NUMBER</u>, STUDENT-NAME, TOTAL-CREDITS, GPA, ADVISOR-NUMBER, ADVISOR-NAME, (<u>COURSE-NUMBER</u>, COURSE-DESC, GRADE))

The record designs for the ADVISOR and COURSE entities are:

> ADVISOR (<u>ADVISOR-NUMBER</u>, ADVISOR-NAME)

> COURSE (<u>COURSE-NUMBER</u>, COURSE-DESC, NUM-CREDITS)

The ADVISOR and COURSE records already are in 3NF. The STUDENT record, however, is unnormalized because it contains a repeating group. To convert the STUDENT record to 1NF, you expand the primary key to include the key of the repeating group and then remove the repeating group, producing:

> STUDENT (<u>STUDENT-NUMBER</u>, STUDENT-NAME, TOTAL-CREDITS, GPA, ADVISOR-NUMBER, ADVISOR-NAME, <u>COURSE-NUMBER</u>, COURSE-DESC, GRADE)

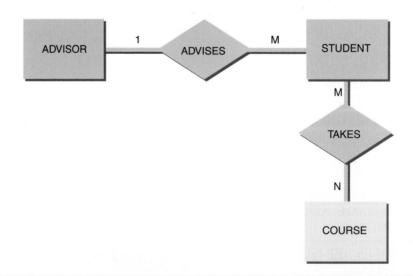

Figure 8-28 shows the 1NF version of the sample STUDENT data. Do any of the fields in the 1NF STUDENT record depend on only a portion of the primary key? The student name, total credits, GPA, advisor number, and advisor name all relate only to the student number and have no relationship to the course number. The course description depends on the course number, but not on the student number. Only the GRADE field depends on the entire primary key.

Creating records for each field and combination of fields in the primary key, then placing the other fields with their appropriate key produces the following record designs:

STUDENT (<u>STUDENT-NUMBER</u>, STUDENT-NAME, TOTAL-CREDITS, GPA, ADVISOR-NUMBER, ADVISOR-NAME)

COURSE (<u>COURSE-NUMBER</u>, COURSE-DESC, NUM-CREDITS)

GRADE (<u>STUDENT-NUMBER</u>, <u>COURSE-NUMBER</u>, GRADE)

STUDENT

STUDENT-NUMBER	STUDENT-NAME	TOTAL-CREDITS	GPA	ADVISOR-NUMBER	ADVISOR-NAME	COURSE-NUMBER	COURSE-DESC	GRADE
1035	Linda	17	3.647	49	Smith	CSC151	Computer Science I	B
						MKT212	Marketing Management	A
						ENG101	English Composition	B
						CHM112	General Chemistry I	A
						BUS105	Introduction to Business	A
3397	Sam	9	3.000	49	Smith	ENG101	English Composition	A
						MKT212	Marketing Management	C
						CSC151	Computer Science I	B
4070	Kelly	14	2.214	23	Jones	CSC151	Computer Science I	B
						CHM112	General Chemistry I	C
						ENG101	English Composition	C
						BUS105	Introduction to Business	C

repeating groups

FIGURE 8-27 Three unnormalized STUDENT records with repeating groups because each student has several classes.

STUDENT

STUDENT-NUMBER	STUDENT-NAME	TOTAL-CREDITS	GPA	ADVISOR-NUMBER	ADVISOR-NAME	COURSE-NUMBER	COURSE-DESC	GRADE
1035	Linda	17	3.647	49	Smith	CSC151	Computer Science I	B
1035	Linda	17	3.647	49	Smith	MKT212	Marketing Management	A
1035	Linda	17	3.647	49	Smith	ENG101	English Composition	B
1035	Linda	17	3.647	49	Smith	CHM112	General Chemistry I	A
1035	Linda	17	3.647	49	Smith	BUS105	Introduction to Business	A
3397	Sam	9	3.000	49	Smith	ENG101	English Composition	A
3397	Sam	9	3.000	49	Smith	MKT212	Marketing Management	C
3397	Sam	9	3.000	49	Smith	CSC151	Computer Science I	B
4070	Kelly	14	2.214	23	Jones	CSC151	Computer Science I	B
4070	Kelly	14	2.214	23	Jones	CHM112	General Chemistry I	C
4070	Kelly	14	2.214	23	Jones	ENG101	English Composition	C
4070	Kelly	14	2.214	23	Jones	BUS105	Introduction to Business	C

FIGURE 8-28 1NF STUDENT records. The repeating group has been eliminated.

You now have expanded the original STUDENT record to three records, all in 2NF. In each record, every nonkey field depends on the entire primary key.

Figure 8-29 shows the 2NF STUDENT, COURSE, and GRADE records for the sample data. Are all three records in 3NF? COURSE and GRADE are in 3NF. STUDENT is not in 3NF, however, because the ADVISOR-NAME field depends on the ADVISOR-NUMBER field, which is not part of the STUDENT primary key. To convert STUDENT to 3NF, you remove the ADVISOR-NAME field from the STUDENT record and place it into a new record

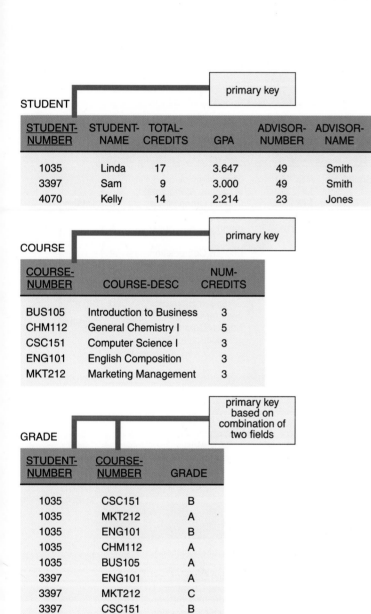

STUDENT

STUDENT-NUMBER	STUDENT-NAME	TOTAL-CREDITS	GPA	ADVISOR-NUMBER
1035	Linda	17	3.647	49
3397	Sam	9	3.000	49
4070	Kelly	14	2.214	23

in 3NF, no nonkey field is dependent on another nonkey field

ADVISOR

ADVISOR-NUMBER	ADVISOR-NAME
23	Jones
49	Smith

COURSE

COURSE-NUMBER	COURSE-DESC	NUM-CREDITS
BUS105	Introduction to Business	3
CHM112	General Chemistry I	5
CSC151	Computer Science I	3
ENG101	English Composition	3
MKT212	Marketing Management	3

GRADE

STUDENT-NUMBER	COURSE-NUMBER	GRADE
1035	CSC151	B
1035	MKT212	A
1035	ENG101	B
1035	CHM112	A
1035	BUS105	A
3397	ENG101	A
3397	MKT212	C
3397	CSC151	B
4070	CSC151	B
4070	CHM112	C
4070	ENG101	C
4070	BUS105	C

FIGURE 8-29 STUDENT, COURSE, and GRADE records in 2NF. All fields are functionally dependent on the primary key.

FIGURE 8-30 STUDENT, ADVISOR, COURSE, and GRADE records in 3NF. When STUDENT records are transformed from 2NF to 3NF, the result is two records: STUDENT and ADVISOR.

with ADVISOR-NUMBER as the primary key. The new record duplicates your original ADVISOR record so a new record is not needed.

Figure 8-30 shows the 3NF versions of the sample data for STUDENT, ADVISOR, COURSE, and GRADE. The final 3NF design for all the entity records is:

STUDENT (<u>STUDENT-NUMBER</u>, STUDENT NAME, TOTAL-CREDITS, GPA, ADVISOR-NUMBER)

ADVISOR (<u>ADVISOR-NUMBER</u>, ADVISOR-NAME)

COURSE (<u>COURSE-NUMBER</u>, COURSE-DESC, NUM-CREDITS)

GRADE (<u>STUDENT-NUMBER</u>, <u>COURSE-NUMBER</u>, GRADE)

Now there are four entities: STUDENT, ADVISOR, COURSE, and GRADE. Figure 8-31 shows the complete ERD after normalization. If you go back to Figure 8-26 on page 8.24 which was drawn before you identified GRADE as an entity, you can see that the M:N relationship between STUDENT and COURSE has been converted into two 1:M relationships: one relationship between STUDENT and GRADE and the other relationship between COURSE and GRADE.

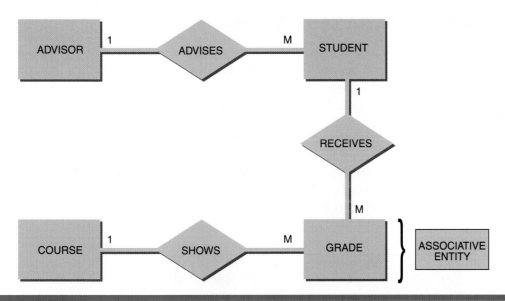

FIGURE 8-31 The entity-relationship diagram for STUDENT, ADVISOR, and COURSE after normalization. The associative entity called GRADE was identified during the normalization process.

To create 3NF designs, you must understand the nature of first, second, and third normal forms. In your work as a systems analyst, you will encounter designs that are much more complex than the examples in this chapter. You also should know that normal forms beyond 3NF exist, but they rarely are used in business-oriented systems.

You handle administrative support for CyberToys, a small chain that sells computer hardware and software and specializes in personal service. The company has four stores located at malls and is planning more. Each store has a manager, a technician, and between one and four sales reps.

Joan Jamison, the owner, wants a personnel records database and she asked you to look over a record design that she developed. She has suggested fields for store number, location, store telephone, manager name, and manager home telephone. She also wants fields for technician name and technician home telephone and fields for up to four sales rep names and sales rep home telephones.

Draw Joan's suggested design and analyze it using the normalization concepts you learned in the chapter. What do you think of Joan's design and why? What would you propose?

STEPS IN DATABASE DESIGN

After normalizing your record designs, you are ready to create the database. The following four analysis and design steps can be used to create database and file designs. To highlight the steps, consider another familiar situation shown in Figure 8-32, which is an information system for a video rental store.

1. *Create the initial ERD.* Start by reviewing DFDs and class diagrams to identify system entities. In addition, consider any data stores shown on DFDs to determine whether they might represent entities. Next, create a draft of the ERD. Carefully analyze each relationship to determine if it is 1:1, 1:M, or M:N. Figure 8-33 shows the initial ERD for the entities MEMBER and VIDEO in the video rental system.

FIGURE 8-32   A video rental involves several entities, including a member, a video, and a rental agreement. In the video store's information system, each entity is represented by a data record that contains various fields.

2. *Assign all data elements to entities.* Verify that every data element in the data dictionary is associated logically with an entity. For the video rental system, the initial record designs with all data elements are listed under the ERD in Figure 8-33.

MEMBER (<u>MEMBER-NUMBER</u>, NAME, ADDRESS, CITY, STATE, ZIP, HOME-TELEPHONE,
    WORK-TELEPHONE, CREDIT-CARD-CODE, CREDIT-CARD-NUMBER, (<u>VIDEO-ID</u>, TITLE,
    DATE-RENTED, DATE-RETURNED))
VIDEO (<u>VIDEO-ID</u>, TITLE)

FIGURE 8-33 The initial entity-relationship diagram and unnormalized record designs for the video rental system.

3. *Create 3NF designs for all records, taking care to identify all primary, secondary, and foreign keys.* Generate the final ERD that will include new entities identified during normalization. Figure 8-34 shows the final ERD and the normalized records. Notice that a new associative entity, RENTAL, was identified during normalization and the M:N relationship became two 1:M relationships.

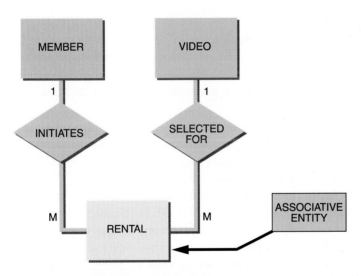

MEMBER (<u>MEMBER-NUMBER</u>, NAME, ADDRESS, CITY, STATE, ZIP, HOME-TELEPHONE,
    WORK-TELEPHONE, CREDIT-CARD-CODE, CREDIT-CARD-NUMBER)
VIDEO (<u>VIDEO-ID</u>, TITLE)
RENTAL (<u>MEMBER-NUMBER</u>, <u>VIDEO-ID</u>, DATE-RENTED, DATE-RETURNED)

FIGURE 8-34 The final entity-relationship diagram and normalized record designs for the video rental system.

4. *Verify all data dictionary entries.* Make sure that the data dictionary entries for all data stores, records, and data elements are documented completely and correctly.

After creating your final ERD and normalized record designs, you can transform them into a database. Your first step will be to consider the design and characteristics of various database models.

DATABASE MODELS

The four basic database models are: hierarchical, network, relational, and object-oriented. Hierarchical and network databases generally are used on mainframes. Relational databases can run on many platforms, including personal computers. Relational databases are well suited to client/server computing because they are so powerful and flexible. Object-oriented databases are modular, cost-effective, and a logical extension of the object-oriented analysis process.

Hierarchical and Network Databases

In a **hierarchical database**, data is organized like a family tree or organization chart, with branches representing parent records and child records. A parent record can have multiple child records, but each child record can have only one parent. The organization is implemented with address pointers linking each parent record with each child record. Hierarchical databases were widely used on mainframe computers in the 1960s, but today they are found only on older systems. The hierarchical model is complex, and application programs that interact with a hierarchical DBMS usually are complicated and difficult to maintain.

A **network database** resembles a hierarchical design, but provides somewhat more flexibility. In a network database, a child record can have relationships with more than one parent. Although the network model is not widely used today, many network databases still exist in older, legacy systems. Network designs represented an advance in database design, but the network model was complex and shared many of the same disadvantages as hierarchical models.

Relational Databases

The **relational model** was introduced during the 1970s and became popular because it was flexible and powerful. Three decades later, the relational design still is the predominate model. Earlier in this chapter, you learned that a relational database uses common fields, which are attributes that appear in more than one table, to establish relationships between the tables and form an overall data structure.

Figure 8-35 shows a relational database for a company that performs on-site computer service. That DBMS uses many of the design concepts described earlier in this chapter and demonstrates the power of a relational model. Separate tables exist for CUSTOMER, TECHNICIAN, SERVICE-CALL, SERVICE-PARTS-DETAIL, SERVICE-LABOR-DETAIL, PARTS, and LABOR-CODE tables. Notice that all the tables use a single field as a primary key, except the SERVICE-LABOR-DETAIL and SERVICE-PARTS-DETAIL tables, in which the primary key requires a combination of two fields to identify each record uniquely.

Because the tables are linked, a user can request data that meets specific conditions. To visualize how a relational DBMS handles complex queries, refer to Figure 8-35 and consider the following three examples. Suppose a user wants to see:

1. All customers who received service after 12/15/2001.

2. All service calls on which technician Marie Johnson put in more than four hours of labor.

3. The number and description of all parts sold to Washington customers.

In the first example, the DBMS looks in the SERVICE-CALL table and finds three records with a date later than 12/15/2001. Then, using CUSTOMER-NUM, which is a foreign key in the SERVICE-CALL table, the DBMS seeks matching primary key values in the CUSTOMER table to identify customers Albert Jones and Mary Belli.

In the second example, the DBMS locates Marie Johnson in the TECHNICIAN table and extracts her technician number, which is a primary key. Using her TECH-NUM value of 21, the DBMS identifies Marie's two service calls by seeking matching values of 21 in the TECH-NUM field in the SERVICE-CALL table. Next, the DBMS uses the CALL-NUM values of 10798 and 10800 to check for matching records with more than four hours in the SERVICE-LABOR-DETAIL table. In the example, only service call 10798 meets all the requirements.

In the third example, the DBMS first locates all records with the value WA in the CUST-STATE field in the CUSTOMER table. The process identifies customer 2836, Juan Gonzalez. Using the value 2836, which is a primary key value in the CUSTOMER table, the DBMS seeks matching values in the CUST-NUM field in the SERVICE-CALL table. After locating service call 10797, the DBMS seeks matching values in the PART-NUM field of the SERVICE-PARTS-DETAIL table. Then using the value AB-6784, the DBMS seeks the matching primary key value in the PARTS table and obtains the description from the PART-DESC field. The results indicate that six meters with part number AB-6784 were sold to Washington customers. Because it is uses a relational model, the DBMS in Figure 8-35 is flexible and powerful.

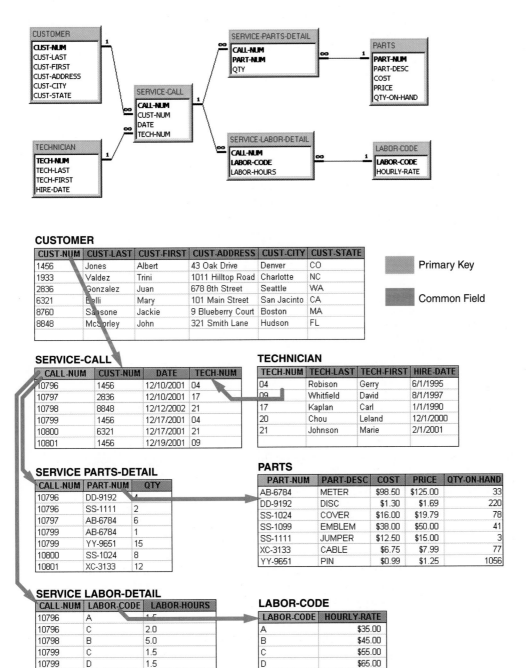

FIGURE 8-35 A relational database for an on-site service company uses common fields to form an overall data structure.

New entities and attributes can be added at any time without restructuring the entire database. If the company wants to add new parts, new service codes, new customers, or new technicians, it can do so without affecting existing data or relationships. Updating information also is simple in a relational design. For example, suppose customer Trini Valdez changes her address from 1011 Hilltop Road to 23 Down Lane. Even though she is listed on 18 separate service calls, only one change is needed in the CUSTOMER table. Because a common field links the CUSTOMER and SERVICE-CALL tables, it is not necessary to make a change in 18 individual records.

Object-Oriented Databases

Ten years ago, virtually all information systems were designed and implemented as relational databases. As object-oriented analysis became popular during the mid-1990s, some analysts began to describe systems in terms of objects, but most systems were constructed as relational DBMSs, regardless of the analysis method.

Today, many systems developers are using **object-oriented database (OODB)** design as a natural extension of the object-oriented analysis process. Some IT professionals believe that OODBs will have a major impact and eventually replace the relational approach. Most object-oriented developers support the **Object Definition Language (ODL)**, which is a design standard set forth by the **Object Database Management Group (ODMG)**, as shown in Figure 8-36.

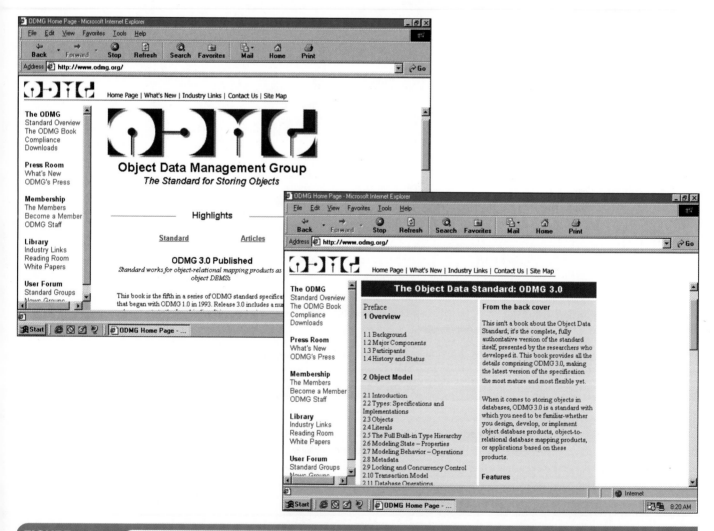

FIGURE 8-36 Many object-oriented developers support OODB design standards set forth by the Object Database Management Group (ODMG).

Each object in an OODB has a unique **object identifier**, which is similar to a primary key in a relational database. The identifier allows the object to interact with other objects and form relationships, as shown in Figure 8-37. Programmers use object-oriented languages, such as C++ to describe and implement object-to-object relationships that resemble the relationships found in a traditional ERD. Objects can have 1:1, 1:M, or M:N relationships with other objects.

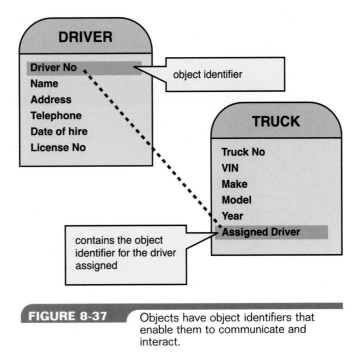

FIGURE 8-37 Objects have object identifiers that enable them to communicate and interact.

DATA STORAGE

Physical design requires an understanding of the difference between logical and physical records, and an understanding of data storage formats, including special characteristics of date fields.

Logical and Physical Records

The smallest unit of data is one binary digit, called a **bit**. A group of eight bits is a called a **byte**, or a **character**. A set of bytes forms a field, which is an individual fact about a person, place, thing, or event. A field also is called a **data element** or a **data item**. Each instance of a field has a specific value. For example, CUSTOMER NUMBER is a field. One customer number might have the three-byte value 823 and another customer number might have the four-byte value 6467. When designing field and record sizes, it is important to provide space for the largest values that can be anticipated, without allocating unnecessarily large storage capacities that will not be used.

A **logical record** contains field values that describe a single person, place, thing, or event. Application programs see a logical record as a set of fields, regardless of how or where the data is stored physically. For example, a logical customer record contains specific field values for a single customer, including the customer's number, name, address, telephone number, credit limit, and so on. The term record usually refers to a logical record. Whenever an application program issues a read or write command, the operating system supplies one logical record to the program or accepts one logical record from the program.

A **physical record**, or a **block**, is the smallest unit of data that is accessed by the operating system. The operating system reads or writes one physical record at a time. When the operating system reads a physical record, it transfers the record from the file or table to a **buffer**, which is a segment of computer memory. Similarly, when the system writes a physical record, all data in the buffer is written to the file.

A physical record consists of one or more logical records. The **blocking factor** is the number of logical records in one physical record. If the blocking factor is more than one, the execution of a read or write command does not always result in the physical action of reading or writing. Sometimes, the read or write command requires only a transfer of data from one memory location to another. Figure 8-38 on the next page shows a data file with fields, logical records, and physical records, or blocks.

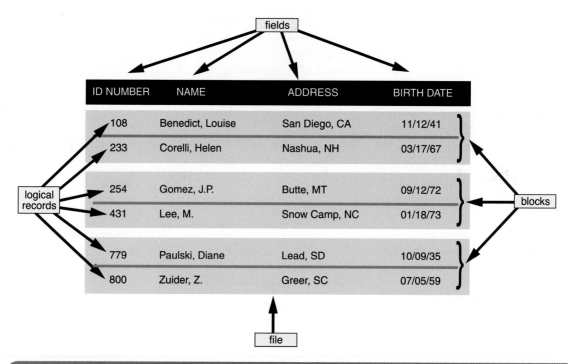

FIGURE 8-38   A data file consists of physical blocks that contain one or more logical records. Each logical record is a set of related field values.

Data Storage Formats

The computer industry uses four primary data storage formats, or codes: EBCDIC, ASCII, Unicode, and binary.

EBCDIC, which stands for **Extended Binary Coded Decimal Interchange Code**, is a data storage method used on most mainframe computers. **ASCII** is an acronym for **American Standard Code for Information Interchange**, which is used on most minicomputers and personal computers. EBCDIC and ASCII require one byte of storage for each character, numeric digit, or symbol. For example, the ASCII code for the number 123456 requires six bytes of storage. Various eight-bit combinations can represent a maximum of 256 characters and symbols.

Unicode is a relatively recent coding method that represents characters as integers. Unlike EBCDIC and ASCII, which use eight bits for each character, Unicode requires 16 bits per character, which allows it to represent more than 65,000 unique characters. That is important as software design becomes global, and large firms require multilingual computer operations. Many IT experts believe that Unicode will become the dominant coding format in the future. The Unicode Consortium maintains standards and support for Unicode, as shown in Figure 8-39.

Compared to character-based coding, **binary storage formats** offer more efficient storage of numeric data. For example, when you specify numeric data types using Microsoft Access 2000, you can choose from a variety of storage formats, including **integer** and **long integer**, among others. The integer format requires two bytes to store numbers from –32,768 to 32,767; the long integer format can store numbers from –2,147,483,647 to 2,147,483,647 using only four bytes of storage. Other binary formats exist for efficient storage of exceedingly long numbers.

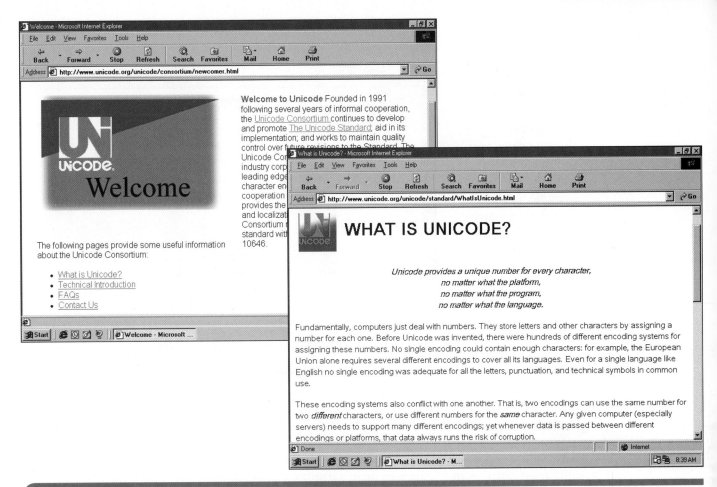

FIGURE 8-39 Unicode is an international coding format that represents characters as integers, using 16 bits per character. The Unicode Consortium maintains standards and support for Unicode.

Date Fields

What is the best way to store date fields? Based on industry-wide experience with Y2K issues, most date formats now are based on the model established by the **International Organization for Standardization (ISO)**, which requires a format of four digits for the year, two for the month, and two for the day (YYYYMMDD). A date stored in that format can be sorted easily and used in comparisons. If a date in ISO form is larger than another date in the same form, then the first date is later. For example, 20010815 is later than 20010131, just as August 15, 2001, is later than January 31, 2001.

But, what if dates must be used in calculations? For example, if a manufacturing order placed on June 23 takes three weeks to complete, when will the order be ready? If a payment due on August 13 is not paid until April 27 of the following year, exactly how late is the payment and how much interest is owed? Julian dates and absolute dates are easier to use in such calculations.

A standard **Julian date** is a five-digit number in which the first two digits represent the year and the last three digits represent the day of the year. Thus, the Julian date form of January 1, 2001, is 01001, while June 23 of that same year is 01174. To provide a full four-digits for the year, an extended Julian date is preferable. An **extended Julian date** is a seven-digit number in which the first four digits represent the year. Thus, the extended Julian date for June 23, 2001, is 2001174; a date three weeks later is represented as 2001195 (2001174 + 21). Julian dates work well for calculations with dates that fall in the same year, but extra steps are needed, for example, to add five weeks to December 3 or to calculate the number of days between one year and the next, such as between August 13 and the following April 27.

An **absolute date** is the total number of days from some specific base date. To calculate the number of days between two absolute dates, you subtract one date from the other. For example, using a base date of January 1, 1900, August 13, 2001 has an absolute date value of 37116 and April 27, 2002 has an absolute date of 37373. If you subtract the earlier date value from the later one, the result is 257 days. You can use a spreadsheet to determine and display absolute dates easily, as shown in Figure 8-40.

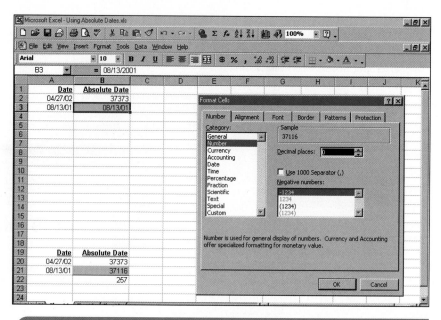

FIGURE 8-40   Microsoft Excel utilizes absolute dates that can be used in calculations. January 1, 1900, is stored with a numeric value of 1. In the example shown, August 13, 2001, can be displayed in number format as 37116.

Which is the best method for storing date fields? The answer depends on how the specific date will be printed, displayed, or used in a calculation. You must consider how the date will be used most often — in calculations or in a display — to determine the right format to use.

W H A T   D O   Y O U   T H I N K ?

SoccerMom Company sells a patented seat that spectators can take to youth soccer games. The seat folds so it is small enough to fit in the glove box of most vehicles. The company operates a factory in Kansas and also contracts its manufacturing projects to small firms in Canada and Mexico.

An unusual problem has occurred for this small multinational company: people are getting confused about dates in internal memos, purchase orders, and e-mail. Towson Hopkins handles all IT functions for SoccerMom. When he designed the company's database, he was not aware that the format for dates in Canada and Mexico was different from the format used in the United States. For example, in Canada and Mexico, the notation 2/1/02 indicates January 2, 2002, whereas in the United States the same notation indicates February 1, 2002. Although it seems like a small point, the date confusion has resulted in several order cancellations.

Towson has asked for your advice. You could suggest writing a simple program to convert the dates automatically or designing a switchboard command that would allow users to select a date format as data is entered. You realize, however, that SoccerMom might want to do business in other countries in the future. What would be the best course of action? Should SoccerMom adapt to the standard of each country, or should it maintain a single international format? What are the arguments for each option?

DATA CONTROL

Just as it is important to secure the physical part of the system, as shown in Figure 8-41, file and database control must include all measures necessary to ensure that data storage is correct, complete, and secure. File and database control also is related to input and output techniques discussed earlier.

A well-designed DBMS must provide built-in control and security features, including subschemas, passwords, encryption, audit trail files, and backup and recovery procedures to maintain data. Your main responsibility is to ensure that the DBMS features are used properly.

Earlier in this chapter, you learned that a subschema can be used to provide a limited view of the database to a specific user, or level of users. Limiting access to files and databases is the most common way of protecting stored data. Users must furnish a proper **user ID** and **password** to access a file or database. Different privileges can be associated with different users, so some employees can be limited to read-only access, while other users might be allowed to update or delete data. For highly sensitive data, additional access codes can be established that restrict specific records or fields within records. Stored data also can be encrypted to prevent unauthorized access. **Encryption** is the process of converting readable data into unreadable characters to prevent unauthorized access to the data.

FIGURE 8-41   System security involves the physical controls shown here and a range of software controls including access codes, data encryption, passwords, and audit trails.

All system files and databases must be backed up regularly and a series of **backup** copies must be retained for a specified period of time. In the event of a file catastrophe, **recovery procedures** can be used to restore the file or database to its current state at the time of the last backup. **Audit log files**, which record details of all accesses and changes to the file or database, can be used to recover changes made since the last backup. You also can include **audit fields**, which are special fields within data records to provide additional control or security information. Typical audit fields include the date the record was created or modified, the name of the user who performed the action, and the number of times the record has been accessed.

SOFTWEAR, LIMITED

At his next meeting with Tom Adams and Becky Evans, Rick Williams shared an e-mail message that Ann Hon had forwarded to him. Attached to Ann's note was the e-mail message shown in Figure 8-42 from Michael Jeremy.

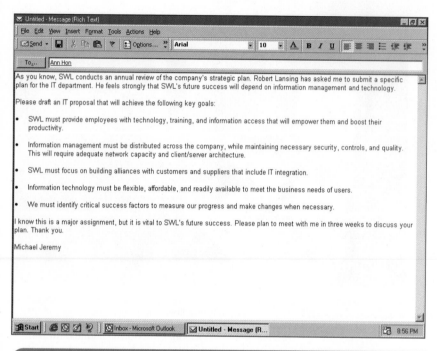

FIGURE 8-42   Michael Jeremy's January 4, 2002 e-mail message to Ann Hon requesting an IT plan for SWL.

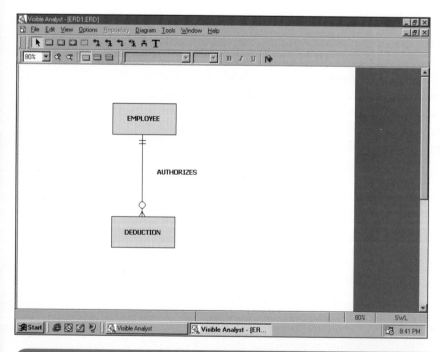

FIGURE 8-43   Initial ERD showing two entities: EMPLOYEE and DEDUCTION. Notice that crow's foot notation shows that one and only one employee can authorize anywhere from zero to many deductions.

After reading the message, Tom and Becky were excited because they would be working on an overall strategy for information technology at SWL. Rick said they would need to study various approaches that could support SWL's current and future business requirements. He said they would examine several alternatives, including a client/server design. Tom and Becky both had heard of client/server design, but neither person had worked on such a system.

Rick also said that Ann Hon wanted to use the ESIP system as a prototype for developing other SWL systems in the future. Ann said that the new design would have to be powerful, flexible, and scalable. With that in mind, the team decided that a DBMS strategy was the best solution for SWL's future information systems requirements.

Meanwhile, work continued on the ESIP system. Rick asked Tom and Becky to draw an entity-relationship diagram with normalized record designs. Tom and Becky used the Visible Analyst, a CASE tool, to produce the diagram shown in Figure 8-43. Rick noticed that only two entities were shown: EMPLOYEE and DEDUCTION. Rick suggested that the ESIP-OPTION and HUMAN RESOURCES entities should be added. Tom and Becky agreed. The second version of their ERD is shown in Figure 8-44.

With the ERD completed, Tom turned to the design of the EMPLOYEE record. He suggested the following design:

EMPLOYEE (<u>SSN</u>, EMPLOYEE-NAME, HIRE-DATE)

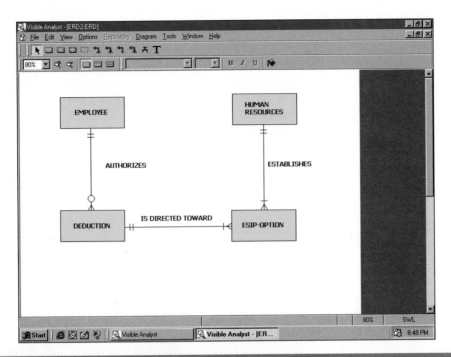

PHASE 3

FIGURE 8-44 Second version of the ERD. Now, DEDUCTION has relationships to two other entities: EMPLOYEE and ESIP-OPTION.

"The record obviously is in 1NF, because it has no repeating groups," Tom said. "It's also in 2NF, because it has a single field as the primary key. And I'm sure it's in 3NF, because the employee name and the hire date both depend on the Social Security number." Everyone agreed that this was the correct design. Tom and Becky turned their attention to designing the ESIP-OPTION record and later suggested the following design:

ESIP-OPTION (<u>OPTION-CODE</u>, OPTION-NAME, DESCRIPTION, DEDUCTION-CYCLE, APPLICATION-CYCLE, MIN-SERVICE, MIN-DEDUCTION, MAX-DEDUCTION)

The design appeared to meet the test for 3NF. Although seven fields existed in addition to the primary key, each field seemed to depend on the entire primary key. Finally, Becky proposed the following design for the DEDUCTION record:

DEDUCTION (<u>SSN</u>, <u>ESIP-OPTION</u>, <u>DATE</u>, EMPLOYEE-NAME, AMOUNT)

This time, Rick felt that the record was in 1NF, but not in 2NF because the EMPLOYEE-NAME field only was dependent on a part of the key rather than the entire key. Becky agreed with him and suggested that the EMPLOYEE-NAME field could be removed and accessed using the EMPLOYEE table. The SSN field could be used as a foreign key to match values in the EMPLOYEE table's primary key. To put the record in 2NF, she rewrote the DEDUCTION record design as follows:

DEDUCTION (<u>SSN</u>, <u>ESIP-OPTION</u>, <u>DATE</u>, AMOUNT)

With that change, everyone agreed that the record also was in 3NF because the AMOUNT field depended on the entire primary key. The next step was to work on a system design to interface with the payroll system and provide support for SWL's long-term information technology goals.

While Rick, Tom, and Becky were working on ERDs and record normalization, Pacific Software delivered the payroll package that SWL ordered. Tom was assigned to work on installing and configuring the package and training users on the new payroll system.

Meanwhile, Rick felt that SWL should get more information about client/server design. With Ann Hon's approval, he contacted several IT consulting firms that advertised their client/server design expertise on the Internet. Rick and Becky met with three firms and recommended that SWL work with True Blue Systems, a consulting group with a local office in Raleigh, not far from SWL's headquarters. In addition to the design for the ESIP system, Rick suggested that the agenda should include a general discussion about a future SWL intranet, with support for Web standards, and the possibility that employees could access their ESIP accounts from home via the Internet.

YOUR TURN

Rick asked you to help him put together a brief progress update for Michael Jeremy and several other top managers. Specifically, Rick wants you to explain the concept of normalization without using a lot of technical jargon with which managers might be unfamiliar. He says that some managers do not understand why it takes so much time to develop the final design for the system. Rick is confident that you will be able to summarize the concept of normalization in a paragraph or two, using plain English and simple examples. You do not have to describe all the details — just the basic idea of normalization and why it is so important.

CHAPTER SUMMARY

Files and tables contain data about people, places, things, or events that affect the information system. File-oriented systems manage data stored in separate files using a method called file processing, which uses master files, table files, transaction files, work files, security files, and history files.

A database consists of linked tables that form an overall data structure. A database management system (DBMS) is a collection of tools, features, and interfaces that enable users to add, update, manage, access, and analyze data in a database.

DBMS designs are more powerful and flexible than traditional file-oriented systems. A database environment offers scalability, support for organization-wide access, economy of scale, data sharing among user groups, balancing of conflicting user requirements, enforcement of standards, controlled redundancy, effective security, flexibility, better programmer productivity, and data independence. Large-scale databases are complex and require extensive security and backup/recovery features.

DBMS components include interfaces for users, database administrators, and related systems; and a data manipulation language, a schema, and a physical data repository. Other data management techniques include data warehousing, which stores data in an easily accessible form for user access; and data mining, which looks for meaningful patterns and relationships among data.

In an information system, an entity is a person, place, thing, or event for which data is collected and maintained. A field, or attribute, is a single characteristic of an entity. A record, or tuple, is a set of related fields that describes one instance of an entity. Records are grouped into files (in a file-oriented system) and tables (in a database environment).

A primary key is the field or field combination that uniquely and minimally identifies a specific record; a candidate key is any field that could serve as a primary key. A foreign key is a field or field combination that must match the primary key of another file or table. A secondary key is a field or field combination used as the basis for sorting or retrieving records.

An entity-relationship diagram (ERD) is a graphic representation of all system entities and the relationships among them. The ERD is based on entities and data stores in DFDs prepared during the systems analysis phase. The three basic relationships represented in an ERD are one-to-one (1:1), one-to-many (1:M), and many-to-many (M:N). In a M:N relationship, the two entities are linked by an associative entity.

The relationship between two entities also is referred to as cardinality. A common form of cardinality notation is called crow's foot notation, which uses various symbols to describe the characteristics of the relationship.

Normalization is a process for avoiding problems in record design. A first normal form (1NF) record has no repeating groups. A record is in second normal form (2NF) if it is in 1NF and all nonkey fields depend on the entire primary key. A record is in third normal form (3NF) if it is in 2NF and if no field depends on a nonkey field.

File and database design tasks include creating an initial ERD; assigning data elements to an entity; normalizing all record designs; and completing the data dictionary entries for files, records, and data elements. Files and database tables should be sized to estimate the amount of storage space they will require.

The four basic database models are hierarchical, network, relational, and object-oriented. The hierarchical and network models generally are used on mainframes and older systems. The relational model, which is currently the dominant form of database design, is powerful, flexible, and provides the best support for client/server architecture. Object-oriented database (OODB) design is becoming more popular as a natural extension of the object-oriented analysis process. Each object in an OODB has a unique object identifier, which is similar to a primary key in a relational database and allows the object to interact with other objects and form relationships.

Data storage involves eight-bit bytes that form fields. Data consists of logical records (which describe instances of an entity) and physical records, or blocks (which represent the smallest unit of data that is accessed by the operating system). A physical record consists of one or more logical records, depending on the blocking factor. Data storage formats include EBCDIC, ASCII, Unicode, and binary. Dates can be stored in several formats, including ISO, Julian, extended Julian, and absolute format.

File and database control measures include limiting access to the data, data encryption, backup/recovery procedures, audit-trail files, and internal audit fields.

Key Terms

absolute date (*8.36*)
ASCII (American Standard Code for Information Interchange) (*8.34*)
attribute (*8.10*)
associative entity (*8.15*)
audit fields (*8.37*)
audit log files (*8.37*)
backup (*8.37*)
binary storage formats (*8.34*)
bit (*8.33*)
block (*8.33*)
blocking factor (*8.33*)
buffer (*8.33*)
byte (*8.33*)
candidate key (*8.12*)
cardinality (*8.16*)
cardinality notation (*8.16*)
character (*8.33*)
client/server (*8.4*)
combination key (*8.11*)
common field (*8.10*)
crow's foot notation (*8.16*)
database (*8.2*)
database administrator (DBA) (*8.5*)
database management system (DBMS) (*8.2*)
data element (*8.33*)
data integrity (*8.3*)
data item (*8.33*)
data manipulation language (DML) (*8.7*)
data mining (*8.8*)
data redundancy (*8.3*)
data warehouse (*8.7*)
dimensions (*8.8*)
EBCDIC (Extended Binary Coded Decimal Interchange Code) (*8.34*)
economy of scale (*8.4*)
encryption (*8.37*)
entity (*8.10*)
entity-relationship diagram (ERD) (*8.14*)
extended Julian date (*8.35*)
field (*8.10*)
file (*8.2*)
file-oriented (*8.2*)
file processing (*8.2*)
first normal form (1NF) (*8.19*)
foreign key (*8.12*)
functionally dependent (*8.21*)
hierarchical database (*8.30*)
history file (*8.4*)
integer (*8.34*)
International Organization for Standardization (ISO) (*8.35*)

Julian date (*8.35*)
key fields (*8.10*)
logical record (*8.33*)
long integer (*8.34*)
many-to-many relationship (M:N) (*8.15*)
master file (*8.3*)
multivalued key (*8.11*)
network database (*8.30*)
nonkey field (*8.12*)
normalization (*8.19*)
Object Database Management Group (ODMG) (*8.32*)
Object Definition Language (ODL) (*8.32*)
object identifier (*8.33*)
object-oriented database (OODB) (*8.32*)
one-to-many relationship (1:M) (*8.14*)
one-to-one relationship (1:1) (*8.14*)
orphan (*8.13*)
password (*8.37*)
physical record (*8.33*)
primary key (*8.11*)
query-by-example (QBE) (*8.6*)
query language (*8.6*)
record (*8.10*)
record design (*8.19*)
recovery procedures (*8.37*)
referential integrity (*8.13*)
relation (*8.14*)
relational model (*8.30*)
relationship (*8.13*)
repeating group (*8.19*)
rigid data structure (*8.3*)
scalability (*8.3*)
schema (*8.7*)
scratch files (*8.3*)
second normal form (2NF) (*8.21*)
secondary key (*8.12*)
security file (*8.3*)
SQL (Structured Query Language) (*8.6*)
subschema (*8.7*)
table file (*8.3*)
tables (*8.2*)
third normal form (3NF) (*8.23*)
transaction file (*8.3*)
tuple (*8.10*)
unnormalized (*8.19*)
Unicode (*8.34*)
user ID (*8.37*)
work file (*8.3*)

Chapter Review

1. Explain the main differences between a file-oriented system and a database environment.

2. What is a DBMS? Briefly describe the components of a DBMS.

3. Define the following terms: primary key, candidate key, secondary key, foreign key, and common field.

4. What are entity-relationship diagrams and how are they used? What symbol is used to represent an entity in an ERD? What symbol is used for a relationship?

5. What is cardinality, and what symbols do you use in the crow's foot notation method?

6. What is the criterion for a record design to be in first normal form? How do you convert an unnormalized record design to 1NF?

7. What are the criteria for a record design to be in second normal form? How do you convert a non-2NF record design to 2NF?

8. What are the criteria for a record design to be in third normal form? How do you convert a non-3NF record design to 3NF?

9. Explain the difference between a logical record and a physical record.

10. What is an extended Julian date? What is an absolute date? How would a specific date, such as March 1, 2001, be represented in each form?

Discussion Topics

1. Are there ethical issues to consider when planning a database? For example, should sensitive personal data (such as medical information) be stored in the same DBMS that manages employee salary and benefits data? Why or why not?

2. Is referential integrity really that important? For example, in a rush situation, you might want to place an order for a customer before you have a chance to enter the customer into the database. Should that be permissible in some cases?

3. Consider an automobile dealership that maintains an inventory system of cars and trucks in stock at its three locations. Data fields exist for stock number, vehicle identification number, make, model, year, color, and invoice cost. Identify the possible candidate keys, the likely primary key, a probable foreign key, and potential secondary keys. Justify your choices.

4. In the discussion of third normal form as shown in Figures 8-23 and 8-24 on page 8.23, the 2NF customer record design was converted to two 3NF records. Verify that the four potential problems identified for non-3NF records were eliminated in the 3NF design.

Apply Your Knowledge

1 Pick and Shovel Construction Company

Situation:

Pick and Shovel Construction Company is a multi-state building contractor specializing in medium-priced town homes. C. T. Scott, the owner, is in your office for the third time today to see how the new relational database project is coming along. Unfortunately, someone mentioned to C. T. that the delay had something to do with achieving "normalization."

"Why is all this normalization stuff so important?" he asks. "The old system worked OK most of the time, and now you are telling me that we need all these special rules. Why is this necessary?"

1. How should you respond to C. T.? Write him a brief memo with your views.

2. Assume that the Pick and Shovel's main entities are its customers, employees, projects, and equipment. A customer can hire the company for more than one project, and employees sometime work on more than one project at a time. Equipment, however, is assigned only to one project. Draw an ERD showing those entities.

3. Add cardinality notation to your ERD.

4. Create 3NF record designs.

2 Puppy Palace

Situation:

Puppy Palace works with TV and movie producers who need dogs that can perform special tricks, such as headstands, somersaults, ladder climbs, and various dog-and-pony tricks. Puppy Palace has about 16 dogs and a list of 50 tricks to choose from. Each dog can perform one or more tricks, and many tricks can be performed by more than one dog. When a dog learns a new trick, the trainer assigns a skill level. Some customers insist on using dogs that score a 10, which is the highest skill level.

As an IT consultant, you have been asked to suggest 3NF record designs. You are fairly certain that a M:N relationship exists between dogs and tricks.

1. Draw an ERD for the Puppy Palace information system.

2. Indicate cardinality.

3. Identify all fields you plan to include in the tables. For example, in the puppy table, you might want breed, size, age, name, and so on. *Hint:* before you begin, review some database design samples in this chapter. You might spot a similar situation to use as a pattern. In addition, remember that numeric values work well in primary key fields.

4. Create 3NF record designs.

3 TopText Publishing

Situation:

TopText Publishing is a textbook publishing company with a headquarters location, a warehouse, and three sales offices that each have a sales manager and sales reps. TopText sells to schools, colleges, and individual customers. Many authors write more than one book for TopText, and some books are written by more than one author. TopText maintains an active list of over 100 books, each identified by a universal code called an ISBN number.

1. Draw an ERD for the TopText information system.

2. Indicate cardinality.

3. Identify all fields you plan to include in the tables.

4. Create 3NF record designs.

4 Mayville Public Library

Situation:

Mayville is a rural village with a population of 500. Until now, Mayville was served by a bookmobile from a larger town. The Mayville Village Council has authorized funds for a small public library, and you have volunteered to set up an information system for the library. Assume that the library will have multiple copies of certain books.

1. Draw an ERD for the Mayville library system.

2. Indicate cardinality.

3. Identify all fields you plan to include in the tables.

4. Create 3NF record designs.

Chapter Assignments

1. Search the Internet to find information about international date formats. Determine whether the date format used in the United States is the most common format.

2. Visit the IT department at your school or at a local business and determine whether the organization uses file processing systems, DBMSs, or both. Write a brief memo with your conclusions.

3. Use Microsoft Access or similar database software to create a DBMS for the imaginary company called TopText, which is described in Assignment 3 in the Apply Your Knowledge section. Add several sample records to each table and report to the class on your progress.

4. Visit the bookstore at your school, or a bookstore in your area. Interview the manager or store employees to learn how the operation works, and what entities are involved in bookstore operations. Remember that an entity is a person, place, thing, or event that affects the information system. Draw an ERD, including cardinality that describes the bookstore operations.

CASE STUDIES

Case Studies offer an opportunity for you to practice specific skills and knowledge learned in the chapter and provide practical experience for you as a systems analyst. Two of the case studies (New Century Health Clinic and Ridgeway Company) are continuing case studies that appear in each chapter. Additionally, one continuing case study (SCR Associates) utilizes the Internet to practice some of the topics covered in this chapter.

NEW CENTURY HEALTH CLINIC

After completing the user interface, input, and output design for the new information system at New Century, you will consider data design issues. Begin by studying the DFDs and object-oriented diagrams you prepared previously and the rest of the documentation from the systems analysis phase. Perform the following tasks:

Assignments

1. Create an initial entity-relationship diagram for the New Century Health Clinic system.

2. Normalize your record designs.

3. If you identified any new entities during normalization, create a final entity-relationship diagram for the system.

4. Write a memo for your documentation file that contains your recommendation about whether a file processing or a database environment should be used. Attach copies of your ERD(s) and normalized designs.

RIDGEWAY COMPANY

The Ridgeway Company requirements were discussed in a Chapter 4 case study. The following assignments are based on the work you did for that case study. Assume that Ridgeway will use a file-oriented design for the information system.

Assignments

1. Create an initial entity-relationship diagram for the Ridgeway Company billing system.

2. Normalize your record designs.

3. For each file, determine the file type (master file, transaction file, and so on) and identify all key fields.

4. Suggest appropriate data controls for Ridgeway Management to consider.

CUTTING EDGE INCORPORATED

Cutting Edge Incorporated is a company engaged in the development of computer-aided design (CAD) software packages. At Cutting Edge, each employee is assigned to a specific department. Employees from several departments often are assigned to special project teams, however. Cutting Edge wants to develop a project management system to track the projects, employees assigned, and accumulated project hours. Systems analyst Penny Binns developed the following initial record design:

> (PROJECT-NUMBER, PROJECT-NAME, START-DATE, PROJECT-STATUS,
> (EMPLOYEE-NUMBER, EMPLOYEE-NAME, JOB-TITLE, DEPT-NUMBER, DEPT-
> NAME, PROJECT-HOURS))

Penny believes that the only entities are PROJECT, DEPT, and EMPLOYEE; but because she is assigned to two other projects, she has not had time to consider the relationships among those system entities or to normalize the record designs, and she has asked for your help.

Assignments

1. Analyze Penny's initial record design and determine its normal form. What is the first step to take? Write a brief recommendation to Penny.

2. Create an ERD, including cardinality, for the project management system using the entities Penny identified. State any assumptions you must make about the Cutting Edge organization to determine the types of the relationships. *Hint*: Penny's situation provides a clue for one of the assumptions you must make.

3. For each of the three entities, design tables and identify the primary key, possible candidate keys, a probable foreign key, and potential secondary keys. Use sample data to populate the fields for three records.

4. Convert the record designs to 3NF.

FASTFLIGHT AIRLINES

FastFlight Airlines is a small air carrier operating in three northeastern states. FastFlight is in the process of computerizing its passenger reservation system. The following data items were identified: reservation number, flight number, flight date, origin, destination, departure time, arrival time, passenger name, and seat number.

For example, flight number 303 leaves Augusta, Maine, at 9:23 a.m. and arrives in Nashua, New Hampshire, at 10:17 a.m. Reservation number AXQ1001 is for passenger Lisa Lane, in seat 4A, on flight 303 on 11/12/2002.

Assignments

1. Create an ERD, including cardinality, for the reservations system.

2. Create 3NF records for the system.

3. For each of the entities identified, design tables and identify the possible candidate keys, the primary key, a probable foreign key, and potential secondary keys.

4. Use sample data to populate the fields for three records.

SCR ASSOCIATES

SCR Associates is an information technology consulting firm that offers IT solutions and training for small- and medium-sized companies. SCR's slogan is "We Know IT!"

Background

As a newly hired systems analyst, you will handle assignments, work on various SCR projects, and apply the skills you learned in the text. SCR needs an information system to manage training operations at the new SCR training center. The new system will be called TIMS (Training Information Management System).

The SCR case is available as an interactive, Web-based case study. You can log on to the Shelly Cashman Series site at www.scsite.com/sad4e/scr for instructions and assignments. If you prefer to complete the case study without using the Internet then you must download the data disk. See the inside back cover for instructions for downloading the data disk or see your instructor for more information on accessing the files required for this book.

Situation

In Part 8 of the SCR case, you will create an ERD and normalized record designs for the new TIMS system.

Before You Begin ...

1. Review the January 11 message from Jesse Baker regarding an ERD for the TIMS system. Open the Document 8-1 from the data disk.

2. Review the January 16 message from Jesse Baker regarding record designs and normalization. Open the Document 8-2 from the data disk.

Assignments

1. Make a list of all the entities that interact with the TIMS system. You might find it helpful to review the DFDs you created in Chapter 4 and the use case diagrams you created in Chapter 5.

2. Draw an ERD that shows cardinality relationships between the entities.

3. For each entity, create a design for a table with a suitable primary key. Include all fields necessary to describe the characteristics of the entity.

4. Create 3NF record designs for the TIMS system. Use sample data to populate the fields for three records in each table.

PHASE 1 Systems Planning
PHASE 2 Systems Analysis
Systems Design **PHASE 3**
PHASE 4 Systems Implementation
PHASE 5 Systems Operation & Support

Application Architecture

In this, the last of three chapters in the systems design phase, you will consider application architecture, which translates the logical design of an information system into a physical plan. As you construct the physical model, you will learn about servers, clients, processing methods, networks, and related issues. At this point in the SDLC, your objective is to determine an overall application architecture that can support the information requirements of the business.

INTRODUCTION

An information system, also called an **application**, requires hardware, software, data, procedures, and people to accomplish an organized set of functions. An effective system combines those elements into an **architecture**, or design, that is flexible, cost-effective, technically sound, and able to support the information needs of the business.

Application architecture translates the logical design of an information system into a physical structure that includes hardware, software, network support, and processing methods. The end product of the systems design phase is the preparation of the system design specification document. If approved, the next step is systems implementation.

OBJECTIVES

When you finish this chapter, you will be able to:

- List the main issues that a systems analyst should consider when selecting an application architecture, including enterprise resource planning, initial costs and TCO (total cost of ownership), scalability, Web integration, legacy interface requirements, security, and processing options

- Describe servers, server-based processing, clients, and client-based processing

- Explain client/server architecture, including the difference between fat and thin clients

- Discuss client/server tiers, cost-benefit issues, and performance considerations

- Explain the impact of the Internet on application architecture

- Describe online and batch processing

- Define network topology, and provide examples of hierarchical, bus, star, and ring network models

- Explain network protocols and licensing issues

- Describe tools for modeling application architecture

- Explain system management tools and techniques, including performance management, system security, fault management, backup, and disaster recovery

- Describe the systems design specification and explain the contents of each section

DESIGN CHECKLIST

Just as an architect begins a project with a list of the owner's requirements, a systems analyst must start with an overall design checklist. Before selecting an application architecture, the analyst must consider the following issues:

- Enterprise resource planning
- Initial cost and TCO
- Scalability
- Web integration
- Legacy interface requirements
- Security
- Processing options

ON THE WEB

For an overview of Enterprise Resource Planning visit scsite.com/sad4e/more.htm, click Systems Analysis and Design Chapter 9 and then click the Enterprise Resource Planning link.

www.scsite.com

Enterprise Resource Planning

Many companies engage in a process called **enterprise resource planning (ERP)**, which establishes an enterprisewide strategy for IT resources. ERP defines a specific architecture, including standards for data, processing, network, and user interface design. A main advantage of ERP is that it describes a specific hardware and software **environment**, also called a **platform**, that ensures hardware connectivity and easy integration of future applications, including in-house software and commercial packages.

As ERP systems become more popular, companies are extending them to suppliers and customers in a process called **supply chain management**. In a totally integrated supply chain, a customer order could cause a production planning system to schedule a work order, which in turn triggers a call for certain parts from one or more suppliers. In a dynamic, highly competitive economy, ERP can help companies achieve faster response, better customer service, and lower operating costs.

Many software vendors offer packages that help companies establish an ERP environment best suited to their business needs. One of the leading ERP providers is SAP, a major software vendor that offers a popular ERP package called SAP R/3, as shown in Figure 9-1.

Initial Costs and TCO

You learned earlier about the importance of considering economic feasibility and TCO during systems planning and analysis. Now, during the final design stage, you make decisions that will have a major impact on the initial costs and TCO for the new system. At this point, you should review all previous cost estimates and ask the following questions:

- If in-house development was selected as the best alternative initially, is it still the best choice? Is the necessary technical expertise available, and does the original cost estimate appear realistic?

- If a specific package was chosen initially, is it still the best choice? Are there newer versions, or competitive products? Have any changes occurred in pricing or support?

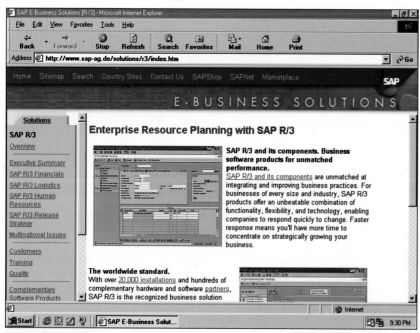

FIGURE 9-1   SAP's R/3 software is a popular ERP package.

- Have any new types of outsourcing become available?

- Have any economic, governmental, or regulatory events occurred that could affect the proposed project?

- Have any significant technical developments occurred that could affect the proposed project?

- Have any major assumptions changed since the company made the build vs. buy decision?

- Are there any merger or acquisition issues to consider, whereby the company might require compatibility with a specific environment?

- Have any new trends occurred in the marketplace? Are new products or technologies on the verge of being introduced?

- Have you updated the original TCO estimate? If so, are there any significant differences?

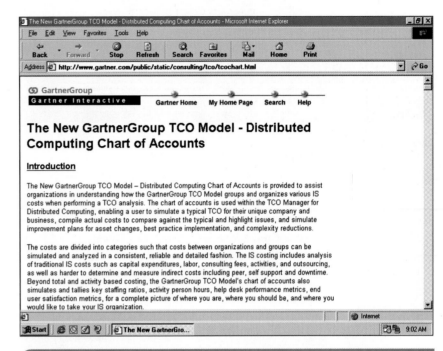

The answers to these questions might affect initial cost and TCO for the proposed system. You should reanalyze system requirements and alternatives now, before proceeding to design the application architecture. To ensure that all costs are considered, you might want to review a suggested chart of accounts published by the Gartner Group, as shown in Figure 9-2.

FIGURE 9-2   The Gartner Group publishes a list of accounts to help firms perform a TCO analysis.

Scalability

Scalability is the measure of a system's ability to expand, change, or downsize easily to meet the changing needs of a business enterprise. Scalability is especially important in implementing systems that are volume-related, such as transaction processing systems. Another term for scalability is extensibility, which refers to a system's ability to support a dynamic, growing business. For example, a scalable network could handle anywhere from a few dozen nodes to thousands of nodes; a scalable DBMS could support the acquisition of a new sales division. When investing large amounts of money in a project, management is especially concerned about scalability issues that could affect the system's life expectancy.

Web Integration

The systems analyst must know if the new application will be part of an e-commerce strategy, and the degree of integration with other Web-based components. A **Web-centric** architecture follows Internet design protocols and enables a company to integrate the new application into its e-commerce strategy. Even where e-commerce is not involved, a Web-centric application can run on the Internet or a company intranet. A Web-based application avoids many of the connectivity and compatibility problems that typically arise when different hardware environments are involved.

In an interesting example of ERP and Web-centric design, Chrysler Corporation worked with IBM to develop its Supply Partner Information Network (SPIN), as shown in Figure 9-3. As the IBM Web site points out, Chrysler found that the Internet was an excellent choice for a supply chain management system that must handle time-sensitive information in a multiplatform setting.

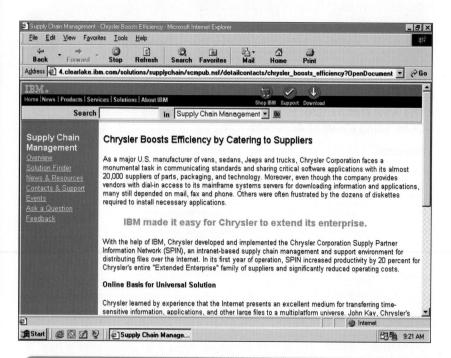

FIGURE 9-3   Working with IBM, Chrysler developed the Supply Partner Information Network (SPIN) as a Web-based application.

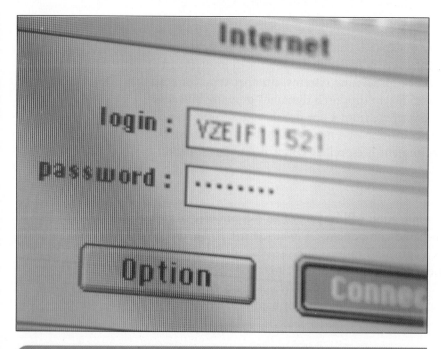

FIGURE 9-4   User login names and passwords are an important part of system security.

Legacy Interface Requirements

The new system might have to interface with one or more **legacy systems**, which are older systems that typically run on mainframe computers. When considering physical design, a systems analyst must determine how the new application will communicate with existing legacy systems. For example, a new marketing information system might need to report sales data to a mainframe-based accounting system, and obtain product cost data from a legacy manufacturing system.

Interface with legacy systems involves analysis of data formats and compatibility. In some cases, a company will need to convert legacy file data, which can be an expensive and time-consuming process. Finally, to select the best application architecture, the analyst must know if the new application will eventually replace the legacy system.

Security

System security is a concern at every stage of application development and design, as shown in Figure 9-4. As the logical and physical design is translated into specific hardware and software, the systems analyst must consider security issues and determine how the company will address them. Web-based systems introduce new security concerns, as critical data must be protected in the Internet environment. E-commerce applications raise additional security concerns as firms seek to reassure customers that their credit card and personal data is safe and secure.

Processing Options

How the new application will process data affects the physical design. For example, a high-capacity transaction processing system, such as an order entry application, requires more network, processing, and data storage resources. If the system must operate online, 24 hours a day and 7 days a week (typically known as **24/7**), provisions must be made for backup and speedy recovery in the event of system failure. If system updates, file maintenance, or batch processing can be done at off-peak times, costs will be lower.

WHAT DO YOU THINK?

You are the IT manager at ABC Systems, a fast-growing company that provides a wide range of consulting services to companies that want to establish e-commerce operations. During the last 18 months, ABC acquired two smaller firms, and set up a new division that specializes in supply chain management. Aligning ABC's internal systems was quite a challenge, and top management was not especially happy with the integration cost or the timetable. To avoid future problems, you have decided to suggest an ERP strategy, and you plan to present your views at the staff meeting tomorrow. ABC's management team is very informal, highly successful, and prefers a loose, flexible style of management. How will you persuade them that ERP is the way to go?

PLANNING THE ARCHITECTURE

Every information system involves three main functions: data storage and access methods, application programs to handle the processing logic, and an interface that allows users to interact with the system. Depending on the architecture, the three functions are performed on a server, on a client, or are divided between the server and the client. As you plan the system design, you must determine where the functions will be carried out, and the advantages and disadvantages of each design approach. This section discusses server and client characteristics, and how each design alternative handles system functions.

Servers

A **server** is a computer that supplies data, processing services, or other support to one or more computers, called **clients**. A system design where the server performs all the processing is described as **mainframe architecture**, and a server that supports a large number of clients at various locations is called a **centralized system**.

Although the actual server does not have to be a mainframe, the terms mainframe architecture and centralized system typically describe a multiuser environment where the server is significantly more powerful than the clients. A systems analyst should know the history of mainframe architecture to understand the server's role in modern system design.

BACKGROUND In the 1960s, mainframe architecture was the only system design available, as shown in Figure 9-5. In addition to centralized data processing, early systems performed all data input and output at a central location, often called a **data processing center**. Physical data was delivered or transmitted in some manner to the data processing center, where it was entered into the system. Users in the organization had no input or output capability, except for printed reports that were distributed by a corporate IT department.

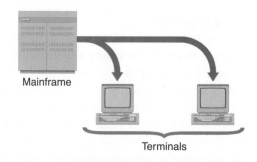

FIGURE 9-5 1960s-style mainframe architecture. A central mainframe at a data processing center handles all data entry, processing, and output.

SERVER-BASED PROCESSING As network technology advanced and became affordable, companies installed terminals at remote locations, so that users could enter and access data from anywhere in the organization, regardless of where the centralized computer was located.

In a centralized design, the remote user's keystrokes are transmitted to the mainframe, which responds by sending screen output back to the user's terminal screen. A main advantage of server-based processing is that various types of terminals can communicate with the mainframe, and the design is not tied to a specific hardware platform. A disadvantage is that server-based processing typically uses character-based terminals that provide a limited interface for users. In a server-based system, all data storage, access, and application programs are located on the mainframe.

Today, mainframe architecture still is used in industries that require large amounts of data processing that can be done in batches at a central location. For example, a credit card company might run monthly statements in a batch, or a bank might use mainframe servers to update customer balances each night. In a blend of old and new technology, an Internet-based retail operation might use centralized data management at a customer service center to support and manage its online sales activity, as shown in Figure 9-6.

FIGURE 9-6 Kozmo.com integrates online shopping with consumer delivery in under-an-hour. The company provides consumers with a wide selection of entertainment and convenience products.

As server technology evolved, terminal technology also has changed dramatically. For example, a company might use a mix of PCs, handheld computers, and other specialized devices that allow users to interact with a centralized server. In most companies, workstations that use powerful GUIs have replaced character-based terminals.

Clients

As PC technology exploded in the mid-1980s, microcomputers quickly appeared on corporate desktops. Users found that they could run their own word processing, spreadsheet, and database applications, without assistance from the IT group, in a mode called stand-alone computing. Before long, most companies linked the stand-alone computers into networks that enabled the clients to exchange data and perform local processing.

STAND-ALONE COMPUTING   When an individual user works in a **stand-alone** mode, the workstation performs all the functions of a server by storing, accessing, and processing data, as well as providing a user interface. Although PCs improved productivity and allowed users to perform tasks that previously required IT department assistance, stand-alone computing is inefficient, expensive, and raises major concerns about data security, integrity, and consistency.

LOCAL AND WIDE AREA NETWORKS   Most companies resolved the problems of stand-alone computing by joining clients into a **local area network (LAN)** that allows sharing of data and hardware resources, as shown in Figure 9-7. One or more LANs, in turn, can connect to a centralized mainframe. Advances in data communication technology made it possible to create powerful networks that could use satellite links, high-speed fiber-optic lines, or the Internet to share data.

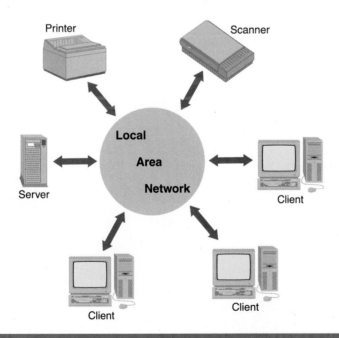

FIGURE 9-7   A LAN allows sharing of data and hardware, such as printers and scanners.

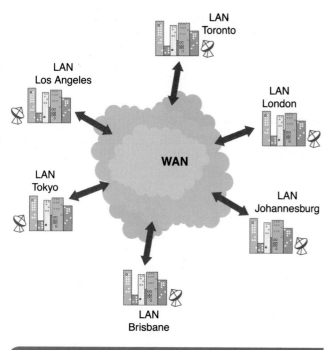

A **wide area network (WAN)** spans long distances and can link users who are continents apart, as shown in Figure 9-8. When a user accesses data on a LAN or WAN, the network is transparent because a user sees the data as if it were stored on his or her own workstation. Companywide systems that connect one or more LANs or WANs are called **distributed systems**. The capabilities of a distributed system depend on the power and capacity of the underlying data communication network. Compared to mainframe architecture, distributed systems increase concerns about data security and integrity because many individual clients require access to perform processing.

CLIENT-BASED PROCESSING   In a typical LAN, clients share data stored on a local server that supports a group of users or a department. As LANs became popular, the most common LAN configuration was a file server design, as shown in Figure 9-9. In a **file server** design, also called a **file sharing architecture**, an individual LAN client has a copy of the application program, but not the data, which is stored on the server. The client requests a copy of the data file and the server responds by transmitting the entire file to the client. After performing the processing,

FIGURE 9-8   A WAN can connect many LANs and link users who are continents apart.

the client returns the data file to the server where it is stored. File sharing designs are efficient only if the number of networked users is low and the transmitted file sizes are relatively small. Because the entire data file is sent to each requesting client, a file server design requires significant network resources.

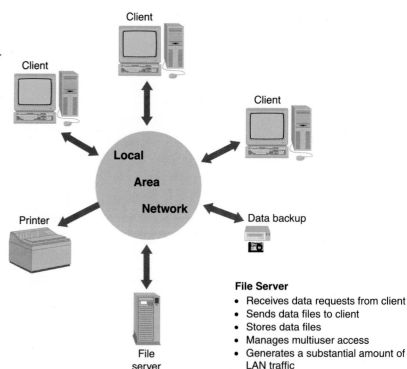

Client
- Handles user interface
- Sends data request to server
- Receives data files from server
- Runs application program locally to process data
- Sends data file back to server

File Server
- Receives data requests from client
- Sends data files to client
- Stores data files
- Manages multiuser access
- Generates a substantial amount of LAN traffic

FIGURE 9-9   Example of a LAN file server design. The server stores and manages the data, while the clients run the application program and perform all the processing.

CLIENT/SERVER ARCHITECTURE

Overview

Although no standard definition exists, the term **client/server architecture** generally refers to systems that divide processing between one or more networked clients and a central server. In a typical client/server system, the client handles the entire user interface, including data entry, data query, and screen presentation logic. The server stores the data and provides data access and database management functions. Application logic is divided in some manner between the server and the clients. In a client/server interaction, the client submits a request for information from the server, which carries out the operation and responds to the client. As shown in Figure 9-10, the data file is not transferred from the server to the client — only the request and the result are transmitted across the network. To fulfill a request from a client, the server might contact other servers for data or processing support, but that process is transparent to the client. The analogy can be made to a restaurant where the customer gives an order to a server, who relays the request to a cook, who actually prepares the meal.

Figure 9-11 lists some major differences between client/server and traditional mainframe systems. Many early client/server systems did not produce expected savings because few clear standards existed, and development costs often were higher than anticipated. Implementation was expensive because clients needed powerful hardware and software to handle shared processing tasks. In addition, many companies had an installed base of mainframe data, called **legacy data**, which was difficult to access and transport to a client/server environment.

ON THE WEB

For an overview of Client/Server Architecture visit scsite.com/sad4e/more.htm, click Systems Analysis and Design Chapter 9 and then click the Client/Server Architecture link.

www.scsite.co

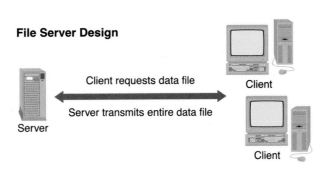

File Server Design

Client requests data file

Server transmits entire data file

Server

Client

Client

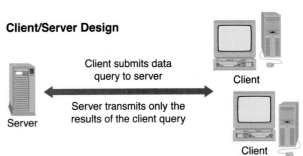

Client/Server Design

Client submits data query to server

Server transmits only the results of the client query

Server

Client

Client

FIGURE 9-10   A file server design compared to a client/server design.

CHARACTERISTICS OF CLIENT/SERVER VERSUS MAINFRAME SYSTEMS

Characteristics	Client/Server	Mainframe
Basic architecture	Very flexible	Very rigid
Application development	Flexible Fast Object-oriented	Highly structured Slow Traditional
User environment	PC-based GUI Empowers the user Improves productivity	Uses terminals Text interface Constrains the user Limited options
Security and control features	Decentralized Difficult to control	Centralized Easier to control
Processing options	Can be shared and configured in any form desired	Cannot be modified
Data storage options	Can be distributed to place data closer to users	All data is stored centrally
Hardware/software integration	Very flexible Multivendor model	Very rigid Single proprietary vendor

FIGURE 9-11   Characteristics of mainframe and client/server systems.

As large-scale networks grew more powerful, client/server systems became more cost-effective. Many companies invested in client/server systems to achieve a unique combination of computing power, flexibility, and support for changing business operations. Today, client/server architecture is the dominant form of systems design, using Internet protocols and traditional network models. As businesses form new alliances with customers and suppliers, the client/server concept continues to expand to include clients and servers outside the organization.

Client/Server Design Styles

Client/server designs can take many forms, depending on the type of server and the relationship between the server and the clients. Figure 9-12 shows the client/server interaction for a database server, a transaction server, an object server, and a Web server. Notice that in each case, the processing is divided between the server and the clients. The nature of the communication depends on the type of server: a database server processes individual SQL commands, a transaction server handles a set of SQL commands, an object server exchanges object messages with clients, and a Web server sends and receives Internet-based communications.

Types of Clients: Fat and Thin

Client/server designs can be based on fat or thin clients. A **fat client**, also called a **thick client**, design locates all or most of the application processing logic at the client. A **thin client** design locates all or most of the processing logic at the server. What are the advantages and disadvantages of each design? Most IT experts agree that thin client designs provide better performance, because program code resides on the server, near the data. In contrast, a fat client handles more of the processing, and must access and update the data more often. Fat client TCO also is higher, because of initial hardware and software requirements, and the ongoing expense of supporting and updating remote client computers, compared with maintaining a central server. A fat client design, however, is simpler and less expensive to develop, because the architecture resembles traditional file server designs where all processing is performed at the client. Figure 9-13 compares the characteristics of fat and thin clients.

Client/server design styles

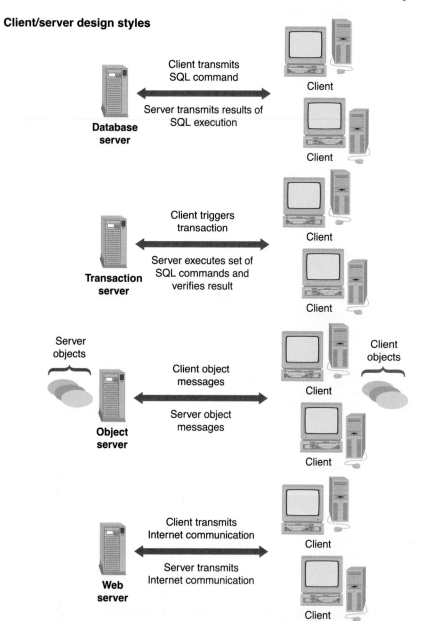

FIGURE 9-12 Client/server interaction for a database server, a transaction server, an object server, and a Web server.

Characteristic	Fat Client	Thin Client
Network traffic	Higher, because the fat client must communicate more often with the server to access data and update processing results	Lower, because most interaction between code and data takes place at the server
Performance	Slower, because more network traffic is required	Faster, because less network traffic is required
Initial cost	Higher — more powerful hardware is required	Lower — workstation hardware requirement are not as stringent
Maintenance cost	Higher, because more program code resides on the client	Lower, because most program code resides on the central server
Ease of development	Easier, because systems resemble traditional file-server designs where all processing was performed at the client	More difficult, because developers must optimize the division of processing logic

FIGURE 9-13 Characteristics of fat and thin clients.

Client/Server Tiers

Early client/server designs were called two-tier designs. In a **two-tier** design, the user interface resides on the client, all data resides on the server, and the application logic can run either on the server, on the client, or be divided between the client and the server.

More recently, another form of client/server design, called three-tier design, has become popular. In a **three-tier** design, the user interface runs on the client and the data is stored on the server, just as with a two-tier design. A three-tier design also has a middle layer between the client and server that processes the client requests and translates them into data access commands that can be understood and carried out by the server, as shown in Figure 9-14. You can think of the middle layer as an **application server**, because it provides the **application logic**, or **business logic**, required by the system. Three-tier designs also are called **n-tier** designs, to indicate that some designs use more than one intermediate layer.

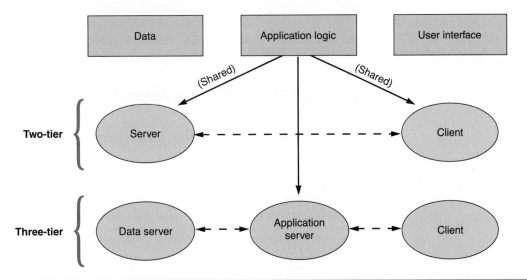

FIGURE 9-14 Characteristics of two-tier versus three-tier client/server design.

Architecture		Data	Application logic	User Interface
Central data processing center	Server Client	X	X	X
Central server with remote terminals	Server Client	X	X	X
Stand-alone client	Server Client	X	X	X
Two-tier client/server	Server Client	X	X X	X
Three-tier client/server	Data server Application server Client	X	X	X

FIGURE 9-15 The table shows where the data, the application logic, and the user interface are located on various types of architecture.

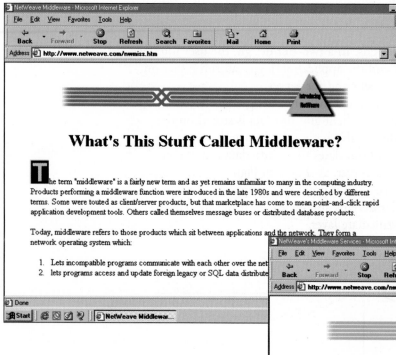

The advantage of the application logic layer is that a three-tier design enhances overall performance by reducing the server's workload. The separate application logic layer also relieves clients of complex processing tasks. Because it can run on a minicomputer that is much more powerful than the typical client workstations, the middle layer is more efficient and cost-effective in large-scale systems. Figure 9-15 shows where the data, the application logic, and the user interface are located on various types of architecture.

Middleware

Middleware is software that connects dissimilar applications and enables them to communicate and exchange data. For example, middleware can link a departmental database to a Web server that can be accessed by client computers via the Internet or a company intranet. Figure 9-16 shows a product named NetWeave, which can integrate legacy systems and Web-based applications. Using middleware, a user enters a customer number on a Web-based inquiry form, and the middleware accesses a legacy accounting system and returns the results.

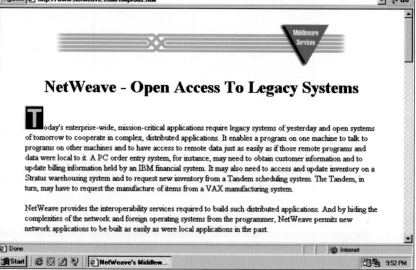

FIGURE 9-16 NetWeave is a middleware product that can integrate legacy systems and Web-based applications.

Cost-Benefit Issues

To support business requirements, information systems need to be scalable, powerful, and flexible. For most companies, client/server systems offer the best combination of features to meet those needs. Whether a business is expanding or downsizing, client/server systems enable the firm to scale the system in a rapidly changing environment. As the size of the business changes, it is easier to adjust the number of clients and the processing functions they perform than it is to alter the capability of a large-scale central server.

Client/server computing also allows companies to transfer applications from expensive mainframes to less expensive client platforms. In addition, using common languages such as SQL, clients and servers can communicate across multiple platforms. That difference is important because many businesses have substantial investments in a variety of hardware and software environments.

Finally, client/server systems reduce network load and improve response times so users have faster access to data. For example, consider a user at a company headquarters who wants information about total sales figures. In a file server design, the system might need to transmit three separate sales transaction files from three regional offices in order to provide sales data that the client would process — but in a client/server system, the server locates the data, performs the necessary processing, and responds immediately to the client's request. The data retrieval and processing functions are transparent to the client because they are done on the server, not the client.

ON THE WEB

To learn more about Middleware visit scsite.com/sad4e/more.htm click Systems Analysis and Design Chapter 9 and then click the Middleware link.

www.scsite.c

Client/Server Performance Issues

Client/server architecture is very different from traditional centralized computing systems, where a server-based program issues a command to the server's CPU, which controls all processing logic, memory, and data. Program instructions and data travel on an internal system bus at multimegahertz speeds. In contrast, client/server architecture locates the application and the data in different places, and clients submit a constant stream of network messages and data requests to the server. Even a high-speed communications network, however, is substantially slower than internal system bus speeds. As a result, when the number of clients and the demand for services increases beyond a certain point, client requests go into a **queue**, which is a waiting line, and system performance declines dramatically.

In the Web site article shown in Figure 9-17, IBM states that most client/server systems run into a wall at some point. The article goes on to state, "... the old mind set of 'open the file and read one record at a time' has gotten many client-server projects and tools into far too much trouble. And it gets very expensive when a business learns this lesson when trying to go from 60 to 90 users, only to find out that the wall is somewhere in between."

What is the answer to enhancing client/server performance? According to IBM, client/server systems must be designed so the client contacts the server only when necessary, and makes as few trips as possible.

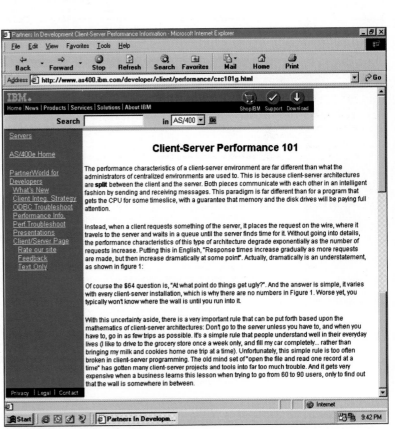

FIGURE 9-17 According to IBM, client/server performance issues are far different than in a centralized environment.

ON THE WEB

For an overview of E-Commerce Strategies visit scsite.com/sad4e/more.htm, click Systems Analysis and Design Chapter 9 and then click the E-Commerce Strategies link.

www.scsite.com

Another issue that affects client/server performance is data storage. Just as processing can be done at various places, data can be stored in more than one location using a **distributed database management system** (DDBMS).

Using a DDBMS offers several advantages: data stored closer to users can reduce network traffic; the system is scalable, so new data sites can be added without reworking the system design; and with data stored in various locations, the system is less likely to experience a catastrophic failure. A potential disadvantage of distributed data storage involves data security. It can be more difficult to maintain controls and standards when data is stored in various locations. In addition, the architecture of a DDBMS is more complex and difficult to manage. As shown in Figure 9-18, Sybase is a leading software vendor that offers products to support distributed data management systems.

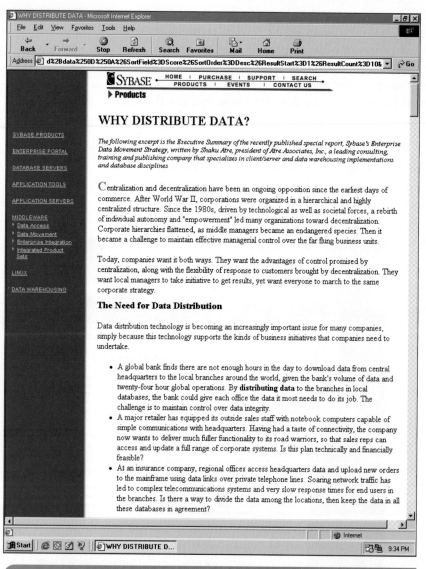

FIGURE 9-18   Sybase is a leading software vendor that offers products to support distributed data management systems.

IMPACT OF THE INTERNET

The Internet has had an enormous impact on application architecture. E-business trends are reshaping the corporate landscape as firms, large and small, learn how to harness the power of the Web and build efficient, reliable, and cost-effective business solutions. To support this trend, systems analysts must suggest e-commerce strategies that apply available technology and meet their company's business requirements.

E-Commerce Strategies

In proposing an e-commerce strategy, an IT group must consider in-house development of e-business systems, the availability of packaged solutions, and the design of corporate portals — all of which are described in detail below.

IN-HOUSE DEVELOPMENT   In Chapter 6, you learned how to analyze advantages and disadvantages of in-house development versus purchasing a software package. The same basic principles apply to application design.

If you decide to proceed with an in-house solution, you must have an overall plan to help achieve your goals. How should you begin? An article in the October 4, 1999, issue of *INFOWORLD* magazine offers suggestions for companies that are moving into the world of e-commerce, and includes a seven-step process summarized in Figure 9-19. The article also points out that an in-house solution usually requires a greater initial investment, but provides more flexibility that helps a company adapt quickly in a dynamic e-commerce environment. By working in-house, a company has more freedom to integrate with customers and suppliers, and is less dependent on vendor-specific solutions.

Guidelines for In-house E-commerce Site Development	
Step	**Actions**
1	Analyze the company's business needs and develop a clear statement of your goals. Consider the experience of other companies with similar projects.
2	Obtain input from users who understand the business and technology issues involved in the project. Plan for future growth, but aim for ease of use.
3	Determine whether the IT staff has the necessary skills and experience to implement the project. Consider training, additional resources, and the use of consultants if necessary.
4	Consider integration requirements for existing legacy systems or enterprise resource planning. Select a physical infrastructure carefully, so it will support the application, now and later.
5	Develop the project in modular form so users can test and approve the functional elements as you go along.
6	Connect the application to existing in-house systems and verify interactivity.
7	Test every aspect of the site exhaustively. Consider a preliminary rollout to a pilot group to obtain feedback before a full launch.

FIGURE 9-19 Seven-step process for in-house development of e-commerce site. (Adapted from *INFOWORLD* magazine, October 4, 1999, page 66.)

PACKAGED SOLUTIONS AND E-COMMERCE SERVICE PROVIDERS If a company is reluctant to take on the complex challenge of developing an Internet commerce site in-house, an alternative might be a packaged solution or an e-commerce service provider. Many vendors offer turnkey systems for companies that want to get an e-business up and running quickly. One example is a product called INTERSHOP, as shown in Figure 9-20 on the next page.

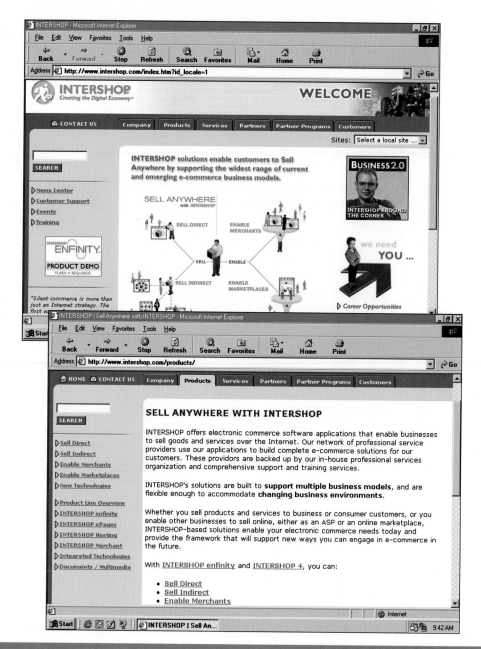

FIGURE 9-20 INTERSHOP offers turnkey systems for companies that want to get an e-business up and running quickly.

For large-scale systems that must integrate with existing applications, packaged solutions might be less attractive. Another alternative is to use an application service provider (ASP). As explained in Chapter 6, an ASP provides applications, or access to applications, by charging a usage or subscription fee. Today, many ASPs offer full-scale Internet business services for companies that decide to outsource those functions. A Web-focused ASP, can develop, maintain, and host a Web site for small- to medium-sized firms as shown in Figure 9-21. As with packaged solutions, a company must consider whether the advantage of lower initial cost outweigh the disadvantage of reduced flexibility later on.

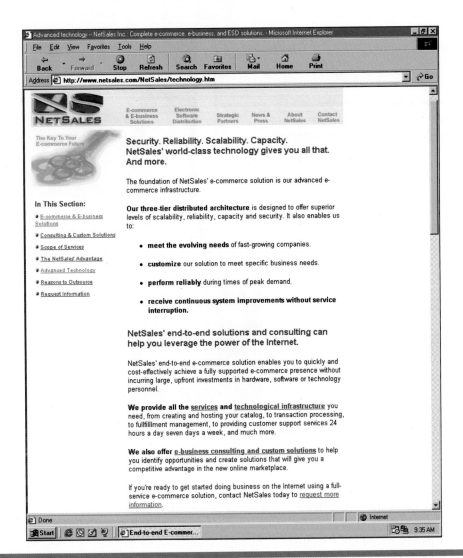

FIGURE 9-21   An e-commerce service provider such as NetSales can develop, maintain, and host a Web site for small- to medium- sized firms.

CORPORATE PORTALS   A **portal** is an entrance to a multifunction Web site. After entering a portal, a user can navigate to a destination, using various tools and features provided by the portal designer. A **corporate portal** provides access for customers, employees, suppliers, and the public. In a Web-based system, portal design provides an important link between the user and the system, and poor design can weaken system effectiveness and value. Figure 9-22 on the next page shows an example of Oracle Corporation's view of how to bring order to what Oracle calls portal chaos. Notice the similarity between portal design and user interface design issues that were discussed in Chapter 7.

ON THE WEB

For more information about Corporate Portals visit scsite.com/sad4e/more.htm click Systems Analysis and Design Chapter 9 and then click the Corporate Portals link.

www.scsite.com

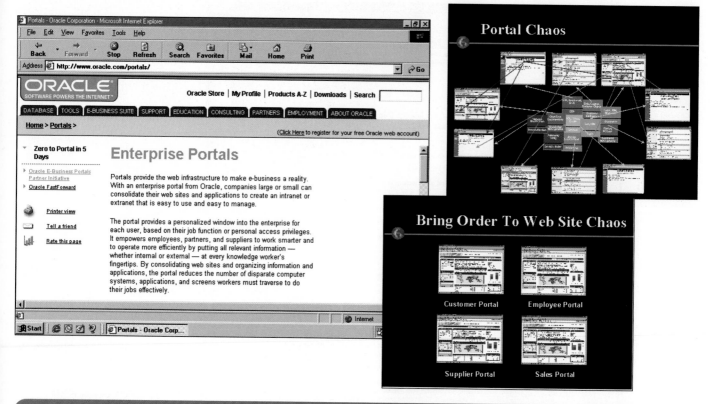

FIGURE 9-22
Oracle Corporation's view of how to bring order to what Oracle calls *PORTAL CHAOS*. Notice the similarity between portal design and user interface design issues that were discussed in Chapter 7.

Industry Experience and Trends

A systems analyst confronts a bewildering array of products and strategies when constructing Internet- or intranet-based systems. A good starting point might be to consider the experience of other companies in the same industry. On their Web sites, firms such as IBM, Microsoft, and Sun Microsystems offer numerous case studies and examples of successful development.

N THE WEB

r an overview of
cessing Methods visit
site.com/sad4e/more.htm,
k Systems Analysis and
sign Chapter 9 and then
k the Processing Methods
:.

w.scsite.com

PROCESSING METHODS

In selecting an application architecture, the systems analyst must determine whether the system will be an online system, a batch processing system, or a combination of the two.

Online versus Batch Processing

Early computer systems relied mainly on batch processing, but the vast majority of systems today use online processing. An **online system** handles transactions when and where they occur and provides output directly to users. Because it is interactive, online processing avoids delays and allows a constant dialog between the user and the system.

An airline reservations system is a familiar example of online processing. When the online customer shown in Figure 9-23 wants to check on flights, she can enter the origin, destination, travel dates, and travel times. The system searches a database and responds by displaying available flights, times, and prices. If the customer makes a reservation, she enters her name, address, credit card information, and other required data and the system creates the reservation, assigns a seat, and updates the flight database immediately.

Online processing also can be used with file-oriented systems. Figure 9-24 shows what happens when a customer uses an ATM to inquire about an account balance. After the ATM verifies the customer's card and password, the customer enters the request (Step 1). Then, the system accesses the account master file using the account number as the primary key and retrieves the customer's record (Step 2). The system verifies the account number and displays the balance (Step 3). Data is retrieved and the system transmits the current balance to the ATM, which prints it for the customer. Online processing systems have four typical characteristics:

1. The system processes transactions completely when and where they occur.

2. Users interact directly with the information system.

3. Users can access data randomly.

4. The information system must be available whenever necessary to support business functions.

Batch Processing

In a **batch processing** system, data is collected and processed in groups, or batches. Although online processing is used for interactive business systems that require immediate data input and output, batch processing can handle other situations more efficiently. For example, batch processing typically is used for large amounts of data that must be processed on a routine schedule, such as paychecks or credit card transactions.

FIGURE 9-23   A Web-based airline reservations system is an example of online processing on the Internet.

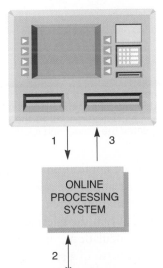

ATM QUERY PROCESS

Step 1:   Customer enters his or her account number and requests an account balance

ONLINE SYSTEM

Step 2:   Retrieves current account balance

Step 3:   Verifies bank account number and displays balance on ATM screen

ACCOUNT MASTER FILE

FIGURE 9-24   When a customer requests a balance, the ATM system verifies the account number, submits the query, retrieves the current balance, and displays the balance on the ATM screen.

In batch processing, input transactions are grouped into a single file and processed together. For example, when a firm produces customer statements at the end of the month, a batch application might process many thousands of records in one run of the program. A batch processing system offers several main characteristics: collect, group, and process transactions periodically; the IT operations group can run batch programs on a predetermined schedule, without user involvement, during regular business hours, at night, or on weekends; and batch programs require significantly less network resources than online systems.

Combined Online and Batch Processing

Even an online system can use batch processing to perform certain routine tasks. Figure 9-25 shows how a retail chain uses both online and batch methods. The system uses online processing to handle data entry and inventory updates, while reports and accounting entries are performed in a batch.

POINT-OF-SALE TERMINAL

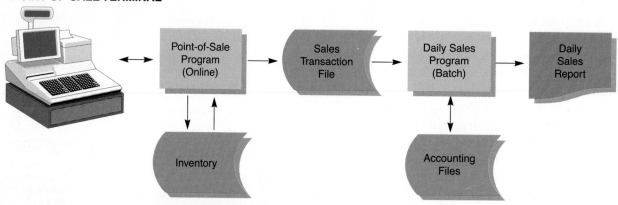

| FIGURE 9-25 | Many retail operations use a combination of online and batch processing. When a salesperson enters the sale on the POS terminal, the online system retrieves data from the item file, updates the quantity in stock, and produces a sales transaction record. At the end of the day, a batch processing program produces a daily sales report and updates the accounting system. |

The retail store application illustrates both online processing and batch processing of data. During business hours, the salesperson enters a sale on a **point-of-sale** (**POS**) terminal, which is part of an information system that handles daily sales transactions and maintains the online inventory file. When the salesperson enters the transaction, online processing occurs. The system performs calculations, updates the inventory file, and produces output on the point-of-sale terminal in the form of a screen display and a printed receipt. At the same time, each sales transaction creates input data for day-end batch processing.

When the store closes, the system uses the sales transactions to produce the daily sales report and related accounting entries, using batch processing. Performing the processing online before all sales transactions are completed does not make sense. In that situation, a batch method provides better routine transaction processing, while an online approach supports point-of-sale processing, which must be done as it occurs.

In the retail store example, both online and batch processing are integral parts of the information system. Online processing offers an inherent advantage because data is entered and validated as it occurs, so the stored data is available sooner and always is up-to-date. Online processing is more expensive, however, and the effects of computer system downtime or slowdown while transactions are processed causes far more disruption than batch processing. In addition, backup and recovery for online processing is more difficult. In many situations, batch processing is cost-effective, less vulnerable to system disruption, and less intrusive to normal operations. Many information systems will continue to use a combination of online and batch processing for some time to come.

You are the new IT manager at R/Way, a small but rapidly growing trucking company head-quartered in Cleveland, Ohio. The company slogan is "Ship It R/Way — State of the Art in Trucking and Customer Service."

R/Way's information system currently consists of a file server and three workstations where freight clerks enter data, track shipments, and prepare freight bills. To perform their work, the clerks obtain data from the server and use database and spreadsheet programs stored on their PCs to process the data.

Unfortunately, your predecessor did not design a relational database. Instead, data is stored in several files, including one for shippers, one for customers, and one for shipments. The system worked well for several years, but cannot handle current volume or support online links for R/Way shippers and customers. The company president is willing to make changes, but he is reluctant to spend money on major IT improvements unless you can convince him that they are necessary.

What would you recommend and why?

NETWORK MODELS

A network allows the sharing of hardware, software, and data resources in order to reduce expenses and provide more capability to users. When planning a network design, you must consider network topology, protocols, and licensing issues, which are covered in this section. You also must consider system performance, security, and interruption issues, which are covered in the following sections.

Network Topology

The way a network is configured is called the **network topology**. LAN and WAN networks typically are arranged in four patterns: hierarchical, bus, star, and ring. The concepts are the same regardless of the size of the network, but the physical implementation is different for a large-scale WAN that spans an entire business enterprise compared with a small LAN in a single department. The four topologies are shown in Figures 9-26 through 9-29 on page 9.22 through 9.24.

ON THE WEB

For a discussion of Network Topology visit scsite.com/sad4e/more.htm click Systems Analysis and Design Chapter 9 and then click the Network Topology link.

www.scsite.c

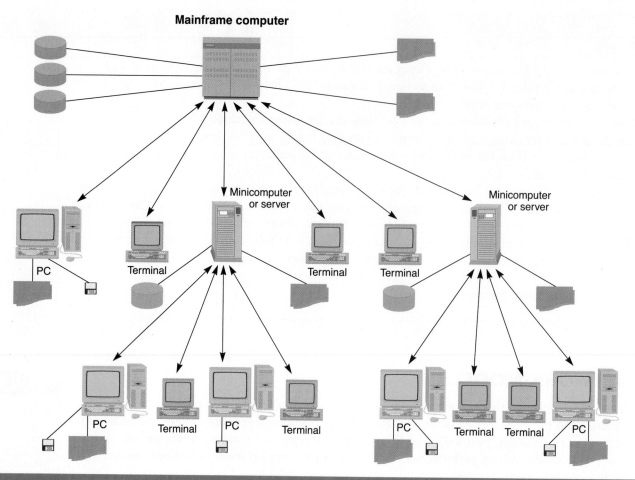

Mainframe computer

Minicomputer
or server

Minicomputer
or server

PC

Terminal

Terminal

Terminal

PC

Terminal

PC

Terminal

PC

Terminal

Terminal

PC

FIGURE 9-26   A hierarchical network with a single computer that controls the network.

HIERARCHICAL NETWORK   In a **hierarchical network**, as shown in Figure 9-26, one computer (typically a mainframe) controls the entire network. Satellite computers or servers control lower levels of processing and network devices.

BUS NETWORK   In a **bus network**, as shown in Figure 9-27, a single communication path connects the mainframe computer, server, workstations, and peripheral devices. Information is transmitted in either direction from any workstation to another workstation, and any message can be directed to a specific device. An advantage of the bus network is that devices can be attached or detached from the network at any point without disturbing the rest of the network. In addition, a failure in one workstation on the network does not necessarily affect other workstations on the network.

STAR NETWORK   A **star network** has a central computer with one or more workstations connected to it that form a star. The central computer could be a mainframe, a minicomputer, or a server. A star configuration, as shown in Figure 9-28, often is used when the central computer contains all data required to process the input from the workstations. The central computer in a star network does not have to serve as the primary data storage point; it also can serve as a network coordinator that enables the other devices to transmit and receive data from each other.

A star network provides efficiency and close control over the data processed on the network. A major disadvantage is that the entire network depends on the central computer. In most large star networks, backup systems are available in case of a failure in the central computer.

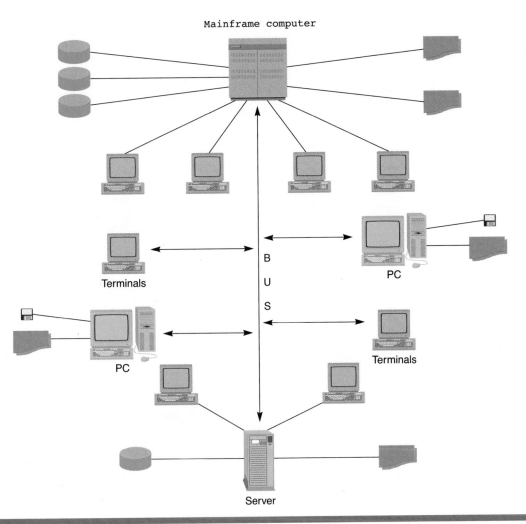

FIGURE 9-27   A bus network with all devices connected to a single communication path.

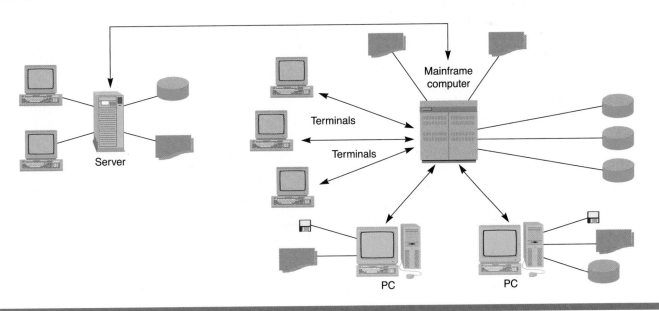

FIGURE 9-28   A star network with a central computer and connected workstations terminals, and servers.

RING NETWORK A **ring network**, as shown in Figure 9-29, resembles a circle of computers that communicate with each other. A ring network often is used when processing is performed at local sites rather than at a central location. For example, users accessing computers in the accounting, personnel, and shipping departments perform the processing for individual functions and then use the ring network to exchange data with other computers on the network. Data flows only in one direction in a ring network.

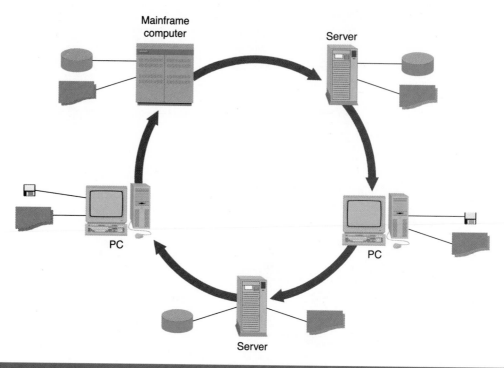

FIGURE 9-29   A ring network with a set of computers that send and receive data flowing in one direction.

Network Protocols

In all cases, the network must use a **protocol**, which is a set of standards that govern network data transmission. A popular network protocol is TCP/IP, which originally was developed by the U.S. Department of Defense to permit interconnection of military computers. Today, TCP/IP is the backbone of the Internet. Other network protocols include NetBIOS, which is a popular protocol for LANs, and IPX/SPX, which is a protocol used by Novell Corporation for its NetWare products.

Licensing Issues

When considering a network design, it is important to take into account software licensing restrictions. Various types of individual and site licenses are available from software vendors. Some vendors limit the number of users or the number of computers that can access the program simultaneously. You also must carefully investigate the capabilities of network software to ensure that it can handle the anticipated system traffic.

MODELING APPLICATION ARCHITECTURE

You learned earlier that CASE tools can be used throughout the systems development process.
Multipurpose drawing tools are especially valuable as you construct the application architecture. One of the most popular tools is Microsoft Visio, which offers a wide variety of drawing types, styles, templates, and shapes. For example, Visio supplies templates for basic network designs, plus manufacturer-specific symbols for firms such as Cisco, IBM, Bay Systems, and Hewlett-Packard, among others.

Figure 9-30 shows how Visio can be used to create a simple network model, using drag-and-drop shapes displayed on the left of the screen. Figure 9-31 shows specific symbols for various products in the left window, and a Cisco 1720 router that a user has dragged into the drawing at the right. By right-clicking the selected shape, a user can get information about the product and enter asset, equipment maintenance, and network data that will be stored in a data repository.

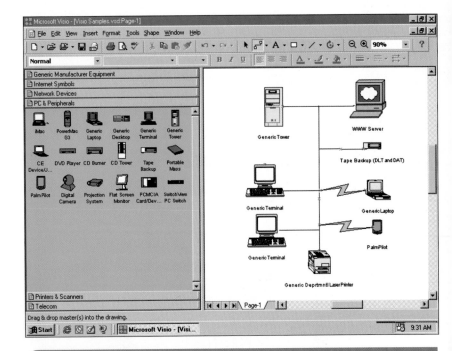

FIGURE 9-30 Visio can be used to create a simple network drawing using drag-and-drop shapes displayed on the left of the screen.

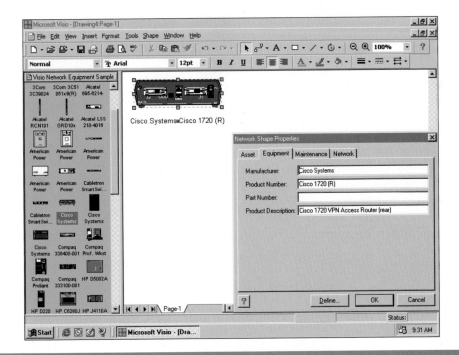

FIGURE 9-31 This Visio screen shows specific shapes for various products. The user has dragged a Cisco 1720 router into the drawing on the right. By right-clicking the selected shape, the user can get more information about the product.

ON THE WEB

To learn more about System Performance Issues visit scsite.com/sad4e/more.htm, click Systems Analysis and Design Chapter 9 and then click the System Performance Issues link.

www.scsite.com

Visio also provides wizards that can walk you through a step-by-step network design process, as shown in Figure 9-32.

SYSTEM MANAGEMENT AND SUPPORT

The information system design must include provision for system management and support tools to monitor system performance, maintain system security, and deal with system interruptions — from fault management to disaster recovery.

Performance Management

Performance management tools are designed to collect information about system resources and activity levels. A performance management tool can monitor system usage, capacity, and trends. Performance management also can include fine-tuning the network configuration or software settings to optimize performance.

In the e-business era, slow performance can be as devastating as no performance at all. Customers expect reliable, fast responses from a Web-based system 24 hours a day, seven days a week. To help meet that need, firms such as NetScout offer comprehensive performance management packages, as shown in Figure 9-33. A NetScout product called nGenius offers detailed, system-wide views of applications, users, and response times.

The NetScout Web site mentions studies that show network delays cost the industry more revenue than actual stoppages, because they occur so frequently. NetScout's conclusion is that network delays and application bottlenecks profoundly affect revenues, productivity, customer satisfaction, communication, and make a company less competitive and profitable.

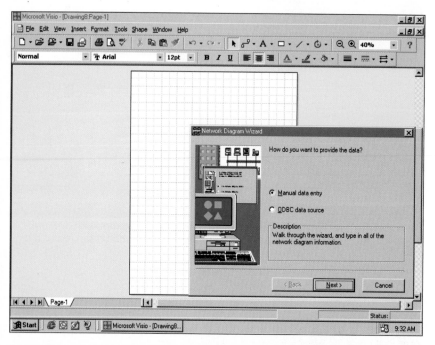

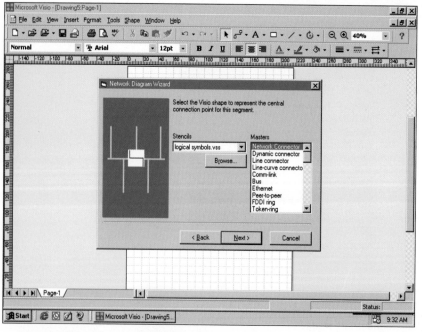

FIGURE 9-32   VISIO also provides wizards that can walk you through a step-by-step network design process.

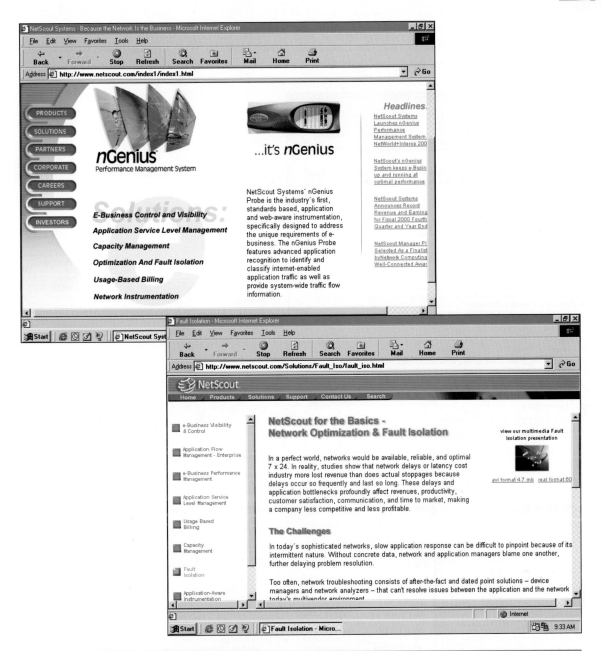

FIGURE 9-33   A performance management tool can monitor system usage, capacity, and trends. A NetScout product called nGenius offers detailed, system-wide views of applications, users, and response times.

System Security

Maintaining system security involves two main tasks. First, there must be provisions to assign and monitor user IDs, passwords, and access levels. Second, the system security tools must handle virus protection and detect any unauthorized access, including attempts by intruders to enter the system.

Many security management software products are available, including the SAFEsuite products shown in Figure 9-34. Notice that the Internet Security Systems Web site mentions three main areas: security assessment, intrusion detection, and security management applications.

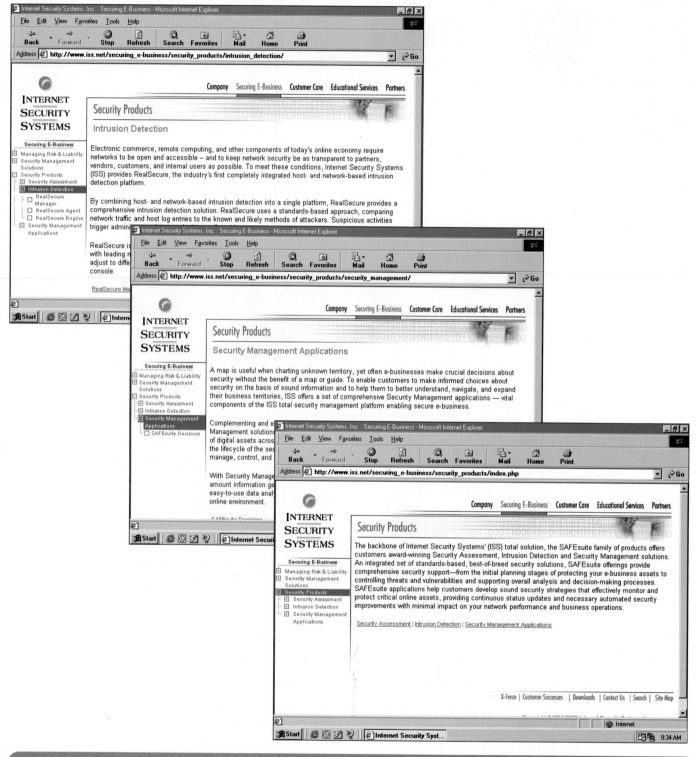

FIGURE 9-34 SAFEsuite is a security management software product offered by Internet Security Systems. The Web site highlights three main functional areas: security assessment, intrusion detection, and security management applications.

In addition to built-in controls and security software, a company can take other steps to enhance system security, such as user training, safeguards for the physical security of hardware and software, security audits, and strong security policies that are well understood and reinforced throughout the organization.

Fault Management, Backup, and Disaster Recovery

No matter how well it is designed, every system will experience some problems, such as hardware failures, software errors, user mistakes, and power outages. Unfortunately, hackers and cyber-vandalism represent a new threat that you also must consider. As part of the systems design, you must anticipate those problems and plan for ways to deal with them.

The best strategy is to prevent problems before they can affect the system. For example, you learned earlier that data validation, audit trail files, security measures, and other control features help ensure that data is entered and processed correctly. You must provide additional means, however, to deal with system faults and interruptions.

FAULT MANAGEMENT   A system administrator's main concern is to detect and resolve operational problems as quickly as possible. That task, often called **fault management**, includes monitoring the system for signs of trouble, logging all system failures, diagnosing the problem, and applying corrective action. The more complex the system, the more difficult it can be to analyze symptoms and isolate a cause. In addition to addressing the immediate problem, it is important to evaluate performance patterns and trends. Automated tools are available to assist system administrators in that task, such as the ProVision Network Monitor offered by Computer Associates, which is shown in Figure 9-35.

BACKUP AND DISASTER RECOVERY

The August 23, 1999 edition of *INFOWORLD* magazine had an article titled "Planning for recovery" by Ted Smalley Bowen, which is shown in Figure 9-36 on the next page. The article suggested a number of strategies for disaster recovery, including disaster recovery service firms that provide backup at secure sites, standby facilities, and systems personnel to assist in recovery.

Every system design must include provisions for data backup and recovery. **Backup** refers to copying data continuously, or at prescribed intervals. **Recovery** procedures involve restoring the data and restarting the system after an interruption. An overall backup and recovery plan often is called a **disaster recovery plan**.

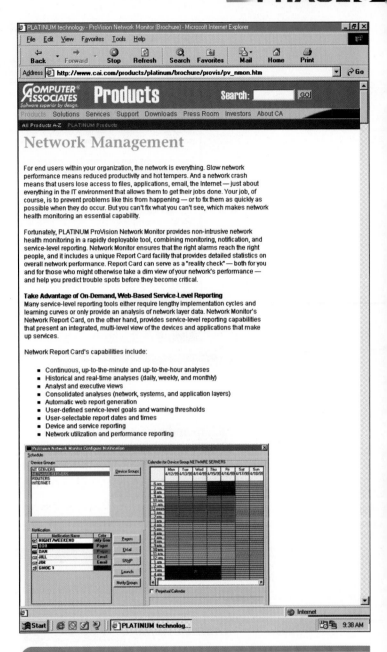

FIGURE 9-35   Fault management includes monitoring the system for signs of trouble, logging all system failures, diagnosing the problem, and applying corrective action. Computer Associates' ProVision Network Monitor can assist system administrators by evaluating performance patterns and trends.

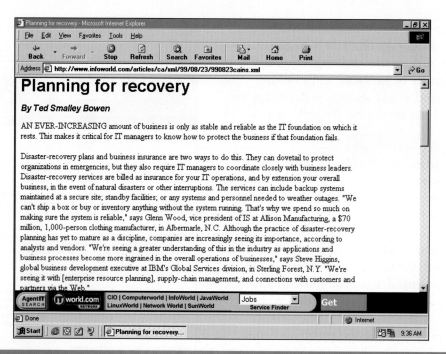

FIGURE 9-36   The August 23, 1999 *INFOWORLD* article by Ted Smalley Bowen suggests a number of strategies for disaster recovery, including disaster recovery service firms that provide backup at secure sites, standby facilities, and systems personnel to assist in recovery.

Backup and recovery planning depends on the type of system involved. The simplest example is a batch processing system, which presents few backup and recovery problems. In this type of system, the batch transaction file and the previous version of the master file are saved as backup files in case the new master file is damaged or the update program execution is interrupted. Any problems are corrected by executing the update program again with the transaction file and the previous master file as inputs.

With online systems, you must either perform backups when the system is inactive, or continuously back up the data during system operation. Most large systems use streaming tape devices that constantly record all processing activity as it occurs. If processing is interrupted, data is recovered by restoring files from the backup media. Another common strategy is to use a **RAID (redundant array of independent disks)** system, which mirrors the data while processing continues. RAID systems are called **fault-tolerant**, because a failure of any one disk does not disable the system.

Web-based system backup can be done over the Internet or an intranet, by using online backup software such as the NovaStor products shown in Figure 9-37. Companies such as Hewlett-Packard also offer automated backup hardware and software solutions, as shown in Figure 9-38.

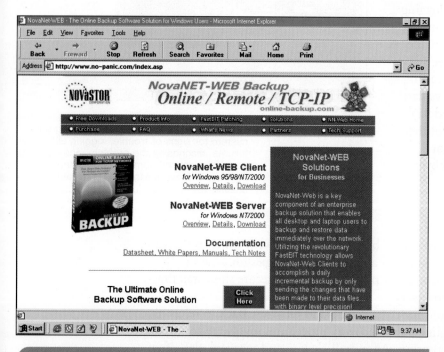

FIGURE 9-37   Web-based system backup can be done over the Internet or an intranet, by using online backup software such as the NovaStor products.

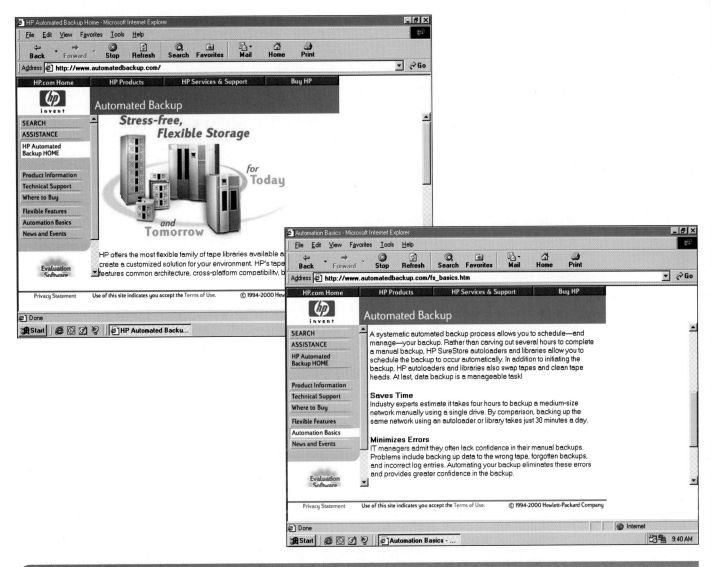

FIGURE 9-38 Hewlett-Packard offers automated backup hardware and software solutions.

Another approach to online system backup uses a special file called a **log file**, or **journal file**, which contains a copy of each record as it appears before and after modification. If data is damaged, the most recent backup is used to recover, or restore, the data file. Then, a special transaction recovery program processes the log file to bring the data file forward to its state at the time the damage occurred. The total recovery time can take many hours for large-scale databases and data files with large numbers of records and transactions. Logging functions are included in most large-scale DBMSs.

In a worst-case scenario, business insurance can help offset expenditures due to system failure and business losses. Those policies can be expensive and require a high deductible amount, however, which must be borne by the company, not the insurer. Many IT professionals feel that their Y2K experience has raised the awareness level for business systems vulnerability, and that will make it easier to obtain top management support for prevention and recovery efforts.

Apart from backup and recovery procedures necessary to sustain business operations, **file retention** laws and regulations apply to company data. If a government rule specifies that a record of all payments to the company must be kept for three years, then your design must retain the data for that period. To satisfy that requirement, you can implement a data warehousing strategy, which was described in Chapter 8, in order to provide easy, cost-effective access to the data.

SYSTEMS DESIGN COMPLETION

Software design involves two distinct stages. The first stage began during the systems analysis phase when all functional primitives were identified and documented with process descriptions. The objective was to identify the system's functions and determine *what* each logical module would do. The second level of software design is performed during the systems implementation phase when programmers determine exactly *how* each program will accomplish its objectives. That process is discussed in Chapter 10, which describes how applications are developed, tested, and documented.

The final activities in the systems design phase are preparing a system design specification, obtaining user approval, and delivering a presentation to management.

System Design Specification

The **system design specification**, also called the **technical design specification**, or the **detailed design specification**, is a document that presents the complete design for the new information system along with detailed costs, staffing, and scheduling for completing the next SDLC phase — systems implementation.

The system design specification is the baseline against which the operational system will be measured. Unlike the system requirements document, which is written for users to understand, the system design specification is oriented toward the programmers who will use it to create the necessary programs. Some sections of the system requirements document are repeated in the system design specification, such as process descriptions, data dictionary entries, and data flow diagrams.

The system design specification varies in length, so you must organize it carefully and number all pages in sequence. You should include a cover page, a detailed table of contents, and an index. The contents of the system design specification depends on company standards and the complexity of the system. A typical system design specification uses a structure similar to Figure 9-39, which is described in the following sections.

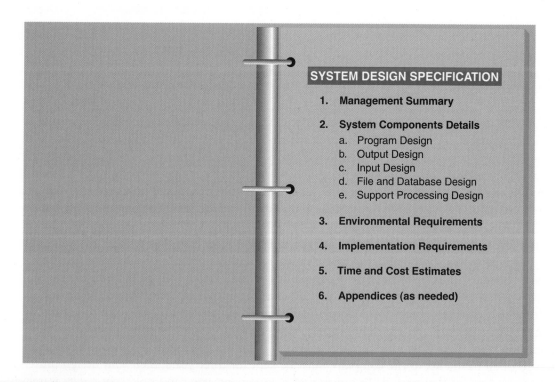

SYSTEM DESIGN SPECIFICATION

1. **Management Summary**

2. **System Components Details**
   a. Program Design
   b. Output Design
   c. Input Design
   d. File and Database Design
   e. Support Processing Design

3. **Environmental Requirements**

4. **Implementation Requirements**

5. **Time and Cost Estimates**

6. **Appendices (as needed)**

FIGURE 9-39   The organization of a typical system design specification.

1. *Management Summary.* The management summary provides a brief overview of the project for company managers and executives. It outlines the development efforts to date, provides a current status report, summarizes current project costs and costs for the remaining phases, reviews the overall benefits of the new system, presents the systems development phase schedule, and highlights any issues that management will need to address.

2. *System Components Details.* This section contains the complete design for the new system, including the user interface, outputs, inputs, files, databases, and network specifications. You should include source documents, report and screen layouts, DFDs, O-O diagrams, and all other relevant documentation. You also should include the requirements for all support processing, such as backup and recovery, startup processing, and file retention. If the purchase of a software package is part of the strategy, you must include any interface information required between the package and the system you are developing. If you use a CASE design tool, you can print design diagrams and most other documentation directly from the tool.

3. *Environmental Requirements.* This section describes the constraints, or conditions, affecting the system, including any requirements that involve operations, hardware, systems software, or security. Examples of operational constraints include transaction volumes that must be supported, data storage requirements, processing schedules, reporting deadlines, and online response times.

4. *Implementation Requirements.* In this section, you specify start-up processing, initial data entry or acquisition, user training requirements, and software test plans.

5. *Time and Cost Estimates.* This section provides detailed schedules, cost estimates, and staffing requirements for the systems development phase and revised projections for the remainder of the SDLC. You also present total costs-to-date for the project and compare those costs with your prior estimates.

6. *Appendices.* Supplemental material can be included in appendices at the end of the system design specification. In this section, you might include copies of documents from the first three phases if they would provide easy reference for readers.

User Approval

Users must review and approve the interface design, report and menu designs, data entry screens, source documents, and other areas of the system that affect them. The review and approval process continues throughout the systems design phase. When you complete the design for a report, you should meet with users to review the prototype, adjust the design if necessary, and obtain written approval.

Securing approvals from users throughout the design phase is very important. That approach ensures that you do not have a major task of collecting approvals at the end, it keeps the users involved with the system's development, and it gives you feedback about whether or not you are on target. Some sections of the system design specification might not interest users, but anything that does affect them should be approved as early as possible.

Other IT department members also need to review the system design specification. IT management will be concerned with staffing, costs, hardware and systems software requirements, network impact, and the effect on the operating environment when the new system is added. The programming team will want to get ready for its role, and the operations group will be interested in processing support, report distribution, network loads, integration with other systems, and any hardware or software issues for which they need to prepare. You must be a good communicator to keep people up-to-date, obtain their input and suggestions, and obtain necessary approvals.

When the system design specification is complete, you distribute the document to a target group of users, IT department personnel, and company management. You should distribute the document at least one week before your presentation to allow the recipients enough time to review the material.

Presentations

Usually, you will give several presentations at the end of the systems design phase. The presentations give you an opportunity to explain the system, answer questions, consider comments, and secure final approval. The first presentation is to the systems analysts, programmers, and technical support staff members who will be involved in future project phases or operational support for the system. Because of the audience, the presentation is technically oriented.

You give the next presentation to department managers and users from departments affected by the system. As in the first presentation, your primary objective is to obtain support and approval for the systems design. This is not a technical presentation; it is aimed at user interaction with the system and management's interest in budgets, schedules, staffing, and impact on the production environment.

The final presentation is given to company management, as shown in Figure 9-40. By the time you give this presentation, you should have obtained all prior approvals from previous presentations, and you should have the support of users and the IT department. Just like the management presentation at the end of the systems analysis phase, this presentation has a key objective: to get management's approval and support for the next development step — systems implementation — including a solid commitment for financial and other resources needed.

Based on the presentation and the data you submitted, management might reach one of three decisions: proceed with systems development, perform additional work on the systems design phase, or terminate the project. The next chapter discusses systems implementation, which is the fourth SDLC phase.

FIGURE 9-40 The management presentation seeks management approval and support for systems implementation, including a solid commitment for financial and other resources needed.

SOFTWEAR, LIMITED

Jane Rossman, manager of applications, and Rick Williams, systems analyst, had several meetings with True Blue Systems, the consulting firm hired to assist SWL in implementing the new ESIP system. Michael Jeremy, SWL's finance vice president, requested that True Blue also make recommendations about a possible SWL intranet to link all SWL locations and support client/server architecture.

The initial report from True Blue indicated that the new ESIP system should be designed as a DBMS so it could interface with the new mainframe payroll package. True Blue suggested that the ESIP system be implemented on a server in the payroll department and developed as a Microsoft Access application. They felt that this approach provided a relational database environment, client/server capability, and SQL command output to communicate with the mainframe. Figure 9-41 shows the proposed design of the system.

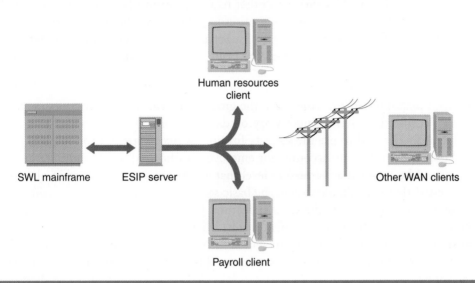

FIGURE 9-41 The proposed ESIP system.

Jane Rossman met with Ann Hon to review True Blue's report and get her approval for training IT staff members. Jane had some prior experience in Access application development, but Rick had none, so Jane suggested that he and Becky Evans attend a one-week workshop. Ann agreed.

Ann, Jane, and Rick met with Michael Jeremy to get his approval before proceeding further. He asked them to develop a specific budget and timetable including all necessary hardware, software, and training costs. They had most of the information, but they needed some help from True Blue to estimate the cost of network implementation, installation, and physical cabling.

The first phase of the project would use a local area network to link the various headquarter departments to the mainframe. A second phase, proposed by True Blue, would connect all SWL locations to a wide area network, with the possibility that employees could access their individual ESIP accounts over the internal network or from outside the company using the Internet.

A week later, Ann received a memo from Mr. Jeremy that said he had approved the project and that she should start work immediately.

System Architecture

The ESIP development team included Jane, Rick, and Becky. The group discovered that Microsoft Access application consists of interactive objects such as tables, queries, forms, reports, macros, and code modules.

They decided to begin by reviewing the entity-relationship diagrams they prepared previously to determine the overall structure of the DBMS design. Then they identified the tables, review the relationship among them, and analyze the record designs they had developed. They also reviewed output requirements, input screen designs, processing considerations, backup and recovery procedures, and controls that must be built into the new system.

As recommended by True Blue Systems, the new ESIP system would be implemented as a client/server design, with the data stored on the payroll department server, which would be linked to clients in the payroll and human resources department.

Planning the System

In their first meeting, Jane asked the team to define all the tasks that the new system would perform, including a list of all reports and other required output. Jane explained that ESIP data would be stored on the server, but the application logic, and objects such as forms, queries and reports would be located on client workstations. Separating the objects from the data would provide better security and reduce the network loads, she explained.

Security

In their next planning session, Jane asked the group to consider all security issues affecting the new system. Because the system contains payroll data, it is important to control user access and updates. The team decided to use the security features in Access for control, including passwords and user and workgroup accounts for employees authorized to use the ESIP application. Each user would be assigned a permission level that grants access only to certain objects.

Rick suggested that they should design the basic security features before proceeding further, but Jane disagreed. "We'll create the security features later, when we create the database. Meanwhile, let's go back to the department heads, Michael Jeremy and Tina Pham, to get their input on security levels," Jane said. "Users will be allowed to create and modify certain forms and reports, but most other actions will be permitted only by authorized IT department members," she added.

Creating the Database Objects

Before creating the database objects, the team reviewed the ERDs and verified that the records designs were in 3NF. In addition, they verified that the new payroll system permitted cross-platform access because the ESIP system required data from the payroll master file. They discovered that the payroll package used a standard data format called **open database connectivity** (**ODBC**) that supported links to the Access database. After planning the system, they started creating the objects.

Planning the User Interface

From earlier interviews, the IT team knew that users in the payroll and human resources departments wanted an interface that would be easy to learn and simple to operate. Jane asked Becky to start designing a main form, or switchboard, that would display automatically when the ESIP application started. All ESIP screen forms would use buttons, menus, and icons as shown in Figure 9-42.

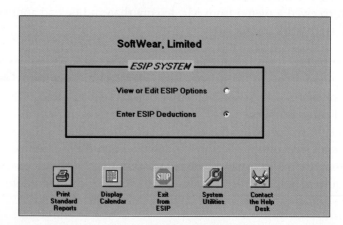

FIGURE 9-42   Sample of a main switchboard that displays when the ESIP system starts.

Becky created a prototype of the input screens to show to users. After securing user approval, the screen designs were added to the system specification document for the ESIP system.

Using Visual Basic and Macros

Because she was a programmer before her assignment as a systems analyst, Becky wanted to know if they would be using Visual Basic as a program development language. Jane told her that they would write many of the procedures in Visual Basic because it allows more powerful data manipulation than macros and makes it easier to customize error messages. They would use macros, however, to speed up the development process and handle simple tasks such as opening and closing forms and running reports.

Completing the Systems Design Phase

The IT team completed the systems design phase by writing the documentation and designing backup and recovery, file retention, and start-up procedures. The final step was to develop a system design specification for the ESIP system.

Rick and Becky showed a draft of the system design specification to Jane and Ann. After incorporating their changes, they e-mailed copies to a distribution list of users, IT staff members, and managers. Their presentations to users and IT staff members went well, and at the management presentation, they received final approval to implement the ESIP system.

YOUR TURN

Rick Williams asked you to suggest software products that can provide security and network management features suitable for a network with 25-50 users. You can use the Internet to research the topic. Rick also wants your input about security issues for a company-wide security policy he is developing. He asked you to respond to a specific question: Who is ultimately responsible for security — users, management, or the IT department? Write a brief memo explaining your views.

CHAPTER SUMMARY

An information system, or application, combines hardware, software, data, procedures, and people into an application architecture. Application architecture translates a system's logical design into a physical structure that includes hardware, software, and processing methods.

Before selecting an application architecture, the analyst must consider enterprise resource planning, initial cost and TCO, scalability, Web integration, legacy interface requirements, security, and processing options.

Enterprise resource planning (ERP) establishes an enterprise-wide strategy for IT resources and specific standards for data, processing, network, and user interface design. Companies can extend ERP systems to suppliers and customers in a process called supply chain management. A systems analyst must assess initial cost and TCO, and ensure that the design is scalable. Scalability means that a system can be expanded, modified, or downsized easily to meet business needs. The analyst also must consider if the system will be Web-centric and follow Internet design protocols, and if it must interface with existing systems, called legacy systems. System security is an important concern throughout the design process, especially for e-commerce applications that involve credit card and personal data. Processing options affect system design and resources required.

An architecture requires servers and clients. Servers are computers that supply data, processing services, or other support to one or more computers called clients. In mainframe architecture, the server performs all processing and terminals communicate with the centralized system. Clients can be connected in distributed systems to form local area networks (LANs) or wide area networks (WANs). A typical LAN design involves file server design, where the client requests a copy of a data file and the server responds by transmitting the entire file to the client.

Client/server architecture divides processing between one or more clients and a central server. In a typical client/server system, the client handles the entire user interface, including data entry, data query, and screen presentation logic. The server stores the data and provides data access and database management functions. Application logic is divided in some manner between the server and the clients. In a typical client/server interaction, the client submits a request for information from the server, which carries out the operation and responds to the client. Compared to file server designs, client/server systems are more scalable and flexible.

A fat, or thick, client design places all or most of the application processing logic at the client. A thin client design places all or most of the processing logic at the server. Thin client designs provide better performance, because program code resides on the server, near the data. In contrast, a fat client handles more of the processing, and must access and update the data more often. Fat client TCO also is higher, because of initial hardware and software requirements, and the ongoing expense of maintaining and updating remote client computers, compared with maintaining a central server. The fat client design is simpler to develop, because the architecture resembles traditional file server designs where all processing is performed at the client.

Client/server designs can be two-tier or three-tier (also called n-tier). In a two-tier design, the user interface resides on the client, all data resides on the server, and the application logic can run either on the server, on the client, or be divided between the client and the server. In a three-tier design, the user interface runs on the client and the data is stored on the server, just as with a two-tier design. A three-tier design also has a middle layer between the client and server that processes the client requests and translates them into data access commands that can be understood and carried out by the server. The middle layer is called an application server, because it provides the application logic, or business logic. Middleware is software that connects dissimilar applications and enables them to communicate and pass data. In planning the system design, a systems analyst also must consider cost-benefit and performance issues.

The Internet has had an enormous impact on application architecture. In implementing a design, an analyst should consider e-commerce strategies, the availability of packaged solutions, and corporate portals, which are entrances to a multifunction Web site.

The primary processing methods are online and batch processing. Users interact directly with online systems that continuously process their transactions when and where they occur and continuously update files and databases. In contrast, batch systems process transactions in groups and execute them on a predetermined schedule. Many online systems also use batch processing to perform routine tasks, such as handling reports and accounting entries.

Networks allow the sharing of hardware, software, and data resources in order to reduce expenses and provide more capability to users. The way a network is configured is called the network topology. Networks typically are arranged in four patterns: hierarchical, bus, star, and ring. A single mainframe computer usually controls a hierarchical network, a bus network connects workstations in a single-line communication path, a star network connects workstations to a central computer, and a ring network connects workstations in a circular communication path.

Case tools can be used to model and document application architecture and network design.

System management and support involves performance management, system security, fault management, backup and disaster recovery, and file retention policies.

The system design specification presents the complete systems design for an information system and is the basis for the presentations that complete the systems design phase. Following the presentations, the project either proceeds on to the systems development phase, requires additional systems design work, or is terminated.

Key Terms

24/7 (*9.5*)
application (*9.1*)
application architecture (*9.1*)
application logic (*9.11*)
application server (*9.11*)
architecture (*9.1*)
backup (*9.29*)
batch processing (*9.19*)
bus network (*9.22*)
business logic (*9.11*)
business-to-business (*9.40*)
business-to-consumer (*9.40*)
centralized system (*9.5*)
client/server architecture (*9.9*)
clients (*9.5*)
corporate portal (*9.17*)
data processing center (*9.6*)
detailed design specification (*9.32*)
disaster recovery plan (*9.29*)
distributed database management system (DDBMS) (*9.14*)
distributed systems (*9.8*)
enterprise resource planning (ERP) (*9.2*)
environment (*9.2*)
fat client (*9.10*)
fault management (*9.29*)
fault-tolerant (*9.30*)
file retention (*9.31*)
file server (*9.8*)
file sharing architecture (*9.8*)
hierarchical network (*9.22*)
journal file (*9.31*)

legacy data (*9.9*)
legacy systems (*9.4*)
local area network (LAN) (*9.7*)
log file (*9.31*)
mainframe architecture (*9.5*)
middleware (*9.12*)
network topology (*9.21*)
n-tier (*9.11*)
online system (*9.18*)
open database connectivity (ODBC) (*9.36*)
platform (*9.2*)
point-of-sale (POS) (*9.20*)
portal (*9.17*)
protocol (*9.24*)
queue (*9.13*)
RAID (redundant array of independent disks) (*9.30*)
recovery (*9.29*)
ring network (*9.24*)
scalability (*9.3*)
server (*9.5*)
stand-alone (*9.7*)
star network (*9.22*)
supply chain management (*9.2*)
system design specification (*9.32*)
technical design specification (*9.32*)
thick client (*9.10*)
thin client (*9.10*)
three-tier (*9.11*)
two-tier (*9.11*)
Web-centric (*9.3*)
wide area network (WAN) (*9.8*)

Chapter Review

1. Define the term application architecture. Define the term scalability and explain why it is important to consider scalability in system design.

2. When selecting an application architecture, what items should a systems analyst consider as part of the overall design checklist?

3. What is enterprise resource planning (ERP) and why is it important? What is supply chain management?

4. Explain the term server and provide an example of server-based processing; explain the term client, and provide an example of client-based processing.

5. Describe client/server architecture, including fat and thin clients, client/server tiers, and middleware.

6. Describe the impact of the Internet on application architecture and provide specific examples.

7. Explain the difference between online processing and batch processing and provide an example of each type.

8. Explain the difference between a LAN and a WAN, define the term topology, and draw a sketch of each network model.

9. Explain system management and support tools and concepts, including performance management, system security, fault management, backup and disaster recovery, and file retention.

10. List the sections of the system design specification, and describe the contents of each section.

Discussion Topics

1. Information technology has advanced dramatically during the last ten years. At the same time, enormous changes took place in the business world as companies confronted global competition and more pressure for quality, speed, and customer service. Some people believe that the new technology inspired the business changes; others believe the opposite, that business requirements drove the technological advances. What do you think and why?

2. In a January 31, 2000 article, *INFOWORLD* magazine reported that the Gartner Group, a market research firm, predicts Internet-based business-to-business sales of $7.3 trillion by 2004. Business-to-business, or B2B, Internet volume is growing even more rapidly than business-to-consumer, or B2C volume. How does B2B interaction differ from consumer-based Internet marketing?

3. This chapter described a seven-item checklist that a systems analyst might use when considering an application architecture. In your view, are all the items of equal weight and importance, or should some be ranked higher than others? If so, which issues would you put at the top of the list and why?

4. One senior manager states, "When a new system is proposed, all I want is a written report, not an oral presentation. I want to see the facts about costs, the time to implement, and the resulting benefits. On that basis, I'll make my decision as to whether or not the system should be implemented. Systems analysts don't get paid to make management-level decisions, and that's exactly what they try to do when they try to sell a system in an oral presentation. I've seen too many systems implemented because smooth-talking analysts convinced management that a system is an absolute necessity when the facts just don't justify it." Do you agree with that point of view? Justify your position.

1 Digital Dynamics

Situation:

After three years as a successful Web design firm in Southern California, Digital Dynamics has decided to add two new business ventures: a group that specializes in supplying qualified employees to hi-tech firms and a training division that offers online courses in advanced Web design and e-commerce skills. As a senior systems analyst, you have been asked to study the situation and make recommendations.

1. Should Digital Dynamics adopt ERP? What specific advantages would ERP offer?

2. How could the concept of supply chain management apply to a company's service-based division? Provide some specific suggestions.

3. Should Digital Dynamics use separate portals for employees, customers, and suppliers? If you follow the example of Oracle Corporation in the text, what type of portal design would you suggest?

4. Is the experience of other companies relevant? Use the Internet to locate examples of Web-based firms that offer personnel services and technical training. How would you evaluate the Web sites you visited? What specific features impressed you favorably or unfavorably?

2 R/Way Trucking

Situation:

As you learned earlier in this chapter, R/Way is a small but rapidly growing trucking company headquartered in Cleveland, Ohio. R/Way's information system currently consists of a file server and three workstations where freight clerks enter data, track shipments, and prepare freight bills. To perform their work, the clerks obtain data from a file server and use database and spreadsheet programs stored on stand-alone PCs to process the data. At your meeting yesterday, R/Way's president approved your recommendation to create a relational database to handle R/Way operations and provide links for R/Way shippers and customers.

1. Review the concept of supply chain management. Although R/Way offers services rather than products, could that concept apply to the design of R/Way's new system? If so, how?

2. What would be the advantages of selecting an Internet-based architecture for R/Way's system?

3. Should R/Way's new system be based on file-server or client/server architecture? Why?

4. What would be the pros and cons of selecting in-house development versus a packaged solution for the R/Way system?

3 Nothing But Net

Situation:

Nothing But Net is an IT consulting firm that specializes in e-commerce solutions. As a newly hired systems analyst, you have been asked to research some current topics.

1. Obtain at least two estimates of how much consumers are projected to spend on Internet purchases during the next three years. Are the estimates similar? If not, which forecast do you believe and why?

2. Many of Nothing But Net's customers are startup firms that must fight hard to attract investment capital, and many traditional lending institutions are skeptical of new Web-based firms. Perform research to determine the mortality rate of new e-commerce firms that use the Web as their primary marketing channel and write a brief memo that describes the results of your research.

3. Some IT professionals predict that traditional companies will increase their Internet marketing efforts, making it even harder for new Web-based firms to compete. Perform research to find out more about the topic and share your results with the class.

4. Suppose you were asked to draft a sales brochure for Nothing But Net. List all the services in which potential customers might be interested.

4 Aunt Ann's Kitchen

Situation:

Aunt Ann's Kitchen offers a line of specialty food products to institutional customers and restaurant chains. The firm prides itself on using only the finest ingredients and preparation methods. The owner, Ann Rose, hired you as an IT consultant to help her plan the application architecture for a new sales and marketing system. She asked you to start with the following questions:

1. What opportunities do you see for building supply chain management features into the new system?

2. What client/server design features might increase network performance for the new system?

3. What are the advantages of developing a Web-centric design for the new system?

4. What security concerns exist and how could you resolve them?

Chapter Assignments

1. Visit the IT department at your school or a local company to determine what type of network they are using. Draw a sketch of the network configuration, either freehand or with a tool such as Visio.

2. Perform research on the Internet or visit a local computer store to find out more about network security products. Write a brief memo with your results and include specific examples.

3. Perform research on the Internet to identify an ASP that offers Web-based business solutions and write a brief memo describing the firm and its services.

4. Perform research on the Internet or visit a local computer store to find out more about fat and thin client hardware and costs. Write a brief memo with your results, and include specific examples.

CASE STUDIES

Case Studies offer an opportunity for you to practice specific skills and knowledge learned in the chapter and provide practical experience for you as a systems analyst. Two of the case studies (New Century Health Clinic and Ridgeway Company) are continuing case studies that appear in each chapter. Additionally, one continuing case study (SCR Associates) utilizes the Internet to practice some of the topics covered in this chapter.

NEW CENTURY HEALTH CLINIC

The New Century clinic associates accepted your interface, output, input, and data designs and your recommendation to install a server and four personal computers as clients on a local area network. The network will include a tape backup unit and Internet access via a modem that can exchange data with insurance companies. A high-speed laser printer and an impact printer for multipart forms will be accessible by any of the four PCs. Now you will determine application architecture for the New Century system.

When you created ERDs and record designs for New Century during the data design process in Chapter 8, you considered whether to use a file-processing or database approach. As you know, each strategy has advantages and disadvantages, depending on the specific hardware and software environment and business requirements. At this point, you must decide which way to proceed, and Dr. Jones will accept your recommendation (with your instructor's approval).

You should start by reviewing the DFDs and O-O diagrams that you prepared in the systems analysis phase (Chapters 4 and 5), and the ERDs and record designs that you created earlier in the systems design phase (Chapter 8). Then review the application architecture checklist at the beginning of this chapter.

Assignments

1. What would be the advantages of selecting an Internet-based architecture for the New Century system?

2. Should the New Century system be based on file-server or client/server architecture? Why?

3. Could the New Century system use both online and batch processing? How?

4. Prepare an outline for a system design specification and describe the contents of each section.

RIDGEWAY COMPANY

The following assignments are based on the Ridgeway Company requirements that were described in Chapters 1, 2, and 3.

Assignments

1. Recommend an overall application architecture for Ridgeway's information system.

2. Suggest a backup and disaster recovery strategy for Ridgeway.

3. Should Ridgeway consider a Web-based design? Why or why not?

4. Should the Ridgeway system use batch processing for certain functions? Why or why not?

SCR ASSOCIATES

SCR Associates is an information technology consulting firm that offers IT solutions and training for small- and medium-sized companies. SCR's slogan is "We Know IT!"

Background

As a newly hired systems analyst, you will handle assignments, work on various SCR projects, and apply the skills you learned in the text. SCR needs an information system to manage training operations at the new SCR training center. The new system will be called TIMS (Training Information Management System).

The SCR case is available as an interactive, Web-based case study. You can log on to the Shelly Cashman Series site at www.scsite.com/sad4e/scr for instructions and assignments. If you prefer to complete the case study without using the Internet then you must download the data disk. See the inside back cover for instructions for downloading the data disk or see your instructor for more information on accessing the files required for this book.

Situation

In Part 9 of the SCR case, you will consider an application architecture for the new TIMS system.

Before You Begin...

1. Review the February 4, 2002 message from Jesse Baker regarding your role in the application architecture phase of the TIMS project. Open the Document 9-1 from the data disk.

2. Review the February 5, 2002 message from Jesse Baker regarding the system requirements document. Open the Document 9-2 from the data disk.

3. Review the current SCR network configuration. Open the Document 9-3 from the data disk.

Assignments

1. Consider an ERP strategy for SCR. Visit Web sites for SAP, Oracle, PeopleSoft, and any others you choose to determine if those firms offer an ERP framework. Based on your research, write a memo to Jesse Baker with your recommendations and reasons.

2. After reviewing SCR's current network configuration, develop a recommendation for the TIMS system. You do not have to select specific hardware or software products, but your proposal should include an overall client/server design, a recommendation regarding the number of tiers, and a network topology. In preparing your recommendation, consider the need to interface with legacy data, the degree of Web-centricity, scalability requirements, security issues, any batch processing that will be required, and any other issues you believe are relevant. You can use facts from previous SCR segments, plus supply your own assumptions when necessary. Write up your proposal in a memo to Jesse Baker.

3. Review at least two network monitoring software products. You can search the Internet, use industry magazines (both online and paper-based), or interview IT staff members at your school or a local firm. Select one of the products and write a brief memo to Jesse Baker supporting your recommendation. Make sure that you include product features, specifications, and price.

4. Visit the Gartner Group site shown in Figure 9-2 on page 9.3, or use an alternative list of accounts as a basis for TCO analysis. Although there are dozens of accounts, select the 10 that you think are most important — because of their magnitude, or potential impact on system operations. Submit your list in the form of a brief memo to Jesse Baker.

Systems Planning **PHASE 1**

Systems Analysis **PHASE 2**

Systems Design **PHASE 3**

Systems Implementation PHASE 4

Systems Operation & Support PHASE 5

Application Development

PHASE 4: SYSTEMS IMPLEMENTATION

Systems implementation is the fourth phase in the systems development life cycle. In the previous phase, systems design, you completed a physical model of the system. Now, in systems implementation, you will perform a series of application development tasks, followed by system installation and evaluation. You will learn about application development in Chapter 10 and about system installation and evaluation in Chapter 11. During application development, all necessary programs and code modules are designed, written, tested, and documented. The system installation and evaluation stage includes user training, file conversion, the actual changeover to the new system, and an evaluation of the results.

Application development begins the systems implementation phase of the SDLC. Chapter 10 is the first of two chapters in this phase. Application development describes the process of constructing the necessary programs and code modules for the new information system.

INTRODUCTION

At the conclusion of the systems design phase, you prepared a system design specification that outlined the physical design for the new information system. Now, in the systems implementation phase, the system design specification serves as a blueprint for constructing the new system. During this phase, the IT department plans, develops, documents, integrates, and tests all new programs and code modules. If the design is based on a commercial software package, IT staff members can add custom features by using the application's built-in development tools or by creating additional programs and modules.

At this point in systems development, programmers and systems analysts assume different responsibilities. An analyst must deliver a clear, accurate set of specifications to a programmer. Depending on the organization, the specifications might be highly detailed or more generalized. A programmer codes, tests, and documents the individual program modules, while the systems analyst plans the integration of the programs and ensures that system components will work together properly. Programmers and analysts often work as a team to test and document the entire system. Chapter 10 stresses the analyst's role during application development and does not cover programming skills, techniques, or activities, which are a separate area of study.

OBJECTIVES

When you finish this chapter, you will be able to:

- Describe the major tasks and activities that are completed during the systems implementation phase

- Discuss the role of the systems analyst during application development

- Explain the importance of quality assurance and the role of software engineering in software development

- Describe top-down and modular design

- Explain cohesion and coupling, and draw a structure chart that illustrates the concepts

- Explain how you can use program flowcharts and pseudocode to document program logic

- Describe the coding process and explain how program code is generated

- Explain object-oriented application development and list the advantages of this approach

- Explain testing phases, including unit testing, integration testing, and system testing

- Describe the types of documentation a systems analyst must prepare

- Explain the importance of management approval at this stage of systems development, and describe the information that systems analysts must provide to management

ON THE WEB

To learn more about software Engineering visit scsite.com/sad4e/more.htm, click Systems Analysis and Design Chapter 10 and then click the Software Engineering link.

www.scsite.com

QUALITY ASSURANCE

In today's competitive business environment, companies are intensely concerned with the quality of their products and services. A successful organization constantly must improve quality in every area, including its information systems. Top management must provide the leadership, encouragement, and support needed for high quality IT resources.

No matter how carefully a system is designed and implemented, some problems can occur, especially in a complex system. Rigorous testing catches errors in the final stages, but it is much less expensive to correct mistakes earlier in the development process. The main objective of **quality assurance** is to avoid problems, or to detect them as soon as possible. Poor quality can result from inaccurate requirements, design problems, coding errors, faulty documentation, and ineffective testing.

In an effort to achieve high standards of quality, software systems developers should consider software engineering concepts and internationally recognized quality standards.

Software Engineering

Because quality is so important, you can use an approach called software engineering to manage and improve the quality of the finished system. **Software engineering** is a software development process that stresses solid design, effective structure, accurate documentation, and careful testing.

The Web site for the **Software Engineering Institute** (SEI) at Carnegie Mellon University is shown in Figure 10-1. SEI is a leader in software engineering and provides quality standards and suggested procedures for software developers and systems analysts. SEI's primary objective is to find better, faster, and less expensive methods of software development. To achieve that goal, SEI designed **Capability Maturity Models** (CMMs)®, which improve quality, reduce development time, and cut costs.

A CMM® tracks an organization's software development goals and practices, using five maturity levels, from Level 1 (relatively unstable, ineffective software) to Level 5 (software that is refined, efficient, and reliable). The five CMMs® levels are shown in Figure 10-2.

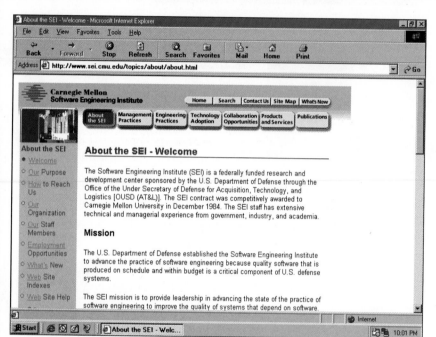

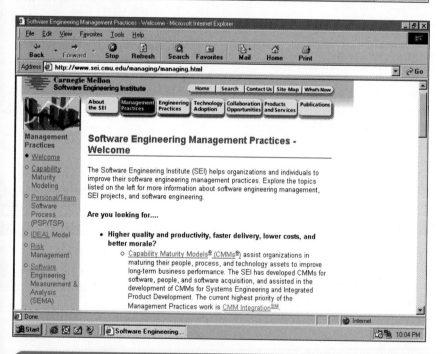

FIGURE 10-1   The Software Engineering Institute (SEI) provides leadership in software engineering that improves the quality of systems that depend on software.

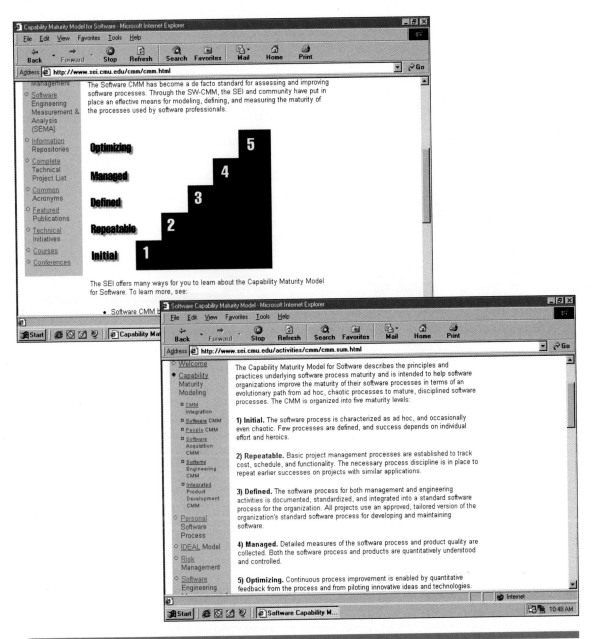

FIGURE 10-2 A CMM® uses five maturity levels, from Level 1 (relatively unstable, ineffective software) to Level 5 (software that is refined, efficient, and reliable).

International Organization for Standardization (ISO)

You learned in Chapter 8 that the International Organization for Standardization (ISO) is a worldwide body that establishes quality standards for products and services. Figure 10-3 on the next page shows that ISO standards include everything from the dashboard symbols in your car to the ISBN number on this textbook. In addition, ISO seeks to offer a global consensus of what constitutes good management practices — practices that can help firms deliver consistently high-quality products and services.

ON THE WEB

To obtain more informati about ISO Standards visit scsite.com/sad4e/more.ht click Systems Analysis an Design Chapter 10 and th click the ISO Standards lir

www.scsite.c

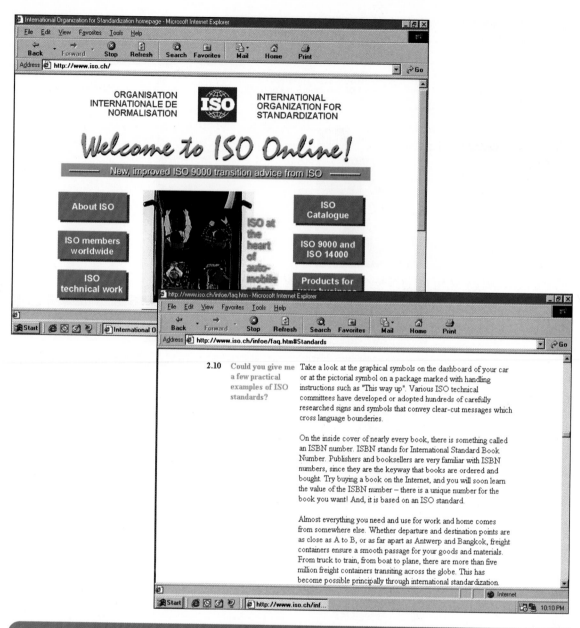

FIGURE 10-3   The International Organization for Standardization (ISO) is an international body that establishes quality standards for products and services, including software development.

Because software is so important to a company's success, many firms seek assurances that software systems, either purchased or developed in-house, will meet rigid quality standards. In 1991, ISO established a set of guidelines called ISO 9000-3, which provided a quality assurance framework for developing and maintaining software. A company can specify ISO 9000-3 standards when it purchases software from a supplier, or use ISO guidelines for in-house software development to ensure that the final result measures up to ISO standards. ISO requires a specific development plan, which outlines a step-by-step process for transforming user requirements into a finished product. ISO standards can be quite detailed. For example, ISO requires that a software supplier document all testing and maintain records of test results. If problems are found, they must be resolved and any modules affected must be retested. Additionally, software and hardware specifications of all test equipment must be documented and included in the test records.

You Call - We Haul, Inc. is a large trucking company with operations in ten midwestern states. As the new IT director, your first priority is to replace the existing freight operations information system, which was designed in the mid-1980s. The company president, Elian Sanchez, recently attended a seminar that explained ISO standards and their importance in global marketing. Now Elian wants to know if the company should use ISO standards, even though it has no international operations at this time. Locate the ISO Web site and see what you can learn about ISO and its background, then write a brief memo to Elian stating your views.

OVERVIEW OF APPLICATION DEVELOPMENT

Whether the application is implemented as a structured or object-oriented design, the process is similar. Structured application development techniques and tools are described first, and object-oriented application development is discussed later in the chapter.

In Chapter 3, during requirements modeling, you learned how to use functional decomposition diagrams (FDDs) to break complex business operations into smaller units, or functions. In Chapter 4, you learned about data and process modeling, and you created DFDs. You also developed process descriptions for functional primitive processes that documented the business logic and processing requirements. In Chapter 5, you learned about object modeling, and how objects could represent an information system. The objects contain both data and processes, called methods, which act on the data. In Chapter 8, you worked with data structures, analyzed relationships between system entities, and constructed ERDs. Those tasks produced a logical design and a plan for physical implementation.

A new system requires planning, construction, and testing. After an overall strategy is established, programs and modules must be designed, coded, tested, and documented, as shown in Figure 10-4. After developing and testing all programs and code modules, systems analysts and programmers ensure that modules will interact properly, test the overall system, and complete all documentation.

Documentation Review

With an overall strategy in place, the next step is to review documentation from prior SDLC phases and create a set of program designs. In addition to the system design specification, the systems analyst can refer to DFDs, process descriptions, object models, class diagrams, ERDs, screen layouts, report layouts, source documents, data dictionary entries, and anything else that helps a programmer understand what functions the program or module must perform and its relationship to other programs and modules. Based on those requirements, the main responsibility for actually coding and constructing the program or module belongs to the programmer.

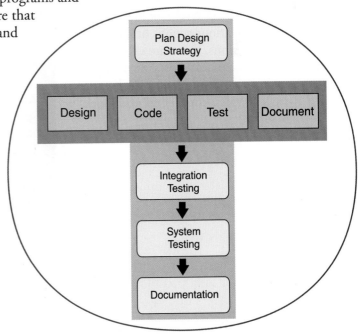

FIGURE 10-4 The main steps in application development.

After reviewing the design, the systems development team develops a step-by-step logical solution. Traditionally, programmers handle application development, but companies often assign a group of analysts to work together with them.

STRUCTURED APPLICATION DEVELOPMENT

During structured application development, a programmer creates modules that perform specific tasks or functions. A **module** consists of related program code organized into small units that are easy to understand and maintain. A complex program could have hundreds or even thousands of modules.

When planning a system, most analysts use a top-down approach, which proceeds from a general design to a detailed structure in a series of logical steps. In a **top-down design**, the systems analyst defines the overall objectives of the system, and then breaks them down into subsystems and modules in a process called **partitioning**. This approach also is called **modular design** and is similar to constructing a leveled set of DFDs that show individual elements in a complete, working structure. By assigning modules to different programmers, several areas of development can proceed at the same time. As explained in the Systems Analyst's Toolkit, you can use project management software to monitor work on each module, forecast overall development time, estimate required human and technical resources, and calculate a critical path for the project.

Although the top-down approach has many advantages, an analyst must proceed carefully, with constant input from programmers and IT management to achieve a sound, modular structure. All modules must function properly as an overall information system, so the analyst must ensure that integration capability is built into each design and thoroughly tested during the development process, as shown in Figure 10-5.

Structure Charts

Structure charts show the relationships among program modules. A **structure chart** consists of rectangles that represent the program modules, with arrows and other symbols that provide additional information. Typically, a higher-level module, called a **control module**, directs lower-level modules, called **subordinate modules**. In a structure chart, symbols represent various actions or conditions. Structure chart symbols represent modules, data couples, control couples, conditions, and loops.

FIGURE 10-5 Careful testing is a critical part of software engineering, especially where a system malfunction could result in serious consequences. Software engineers must test a system or program thoroughly before releasing it for use.

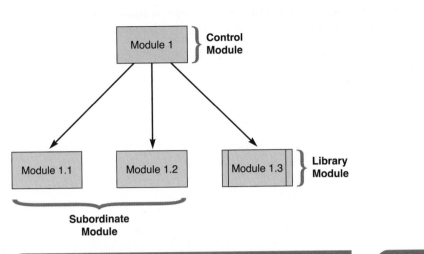

FIGURE 10-6   An example of structure chart modules.

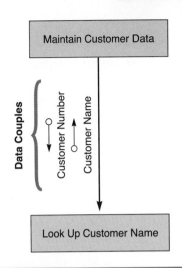

FIGURE 10-7   An example of a structure chart data couple.

MODULE   A rectangle represents a module, as shown in Figure 10-6. Vertical lines at the edges of a rectangle indicate that module 1.3 is a library module. A **library module** is reusable and can be invoked from more than one point in the chart.

DATA COUPLE   An arrow with an empty circle represents a data couple. A **data couple** shows data that one module passes to another. In the data couple example shown in Figure 10-7, the Look Up Customer Name module exchanges data with the Maintain Customer Data module.

CONTROL COUPLE   An arrow with a filled circle represents a control couple. A **control couple** shows a message, also called a **flag**, which one module sends to another. In the example shown in Figure 10-8, the Update Customer File module sends an Account Overdue flag back to the Maintain Customer Data module. A module uses a flag to signal a specific condition or action to another module.

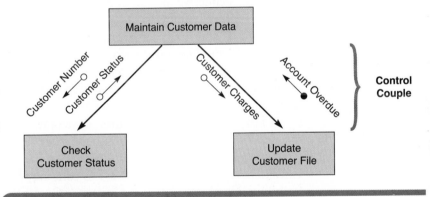

FIGURE 10-8   An example of a structure chart control couple.

CONDITION   A line with a diamond on one end represents a con dition. A **condition** line indicates that a control module determines which subordinate modules will be invoked, depending on a specific condition. In the example shown in Figure 10-9, Sort Inventory Parts is a control module with a condition line that triggers one of the three subordinate modules.

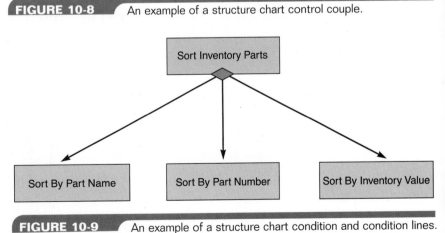

FIGURE 10-9   An example of a structure chart condition and condition lines.

LOOP   A curved arrow represents a loop. A **loop** indicates that one or more modules are repeated. In the example shown in Figure 10-10, the Get Student Grades and Calculate GPA modules are repeated.

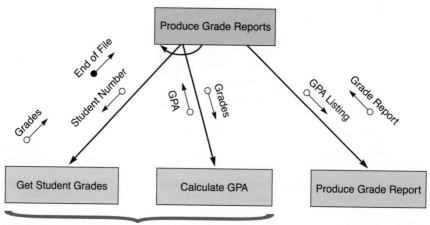

The curved arrow indicates that these modules are repeated.

FIGURE 10-10   An example of a structure chart loop.

Cohesion and Coupling

Cohesion measures a module's scope and processing characteristics. A module that performs a single function or task has a high degree of cohesion, which is desirable. Because it focuses on a single task, a cohesive module is much easier to code and reuse. For example, a process named Verify Customer Number is more cohesive than a process named Calculate And Print Statements. If you notice the word *and* in a module name, you know that more than one task is involved. If a module must perform multiple tasks, more complex coding is required and the module will be more difficult to create and maintain.

Another way to understand cohesion is to remember what you did during data and process modeling. To create a leveled set of DFDs, you identified functional primitives that performed a single task. Now, during application development, you must translate those functional primitives into cohesive modules. If you need to make a module more cohesive, you can split it into separate units that each performs a single function. In the example shown in Figure 10-11, the Check Customer Status module is less cohesive, because it consists of two separate tasks: Check Customer Number and Check Customer Credit Limit. By treating the tasks as separate modules, you achieve more cohesion and better program quality.

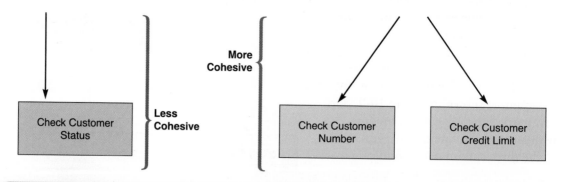

FIGURE 10-11   An example of structure chart cohesion.

Coupling measures relationships and interdependence among modules. Modules that are relatively independent are **loosely coupled**, which is desirable. Loosely coupled modules are easier to maintain and modify, because the logic in one module does not affect other modules. If a programmer needs to update a loosely coupled module, he or she can accomplish the task in a single location. If modules are **tightly coupled**, one module refers to internal logic contained in another module. For example, a Calculate GPA module might refer to an internal variable, such as Student Status, contained in another module called Update Student Status. In that case, a logic error in the second module affects the first module's processing sequence.

Figure 10-12 shows two examples of coupling. In the tightly coupled example on the left, notice that the subordinate module, Calculate Current Charges, depends on a status flag that it receives from the control module, Update Customer Balance. Passing status flags down from a control module generally is regarded as poor design, because logic problems in the control module can affect logic and coding in the subordinate module. In contrast, the loosely coupled modules on the right are logically independent. Rather than passing a flag down to the subordinate module, the control module allows the Apply Discount module to handle discount processing independently. Logic errors, if any, are confined to the Apply Discount module, where they can be detected and resolved more easily.

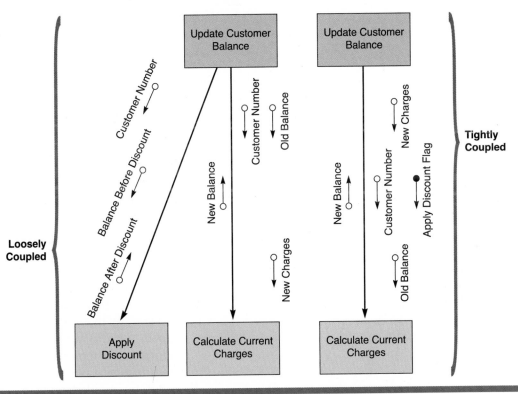

FIGURE 10-12 An example of loosely coupled and tightly coupled structure charts.

Structure Chart Examples

Figure 10-13 shows the initial design for the Sales Commission structure chart that was described in structured English in Chapter 4. Process Sales Commission is a control module, and there are five subordinate modules. Data couples and control couples have not yet been added. Notice the loop symbol, which represents repetitive processing.

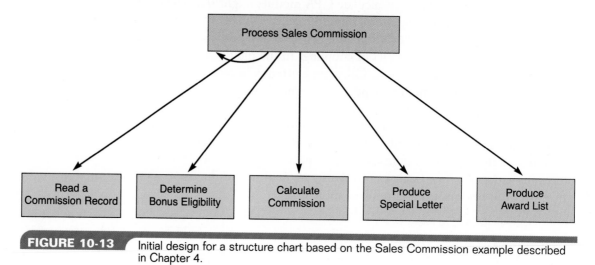

FIGURE 10-13 Initial design for a structure chart based on the Sales Commission example described in Chapter 4.

Figure 10-14 shows a structure chart based on a Grading System example that was described in Chapter 4. Notice that each subordinate module exchanges data with a higher-level control module. Each module appears to perform a single task, and is cohesive. The modules are independent, and are loosely coupled.

Steps in Drawing a Structure Chart

Structure charts are based on the DFDs you constructed during data and process modeling, and object models that you developed. Typically, you follow four steps when you create a structure chart. You review DFDs and object models to identify the processes and methods, identify the program modules and determine control-subordinate relationships, add symbols for couples and loops, and analyze the structure chart to ensure that it is consistent with your system documentation.

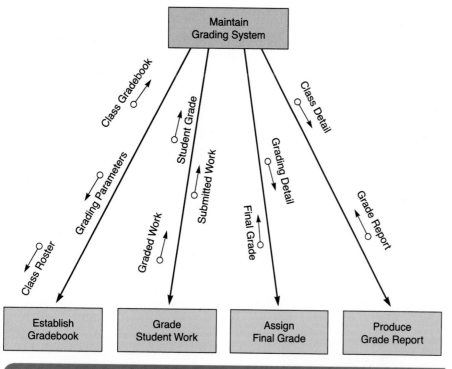

FIGURE 10-14 A structure chart based on the Grading System example described in Chapter 4.

REVIEW THE DFDS AND OBJECT MODELS The first step is to review the DFDs to ensure that you have a leveled, balanced set of diagrams. You should check for accuracy and completeness, especially if changes have occurred since the systems analysis phase. For example, Figure 10-15 shows a DFD for the order system you studied in Chapter 4. If object models were developed, you should analyze them to identify the objects, the methods that each object must perform, and the relationships among the objects.

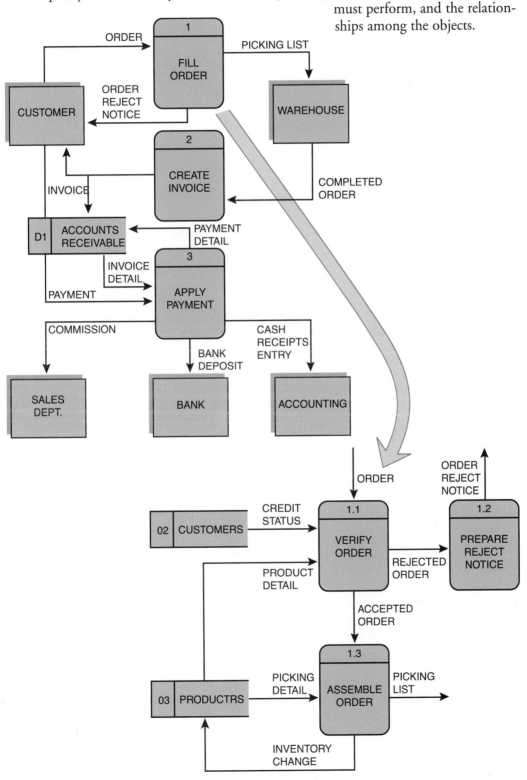

IDENTIFY MODULES AND RELATIONSHIPS   Working from the logical model, you transform functional primitives and object methods into program modules. When analyzing a set of DFDs, remember that each DFD level represents a processing level. You work your way down from the context diagram to the lower-level diagrams, identifying control modules and subordinate modules, until you reach functional primitives. If more cohesion is desired, you can divide processes into smaller modules that handle a single task. Figure 10-16 shows a structure chart based on the DFDs in Figure 10-15 on the previous page. Notice how the chart relates to the various DFD levels.

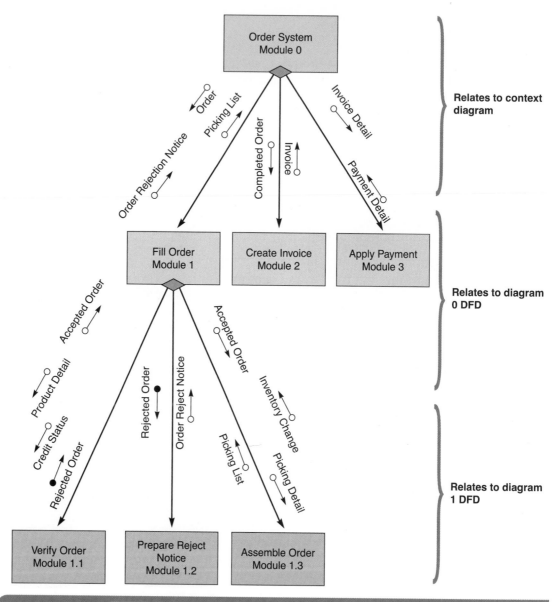

FIGURE 10-16   A structure chart based on the Order System DFDs shown in Figure 10-15.

ADD COUPLES, LOOPS, AND CONDITIONS   Next, you add couples, loops, and conditions to the structure chart. You can review the DFD data flows and the data dictionary to identify the data elements that pass from one module to another. In addition to adding the data couples, you add control couples where a module is sending a control parameter, or flag, to another module. You also add loops and condition lines that show repetitive or alternative processing steps.

ANALYZE THE STRUCTURE CHART, THE DFDs, AND THE DATA DICTIONARY

At this point, the structure chart is ready for careful analysis. You should check each process and data element to ensure that the chart reflects all previous documentation, and that the logic is correct. You also should determine that modules are cohesive and loosely coupled. Often, you must draw several versions of the chart. Some CASE tools can help you analyze the chart and identify problem areas.

OTHER APPLICATION DEVELOPMENT TOOLS

In addition to structure charts, other application development tools include program flowcharts and pseudocode.

Program Flowcharts

Program flowcharts graphically represent the logic and interaction between program modules, using a series of symbols connected by arrows. Using program flowcharts, programmers can break large systems into subsystems that are easier to understand and code. Figure 10-17 illustrates a program flowchart for calculating sales commissions. Notice that each diamond-shaped symbol represents a specific decision that determines the actions the program will perform next.

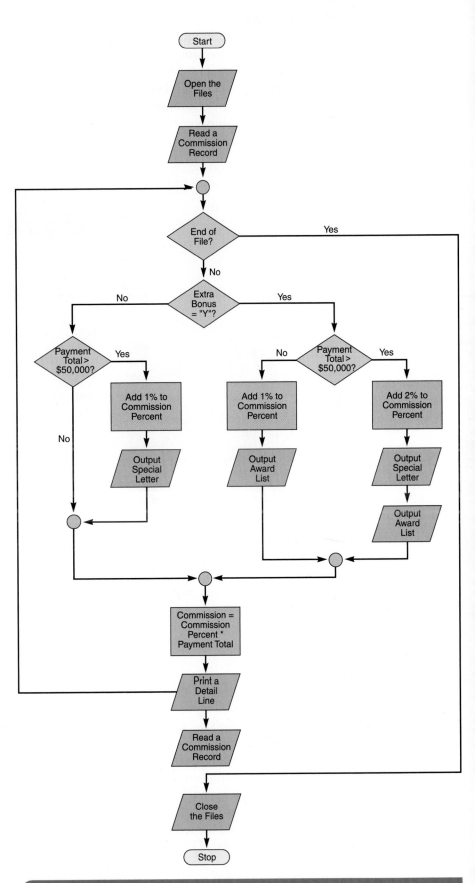

FIGURE 10-17 A program flowchart shows the logic needed to calculate commissions and perform related tasks.

Pseudocode

Pseudocode is a technique for representing program logic. Pseudocode is similar to structured English, which was explained in Chapter 4. Pseudocode is not language-specific, so you can use it to describe a software module in plain English without requiring strict syntax rules. Using pseudocode, a systems analyst or a programmer can describe program actions that they can implement in any programming language. Figure 10-18 illustrates the pseudocode used to document the sales commission module.

```
Open the files
Read a COMMISSION record
Do until end of file
       If EXTRA BONUS equals Y
              If PAYMENT TOTAL is greater than $50,000
                     Add 2% to COMMISSION PERCENT
                     Output SPECIAL LETTER
                     Output AWARD LIST
                  Else
                     Add 1% to COMMISSION PERCENT
                     Output AWARD LIST
              ENDIF
           Else
              If PAYMENT TOTAL is greater than $50,000
                     Add 1% to COMMISSION PERCENT
                     Output SPECIAL LETTER
              ENDIF
       ENDIF
       Calculate COMMISSION = COMMISSION PERCENT times PAYMENT TOTAL
       Print a detail line
       Read a COMMISSION record
ENDDO
Close the files
End the program
```

FIGURE 10-18 An example of pseudocode that documents the logical steps in the Sales commission flowchart shown in Figure 10-17 on the previous page.

If a programmer believes that changes are needed in the design, he or she contacts the systems analyst to review the suggested revisions. For example, a programmer notices that certain information is duplicated in a report design. If the changes could affect users, the analyst must inform them in advance, and document all modifications and user approvals in the system design specification.

CODING

Coding is the process of turning program logic into specific instructions that the computer system can execute. Working from a specific design, a programmer uses a programming language to transform program logic into code statements. An individual programmer might create a small program, while larger programs typically are divided into modules that several individuals or groups can work on simultaneously.

Each IT department has its own programming environment and standards. Visual C++, Visual Basic, and SQL are examples of commonly used programming languages, and many commercial packages use a proprietary set of commands. As more companies use Internet applications and protocols, HTML, Java, and other Web-centric languages will be used extensively.

You learned in earlier chapters that systems analysts use application generators, report writers, screen generators, fourth-generation languages, and other CASE tools that produce code directly from program design specifications. Some commercial applications can generate editable program code directly from macros, keystrokes, or mouse actions. Figure 10-19 shows an example of a Visual Basic code module in Microsoft Access that opens a customer order form and produces a beep sound. A macro automatically generated the code; the macro itself was created by a series of keystrokes and mouse actions. Notice that the module shown in Figure 10-19 includes program commands, comments, and error-handling procedures.

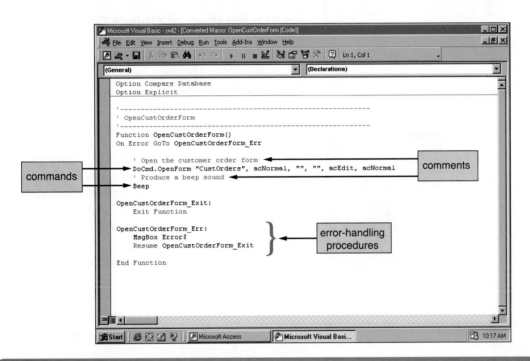

FIGURE 10-19 A Visual Basic code module that opens a customer order form and produces a beep sound. First, the programmer creates a Microsoft Access macro by using keystrokes and mouse actions, and then Access converts the macro to editable code — complete with commands, comments, and error-handling procedures.

OBJECT-ORIENTED APPLICATION DEVELOPMENT

Object-oriented application development translates an object model directly into an object-oriented programming language. An important reason for the popularity of O-O methodology is that the implementation process is easier and faster than structured design because much of the work has been done already. Although many of the concepts described earlier in this chapter also apply to an object-oriented methodology, there are some differences.

Overview of Object-Oriented Application Development

You learned in Chapter 5 that objects contain both data and program logic, called methods. Individual object instances belong to classes of objects with similar characteristics. The relationship and interaction among classes are described using a class diagram, such as the one shown in Figure 10-20 on the next page. A class diagram includes class attributes, which describe the characteristics of objects in the class, and methods, which represent program logic. For example, the Customer class describes customer objects. Customer attributes include Number, Name, Address, and so on. Methods for the Customer class include Place order, Modify order, and Pay invoice, among others. The Customer class can exchange messages with the Order class.

ON THE WEB

For an overview of Object-Oriented Application Development (OOAD) visit scsite.com/sad4e/more.htm click Systems Analysis and Design Chapter 10 and then click the Object-Oriented Application Development (OOAD) link.

www.scsite.c

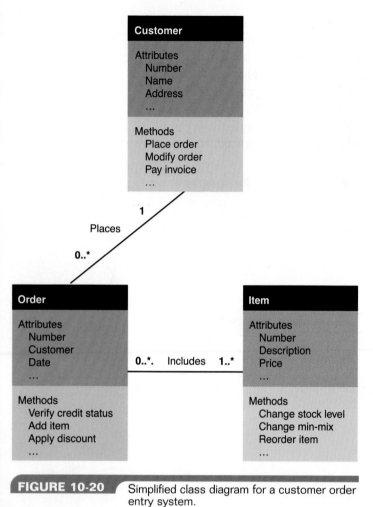

FIGURE 10-20 Simplified class diagram for a customer order entry system.

When implementing a structured design, a structure chart is used to control the interaction between program modules, as described earlier in this chapter. In contrast, when implementing an object-oriented design, relationships between objects already exist. Because the interaction was defined during the O-O analysis and design process, the application structure is imbedded in the object model itself.

Implementation of Object-Oriented Designs

When a programmer translates an object-oriented design into an application, he or she analyzes the classes, attributes, methods, and messages that are documented in the object model. During this process, the programmer makes necessary revisions and updates to class diagrams, sequence diagrams, state transition diagrams, and activity diagrams.

The programmer's main objective is to translate object methods into program code modules and determine what event or message will trigger the execution of each module. To accomplish the task, the programmer analyzes sequence and state transition diagrams that show the events and messages that trigger changes to an object. Each event or message must have a corresponding action. The programmer can represent the program steps in pseudocode initially, or use application development or CASE tools to create object-oriented code directly from the object model.

Because the application development process is modular, individual programmers or teams can be assigned various tasks within the overall project framework and timetable. In addition to coordinating the programming effort, systems analysts must ensure that code modules are properly tested and documented. At this stage in systems development, project management becomes especially important. Users are looking forward to the new system, and pressures may come from management. The systems analyst or project manager should use project management tools and techniques similar to those described in the Systems Analyst's Toolkit to monitor and control the overall project.

TESTING THE APPLICATION

After coding, a programmer must test the program to make sure that it functions correctly. Later, programs are tested in groups, and finally the programmer must test the entire system. The first step is to compile the program using a CASE tool or a language compiler. This process detects **syntax errors**, which are language grammar errors. The programmer corrects the errors until the program executes properly.

Next, the programmer desk checks the program. **Desk checking** is the process of reviewing the program code to spot **logic errors**, which produce incorrect results. This process can be performed by the person who wrote the program or by other programmers. Many organizations require a more formal type of desk checking called a **structured walkthrough**, or **code review**, as shown in Figure 10-21.

Typically, a group of three to five IT staff members participate in code review. The group usually consists of project team members and might include other programmers and analysts who did not work on the project. The objective is to have a peer group identify errors, apply quality standards, and verify that the program meets the requirements of the system design specification. Errors found during a structured walkthrough are easier to fix while coding is still in the developmental stages.

In addition to analyzing logic and program code, the project team usually holds a session with users called a **design walkthrough**, to review the interface with a cross-section of people who will work with the new system. This is a continuation of the modeling and prototyping effort that began early in the systems development process.

The next step in application development is to initiate a sequence of unit testing, integration testing, and system testing, as shown in Figure 10-22.

FIGURE 10-21 Teamwork is important in all phases of the SDLC, including program development. Both programmers and systems analysts, for example, participate in the process of code review, or structured walkthrough.

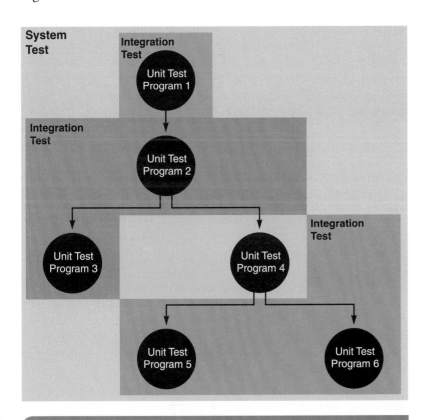

FIGURE 10-22 The first step in testing is unit testing, followed by integration testing, and then system testing.

Unit Testing

The testing of an individual program or module is called **unit testing**. The objective is to identify and eliminate execution errors that could cause the program to terminate abnormally, and logic errors that could have been missed during desk checking.

Test data should contain both correct data and erroneous data and should test all possible situations that could occur. For example, for a field that allows a range of numeric values, the test data should contain minimum values, maximum values, values outside the acceptable range, and alphanumeric characters. During testing, programmers can use software tools to determine the location and potential causes of program errors.

During unit testing, programmers must test programs that interact with other programs and files individually, before they are integrated into the system. This requires a technique called stub testing. In **stub testing**, the programmer simulates each program outcome or result and displays a message to indicate whether or not the program executed successfully. Each stub represents an entry or exit point that will be linked later to another program or data file.

To obtain an independent analysis, someone other than the programmer who wrote the program usually creates the test data and reviews the results. Systems analysts frequently create test data during the systems design phase as part of an overall test plan. A **test plan** consists of detailed procedures that specify how and when the testing will be performed, who will participate, and what test data will be used. A comprehensive test plan should include scenarios for every possible situation the program could encounter.

Regardless of who creates the test plan, the project manager or a designated analyst also reviews the final test results. Some organizations also require users to approve final unit test results.

Integration Testing

Testing two or more programs that depend on each other is called **integration testing**, or **link testing**. For example, consider an information system with a program that checks and validates customer credit status, and a separate program that updates data in the customer master file. The output from the validation program becomes input to the master file update program. Testing the programs independently does not guarantee that the data passed between them is correct. Only by performing integration testing for this pair of programs can you make sure that the programs work together properly. Figure 10-22 on the previous page shows integration testing for several groups of programs. Notice that a program can have membership in two or more groups.

Systems analysts usually develop the data they use in integration testing. As is the case with all forms of testing, integration test data must consider both normal and unusual situations. For example, integration testing might include passing typical records between two programs, followed by blank records, to simulate an unusual event or an operational problem. You should use test data that simulates actual conditions because you are testing the interface that links the programs. A testing sequence should not move to the integration test stage unless it has performed properly in all unit tests.

System Testing

After completing integration testing, you must perform **system testing**, which involves the entire information system, as shown in Figure 10-22. A system test includes all typical processing situations. During a system test, users enter data, including samples of actual, or live data, perform queries, and produce reports to simulate actual operating conditions. All processing options and outputs are verified by users and the IT project development team to ensure that the system functions correctly. Commercial software packages must undergo system testing similar to that of in-house developed systems, although unit and integration testing usually are not performed. Regardless of how the system was developed, system testing has the following major objectives:

- Perform a final test of all programs.
- Ensure that the IT staff has the documentation and instructions needed to operate the system properly and that backup and restart capabilities of the system are adequate (the details of creating this sort of documentation are discussed later in this chapter).
- Demonstrate that users can interact with the system successfully.
- Verify that all system components are integrated properly and that actual processing situations will be handled correctly.
- Confirm that the information system can handle predicted volumes of data in a timely and efficient manner.

Successful completion of system testing is the key to user and management approval, which is why system tests sometimes are called **acceptance tests**. Final acceptance tests, however, are performed during systems installation and evaluation, which is described in Chapter 11.

How much testing is necessary? The answer depends on the situation and requires good judgment and input from other IT staff members, users, and management, as shown in Figure 10-23. Unfortunately, IT project managers often are pressured to finishing testing quickly and hand the system over to users. Common

FIGURE 10-23   Determining the duration of system testing requires good judgment and input from other IT staff members, users, and IT management.

reasons for premature or rushed testing are demands from users, tight systems development budgets, and demands from top management to finish projects early. Those demands hinder the testing process and often have detrimental effects on the final product.

You should regard thorough testing as a cost-effective means of providing a quality product. Every error caught during testing eliminates potential expenses and operational problems. No system is 100 percent error-free, however. Often, errors go undetected until the system becomes operational. Errors that affect the integrity or accuracy of data must be corrected immediately. Minor errors, such as typographical errors in screen titles, can be corrected later.

Some users want a system that is a completely finished product, while others realize that minor changes can be treated as maintenance items after the system is operational. In the final analysis, you must decide whether or not to postpone system installation if problems are discovered. If conflicting views exist, management will decide whether or not to install the system after a full discussion of the options.

W H A T   D O   Y O U   T H I N K ?

You are a systems analyst at Global Cooling, a leading manufacturer of air conditioning units. You are leading a team that is developing a new inventory management system. The project is now in the application development stage. Unit testing has been completed, and you are in the final stages of integration testing. Your supervisor is eager to implement the new application ahead of schedule and asked if you could trim system testing from two weeks to three days. Write a brief memo expressing your views.

ON THE WEB

o learn more about
oftware Documentation visit
csite.com/sad4e/more.htm,
lick Systems Analysis and
esign Chapter 10 and then
lick the Software
ocumentation link.

w.scsite.com

DOCUMENTATION

Documentation is essential for successful system operation and maintenance. Accurate documentation helps a programmer who needs to carry out a future program change and makes maintenance easier, faster, and less expensive. **Documentation** explains the system, helps people interact with it, and includes program documentation, system documentation, operations documentation, and user documentation.

Program Documentation

Program documentation starts in the systems analysis phase and continues during systems implementation. Systems analysts prepare overall documentation, such as process descriptions and report layouts, early in the SDLC. Programmers provide documentation by constructing modules that are well supported by internal and external comments and descriptions that can be understood and maintained easily. A systems analyst usually verifies that program documentation is complete and accurate.

System Documentation

System documentation describes the system's functions and how they are implemented. The analyst prepares most of the system documentation during the systems analysis and systems design phases. System documentation includes data dictionary entries, data flow diagrams, object models, screen layouts, source documents, and the systems request that initiated the project.

During systems implementation, an analyst must review system documentation to verify that it is complete, accurate, and up-to-date, including any changes made during the implementation process. For example, if a screen or report is modified, the analyst must update the documentation. Updates to the system documentation should be made in a timely manner to prevent oversights.

Operations Documentation

If the information system environment involves a minicomputer or mainframe, the analyst must prepare documentation for the IT group that supports centralized operations. A mainframe installation might require the scheduling of batch jobs and the distribution of printed reports. In this type of environment, the IT operations staff serves as the first point of contact when users experience problems with the system.

Operations documentation contains all the information needed for processing and distributing printed output. Typical operations documentation includes the following information:

- Program, systems analyst, programmer, and system identification
- Scheduling information, such as report run frequency and deadlines
- Input files and where they originate; and output files and destinations
- Report distribution
- Special forms required
- Error and informational messages to operators and restart procedures
- Special instructions, such as security requirements

Operations documentation should be clear, concise, and available online if possible. If the IT department has an operations group, you should review the documentation with them, early and often, to identify any problems. If you keep the operations group informed at every phase of the SDLC, you can develop operations documentation as you go along.

User Documentation

User documentation consists of instructions and information to users who will interact with the system and includes user manuals, Help screens, and tutorials. Programmers or systems analysts usually create program documentation and system documentation. To produce effective and clear user documentation — and hence have a successful project — you need someone with expert skills in this area doing the development, just as you need someone with expert skills developing the software. The skill set required to develop documentation usually is not the same as that to develop a system. This is particularly true as you move into the world of online documentation, which needs to coordinate with print documentation and intranet and Internet information.

Just as you cannot throw a system all together in a couple days, you cannot just add documentation at the end. That is a common misconception and often proves fatal to a project. While that has always been true of software user documentation, this is an even more critical issue now that online Help and context-sensitive Help are so often needed. Context-sensitive Help is part of the program. You have to put coded call-outs in the text that link to the correct page of information in the documentation. To try to go back and add this after the fact would take a great deal of time, and depending on the project size it could take months! Additionally, it could introduce other coding errors — and it all has to be tested as well.

If the analysts are responsible for preparing documentation to help users learn the system, as shown in Figure 10-24, and there are no on-staff technical writers or information developers with which to work, the company could hire a technical writer to prepare the documentation. Producing good documentation is essential to the success and acceptance of a system, and if a systems analyst has not been trained in software documentation or technical writing, it is better to bring in outside resources rather than risk the success of the project.

User documentation includes the following:

- System overview that clearly describes all major system features, capabilities, and limitations
- Source document content, preparation, processing, and samples
- Menu and data entry screen options, contents, and processing instructions
- Reports that are produced regularly or available at the user's request, including samples
- Security and audit trail information
- Responsibility for specific input, output, or processing requirements
- Procedures for requesting changes and reporting problems
- Examples of exceptions and error situations
- Frequently asked questions (FAQs)
- Explanations of how to get Help and procedures for updating the manual

Most users prefer **online documentation**, which provides immediate Help when they have questions or encounter problems. Many users are accustomed to context-sensitive Help screens, hints and tips, hypertext, on-screen demos, and other user-friendly features commonly found in popular software packages; they expect the same kind of support for in-house developed software.

FIGURE 10-24 Whether written or online, clear user documentation helps users learn the system. Systems analysts are responsible for preparing the documentation, but often invite users to participate in developing the material.

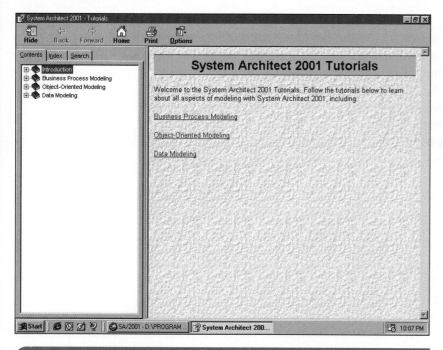

FIGURE 10-25 Interactive tutorials are especially popular with users who like to learn by doing.

If the system is going to have online documentation, that fact needs to be identified well before the coding is started. If the documentation is going to be created by someone other than the systems analysts who are developing the software, that person(s) needs to be involved as early as possible to familiarize themselves with the software, begin developing the documents that will be required, and begin setting up the structure of the documents. In addition, it needs to be determined if the documentation is going to be a separate, stand-alone entity, such as in a separate directory, on a CD, or on an intranet; or, if available from within the program, links need to be set up within the program that will take the user to the appropriate documentation. This has to be done in coordination with and during development.

Powerful online documentation actually is a productivity tool because it helps users take full advantage of the program and reduces the time that IT staff members must spend in providing telephone, e-mail, or face-to-face assistance. Interactive tutorials are especially popular with users who like to learn by doing. Many packages provide tutorials, as shown in Figure 10-25.

In addition to program-based assistance, the Internet offers an entirely new level of comprehensive, immediate support. Many programs include links to Web sites, intranet sites, and Internet-based technical support, as shown in Figure 10-26. The sites usually include up-to-date information, tips, and FAQs.

Although online documentation is essential, written documentation material also is valuable, especially in training users and for reference purposes. A sample page from a user manual is shown in Figure 10-27. Systems analysts or technical writers usually prepare the manual but many companies invite users to review the material and participate in the development process.

FIGURE 10-26 Many programs include links to technical support sites that offer up-to-date information, tips, and frequently asked questions (FAQs).

PHASE 4

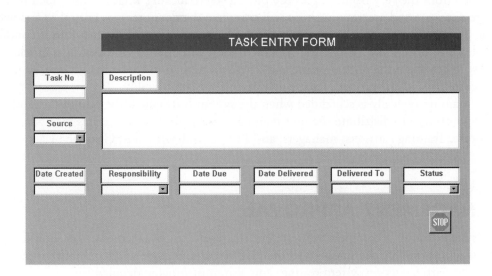

HOW TO ADD A NEW TASK TO THE SYSTEM

Task No: Press the TAB key to generate a task number. The system automatically will assign a sequential number. Then press the TAB key again to advance to the next data field. Continue to do this until all data is entered. Then click the STOP symbol to return to the main menu.

Description: Enter a task description of up to 256 characters.

Source: Click the arrow to display the selections and click one of the choices.

Date Created: Enter the date in MM/DD/YYYY format.

Responsibility: Click the arrow to display the selections and click one of the choices.

Date Due: Enter the due date in MM/DD/YYYY format.

Date Delivered: Enter the delivered date in MM/DD/YYYY format.

Status: Click the arrow to display the selections and click one of the choices.

FIGURE 10-27   A sample page from a user manual. The instructions explain how to add a new task to the system.

No matter what form of user documentation your system will require, you must keep in mind that it can take a good deal of time to develop. The time between finishing software coding and the time when a complete package — including documentation — can be released to users is entirely dependent on how well the documentation is thought out in advance. If the completion of your project includes providing user documentation, this issue needs to be addressed from the very beginning of the project. Determining what the user documentation requirements are and ascertaining who will complete the documents is critical to a timely release of the project. Neglecting user documentation issues until after all the program is complete often leads to one of two things: the documentation will be thrown together as quickly as possible just to get it out the door on time and it will more than likely be inadequate, or it will be done correctly and the product release will be delayed considerably.

User training typically is scheduled when the system is installed; the training sessions offer an ideal opportunity to distribute the user manual and explain the procedures for updating it in the future. Training for users, managers, and IT staff is described in Chapter 11.

MANAGEMENT APPROVAL

After system testing is complete, you present the results to management. You should describe the test results, update the status of all required documentation, and summarize input from users who participated in system testing. You also must provide detailed time schedules, cost estimates, and staffing requirements for making the system fully operational. If system testing produced no technical, economical, or operational problems, management determines a schedule for system installation and evaluation, which is discussed in Chapter 11.

SOFTWEAR, LIMITED

The ESIP development team of Jane Rossman, Tom Adams, and Becky Evans started work on the ESIP system, which they would develop as a Microsoft Access application in a client/server environment. Jane and Tom scheduled additional meetings with the consulting firm, True Blue Systems, while Becky started designing the main switchboard and the data input screens.

The ESIP system design included a server to interact with various SWL clients and an interface with the new payroll package from Pacific Software. The payroll package was implemented successfully on SWL's mainframe, and several payroll cycles were completed without any processing problems.

When the ESIP development team met on Monday morning, the members studied the overview that True Blue submitted, shown in Figure 10-28. Jane said they would use a top-down design approach. Their first step was to partition the system and break it down into a set of modules on a structure chart. Each module would represent a program or function to be performed by one or more macros or Visual Basic procedures.

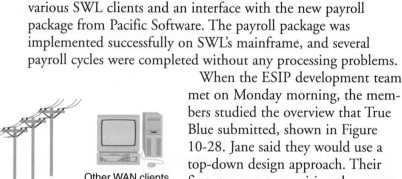

FIGURE 10-28 The ESIP system plan as submitted by True Blue Systems.

The team reviewed the documentation carefully, using the DFDs they prepared during the systems analysis phase. The team determined that the ESIP system needed to perform five main tasks: extract the ESIP deductions during payroll processing; apply the extracted deductions to specific ESIP options; update employee deduction selections; update ESIP option choices; and handle fund transfers to internal and external ESIP entities. To accomplish those tasks, the system would need a variety of reports, controls, query and display capabilities, input screens, security provisions, and other features.

Of the five main ESIP processes, only the extracting of payroll deductions would be done on SWL's mainframe. Jane said they would need to develop an interface program to control the extraction processing, but all the other functions would run on the ESIP server and clients. By afternoon, they had produced the draft structure chart shown in Figure 10-29.

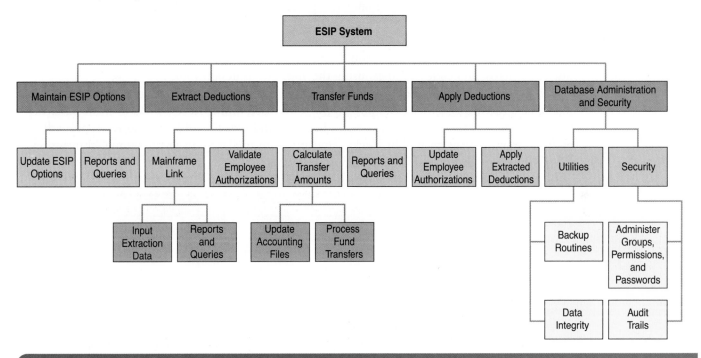

FIGURE 10-29 Draft of a structure chart for the ESIP system.

After studying the tasks and requirements, Jane estimated the time needed to design, code, unit test, and document each module. She also estimated time needed for integration and system testing, completing the ESIP system documentation, and receiving management approval. Jane used Microsoft Project software to create a Gantt chart, which is explained in the Systems Analyst's Toolkit, to manage and track the project and show the individual assignments. The chart indicated that many tasks could be performed concurrently and displayed the critical path. The development team agreed that they would meet daily to review their progress and discuss any problems.

Mainframe Interface

Jane's next step was to meet with Rick Williams, who was familiar with the new payroll package, to discuss the ESIP deduction extraction program that executes when the mainframe runs the weekly payroll. Jane learned that the new payroll package was developed as a database application and she could write the extract module in Visual Basic.

Working together, Jane and Becky prepared a design, wrote the commands, and unit tested the ESIP program modules with test files they created. They used stubs to indicate inputs and outputs to files with which the extraction program would interact. After verifying the results, Jane created a procedure for downloading the deduction file from the mainframe to the ESIP server in the payroll department. She tested the download procedure and updated the documentation.

ESIP Server

The team started developing the Access database application that would handle the other ESIP functions. The plan was for Becky to finish the basic switchboard and screen designs, then add features that users had requested, including custom menus and icons for frequently used functions. Becky also would design all the reports documented in the data dictionary.

Meanwhile, Jane and Tom worked on the other modules. Their first task was to examine the ERDs developed in the systems design phase to ensure that the entities and normalized record designs still were valid. Then they would start creating individual objects, including tables, queries, macros, and code modules, using the application design tools in Access.

Jane and Tom defined the data tables, identified primary keys, and linked the tables into a relational structure as shown in Figure 10-30. They used online Access Help to make sure they were using the correct field types, sizes, and names, and that the tables would work properly with the input screens created by Becky. Jane and Tom used an agreed-on naming convention for all objects to ensure consistency among the systems.

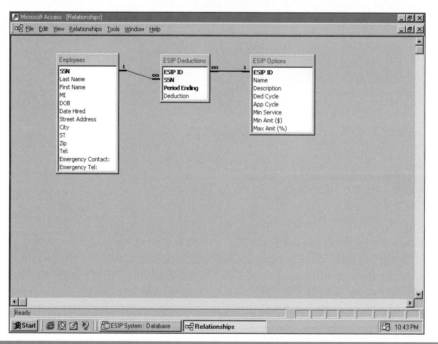

FIGURE 10-30 Relational structure for the ESIP system tables. Notice that the field or fields that comprise the primary key are shown in bold. Common fields link the tables, and referential integrity is indicated by the *1* (one) and ∞ (many) symbols.

After they designed and loaded the tables with test data, Jane and Tom developed queries that would allow users to retrieve, display, update, and delete records. Some queries affected only individual records, such as ESIP options, while they designed other queries for specific reports, such as the ESIP Deduction Register query shown in Figure 10-31, which displays deductions first in date order, then by employee SSN. This query produces SQL commands, also shown in Figure 10-29 on page 10.25 that will be transmitted to the ESIP server.

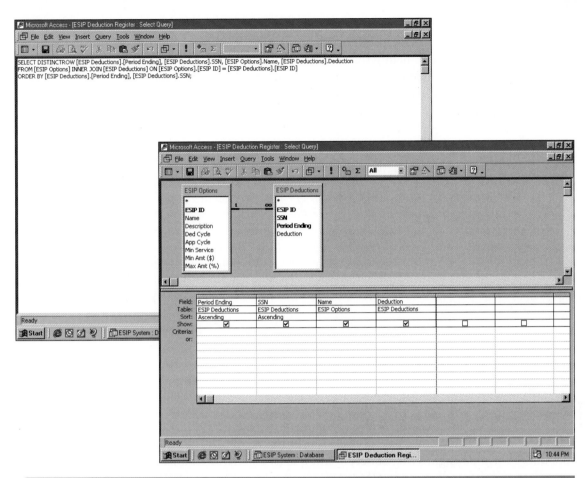

FIGURE 10-31 Example of a query that will provide data for the ESIP Deduction Register. Notice that the query sorts deductions by date, then by employee SSN. The query produces SQL commands that will be transmitted to the ESIP server.

Jane and Tom also developed macros that performed specific actions when certain events occurred. They tested each macro by stepping through it to make sure the commands executed properly. The macros later would be linked to various buttons and menus that Becky was designing into her switchboard and input screens. To save coding time, Tom converted several macros to Visual Basic in order to work on additional features and capabilities.

Jane and Tom also completed work on various security features, including password protection and several levels of permission required to view, modify, or delete specific objects. Later, when the system became operational, management would authorize specific permission levels, and Jane would designate a system administrator to maintain security and system policies.

Completing Application Development

In three weeks, the ESIP development team finished unit testing. Becky tested the switchboard, macros, queries, screen forms, menus, submenus, and code modules to ensure that they functioned correctly. Next, they linked the modules and performed integration testing. The testing ran smoothly and they encountered no significant problems.

After integration testing, the analysts asked several principal users to participate in system testing. During this process, some minor screen changes were suggested and implemented after checking with users who would be affected by those changes. In addition, it turned out that one of the reports did not include a federally required Employer Identification Number (EIN). Because the reports had been designed using the Access report generator, the development team easily implemented this change.

The team members prepared user documentation as they completed each task. To produce a clear, understandable user manual, they decided to ask Amy Calico, SWL's payroll director, to review their notes and help them write a draft for current and future users. They wanted to explain the system in nontechnical terms, with adequate illustrations, screen shots, and a set of frequently asked questions. Jane said that the entire manual could be put online after SWL's intranet was developed.

YOUR TURN

Although the systems testing at SWL resulted in no major problems, Rick asked you to help him develop a recommendation for future testing of this type. One of his concerns is that in systems testing, it is virtually impossible to simulate every system transaction and function. Specifically, Rick wants you to suggest some guidelines that will produce the most reliable test results.

He suggested that you should consider who should be involved in the testing, what types of transactions should be tested, and when the testing should be done. Based on what you already have learned about the ESIP system in prior chapters, what would you recommend? Write a brief memo to Rick with your suggestions.

CHAPTER SUMMARY

The systems implementation phase consists of application development, followed by installation and evaluation of the new system. During application development, analysts determine the overall design strategy and work with programmers to complete design, coding, testing, and documentation. Quality assurance is essential during the implementation phase. Many companies utilize software engineering concepts and quality standards established by the International Organization for Standardization (ISO).

During application development, large systems can be broken down into subsystems and modules that represent a particular transaction or process described in a DFD or object model. Programmers and systems analysts use structure charts, program flowcharts, and pseudocode to represent the program module logically.

A structure chart consists of symbols that represent program modules, data couples, control couples, conditions, and loops. A rectangle represents a program module, which consists of program code that accomplishes a specific function. An arrow with an empty circle represents a data couple, which shows data that one module passes to another. An arrow with a filled circle represents a control couple, which shows a message, also called a flag, which one module sends to another. A line with a diamond on one end represents a condition, which indicates a control module that determines which subordinate modules are invoked, depending on a specific condition. A curved arrow represents a loop, which indicates that one or more modules are repeated.

Cohesion measures a module's scope and processing characteristics. A module that performs a single function or task has a high degree of cohesion, which is desirable. Coupling measures relationships and interdependence among modules. Modules that are relatively independent are loosely coupled, which is desirable.

Typically, you follow four steps when you create a structure chart. You review DFDs and object models to identify the processes and methods, identify the program modules and determine control-subordinate relationships, add symbols for couples and loops, and analyze the structure chart to ensure that it is consistent with your system documentation.

Programmers perform desk checking, code review, and unit testing tasks during application development. Systems analysts design the initial test plans, which include test steps and test data for integration testing and system testing. Integration testing is necessary for programs that interact. The final step is system testing for the completed system. System testing includes users in the testing process.

In addition to system documentation, analysts also prepare operations documentation and user documentation. Operations documentation provides instructions and information to the IT operations group. User documentation consists of instructions and information for users who interact with the system and includes user manuals, Help screens, and tutorials.

The application development stage ends with a presentation to management. If management approves the results, the development team can begin system installation.

Key Terms

acceptance tests (*10.19*)
Capability Maturity Models (CMMs)® (*10.2*)
code review (*10.16*)
coding (*10.14*)
cohesion (*10.8*)
condition (*10.7*)
control couple (*10.7*)
control module (*10.6*)
coupling (*10.9*)
data couple (*10.7*)
design walkthrough (*10.17*)
desk checking (*10.16*)
documentation (*10.20*)
flag (*10.7*)
integration testing (*10.18*)
library module (*10.7*)
link testing (*10.18*)
logic errors (*10.16*)
loop (*10.8*)
loosely coupled (*10.9*)
modular design (*10.6*)

module (*10.6*)
operations documentation (*10.20*)
online documentation (*10.21*)
partitioning (*10.6*)
program documentation (*10.20*)
quality assurance (*10.2*)
software engineering (*10.2*)
Software Engineering Institute (SEI) (*10.2*)
structure chart (*10.6*)
structured walkthrough (*10.16*)
stub testing (*10.18*)
subordinate modules (*10.6*)
syntax errors (*10.16*)
system documentation (*10.20*)
system testing (*10.18*)
test plan (*10.18*)
tightly coupled (*10.9*)
top-down design (*10.6*)
unit testing (*10.17*)
user documentation (*10.21*)

Chapter Review

1. Where does systems implementation fit in the SDLC, and what tasks typically are performed during systems implementation?

2. Why is quality assurance an important part of application development?

3. Describe top-down design and modular design?

4. Describe structure charts and explain structure chart symbols.

5. Define cohesion and coupling.

6. List the steps in drawing a structure chart.

7. Describe program flowcharts and pseudocode.

8. Explain the coding process and give an example of how code can be generated by application packages.

9. Define unit testing, integration testing, and system testing.

10. What types of documentation does a systems analyst prepare, and what would be included in each type?

Discussion Topics

1. A supervisor states, "Integration testing is a waste of time. If each program is tested adequately and if program specifications are prepared properly, integration testing is not needed. Instead, we should move on to system testing as soon as possible. If modules don't interact properly, we'll handle it then." Do you agree or disagree with this comment? Justify your position.

2. Discuss the importance of documentation in application development. Why are the four types of documentation important regardless of the size of the project?

3. Programmers use a variety of methods to represent program logic. Which technique is best? Why?

4. Suppose you are a systems analyst developing a detailed test plan. Explain the testing strategies you will use in your plan. Will you use live or simulated data? Justify your decisions.

Apply Your Knowledge

1 ACE Consultants

Situation:

ACE Consultants is a small consulting firm with a history of designing application software for government agencies. ACE Consultants is currently engaged in developing high-level information systems for the military. The project team recently started application development of a new system. Programmers have completed several modules and have started unit testing the modules. You have been designated as the lead systems analyst to oversee testing for this project.

1. What steps would you take to develop a test plan for the project? *(10.16)*

2. Should you use real or simulated test data? Explain your decision.

3. Would you want the programmer who wrote the original code to perform integration and system testing? Why or why not? *(10.19)*

4. Your supervisor informs you that the project is behind schedule. What are your options? *(10.21)*

2 Fanciful Crystal, LTD

Situation:

Fanciful Crystal, LTD has produced fine crystal for over 10 years. The company once dominated the global market with their merchandise; however, the company's status has declined in the last few years. Last year Fanciful Crystal, LTD implemented a new Web-based ordering system to boost sagging sales. Unfortunately, the online system had start-up problems. Customers complained about order mix-ups and overcharges for deliveries. You are a new systems analyst with the company and your supervisor asked you to investigate the problems.

1. Based on what you know about e-commerce, how would you have tested a new Web-based system?

2. Should ISO standards have been considered? Why or why not?

3. What kind of documentation should this system have?

4. What would you advise that Fanciful Crystal, LTD do in the future to avoid similar problems in new systems development?

3 Sand and Surf Retailers

Situation:

Sand and Surf Retailers recently acquired several smaller companies to expand their chain of clothing outlets. To establish consistency for the current organization and future acquisitions, Sand and Surf decided to develop an in-house application called UPS (Universal Purchasing System). The UPS system would standardize purchasing practices for each Sand and Surf subsidiary and manage all purchasing information. System testing will be completed by the end of the week.

1. What types of documentation are needed for this application?

2. During application development, what steps should the IT staff follow to develop a structure chart?

3. What suggestions do you have for Help screens and online tutorials?

4. What types of testing should be performed? What types of test data should be used?

4 Albatross Airfreight

Situation:

Albatross Airfreight specializes in shipping cargo via air across North America. In an effort to modernize, the company has begun to computerize manual business processes. The new IT infrastructure includes a computer system that tracks cargo from departure point to destination. At this point, the new system is ready for implementation. Systems analysts are modularizing the system, and programmers are ready to start coding the first modules.

1. What issues should systems analysts and programmers discuss before they proceed with the project?

2. As a systems analyst on this project, how would you describe your primary responsibilities, and how could you contribute to the quality of the finished product?

3. As a programmer, how would you describe your primary responsibilities, and how could you contribute to the quality of the finished product?

4. Will the use of structure charts be beneficial during this stage of development? Discuss the advantages of structure charts compared with program flowcharts and pseudocode.

Chapter Assignments

1. In this chapter you learned about the importance of testing. Design a generic test plan that describes the testing for an imaginary system.

2. Perform research to find examples of Internet-based user support and documentation. Write a brief report with at least three examples.

3. Refer to the context diagram and diagram 3 DFD for the Order System shown in Chapter 4 on pages 4.7 and 4.8. Draw a sample structure chart that represents the program logic shown in the DFDs.

4. Use the Internet to research ISO standards generally. Are the standards important? Why? Do they affect businesses and customers? How?

CASE STUDIES

Case Studies offer an opportunity for you to practice specific skills and knowledge learned in the chapter and provide practical experience for you as a systems analyst. Two of the case studies (New Century Health Clinic and Ridgeway Company) are continuing case studies that appear in each chapter. Additionally, one continuing case study (SCR Associates) utilizes the Internet to practice some of the topics covered in this chapter.

NEW CENTURY HEALTH CLINIC

You completed the systems design for the insurance system at New Century Health Clinic. The associates at the clinic have approved your design specification, and you hired two programmers, Bill Miller and Celia Goldring, to assist you with the programming and testing of the insurance system.

Assignments

1. Design the testing required for the system. You should consider unit, integration, and system testing in your test plan and determine who should participate in the testing.

2. Design the test data that you will use. You should include data for all tests that will be performed on the system in all phases of testing.

3. Prepare a structure chart that shows the main program functions for the New Century system.

4. You have asked Anita Davenport, New Century's office manager, to contribute to the user manual for the insurance system. She suggested that you include a section of frequently asked questions (FAQs), which you also could include in the online documentation. Prepare 10 FAQs and answers for use in the printed user manual and context-sensitive Help screens.

RIDGEWAY COMPANY

The Ridgeway Company requirements were described in a Chapter 4 case study. The following assignments are based on the work you did for that case study.

Assignments

1. Design the testing required for the billing system. You should consider program, integration, and system testing in your test plan.

2. Design the test data for the billing system tests. You should include data for all tests that will be performed on the system in all phases of testing.

3. During systems testing, team members found several errors in the billing system report, including one subtotal field that calculated incorrectly. Thomas McGee wanted to proceed with system installation and correct this error later. As lead analyst on the project, what would be your recommended course of action? Why?

4. Design three sample context-sensitive online Help screens to assist a user who wants to add a new customer to the billing system.

SCR ASSOCIATES

SCR Associates is an information technology consulting firm that offers IT solutions and training for small- and medium-sized companies. SCR's slogan is "We Know IT!"

Background

As a newly hired systems analyst, you will handle assignments, work on various SCR projects, and apply the skills you learned in the text. SCR needs an information system to manage training operations at the new SCR training center. The new system will be called TIMS (Training Information Management System).

The SCR case is available as an interactive, Web-based case study. You can log on to the Shelly Cashman Series site at www.scsite.com/sad4e/scr for instructions and assignments. If you prefer to complete the case study without using the Internet then you must download the data disk. See the inside back cover for instructions for downloading the data disk or see your instructor for more information on accessing the files required for this book.

Situation

In Part 10 of the SCR case, you will work on application development for the new TIMS system. You will review background material, draw a structure chart, propose a testing plan, and consider documentation and ISO standards issues.

Before You Begin ...

1. Review the March 1 message from Jesse Baker regarding structure charts. Open the Document 10-1 from the data disk.

2. Review the March 4 message from Jesse Baker regarding application development tasks. Open the Document 10-2 from the data disk.

Assignments

1. Follow the suggestions in Jesse Baker's March 1 message, and create a structure chart as requested. The program modules should represent processes and object methods that were identified earlier. Modules should be cohesive and loosely coupled.

2. Develop a testing plan, as requested in Jesse Baker's March 4 message, and make sure that you include unit testing, integration testing, and system testing. Write up your suggestions in a memo to Jesse.

3. Draft a reminder to all IT staff members about the importance of careful documentation. Make sure to include all types of documentation referred to in this chapter.

4. Locate the ISO Web site and determine if general information about ISO standards is available. In addition, find out if you can purchase or download over the Internet specific information about ISO standards. Write a brief memo with the results of your efforts.

ON THE WEB

The SCR case is available as an interactive, Web-based case study. You can log on to the Shelly Cashman Series site at www.scsite.com/sad4e/scr for instructions and assignments.

PHASE 1 Systems Planning

PHASE 2 Systems Analysis

PHASE 3 Systems Design

PHASE 4 Systems Implementation

PHASE 5 Systems Operation & Support

Installation and Evaluation

Installation and evaluation is the second of two chapters in the systems implementation phase. Chapter 11 describes the actual installation of the information system and its initial evaluation by users.

INTRODUCTION

Chapter 11 describes the actual installation of the new system and the evaluation that follows. The tasks in this chapter complete the implementation phase of the SDLC and are performed for every information systems project, whether you develop the application in-house or purchase it as a commercial package. The end product of the systems implementation phase is a fully operational information system that meets design specifications and user requirements.

The new system now is ready to go to work. Your earlier design activities produced the overall architecture and processing strategy, and you consulted users at every stage of development. You developed and tested programs individually, in groups, and as a complete system. You prepared the necessary documentation and checked it for accuracy, including support material for IT staff and users. Now, you will carry out the remaining steps in systems implementation:

- Prepare an operational environment and install the new system

- Provide training for users, managers, and IT staff

- Perform data conversion and system changeover

- Carry out a post-implementation evaluation of the system

- Present a final report to management

OBJECTIVES

When you finish this chapter, you will be able to:

- Describe the main tasks in the installation and evaluation process

- Explain why it is important to maintain separate operational and test environments

- Develop an overall training plan with specific objectives for each group of participants

- Explain three typical ways to provide training, including vendors, outside resources, and in-house staff

- Describe online tutorials and other user training techniques

- Describe the data conversion process

- Identify four system changeover methods and discuss the advantages and disadvantages of each

- Explain the purpose of a post-implementation evaluation and list the specific topics covered during the evaluation

- Describe the contents of the final report to management

ON THE WEB

To learn more about
Operational and Test
Environments visit
scsite.com/sad4e/more.htm,
click Systems Analysis and
Design Chapter 11 and then
click the Operational and Test
Environments link.

www.scsite.com

OPERATIONAL AND TEST ENVIRONMENTS

In Chapter 9, you learned that an environment, or platform, is a specific combination of hardware and software. The environment for the actual system operation is called the **operational environment** or **production environment**. The environment that analysts and programmers use to develop and maintain programs is called the **test environment**. A separate test area is necessary to maintain system security and integrity and protect the operational environment. An effective testing process is essential, whether you are examining an information system or a batch of computer chips, as shown in Figure 11-1.

Access to the operational environment is limited to users and must be controlled strictly. Systems analysts and programmers should not have access to the operational environment except to correct a system problem or to make authorized modifications or enhancements. Otherwise, IT department members have no reason to access the day-to-day operational system.

The test environment for an information system contains copies of all programs, procedures, and test data files. Before making any changes to an operational system, you must verify them in the test environment and obtain user approval. Figure 11-2 shows the differences between test environments and operational environments.

Every experienced systems analyst can tell you a story about an apparently innocent program change that was introduced without being tested properly. In those stories, the innocent change invariably ends up causing some unexpected and unwanted changes to the program. After any modification, you should repeat the same acceptance tests you ran when the system was developed. By restricting access to the operational area and performing all tests in a separate environment, you can protect the system and avoid problems that could damage data or interrupt operations.

The operational environment includes hardware and software configurations and settings, system utilities, telecommunications resources, and any other components that might affect system performance. Because network capability is critically important in a client/server environment, you must verify connectivity, specifications, and performance before installing any applications. You should check all communications features in the test environment carefully, and then check them again after loading the applications into the operational environment. Your documentation should identify all network specifications and settings, including technical and operational requirements for communications hardware and software. If you have to build or upgrade network resources to support the new system, you must test the platform rigorously before system installation begins.

FIGURE 11-1 The basic concepts of testing are the same regardless of whether hardware or information systems are being evaluated. The objective is to verify that the product meets all specifications.

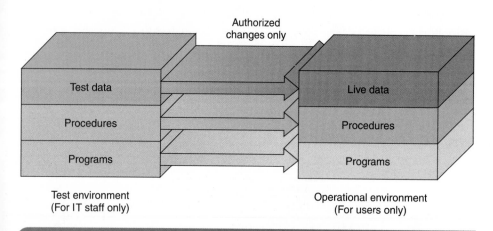

FIGURE 11-2 The test environment versus the operational environment. Notice that access to the test environment is limited to IT staff, while the operational environment is restricted to users.

TRAINING

No system can be successful without proper training, whether it involves software, hardware, or manufacturing, as shown in Figure 11-3. A successful information system requires training for users, managers, and IT staff members. The entire systems development effort can depend on whether or not people understand the system and know how to use it effectively.

ON THE WEB

For an overview of Training visit scsite.com/sad4e/more.htm, click Systems Analysis and Design Chapter 11 and then click the Training link.

www.scsite.c

FIGURE 11-3 In any situation, training must fit the needs of users and help them carry out their job functions.

Training Plan

You should start to consider a **training plan** early in the systems development process. As you create documentation, you should think about how to use the material in future training sessions. When you implement the system, it is essential to provide the right training for the right people at the right time. The first step is to identify who should receive training and what training is needed. You must look carefully at the organization, how the system will support business operations, and who will be involved or affected. Figure 11-4 shows specific training topics for users, managers, and IT staff. Notice that each group needs a mix of general background and detailed information to understand and use the system.

USERS
System overview
Key terms
Start-up and shut down
Main menu and submenus
Icons and shortcut keys
Major system functions
Online and external Help
Frequently asked questions
Troubleshooting guide
Handling emergencies

MANAGERS
Project origin
Cost-benefit analysis
Support for business goals
Key IT contact people
Handling system charges
Major reports and displays
Requesting enhancements
User training

TRAINING

Project history and justification
System architecture
System documentation
Typical user questions
Vendor support
Logging and resolving problems
Technical training for IT staff
User and management training

IT STAFF

FIGURE 11-4 Examples of training topics for three different groups. Users, managers, and IT staff members have different training needs.

As shown in Figure 11-4 on the previous page, the three main groups for training are users, managers, and IT staff. A manager does not need to understand every submenu or feature, but he or she does need a system overview to ensure that users are being trained properly and are using the system correctly. Similarly, users need to know how to perform their day-to-day job functions, but do not need to know how the company allocates system operational charges among user departments. IT staff people probably need the most information. To support the new system, they must have a clear understanding of how the system functions, how it supports business requirements, and the skills that users need to operate the system and perform their tasks.

After you identify the objectives, you must determine how the company will provide training. The main choices are to obtain training from vendors, outside training firms, or use IT staff and other in-house resources.

Vendor Training

If the system includes the purchase of software or hardware, then vendor-supplied training is one of the features you should investigate or request in the RFPs (requests for proposal), RFQs (requests for quotation), or RFIs (requests for information) that you send to potential vendors.

Many hardware and software vendors offer training programs free or at a nominal cost for the products they sell. In other cases, the company might negotiate the price for training, depending on their relationship with the vendor and the prospect of future purchases. The training usually is conducted at the vendor's site by experienced trainers who provide valuable hands-on experience. If a large number of people need training, you might be able to arrange classes at your location.

Vendor training, as shown in Figure 11-5, often gives the best return on your training dollars because it is focused on products that the vendor developed. The scope of vendor training, however, usually is limited to a standard version of the vendor's software or hardware. You might have to supplement the training in-house, especially if your IT staff customized the package.

Outside Training Resources

You also can look into an independent training firm to provide in-house hardware or software training. If vendor training is not practical and your organization does not have the internal resources to perform the training, you might find that outside training consultants are a desirable alternative.

N THE WEB

r more information
bout Outside Training
esources visit
csite.com/sad4e/more.htm,
ick Systems Analysis and
esign Chapter 11 and then
ck the Outside Training
esources link.

w.scsite.com

FIGURE 11-5   Users must be trained on the new system. Training sessions might be one-on-one or group situations such as the one shown here. Many vendors provide product training as part of an overall service to customers.

The rapid expansion of information technology has produced tremendous growth in the computer-training field. Many training consultants, institutes, and firms are available that provide either standardized or customized training packages. IT industry leaders such as Hewlett Packard and IBM offer a wide variety of training solutions, as shown in Figure 11-6.

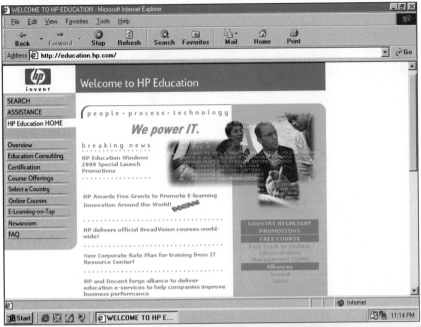

FIGURE 11-6 IT industry leaders such as Hewlett Packard and IBM offer a wide variety of training solutions.

If you decide to investigate outside training resources, you can contact a training provider and obtain references from clients. You also can seek assistance from nonprofit sources with an interest in training, including universities, industry associations, and information management organizations. For example, Figure 11-7 shows the Web site for the **Center for the Application of Information Technology (CAIT)** that describes a variety of information technology (IT) education and training resources.

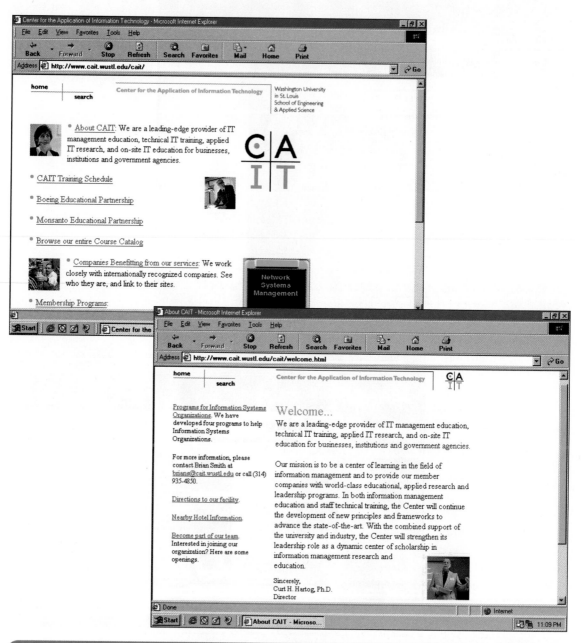

FIGURE 11-7   The Center for the Application of Information Technology (CAIT) uses its Web site to present information technology education and training and describes the organization's mission.

In-House Training

The IT staff and user departments often share responsibility for developing and conducting training programs for internally developed software. If your organization has a help desk, the staff might be able to handle user training.

Multimedia is an effective training method. Presentation software such as Microsoft PowerPoint or Corel Presentations allows you to design training sessions that combine slides, animation, and sound. You also can use programs that capture actual keystrokes and mouse actions, and then replay the screens as a demonstration for users. If your firm has a media or graphic arts group, they can help you prepare training aids such as videotapes, charts, and other instructional materials. When developing a training program, you should keep the following guidelines in mind.

Train people in groups, with separate training programs for distinct groups. Group training makes the most efficient use of time and training facilities. In addition, if the group is small, trainees can learn from the questions and problems of others. A training program must address the job interests and skills of a wide range of participants. For example, IT staff personnel and users require very different information. Problems often arise when some participants have technical backgrounds and others do not. A single program will not meet everyone's needs.

Select the most effective place to conduct the training. Training employees at your company's location offers several advantages. Employees incur no travel expense, they can respond to local emergencies that require immediate attention, and training can take place in the actual environment where the system will operate. You can encounter some disadvantages, however. Employees who are distracted by telephone calls and other duties will not get the full benefit of the training. In addition, using the organization's computer facilities for training can disrupt normal operations and limit the amount of actual hands-on training.

Provide for learning by hearing, seeing, and doing. Some people learn best from lectures, discussions, and question-and-answer sessions. Others learn best from viewing demonstrations or from reading documentation and other material. Most people learn best from hands-on experience. You should provide training that supports each type of learning.

Prepare effective training materials, including interactive tutorials. User-friendly training materials contribute to training effectiveness and provide a valuable resource for users. You can prepare the material in various forms, including traditional training manuals, printed handouts, or online material. The main goal is to deliver user-friendly, cost-effective training. Regardless of the instructional method, the training lessons should include step-by-step instructions for using all the features of the information system.

Most people learn best when they participate actively in the training process. A **tutorial** is a series of online interactive lessons that present material and provide a dialog with users. Figure 11-8 on page 11.8 shows a sample tutorial lesson for a sales prospect management system. In Lesson 1, the user learns how to enter and exit the system. In Lesson 2, as shown in Figure 11-9 on page 11.9, the user learns how to add a sales prospect and return to the main menu.

A training package also should include a reference section that summarizes all options and commands, and a listing of all error messages and what action the user should take when a problem occurs. More sophisticated tutorials might offer interactive sessions where users practice various tasks and get feedback on their progress. Even if you lack the resources to develop interactive tutorials, you can design a series of dialog boxes that respond with Help information and suggestions when users select various menu topics.

Rely on previous trainees. After one group of users has been trained, they can assist others. Users often learn more quickly from coworkers who share common experience and job responsibilities. Using a **train-the-trainer** strategy, you can select knowledgeable users who then conduct sessions for others. When utilizing train-the-trainer techniques, the initial training must include not only the use of the application or system but some instruction on how to present the materials effectively.

When training is complete, many organizations conduct a full-scale test, or **simulation**, which is a dress rehearsal for users and IT support staff. Organizations include all procedures, such as those that they execute only at the end of a month, quarter, or year, in the simulation. As questions or problems arise, the participants consult the system documentation, Help screens, or each other to determine appropriate answers or actions. This full-scale test provides valuable experience and builds confidence for everyone involved with the new system.

Sales Prospect Management System
Lesson 1: Entering and Exiting the System

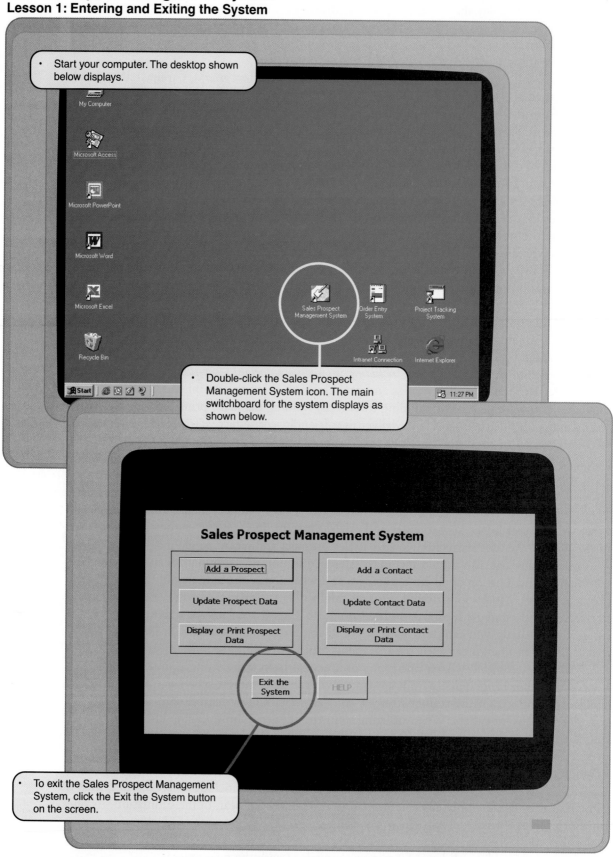

FIGURE 11-8 A sample tutorial for a sales prospect management system. In the first lesson, the user learns how to enter and exit the system.

Sales Prospect Management System
Lesson 2: Adding a Sales Prospect

- Start your computer and enter the Sales Prospect Management System as explained in Lesson 1. Click the Add a Prospect button on the main switchboard. The blank form shown below displays.

Add a Sales Prospect

First Name		Prospect ID	
Last Name		Title	
Company		Work Phone	
Dear		Work Extension	
Address		Fax Number	
City			
State/Province			
Postal Code			
Country			
Email Address			
Referred By			
Notes			

Dial Phone Number
Contact Via E-mail
Generate Memo
Add Another Prospect
Return to Main Menu
HELP

- Enter the data into the fields as shown on the screen below. The system will add the Prospect ID automatically. Press the Enter key to move to the next field.

Add a Sales Prospect

First Name	Samuel	Prospect ID	10343
Last Name	Rose	Title	Tech Support Manager
Company	Last Resort Systems, Inc.	Work Phone	(555) 123-4567
Dear	Sam	Work Extension	2219
Address	1303 Van Buren Drive	Fax Number	(555) 123-9999
City	Annapolis		
State/Province	MD		
Postal Code	21403-9999		
Country	US		
Email Address	sam_rose@lrs.com		
Referred By	Emma Nell		
Notes	Sam's company might be merging with SuperSystems. This would be a great time to get our foot in the door.		

Dial Phone Number
Contact Via E-mail
Generate Memo
Add Another Prospect
Return to Main Menu
HELP

- When you have entered all the data, compare your screen to the one shown above. If it matches, you have entered a sales prospect successfully. Click the Return to Main Menu button. You now are ready for Lesson 3, Updating Prospect Data.

FIGURE 11-9 A second sample lesson in the online tutorial.

W H A T   D O   Y O U   T H I N K ?

As IT manager at a 300-person manufacturing firm, you are responsible for training employees on the new production management system that will become operational in 60 days. Based on input from production workers, the new system will schedule the work and submit orders for the necessary material. Some employees are computer-literate, but most have never used a business information system. What kind of training methods and materials would you suggest, and why?

ON THE WEB

To learn more about Data Conversion visit scsite.com/sad4e/more.htm, click Systems Analysis and Design Chapter 11 and then click the Data Conversion link.

www.scsite.com

DATA CONVERSION

Data conversion is an important part of the system installation process. During **data conversion**, existing data is loaded into the new system. Depending on the system, data conversion can be done before, during, or after the operational environment is complete. You should develop a data conversion plan as early as possible, and the conversion process should be tested when the test environment is developed.

When a new system replaces an existing system, you should automate the data conversion process, if possible. The old system might be capable of **exporting** data in an acceptable format for the new system or in a standard format, such as ASCII or ODBC. ODBC (Open Database Connectivity) is an industry-standard protocol that allows DBMSs from various vendors to interact and exchange data. Most database vendors provide ODBC drivers, which are a form of middleware. As you learned in Chapter 9, middleware connects dissimilar applications and enables them to communicate.

If a standard format is not available, you must develop a program to extract the data and convert it to an acceptable format. Data conversion is more difficult when the new system replaces a manual system because all data must be entered manually, unless it can be scanned. Even when you can automate data conversion, a new system often requires additional data items, which might require manual entry.

You should maintain strict input controls during the conversion process, when data is extremely vulnerable. You must ensure that all system control measures are in place and operational to protect data from unauthorized access and to help prevent erroneous input.

Even with careful data conversion and input controls, some errors will occur. Most organizations require that users verify all data, correct all errors, and supply every missing data item during conversion. Although automated methods can make data conversion easier, the process can be time-consuming and expensive.

SYSTEM CHANGEOVER

ON THE WEB

For an overview of Changeover Methods visit scsite.com/sad4e/more.htm click Systems Analysis and Design Chapter 11 and then click the Changeover Methods link.

www.scsite.c

System changeover is the process of putting the new information system online and retiring the old system. Changeover can be rapid or slow, depending on the method. The four changeover methods are direct cutover, parallel operation, pilot operation, and phased operation.

Direct cutover is similar to throwing a switch that instantly changes over from the old system to the new. Parallel operation requires that both systems run simultaneously for a specified period, resulting in the slowest method. The other methods, phased and pilot operation, fall somewhere between direct cutover and parallel operation. Figure 11-10 illustrates the four system changeover methods.

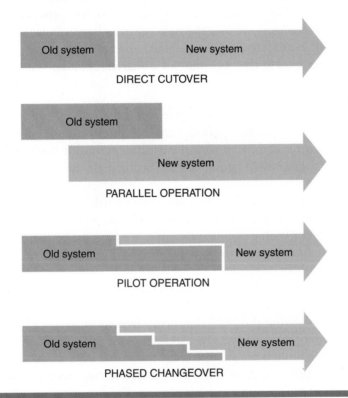

FIGURE 11-10 The four system changeover methods.

Direct Cutover

The **direct cutover** approach causes the changeover from the old system to the new system to occur immediately when the new system becomes operational. Direct cutover usually is the least expensive changeover method because the IT group has to operate and maintain only one system at a time.

Direct cutover, however, involves more risk than other changeover methods. Regardless of how thoroughly and carefully you conduct testing and training, some difficulties can arise when the system goes into operation. Problems can result from data situations that were not tested or anticipated or from errors caused by users or operators. A system also can encounter difficulties because live data typically occurs in much larger volumes than test data.

Although initial implementation problems are a concern with all four changeover methods, they are most significant when the direct cutover approach is used. Detecting minor errors also is more difficult with direct cutover because users cannot verify current output by comparing it to output from the old system. Major errors can cause a system process to terminate abnormally, and with the direct cutover method, you cannot revert to the old system as a backup option.

Companies often choose the direct cutover method for implementing commercial software packages because those packages involve less risk of total system failure. For systems developed in-house, most organizations use direct cutover only for noncritical situations. Direct cutover might be the only choice, however, if the operating environment cannot support both the old and new systems or if the old and new systems are incompatible.

Timing is very important when using a direct cutover strategy. Most systems operate on weekly, monthly, quarterly, and yearly cycles. For example, consider a payroll system that produces output on a weekly basis. Some employees are paid twice a month, however, so the system also operates semimonthly. Monthly, quarterly, and annual reports also require the system to produce output at the end of every month, quarter, and year. When a cyclical information system is implemented in the middle of any cycle, complete processing for the full cycle requires information from both the old and the new systems. To minimize the need to require information from two different systems, cyclical information systems usually are converted using the direct cutover method at the beginning of a quarter, calendar year, or fiscal year.

Parallel Operation

The **parallel operation** changeover method requires that both the old and the new information systems operate fully for a specified period. Data is input into both systems, and output generated by the new system is compared with the equivalent output from the old system. When users, management, and the IT group are satisfied that the new system operates correctly, the old system is terminated.

The most obvious advantage of parallel operation is lower risk. If the new system does not work correctly, the company can use the old system as a backup until appropriate changes are made. It is much easier to verify that the new system is working properly under parallel operation than under direct cutover, because the output from both systems is compared and verified during parallel operation.

Parallel operation, however, does have some disadvantages. First, it is the most costly changeover method. Because both the old and the new systems are in full operation, the company pays for both systems during the parallel period. Users must work in both systems and the company might need temporary employees to handle the extra workload. In addition, running both systems might place a burden on the operating environment and cause processing delays.

Parallel operation is not practical if the old and new systems are incompatible technically, or if the operating environment cannot support both systems. Parallel operation also is inappropriate when the two systems perform different functions or if the new system involves a new method of business operations. For example, until a company installs new data scanners in a factory, it is impractical to launch a new production tracking system that requires that technology.

Pilot Operation

The **pilot operation** changeover method involves implementing the complete new system at a selected location of the company. A new sales reporting system, for instance, might be implemented only in one branch office, or a new payroll system might be installed only in one department. In these examples, the group that uses the new system first is called the **pilot site**. During pilot operation, the old system continues to operate for the entire organization, including the pilot site. After the system proves successful at the pilot site, it is implemented in the rest of the organization, usually using the direct cutover method. Therefore, pilot operation is a kind of semiparallel operation that combines the parallel operation and direct cutover methods.

Restricting the implementation to a pilot site reduces the risk of system failure, compared with a direct cutover method. Operating both systems for only the pilot site is less expensive than a parallel operation for the entire company. In addition, if you later use a parallel approach to complete the implementation, the changeover period can be much shorter if the system proves successful at the pilot site.

Phased Operation

The **phased operation** method allows you to implement the new system in stages, or modules. For example, instead of implementing a new manufacturing system all at once, you might first install the materials management subsystem, then the production control subsystem, then the job cost subsystem, and so on. You can implement each subsystem by using any of the other three changeover methods.

Analysts sometimes confuse phased and pilot operation methods. Both methods combine direct cutover and parallel operation to reduce risk and costs. With phased operation, however, you give a part of the system to all users, while pilot operation provides the entire system, but only to some users.

One advantage of a phased approach is that the risk of errors or failures is limited to the implemented module only. For instance, if a new production control subsystem fails to operate properly, that failure might not affect the new purchasing subsystem or the existing shop floor control subsystem.

Phased operation is less expensive than full parallel operation because you have to work with only one part of the system at a time. A phased approach is not possible, however, if the system cannot be separated easily into logical modules or segments. In addition, if the system involves a large number of separate phases, phased operation can cost more than a pilot approach.

Figure 11-11 shows that each changeover method has risk and cost factors. As a systems analyst, you must weigh the advantages and disadvantages of each method and recommend the best choice in a given situation. The final changeover decision will be based on input from the IT staff, users, and management.

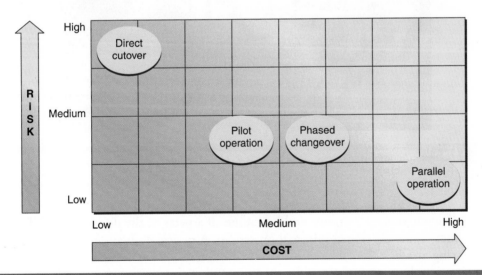

FIGURE 11-11 Relative risk and cost characteristics of the four changeover methods.

ON THE WEB

To learn more about Post-implementation Evaluation visit scsite.com/sad4e/more.htm, click Systems Analysis and Design Chapter 11 and then click the Post-Implementation Evaluation link.

www.scsite.com

POST-IMPLEMENTATION TASKS

Once the new system is operational, you must perform two additional tasks: prepare a post-implementation evaluation and deliver a final report to management.

Post-implementation Evaluation

A **post-implementation evaluation**, as shown in Figure 11-12, assesses the overall quality of the information system. The evaluation verifies that the new system meets specified requirements, complies with user objectives, and achieves the anticipated benefits. In addition, by providing feedback to the development team, the evaluation also helps improve IT development practices for future projects.

FIGURE 11-12 An important function of the post-implementation phase is an evaluation. This task requires one-to-one communication with users so the IT staff can learn as much as possible about the strengths and possible weaknesses of the new system.

A post-implementation evaluation should examine all aspects of the development effort and the end product — the developed information system. A typical evaluation includes feedback for the following areas:

- Accuracy, completeness, and timeliness of information system output
- User satisfaction
- System reliability and maintainability
- Adequacy of system controls and security measures
- Hardware efficiency and platform performance
- Effectiveness of database implementation
- Performance of the IT team
- Completeness and quality of documentation
- Quality and effectiveness of training
- Accuracy of cost-benefit estimates and development schedules

You can apply the same fact-finding techniques in a post-implementation evaluation that you used to determine the system requirements during the systems analysis phase. When evaluating a system, you should:

- Interview members of management and key users.

- Observe users and computer operations personnel actually working with the new information system.

- Read all documentation and training materials.

- Examine all source documents, output reports, and screen displays.

- Use questionnaires to gather information and opinions from a large number of users.

- Analyze maintenance and help desk logs.

Figure 11-13 shows the first page of a sample user evaluation form for the new information system where users evaluate 18 separate elements on a numerical scale, so the results can be tabulated easily. Following that section, the form provides space for open-ended comments and suggestions.

1 of 2

USER EVALUATION FORM

System: Evaluator: Date:

Please evaluate the information system project by circling the one number for each factor that best represents your assessment.

	Unsatisfactory		Acceptable		Excellent

SYSTEM OUTPUT

1. Accuracy of information	1	2	3	4	5	6
2. Completeness of information	1	2	3	4	5	6
3. Ease of use	1	2	3	4	5	6
4. Timeliness of information	1	2	3	4	5	6

USER INTERFACE

5. Clarity of instructions	1	2	3	4	5	6
6. Quality of Help messages	1	2	3	4	5	6
7. Ease of use	1	2	3	4	5	6
8. Appropriateness of options	1	2	3	4	5	6
9. Clarity of error messages	1	2	3	4	5	6
10. Prevention of input errors	1	2	3	4	5	6

INFORMATION TECHNOLOGY STAFF

11. Cooperation	1	2	3	4	5	6
12. Availability	1	2	3	4	5	6
13. Knowledge	1	2	3	4	5	6
14. Reporting of progress	1	2	3	4	5	6
15. Communication skills	1	2	3	4	5	6

TRAINING

16. Completeness	1	2	3	4	5	6
17. Appropriateness	1	2	3	4	5	6
18. Schedule	1	2	3	4	5	6

FIGURE 11-13 Sample user evaluation form. The numerical scale allows easy tabulation of results. Following this section, the form provides space for open-ended comments and suggestions.

Whenever possible, people who were not directly involved in developing the system should conduct the post-implementation evaluation. IT staff and users usually perform the evaluation, although some firms use an internal audit group or independent auditors to ensure the accuracy and completeness of the evaluation.

When should post-implementation evaluation occur? Is it better to wait until the new system has been in operation for one month, six months, one year, or longer? Users can forget details of the developmental effort if too much time elapses before the evaluation. After several months or a year, for instance, users might not remember whether they learned a procedure through training, from user documentation, or by experimenting with the system on their own.

Users also might forget their impressions of IT team members over time. An important purpose of the post-implementation evaluation is to improve the quality of IT department functions, including interaction with users, training, and documentation. Consequently, the evaluation team should perform the assessment while users are able to recall specific incidents, successes, and problems so they can offer suggestions for improvement. Post-implementation evaluation primarily is concerned with assessing the quality of the new system. If the team performs the evaluation too soon after implementation, users will not have enough time to learn the new system and appreciate its strengths and weaknesses. Although many IT professionals recommend conducting the evaluation after at least six months of system operation, pressure to finish the project sooner usually results in an earlier evaluation in order to allow the IT department to move on to other tasks.

Ideally, conducting a post-implementation evaluation should be standard practice for all information systems projects. Sometimes, evaluations are skipped because users are eager to work with the new system, or because IT staff members have bigger priorities. In some organizations, management might not recognize the importance and benefits of a post-implementation evaluation. The evaluations are extremely important, however, because they enable the development team and the IT department to learn what worked and what did not work. Otherwise, developers might commit the same errors in another system.

W H A T   D O   Y O U   T H I N K ?

Cindy Winslow liked her new job as lead systems analyst at Yorktown Industries. She was pleased that her development team completed the new human resources system ahead of schedule and under budget. Cindy looked forward to receiving the post-implementation evaluation because she was confident that both the system and the development team would receive high marks from users and managers.

After the system operated for one month, Cindy received a call from her supervisor, Ted Haines. Ted told her that she would have to handle the evaluation, even though she headed the development effort. Cindy told Ted that she did not feel comfortable evaluating her own team's work. She explained that someone who was not involved in its development should do an independent evaluation. Ted responded that he had full confidence in Cindy's ability to be objective. He explained that no one else was available and he needed the evaluation quickly so he could move forward with the next stage in the corporate development plan.

Cindy was troubled about the situation and she called you, a professional acquaintance, for your advice. What would you tell her and why?

FINAL REPORT TO MANAGEMENT

At the end of each SDLC phase, you produce a **final report to management**, and the systems implementation phase is no exception. Your report should include the following:

- Final versions of all system documentation.
- Planned modifications and enhancements to the system that have been identified.
- A recap of all systems development costs and schedules.
- A comparison of actual costs and schedules to the original estimates.
- The post-implementation evaluation, if it has been performed.

The final report to management marks the end of systems development work. In the next chapter, you will study the role of a systems analyst during systems operation and support, which is the final phase of the SDLC.

SOFTWEAR, LIMITED

After a successful period of parallel processing, SWL fully implemented the payroll package purchased from Pacific Software and was ready to start installation of the ESIP system.

In preparation, the IT development team of Jane Rossman, Tom Adams, and Becky Evans confirmed that SWL's existing network could handle the additional traffic generated by the new system. True Blue Systems, the outside consulting firm, noted in its report that the network might need to be upgraded in the future, especially if SWL expanded the number of networked applications and users.

Tom's first task was to install the ESIP application on the server in the payroll department, and to verify that the system could communicate properly with SWL's mainframe. Then he installed and tested a new high-speed tape cartridge backup system for the ESIP system.

Next, Tom loaded the ESIP application on a client PC in the human resources department. He checked all hardware and system software settings and used several test files to ensure that the client communicated with the ESIP server in the payroll department.

Meanwhile, Becky Evans and Rick Williams worked together on the interface between the ESIP system and the mainframe. They previously created a module called an extract program that directed the mainframe payroll system to capture the ESIP payroll deductions, store them in a file, and transmit the file back to the ESIP system. They already tested the interface using stubs to represent actual input and output files. Next, they would use a test data file with examples of every possible combination of permissible deductions, and several improper deductions that testing should detect.

As soon as Rick confirmed that the payroll package was ready for the interface test, Tom set up the ESIP server and sent the test file to the mainframe. Then he ran the module that sent processing commands to the payroll system. Everyone was pleased to see that the mainframe handled the test data properly and generated an extracted deduction file, which it downloaded to the ESIP server.

Becky and Rick were ready to conduct hands-on training with the payroll group, so they arranged an early morning session with Amy Calico, Nelson White, Britton Ellis, and Debra Williams. Becky walked them through the steps, which were described clearly in the user manual and then answered several questions. The payroll employees seemed pleased with the explanation and commented on how much easier the new system would be for them to use.

Next, Becky went to see Mike Feiner, director of human resources. Mike would be the only person allowed to add, change, or delete any of the ESIP options. Based on written authorization from Tina Pham, vice president of human resources, Mike would have a special password and permission level to allow him to perform those actions. Becky described to Mike how the system worked and then showed him how to enter, modify, and delete a test option she prepared. For security reasons, the special documentation for those functions would not be printed in the user manual itself, but would be retained in the IT department files.

Becky and Tom met again with the payroll group to show users how to enter the deduction authorizations for individual employees. Although the new payroll system was operational, the company still handled ESIP deductions manually. Using the ESIP server and another networked payroll PC, the payroll clerks were able to enter actual payroll data during a three-day test period. The built-in edit and validation features detected the errors that the team purposely inserted as test data and even identified several invalid authorizations that they had not noticed previously. The group produced printed reports and asked other payroll department members to review and verify the output.

Jane Rossman had a last minute idea: perhaps they should send a notice to all SWL employees describing the new ESIP system. The flyer also could remind employees how to select options and invite their questions or comments. Michael Jeremy, vice president of finance, thought that Jane's idea was excellent.

Up to that point, the company had made no final decision about the changeover method for the new system. Because the ESIP system replaced a series of manual processing steps, the main question was: Should they run the manual system in parallel operation for a specified period? Managers in the payroll, human resources, and accounting departments all wanted the new system operational as soon as possible and everyone agreed that a direct cutover was the best method and should take place on Friday, May 3, 2002, when the first weekly payroll in May was processed.

Starting on Monday, April 29, the IT team met again with each of the users and reviewed a final checklist. No problems appeared and the system was ready to interface with the mainframe and handle live data in an operational environment. On Friday morning, May 3, the payroll department ran the ESIP module that sent the processing commands to the payroll system. Later that morning, during the weekly processing cycle, the payroll package created a file with the extracted deductions and passed it back to the ESIP server.

With the ESIP system using real input data, IT department members visited each of the recently trained users to make sure they were experiencing no difficulties. They received good reports — users in the payroll and human resources departments seemed pleased with the new system. They were able to access the ESIP data, enter new deductions, and had no problems with screen output or printed reports.

The direct cutover to the ESIP system occurred without major problems. By the end of June, 2002, the system had completed nine weekly payroll cycles, produced all required reports and outputs, and properly handled the monthly transfer of funds to the credit union and the SWL stock purchase plan.

During the first part of July, the IT department conducted a post-implementation evaluation with a team that consisted of two people: Katie Barnes, a systems analyst who had not been involved in the ESIP system development and Ben Mancuso, a member of the finance department designated by Michael Jeremy. The evaluation team reviewed system operations, conducted interviews, and asked users to complete a brief questionnaire. The results were favorable, and it appeared that users were very satisfied with the new ESIP system. When the evaluation was completed in mid-July, Ann Hon sent the email message shown in Figure 11-14 to Michael Jeremy. The systems development effort for the ESIP system was completed successfully.

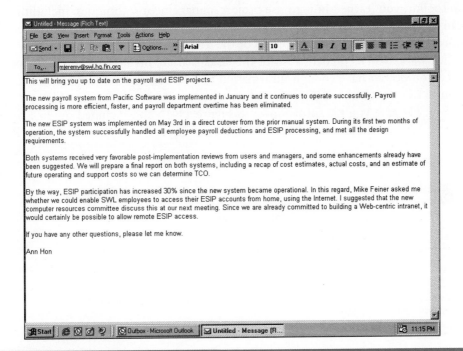

FIGURE 11-14 E-mail message from Ann Hon to Michael Jeremy regarding the payroll and ESIP systems.

YOUR TURN

During the systems analysis phase, you learned how to use fact-gathering techniques to determine system requirements. Before completing this assignment, you should review the material on interviews and questionnaires in Chapter 3.

Suppose you are selected as a member of the post-implementation evaluation team at SWL, with two specific assignments: you must prepare a list of interview questions for users and design a brief questionnaire that measures the effectiveness of the new system. Develop the interview questions and questionnaire by following the guidelines suggested in this chapter and in the Systems Analyst's Toolkit.

In the Systems Analyst's Toolkit, you learned how to use project management techniques, including PERT/CPM charts, to plan a project and make sure it stays on schedule. Before completing this assignment, you should review the project management section in part 3 of the Toolkit.

To practice your skills, Rick wants you to prepare a list of the tasks that are involved in this phase of the project. He understands that you do not have enough information to make an accurate estimate of the task durations, but he wants you to use your best judgment based on what you know about the ESIP system and the capabilities of the IT team. He gave you the form shown in Figure 11-15 and included the first four tasks as examples to get you started. You should examine the SWL case carefully and complete the list for Rick.

ESIP System: Systems Installation and Evaluation Tasks			
Task	Description	IT people assigned	Duration in hours
1	Install the ESIP application on the server	Tom	3
2	Verify that the ESIP server can communicate properly with the mainframe	Tom	1
3.	Install and test tape backup system	Tom	4
4	Load the ESIP application on the client PCs in the payroll and human resources departments	Tom	4
5	...	...	...

FIGURE 11-15   Systems installation and evaluation tasks for the ESIP system.

CHAPTER SUMMARY

During installation and evaluation, you establish an operational, or production, environment for the new information system that is completely separate from the test environment.

The operational environment contains live data and is accessible only by authorized users. Once the operational environment is established, members of the IT department can access that environment only to apply authorized corrections, modifications, and enhancements. The test environment, which the project team created to develop and test the new system, continues to exist after the operational environment is established. All future changes to the system must be verified in the test environment before any changes are applied to the operational environment.

Everyone who interacts with the new information system should receive training appropriate to his or her role and skills. The IT department usually is responsible for training. Software or hardware vendors or professional training organizations also can provide training.

When you develop a training program, remember the following guidelines: train people in groups; utilize people already trained to help train others; develop separate programs for distinct employee groups; and provide for learning by using discussions, demonstrations, documentation, training manuals, and interactive tutorials.

Data conversion often is necessary when installing a new information system. When a new system replaces a computerized system, you should automate the data conversion process if possible. The old system might be capable of exporting data in a format that the new system can use, or you might have to extract the data and convert it to an acceptable format. Data conversion from a manual system often requires labor-intensive data entry or scanning. Even when data conversion can be automated, a new system often requires additional data items, which might require manual entry. Strict input controls are important during the conversion process to protect data integrity and quality. Typically, data is verified, corrected, and updated during the conversion process.

System changeover is the process of putting the new system into operation. Four changeover methods exist: direct cutover, parallel operation, pilot operation, and phased operation.

With direct cutover, the old system stops and the new system starts simultaneously; direct cutover is the least expensive, but the most risky changeover method. With parallel operation, users operate both the old and new information systems for some period of time; parallel operation is the most expensive and least risky of the changeover methods. Pilot operation and phased operation represent compromises between direct cutover and parallel operation; both methods are less risky than direct cutover and less costly than parallel operation. With pilot operation, a specified group within the organization uses the new system for a period of time, while the old system continues to operate for the rest of the users. After the system proves successful at the pilot site, it is implemented throughout the organization. With phased operation, you implement the system in the entire organization, but only one module at a time, until the entire system is operational.

A post-implementation evaluation assesses and reports on the quality of the new system and the work done by the project team. Although it is best if people who were not involved in the systems development effort perform the evaluation, that is not always possible. The evaluation should be conducted early so users have a fresh recollection of the development effort, but not before users have experience using the new system.

The final report to management includes the final system documentation, describes any future system enhancements that already have been identified, and details the project costs. The report represents the end of the development effort and the beginning of the new system's operational life.

Key Terms

Center for the Application of Information Technology (CAIT) (*11.6*)	pilot site (*11.12*)
data conversion (*11.10*)	post-implementation evaluation (*11.14*)
direct cutover (*11.11*)	production environment (*11.2*)
exporting (*11.10*)	simulation (*11.7*)
final report to management (*11.17*)	system changeover (*11.11*)
operational environment (*11.2*)	test environment (*11.2*)
parallel operation (*11.12*)	training plan (*11.3*)
phased operation (*11.13*)	train-the-trainer (*11.7*)
pilot operation (*11.12*)	tutorial (*11.7*)

Chapter Review

1. What is the purpose of an operational environment and a test environment?

2. Who must receive training before a new information system is implemented?

3. What factors should you consider when developing a training plan for a new system?

4. What security concerns exist during the data conversion process?

5. List and describe the four system changeover methods.

6. Which of the system changeover methods generally is the most expensive? Why?

7. Which of the system changeover methods generally is the most risky? Why?

8. Who should be responsible for performing a post-implementation evaluation?

9. List four investigative techniques that can be used when performing a post-implementation evaluation.

10. List the information usually included in the final report to management.

Discussion Topics

1. Using the Internet, locate an example of vendor training for a software or hardware product. Write a brief summary of the vendor, the product, the type of training offered, the cost of training (if available), and discuss your findings with the class.

2. Suppose that you designed a tutorial to train a person in the use of specific software or hardware, such as a Web browser or an ATM machine. What specific information would you want to know about the recipient of the training? How would that information affect the design of the training material?

3. Suggest specific examples of information systems well suited to each of the changeover methods described in the chapter and suggest examples of systems not suited to a specific method.

4. This chapter discusses the timing of a post-implementation review, and several advantages and disadvantages are mentioned. In your view, which carries the greater risk: having the review too early, or having it too late? Justify your position.

Apply Your Knowledge

Victorian Creations

Situation:

Victorian Creations is a growing business that specializes in the reproduction of furniture from the Victorian era. Since 1998, sales have increased steadily. The original accounting system was a package from Peachtree Software, which initially ran on a stand-alone PC and later on a LAN. Now, the firm is preparing to install a powerful, scalable accounting package that can support the company's current and future operations. You have been asked to develop a training plan for users.

1. Who should receive training on the new software, and what topics should the training cover?

2. Investigate an accounting package such as Peachtree or QuickBooks to learn if the product can export data, and in what formats.

3. What changeover strategy would you suggest for the new accounting system? Explain your answer.

4. When should a post-implementation review be scheduled? Explain your answer.

2 GrayRock Games

Situation:

GrayRock Games is a leading seller of computer games that feature virtual reality and interactive scripts. The firm maintains a Web site where customers can review an online catalog and order products. GrayRock wants to upgrade the Web site with a new system that will allow customers to run demos and experience the technology that made GrayRock a leader in its field. Currently, the upgrade is running in a test environment. Unfortunately, the project is behind schedule and well over budget. GrayRock's top management wants the new system implemented as soon as possible, but has left the decision up to you.

1. What changeover methods would you consider and why? (11.11)

2. After the upgrade is implemented, should the test environment be maintained? Why or why not? (11.2)

3. If the test environment is maintained after the new system becomes operational, what guidance should be given to IT staff members? Draft a brief memo that provides specific guidelines regarding the separation between the two environments. (11.3)

4. Suggest post-implementation evaluation methods, and draft an evaluation checklist that might be used by GrayRock's customers. (11.4)

3 Calico Prints

Situation:

Calico Prints creates a wide range of fabrics and wallpapers. Recently the company updated their payroll software as an in-house development project. Users and IT staff members have completed a comprehensive training curriculum. The system has been in the operational environment for approximately six weeks, and no major problems have occurred. You are responsible for the post-implementation evaluation.

1. What are some techniques you might use to obtain an accurate evaluation?

2. What are some specific questions you would include in a questionnaire? Who should receive the questionnaire?

3. Are there general guidelines that apply to the timing of a post-implementation evaluation? What are they?

4. In your view, should the company schedule a post-implementation evaluation for the payroll system at this time? Give specific reasons for your answer.

Apply Your Knowledge

Bayview College

Situation:

Bayview College is a small community college in Northern California. Bayview recently decided to develop an online student registration system to replace a manual system. Using the new system, students will visit their advisors to discuss their schedules for the next semester. The advisor then will input the data into the registration system. After the new system has been operational for a year, Bayview plans to allow students to submit a proposed schedule, have it reviewed by an advisor, and enter the data directly — all on the Internet. Application development and testing has been completed for the new system. You are the lead systems analyst for the project.

1. What types of training would you suggest? Should the training process involve students?

2. Is data conversion necessary for this project? Why or why not?

3. Assume that today is May 1, and that Fall registration does not begin until the end of July. When is the best time to implement the system changeover?

4. What type of system changeover method would you use and why?

Chapter Assignments

1. One effective way to train employees is through a method called train-the-trainer. Research this training method using the Internet. What are some of the advantages and disadvantages of the program? What types of organizations might want to use train-the-trainer? Write a brief report on your findings.

2. Design a generalized post-implementation evaluation form. The form should consist of generic questions that you could use to evaluate any information system. The form should evaluate the training received on the project, and any problems associated with the program.

3. Create a one-page questionnaire to distribute to users in a post-implementation evaluation of a recent information system project. Include at least 10 questions that cover the important information you want to obtain.

4. On the Internet, locate an example of an online tutorial and reference material for a software product. Are the instructions and lesson steps clear and effective? Does the manual assume that the user is an expert or novice? What are your suggestions for improving the training material?

CASE STUDIES

Case Studies offer an opportunity for you to practice specific skills and knowledge learned in the chapter and provide practical experience for you as a systems analyst. Two of the case studies (New Century Health Clinic and Ridgeway Company) are continuing case studies that appear in each chapter. Additionally, one continuing case study (SCR Associates) utilizes the Internet to practice some of the topics covered in this chapter.

NEW CENTURY HEALTH CLINIC

All the programs and procedures for the new computerized office information system for New Century Health Clinic have been prepared, tested, and approved. A server and six client workstations have been purchased, installed, and networked in the clinic offices. You now are ready to begin installation and evaluation of the system.

Assignments

1. Identify the specific people who will require training on the new system. Describe the type and level of training you recommend for each person or group.

2. Recommend a changeover method for New Century's system and justify your recommendation. If you suggest phased changeover or pilot operation, specify the order in which you would implement the modules or how you would select a pilot workstation or location.

3. Develop a data conversion plan that identifies what data must be entered during the conversion process, and the order in which data should be entered.

4. Should the associates perform a post-implementation evaluation? If an assessment is done, who should perform it? What options are available and which would you recommend?

RIDGEWAY COMPANY

The Ridgeway Company requirements for the new billing system for the Lake View Country Club were described in case studies in Chapters 4, 8, 9, and 10. The following assignments are based on the work you already have done in those chapters.

Assignments

1. Identify the specific groups of people who need training on the new system. For each group, describe the type of training you would recommend and list the topics you would cover.

2. Suggest a changeover method for the new billing system and provide specific reasons to support your choice. If you recommend phased changeover, specify the order in which you would implement the modules. If your recommendation is for pilot operation, specify the department or area you would select as the pilot site and justify your choice.

3. Develop a data conversion plan that specifies which data items must be entered, the order in which the data should be entered, and which data items are the most time-critical.

4. You decide to perform a post-implementation evaluation to assess the quality of the system. Who would you involve in the process? What investigative techniques would you use and why?

OVER THE LINE INVESTMENTS

You are the project manager for a new investment analysis system at Over The Line Investments, a Web-based firm that offers financial and investment advice to clients. The new system calculates the performance of stocks and mutual funds recommended by the firm. Previously, the information was collected manually and entered into a DBMS. The new system will obtain data automatically using links to major securities exchanges, and allow Internet access for Over The Line's clients.

During the development process for the new system, you used project management techniques that you learned in Part 3 of the Systems Analyst's Toolkit. Now, you will use those skills to plan the installation and evaluation of the new system. Before the system changeover takes place, two activities must be completed: training and data conversion. Based on the following facts, you must prepare a training plan, which will take about a day to complete. In developing your plan, use the following assumptions:

- You must train 30 investment advisors (who will be the primary users), three managers, and three IT staff people. Each group will be trained separately, using training material that you developed for that group.
- All training will be scheduled on weekdays.
- All IT staff training must be completed before any other training is done.
- All IT staff members can attend training sessions in a group.
- Training for IT staff members will require 16 hours (in 4-hour blocks) with a maximum of one 4-hour block per day.
- No more than five users can be trained in a group.
- Each user training session will require eight hours. To maintain operations, however, a user only can spend up to four hours per day in training.
- Managers will receive a two-hour overview session. Managers will be trained one-on-one on three different days.
- Data conversion will be handled by the IT staff and can begin as soon as user and manager training are finished. The data conversion process will require three days (a Friday, Saturday, and Sunday) before the system becomes operational on a Monday morning, using a direct cutover method.

Assignments

1. Prepare a training and data conversion plan that will result in the earliest possible implementation. Analyze the facts, break the process down into a series of tasks, and estimate the time required for each task. Then use the project management tools in the Systems Analyst's Toolkit to create a Gantt chart and a PERT/CPM chart.

2. Develop a cost estimate for training. First, estimate the total number of person-hours that will be required for training. Assume that one person in training for one hour equals one person-hour. To calculate a dollar figure, use the following hourly costs: $100/hour for users and IT staff members and $200/hour for managers. Make sure that you include a figure for the trainer's time at $150/hour.

3. One of the managers is nervous about using the direct cutover method, and she asked you to clarify why you chose this approach. Draft a memo outlining the reasons for using a direct cutover approach.

4. Three months after the system changeover, the system is operating largely error-free. To assess the system's overall quality, you perform a post-implementation evaluation. Prepare three evaluation forms for the new information system: one for users, one for managers, and one for the IT operations staff.

SCR ASSOCIATES

SCR Associates is an information technology consulting firm that offers IT solutions and training for small- and medium-sized companies. SCR's slogan is "We Know IT!"

Background

As a newly hired systems analyst, you will handle assignments, work on various SCR projects, and apply the skills you learned in the text. SCR needs an information system to manage training operations at the new SCR training center. The new system will be called TIMS (Training Information Management System).

The SCR case is available as an interactive, Web-based case study. You can log on to the Shelly Cashman Series site at www.scsite.com/sad4e/scr for instructions and assignments. If you prefer to complete the case study without using the Internet then you must download the data disk. See the inside back cover for instructions for downloading the data disk or see your instructor for more information on accessing the files required for this book.

Situation

In Part 11 of the SCR case, you will plan the installation and evaluation of the TIMS system.

Before You Begin ...

1. Review the March 15, 2002, message from Jesse Baker regarding TIMS installation tasks. Open the Document 11-1 from the data disk.

2. Review the March 22, 2002, message from Jesse Baker regarding post-implementation evaluation for the TIMS system. Open the Document 11-2 from the data disk.

Assignments

1. During TIMS installation, it is important for SCR support staff and users to understand the difference between the test environment and the operational environment. Draft a message that explains the installation process and provides guidelines for all concerned.

2. Using Jesse Baker's March 15 message as a guide, develop a training plan for the TIMS system. Identify the groups that should receive training, list topics that should be covered, and suggest training methods that might be used.

3. Before TIMS, training data was stored in a Microsoft Access database. To learn more about data conversion options, research Microsoft Access online Help and determine what data formats are supported. Notice if ODBC (Open Database Connectivity) is listed as an export format, and use online Help to learn more about ODBC. Summarize your findings in a brief memo.

4. Develop a plan for post-implementation review of the TIMS system. Include fact-gathering methods and a list of topics to be covered. Suggest the best time to conduct the review, and who should perform it.

ON THE WEB

The SCR case is available as an interactive, Web-based case study. You can log on to the Shelly Cashman Series site at www.scsite.com/sad4e/scr for instructions and assignments.

PHASE 1 — Systems Planning
PHASE 2 — Systems Analysis
PHASE 3 — Systems Design
PHASE 4 — Systems Implementation
PHASE 5 — Systems Operation & Support

Systems Operation and Support

Systems operation and support is the last phase in the systems development life cycle. The systems operation and support phase begins after the system becomes operational and continues throughout the useful life of the system. In addition to user support, this phase includes system maintenance, improvement, and performance measurement.

INTRODUCTION

Now that the system is operational, the real test begins. The key question is whether or not the system meets user expectations and provides support for business objectives. Systems must be maintained and improved continuously to meet changing business demands, and users constantly require assistance. Chapter 12 describes how companies meet those needs.

In addition to performing maintenance, a systems analyst is like an internal consultant who provides guidance, support, and training. Successful, robust systems often need the most support because users want to learn the features, try all the capabilities, and discover how the system can help them perform their business functions. Higher levels of system activity cause users to want more features, more enhancements, more maintenance, and more support. In most organizations, more than half of all IT department effort goes into supporting existing systems and making them more valuable to users.

This chapter begins with a discussion of systems support, including user training and help desks. You will study the four main types of maintenance: corrective, adaptive, perfective, and preventive. You also will learn how the IT group delivers operational support, including maintenance teams, configuration management, and maintenance releases. Finally, you will examine system performance issues, CASE maintenance tools, and how to recognize system obsolescence.

OBJECTIVES

When you finish this chapter, you will be able to:

- Explain how the systems operation and support phase relates to the rest of the system development process

- Describe user support activities, including user training and help desks

- Discuss the four main types of system maintenance: corrective, adaptive, perfective, and preventive

- Explain techniques for managing systems operation and support, including maintenance teams, maintenance request procedures, configuration management, maintenance releases, version control, and baselines

- Describe techniques for managing system performance, including performance and workload measurement, and capacity planning

- List factors indicating that a system has reached the end of its useful life

OVERVIEW OF SYSTEMS SUPPORT AND MAINTENANCE

The systems operation and support phase begins when a system becomes operational and continues until the system reaches the end of its useful life. Throughout the development process, the objective has been to create an information system that is efficient, easy to use, and affordable. After delivering the system, the analyst has two other important tasks: he or she must support users and provide necessary maintenance to keep the system operating properly.

N THE WEB

learn more about
lp Desk Activities visit
site.com/sad4e/more.htm,
ck Systems Analysis and
sign Chapter 12 and then
ck the Help Desk Activities
k.

w.scsite.com

USER SUPPORT ACTIVITIES

User support includes training and the use of a help desk, also known as an information center, that provides technical support.

User Training

You already are familiar with initial user training that is performed when a new system is introduced. For example, an airline provides training for mechanics when they have new aircraft delivered, as shown in Figure 12-1. In addition, new employees must learn how to use the company's information systems. In most firms, newly hired employees are trained by user departments, rather than IT staff members.

If significant changes take place in the existing system or if a new version is released, the IT department might develop a **user training package**. Depending on the nature of the changes, the package could include special online Help via e-mail or the company's intranet, a revision to the user guide, a training manual supplement, or formal training sessions. Training users about system changes is similar to initial training. The main objective is to show users how the system can help them perform their jobs.

Help Desks

As systems and data structures become more complex, users need constant support and guidance. To make data more accessible and to empower users, many IT departments create help desks. A **help desk** has three main objectives: to show people how to use system resources more effectively, to provide answers to technical or operational questions, and to make users more productive by teaching them how to meet their own information needs. A help desk also is often called an **information center** (IC) because it is the first place users turn when they need assistance.

A help desk does not replace traditional IT maintenance and support activities. Instead, help desks enhance productivity and improve utilization of a company's information resources.

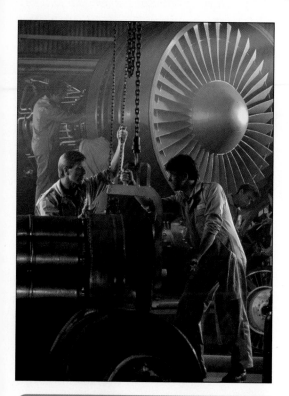

FIGURE 12-1 The training process for any type of organization, whether the users are data entry staff, customer service reps, airline mechanics, or NASA technicians, is essentially the same. The main objective is to give users the best possible support so they can use the system efficiently to perform their job functions.

Help desk representatives need strong inter-personal and technical skills plus a solid understanding of the business, because they interact with users in many departments. During a typical day, the help desk staff shown in Figure 12-2 might have to perform the following tasks:

- Show a user how to create a data query or report that displays specific business information
- Resolve network access or password problems
- Demonstrate an advanced feature of a system or a commercial package
- Help a user recover damaged data
- Offer tips for better operation
- Explain an undocumented software feature
- Show a user how to write a macro
- Explain how to access the company's intranet or the Internet
- Assist a user in developing a simple database to track time spent on various projects
- Answer questions about software licensing and upgrades
- Provide information about system specifications and the cost of new hardware or software
- Recommend a system solution that integrates data from different locations to solve a business problem

In addition to functioning as a valuable link between IT staff and users, the help desk is a central contact point for all IT maintenance activities. The help desk is where users report system problems, ask for maintenance, or submit new systems requests. A help desk can utilize many types of automated support, just as outside vendors do, including e-mail responses, on-demand fax capability, an online knowledge base, frequently asked questions (FAQs), discussion groups, bulletin boards, and automated voice mail.

Interactive support also can be delivered in the form of an online chat, as shown in Figure 12-3. In the example, CyberClass offers software that enables college instructors to deliver Internet-based courses. In addition to FAQs and other forms of support, the CyberClass chat room feature allows one or more instructors to discuss technical problems and questions online with a technical support representative.

FIGURE 12-2   A help desk, also called an information center (IC), provides guidance and assistance to system users. When a user contacts a help desk, the response should be prompt and effective.

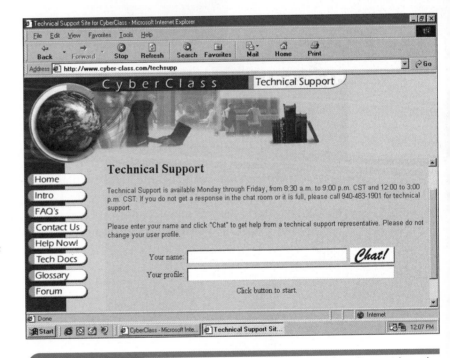

FIGURE 12-3   CyberClass enables instructors to deliver Internet-based courses and offers a chat room feature that allows one or more instructors to discuss technical problems and questions online with a technical support representative.

A help desk should document all inquiries, support tasks, and activity levels carefully. The information can identify trends, common problems, and help build a technical support knowledge base. Whether a system involves computer applications or building high-performance automobile engines, it is essential to monitor, measure, and analyze performance, as shown in Figure 12-4.

FIGURE 12-4 Regardless of the type of system, performance must be monitored carefully, measured, and analyzed.

MAINTENANCE ACTIVITIES

An important component of TCO is the systems operation and support phase. Figure 12-5 shows a typical pattern of operational and maintenance expenses during the useful life of a system. **Operational costs** include items such as supplies, equipment rental, and software leases. Notice that the lower area shown in Figure 12-5 represents fixed operational expenses, while the upper area represents maintenance expenses.

Maintenance expenses vary significantly during the system's operational life and include

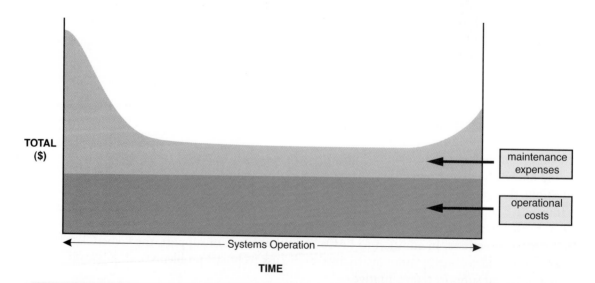

FIGURE 12-5 The total cost of operating an information system includes operational and maintenance costs. Operational costs are relatively constant, while maintenance expenses vary over time.

spending to support maintenance activities. **Maintenance activities** include changing programs, procedures, or documentation to ensure correct system performance; adapting the system to changing requirements; and making the system operate more efficiently. Those needs are met by corrective, adaptive, perfective, and preventive maintenance. **Corrective maintenance** is performed to fix errors, **adaptive maintenance** adds new capability and enhancements, **perfective maintenance** improves efficiency, and **preventive maintenance** reduces the possibility of future system failure. Some analysts use the term maintenance to describe only corrective maintenance that fixes problems. It is helpful, however, to view the maintenance concept more broadly, and differentiate among the different types of tasks. Although some overlap exists, four types of maintenance tasks can be identified, as shown by the examples in Figure 12-6.

Examples of Maintenance Tasks

Corrective Maintenance
- Diagnose and fix logic errors
- Replace defective network cabling
- Restore proper configuration settings
- Debug program code
- Update drivers
- Install software patch

Adaptive Maintenance
- Add online capability
- Create new reports
- Add new data entry field to input screen
- Install links to Web site
- Create employee portal

Perfective Maintenance
- Install additional memory
- Write macros to handle repetitive tasks
- Compress system files
- Optimize user desktop settings
- Develop library for code reuse
- Install more powerful network server

Preventive Maintenance
- Install new antivirus software
- Develop standard backup schedule
- Implement regular defragmentation process
- Analyze problem report for patterns
- Tighten all cable connections

ON THE WEB

For an overview of Software Maintenance visit scsite.com/sad4e/more.htm click Systems Analysis and Design Chapter 12 and then click the Software Maintenance link.

www.scsite.c

FIGURE 12-6 Corrective maintenance fixes errors and problems. Adaptive maintenance provides enhancements to a system. Perfective maintenance improves a system's efficiency, reliability, or maintainability. Preventive maintenance avoids future problems.

Maintenance expenses usually are high when a system is implemented because problems must be detected, investigated, and corrected. Afterward, costs usually remain low and involve minor adaptive maintenance. Eventually, both adaptive and perfective maintenance activities increase in a dynamic business environment.

Near the end of a system's useful life, maintenance expenses increase rapidly due to adaptive maintenance and a higher level of perfective maintenance. Figure 12-7 shows the typical patterns for each of the four classifications of maintenance activities over a system's life span.

	Immediately After Implementation	Early Operational Life	Middle Operational Life	Later Operational Life
Corrective Maintenance	High	Low	Low	High
Adaptive Maintenance (Minor Enhancements)	None	Medium	Medium	Medium
Adaptive Maintenance (Major Enhancements)	None	None	Medium to High	Medium to High
Perfective Maintenance	Low	Low to Medium	Medium	Low
Preventive Maintenance	Low	Medium	Medium	Low

FIGURE 12-7   Information systems maintenance depends on two major factors: the type of maintenance and the age of the system.

Corrective Maintenance

Corrective maintenance diagnoses and corrects errors in an operational system. In addition to errors in the original version of the system, corrective maintenance often is needed to resolve issues created by previous maintenance changes. To avoid introducing new problems, all maintenance work requires careful analysis before making changes. The best maintenance approach is a scaled-down version of the SDLC itself, where investigation, analysis, design, and testing are performed before implementing any solution.

You can respond to errors in various ways, depending on the nature and severity of the problem. Most organizations have standard procedures for minor errors, such as an incorrect report title or an improper format for a data element. In a typical procedure, a user submits a systems request that is evaluated, prioritized, and scheduled by the systems review committee. If the request is approved, a maintenance team designs, tests, documents, and implements a solution. Figure 12-8 shows a systems request to correct a relatively minor error in a monthly sales report.

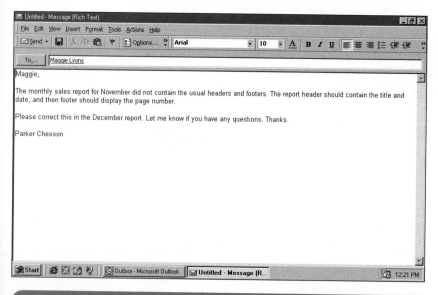

FIGURE 12-8   Example of an e-mail request for the correction of a formatting error in a report.

For more serious situations, such as incorrect report totals or inconsistent data, a user submits a systems request with supporting evidence. Those requests receive a high priority and a maintenance team begins work on the problem immediately. Severe errors sometimes occur because the systems developers did not test for certain data combinations or processing situations.

The worst-case situation is a total system failure. If that type of emergency occurs, the maintenance team bypasses the initial steps and tries to correct the failure immediately. Meanwhile, a written systems request is prepared by a user or a member of the IT department and added to the maintenance log. When the system is operational again, the maintenance team determines the cause, analyzes the problem, and designs a permanent solution. The IT response team updates the test data files, thoroughly tests the system, and prepares full documentation.

Adaptive Maintenance

Adaptive maintenance adds enhancements to an operational system and makes the system easier to use. An **enhancement** is a new feature or capability. The need for adaptive maintenance usually arises from business environment changes such as new products or services, new manufacturing technology, or support for a new Web-based operation.

The procedure for minor adaptive maintenance is similar to routine corrective maintenance. A user submits a systems request that is evaluated and prioritized by the systems review committee. A maintenance team then analyzes, designs, and implements the enhancement. Although the procedures for the two types of maintenance are alike, adaptive maintenance requires more IT department resources than minor corrective maintenance.

A major adaptive maintenance project is like a small-scale SDLC project because the development procedure is similar. Adaptive maintenance can be more difficult than new systems development because the enhancements must work within the constraints of an existing system.

Perfective Maintenance

Perfective maintenance involves changing an operational system to make it more efficient, reliable, or maintainable. Requests for corrective and adaptive maintenance normally come from users, while the IT department usually initiates perfective maintenance.

During system operation, changes in user activity or data patterns can cause a decline in efficiency and perfective maintenance might be needed to restore performance. When users are concerned about performance, you should determine if a perfective maintenance project could improve response time and system efficiency.

Perfective maintenance also can improve system reliability. For example, input problems might cause a program to terminate abnormally. By modifying the data entry process, you can highlight errors and notify the user that they must enter proper data. When a system is easier to maintain, support is less costly and less risky. In many cases, you can simplify a complex program to improve maintainability.

In many organizations, perfective maintenance is not performed frequently enough. Companies with limited resources often consider new systems development, adaptive maintenance, and corrective maintenance more important than perfective maintenance. Managers and users constantly request new projects so few resources are available for perfective maintenance work. As a practical matter, perfective maintenance can be performed as part of another project. For example, if a new function must be added to a program, you can include perfective maintenance in the adaptive maintenance project.

Perfective maintenance usually is cost-effective during the middle of the system's operational life. Early in systems operation, perfective maintenance usually is not needed. Later, perfective maintenance might be necessary, but have a high cost. Most benefits of perfective maintenance are less valuable if the company already plans to discontinue the system.

Two techniques you can use in perfective maintenance are reverse engineering and re-engineering. Some CASE tools offer **reverse engineering,** which translates an existing application or relational databases into a series of logic diagrams, structure charts, and text descriptions that allow the analyst to study the application from a design viewpoint. Figure 12-9 shows examples of CASE reverse engineering tools.

Re-engineering analyzes an application's quality or performance, as shown in Figure 12-10. Depending on the results, an IT consultant might recommend that the program be updated, translated to another programming environment, or replaced altogether. Programs that need a large number of maintenance changes usually are good candidates for re-engineering. The more a program changes, the more likely it is to become inefficient and difficult to maintain. Detailed records of all maintenance work help identify systems with a history of frequent corrective, adaptive, or perfective maintenance.

Preventive Maintenance

Reverse engineering includes changes to an operational system that reduce the possibility of future problems. To avoid problems before they happen, preventive maintenance requires analysis of areas where trouble is likely to occur. Like perfective maintenance, the IT department normally initiates preventive maintenance. Preventive maintenance often results in increased user satisfaction, decreased downtime, and reduced TCO. Preventive maintenance competes for IT resources along with other projects, and sometimes does not receive the high priority that it deserves.

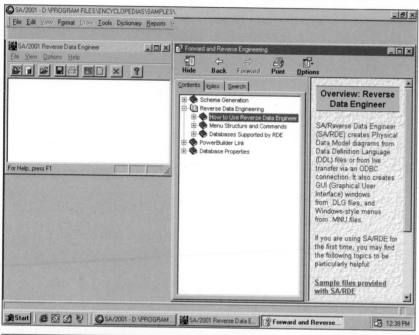

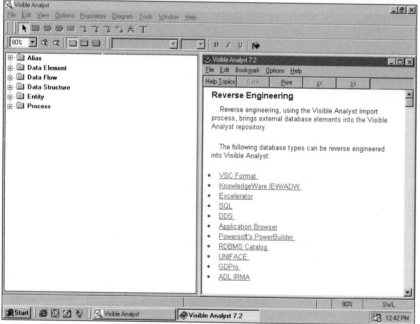

FIGURE 12-9 Examples of CASE reverse engineering tools that allow an analyst to study an application or database from a design viewpoint.

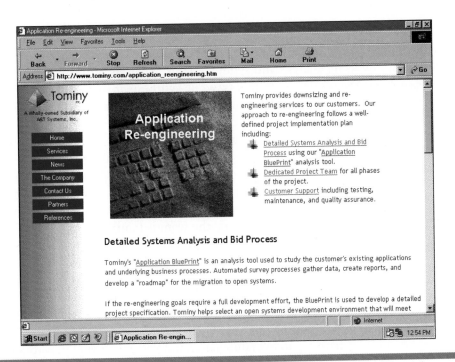

FIGURE 12-10 Re-engineering analyzes an application's quality or performance. Depending on the results, an IT consultant might recommend that the application be updated, translated to another programming environment, or replaced altogether.

WHAT DO YOU THINK?

You are a systems analyst at Outback Outsourcing, a firm that handles payroll processing for many large companies. Outback Outsourcing uses a combination of payroll package programs and in-house developed software to deliver custom-made payroll solutions for its clients. Lately, users have flooded you with requests for more new features and Web-based capability to meet customer expectations. Your boss, the IT manager, comes to you with a question. She wants to know when to stop trying to enhance the old software and develop a totally new version better suited to the new marketplace. How would you answer her?

MANAGING SYSTEMS OPERATION AND SUPPORT

Systems operation, like all other phases in the SDLC, requires effective management. During the operational phase, many companies use a maintenance team, have a process for managing maintenance requests and for establishing priorities, as well as a configuration management process, and a maintenance release procedure. In addition, they may choose to use version control and baselines to track system releases and the system's life cycle.

Maintenance Team

A **maintenance team** consists of one or more systems analysts and programmers. The analysts must have a solid background in information technology, strong analytical abilities, and a solid understanding of business operations and management functions. Analysts also need effective interpersonal and communications skills and they must be creative, energetic, and eager for new knowledge.

Maintenance systems analysts are like skilled detectives who investigate and rapidly locate the source of a problem by using analysis and synthesis skills. **Analysis** means examining the whole in order to learn about the individual elements, while **synthesis** involves studying the parts to understand the overall system. A systems analyst must understand the system elements and how to maintain them without affecting the overall system.

IT managers often divide systems analysts and programmers into two groups: one group performs new system development and the other group handles all maintenance. One advantage of this approach is that the maintenance group develops strong support skills. Some organizations, however, use a more flexible approach and assign IT staff members to various projects as they occur. By integrating development and support work, the people developing the system also assume responsibility for maintaining it. Because the team is familiar with the project, additional training or expense is unnecessary and members are likely to have a sense of ownership from the onset.

Unfortunately, many analysts feel that maintenance work is less attractive than developing new systems, which they see as more interesting and creative. In addition, an analyst might find it more challenging to troubleshoot and support someone else's work that might have been poorly documented and organized.

Some organizations that have separate maintenance and new systems groups rotate people from one area to the other. When analysts learn different skills, the organization is more versatile and people can shift to meet changing business needs. For instance, systems analysts working on maintenance projects learn why it is important to design easily maintainable systems. Similarly, analysts working on new systems get a better appreciation of the development process and the design compromises necessary to meet business objectives. That knowledge can help them become better maintenance systems analysts.

One disadvantage of rotation is that it increases overhead costs because time is lost when people move from one job to another. When systems analysts constantly shift between maintenance and new development, they have less opportunity to become highly skilled at any one job. Another disadvantage is that with the rotation method, some analysts must spend a substantial amount of time in a job that is less desirable to them personally.

Newly hired and recently promoted IT staff members sometimes are assigned to maintenance projects because most IT managers believe that maintenance work offers the best learning experience. Studying existing systems and documentation is an excellent way to learn program and documentation standards. In addition, the mini-SDLC used in many adaptive maintenance projects is good training for the full-scale systems development life cycle. Some disadvantages exist, however. For a new systems analyst, maintenance work often is more difficult than new systems development, and it might make more sense to assign a new person to a development team where more experienced analysts are available to provide training and guidance.

In most organizations, the training value of maintenance work outweighs the other factors and IT managers usually assign new employees to maintenance activities.

Managing Maintenance Requests

Typically, maintenance requests involve a series of steps, as shown in Figure 12-11. A user submits a request, a **system administrator** makes an initial decision, a systems review committee renders a final determination, maintenance tasks are assigned, and the user is notified of the outcome.

1. **Maintenance request.** Users submit most requests for corrective and adaptive maintenance when the system is not performing properly or if they want new features. IT staff members usually initiate requests for perfective and preventive maintenance. To keep a complete maintenance log, all work must be covered by a specific request that users submit in writing or by e-mail.

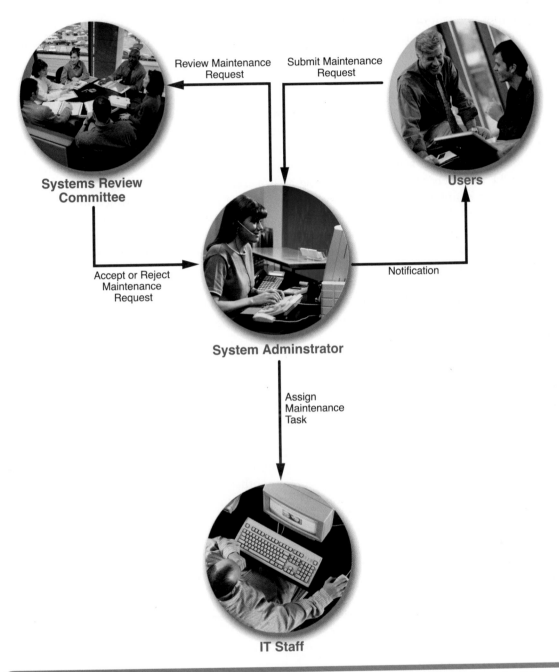

Review Maintenance
Request

Submit Maintenance
Request

**Systems Review
Committee**

Users

Accept or Reject
Maintenance
Request

Notification

System Adminstrator

Assign
Maintenance
Task

IT Staff

FIGURE 12-11 A user submits a maintenance request to the system administrator, who routes it to the systems review committee. Once the committee has reviewed the request the user is notified of the decision. If the change is accepted the system administrator assigns the task to IT staff members.

2. **Initial determination.** Most organizations designate a system administrator with responsibility for configuration management on specific systems. When a user submits a maintenance request, the administrator makes an initial decision. If the request involves a severe problem, a team is assigned immediately to perform corrective maintenance. In noncritical situations, the administrator either accepts or rejects the request or postpones action pending further study. The administrator notifies the requester and the systems review committee of the decision and the reasons for the determination.

3. **Final disposition of the request.** The systems review committee evaluates the request and either rejects it or assigns it a priority and schedules the maintenance work. To reduce paperwork and unnecessary effort, the committee often delegates final authority to the system administrator for requests that fall within a certain cost range.

Establishing Priorities

In many companies, the systems review committee separates maintenance requests from new systems development requests when evaluating requests and setting priorities. In other organizations, all requests for systems services are put into one group and considered together and the most important project is given top priority, whether it is maintenance or new development.

Many IT managers believe that evaluating all projects together leads to the best possible decisions because maintenance and new development require similar IT department resources. In IT departments where systems analysts and programmers are organized into separate maintenance and new development groups, however, it might make sense to evaluate requests separately. Another advantage of a separate approach is that maintenance is more likely to receive a proportional share of IT department resources.

Neither approach guarantees an ideal allocation between maintenance and new systems development. The most important objective is to have a procedure that balances new development and necessary maintenance work to provide the best support for business requirements and priorities.

W H A T   D O   Y O U   T H I N K ?

As IT manager at Brightside Insurance Company, you organized your IT staff into two separate groups — one team for maintenance projects and the other team for new systems work. That arrangement worked well in your last position at another company. Brightside, however, previously made systems assignments with no particular pattern.

At first, the systems analysts in your group did not comment about the team approach. Now, one of your best analysts might quit if he is assigned to work on the maintenance team because he is not interested in that type of work. You decide that if you match the right analyst with the right assignment, there would be no problems. What could you do? Should assignments be voluntary? Why or why not? If you have to make assignments, what criteria should you use?

N THE WEB

earn more about
figuration
nagement visit
te.com/sad4e/more.htm,
k Systems Analysis and
ign Chapter 12 and then
k the Configuration
nagement link.

v.scsite.com

Configuration Management

Configuration management (CM) is a process for controlling changes in system requirements during the development phases of the SDLC. Configuration management also is an important tool for managing system changes and costs after a system becomes operational. Most companies establish a specific process that describes how system changes must be requested and documented. As enterprise-wide information systems grow more complex, configuration management becomes critical. Industry standards have emerged, and many vendors offer configuration management software and techniques. One resource for information is a Web site called CM Today, as shown in Figure 12-12.

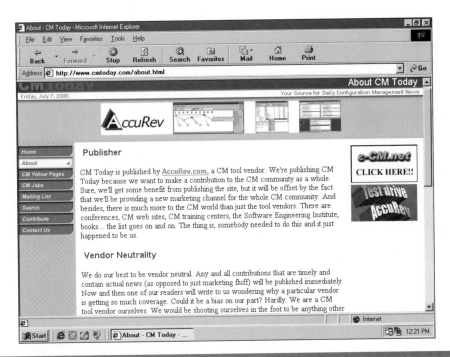

FIGURE 12-12 CM Today is published by AccuRev, a CM tool vendor. The CM Yellow Pages feature on the left-hand menu bar provides a source of information and resources that relate to configuration management.

A system implemented in multiple environments often has different versions for each platform and thus requires different maintenance updates. Configuration management is an effective tool for managing that type of situation. Using a specific configuration management process, the IT staff keeps track of all system versions, installs all maintenance updates, and ensures that all versions of the system work correctly.

Configuration management also helps to organize and handle documentation. An operational system has extensive documentation that covers development, modification, and maintenance for all versions of the installed system. Most documentation material, including the initial systems request, project management data, end-of-phase reports, data dictionary, and the IT operations and user manuals, is stored in the IT department.

Most maintenance projects require documentation changes. You must be especially careful to issue updates whenever you make adaptive changes or perform major corrective maintenance. It is important to avoid surprises for users and IT staff members. Keeping track of all documentation and ensuring that updates are distributed properly is an important part of configuration management.

Maintenance Releases

Coordinating maintenance changes and updates can be difficult, especially for a complex system with several versions. Many organizations, and especially software vendors, use numbered releases to designate different versions. When a **maintenance release methodology** is used, all noncritical changes are held until they can be implemented at the same time. Each change is documented and installed as a new version of the system called a **maintenance release**.

For an in-house developed system, the time between releases usually depends on the level of maintenance activity. A new release to correct a critical error, however, might be implemented immediately rather than saved for the next scheduled release. The decision depends on the nature of the error and the possible impact of the release.

When a release method is used, a numbering pattern distinguishes the different releases. In a typical system, the initial version of the system is 1.0, and the release that includes the first set of maintenance changes is version 1.1. A change, for example, from version 1.4 to 1.5 indicates relatively minor enhancements, while whole number changes, such as from version 1.0 to 2.0, or from version 3.4 to 4.0, indicate a significant upgrade.

The release methodology offers several advantages, especially if two teams perform maintenance work on the same system. When a release methodology is used, all changes are tested together before a new system version is released. The release methodology also reduces costs because only one set of system tests is needed for all maintenance changes. This approach results in fewer versions, less expense, and less interruption for users.

Using a release methodology also reduces the documentation burden. Every time a new version of a system is implemented, all documentation must be updated, and some users feel that they spend too much time filing documentation changes. Even worse, some users let the upgrades pile up and eventually ignore them. With a release methodology, all documentation changes are coordinated and become effective simultaneously. Users and IT staff members integrate a package of updates into their documentation for each release.

The release methodology also has some potential disadvantages. Users expect a rapid response to their problems and requests, but with a release methodology, new features or upgrades are available less often. Even when changes would improve system efficiency or user productivity, the potential savings must wait until the next release date, which might increase operational costs.

Commercial software suppliers also provide maintenance releases, often called **service packs**, to purchasers. *INFOWORLD* magazine reported in its February 21, 2000 issue that Microsoft planned to release Windows 2000 service packs on a regular six-month basis. As the article shown in Figure 12-13 suggests, there are pros and cons to that type of policy.

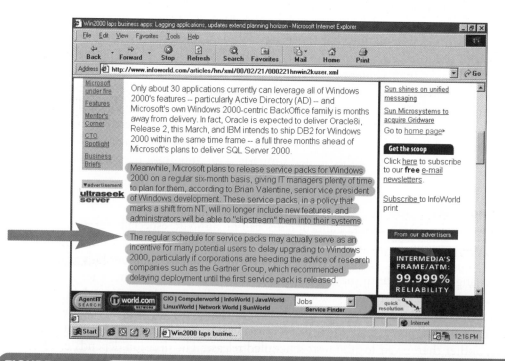

FIGURE 12-13   *INFOWORLD* magazine reported that Microsoft would release Windows 2000 service packs on a regular six-month basis. As the article suggests, there are pros and cons to this type of policy.

Version Control

Version control is the process of tracking system releases. When a new version of a system is released into production, the release is archived by a **systems librarian**. The systems librarian is responsible for archiving current and previously released versions of the system. In the event of major system failure, the company can reinstate the prior version for system recovery. In addition, librarians are responsible for configuring systems that have several modules at various release stages. That allows one individual to have the responsibility for tracking version changes and building the new system using the appropriate releases. Many companies use software such as Merant's PVCS Professional to automate and track the version control process, as shown in Figure 12-14.

Baselines

A **baseline** is a formal reference point that measures system characteristics at a specific time. Systems analysts use baselines as yardsticks to document features and performance during the systems development process.

There are three types of baselines: functional, allocated, and product. The **functional baseline** is the configuration of the system documented at the beginning of the project. It consists of all the necessary system requirements and design constraints. The **allocated baseline** documents the system at the end of the design phase and identifies any changes since the functional baseline. The allocated baseline includes testing and verification of all system requirements and features. The **product baseline** describes the system at the beginning of system operation. The product baseline incorporates any changes made since the allocated baseline and includes the results of performance and acceptance tests for the operational system.

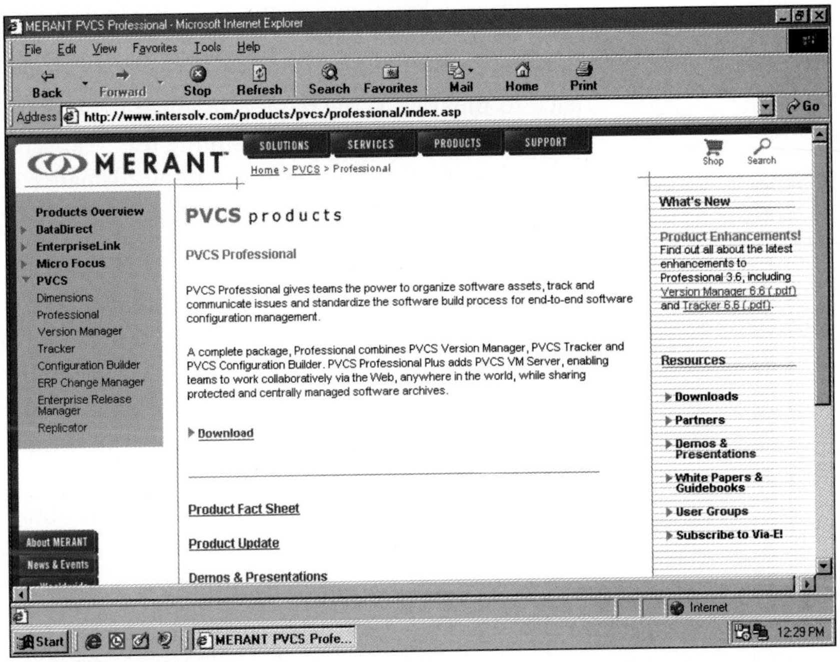

FIGURE 12-14 Many companies use software such as PVCS Professional to automate and track the version control process.

MANAGING SYSTEM PERFORMANCE

A system's performance directly affects users who rely on it to perform their job functions. To ensure satisfactory support for business operations, the IT department monitors current system performance and anticipates future needs.

When most firms used a central computer for processing data, it was relatively simple to measure the efficiency of the system. Today, companies use complex networks and client/server systems to support business information needs. A user at a client workstation often interacts with an information system that depends on other clients, servers, networks, and data located throughout the company. Rather than a single computer, it is the integration of all those system components that determines the system's capability and performance.

Various statistics are available to assess system performance, including capacity planning, which is a process that uses operational data to forecast system capabilities and future needs.

N THE WEB

r more information about
ystems Performance and
orkload Management visit
site.com/sad4e/more.htm,
ck Systems Analysis and
esign Chapter 12 and then
ck the Systems Performance
d Workload Management
k.

Performance and Workload Measurement

You already are familiar with several **workload measurements**, including the number of lines printed, the number of records accessed, and the number of transactions processed in a given time period. To measure performance of network-based systems, an analyst also needs to consider response time, bandwidth, and throughput. Analysts also consider turnaround time as a way to measure system performance and user support.

RESPONSE TIME   **Response time** is the overall time between a request for system activity and the delivery of the response. In the typical online environment, response time is measured from the instant the user presses the ENTER key or clicks a mouse button until the requested screen display appears or printed output is ready. Response time is affected by the system design, capabilities, and processing methods. If a user requests a batch-processed report, for example, the batch processing schedule determines the response time. Response time includes three elements: the time necessary to transmit or deliver the request to the system, the time that the system needs to process the request, and the time it takes to transmit or deliver the result back to the user. If the request involves network or Internet access, response time is affected by data communication factors. Online users expect an immediate response and they are frustrated by any apparent lag or delay. Of all performance measurements, response time is the one that users notice and complain about most.

BANDWIDTH AND THROUGHPUT   Bandwidth and throughput are closely related terms, and many analysts use them interchangeably. **Bandwidth** describes the amount of data that the system can handle in a fixed time period. Bandwidth requirements are expressed in bits per second. Depending on the system, you might measure bandwidth in **kbps (kilobits per second)**, **mbps (megabits per second)**, or **gbps (gigabits per second)**. Analyzing bandwidth is similar to forecasting the hourly number of vehicles that will use a highway in order to determine the number of lanes required.

Throughput measures actual system performance under specific circumstances and is affected by network loads and hardware efficiency. Throughput, like bandwidth, is expressed as a data transfer rate, such as kbps, mbps, or gbps. Just as traffic jams delay highway traffic, throughput limitations can slow system performance and response time. That is especially true with graphics-intensive systems and Web-based systems that are subject to Internet-related conditions.

TURNAROUND TIME   **Turnaround time** applies to centralized batch processing operations, such as customer billing or credit card statement processing. Turnaround time measures the time between submitting a request for information and the fulfillment of the request. Turnaround time also can be used to measure the quality of IT support or services by measuring the time from a user request for help to the resolution of the problem.

The IT department often measures response time, bandwidth, throughput, and turnaround time to evaluate system performance both before and after changes to the system or business information requirements. Performance data also is used for cost-benefit analyses of proposed maintenance and to evaluate systems that are nearing the end of their economically useful lives. Finally, management uses current performance and workload data as input for the capacity planning process.

Capacity Planning

Capacity planning is a process that monitors current activity and performance levels, anticipates future activity, and forecasts the resources needed to provide desired levels of service. Capacity planning information and resources are available on the Web, as shown in Figure 12-15.

As the first step in capacity planning, you develop a current model based on the system's present workload and performance specifications. Then you project demand and user requirements over a one- to three-year time period and analyze the model to see what is needed to maintain satisfactory performance and meet requirements. To assist you in the process, you can use a technique called what-if analysis.

What-if analysis allows you to vary one or more elements in a model in order to measure the effect on other elements. For example, you might use what-if analysis to answer questions such as: How will response time be affected if we add more PC workstations to the network? Will our client/server system be able to handle the growth in sales from the new Web site? What will be the effect on server throughput if we add more memory?

Powerful spreadsheet tools also can assist you in performing what-if analysis.

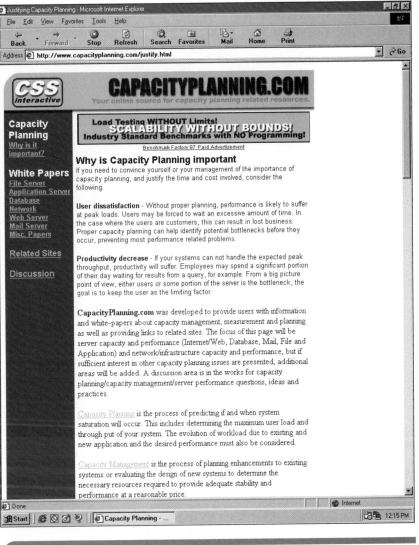

FIGURE 12-15 Capacity planning information and resources are available on the CSS Web site.

For example, Microsoft Excel contains a feature called Goal Seek that determines what changes are necessary in one value to produce a specific result for another value. In the example shown in Figure 12-16, a capacity planning worksheet indicates that the system can handle 3,840 Web-based orders per day, at 22.5 seconds each. The user wants to know the effect on processing time if the number of transactions increases to 9,000. As the Goal Seek solution in the bottom figure shows, order processing will have to be performed in 9.6 seconds to achieve that goal.

When you plan capacity, you need detailed information about the number of transactions; the daily, weekly, or monthly transaction patterns; the number of queries; and the number, type, and size of all generated reports. If the system involves a LAN, you need to estimate network traffic levels to determine whether or not the existing hardware and software can handle the load. If the system uses a client/server design, you need to examine performance and connectivity specifications for each platform.

Most important, you need an accurate forecast of future business activities. If new business functions or requirements are predicted, you should develop contingency plans based on input from users and management. The main objective is to ensure that the system meets all future demands and provides effective support for business operations.

ON THE WEB

To learn more about Capacity Planning visit scsite.com/sad4e/more.ht click Systems Analysis and Design Chapter 12 and the click the Capacity Planning link.

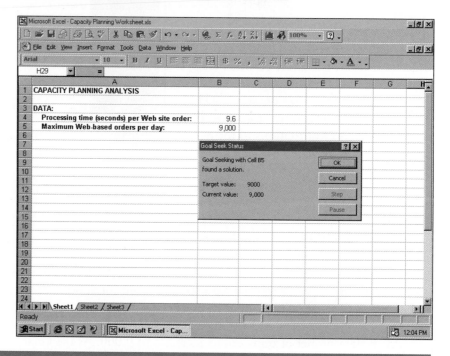

FIGURE 12-16 Microsoft Excel provides a Goal Seek feature that permits what-if analysis. In the first example, the Web site order processing time is 22.5 seconds per order, and 3,840 orders per day. The analyst asks the program to calculate how much faster the processing must be to handle 9,000 transactions per day rather than 3,840. The second figure shows that the new processing time must be 9.6 seconds per order.

CASE Tools for Systems Maintenance

You can use automated tools that provide valuable assistance during the operation and support phase. A typical CASE maintenance toolkit provides various tools for systems evaluation and maintenance, including the following:

- A performance monitor that provides data on program execution times.
- A program analyzer that scans source code, provides data element cross-reference information, and helps evaluate the impact of a program change.

- An interactive debugging analyzer that locates the source of a programming error.
- A restructuring tool or a reengineering tool.
- An automated documentation tool.
- A network activity monitor.
- Software that forecasts workloads.

In addition to CASE tools, you also can use spreadsheet and presentation software to calculate trends, perform what-if analyses, and create attractive charts and graphs to display the results. Information technology planning is an essential part of the business planning process, and you probably will deliver presentations to management. You can use the Systems Analyst's Toolkit for more information on using spreadsheet and presentation software to help you communicate effectively.

SYSTEM OBSOLESCENCE

Even with solid support, at some point every system becomes obsolete. For example, you might not remember the punch cards shown in Figure 12-17, which represented the cutting edge of IT in the 1960s. Constantly changing technology means that every system has a limited economic life span, some longer than others. Analysts and managers must realize that they can anticipate system obsolescence in several ways and it should never come as a complete surprise.

A system becomes **obsolete** when users no longer require its functions or when the platform becomes outmoded. The most common reason for discontinuing a system is that it has reached the end of its economically useful life, as indicated by the following signs:

1. The system's maintenance history indicates that adaptive and corrective maintenance is increasing steadily.

2. Operational costs or execution times are increasing rapidly and routine perfective maintenance does not reverse or slow the trend.

3. A software package is available that provides the same or additional services faster, better, and less expensively than the current system.

4. New technology offers a way to perform the same or additional functions more efficiently.

5. Maintenance changes or additions are difficult and expensive to perform.

6. Users request significant new features to support business requirements.

ON THE WEB

For examples of System Obsolescence visit scsite.com/sad4e/more.htm, click Systems Analysis and Design, Chapter 12 and then click System Obsolescence link.

www.scsite.com

FIGURE 12-17 At one time, punch cards represented the cutting edge of IT. As technology evolved, punch cards quickly became obsolete. To maintain a competitive edge, companies must use the newest, most efficient IT available, and obsolescence should never be a surprise.

Systems operation and support continues until a replacement system is installed. Toward the end of a system's operational life, users are unlikely to submit new requests for adaptive maintenance because they are looking forward to the new release. Similarly, the IT staff usually does not perform much perfective or preventive maintenance because the system will not be around long enough to justify the cost. A system in its final stages only requires corrective maintenance to keep the system operational. Figure 12-18 shows typical levels of maintenance for a system at the obsolescence stage in the SDLC.

Type	Activity level
Corrective Maintenance	Low
Adaptive Maintenance (Minor Enhancements)	None
Adaptive Maintenance (Major Enhancements)	None
Perfective Maintenance	None
Preventive Maintenance	None

FIGURE 12-18 All maintenance activities decrease significantly during the final phase of operations as a replacement system is being developed.

User satisfaction typically determines the life span of a system. The critical success factor for any system is whether or not it helps users achieve their operational and business goals. As an IT staff member, you should expect to receive input from users and managers throughout the systems development process. You should investigate and document all negative feedback, because it can be the first signal of system obsolescence.

At some point in a system's operational life, maintenance costs start to increase, users begin to ask for more features and capability, new systems requests are submitted, and the SDLC begins again.

SOFTWEAR, LIMITED

In mid-December, 2002, five months after the final report to management, the payroll package and the ESIP system were operating successfully and users seemed satisfied with both systems.

During that time, users requested minor changes in reports and screen displays, which the IT staff handled easily. Jane Rossman, manager of applications, continued to assign a mixture of new systems and maintenance tasks to the IT team, and the members indicated that they enjoyed the variety and challenge of both types of work.

Debra Williams, the payroll clerk who prints the ESIP checks, reported the only operational problem. She could not load and align the special check stock in the printer correctly. Becky Evans visited Debra to study the situation, and then wrote a specific procedure to solve the problem.

No overtime had been paid in the payroll department since the new system was implemented and errors in payroll deductions had stopped. Michael Jeremy, SWL's vice president of finance, who initiated the payroll and ESIP projects, is very pleased with the system's operation and output. He recently visited an IT department staff meeting to congratulate the entire group personally.

Some requests for enhancements also occurred. Mike Feiner recently submitted a systems request for the ESIP system to produce an annual employee benefits statement with the current value of all savings plan deductions, plus information on insurance coverage and other benefits data. Mike also indicated that the company would offer several new ESIP choices during 2003, including various mutual funds.

On December 15, Pacific Software announced the latest release of its payroll package. The new version supported full integration of all payroll and human resources functions and data. Ann Hon, director of information systems, was interested in the announcement because she knew that Tina Pham, SWL's vice president of human resources, wanted a human resources information system (HRIS) to support SWL's long-term needs. At Ann's request, Jane Rossman assigned Becky Evans to analyze the new payroll package to determine if SWL could implement the latest version as a companywide client/server application.

Becky began the preliminary investigation by reviewing the current system and meeting with Mike Feiner to learn more about the new ESIP options. Next, she met with Marty Hoctor, a representative from Pacific Software, to review the features of the new release. After describing the new software, Marty mentioned that a large midwestern retail chain recently implemented the package and he invited Becky to contact Fred Brown, director of IT at that company, to discuss the new release. Becky spoke with Fred and he agreed to e-mail her a summary of comments that users had made about the new software.

Becky completed her preliminary investigation, including a cost-benefit analysis, and worked with Jane Rossman and Ann Hon to prepare a report and presentation to SWL's newly formed systems review committee, which was created at Ann's suggestion. In their presentation, the IT team recommended that SWL upgrade to the new release of the payroll package and build a client/server application for all of SWL's payroll and personnel functions, including the ESIP system. They also suggested that a team of IT and human resources people get together to study preliminary economic, technical, and operational factors involved in a human resources information system, and report back to the systems review committee. They pointed out that if the project was approved, the same team could handle the systems development using JAD or RAD techniques. After the presentation, the committee approved the request and Ann called an IT department staff meeting for the next morning to start planning the systems analysis phase.

During the meeting, Ann and Jane thanked the entire department for its efforts on the payroll and ESIP projects. Ann pointed out that although the payroll package and the ESIP system support SWL's current needs, the business environment changes rapidly and a successful, growing company must investigate new information management technology constantly. At this point, the systems development life cycle for SWL begins again.

Now that the new ESIP system is operational, Jane Rossman wants you to track system performance using various measurements. At a minimum, she expects you to monitor operational costs, maintenance frequency, technical issues, and user satisfaction. You can add other items if you choose. Write a proposal for Jane that lists each factor you will measure and make sure that you explain why the item is important and how you plan to obtain the information.

Jane also wants you to learn more about human resources information systems (HRIS) that help a company manage information about its people. Many firms have replaced older personnel record-keeping systems with powerful, state-of-the-art HRIS products. You will be assigned to the SWL team that will study the feasibility of a human resources information system. Using the Internet, your task is to identify several commercial packages and the names of firms or consultants who specialize in HRIS implementation. Write a brief memo to Jane with your findings.

CHAPTER SUMMARY

Systems operation and support covers the entire period from the implementation of an information system until the system is no longer used. A systems analyst's primary involvement with an operational system is to manage and solve user support requests.

Corrective maintenance includes changes to correct errors. Adaptive maintenance satisfies new systems requirements, and perfective maintenance makes the system more efficient. Adaptive and perfective maintenance changes often are called enhancements. Preventive maintenance is performed to avoid future problems.

The typical maintenance process resembles a miniature version of the systems development life cycle. A systems request for maintenance work is submitted and evaluated. If it is accepted, the request is prioritized and scheduled for the IT group. The maintenance team then follows a logical progression of investigation, analysis, design, development, testing, and implementation.

Corrective maintenance projects occur when a user or an IT staff member reports a problem. Standard maintenance procedures usually are followed for relatively minor errors, but work often begins immediately when users report significant errors.

In contrast to corrective maintenance, adaptive, perfective, and preventive maintenance projects always follow the organization's standard maintenance procedures. Adaptive maintenance projects occur in response to user requests for improvements to meet changes in the business or operating environments. The IT staff usually initiates perfective maintenance projects to improve performance or maintainability. Automated program restructuring and re-engineering are forms of perfective maintenance. In order to avoid future problems, IT staff performs preventive maintenance, which involves analysis of areas where trouble is likely to occur.

A maintenance team consists of one or more systems analysts and programmers. Systems analysts need the same talents and abilities for maintenance work as they use when developing a new system. Many IT departments are organized into separate new development and maintenance groups where staff members are rotated from one group to the other.

Configuration management is necessary to handle maintenance requests, to manage different versions of the information system, and to distribute documentation changes. Maintenance changes can be implemented as they are completed or a release methodology can be used in which all noncritical maintenance changes are collected and implemented simultaneously. A release methodology usually is cost-effective and advantageous for users because they do not have to work with a constantly changing system. Systems analysts use functional, allocated, and product baselines as formal reference points to measure system characteristics at a specific time.

System performance measurements include response time, bandwidth, throughput, and turnaround time. Capacity management uses those measurements to forecast what is needed to provide future levels of service and support.

CASE tools are available to assist you in many aspects of systems operation and support. Maintenance toolkits provide a wide selection of systems evaluation and maintenance support tools.

All information systems eventually become obsolete. The end of a system's economic life usually is signaled by rapidly increasing maintenance or operating costs, the availability of new software or hardware, or new requirements that cannot be achieved easily by the existing system. When a certain point is reached, an information system must be replaced, and the entire systems development life cycle begins again.

Key Terms

adaptive maintenance (*12.5*)	mbps (megabits per second) (*12.16*)
allocated baseline (*12.15*)	obsolete (*12.19*)
analysis (*12.10*)	operational costs (*12.4*)
bandwidth (*12.16*)	perfective maintenance (*12.5*)
baseline (*12.15*)	preventive maintenance (*12.5*)
capacity planning (*12.17*)	product baseline (*12.15*)
configuration management (CM) (*12.12*)	re-engineering (*12.8*)
corrective maintenance (*12.5*)	response time (*12.16*)
enhancement (*12.7*)	reverse engineering (*12.8*)
functional baseline (*12.15*)	service packs (*12.14*)
gbps (gigabits per second) (*12.16*)	synthesis (*12.10*)
help desk (*12.2*)	system administrator (*12.10*)
information center (*12.2*)	systems librarian (*12.15*)
kbps (kilobits per second) (*12.16*)	throughput (*12.16*)
maintenance activities (*12.5*)	turnaround time (*12.16*)
maintenance expenses (*12.5*)	user training package (*12.2*)
maintenance release (*12.13*)	version control (*12.15*)
maintenance release methodology (*12.13*)	what-if analysis (*12.17*)
maintenance team (*12.9*)	workload measurements (*12.16*)

Chapter Review

1. List and describe the four classifications of maintenance.

2. Which of the four types of maintenance is most likely to generate changes to user documentation?

3. Why are newly hired systems analysts and programmers often assigned to maintenance projects?

4. What is configuration management and why is it important?

5. List the typical steps in requesting system maintenance.

6. What is a release methodology? What are the advantages and disadvantages of using this approach?

7. What is the purpose of version control?

8. Define the following terms: response time, bandwidth, throughput, and turnaround time. How are the terms related?

9. What is the purpose of capacity planning, and how is what-if analysis used in capacity planning?

10. List six indications that an information system is approaching obsolescence.

Discussion Topics

1. Assume that updates to your company's inventory control system are controlled with a release methodology. The current version of the system is version 4.5. For each of the maintenance changes listed below, decide whether you should number the release including only that change as version 4.6 or version 5.0.

   a. Deleted obsolete report

   b. Added graphical screen display

   c. Added input validation check

   d. Added interface to the budget control system

   e. Additional valid product classification code

   f. Additional level in the inventory classification scheme

   g. Added capability for producing graphical output on a laser printer

   h. Changed order of the printed fields in an existing report

   i. Made sort procedure more efficient

   j. Added new supply module

   k. Renamed several data elements

   l. Rewrote a program to streamline its execution

2. The four types of IT system maintenance also could apply to other industries. Suppose you were in charge of aircraft maintenance for a small airline. What would be an example of each type of maintenance — corrective, adaptive, perfective, and preventive — in this situation?

3. An IT manager assigns programmers and systems analysts to maintenance projects if they have less than two years of experience or if they received an average or below average rating in their most recent performance evaluation. What misconceptions do you suspect that manager holds?

4. User documentation is essential to a successful operation. Think of examples of especially good or bad user documentation that you have encountered. How could the poor examples have been improved?

1 Premium Publishers

Situation:

Premium Publishers is a small publishing firm that specializes in reprinting classic literature. A year ago the IT staff developed a Web-based order entry system. The system has performed well, but the company would like to add more features and improve performance. So far, most of the maintenance has involved correcting minor errors.

1. What type of maintenance has the IT staff performed? What types of maintenance will they perform if the existing system is retained?

2. If new features are added, what methodology should the IT staff use to add new functions and enhancements?

3. Does a Web-based order entry system require special preventive maintenance? Explain your answer.

4. Even though the new system is only a year old, e-commerce changes constantly. At what point should Premium Publishers consider replacing the Web-based system with a new system, and why?

2 Oceanside Furniture

Situation:

Oceanside Furniture produces indoor and outdoor wicker furniture. The company grew from one store in 1995 to eight locations today. Two years ago, the company's IT department developed an inventory control system to keep track of products and reorder out-of-stock items. The new system was well received by users, and inventory problems have decreased significantly. However, since the inventory system became operational, users have steadily requested increased functionality and changes in screen forms and reports.

1. Should Oceanside have a specific process to manage future changes and enhancements? What should it be?

2. What about version control? Should Oceanside institute a maintenance release methodology? Why or why not?

3. Suppose that you had to assign specific IT staff members to maintain the inventory control system. How would you accomplish the task? Describe your strategy in a brief memo.

4. What should Oceanside watch for to detect possible obsolescence in the future? Develop a checklist with specific examples that Oceanside management could use.

Apply Your Knowledge

3 Robin Hood Associates

Situation:

Robin Hood Associates is an IT consulting firm that develops new systems and maintains older systems for its clients. Robin Hood recently was awarded a contract to correct problems with an existing system. The system is three years old and the consulting firm that initially designed the system did a poor job of documentation. The data dictionary, user manuals, and other reference material have never been updated, and no process exists for version control.

1. As one of the Robin Hood team members, how should you proceed? What steps would you take, and what would be your priorities?

2. Are CASE tools available that you could use on this assignment? What are they?

3. What advice would you give to the client regarding capacity planning for the future?

4. If the existing system remains in place over a long period, what are some obsolescence symptoms that the client might notice?

4 Economy Travel

Situation:

Economy Travel specializes in personalized travel packages at popular prices, and the firm operates 12 offices in major U.S. cities. A key selling point is the firm's client management database, which includes preferences such as airline seating choices and favorite hotels. Economy Travel purchased the client management software as an off-the-shelf vendor package and modified the program to meet the company's needs. The package has been operational for one year and has performed well. Economy Travel, however, is in the process of expanding their operation to include six additional locations. You have been called in as a consultant to help the company make some decisions about IT support.

1. What performance and workload measurement issues should the company consider at the present time?

2. What capacity planning issues should the company consider at the present time?

3. Should the company establish a system baseline before the integration of the six new sites? Explain your answer.

4. As an IT consultant, you must understand the client's business. From that perspective, consider the impact of the Internet on the travel agency business. Investigate this topic, using the Internet and other sources of information, and decide what issues to discuss with Economy Travel.

Chapter Assignments

1. Using the Internet, identify at least two software packages designed to automate version control. List some of the key features and benefits of version control software, and describe your findings in a brief memo.

2. Develop a process for handling change requests and design a form that would handle a generic change request. The process should contain procedures for corrective, adaptive, perfective, and preventive maintenance requests. The process also should include a contingency plan for changes that the organization must resolve immediately.

3. Visit the IT department at your college or at a local company and investigate whether or not performance measurements are used for operational systems. Write a brief report describing your findings. If the department does not use performance measurements, explain the reason for not doing so.

4. Using a spreadsheet package, print out the Help explanation for the what-if analysis feature (which is called Goal Seek in Microsoft Excel) and create a worksheet that demonstrates this feature. You can use the sample shown in Figure 12-16 on page 12.18, or create your own example.

CASE STUDIES

Case Studies offer an opportunity for you to practice specific skills and knowledge learned in the chapter and provide practical experience for you as a systems analyst. Two of the case studies (New Century Health Clinic and Ridgeway Company) are continuing case studies that appear in each chapter. Additionally, one continuing case study (SCR Associates) utilizes the Internet to practice some of the topics covered in this chapter.

NEW CENTURY HEALTH CLINIC

You implemented the new system at New Century Health Clinic successfully, and the staff has used the system for nearly four months. New Century is pleased with the improvements in efficiency, office productivity, and patient satisfaction.

Some problems have surfaced, however. The office staff members call you almost daily to request assistance and changes in the way certain reports and forms are organized. You try to be helpful, but now you are busy with a major project for a local distributor of exercise equipment. Actually, your contract with New Century only required you to provide support during the first three months of operation. Anita Davenport, New Century's office manager, reported that the system seems to slow down at certain times during the day, making it difficult for the staff to keep up with its workload.

Assignments

1. You are willing to charge a lower rate for ongoing support services because you designed the system. You want New Century to use a specific procedure for requesting assistance and changes, however, so that you can efficiently plan your activities. Prepare a complete, written procedure for New Century Health Clinic maintenance change requests. Include appropriate forms with your procedure.

2. What could be causing the periodic slowdowns at New Century? If a problem does exist, which performance and workload measures would you monitor to pinpoint the problem?

3. At the end of the systems analysis phase you studied the economic feasibility of the system and estimated the future costs and benefits. Now that the system is operational, should those costs and benefits be monitored? Why or why not?

4. To your surprise, you receive a call from a large IT consulting firm that wants to interview you for a systems analyst position. The position would involve handling projects for several major corporations, and you are quite excited about the opportunity. You know that the firm will ask you about your experiences on the New Century project. To prepare for the meeting, write a memo that describes the highlights of your work at New Century. You should list any significant experiences, including the following:

- What was the most difficult part of the project and why?
- What was the easiest part of the project and why?
- If you had the project to do again, what would you do differently?
- List the most important skills you gained during the project.
- Will this project help you in your future IT career? How?
- Suppose that three years from now you are in an IT management position. Will your experiences on the New Century project be of value to you? Why or why not?

RIDGEWAY COMPANY

System changeover and data conversion were successful for the Ridgeway Company billing system. The post-implementation evaluation indicated that users were pleased with the system. The evaluation also confirmed that the system was operating properly. Several users commented, however, that system response seemed slow. Ridgeway wants to meet with you to discuss the new system.

Assignments

1. What might be causing the slow response time? Prepare a brief memo explaining system performance and workload measurement, using nontechnical language that Ridgeway users can understand easily.

2. Ridgeway's top management asked you to provide ongoing maintenance for the new system. In order to avoid any misunderstanding, you want to provide a brief description of the various types of maintenance. Prepare a brief memo that does this, and include at least two realistic examples of each type of maintenance.

3. Although the system has been operational for a short time, users already have submitted several requests for enhancements and noncritical changes. Should Ridgeway use a maintenance release methodology to handle the requests? Why or why not?

4. There is some talk that Ridgeway will expand in the future by acquiring several smaller operations. Prepare a brief memo to Ridgeway management that explains the concept of capacity planning and suggests some specific information that they might need in order to plan capacity.

TARGET INDUSTRIES

The online production support system runs 24 hours a day in all manufacturing facilities at Target Industries. They developed the current system in-house and implemented it less than two months ago. Last Monday morning, the system developed a problem. When a screen display for certain parts was requested, the displayed values were garbled.

When she was alerted to the situation, Marsha Stryker, Target's IT manager, immediately assigned a systems analyst to investigate the problem. Marsha instructed the analyst, Eric Wu, to resolve the problem and get the system up and running as soon as possible. Eric previously worked on two small maintenance projects for the production control system so he was somewhat familiar with the application.

Eric worked the rest of the day on the problem and by 6:30 in the evening, he developed and implemented a fix. After verifying that the production support system again was capable of producing correct part displays, Eric went home. Early the following morning, Marsha called Eric and two other members of the applications maintenance group to a meeting in her office, where she briefed them on a new adaptive maintenance project for another high-priority system. She asked them to begin work on the new project immediately.

Several nights later, the production control system crashed shortly after midnight. Every time the system was reactivated, it crashed again. Finally, around 2:30 a.m., all production lines were shut down and third-shift production workers were sent home. The production support system finally was corrected and full production was restored the following day, but by that time, Target Industries had incurred thousands of dollars in lost production costs. The cause of the production support system crash was identified as a side effect of the fix that Eric made to the system.

Assignments

1. Is the second production support system failure entirely unexpected?

2. Who is most to blame for the second system failure?

3. What might Marsha have done differently to avoid the situation? What might Eric have done differently?

4. Outline a new set of maintenance procedures that will help Target Industries avoid such problems in the future.

GALLAGHER IMPORTS

Gallagher Imports recently developed and implemented an online sales information system. Using a client/server design, the PCs in each of Gallagher's 12 retail stores were networked with an AS/400 server located in the sales support center at the main office. Salespeople in the retail stores use the customer sales information system to record sales transactions; to open, close, or query customer accounts; and to print sales receipts, daily sales reports by salesperson, and daily sales reports by merchandise code. The sales support staff uses the system to query customer accounts and print various daily, weekly, and monthly reports.

When the customer sales system was implemented, the IT department conducted extensive training for the salespeople and the sales support center staff. One member of the systems development team also prepared a user manual, but users are familiar with the system so the manual rarely is used.

Two weeks ago, Gallagher Imports opened two additional stores and hired six new sales representatives. Gallagher gave the new sales representatives the user manual and asked them to read it and experiment with the system. Now, the salespeople in both new stores are having major problems using the sales system. When a representative from the main office visited the stores to investigate the problem, she discovered that the new people could not understand the user manual. When she asked for examples of confusing instructions, several salespeople pointed to the following examples:

- *Obtaining the authorization of the store manager on Form RBK-23 is required before the system can activate a customer charge account.*
- *Care should be exercised to ensure that the BACKSPACE key is not pressed when the key on the numeric keypad with a left-facing arrow is the appropriate choice to accomplish nondestructive backspacing.*
- *To prevent report generation interruption, the existence of sufficient paper stock should be verified before any option that requires printing is selected. If not, the option must be reselected.*
- *The F2 key should be pressed in the event that a display of valid merchandise codes is required. That same key terminates the display.*

Assignments

1. What policies or procedures could Gallagher have established to avoid the situation?

2. Should the sales support staff ask the IT department to rewrite the user manual as a maintenance project, or should they request a training session for the new salespeople? Can you offer any other suggestions?

3. Rewrite the user manual instructions so they are clear and understandable for new users. What steps might you take to ensure the accuracy of the new user manual instructions?

4. In the process of rewriting the user manual instructions, you discover that some of the instructions were not changed to reflect system maintenance and upgrade activities. A request form on the firm's intranet, for example, has replaced Form RBK-23. Gallagher also has phased out printed reports in favor of online reports, which users can view by entering a user name and password. Rewrite the user manual instructions to reflect the changes.

SCR ASSOCIATES

SCR Associates is an information technology consulting firm that offers IT solutions and training for small- and medium-sized companies. SCR's slogan is "We Know IT!"

Background

As a newly hired systems analyst, you will handle assignments, work on various SCR projects, and apply the skills you learned in the text. SCR needs an information system to manage training operations at the new SCR training center. The new system will be called TIMS (Training Information Management System).

The SCR case is available as an interactive, Web-based case study. You can log on to the Shelly Cashman Series site at www.scsite.com/sad4e/scr for instructions and assignments. If you prefer to complete the case study without using the Internet then you must download the data disk. See the inside back cover for instructions for downloading the data disk or see your instructor for more information on accessing the files required for this book.

Situation

In Part 12 of the SCR case, you will consider system operation and support activities for the newly implemented TIMS system.

Before You Begin ...

1. Review the September 16, 2002 messages from Jesse Baker regarding systems operation and support tasks. Open the Documents 12-1 and 12-2 from the data disk.

2. Review the October 16, 2002 message from Smith, Campbell, and Richards regarding completion of the TIMS system project. Open the Document 12-3 from the data disk..

3. Review the October 17, 2002 message from Jesse Baker regarding important changes at SCR. Open the Document 12-4 from the data disk.

Assignments

1. Perform research to find out all you can about help desks. Try to determine why they are successful and why they are not. Write a brief memo describing the results of your research, and suggest an approach that SCR should follow in building a help desk for its users.

2. How should SCR manage the TIMS system in the future? Use the Internet to learn more about version control and configuration management and write a brief memo with your recommendations.

3. When and how should capacity planning be considered during the systems development life cycle? Is it possible to plan for potential mergers and acquisitions when considering the information system capacity? Why or why not? Write a brief memo explaining your views.

4. Create a checklist that SCR might use to detect TIMS obsolescence as early as possible. Propose a specific strategy that SCR can use to avoid surprises and problems relating to system obsolescence.

ON THE WEB

The SCR case is available as an interactive, Web-based case study. You can log on to the Shelly Cashman Series site at www.scsite.com/sad4e/scr for instructions and assignments.

The Systems Analyst's Toolkit

Communication Tools

Feasiblity and Cost Analysis Tools

Project Management Tools

Alternative Systems Development Methodologies

The Systems Analyst's Toolkit presents a valuable set of cross-phase skills and concepts that you can use throughout the systems development process. Part 1 describes communication tools that can help you write clearly, speak effectively, and deliver powerful presentations. Part 2 demonstrates economic analysis tools you can use to measure project feasibility, develop accurate cost-benefit estimates, and make sound decisions. Part 3 explains project management tools that can help you organize, plan, and manage IT projects to a successful conclusion. Part 4 describes two popular systems development methodologies: rapid application development (RAD) and Microsoft Solutions Framework (MSF).

Communication Tools PART 1

Communication Tools

In Part 1 of the Toolkit, you will learn about communication skills that are important to the systems analyst.

INTRODUCTION

A successful systems analyst must have good written and oral communication skills to perform his or her job effectively. Never underestimate the importance of effective communications whether you are using a memo, e-mail, or an oral presentation to convey your ideas. The following guidelines will help you prepare and deliver effective presentations. Remember, however, that nothing increases your ability to communicate better than practicing these skills.

OBJECTIVES

When you finish this Part of the Toolkit, you will be able to:

- List the guidelines for successful communications

- Explain the importance of effective letters, memos, and e-mail communication

- Describe the organization of written reports that are required during the SDLC and explain each report section

- List the guidelines for effective oral communication

- Organize and plan an oral presentation

- Use speaking techniques to achieve your objectives

GUIDELINES FOR SUCCESSFUL COMMUNICATIONS

When you are planning your communications, concentrate on making sure that your communication answers the questions of **why, who, what, when,** and **how.**

1. Know why you are communicating, and what you want to accomplish. Ask yourself the question, "Is this communication necessary, and what specific results am I seeking?" Your entire communication strategy depends on the results that you need.

2. Know who your targets are. Chapter 1 describes how the information needs of managers depend on their organizational and knowledge levels. When communicating with management, sometimes a fine line exists between saying enough and saying too much. Each situation is different, so you must use good judgment. You should plan a communication strategy and be alert for feedback from your audience.

3. Know what is expected of you, and when to go into detail. This is directly related to knowing who your targets are and the organizational and knowledge levels of your audience. For example, a vice president might expect less detail and more focus on how a project supports the company's strategic business goals. You must design your communications just as carefully as your systems project. For example, will the recipients expect you to address a specific issue or topic? Will they expect cost estimates or charts? Design your communications based on the answers to those questions.

4. Know how to communicate effectively. Use the Toolkit and your own experiences and observations of successful and unsuccessful techniques used by others to become a better communicator.

Most important, know your subject. Before any presentation, consider what others expect you to know and what questions they will ask. No matter how well you prepare, you will not have an answer for every question. Remember that it is better to say, "I don't know, but I'll find out," rather than to guess.

WRITTEN COMMUNICATIONS

Good writing is important because others often judge you by your writing. If you make a mistake while speaking, your audience probably will forget it. Your written errors, however, might stay around for a long time. Grammatical, typographical, and spelling errors distract readers from your message.

If you have not taken a writing course, you should consider doing so. If you have a choice of courses, select one that focuses on business writing or technical writing. Any writing class, however, is worth the effort. Bookstores and libraries have many excellent books on communicating effectively. As you prepare written documents, keep in mind the following suggestions:

1. Know your audience. If you are writing for nontechnical readers, use terms that readers will understand.

2. Use active voice whenever possible. For example, "Tom designed the system," is better than, "The system was designed by Tom."

3. Keep your writing concise.

4. Use one paragraph to convey a single idea.

5. Use the right style. Use a conversational tone in informal documents and a business tone in formal documents.

6. Use lists. When you must enumerate a number of subtopics related to the same topic, lists are an organized way to present them.

7. Use short, easy-to-understand words. Your objective is not to impress your audience with the size of your vocabulary.

8. Check your work. Look for grammatical and typographical mistakes and correct them.

9. Avoid repeating the same word too often. Use a thesaurus to locate synonyms for frequently repeated words. Many word processing programs include a thesaurus and other tools to help you write better.

10. Check your spelling. You can use the **spell checker** in your word processing program to check your spelling, but remember that a spell checker identifies only those words that do not appear in the program's dictionary. You should proofread your documents. For example, the spell checker will not identify instances when you use the word *their*, instead of the word *there*.

E-mail, Memos, and Letters

Although e-mail and workgroup software have become the main form of internal communication, in-house memos still are important, and external communications often require letters printed on company letterhead.

Most companies have a standard format, or template, for internal memos and external letters. If your company stores those on a network, you can download and use the templates. If you want to create your own designs, you can use a word processor to create templates with specific layouts, fonts, and margin settings. **Templates** give your work a consistent look and make your job easier. Word processing programs also provide a feature that allows you to design your memos as forms and fill in the blanks as you work.

Most companies now use **e-mail** as the standard form of written correspondence. E-mail usually is less formal than other written communication, but you still must follow the rules of good grammar, spelling, and clear writing. Although many authors use a more conversational style for e-mail, you should remember that e-mail messages often are forwarded to other recipients or groups, and so they are as important as any other form of written communication. If you regularly exchange messages with a specific group of users, most e-mail programs allow you to create a distribution list that includes the members and their e-mail addresses. For example, Figure TK 1-1 shows how to use Microsoft Outlook to send an e-mail to a four-person systems development team.

ON THE WEB

To learn more about using E-mail visit scsite.com/sad4e/more.htm click Systems Analysis and Design Toolkit and then click the E-mail link.

www.scsite.c

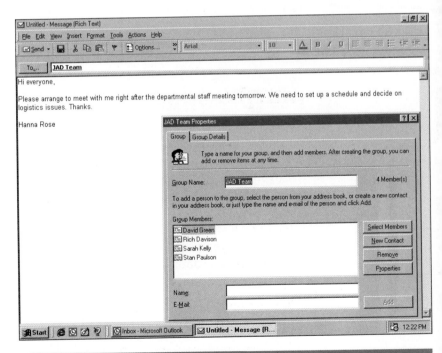

FIGURE TK 1-1 Microsoft Outlook is a desktop information management program that allows users to create distribution lists for sending e-mail messages.

The System's Analyst's Toolkit

Reports

You must prepare many reports during the SDLC, including the preliminary investigation report, the system requirements document at the end of the systems analysis phase, the system design specification at the end of the system design phase, and the final report to management when the system goes into operation. You also might submit other reports such as status reports, activity reports, proposals, and departmental business plans. You will create those reports as electronic documents, so you can attach them to e-mails and print them out, if desired.

In some cases, you must present reports more formally. The example in Figure TK 1-2 shows a binder for a system requirements document, which includes an introduction, summary, findings, recommendations, time and cost estimates, expected benefits, and an appendix.

You can use a **cover letter** or e-mail to identify an attached report and set a date, time, and place for an oral presentation. You also can request that the recipients read the report in advance of the presentation.

The **introduction** usually includes a title page, table of contents, and brief description of the proposal. The **title page** should be clean and neat and contain the name of the proposal, the subject, the date, and the names of the development team members. If the project already has a recognized name or acronym, use it. Include a **table of contents** when the report is long or includes many exhibits. Many word processing programs include a tool that can generate a table of contents automatically.

SYSTEM REQUIREMENTS DOCUMENT

Proposal for Material Ordering Management System (MOMS)

COA Industries, Inc.
September 17, 2001

Tabs: Introduction | Summary | Findings | Recommendations | Time & Cost Estimates | Expected Benefits | Appendix

FIGURE TK 1-2 Typical binder for a system requirements document.

The **summary** is used to summarize the entire project, including your recommendations, in several paragraphs. Generally, the summary should not exceed 200 words or one page.

Use the **findings** section to describe the major conclusions that you or the team reached during the systems analysis phase. You can make the findings section detailed or summarized, depending on the project. You must explain the logical design of the new system in a way that nontechnical managers can understand clearly. With a management audience, the most important task is to explain how the proposed system supports the company's business needs.

The **recommendations** section presents the best system alternative, with a brief explanation that does not disparage anyone who favors a different alternative. Your recommendation should mention the essential factors of economic, technical, and operation feasibility.

The **alternatives** section can be a separate section, or part of the recommendations section. The alternatives section identifies various strategies and alternatives, as discussed in Chapter 6. In the alternatives section, you should list the advantages and disadvantages of each major system alternative. In this section, you should include the cost-benefit results, with a clear description of the economic analysis techniques that were used. You can use tables or graphs to support and clarify your alternatives when necessary.

When you have a large number of supporting documents such as questionnaires or sampling results, you should put those items in an **appendix** located at the end of the document. Make sure you include only relevant information, and provide references for interested readers.

ORAL COMMUNICATION

An **oral presentation** is required at the end of the preliminary investigation and again at the conclusion of the systems analysis phase. You might need to give more than one presentation in some situations to present technical material to members of the IT department or to present an overview for top managers. When preparing an oral presentation, keep in mind the following suggestions: define the audience, define the objectives for your presentation, organize the presentation, define any technical terms you will use, prepare your presentation aids, and practice your material.

Define the Audience

Before you develop a detailed plan for a management presentation, you must define the audience. For vice presidents and senior managers, you should provide less detail and include a strategic overview.

Define the Objectives

When you communicate, you should focus on your objectives. In the management presentation for the systems analysis phase, your goals are the following:

- Inform management of the status of the current system.
- Describe your findings concerning the current system problems.
- Explain the alternative solutions that you developed.
- Provide detailed cost and time estimates for the alternative solutions.
- Recommend the best alternative and explain the reasons for your selection.

Organize the Presentation

Plan your presentation in three stages: the introduction, the information, and the summation. First, you should introduce yourself and describe your objectives. During the presentation, make sure that you discuss topics in a logical order. You should be as specific as possible when presenting facts — your listeners want to hear your views about what is wrong, how it can be fixed, and how much it will cost. In your conclusion, or summation, briefly summarize the main points, and then ask for questions.

Define Any Technical Terms

You should avoid specialized or technical terminology whenever possible. If your audience might be unfamiliar with a term that you plan to use, either define the term or find another way to say it so they will understand your material.

Prepare Presentation Aids

Much of what people learn is acquired visually, so you should use helpful, appropriate **visual aids** to help the audience follow the logic of your presentation and hold their attention. Visual aids also can direct audience attention away from you, which is helpful if you are nervous when you give the presentation. You can use a visual aid with an outline of topics that will help you stay on track.

Visual aids can help you display a graphical summary of performance trends, a series of cost-benefit examples, or a bulleted list of important points. You can use whiteboards, flip charts, overhead transparencies, slides, films, and videotapes to enhance your presentation. When preparing your visual aids, make sure that the content is clear, readable, and easy to understand. Verify ahead of time that the audience can see the visual material from anywhere in the room. Remember that equipment can fail unexpectedly, so be prepared with an alternate plan.

With a computer and a projection system, you can use presentation graphics software, such as Microsoft PowerPoint, to create slides with sounds, animation, and graphics. A sample PowerPoint slide is shown in Figure TK 1-3, along with tips for broadcasting your presentation on the Internet. Notice that you can take questions and gather feedback during the presentation by specifying an e-mail address.

When you create a slide show, you should concentrate on preparing the content of your presentation first, and then focus on visual aids. You should select special effects carefully — too many graphics, colors, special effects, or audio will distract the audience.

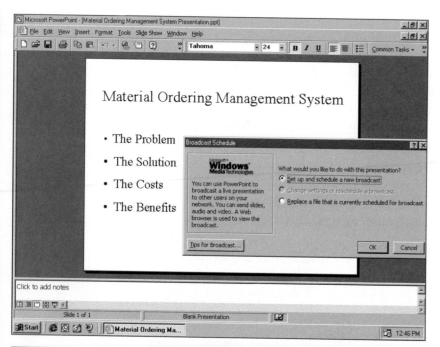

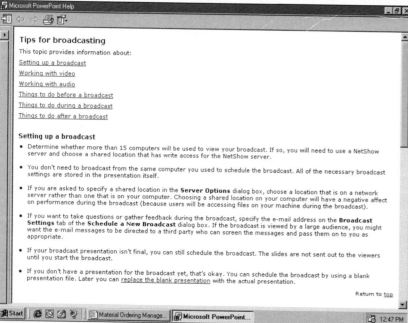

FIGURE TK 1-3 You can broadcast your PowerPoint presentation on the Internet. During the presentation, you can take questions and gather feedback by specifying an e-mail address.

Practice

The most important part of your preparation is **practice**. You should rehearse several times to ensure that the presentation flows smoothly and the timing is correct. Practicing will make you more comfortable and build your confidence.

Do not be tempted to write a script. If you read your presentation, you will be unable to interact with your audience and adjust your content based on their reactions. Instead, prepare an outline of your presentation and practice from the outline. Then, when you deliver the actual presentation, you will not have to struggle to remember the exact words you planned to say, and you will be able to establish a good rapport with your audience.

The Presentation

When you give the presentation, the following points will help you succeed:

SELL YOURSELF AND YOUR CREDIBILITY   To have a successful presentation, you must sell yourself and your credibility. A brilliant presentation will not convince top managers to approve the system if they are not sold on the person who gave the presentation. On the other hand, many systems projects are approved because the systems analyst did an excellent sales job.

Your presentation must show confidence about the subject and your recommendations. You should avoid any conflicts with the people attending the presentation. If anyone directs critical remarks to you, address the criticisms honestly and directly. You will have a successful presentation only if you know the material thoroughly, prepare properly, and sell yourself and your credibility effectively.

CONTROL THE PRESENTATION   During the presentation, you must control the discussion, maintain the pace of the presentation, and stay focused on the agenda — especially when answering questions. Although you might be more familiar with the subject material, you must not appear to have a superior attitude toward your listeners. Maintain eye contact with the audience and use some humor, but do not insert irrelevant jokes or make a joke at someone else's expense.

ANSWER QUESTIONS APPROPRIATELY   Let your audience know whether you would prefer to take questions as you go along or have a question and answer session at the end. Sometimes the questions can be quite difficult. You must listen carefully and respond with a straightforward answer. Try to anticipate the questions your audience will ask so you can prepare your responses ahead of time.

When answering a difficult or confusing question, repeat the question in your own words to make sure that you understand it. For example, you can say, "If I understand your question, you are asking if …" This will help avoid confusion and give you a moment to think on your feet. To make sure that you gave a clear answer, you can say, "Have I answered your question?" Allow follow-up questions when necessary.

USE GOOD SPEAKING TECHNIQUES   The delivery of your presentation is just as important as its content. You can strengthen your delivery by speaking clearly and confidently and projecting a relaxed approach. You also must control the pace of your delivery. If you speak too fast, you will lose the audience and if the pace is too slow, people lose their concentration and the presentation will not be effective.

ON THE WEB

For more information about Developing Presentations v scsite.com/sad4e/more.htm click Systems Analysis and Design Toolkit and then clic the Developing Presentatio link.

www.scsite.c

ON THE WE

To learn more about Speaking Skills visit scsite.com/sad4e/more.h click Systems Analysis an Design Toolkit and then c the Speaking Skills link.

www.scsite.c

Many speakers are nervous when facing an audience. If this is a problem for you, keep the following suggestions in mind.

1. **Control your environment.** If you are most nervous when the audience is looking at you, use visual aids to direct their attention away from you. If your hands are shaking, do not hold your notes. If you are delivering a computer slide show, use the keyboard to advance to the next slide instead of using the mouse. Concentrate on using a strong, clear voice. If your nervousness distracts you, take a deep breath and remind yourself that you really do know your subject.

2. **Turn your nervousness to your advantage.** Many people do their best work when they are under a little stress. Think of your nervousness as normal pressure.

3. **Avoid meaningless filler words and phrases.** Using words and phrases such as okay, all right, you know, like, um, and ah are distracting and serve no purpose.

4. **Practice! Practice! Practice!** Some people are naturally gifted speakers, but most people need lots of practice. You must work hard at practicing your presentation and building your confidence. Many schools offer speech or public speaking courses that are an excellent way of practicing your skills.

TOOLKIT PART 1 SUMMARY

Your success as a systems analyst depends on your ability to communicate effectively. You must know why you are communicating, what you want to accomplish, who your targets are, what is expected of you, and when to go into detail. You must know your subject and how to use good written and oral communications techniques.

You will be judged by your written work, so it must be free of grammatical, spelling, and punctuation errors. You should write e-mail, letters, and memos clearly, and the writing style should match the situation. Many companies have standard formats for letters and memos, and you can use word processing templates to achieve consistency.

You will prepare various reports during the SDLC and the format will vary depending on the nature of the report. Your reports should have a cover memo and might include a title page, table of contents, summary or abstract, description of alternatives, your recommendations, and an appendix.

In addition to written communications, you must communicate effectively in person. You might have to deliver several presentations to different audiences at different times during the SDLC. Presentations are an important form of oral communication and you should follow specific guidelines in preparing your presentation. You prepare by defining your audience, identifying your objectives, and organizing the presentation itself. You also need to define technical terms and prepare visual aids to help your audience understand the material. Most important, you must practice your delivery to gain confidence and strengthen your presentation skills.

When you give the presentation, you are selling your ideas and your credibility. You must control the discussion, build a good rapport with the audience, answer all questions clearly and directly, and try to use good speaking techniques. Again, the best way to become a better speaker is to practice.

Toolkit Part 1 Key Terms

alternatives (*TK 1.5*)
appendix (*TK 1.5*)
cover letter (*TK 1.4*)
e-mail (*TK 1.3*)
findings (*TK 1.5*)
introduction (*TK 1.4*)
oral presentation (*TK 1.5*)
practice (*TK 1.7*)
recommendations (*TK 1.5*)

spell checker (*TK 1.3*)
summary (*TK 1.5*)
table of contents (*TK 1.4*)
templates (*TK 1.3*)
title page (*TK 1.4*)
visual aids (*TK 1.6*)
why, who, what, when, and how (*TK 1.2*)

Toolkit Part 1 Review

1. Describe the why, who, what, when, and how of communications. Explain each term and give an example.

2. Mention five specific techniques you can use to improve your written documents.

3. What is the role of e-mail communication? What techniques can you use to become an effective e-mail communicator?

4. What are the main sections of a written report to management, and what is the purpose of each section?

5. What are six things you can do to prepare an effective oral presentation?

6. When you organize your presentation, what three main stages do you plan?

7. Why are visual aids important? Give at least three examples of different types of visual aids, with a specific example of how you would use each type in an actual presentation. You can use the SWL case or make up your own scenario.

8. What should you do during the delivery of your presentation to improve the success of the presentation?

9. Name three specific strategies you can use if you get nervous during a presentation.

10. Why is practice so important when preparing a presentation?

Feasibility and Cost
Analysis Tools **PART 2**

Feasibility and Cost Analysis Tools

In Part 2 of the Toolkit, you will learn about the feasibility and cost analysis tools that are used in the preliminary investigation and during the systems analysis phase.

INTRODUCTION

Chapter 2 contains a brief overview of economic feasibility. A project is economically feasible if the future benefits outweigh the estimated costs of developing or acquiring the new system. In Part 2 of the Systems Analyst's Toolkit, you will learn how to calculate a project's costs and benefits. As a systems analyst, you need to know how to calculate a project's costs and benefits when conducting a preliminary investigation, evaluating projects, and making recommendations to management.

OBJECTIVES

When you finish this Part of the Toolkit, you will be able to:

- Define economic feasibility

- Identify the cost considerations that analysts consider throughout the SDLC

- Understand chargeback methods and how they are used

- Use cost-benefit analysis, payback analysis, return on investment analysis, and present value analysis

DESCRIBING COSTS AND BENEFITS

As a systems analyst, you must analyze a project's costs and benefits at the end of each SDLC phase so management can decide whether or not to continue the development effort. Before you can use the economic analysis tools described in this section of the Toolkit, you must learn how to identify and classify all costs and benefits.

Cost Classifications

Costs can be classified as tangible or intangible, direct or indirect, fixed or variable, and developmental or operational. **Tangible costs** are costs for which you can assign a specific dollar value. Examples of tangible costs include employee salaries, hardware and software purchases, and office supplies. In contrast, **intangible costs** are costs whose dollar value cannot be calculated easily. The cost of customer dissatisfaction, lowered employee morale, and reduced information availability are examples of intangible costs.

If the analyst examines an intangible item carefully, however, it sometimes is possible to estimate a dollar value. For example, users might dislike a system because it is difficult to learn. Their dissatisfaction is an intangible cost, but if it translates into an increase in errors that must be corrected, you probably could assign a tangible dollar cost. You should try to work with tangible costs whenever possible.

Direct costs are costs that can be associated with the development of a specific system. Examples of direct costs include the salaries of project team members and the purchase of hardware that is used only for the new system. In contrast, **indirect costs**, or **overhead expenses**, cannot be attributed to the development of a particular information system. The salaries of network administrators, copy machine rentals, and insurance expenses are examples of indirect costs.

Fixed costs are costs that are relatively constant and do not depend on a level of activity or effort. Many fixed costs recur regularly, such as salaries and hardware rental charges. **Variable costs** are costs that vary depending on the level of activity. The costs of printer paper, supplies, and telephone line charges are examples of variable costs.

Developmental costs are incurred only once at the time the system is developed or acquired. Those costs might include salaries of people involved in systems development, software purchases, initial user training, and the purchase of necessary hardware or furniture. **Operational costs** are incurred after the system is implemented and continue while the system is in use. Examples of operational costs include system maintenance, ongoing training, annual software license fees, and communications expense.

Some costs apply to more than one category of expenses. For example, overtime pay for clerical help during the systems analysis phase might be developmental, variable, and direct; or a monthly fee for maintaining the company's Web site might be operational, fixed, and indirect.

Managing Information Systems Costs and Charges

Management wants to know how much an information system costs, so it is important for the systems analyst to understand direct costs, indirect costs, and methods of allocating IT charges within the company.

Direct costs usually are easier to identify and predict than indirect costs. For example, the salaries of project team members and the purchase of hardware, software, and supplies for the new system are direct costs. After a new information system goes into operation, other direct costs might include the lease of system-specific hardware or software.

Many IT department costs cannot be attributed directly to a specific information system or user group. Those indirect costs can include general hardware and software acquisition expenses; facility maintenance, air conditioning, security, rent, insurance, and general supplies; and the salaries of operations, technical support, and information center personnel.

A **chargeback method** is a technique that uses accounting entries to allocate the indirect costs of running the IT department. Most organizations adopt one of four chargeback methods: no charge, a fixed charge, a variable charge based on resource usage, or a variable charge based on volumes.

1. **No charge.** Some organizations treat information systems department indirect expenses as a necessary cost of doing business, and IT services are seen as benefiting the entire company. Thus, indirect IT department costs are treated as general organizational costs and are not charged to other departments. In this case, the information systems department is called a **cost center** because it generates accounting charges with no offsetting credits for IT services.

2. **Fixed charge.** With this method, the indirect IT costs are divided among all the other departments in the form of a fixed monthly charge. The monthly charge might be the same for all departments or based on a relatively constant factor such as department size or number of workstations. By using a fixed charge approach, all indirect costs are charged to other departments and the IT group is regarded as a profit center. A **profit center** is a department that is expected to break even or show a profit. Under the profit center concept, company departments purchase services from the IT department and receive accounting charges that represent the cost of providing the services.

3. **Variable charge based on resource usage. Resource allocation** is the charging of indirect costs based on the resources used by an information system. The allocation might be based on connect time, server processing time, network resources required, printer use, or a combination of similar factors. **Connect time** is the total time that a user is connected actively to a remote server — some Internet service providers use this as a basis for charges. In a client/server system, **server processing time** is the time that the server actually responds to client requests for processing. The amount a particular department is charged will vary from month to month, depending not only on that department's resource usage, but also on the total resource usage. The information systems department is considered a profit center when an organization uses the resource allocation method.

4. **Variable charge based on volume.** The indirect information systems department costs are allocated to other departments based on user-oriented activity, such as the number of transactions or printing volume. As with the resource allocation method, a department's share of the costs varies from month to month, depending on the level of activity. In this case, the information systems department is considered a profit center.

Benefit Classifications

In addition to classifying costs, you must classify the benefits that the company expects from a project. Like costs, benefits can be classified as tangible or intangible, fixed or variable, and direct or indirect. Another useful benefit classification relates to the nature of the benefit: positive benefits versus cost-avoidance benefits. **Positive benefits** increase revenues, improve services, or otherwise contribute to the organization as a direct result of the new information system. Examples of positive benefits include improved information availability, greater flexibility, faster service to customers, higher employee morale, and better inventory management.

In contrast, **cost-avoidance benefits** refer to expenses that would be necessary if the new system is not installed. Examples of cost-avoidance benefits include handling the work with current staff instead of hiring additional people, not having to replace existing hardware or software, and avoiding problems that otherwise would be faced with the current system. Cost-avoidance benefits are just as important as positive benefits, and you must consider both types when performing cost-benefit analysis.

COST-BENEFIT ANALYSIS

Cost-benefit analysis is the process of comparing the anticipated costs of an information system to the anticipated benefits. Cost-benefit analysis is performed throughout the SDLC to determine the economic feasibility of an information system project and to compare alternative solutions. Many cost-benefit analysis techniques exist. This section covers discussion of only the three most common methods: payback analysis, return on investment analysis, and present value analysis. Each of the approaches analyzes cost-benefit figures differently, but the objective is the same: to provide reliable information for making decisions.

Payback Analysis

Payback analysis is the process of determining how long it takes an information system to pay for itself. The time it takes to recover the system's cost is called the **payback period**. To perform a payback analysis, you carry out the following steps:

1. Determine the initial development cost of the system.

2. Estimate annual benefits.

3. Determine annual operating costs.

4. Find the payback period by comparing total development and operating costs to the accumulated value of the benefits produced by the system.

When you plot the system costs over the potential life of the system, you typically see a curve such as the one shown in Figure TK 2-1. After the system is operational, costs decrease rapidly and remain relatively low for a period of time. Eventually, as the system requires more maintenance, costs begin to increase. The period between the beginning of systems operation and the point when operational costs are rapidly increasing is called the **economically useful life** of the system.

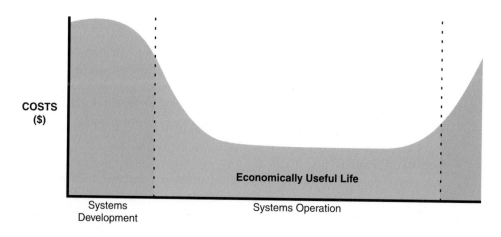

COSTS
($)

Economically Useful Life

Systems
Development

Systems Operation

TIME

FIGURE TK 2-1 The costs of a typical system vary over time. At the beginning, system costs are high due to initial development expense. Costs then drop during systems operation. Maintenance costs begin to increase until the system reaches the end of its economically useful life. The area between the two dashed lines shows the economically useful life of this system.

When you plot the benefits provided by an information system against time, the resulting curve usually resembles the one shown in Figure TK 2-2. Benefits start to appear when the system becomes operational, might increase for a time, and then level off or begin to decline.

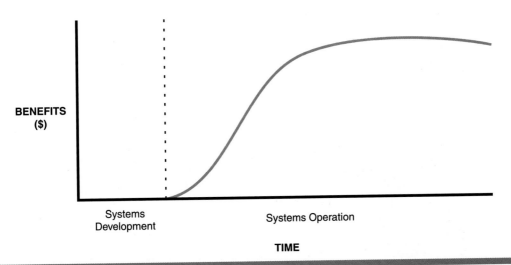

BENEFITS
($)

Systems
Development

Systems Operation

TIME

FIGURE TK 2-2 The benefits of an information system change over time. Benefits are not realized until the system becomes operational. Then, benefits usually increase rapidly at first before leveling off.

When conducting a payback analysis, you calculate the time it takes for the accumulated benefits of an information system to equal the accumulated costs of developing and operating the system. In Figure TK 2-3, the cost and benefit curves are plotted on the same graph. The dashed line indicates the payback period. Notice that the payback period is not the point when current benefits equal current costs, where the two lines cross. Instead, the payback period compares accumulated costs and benefits. If you graph current costs and benefits, the payback period corresponds to the time at which the areas under the two curves are equal.

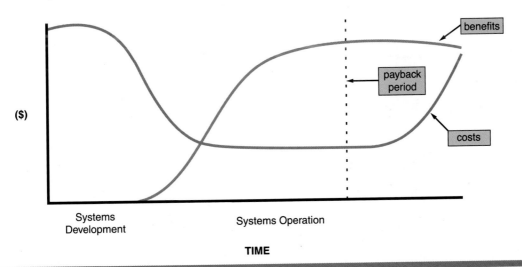

($)

benefits

payback
period

costs

Systems
Development

Systems Operation

TIME

FIGURE TK 2-3 A system's costs and benefits are plotted on the same graph. The dashed line indicates the payback period, when accumulated benefits equal accumulated costs.

Figure TK 2-4 contains two cost-benefit tables. The tables show the anticipated annual costs, cumulative costs, annual benefits, and cumulative benefits for two information systems projects. Year 0 (zero) corresponds to the year in which systems development begins. The development of Project A takes less than one year, so some benefits are realized in Year 0. Systems development for Project B requires more than one year, so the benefits do not begin until some time in Year 1.

PROJECT A:

YEAR	COSTS	CUMULATIVE COSTS	BENEFITS	CUMULATIVE BENEFITS
0	60,000	60,000	3,000	3,000
1	17,000	77,000	28,000	31,000
2	18,500	95,500	31,000	62,000
3	19,200	114,700	34,000	96,000
4	21,000	135,700	36,000	132,000
5	22,000	157,700	39,000	171,000
6	23,300	181,000	42,000	213,000

Payback period is approximately 4.2 years

PROJECT B:

YEAR	COSTS	CUMULATIVE COSTS	BENEFITS	CUMULATIVE BENEFITS
0	80,000	80,000	—	—
1	40,000	120,000	6,000	6,000
2	25,000	145,000	26,000	32,000
3	22,000	167,000	54,000	86,000
4	24,000	191,000	70,000	156,000
5	26,500	217,500	82,000	238,000
6	30,000	247,500	92,000	330,000

Payback period is approximately 4.7 years

FIGURE TK 2-4 Payback analysis data for two information systems proposals: Project A and Project B.

In Project A, by the end of Year 4, the cumulative costs are $135,700, which slightly exceeds the $132,000 cumulative benefits through that year. By the end of Year 5, however, the $171,000 cumulative benefits far exceed the cumulative costs, which are $157,700. At some point in time, closer to the beginning of Year 5, the accumulated costs and benefits are equal. The payback period for Project A is, therefore, approximately 4.2 years. Using a similar process, the payback period for Project B is determined to be approximately 4.7 years.

Some managers are critical of payback analysis because it places all the emphasis on early costs and benefits and ignores the benefits received after the payback period. Even if the benefits for Project B in Year 6 soared as high as $500,000, the payback period for that project still is 4.7 years. In defense of payback analysis, the earlier cost and benefit predictions usually are more certain. In general, the further out in time that you extend your projections, the more unsure your forecast will be. Thus, payback analysis uses the most reliable of your cost and benefit estimates.

Payback analysis rarely is used to compare or rank projects because later benefits are ignored. You would never decide that Project A is better than Project B simply because the payback period for A is less than that for B; considering all the costs and all the benefits when comparing projects makes more sense.

Even with its drawbacks, payback analysis is a widely used tool. Many business organizations establish a minimum payback period for approved projects. If company policy requires a project to begin paying for itself within three years, then neither project in Figure TK 2-4 would be approved, though both are economically feasible.

Using a Spreadsheet to Compute Payback Analysis

You can use a spreadsheet to record and calculate accumulated costs and benefits, as shown in Figure TK 2-5. The first step is to design the worksheet and label the rows and columns. After entering the cost and benefit data for each year, you enter the formulas. For payback analysis, you will need a formula to display cumulative totals, year by year. For example, the first year in the CUMULATIVE COSTS column is the same as Year 0 costs, so the formula in cell C6 is =B6. The cumulative cost total for the second year is Year 0 cumulative total + Year 1 costs, so the formula for cell C7 is =C6+B7, and so on. The first worksheet shows the initial layout and the second worksheet shows the finished spreadsheet.

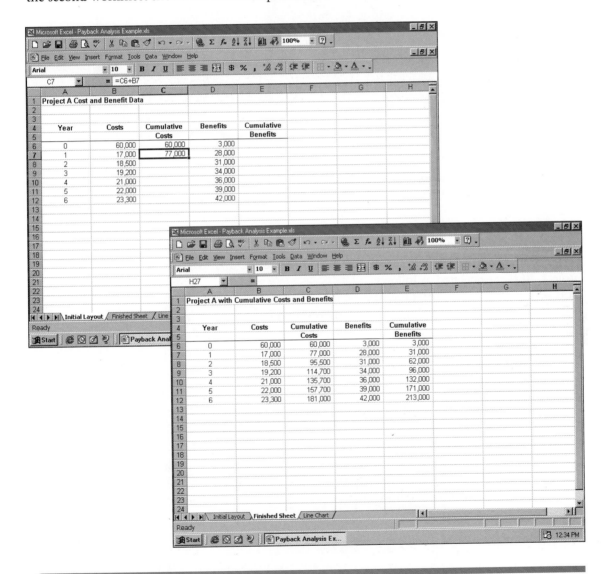

FIGURE TK 2-5 A Microsoft Excel worksheet showing payback analysis data for Project A, and the finished payback analysis worksheet.

After you verify that the spreadsheet operates properly, you can create a line chart (again using the spreadsheet program) that displays the cumulative costs and benefits, as shown in Figure TK 2-6.

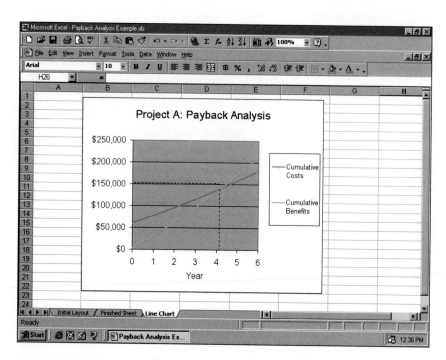

FIGURE TK 2-6   A Microsoft Excel chart showing cumulative costs and benefits.

N THE WEB

r information about Return
Investment (ROI) visit
site.com/sad4e/more.htm,
ck Systems Analysis and
sign Toolkit and then click
e Return on Investment
OI) link.

w.scsite.com

Return on Investment Analysis

Return on investment (ROI) is a percentage rate that measures profitability by comparing the total net benefits (the return) received from a project to the total costs (the investment) of the project. ROI is calculated as follows:

ROI = (total benefits – total costs) / total costs

Return on investment analysis considers costs and benefits over a longer time span than payback analysis. ROI calculations usually are based on total costs and benefits for a period of five to seven years. For example, Figure TK 2-7, shows the ROI calculations for Project A and Project B. The ROI for Project A is 17.7 percent and the ROI for Project B is 33.3 percent.

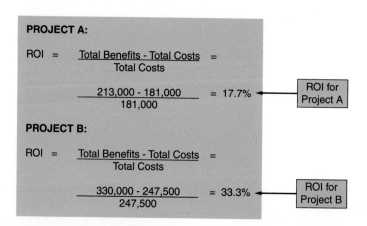

FIGURE TK 2-7   Return on investment analysis for Project A and Project B shown in Figure TK 2-4 on page TK 2.6.

In many organizations, projects must meet or exceed a minimum ROI. This minimum ROI can be an estimate of the return the organization would receive from investing its money in other investment opportunities such as treasury bonds, or it can be a higher rate that the company requires for all new projects. If a company requires a minimum ROI of 15 percent, for example, then both Projects A and B would meet the criterion.

You also can use ROI for ranking projects. If Projects A and B represent two different proposed solutions for a single information systems project, then the solution represented by Project B is better than the Project A solution. If Projects A and B represent two different information systems projects, and if the organization has sufficient resources to pursue only one of the two projects, then Project B is the better choice.

Critics of return on investment analysis raise two points. First, ROI measures the overall rate of return for the total period, and annual return rates can vary considerably. Two projects with the same ROI might not be equally desirable if the benefits of one project occur significantly earlier than the benefits of the other project. The second criticism is that the ROI technique ignores the timing of the costs and benefits. This concept is called the time value of money, and is explained in the section on the present value analysis method.

Using a Spreadsheet to Compute ROI

You also can use spreadsheet programs to calculate the ROI. To do so for Project A, first set up the worksheet and enter the cost and benefit data. You can use cumulative columns (as you did in payback analysis) but you also will need two overall totals (one for costs and one for benefits), as shown in Figure TK 2-8.

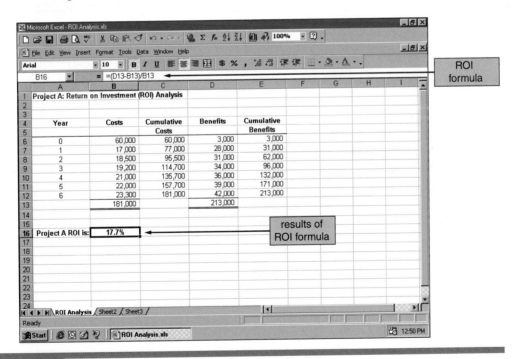

FIGURE TK 2-8 The worksheet for ROI analysis for Project A.

The last step is to add a formula to calculate the ROI percentage rate, which is displayed in cell B16 in Figure TK 2-8. As stated previously, the ROI calculation is total benefits minus total costs, divided by total costs. Therefore, the formula that displays the ROI percentage in cell B16 is =(D13-B13)/B13.

A major advantage of using a spreadsheet is if your data changes, you can modify your worksheet and calculate a new result instantly.

Present Value Analysis

A dollar you have today is worth more than a dollar you do not receive until one year from today. If you have the dollar now, you can invest it and it will grow in value. For example, would you rather have $100 right now or a year from now? The answer should be obvious. If you receive the $100 now, you can invest it in a mutual fund that has an annual return of 8 percent. One year from now, you will have $108 instead of $100.

Alternatively, you might start from a different point of view. Instead of asking, "How much will my $100 be worth a year from now?" you can ask, "How much do I need to invest today, at 8 percent, in order to have $100 a year from now?" This concept is known as the **time value of money**, and it is the basis of the technique called **present value analysis**.

The **present value** of a future dollar is the amount of money that, when invested today at a specified interest rate, grows to exactly one dollar at a certain point in the future. The specified interest rate is called the discount rate. In present value analysis, a company uses a discount rate that represents the rate of return if the money is put into relatively risk-free investments, such as bonds, instead of being invested in the project.

Most companies require a rate of return that is higher than the discount rate because of the degree of risk in any project compared with investing in a bond. Companies often reject projects that seem attractive because the risk is not worth the potential reward.

To help you perform present value analysis, adjustment factors for various interest rates and numbers of years are calculated and printed in tables called **present value tables**. Figure TK 2-9 shows a portion of a present value table, including values for 10 years at various discount rates.

N THE WEB

learn more about
resent Value Analysis visit
csite.com/sad4e/more.htm,
ick Systems Analysis and
esign Toolkit and then click
e Present Value Analysis
nk.

w.scsite.com

PERIODS	6%	8%	10%	12%	14%
1	0.943	0.926	0.909	0.893	0.877
2	0.890	0.857	0.826	0.797	0.769
3	0.840	0.794	0.751	0.712	0.675
4	0.792	0.735	0.683	0.636	0.592
5	0.747	0.681	0.621	0.567	0.519
6	0.705	0.630	0.564	0.507	0.456
7	0.665	0.583	0.513	0.452	0.400
8	0.627	0.540	0.467	0.404	0.351
9	0.592	0.500	0.424	0.361	0.308
10	0.558	0.463	0.386	0.322	0.270

FIGURE TK 2-9 Portion of a present value table showing adjustment factors for various time periods and discount rates. Values in the table are calculated using the formula shown in the text. Notice how the factors decrease as time and percentages increase.

Many finance and accounting books contain comprehensive present value tables, or you can obtain this information on the Internet, as shown in Figure TK 2-10.

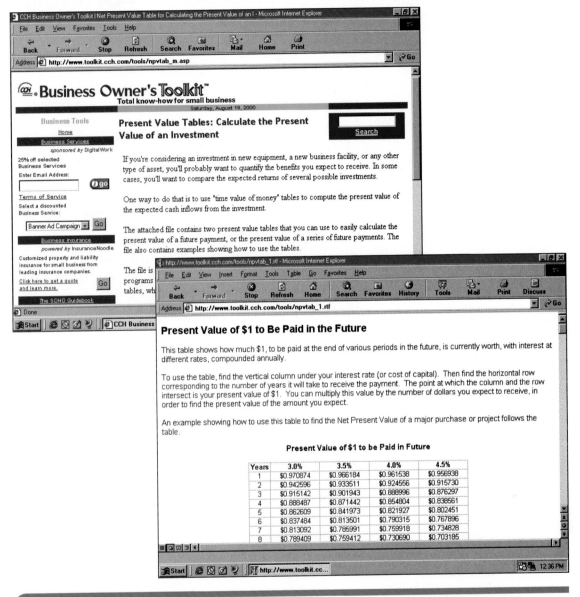

FIGURE TK 2-10 The CCH Web site provides a variety of information to the business community, including present value tables.

To use a present value table, you locate the value in the column with the appropriate discount rate and the row for the appropriate number of years. For example, to calculate the present value of $1 at 12 percent for five years, you look down the 12 percent column in Figure TK 2-9 until you reach the row representing five years. The table value is 0.567. To determine what the present value of $3,000 will be in five years with a discount rate of 12 percent, multiply the present value factor from the table by the dollar amount; that is, PV = $3,000 x 0.567 = $1,701.

To perform present value analysis, you must time-adjust the cost and benefit figures. First, you multiply each of the projected benefits and costs by the proper present value factor, which depends on when the cost will be incurred or the benefit will be received. The second step is to sum all the time-adjusted benefits and time-adjusted costs. Then, you calculate the **net present value (NPV)** of the project, which is the total present value of the benefits minus the total present value of the costs. Figure TK 2-11 shows the calculation of net present value for two sample projects.

PROJECT A: **PRESENT VALUE ANALYSIS**

	Year 0	Year 1	Year 2	Year 3	Year 4	Year 5	Year 6	Total
Benefits:	3,000	28,000	31,000	34,000	36,000	39,000	42,000	
Present Value Factor (12%):	1.000	0.893	0.797	0.712	0.636	0.567	0.507	
Present Value:	3,000	25,004	24,707	24,208	22,896	22,113	21,294	143,222
Costs:	60,000	17,000	18,500	19,200	21,000	22,000	23,300	
Present Value Factor (12%):	1.000	0.893	0.797	0.712	0.636	0.567	0.507	
Present Value:	60,000	15,181	14,745	13,670	13,356	12,474	11,813	141,239
Net Present Value:					net present value of Project A →			1,983

PROJECT B: **PRESENT VALUE ANALYSIS**

	Year 0	Year 1	Year 2	Year 3	Year 4	Year 5	Year 6	Total
Benefits:	——	6,000	26,000	54,000	70,000	82,000	92,000	
Present Value Factor (12%):	——	0.893	0.797	0.712	0.636	0.567	0.507	
Present Value:	——	5,358	20,722	38,448	44,520	46,494	46,644	202,186
Costs:	80,000	40,000	25,000	22,000	24,000	26,500	30,000	
Present Value Factor (12%):	1.000	0.893	0.797	0.712	0.636	0.567	0.507	
Present Value:	80,000	35,720	19,925	15,664	15,264	15,026	15,210	196,809
Net Present Value:					net present value of Project B →			5,377

FIGURE TK 2-11 Present value analysis for Project A and Project B.

In theory, any project with a positive NPV is economically feasible because the project will produce a larger return than would be achieved by investing the same amount of money in a discount rate investment. Remember that risks are associated with any project, however, and management typically insists on a substantially higher return for high-risk projects. For example, both projects in Figure TK 2-11 have positive net present values and appear economically worthwhile. Suppose, however, that you knew one of the projects had a 90 percent probability of achieving its goals, while the other project had only a 70 percent chance. To be attractive, the project with the higher risk would have to offer a corresponding higher reward.

Net present value also can be used to compare and rank projects. All things being equal, the project with the highest net present value is the best investment. Figure TK 2-11 shows that Project B is a better investment than Project A because it has a higher net present value.

Present value analysis provides solutions to the shortcomings of payback analysis and return on investment analysis. Unlike payback analysis, present value analysis considers all the costs and benefits, and not just the earlier values. In addition, present value analysis takes into account the timing of costs and benefits, so their values can be adjusted by the discount rate that provides a common yardstick and recognizes the time value of money. Even so, companies often use all three methods to get more input for making decisions. Sometimes a project will score higher on one method of analysis and lower on another.

Using a Spreadsheet to Calculate Present Value

You can use a worksheet such as the one shown in Figure TK 2-12 to calculate the present value based on the data for Project A. You begin by entering the unadjusted cost and benefit values and the discount factors for each year. Next, enter a formula to produce an adjusted value for each cost and benefit entry. To produce an adjusted value, you multiply the cost or benefit value times the discount factor. You start with cell B12 by entering the formula =B10*B11. Because the factor is 1.000, the 3,000 amount remains unchanged.

	Year 0	Year 1	Year 2	Year 3	Year 4	Year 5	Year 6	Total
Benefits	3,000	28,000	31,000	34,000	36,000	39,000	42,000	
Factor	1.000	0.893	0.797	0.712	0.636	0.567	0.507	
PV of Benefits	3,000	25,004	24,707	24,208	22,896	22,113	21,294	143,222
Costs	60,000	17,000	18,500	19,200	21,000	22,000	23,300	
Factor	1.000	0.893	0.797	0.712	0.636	0.567	0.507	
PV of Costs	60,000	15,181	14,745	13,670	13,356	12,474	11,813	141,239
Net Present Value of Project A:			1,983					

FIGURE TK 2-12 A Microsoft Excel worksheet can be used to calculate present value (PV) and net present value (NPV).

Now, you copy the formula from cell B12 to cells C12 through H12, and the adjusted values will display. You total the adjusted benefits in cell I12 with the formula =SUM(B12:H12), and then use the same method for the cost figures. Your final step is to calculate the net present value in cell D18 by subtracting the adjusted costs in cell I16 from the adjusted benefits in cell I12.

There is one more way to use a worksheet in present value analysis. Most spreadsheet programs include a built-in present value function that calculates present value and other time-adjusted variable factors. The program inputs the formula, and then you input the investment amount, discount rate, and number of time periods. Use your spreadsheet's Help function to find out more about using this automatic calculation feature.

TOOLKIT PART 2 SUMMARY

As a systems analyst, you must be concerned with economic feasibility throughout the SDLC, and especially during the systems planning and systems analysis phases. A project is economically feasible if the anticipated benefits exceed the expected costs. When you review a project, you work with various feasibility and cost analysis tools.

You must classify project costs as either tangible or intangible, direct or indirect, fixed or variable, and developmental or operational. Tangible costs are those that have a specific dollar value, whereas intangible costs involve items that are difficult to measure in dollar terms, such as employee dissatisfaction. Direct costs can be associated with a particular information system, while indirect costs refer to overhead expenses that cannot be allocated to a specific project. Fixed costs remain the same regardless of activity levels, while variable costs are affected by the degree of system activity. Developmental costs are one-time systems development expenses, while operational costs continue during the systems operation and use phase.

Every company must decide how to charge or allocate information systems costs and the chargeback method. Common chargeback approaches are no charge, a fixed charge, a variable charge based on resource usage, or a variable change based on volume.

Some companies use a no charge approach because IT services benefit the overall organization. This method treats the IT group for accounting purposes as a cost center that offers services without charge. In contrast, if management imposes charges on other departments, the IT department is regarded as a profit center that sells services that otherwise would have to be purchased from outside the company.

You also must classify system benefits. Many benefit categories are similar to costs: tangible or intangible, fixed or variable, and direct or indirect. Benefits also can be classified as positive benefits that result in direct dollar savings or cost-avoidance benefits that allow the firm to avoid costs that they would otherwise have incurred.

Cost-benefit analysis involves three common approaches: payback analysis, return on investment (ROI) analysis, and present value analysis. You can use spreadsheet programs to help you work with those tools.

Payback analysis determines the time it takes for a system to pay for itself, which is called the payback period. In payback analysis, you compare total development and operating costs to total benefits. The payback period is the point at which accumulated benefits equal accumulated costs. A disadvantage of this method is that payback analysis only analyzes costs and benefits incurred at the beginning of a system's useful life.

Return on investment (ROI) analysis measures a system by comparing total net benefits (the return) to total costs (the investment). The result is a percentage figure that represents a rate of return that the system offers as a potential investment. Many organizations set a minimum ROI that all projects must match or exceed and use ROI to rank several projects. Although ROI provides additional information compared with payback analysis, ROI only expresses an overall average rate of return that might not be accurate for a given time period, and ROI does not recognize the time value of money.

Present value analysis adjusts the value of future costs and benefits to account for the time value of money. By measuring all future costs and benefits in current dollars, you can compare systems more accurately and consistently. Present value analysis uses mathematical factors that you can derive or look up in published tables. You also can use a spreadsheet function to calculate present value. Many companies use present value analysis to evaluate and rank projects.

Toolkit Part 2 Key Terms

chargeback method, (TK 2.3)
connect time, (TK 2.3)
cost center, (TK 2.3)
cost-avoidance benefits, (TK 2.3)
cost-benefit analysis (TK 2.4)
developmental costs, (TK 2.2)
direct costs, (TK 2.2)
economically useful life, (TK 2.4)
fixed costs, (TK 2.2)
indirect costs, (TK 2.2)
intangible costs, (TK 2.2)
net present value (NPV), (TK 2.12)
operational costs, (TK 2.2)
overhead expenses, (TK 2.2)

payback analysis, (TK 2.4)
payback period, (TK 2.4)
positive benefits, (TK 2.3)
present value, (TK 2.10)
present value analysis, (TK 2.10)
present value tables, (TK 2.10)
profit center, (TK 2.3)
resource allocation, (TK 2.3)
return on investment (ROI), (TK 2.8)
server processing time, (TK 2.3)
tangible costs, (TK 2.2)
time value of money, (TK 2.10)
variable costs, (TK 2.2)

Toolkit Part 2 Review

1. What is economic feasibility? How do you know if a project is economically feasible?

2. How can you classify costs? Describe each cost classification and provide a typical example for each category.

3. What is a chargeback method? What are four common chargeback approaches?

4. How can you classify benefits? Describe each benefit classification and provide a typical example for each category.

5. What is payback analysis and what does it measure? What is a payback period and what is the formula to calculate the payback period?

6. What is return on investment (ROI) analysis and what does it measure? What is the formula to calculate ROI?

7. What is present value analysis and what does it measure?

8. What is the meaning of the phrase, time value of money?

9. Present value analysis can be a handy tool for the analyst in many situations. Suppose you are studying two hardware lease proposals, as shown in Figure TK 2-13 on the next page.

Lease Option 1 costs only $4,000 but requires that the money be paid up front. Option 2 costs $5,000, but the payments stretch out over a longer period. You performed a present value analysis using a 14 percent discount rate. What happens if you use an 8 percent rate? What if you use a 12 percent rate?

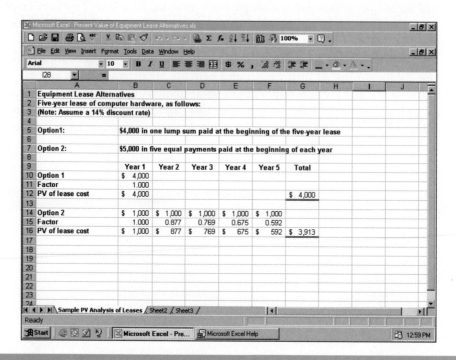

FIGURE TK 2-13 You can use a spreadsheet to evaluate two lease options by applying the present value factors in rows 11 and 15. Even though Option 2 requires the payment of $5,000, it is less expensive when present value is considered.

10. What are two specific advantages of present value analysis compared to other approaches?

Project Management Tools **PART 3**

Project Management Tools

In Part 3 of the Toolkit, you will learn about project management tools that are important to the systems analyst.

INTRODUCTION

In Part 3 of the Systems Analyst's Toolkit, you will learn about project management, cost estimating, and change control for information systems projects. Part 3 discusses planning, estimating, scheduling, monitoring, control, reporting, and the use of project management software. You will learn how to use Gantt charts and PERT/CPM to schedule and monitor projects and how to control and manage project changes.

OBJECTIVES

When you finish this Part of the Toolkit, you will be able to:

- Describe project management tools and how they are used

- Describe the steps used in project planning

- Explain the project estimating process

- Describe the different scheduling tools, including Gantt charts and PERT/CPM charts

- Calculate completion times, start dates, and end dates for a project

- Explain the tasks of project monitoring, control, and reporting

- Explain the steps involved in software change control

- Understand the reasons why projects sometimes fail

PROJECT MANAGEMENT

Project management is the process of defining, planning, organizing, leading, and controlling the development of an information system. Project management is important throughout the entire SDLC but is especially vital during systems implementation, which usually is the longest and most costly phase.

Project Management Overview

The goal of project management is to deliver an information system that is acceptable to users and is developed on time and within budget. The acceptability, deadline, and budget criteria all must be met for a project to be considered successful. To meet those requirements, you must manage the project carefully and effectively.

Every successful project must have a leader. The **project manager**, or **project leader**, usually is a senior systems analyst or an IT department manager if the project is large. An analyst or a programmer/analyst might manage smaller projects.

In addition to the project manager, most large projects also have a project coordinator. The **project coordinator** handles administrative responsibilities for the development team and negotiates with users who might have conflicting requirements or want changes that would require additional time or expense.

Management Functions

The **management functions** are planning, organizing, leading, and controlling. The activities apply to all types of managers, including IT project managers. A project manager's **planning** work includes identifying and planning project tasks and estimating completion times and costs. The **organizing** function consists of staffing, which includes selecting the project team and assigning specific tasks to team members. Organizing also requires structuring and scheduling the project work. **Leading**, or directing, involves guiding, supervising, and coordinating the team's workload. Finally, **controlling** activities include monitoring the progress of the project, evaluating results, and taking corrective action when necessary to stay on target.

Project Planning

The project plan provides an overall framework for managing costs and schedules. Project planning takes place at the beginning and end of each SDLC phase to develop a plan and schedule for the phases that follow.

The planning process starts with a list of activities, or tasks. An **activity**, or **task**, is any work that has a beginning and an end, and requires the use of company resources including people, time, and/or money. Examples of activities include conducting a series of interviews, designing a report, selecting software, waiting for the delivery of equipment, or training users.

Activities are basic units of work that the project manager plans, monitors, and tracks, so tasks should be relatively small and manageable. For instance, if your project team needs to code five programs, you identify five separate tasks — one for each program — rather than one activity for all five programs.

In addition to activities, every project has events, or milestones. An **event**, or **milestone**, is a reference point that marks a major occurrence. Events are used to monitor progress and manage the project. Every activity has two events: one represents the beginning of the task, and the other marks the end of the task. Figure TK 3-1 shows a plan for creating and analyzing a questionnaire, with specific activities and events.

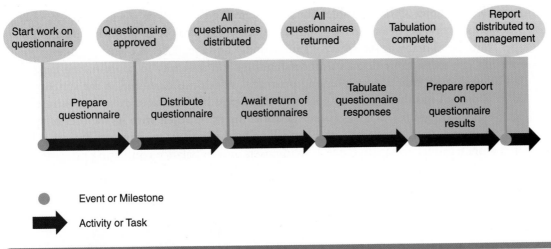

FIGURE TK 3-1 Using a questionnaire requires a series of activities and events to track the progress. The illustration shows the relationship between the activities and the events, or milestones that mark the beginning and end of each task.

All events must be recognizable. Delivery of equipment, beginning the design of a report, obtaining user approval, completing user training, and completing the tabulation of returned questionnaires are good examples of recognizable events. Completing 50 percent of a program's testing would not be a good milestone, however, unless you could determine exactly when that event occurs.

Project managers must define all activities and events, with estimates of time and costs for each task. Then they stipulate the order of the tasks and develop a work schedule. The final step is to assign tasks to specific members of the project team. As the work is performed, the project manager leads and coordinates the team, monitors events, and reports on progress.

PROJECT ESTIMATING

Determining precise time estimates for a project is not an easy task, because of the many factors a project manager must consider. One of the most important variables is the size of the project, because the amount of work does not relate directly to the size of the project. If one project is twice the size of another project, the larger project will take more than twice as many resources to develop. Why is this so?

As an example, Figure TK 3-2 shows two projects. Project A has two development team members working on a system with three main programs and four end users. Project B has four people assigned to a system with six programs and eight end users. It appears that Project B is twice as large as Project A. Will Project B require twice as many resources as Project A?

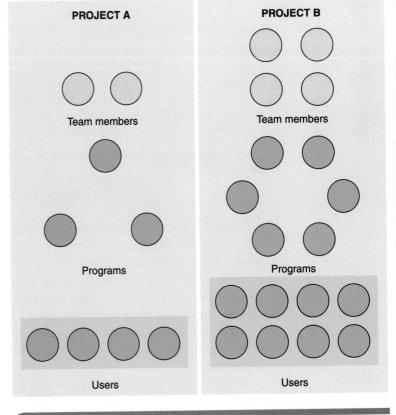

FIGURE TK 3-2 Project A has two team members, three programs, and four end users. Project B has twice as many team members, programs, and users. Is Project B twice as large as Project A?

Figure TK 3-3 shows all the possible interactions among the analysts. As you can see, only one interaction exists between the two analysts in Project A. Project B, however, has a four-member team, so as many as six different interactions can take place. Six times as many relationships can mean more delay, misunderstanding, and difficulty in coordinating tasks.

In addition, look at the interfaces among programs, which was discussed in the systems analysis phase. Project A has three programs, so only three possible interfaces exist. In contrast, Project B has six programs, so it has fifteen possible interfaces, each with its own set of specifications, requirements, and potential problems. Finally, the analysts working on Project B know that it is more complex to satisfy twice as many users and to balance conflicting priorities.

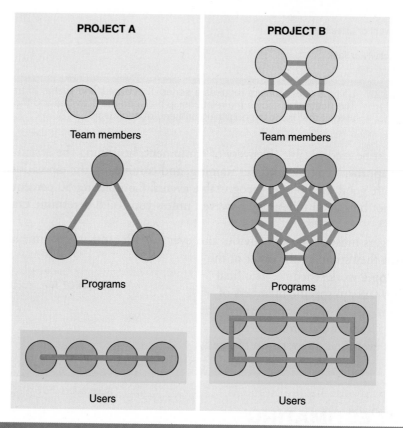

FIGURE TK 3-3 The relationships have been drawn. Notice that Project B has six team-member interactions, 15 possible program interfaces, and eight users to satisfy. Project B clearly is more than twice as large as Project A.

Figure TK 3-4 shows the relationship between project resources and project size. If doubling the project size requires exactly twice as many resources, then you would draw the dashed line to show a linear relationship. The solid line that shows the required resources, however, will increase much faster than the dashed line that represents project size.

The capabilities of project team members also affect time requirements. A less experienced analyst usually will need more time to complete a task than an experienced team member will. Other factors that can affect project time requirements include the attitudes of users, the degree of management support, and the priority of the project compared with other projects within the organization.

Time estimates usually are expressed in **person-days** that represent the amount of work that one person can complete in one day. This approach, however, can present some problems. For example, if it will take one person 20 days to perform a particular task, it might not be true that two people could complete the same task in 10 days or that 10 people could perform the task in two days.

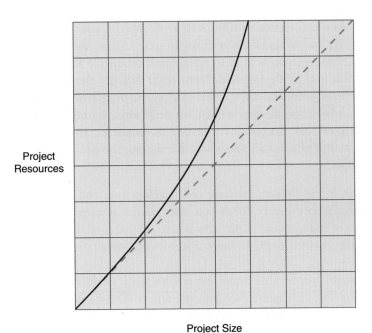

Project Resources

Project Size

FIGURE TK 3-4 As the size of a project grows, the resources needed to develop it will grow even faster.

Some tasks can be divided evenly so it is possible to use different combinations of time and people, up to a point. For instance, if it takes two person-days to install the cables for a new local area network, one person might do the task in two days, two people in one day, or four people in half a day. In most systems analysis tasks, however, time and people are not interchangeable. If one analyst needs two hours to interview a user, two analysts also will need two hours to do the same interview.

Developing Time and Cost Estimates

Because programming activities represent a significant part of the project, it is important to estimate the time required for those tasks and develop a budget. Project managers must consider four main factors: project size and scope, IT resources, prior experience with similar projects or systems, and applicable constraints.

PROJECT SIZE AND SCOPE You learned in Chapter 1 that information systems have various characteristics that affect their complexity and cost. Those characteristics include relationships with other systems, boundaries, specialized business needs, and size of the company. In addition to considering those factors, a project manager must estimate the time required to complete each project phase, including systems analysis, systems design, and systems implementation. To develop accurate time estimates, as a project manager you must identify all project activities and tasks, from initial fact-finding to application development. Regardless of which systems development methodology you use, you must determine how much time will be needed to perform each task. In developing your estimate, you must allow time for meetings, project reviews, training, and any other factors that could affect the productivity of the development team.

IT RESOURCES   As e-commerce continues to grow rapidly, companies must invest heavily in cutting-edge technology and Web-based systems. In many areas, skilled IT professionals are in great demand, and firms must work hard to attract and retain the talent they need. A project manager must assemble and guide a development team that has the skill and experience to handle the project. If necessary, additional systems analysts or programmers must be hired or trained, and this must be accomplished within a specific time frame. After a project gets underway, the project manager must deal with turnover, job vacancies, and escalating salaries in the technology sector — all of which can affect whether or not the project can be completed on time and within budget.

PRIOR EXPERIENCE   A project manager can develop time and cost estimates based on the resources used for similar, previously developed information systems. The experience method works best for small- or medium-sized projects where the two systems are similar in size, basic content, and operating environment. In large systems with more variables, the estimates are less reliable.

In addition, you might not be able to use experience from projects that were developed in a different environment. For example, when you use a new Web-based database application, you might not have previous experience to measure in this environment. In this situation, you can design a prototype or pilot system to gain technical and cost estimating experience. A **pilot system** is a small system that is developed as a basis for understanding a new environment. The concept is similar to pilot operation, which is one of the four system changeover methods that you learned about in Chapter 11, but it takes place much earlier in the systems development life cycle.

CONSTRAINTS   You learned in Chapter 2 that constraints must be defined as part of the preliminary investigation of a project. A constraint is a condition, restriction, or requirement that the system must satisfy. For example, a constraint might involve maximums for one or more resources, such as time, dollars, or people. Given those limitations, the project manager must define the system requirements that can be achieved realistically within the required constraints. In the absence of constraints, the project manager calculates the resources needed. In contrast, if constraints are present, the project manager either must adjust other resources or change the scope of the project. This approach is similar to the what-if analysis that was discussed in Chapter 12.

PROJECT SCHEDULING

When **project scheduling**, the project manager must know the duration of each activity, the order in which the activities will be performed, the start and end times for each activity, and who will be assigned to each specific task.

Once the time for each activity is estimated, the project manager determines if certain tasks are dependent on other activities. A **dependent activity** cannot be started until one or more other tasks are completed. You cannot tabulate questionnaires, for example, until they have been developed, tested, approved, distributed, and returned. After the project manager identifies all the activity dependencies, he or she arranges the tasks in a logical sequence.

The next step is to set starting and ending times for each activity. An activity cannot start until all preceding activities on which it depends are completed. The ending time for an activity is its start time plus whatever time it takes to complete the task.

When scheduling a project, project managers must decide how they will assign people to the work. Assignments should not overload or underutilize team members, and alternate periods of inactivity followed by intense effort can cause problems and should be avoided. Although scheduling can be a difficult task, a project manager must balance activity time estimates, sequences, and personnel assignments to achieve a workable schedule.

Several graphical planning aids can help a project manager in the scheduling process. We will examine two of those tools: Gantt charts and PERT/CPM charts.

Gantt Charts

Gantt charts were developed many years ago by Henry L. Gantt as a production control technique and are still in common use. A **Gantt chart** is a horizontal bar chart that illustrates a schedule. In the Gantt chart shown in Figure TK 3-5, the analyst displays time on the horizontal axis and arranges the activities vertically, from top to bottom, in the order of their start dates. The horizontal position of the bar shows the start and end of the activity, and the length of the bar indicates its duration.

ON THE WEB

To learn more about working with Gantt Charts visit scsite.com/sad4e/more.htm, click Systems Analysis and Design Toolkit and then click the Gantt Charts link.

www.scsite.c

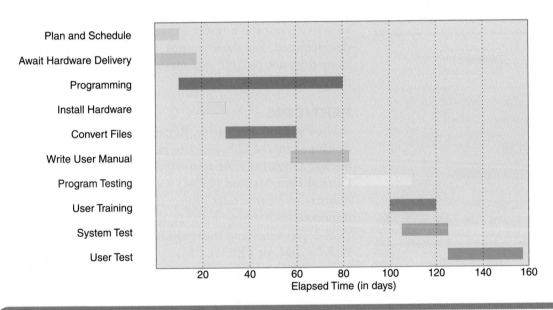

FIGURE TK 3-5 A Gantt chart for the implementation phase of a project. The chart shows 10 activities on the vertical axis and the elapsed time on the horizontal axis.

Medium-sized projects can have dozens of activities, and larger projects might have hundreds, or even thousands, of activities. A detailed Gantt chart for a very large project might be quite complex and hard to understand. To simplify the chart, the project manager can combine related activities into one task. Figure TK 3-6 on the next page shows a Gantt chart for systems development tasks. The activities labeled Programming, Write User Manual, and Program Testing actually are **activity groups**, where each activity represents several tasks. For larger projects, project managers can create multiple Gantt charts. A master chart displays the major activity groups and is followed by individual Gantt charts that show the tasks assigned to team members.

For future project phases, the time axis usually is shown as elapsed time from a zero point. For work currently in progress, the actual dates are shown on the horizontal axis.

A Gantt chart also can be used to track and report progress in several ways. First, bars can be fully or partly darkened to show completed activities, as shown in Figure TK 3-6a. Arrowheads can be used to indicate the completed portion of an activity, as shown in Figure TK 3-6b. Finally, progress can be shown by including a second bar under the schedule bar, as shown in Figure TK 3-6c.

In all cases, a vertical line indicates the current, or reporting, date. Notice that all three charts show how much of the activity has been completed, and from that you can infer if the work is on schedule. In Figure TK 3-6c, for example, Activity 2 is about 80 percent complete, although 100 percent of the time allotted for the task has passed. Similarly, Activity 4 appears to be almost half done, although the activity has used about only 5 percent of the time allotted for the task.

Gantt charts often are used to report progress because they present a clear picture of project status, but they are not an ideal tool for project control. One problem with Gantt charts is that they do not show activity dependencies. You cannot determine from a Gantt chart the impact on the entire project caused by a single activity that falls behind schedule. In addition, a Gantt chart does not show the number of hours or days required to complete an activity. The length of a bar indicates only the time span for completing an activity, not the number of people assigned or the person-days required. For those reasons, looking at a Gantt chart alone does not provide enough detail for effective project management.

PERT/CPM

The **Program Evaluation Review Technique (PERT)** was developed by the U.S. Navy to manage the construction of nuclear submarines. At approximately the same time, the **Critical Path Method (CPM)** was developed by private industry to meet similar project management needs. The important distinctions between the two methods have disappeared over time, and today the technique is called either PERT, CPM, or PERT/CPM.

PERT/CPM CHARTING CONVENTIONS   A PERT/CPM chart shows a project as a network diagram. The activities are shown as **vectors**, and the events are displayed graphically as **nodes**. Figure TK 3-7a shows the event nodes drawn as circles, although rectangles also can be used. Activity vectors, or lines, connect one node to another. Vectors on a PERT/CPM chart are like bars on a Gantt chart, with one important difference — the length of the line has nothing to do with the duration of the activity it represents. Figure TK 3-7a shows two events connected by an activity vector. Each event is identified by a number — event 1 is the beginning of the activity, and event 2 marks the end. Each activity is identified by a short description above the vector, or with a letter or code explained in a table. The estimated duration of the activity appears below the vector.

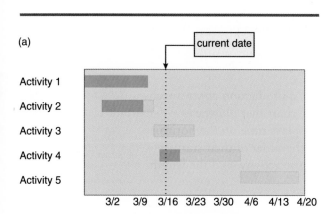

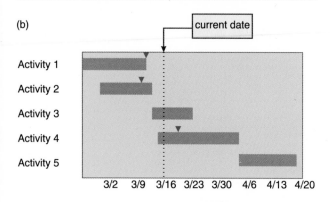

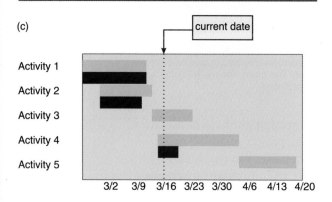

FIGURE TK 3-6   Three different ways to show the status of a project on a Gantt chart. In Figure TK 3-6a, the completed portion of each bar is shaded. In Figure TK 3-6b, a triangle or arrowhead, indicator is used. In Figure TK 3-6c, a second bar shows the completed work. All three methods show that Activity 1 is completed, Activity 2 is about 80 percent finished but behind schedule, Activity 3 has not yet started, Activity 4 is ahead of schedule, and Activity 5 has not yet begun.

FIGURE TK 3-7a In a PERT/CPM chart, a circle, or node, represents an event, or milestone, and is identified by a number. The vector line connecting the events represents an activity, or task, and is identified by a description or code letter. The estimated duration is placed below the activity.

FIGURE TK 3-7b To show that one event depends on another, a dummy activity is used. The dummy activity is shown as a dashed vector line to illustrate that Event 4 cannot occur until event 3 takes place. Because their only purpose is to show event dependencies, dummy activities do not have descriptions or durations.

The activity connecting events 3 and 4 in Figure TK 3-7b is a **dummy activity**, which is shown by a dashed vector line. A dummy activity in a PERT/CPM chart indicates an **event dependency**, but does not require any resources or completion time. For example, the dummy activity connecting events 3 and 4 identifies that event 4 cannot take place until event 3 occurs.

When tasks must be completed in sequence, they are called **dependent**, or **serial**, activities. When activities can be completed at the same time, they are called **concurrent**, or **parallel**, activities. Figure TK 3-8 shows three dependent activities: A, B, and C. Notice that activity A must end before activity B can begin. Event 3, which marks the end of activity B, must occur before activity C can start.

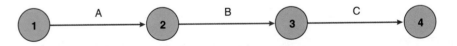

FIGURE TK 3-8 Activities A, B, and C are sequential, or serial, tasks that must be completed in order. Activity A must be finished before activity B can start, and activity C cannot start until activity B is completed.

In Figure TK 3-9, activities D and E are parallel activities that can be done at the same time, but the length of the two tasks may be different. Activity D could represent a two-week series of interviews, while activity E might show a one-day training session. Notice that activity F depends on D and E, and it cannot start until both D and E are completed. The dummy activity between events 6 and 7 connects activities D and E into a single path that leads to activity F and shows that they both must be completed before F can begin.

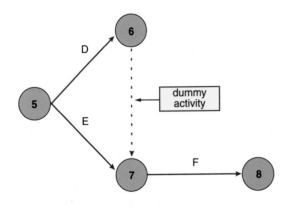

FIGURE TK 3-9 Activities D and E are parallel tasks that can be worked on at the same time. Both activities D and E must be finished, however, before activity F can begin. Therefore, it is necessary to show a dummy activity leading to event 7. Event 7, which marks the start of activity F, cannot begin until activities D and E are done.

Figure TK 3-10 shows a Gantt chart and a PERT/CPM chart. The Gantt chart shown in Figure TK 3-10a includes 10 activities, some of which are groups of related activities. To keep the PERT/CPM chart simple, the same 10 activities are included. In an actual PERT/CPM chart, individual tasks are shown in more detail and all the activity dependencies are displayed.

In addition to the 10 activities, the PERT/CPM chart shown in Figure TK 3-10b includes 11 events and three dummy activities that are used to reconnect parallel paths.

(a)

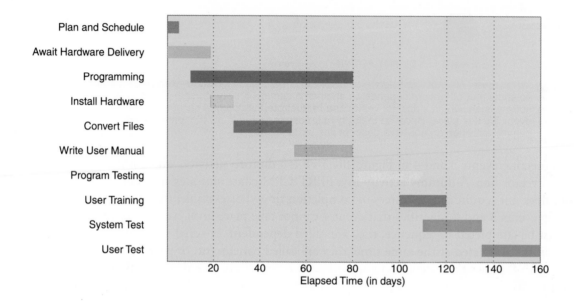

(b)

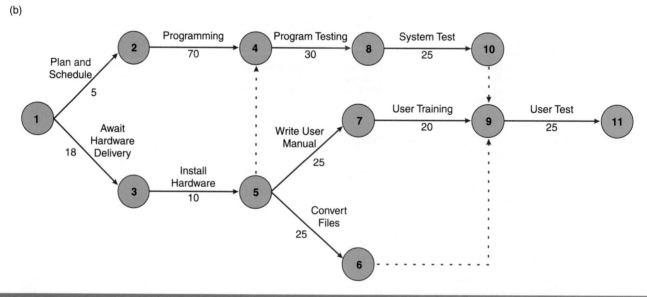

FIGURE TK 3-10 A Gantt chart and a PERT/CPM chart for the implementation phase of the same project shown in Figure TK 3-5 on page TK 3.7.

ACTIVITY DURATION   Traditional PERT techniques use a weighted formula for calculating the estimated **duration** of each activity. The project manager first makes three time estimates for each activity: an optimistic, or **best case,** estimate (B), a **probable case** estimate (P), and a pessimistic, or **worst case,** estimate (W). The manager then assigns a weight, or importance value to each estimate. The weight can vary, but a common approach is to use a ratio of B = 1, P = 4, and W = 1. The expected activity duration is calculated as follows:

$$\frac{(B+4P+W)}{6}$$

For example, a project manager might estimate that a file-conversion activity could be completed in as few as 20 days or could take as many as 34 days, but most likely will require 24 days. Using the formula, the expected activity duration is 25 days, calculated as follows:

$$\frac{(20+4*24+34)}{6} =25$$

EARLIEST COMPLETION TIMES   After identifying the tasks and durations, the project manager determines the overall length of the project. The first step is to determine the **earliest completion time (ECT)** for each event, which is the minimum amount of time necessary to complete all the activities that precede the event, as shown in Figure TK 3-11. The number in the left half of each node is the event number. The ECT is the number entered in the upper-right section of the event node.

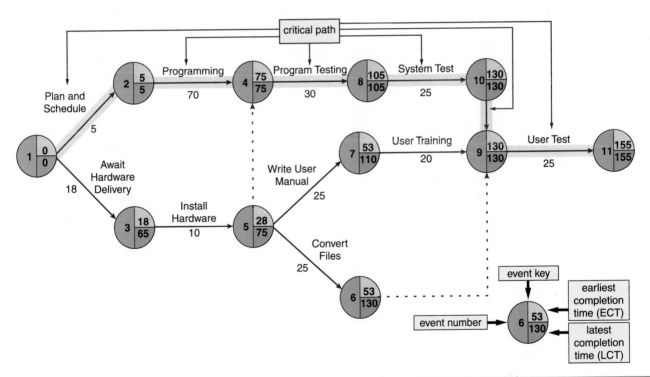

FIGURE TK 3-11 After doing the calculations, the PERT/CPM chart now shows the ECTs, LCTs, and the critical path.

You calculate earliest completion times by working from left to right across the chart. Event 1 always is given an ECT of zero days because no preceding events exist. The ECT for event 2 is five days, because the expected duration of the Plan and Schedule activity is five days. Similarly, the ECT for event 3 is 18 days.

To calculate the ECT for event 5, you take the ECT for the preceding event 3 and add 10 days, which is the duration of the Install Hardware activity. In these cases, the ECT for an event is determined by adding the duration of the immediately preceding activity to the ECT of the immediately preceding event.

How do you calculate the ECT for an event, such as event 4, that has more than one preceding event? Here you see a dummy activity leading into the event, showing that both events, 2 and 5, must be completed before event 4 can occur. This shows that the ECT for event 4 will be the largest of the earliest completion times for each path into the event. You could say that an event must await the completion of the latest event that precedes it. For example, if you cannot start a meeting until all four people arrive, then the meeting cannot begin until the last person arrives, although the other three already are present. Now, apply that concept to the PERT/CPM chart shown in Figure TK 3-11 on the previous page.

As previously mentioned, two paths lead into event 4. One of the paths is 1-2-4, meaning event 1, followed by event 2, followed by event 4. The earliest completion time for this path is 75 days (5 + 70). The other path leading to event 4 is 1-3-5-4, where the dummy activity is shown. The earliest completion time for this path is 28 days (18 + 10 + 0). Because event 4 cannot occur until all preceding events have occurred, the ECT for event 4 is the largest of 75 and 28, which is 75 days. A general rule now can be stated: the ECT for any event is the largest of the paths leading into that event.

When you have determined ECTs for all the nodes in the PERT/CPM network, the ECT of the last node is the **expected project duration**. Because the ECT for event 11 is 155 days, this systems development phase is expected to take 155 days to complete.

LATEST COMPLETION TIMES   The project manager also must determine the latest completion time for each event. The **latest completion time (LCT)** for an event is the latest time at which the event can occur without delaying the project. To determine LCTs, you work backward through the chart, from right to left. Just like ECTs, with only one path into an event, the calculation is simple. To determine the LCT of an event, you subtract the last activity from the LCT of the following event, starting with the rightmost, or final, event. The first rule is that the LCT of the final event always is the same as its ECT. That is because the last event is the overall project completion date, which is like a specific target date with no room for slippage.

Look at the example of event 9, which has only one following path connected to the right. As explained above, the final event has an LCT of 155 days, which means that it must be completed by that time. Because the connecting activity will take 25 days, the latest that event 9 can occur without delaying the project is 130 days (155 − 25). As Figure TK 3-11 shows, the LCT is entered in the lower-right section of the event node.

The process for finding the LCT for an event with more than one path is the same as you used for determining ECTs, except for three points: you work from right to left, you work with LCTs rather than ECTs, and you subtract the next activity from the following LCT, rather than add it. Therefore, the LCT of an event with more than one following path is the smallest of the paths connected to the event.

Figure TK 3-11 shows the results of the calculations. The LCT of the last event, event 11, is equal to its ECT of 155 days. As explained earlier, the LCT for event 9 is 130 days, which is calculated by subtracting the 25 days for the User Test activity from 155 days. Events 6 and 10 both are connected to event 9 by dummy activities, which have no duration; therefore, the LCT also is 130 days for both events 6 and 10. Continuing to work from right to left, the LCT for event 7 is 110 days (130 − 20), the LCT for event 8 is 105 days (130 − 25), and the LCT for event 4 is 75 days (105 − 30).

What about the LCT for event 5? Event 5 connects to three other events (4, 6, and 7) so you must calculate all three to see which is the smallest. You would proceed as follows:

Event 4:   75 days (75 − 0)
Event 7:   105 days (130 − 25)
Event 6:   85 days (110 − 25)

Thus, the LCT for event 5 is 75 days, the smallest of 75, 85, and 105.

The slack time for an event is the amount of time by which an event can be late without delaying the project. The **slack time** for an event is the difference between its LCT and ECT. You can see that the Convert Files activity could be completed as early as 53 days (ECT) and as late as 130 days (LCT). Therefore, the slack time is 77 days (130 − 53). That means that this event could be as many as 77 days behind schedule without delaying the project schedule or affecting the project completion date.

CRITICAL PATH At least one complete path will exist through a PERT/CPM network for which every node has equal ECTs and LCTs. In Figure TK 3-11, the ECTs and LCTs are equal for every event in the path 1-2-4-8-10-9-11. That path is called the critical path and has been highlighted in the figure. A **critical path** is a series of events and activities with no slack time. If any activity along the critical path falls behind schedule, the entire project schedule is similarly delayed. As the name implies, a critical path includes all activities that are vital to the project schedule. Project managers always must know what the critical path is, so they can monitor progress and make prompt decisions, if necessary, to keep the project on track.

Comparing Gantt Charts and PERT/CPM

One significant advantage of PERT/CPM charts is that, unlike Gantt charts, all individual activities and dependencies are shown. Most project managers find PERT/CPM charts very helpful for scheduling, monitoring, and controlling projects. A project manager would convert all ECTs and LCTs to actual dates by laying out the entire project on a calendar. Then, on any given day, the manager can compare what should be happening to what is taking place, and react accordingly.

PERT/CPM charts differ from Gantt charts in two respects. First, a PERT/CPM chart for even a small project can be rather complicated, and the degree of complexity increases significantly for larger projects. Second, the picture presented by a PERT/CPM chart is not as clear as a Gantt chart, which graphically displays the timing and duration of the activities.

PERT/CPM and Gantt charts are not mutually exclusive techniques. Project managers often use both methods. Neither Gantt charts nor PERT/CPM, however, handle the scheduling of personnel and the allocation of resources. To achieve efficient utilization of people, time, and company resources, you must use other techniques and software tools such as Microsoft Project, which is described in a later section of the Toolkit.

PROJECT MONITORING AND CONTROLLING

A project must be planned, organized, and scheduled before the work actually starts. After the project activities begin, the project manager concentrates on monitoring and controlling the project.

Project Monitoring and Control

The project manager must set standards and ensure that they are followed, keep track of the activities and progress of team members, compare actual progress to the project plan, and verify the completion of project milestones. To help ensure that quality standards are met, many project managers institute structured walkthroughs. A **structured walkthrough** is a review of a project team member's work by other members of the team. Generally, systems analysts review the work of other systems analysts, and programmers review the work of other programmers, as a form of peer review. Structured walkthroughs should take place throughout the SDLC and are called **requirements reviews**, **design reviews**, **code reviews**, or **testing reviews**, depending on the phase in which they occur.

Project Scheduling

Maintaining a project schedule can be a challenging task, and most projects run into at least some problems or delays. By monitoring and controlling the work, the project manager tries to anticipate problems, avoid them or minimize their impact, identify potential solutions, and select the best way to solve the problem.

The better the original plan, the easier it will be to control the project. If clear, verifiable milestones exist, it will be simple to determine if and when those targets are achieved. If enough milestones and frequent checkpoints exist, problems will be detected rapidly.

A project that is planned and scheduled with PERT/CPM techniques can be tracked and controlled using the same tools. As work continues, the project manager revises the network to record actual times for completed activities and revises times for tasks that are not yet finished. Project managers often spend most of their time tracking the activities along the critical path, because delays in those tasks have the greatest potential to delay or jeopardize the project. Other activities cannot be ignored, however. If some activity off the critical path takes too long, the slack time for that task will be exceeded. At that point, the activity actually becomes part of the critical path and any further delay will push back the overall project.

PROJECT REPORTING

Members of the project team regularly report their progress to the project manager, who in turn reports to management and users. The project manager first collects, verifies, organizes, and evaluates the information he or she receives from the team. Then the manager decides which information needs to be passed along, prepares a summary that can be understood easily, adds comments and explanations if needed, and submits it to management and users.

Project Status Meetings

Although team members constantly use e-mail to communicate, most project managers schedule regular status meetings with the entire project team. At those meetings, each team member updates the group and identifies any problems or delays. Although meetings can be time-consuming, most project managers believe it is worth the effort. The sessions give team members an opportunity to share information, discuss common problems, explain new techniques, and offer comments that can be extremely valuable to team members working on other areas of the project. The meetings also give the project manger an opportunity to update the entire group, seek input, and conduct brainstorming sessions.

Project Status Reports

A project manager must report regularly to his or her immediate supervisor, upper management, and users. Although a progress report might be given verbally to an immediate supervisor, reports to management and users usually are written. Gantt charts often are included in progress reports to show project status graphically.

Deciding how to handle potential problems can be difficult. At what point should you inform management about the possibility of cost overruns, schedule delays, or technical problems? At one extreme is the overly cautious project manager who alerts management to every potential snag and every slight delay. The danger here is that the manager loses credibility over a period of time, and management might ignore potentially serious situations. At the other extreme is the project manager who tries to handle all situations single-handedly and does not alert management until a problem is serious. By the time management learns of the problem, little time might remain in which to react or come up with a solution.

A project manager's best course of action lies somewhere between the two extremes, but probably closer to the first. If you are unsure of the consequences, you should be cautious and warn management about the possibility of a problem. When you report the situation, you also should explain what you are doing to handle and monitor the problem. If you believe the situation is beyond your control, you might want to suggest possible actions that management can take to resolve the situation. Most managers recognize that problems do occur on most projects; it is better to alert management sooner rather than later.

ON THE WEB

For more information about Project Management Software visit scsite.com/sad4e/more.htm click Systems Analysis and Design Toolkit and then clic the Project Management Software link.

www.scsite.c

PROJECT MANAGEMENT SOFTWARE

Project management software can assist you in project planning, estimating, scheduling, monitoring, and reporting. Powerful project management packages offer many features, including PERT/CPM, Gantt charts, resource scheduling, project calendars, cost tracking, and cost-benefit analysis. The analyst can select output in the form of printed reports, screen displays, or graphical plots.

The top screen in Figure TK 3-12 shows a Gantt chart produced by Microsoft Project, a project management program. The display includes 12 systems planning tasks, beginning with a review of the systems request and ending with a review of Internet access delays. The display is similar to the Gantt chart in Figure TK 3-10a on page TK 3.10 that was developed manually, although some differences exist. Notice that Saturdays and Sundays are shown as shaded areas, and that arrows indicate task dependencies.

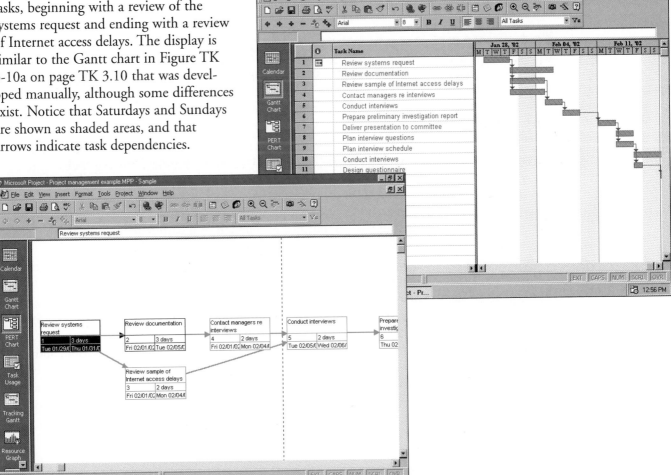

FIGURE TK 3-12 The Microsoft Project screen at the top of the figure shows an example of a systems development project in the form of a GANTT chart. The same information also is displayed in the form of a PERT/CPM chart, as shown in the bottom screen.

Using Microsoft Project, you also can produce a PERT/CPM chart, as shown in the bottom screen in Figure TK 3-12 on the previous page, which is based on the same information (without re-entry) as the Gantt chart shown in the top screen. Notice that there are several differences in the computer-generated PERT/CPM chart compared with the chart that appears in Figure TK 3-11 on page TK 3.11. In traditional PERT/CPM charts, events are shown as nodes and activities are shown as vectors. Computer-generated PERT/CPM charts use a reverse style, showing activities as nodes, with vectors to connect the activities. The vectors also show task dependencies, so it is unnecessary to use dummy activities with dashed lines as in the traditional PERT/CPM method.

The activity nodes in Microsoft Project are rectangular instead of circular, which is typical of PERT/CPM charts produced by project management software packages. Each node contains the activity description, activity identification number, task duration, start date, and end date. The critical path is indicated by a bold vector line and thicker borders that outline critical path activity nodes.

You learned that project schedules, activity estimates, and personnel assignments all are interrelated. Therefore, project planning is a dynamic task and involves constant change. One significant advantage of integrated interactive project management software is that it allows the project manager to adjust schedules, estimates, and resource assignments rapidly to develop a workable plan.

SOFTWARE CHANGE CONTROL

Software change control is the process of managing and controlling changes requested after the system requirements document has been submitted and accepted. Software change control can be a real problem because the development process involves many compromises, and users are never entirely satisfied with the results. Changes to an information system's requirements are inevitable. The issue, therefore, is how to create an effective process for controlling changes that protects the overall project, but allows those changes that are necessary and desirable.

The project coordinator, rather than the project manager, has primary responsibility for change control because requests for change most often are initiated by someone outside the information systems department. There must be a specific process for handling requested changes. The process must be formal, but flexible enough to incorporate desired changes promptly with minimal impact to the overall project.

A procedure for processing requests for changes to an information system's requirements consists of four steps: complete a change request form, take initial action on the request, analyze the impact of the requested change, and determine the disposition of the requested change.

1. **Complete a change request form.** The person requesting the change completes a System Requirements Change Request form similar to the one shown in Figure TK 3-13. On the form, which can be stored in an online network library, the requester describes and justifies the desired changes. The requester attaches helpful documents and pertinent information, such as new calculations, copies of government regulations, and memos from executives specifying new strategies and directions.

SYSTEM REQUIREMENTS CHANGE REQUEST

PRINT THE FOLLOWING INFORMATION:

NAME	
DEPARTMENT	JOB TITLE

DESCRIPTION OF CHANGE:

REASON FOR CHANGE:

ATTACH ADDITIONAL INFORMATION AND DOCUMENTS AS NEEDED:
CHECK THIS BOX IF ATTACHMENTS ARE INCLUDED: ☐

SIGNED _____ DATE _____

TO BE COMPLETED BY THE PROJECT COORDINATOR:

CONTROL NUMBER	DATE RECEIVED

IMPACT ANALYSIS:

Include an estimate of resources needed, with specific costs and timetables.

ACTION:

_____ ACCEPT

_____ DEFER UNTIL _____ (DATE)

_____ REJECT FOR THE FOLLOWING REASONS:

SIGNED _____ DATE _____

FIGURE TK 3-13 Sample of a Change Request form. Notice the Impact Analysis section. If a system has a great number of changes, what does that indicate?

2. **Take initial action on the request.** The project coordinator completes a sequential control number and the date on the change request form, reviews the specific change, and then determines if the change should be deferred to a later date, rejected for specific reasons, or investigated further. If the request is deferred or rejected, the project coordinator sends a copy of the request back to the requester. If the change is to be investigated further, then the request is reviewed for impact by the project manager or a systems analyst.

3. **Analyze the impact of the requested change.** The project manager or a systems analyst must review the request and determine the impact of incorporating the change into the information system's requirements. Then, the manager or analyst prepares an impact analysis that describes the effect of the change on the information system's requirements and on costs and schedules. The analysis should address the impact of incorporating the change immediately versus incorporating the change after the currently configured information system has been implemented.

4. **Determine the disposition of the requested change.** Based on the impact analysis and the project coordinator's recommendation, the change might be accepted, deferred, or rejected. In each of the three cases, the project coordinator informs the requester of the action taken.

KEYS TO PROJECT SUCCESS

To be successful, an information system must satisfy business requirements, meet users' needs, stay within its budget, and be completed on time. What happens when those goals are not achieved?

The major objective of every system is to provide a solution to a business problem or opportunity. If the system fails to do this, then it is a failure — regardless of positive reaction from users, acceptable budget performance, or timely delivery.

When the final information system does not meet business requirements, the most likely causes include unidentified or unclear requirements, inadequately defined scope, imprecise targets, shortcuts or sloppy work during systems analysis, poor design choices, insufficient testing or inadequate testing procedures, and lack of appropriate change control. Systems also fail because of changes in the organization's culture, funding, or objectives. A system that falls short of business needs also produces problems for users, and reduces morale and productivity.

Cost overruns typically result from unrealistic estimates that either were too optimistic or were based on incomplete definitions of work to be done, from poor monitoring of progress and inadequate reaction to early signs of problems, or from schedule delays due to unanticipated factors.

Overdue or late completion of projects can indicate a failure to recognize activity interdependencies, confusing effort with progress, poor monitoring and control of progress, personality conflicts among the team members, or turnover of project personnel.

The failure of an information system usually is due to a failure in project management. If the project manager fails to plan, staff, organize, supervise, communicate, motivate, evaluate, direct, and control properly, then the project is certain to fail. Even when factors outside the project manager's control contribute to the failure, the project manager is responsible if those factors were not recognized quickly and handled appropriately.

When the project manager first recognizes that a project is in trouble, behind schedule, or out of control, what options are available? In general, the four options are: trimming the project requirements, adding to the project resources, delaying the project deadline, and improving the quality of the project management.

Sometimes, when a project experiences delays or cost overruns, the system still can be delivered on time and within budget if several less critical requirements are trimmed. The system can be delivered to satisfy the most necessary requirements, and additional features can be added later as a part of a maintenance or enhancement project.

If a project is in trouble because of a lack of resources or organizational support, management might be willing to give the project a higher priority for computer turnaround times, clerical support, end user attention, and management decisions. If more project work needs to be completed than there are people to perform it, adding more people to the project team might help. Adding staff, however, will reduce the time necessary to complete the work only if the work to be done can be divided into separate tasks on which different people can work.

If the problem is that current team members lack experience or technical proficiency, you might obtain expert temporary help, such as consultants, contract programmers or analysts, or service bureau personnel. Adding staff might require time for training and orienting new people, however. At some point, adding more people to a project actually increases the time necessary to complete the project. Adding new staff also means adding costs, with the potential for going over the budgeted project costs.

The action most often taken when a project is behind schedule is to add more time to the schedule. Additional time is an alternative only if the original target date is not an absolute deadline that you must meet and if extending the target date will not result in excessive costs.

When a project is in trouble for whatever reason, the project manager must try to get the project back under control and keep it under control.

TOOLKIT PART 3 SUMMARY

Project management is the process of defining, planning, organizing, leading, and controlling the development of an information system. Project management is important throughout the SDLC, but is especially vital during the implementation phase of a project. The primary objective of project management is to deliver a system that meets all requirements on time and within budget. Although the project manager can use a variety of software tools that make the job easier, he or she must have a clear understanding of project management concepts and techniques.

Project management begins with identifying and planning all specific activities or tasks. Projects also have events or milestones that provide major reference points to monitor progress. After identifying the tasks, project managers must develop a work schedule that assigns specific tasks to project team members.

Time estimates for tasks usually are made in person-days. A person-day represents the work that one person can accomplish in one day. Estimating the time for project activities is more difficult with larger systems. Project managers must consider project size and scope, IT resources, prior experience with similar projects or systems, and applicable constraints.

In project scheduling, the project manager develops a specific time for each activity, based on available resources and whether or not the task is dependent on other activities being accomplished earlier. The project manager can use graphical tools such as Gantt charts and PERT/CPM charts to assist in the scheduling process.

A Gantt chart is a horizontal bar chart that represents the project schedule, with time on the horizontal axis and tasks arranged vertically. It shows individual tasks and activity groups, which include several tasks. In a Gantt chart, the length of the bar indicates the duration of the tasks. A Gantt chart can display progress, but does not show task dependency details or resource assignment unless the chart was created with a project management program that supports dependency linking and the entry of other information.

A PERT/CPM chart shows the project as a network diagram, with activities shown as vectors and events displayed as nodes. Using a prescribed calculation method, the project manager uses a PERT/CPM chart to determine the overall duration of the project, and provide specific information for each activity, including the earliest completion time (ECT) and the latest completion time (LCT). With this information, the manager can determine the critical path, which is the sequence of tasks that must be performed on time in order to meet the overall project deadline.

A project manager uses a variety of techniques to monitor, control, and report project tasks. The methods include structured walkthroughs, which are reviews of a team member's work by other team members. A project manager also keeps team members and others up-to-date with regular reports and periodic meetings.

Software change control is concerned with change requests that arise after the system requirements document has been approved, and most companies establish a specific procedure for managing such requests. A typical change control procedure consists of four steps: completion of a change request form, initial determination, impact analysis, and final disposition.

In the end, every successful information system must support business requirements, satisfy users, stay within budget, and be available on time. Sound project management involves the same skills as any type of management. The project manager must be perceptive, analytical, well-organized, and a good communicator. If the project manager senses that the project is off-track, he or she must take immediate steps to diagnose and solve the problem.

Toolkit Part 3 Key Terms

activity (*TK 3.2*)
activity groups (*TK 3.7*)
best case (*TK 3.11*)
code reviews (*TK 3.13*)
concurrent (*TK 3.9*)
controlling (*TK 3.2*)
critical path (*TK 3.13*)
Critical Path Method (CPM) (*TK 3.8*)
dependent (*TK 3.9*)
dependent activity (*TK 3.6*)
design reviews (*TK 3.13*)
dummy activity (*TK 3.9*)
duration (*TK 3.11*)
earliest completion time (ECT) (*TK 3.11*)
event (*TK 3.2*)
event dependency (*TK 3.9*)
expected project duration (*TK 3.12*)
Gantt chart (*TK 3.7*)
latest completion time (LCT) (*TK 3.12*)
leading (*TK 3.2*)
management functions (*TK 3.2*)
milestone (*TK 3.2*)
nodes (*TK 3.8*)

organizing (*TK 3.2*)
parallel (*TK 3.9*)
person-days (*TK 3.4*)
pilot system (*TK 3.6*)
planning (*TK 3.2*)
probable case (*TK 3.11*)
Program Evaluation Review Technique (PERT) (*TK 3.8*)
project coordinator (*TK 3.2*)
project leader (*TK 3.2*)
project management software (*TK 3.15*)
project manager (*TK 3.2*)
project scheduling (*TK 3.6*)
requirements reviews (*TK 3.13*)
serial (*TK 3.9*)
slack time (*TK 3.13*)
software change control (*TK 3.16*)
structured walkthrough (*TK 3.13*)
task (*TK 3.2*)
testing reviews (*TK 3.13*)
vectors (*TK 3.8*)
worst case (*TK 3.2*)

Toolkit Part 3 Review

1. What is project management and what are its main objectives?

2. What is the relationship among activities (or tasks) and events (or milestones)?

3. If Project A has twice as many resources as Project B, will Project A be twice as complex as Project B? Why or why not?

4. What is the difference between dependent (or serial) and concurrent (or parallel) activities?

5. Compare the characteristics, advantages, and disadvantages of a Gantt chart to a PERT/CPM chart.

6. Define the following terms: best case, probable case, and worst case, and describe how a project manager could use these concepts to estimate activity duration?

7. How does a project manager calculate earliest completion time (ECT) and latest completion time (LCT) for the tasks in a project?

8. What is a critical path and why it important to project managers?

9. What is software change control and what are the four steps typically involved?

Background:

You have been asked to conduct user training sessions during the implementation phase for a new information system. Your first step was to prepare an overall plan. Now you must develop a specific schedule for the tasks listed below. The following steps must be followed (the estimated time is shown in parentheses).

Tasks:

First, you will send an e-mail message to all department managers announcing the training sessions (1 day). After the e-mail message goes out, two tasks can begin at the same time: you can develop the training material (5 days) and confirm arrangements for the training facility you plan to use (3 days). As soon as the training material is complete, you can work on two tasks at once: arrange to have copies of handout material printed (3 days) and develop a set of PowerPoint slides (4 days). As soon as the PowerPoint slides are ready, you conduct a practice training session with the instructor who will assist you (1 day). Finally, when the practice session is over, the handout material is ready, and the training facility is confirmed, you conduct the sessions (3 days).

Assignment:

Using the PERT/CPM techniques described in the Toolkit, develop a chart that shows ECTs, LCTs, project duration, and the critical path for this project. Use the format shown in Figure TK 3-11 on page TK 3.10 for your chart. If project management software is available, use it to develop the same information.

PART 4

Alternative
Systems Development
Methodologies **PART 4**

Alternative System
Development
Methodologies

In Part 4 of the Toolkit, you will learn about two popular systems development methodologies: rapid application development (RAD) and Microsoft Solutions Framework (MSF).

INTRODUCTION

As you learned in the text, several systems development strategies exist. Although traditional structured analysis is still common, the use of object-oriented analysis and design is growing rapidly. Systems developers find it advantageous to translate O-O designs directly into O-O programming languages such as C++ and Java, which are extremely popular. In addition to understanding structured analysis and O-O methodologies, systems analysts should know about two other systems development strategies: rapid application development (RAD) and Microsoft Solutions Framework (MSF).

OBJECTIVES

When you finish this Part of the Toolkit, you will be able to:

- Describe RAD methodology and explain its main features

- List the four RAD phases and describe the activities performed in each phase

- Identify potential disadvantages of RAD

- Describe Microsoft Solutions Framework and explain its main features

- Explain the objectives of the seven Microsoft Solutions Framework models

- Describe Microsoft solution architecture certification opportunities

N THE WEB

learn more about
pid Application
velopment (RAD) visit
site.com/sad4e/more.htm,
ck Systems Analysis and
sign Toolkit and then click
 Rapid Application
velopment (RAD) link.

w.scsite.com

RAPID APPLICATION DEVELOPMENT

Rapid application development (RAD) is a team-based technique that speeds up information systems development and produces a functioning information system.

Overview

Like joint application development (JAD), RAD uses a group approach, but goes much further. While JAD focuses on the requirements modeling process, RAD is a complete methodology, with a four-phase life cycle that parallels the traditional SDLC phases. The end product of RAD is the new information system. Companies use RAD to reduce cost and systems development time, and increase the probability of success.

James Martin pioneered the RAD technique during the 1980s. RAD soon became popular, and many companies and IT consultants developed their own versions of RAD. Figure TK 4-1 shows two examples of IT consultants that offer RAD development strategies and support.

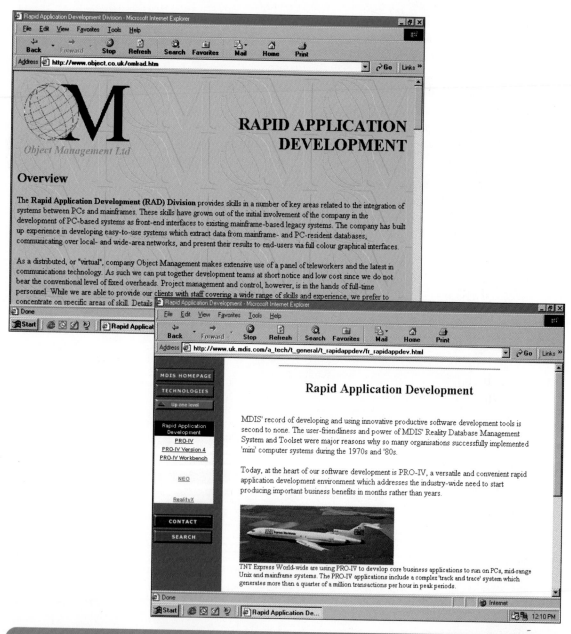

FIGURE TK 4-1 Two examples of IT consultants that offer RAD development strategies and support.

RAD relies heavily on prototyping and user involvement. The RAD process allows users to examine a working model as early as possible, determine if it meets their needs, and suggest necessary changes. Based on user input, the prototype is modified and the interactive process continues until the system is completely developed and users are satisfied. The project team uses CASE tools to build the prototypes and create a continuous stream of documentation.

RAD Phases and Activities

The RAD model consists of four phases: requirements planning, user design, construction, and cutover, as shown in Figure TK 4-2. Notice the continuous interaction between the user design and construction phases. The RAD team performs the following activities in each phase: requirements planning, user design, construction, and cutover.

REQUIREMENTS PLAN-NING The **requirements planning phase** combines elements of the systems planning and systems analysis phases of the SDLC. Users, managers, and IT staff members discuss and agree on business needs, project scope, constraints, and system requirements. The requirements planning phase ends when the team agrees on the key issues and obtains management authorization to continue.

USER DESIGN During the **user design phase**, users interact with systems analysts and develop models and prototypes that represent all system processes, outputs, and inputs. The RAD group, or subgroups typically use a combination of JAD techniques and CASE tools to translate user needs into work-

Task:
- Users, managers, and IT staff agree upon business needs, project scope, and systems requirements
- Obtain approval to continue

Requirements Planning

Task:
- Interact with users
- Build models and prototypes
- Conduct intensive JAD-type sessions

User Design

Construction

Task:
- Program and application development
- Coding
- Unit, integration, and system testing

Task:
- Data conversion
- Full-scale testing
- System changeover
- User training

Cutover

FIGURE TK 4-2 In the RAD model suggested by James Martin, the four phases are requirements planning, user design, construction, and cutover. Notice the continuous interaction between the user design and construction phases.

ing models. User design is a continuous, interactive process that allows users to understand, modify, and eventually approve a working model of the system that meets their needs.

CONSTRUCTION The **construction phase** focuses on program and application development tasks similar to the SDLC. In RAD, however, users continue to participate and can still suggest changes or improvements as actual screens or reports are developed.

CUTOVER The **cutover phase** resembles the final tasks in the SDLC implementation phase, including data conversion, testing, changeover to the new system, and user training. Compared with traditional methods, the entire process is compressed. As a result, the new system is built, delivered, and placed in operation much sooner.

RAD Objectives

The main objective of all RAD approaches is to cut development time and expense by involving users in every phase of systems development. Because it is a continuous process, RAD allows the development team to make necessary modifications quickly, as the design evolves. The **Rapid Application Development Technologies Design Group (RADTDG)** is a forum for systems developers and others with an interest in RAD, as shown in Figure TK 4-3. Notice that the Sun Microsystems article cited by RADTDG stresses the importance of maintaining a short development cycle and limiting the cost of change before a company makes large investments in development and testing.

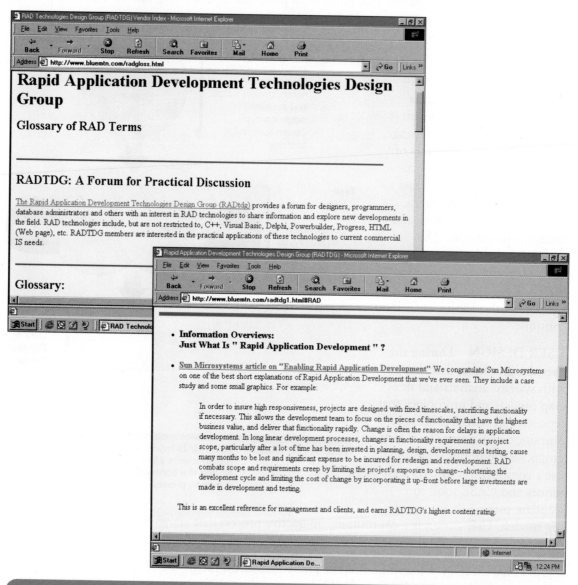

FIGURE TK 4-3 The Rapid Application Development Technologies Design Group (RADTDG) is a forum for systems developers and others with an interest in RAD. Notice the Sun Microsystems article, which stresses the importance of a short development cycle.

In addition to user involvement, a successful RAD team must have IT resources, skills, and management support. Because it is a dynamic, user-driven process, RAD is especially valuable when a company needs an information system to support a new business function. By obtaining user input from the beginning, RAD also helps a development team design a system that requires a highly interactive or complex user interface.

RAD Advantages and Disadvantages

RAD has advantages and disadvantages compared with traditional structured analysis methods. The primary advantage is that systems can be developed more quickly with significant cost savings. A disadvantage is that RAD stresses the mechanics of the system itself and does not emphasize the company's strategic business needs. The risk is that a system might work well in the short term, but the corporate and long-term objectives for the system might not be met. Another potential disadvantage is that the accelerated time cycle might allow less time to develop quality, consistency, and design standards. RAD can be an attractive alternative, however, if an organization understands the possible risks.

OVERVIEW OF MICROSOFT SOLUTIONS FRAMEWORK

ON THE WEB

For more information about Microsoft Solution Framework (MSF) visit scsite.com/sad4e/more.htm click Systems Analysis and Design Toolkit and then click the Microsoft Solution Framework (MSF) link.

www.scsite.c

You learned in Chapter 1 that Microsoft offers an approach to systems development called the **Microsoft Solutions Framework (MSF)**. The objective of MSF is to define and analyze business requirements and provide IT solutions. In Microsoft's view, MSF is only one component of the **Enterprise Services Framework**, which is an overall model of how to prepare, plan, build, and manage information systems, as shown in Figure TK 4-4.

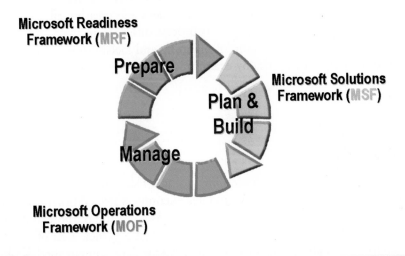

FIGURE TK 4-4   According to Microsoft, MSF is the plan and build phase of the Enterprise Services Framework, which is Microsoft's version of a systems development life cycle. Microsoft Readiness Framework (MRF) is the prepare phase, and Microsoft Operations Framework (MOF) is the manage phase of the model.

According to Microsoft, MSF is the plan and build phase of the Enterprise Services Framework, which is Microsoft's version of a systems development life cycle. **Microsoft Readiness Framework (MRF)** is the prepare phase, and **Microsoft Operations Framework (MOF)** is the manage phase of the model. Microsoft also refers to a **BAIT model**, as shown in Figure TK 4-5 on the next page, which looks at a system from four separate, but interdependent viewpoints: business, applications, information, and technology.

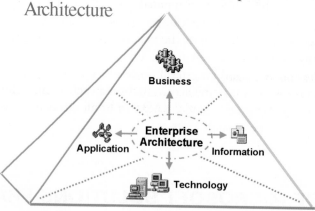

Four Perspectives of an Enterprise Architecture

FIGURE TK 4-5   Microsoft's BAIT model views a system from four separate, but interdependent perspectives: business, applications, information, and technology.

Microsoft developed MSF by documenting the experience of its own IT teams in analyzing information system requirements and creating solution architectures. A **solution architecture** is a specific strategy for understanding business IT needs and creating effective systems that satisfy those requirements. Although the Microsoft process differs from the SDLC phase-oriented approach, MSF requires the same kind of planning and fact-finding. MSF, which uses O-O analysis and design concepts, starts by examining the business and organizational context for the information system.

MSF MODELS

Using MSF, you build a series of models, including a risk management model, a team model, and a process model. Those three basic models encompass several other models, which are described in the sections that follow. Each model has a specific purpose and contributes to the overall design and implementation of the system. Taken together, a set of MSF models describes an information system and provides an overall systems development methodology.

Risk Management Model

The MSF **risk management model** is based on the concept that every project involves risk, and managing risk effectively is crucial to the project's success. Microsoft states that the risk management model is built on the following key principles:

- Risk is inherent in every project. The result might involve product quality, cost overruns, missed deadlines, or project failure.

- Risk is neither intrinsically good nor bad. Risk should be identified and assessed, rather than avoided.

- Risk should be managed rather than feared. Successful systems developers handle uncertainty by dealing with each identified risk in a proactive manner.

- Risk involves not only technology, but also people and processes.

Microsoft suggests several specific guidelines for teams involved in risk management:

- Assess risks continuously throughout the project life cycle. Some risks can be identified at the beginning of a project; others cannot be detected until the project is underway.

- Use risk-based decision making. Decisions must be made with the risk factor in mind. Microsoft suggests that teams address the highest risk items first.

- Establish a process that the team can understand and use. The process should be reasonably structured, but flexible enough to accommodate varying situations.
- Use a broad focus. Successful risk management requires the team to look for risk almost everywhere in the project, including the technology, processes, and people that the risk might involve or affect.
- Treat risk identification as a positive factor. For risk management to be effective, team members must be willing to speak out freely. Risk identification avoids unpleasant surprises. When a risk is identified, the team can prepare for it and attempt to minimize it or avoid it altogether.

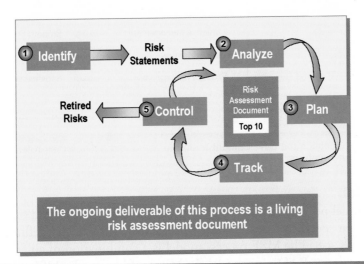

FIGURE TK 4-6 In the MSF risk management model, the team identifies, analyzes, plans, tracks, and controls risks associated with new system development.

The model shown in Figure TK 4-6 shows the risk management model and how the team identifies, analyzes, plans, tracks, and controls risks associated with the project.

Team Model

The **team model** identifies the development team members and defines their roles. MSF suggests six separate roles for team members, as shown in Figure TK 4-7 on the next page. Team roles are performed by individuals or sub-teams each with a specific focus. The roles include the following:

Product management. The product management role views the project from a customer's perspective and expectations, and becomes highly familiar with the business needs and processes that must be supported.

Development. The development role translates the business requirements into a fully tested, functioning system. Programmers and systems analysts work together to create the logical and physical design for the system, construct the system, and assure that specifications are met.

Testing. The testing role is performed by IT staff members who develop a comprehensive test plan and perform rigorous testing and assessment.

Logistics Management. When development and testing are complete, the logistics management role distributes the system to users and handles any tasks necessary to make the system fully operational.

User Education. The user education role is responsible for planning and implementing user support and training.

Program Management. The program management role is responsible for overall management of the project, including budgets, schedules, staff assignments, and necessary approvals.

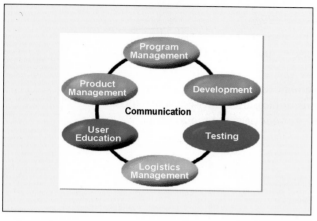

Team role		Goal
Program management	⟹	Delivery within project constraints
Development	⟹	Delivery to product specifications
Testing	⟹	Release after addressing all known issues
Logistics management	⟹	Smooth product deployment
User education	⟹	Enhanced user performance
Product management	⟹	Satisfied customers

FIGURE TK 4-7 The MSF team model identifies the development team members and defines their roles. MSF suggests six separate roles for team members.

Process Model

The **process model** provides a framework for systems development and organizes development tasks into four specific phases, each of which ends with a clearly defined milestone, as shown in Figure TK 4-8. The MSF process model is a combination of an SDLC-type waterfall model and an interactive RAD-type model. In Microsoft's view, the MSF process model has the best features of both: the predictability of milestone-based planning, and the feedback and creativity of an interactive model. The following are the four process model phases:

- **Envisioning phase.** The development team creates a vision statement that provides overall direction and spells out the scope and limits for this version of the system. The envisioning phase ends with approval to proceed with the project.

- **Planning phase.** Systems developers and users create a set of specific requirements, called a **functional specification**, and a development schedule. The planning phase ends with a project plan approval milestone.

- **Developing phase.** The development team translates the functional specification into an operational system. During this phase, the system is tested initially and modified as necessary to assure that it meets all functional requirements. The developing phase ends with a milestone called scope complete.

- **Stabilizing phase.** At this point, the project undergoes full-scale user testing that simulates all operational conditions. Any problems are analyzed, resolved, and documented. If additional features are requested, a record is kept for the next version. The stabilization phase ends with a release milestone to indicate that the operational system is available to users.

The process model includes an overall conceptual solution; a logical design similar to a DFD; and a physical design that includes hardware, software, and network specifications and requirements. The objective of the process model is to translate business requirements into a set of specifications that systems developers can use as a blueprint for building and coding the new system.

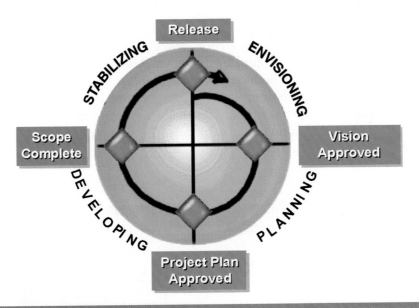

FIGURE TK 4-8   The MSF process model organizes development tasks into four specific phases. Each phase ends with a clearly defined milestone.

Other MSF Models

The three basic models can contain a series of other models, including an enterprise architecture model, an application model, an infrastructure model, and a TCO model.

ENTERPRISE ARCHITECTURE MODEL   The **enterprise architecture model** focuses on underlying business requirements and how IT must support the company's mission, goals, and objectives. Microsoft lists four key principles for a successful enterprise architecture:

- **Clear vision.** Businesses need to know where they are and where they are heading.
- **Alignment of business and technology.** The starting point is to define business goals and objectives so that the necessary systems and technologies can be applied.
- **Versioned releases.** The MSF concept allows companies to plan future releases and features while the current system is being built.
- **Proactive risk management.** MSF includes a process for risk assessment and decision making throughout the project.

APPLICATION MODEL   The **application model** provides another way of viewing the system by defining user services, business services, and data services. A **service** is a specific process or function that must be provided by the system. **User services** include the user interface, **business services** include the business logic and rules that support company operations, and **data services** include methods of maintaining and accessing system data. As Figure TK 4-9 shows, MSF views an application as a logical network of modular services that can be provided across physical and functional boundaries. As modular components, they can be reused to support different business applications.

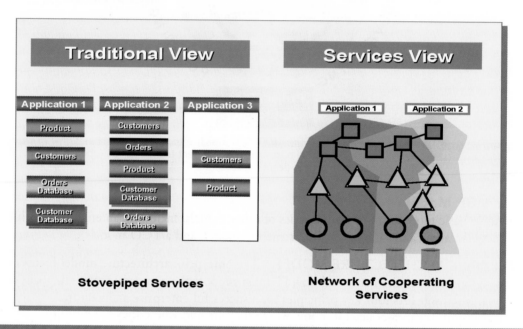

FIGURE TK 4-9   MSF views an application as a logical network of modular services that can be provided across physical and functional boundaries. As modular components, they can be reused to support different business applications.

INFRASTRUCTURE MODEL   The **infrastructure model** describes the resources required to develop and support the system, within budget and on schedule. The resources include necessary technology, people, financial support, and management. The infrastructure model provides a checklist that can be used in TCO analysis.

TCO MODEL   The **TCO model** identifies and analyzes all costs associated with the project. Systems developers use this model to minimize TCO and obtain the greatest possible return on investment. In addition to hardware and software costs, the TCO model includes all expenses associated with training, support, downtime, and telecommunications.

MICROSOFT CERTIFICATION FOR SOLUTION ARCHITECTURES

As part of its certification programs, Microsoft has created an examination called Analyzing Requirements and Defining Solution Architectures (Exam 70-100). Individuals who pass this exam achieve Microsoft Certified Professional status, and earn credit toward Microsoft Certified Solution Developer certification. The exam uses case studies, interactive questions, online systems development tools, and simulation techniques. You can try a sample version of the exam at the Microsoft Web site, as shown in Figure TK 4-10.

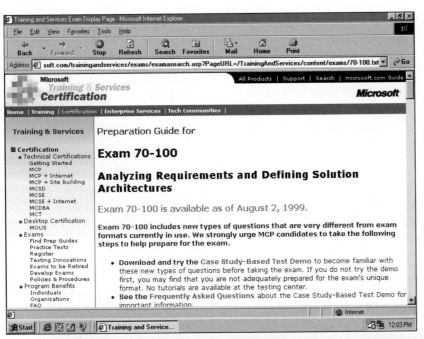

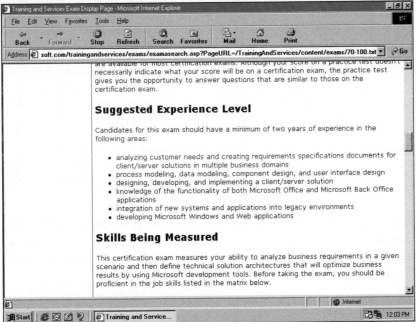

FIGURE TK 4-10 Microsoft's 70-100 examination is called Analyzing Requirements and Defining Solution Architectures. Individuals who pass this exam achieve Microsoft Certified Professional status and earn credit toward Microsoft Certified Solution Developer certification. The exam uses case studies, interactive questions, online systems development tools, and simulation techniques. You can try a sample version of the online exam at the Microsoft Web site.

Microsoft suggests that two years of experience is necessary for the 70-100 exam, and offers several courses that can help you prepare for this exam. Although this text alone will not prepare you for the exam, many of the exam topics are covered in this book. To help you review your knowledge and develop your preparation plan, Figure TK 4-11 on the next page lists the specific topics and objectives included in the 70-100 exam.

SKILLS MEASURED BY EXAM 70-100

I. ANALYZING BUSINESS REQUIREMENTS

Analyze the scope of a project. Considerations include:
- existing applications
- anticipated changes in environment
- expected lifetime of solution
- time, cost, budget, and benefit trade offs

Analyze the extent of a business requirement.
- Establish business requirements.
- Establish type of problem, such as messaging problem or communication problem.
- Establish and define customer quality requirements.
- Minimize Total Cost of Ownership (TCO).
- Increase Return on Investment (ROI) of solution.
- Analyze current platform and infrastructure.
- Incorporate planned platform and infrastructure into solution.
- Analyze impact of technology migration.
- Plan physical requirements, such as infrastructure.
- Establish application environment, such as hardware platform, support, and operating system.
- Identify organizational constraints, such as financial situation, company politics, technical acceptance level, and training needs.
- Establish schedule for implementation of solution.
- Identify audience.

Analyze security requirements.
- Identify roles of administrator, groups, guests, and clients.
- Identify impact on existing environment.
- Establish fault tolerance.
- Plan for maintainability.
- Plan distribution of security database.
- Establish security context.
- Plan for auditing.
- Identify level of security needed.
- Analyze existing mechanisms for security policies.

Analyze performance requirements. Considerations include:
- transactions per time slice
- bandwidth
- capacity
- interoperability with existing standards
- peak versus average requirements
- response-time expectations
- existing response-time characteristics
- barriers to performance

Analyze maintainability requirements. Considerations include:
- breadth of application distribution
- method of distribution
- maintenance expectations
- location and knowledge level of maintenance staff
- impact of third-party maintenance agreements

Analyze extensibility requirements. Solution must be able to handle the growth of functionality.

Analyze availability requirements. Considerations include:
- hours of operation
- level of availability
- geographic scope
- impact of downtime

Analyze human factors requirements. Considerations include:
- target users
- localization
- accessibility
- roaming users
- Help
- training requirements
- physical environment constraints
- special needs

Analyze the requirements for integrating a solution with existing applications. Considerations include:
- legacy applications
- format and location of existing data
- connectivity to existing applications
- data conversion
- data enhancement requirements

Analyze existing methodologies and limitations of a business. Considerations include:
- legal issues
- current business practices
- organization structure
- process engineering
- budget
- implementation and training methodologies
- quality control requirements
- customer's needs

Analyze scalability requirements. Considerations include:
- growth of audience
- growth of organization
- growth of data
- cycle of use

FIGURE TK 4-11 To help you review your knowledge and develop your preparation plan, the specific topics and objectives of the 70-100 exam are listed here. The material is accurate as of the text publication date, but the content of this exam might change in the future. To ensure that your exam preparation plan is up-to-date, you should visit Microsoft's Web site.

Continued

II. DEFINING THE TECHNICAL ARCHITECTURE FOR A SOLUTION

Given a business scenario, identify which solution type is appropriate. Solution types are single-tier, two-tier, and n-tier.

Identify which technologies are appropriate for implementation of a given business solution. Considerations include:
- technology standards such as EDI, Internet, OSI, COMTI, and POSIX
- proprietary technologies
- technology environment of the company, both current and planned
- selection of development tools
- type of solution, such as enterprise, distributed, centralized, and collaborative

Choose a data storage architecture. Considerations include:
- volume
- number of transactions per time increment
- number of connections or sessions
- scope of business requirements
- extensibility requirements
- reporting requirements
- number of users
- type of database

Test the feasibility of a proposed technical architecture.
- Demonstrate that business requirements are met.
- Demonstrate that use case scenarios are met.
- Demonstrate that existing technology constraints are met.
- Assess impact of shortfalls in meeting requirements.

Develop appropriate deployment strategy.

III. DEVELOPING THE CONCEPTUAL AND LOGICAL DESIGN FOR AN APPLICATION

Construct a conceptual design that is based on a variety of scenarios and that includes context, workflow process, task sequence, and physical environment models. Types of applications include:
- SDI, MDI, console, and dialog desktop applications
- two-tier, client/server, and Web applications
- n-tier applications
- collaborative applications

Given a conceptual design, apply the principles of modular design to derive the components and services of the logical design.

Incorporate business rules into object design.

Assess the potential impact of the logical design on performance, maintainability, extensibility, scalability, availability, and security.

IV. DEVELOPING DATA MODELS

Group data into entities by applying normalization rules.

Specify the relationships between entities.

Choose the foreign key that will enforce a relationship between entities and will ensure referential integrity.

Identify the business rules that relate to data integrity.

Incorporate business rules and constraints into the data model.

Identify appropriate level of de-normalization.

Develop a database that uses general database development standards and guidelines.

V. DESIGNING A USER INTERFACE AND USER SERVICES

Given a solution, identify the navigation for the user interface.

Identify input validation procedures that should be integrated into the user interface.

Evaluate methods of providing online user assistance, such as status bars, ToolTips, and Help files.

Construct a prototype user interface that is based on business requirements, user interface guidelines, and the organization's standards.
- Establish appropriate and consistent use of menu-based controls.
- Establish appropriate shortcut keys (accelerated keys).

Establish appropriate type of output.

VI. DERIVING THE PHYSICAL DESIGN

Assess the potential impact of the physical design on performance, maintainability, extensibility, scalability, availability, and security.

Evaluate whether access to a database should be encapsulated in an object.

Design the properties, methods, and events of components.

TOOLKIT PART 4 SUMMARY

In addition to understanding structured analysis and O-O methodologies, systems analysts should know about rapid application development (RAD) and Microsoft Solutions Framework (MSF).

RAD is a team-based technique that speeds up information systems development and produces a functioning information system. Like JAD, RAD uses a group approach, but goes much further. While JAD focuses on the requirements modeling process, RAD is a complete methodology, with a four-phase life cycle that parallels the traditional SDLC phases. RAD can reduce cost and systems development time, and increase the probability of success.

RAD relies heavily on prototyping and user involvement, as early as possible. Based on user input, the prototype is modified and the interactive process continues until the system is completely developed and users are satisfied. The project team uses CASE tools to build the prototypes and create a continuous stream of documentation.

The four RAD phases are: requirements planning, user design, construction, and cutover. During the requirements planning phase, users, managers, and IT staff members discuss and agree on business needs, project scope, constraints, and system requirements. During the user design phase, the team uses JAD techniques and CASE tools to develop a series of models and prototypes. The user design phase is a continuous, interactive process. The construction phase focuses on program development, and includes application development tasks similar to the SDLC. The cutover phase includes data conversion, testing, changeover to the new system, and user training.

Compared with traditional methods, the entire RAD process is compressed. As a result, the new system is built, delivered, and placed in operation much sooner. A successful RAD team must have IT resources, skills, and management support, which are especially valuable when a company needs an information system to support a new business function.

RAD's primary advantage is that systems can be developed more quickly with significant cost savings. A disadvantage is that RAD stresses the mechanics of the system itself, and does not emphasize the company's strategic business needs. The risk is that a system might work well in the short-term, but the corporate and long-term objectives for the system might not be met. In addition, the accelerated time cycle might allow less time to develop quality, consistency, and design standards.

Microsoft offers a systems development approach called the Microsoft Solutions Framework (MSF), which helps companies define and analyze business requirements and provide IT solutions. MSF is the plan and build phase of the Enterprise Services Framework, which also includes the Microsoft Readiness Framework (MRF) and the Microsoft Operations Framework (MOF). The BAIT model looks at a system from four separate, but interdependent viewpoints: business, applications, information, and technology.

Microsoft developed MSF based on its own experience in creating solution architectures, which are specific strategies for understanding business IT needs and creating effective systems that satisfy those requirements.

Using MSF, you build a series of basic models, including a risk management model, a team model, and a process model. Those three models encompass other models, including an enterprise architecture model, an application model, an infrastructure model, and a TCO model. The MSF models provide an overall framework for systems development.

The risk management model identifies and assesses risks that are inherent in all projects. This model is based on the concept that effective risk management is crucial to a project's success.

The team model identifies the development team members and defines their roles, which are product management, program management, development, testing, user education, and logistics management.

The process model organizes development tasks into four specific phases, each of which ends with a clearly defined milestone. The phases include envisioning, planning, developing, and stabilizing. The MSF process model is a combination of an SDLC-type waterfall model and an interactive RAD-type model. The process model encompasses a solutions design model, which translates business requirements into a set of specifications that represent a blueprint for building and coding the new system.

The enterprise architecture model focuses on underlying business requirements and how IT must support the company's mission, goals, and objectives.

The application model provides another way of viewing the system by defining user services, business services, and data services. A service is a specific process or function that must be provided by the system. Services are modular components that can be reused to support different business applications.

The infrastructure model describes the resources required to develop and support the system, within budget and on schedule. The resources include necessary technology, people, financial support, and management. The infrastructure model provides a checklist that can be used in connection with the TCO model, which analyzes all costs associated with the project.

As part of its certification programs, Microsoft has created a case study-based examination called Analyzing Requirements and Defining Solution Architectures (Exam 70-100). Individuals who pass this exam achieve Microsoft Certified Professional status, and earn credit toward Microsoft Certified Solution Developer certification. Microsoft suggests that two years of experience is necessary for the 70-100 exam, and offers several courses that can help you prepare for this exam.

Toolkit Part 4 Key Terms

application model (*TK 4.10*)
BAIT model (*TK 4.5*)
business services (*TK 4.10*)
construction phase (*TK 4.3*)
cutover phase (*TK 4.3*)
data services (*TK 4.10*)
enterprise architecture model (*TK 4.9*)
Enterprise Services Framework (*TK 4.5*)
functional specification (*TK 4.9*)
infrastructure model (*TK 4.10*)
Microsoft Operations Framework (MOF) (*TK 4.5*)
Microsoft Readiness Framework (MRF) (*TK 4.5*)

Microsoft Solutions Framework (MSF) (*TK 4.5*)
process model (*TK 4.8*)
rapid application development (RAD) (*TK 4.2*)
Rapid Application Development Technologies Design Group (RADTDG) (*TK 4.4*)
requirements planning phase (*TK 4.3*)
risk management model (*TK 4.6*)
service (*TK 4.10*)
solution architecture (*TK 4.6*)
TCO model (*TK 4.10*)
team model (*TK 4.7*)
user design phase (*TK 4.3*)
user services (*TK 4.10*)

Toolkit Part 4 Review

1. Explain the main features of the RAD methodology.

2. List the four RAD phases and explain the tasks that are performed during each phase.

3. Compare RAD to the traditional SDLC strategy. What are the similarities? What are the differences?

4. Describe the MSF strategy for application development.

5. Explain Microsoft's BAIT model.

6. Describe the MSF risk management model and list the key principles.

7. Describe the MSF team model and list the six roles.

8. Describe the MSF process model and list the four phases.

9. Describe the MSF enterprise architecture model and list the four key principles.

10. What Microsoft examination relates to solution architectures? Provide a sample of the skills involved in this exam.

INDEX